Article 10.

The solemn Ratifications of the present Treaty expedited in good and due Form shall be exchanged between the contracting Parties in the Space of Six Months or sooner, if possible, to be computed from the Day of the Signature of the present Treaty In Witness whereof We the undersigned, their Ministers Plenipotentiary have in their Name and in Virtue of our full Powers, signed with our Hands the present Definitive Treaty, and caused the Seals of our Arms to be affixed thereto.

Done at Paris, this third Day of September In the Year of our Lord, one thousand, seven hundred and Eighty three.

D Hartley

John Adams.

B Franklin

John Jay

TO PRESERVE THE REPUBLIC

United States Foreign Policy

Frederick H. Hartmann

Alfred Thayer Mahan Professor, Naval War College

Robert L. Wendzel

Professor of Political Science, University of Maine, Orono

Macmillan Publishing Company
New York

Collier Macmillan Publishers
London

Macmillan Publishing Company
866 Third Avenue, New York, New York 10022

Collier Macmillan Canada, Inc.

Library of Congress Cataloging in Publication Data

Hartmann, Frederick H.
　To preserve the Republic.

　Includes index.
　1. United States—Foreign relations—1945–　　　.
I. Wendzel, Robert L.,　　　.　II. Title.
JX1417.H37 1985　　　　327.73　　　　84-5708
ISBN 0-02-351300-4

Printing: 1 2 3 4 5 6 7 8　　　Year: 5 6 7 8 9 0 1 2 3

ISBN　0-02-351300-4

PREFACE

Many books on American foreign policy are preoccupied with the internal or domestic American political process. Some of these examine in detail the swing from a Nixon to a Carter, from a Carter to a Reagan, as these swings produce divergent interpretations by administrations of America's role in foreign affairs. Others of these look minutely at the (internal) bureaucratic process by which decisions are reached or at American interest groups as they try to influence policy—such as limiting the imports of Japanese autos or foreign steel. Both such emphases are desirable—the question is one of degree, and what gets left out if these emphases take up too much of the available space. The question is also one of the impression it may leave on the student: that the fundamental and really only important problem of foreign policy is making up our minds what *we* want to do.

There is, of course, also a world out there beyond the American frontiers, a world composed in nation-state terms of about one hundred sixty sovereign entities. Each is affected by what the United States does; most have some effect individually on what the United States decides to do. Certainly collectively, as a state system, they have to be taken into account. Yet the tendencies of this nation-state system are rarely taken adequately into account in the usual book on U.S. foreign policy. Partly this lack may occur because it is extremely difficult to portray American foreign policy in its real complexity. That complexity includes not only how the American internal or domestic political process influences the nature and scope of policy, or how the American governmental (bureaucratic) process results in one emphasis over another. It includes also how nations far from American norms and values approach problems in which the United States is involved and how foreign nations generally, as a system, behave. It includes, clearly, some adequate discussion of the ways in which American conditions and American experiences differ from the norm and have, for better or worse, given us a rather unusual set of lenses through which Americans contemplate foreign policy problems in the first place.

Gathering all of this into one book of modest size is a difficult challenge. It certainly tapped both our skills, not only in extent of coverage but also in balancing all these emphases. But we have nonetheless attempted exactly that. Believing as we do that the American way of thinking about foreign policy, especially as it derives from the U.S. national experience, requires a strong initial emphasis, we have devoted Part One to the American cultural background within the context of a set of conceptual tools by which the validity and utility of American attitudes toward foreign policy can be assessed. (These conceptual tools are applied systematically later to the problems and issues facing the United States.)

Part Two then looks at how Washington makes foreign policy, including an assessment of both bureaucratic politics and interest groups, together with an analysis of how the executive branch and Congress affect foreign policy. Part Two culminates in a description of the national security system.

In Part Three, building on this background, we have two connected purposes in mind: to give a résumé of American experience by looking at the foreign policy record, and also evaluating that record through the use of our conceptual tools. Part Three, in chronological terms, brings us roughly to the Vietnam conflict and the era of détente.

In Part Four we begin to look systematically at the alternatives we can choose among to resolve the main contemporary American foreign policy problems, and what their major advantages and disadvantages are, given the nature of the world in which those problems arise and the nature of the American outlook and interests. We begin with the fundamental relationship to the Soviet Union, then look at divided Europe in this perspective, the prospects for stability in Asia, the problems of bringing peace to the troubled Middle East, and the problems of the United States in dealing with Africa and Latin America.

Having looked at the regional problems we turn in the final chapter of Part Four to the overarching, functional problems now confronting the United States (as well as the rest of the world) as the consequence of technological change and an altering world environment. Here we look at such problems as the uses of space and of the seas, problems involving terrorism, and problems involving the availability of energy and resources. These are the most complicated problems for U.S. policy of any—which is why we left them to last.

Part Five then concludes with a final chapter, summing up the problems and issues, and recommending responses.

To achieve these objectives in these five parts we have deliberately and systematically varied both focus and pace. Especially on focus, there is always an important trade-off. "Close-up" gives detail but blurs the overall perspective by eliminating the setting. And vice versa. So in Part One we have been concerned with the large perspectives: the broad viewpoints, the major influences, the overall setting in which policy must be designed. There we have noted the historical alternation of periods of policy consensus (such as pre-Vietnam) with periods of dissension (such as now, since Vietnam). Part Two moves our "camera" much closer as we look at the tremendous, detailed activity associated with the implementation of policy. We take care there to show the subtle ways in which the bureaucracy changes its functioning when there is or is not a foreign policy consensus. Part Three again takes a large view of events, examining the history of U.S. policy from the special perspective of how well we have handled our problems in dealing with security issues but covering much ground in little space. Parts Four and Five take a mid-range focus, specific as to problems and issues, but not so immersed in detail as to jeopardize a sense of relationships between problems—*interlinked* problems, as we call them there. The pace is, accordingly, slower to permit full and accurate appraisal.

These changes in focus and pace should be kept in mind, for particular generalizations will seem more or less meaningful as the focus changes. Examine the tragedy of Vietnam very close up and you get a strong sense of inevitability about the sequence. But stand way back and what strikes you is a sense of wonder that anyone would consider it worth the effort there.

To sum up, in this book foreign policy is systematically examined from three perspectives that can best be explained by continuing our camera analogy. We already mentioned *focus and pace*. We have varied our focus from macro to micro as the material dictated, much as a zoom lens would do, looking at the policy scene closer up (more bureaucratic detail) or further away (the overall conceptual approach to the problem), speeding the action or slowing it down for detail. We have also *changed our lens* as necessary from one capable of showing the United States as the center of the universe, looking out on the rest of the world, to one capable of giving a moon-view or systems perspective (with the United States as one nation among many). We have also taken our "pictures" *under various degrees of consensus* (showing the contrast between a policy time when "everyone" knows what the problem is and concentrates on handling it, and a time when the big debate is over defining the problem to be handled).

In writing this book we have used parts of two chapters from a book written by one of us some years ago and now out of print. We did not think we could improve upon what was first published in *The New Age of American Foreign Policy.*

Certain parts of the manuscript were read by specialists, for their advice. We wish to thank, in particular, Professor Nathaniel Davis, now of Harvey Mudd College, the Associated Colleges of Claremont, but formerly Director-General of the Foreign Service and Assistant Secretary of State. Also, Professor Jon L. Jacobson, the University of Oregon, for comments on the law of the sea and the open oceans regime.

Frederick H. Hartmann
Robert L. Wendzel

CONTENTS

PART TWO
How Washington Makes Foreign Policy

PART FOUR
Problems and Issues Facing the United States

DIAGRAMS, MAPS, AND TABLES

TABLES

GLOSSARY

The following terms are used in a specific and technical sense in this book. They are cross-referenced.

Alternatives   Term used to describe the choices available in deciding foreign policy issues. (See also *Issues* and *Problems*.)

Analyze Capability Available   Step three of four operational steps in the implementation of policy.

Cardinal Principles   Four principles useful in the design of policy. They are (1) past-future linkages, (2) third-party influences, (3) counterbalancing national interests, (4) the conservation of enemies.

Choose Orientation   Step four of four operational steps in the implementation of policy.

Cold War   Name for period of high tension between the United States and the Soviet Union after World War II and until at least the Sino-Soviet split of 1963; the period before détente.

Concept   First of three policy parts, the intellectual analysis of likely outcomes; important to phase 1 of policy (its design).

Consensus Periods   Periods in foreign policy when substantial agreement exists on the problems faced and the issues to be resolved.

Conservation of Enemies   One of the four cardinal principles. It reminds us of the importance of controlling the amount of enmity confronted, through adjustments in policy, thereby keeping danger to a safer level.

Content   Second of three policy parts; reflects results of phase 1 of policy; forms substance of what is implemented in phase 2; consists of national interests chosen.

Counterbalancing National Interests   One of the four cardinal principles. It calls attention to the nature of important choices of national interests in foreign policy, each alternative interest having advantages and disadvantages but only one of which will be chosen as the content of policy, the other alternative being "shelved." From a systems perspective, the term is used to examine sets of bilateral relations in a multilateral context, showing how various rearrangements such as the "China card" are implicit in the "shelved" interests in the system.

Design   Phase 1 of policy, in which plans made reflect the conception of the problem (reflect the perspective of the decision makers) and lead to choice of policy contents. Involves first and second of three policy parts.

Détente   Period after the playing of the "China card"; three-sided relations begin for the United States, Russia, and China.

Dissension Periods   Periods when substantial conceptual agreement does not exist on foreign policy.

"Domino Effect"   Theory that the loss of one nation to aggression makes resistance by others progressively less. A presumed snowball effect occurs.

Determine Objectives   Step two of four in policy implementation.

Exterior Environment   The world outside United States frontiers.

Foreign Policy   As pieces, has two phases and three parts. As goals, focused on preserving the Republic—its values, way of life, material prosperity, and, above all, its security.

"Free World"   A term popular in the United States, especially in the Cold War period of policy consensus, used to distinguish non-Communist states and to refer to them as a group. Used very loosely for "democratic."

Idealism   As it affects American approaches to policy: a fixed method for problem solving; a belief in law and principle as applied both to domestic and international affairs.

Identify Actors   Step one of four in policy implementation.

Implementation   Phase 2 of foreign policy. Involves second and third of three policy parts.

Issues   Term used for responses made to problems faced. Issues involve choices between (among) alternative foreign policy contents in decision making.

National Interests   During debates over policy content, items put forward as proposed content. In this sense, "claims" on policy. Once debate is over and the decision is made, the chosen items form policy content (become the "official" national interests).

Operational Steps   Four steps in policy implementation: (1) identifying the actors, (2) determining their objectives, (3) analyzing the capability available, and (4) choosing an orientation (i.e., degree and kind of involvement or commitment required).

Overarching Problems   Fundamental questions (problems) in foreign policy of universal relevance.

Past-Future Linkages   One of the four cardinal principles. It calls attention to the fact that the perception of what will happen in the future is linked to one's understanding of the past.

Phase 1 of Policy   Design, leading to content.

Phase 2 of Policy   Content, implemented.

Policy Process   A three-part process: concept, content, implementation.

Policy's Three Parts   Concept, content, implementation.

Policy's Two Phases   Design and implementation.

Power   Used as a measure of resources. Used also as a measure of threat.

Power Problem   Power as threat; those states whose attack is feared or against which military plans are made.

Pragmatism   As it affects American policy: involves open-mindedness and flexibility in approaching potential problem solutions.

Problems   Fundamental questions faced in foreign policy, to which some response is necessary.

Sovereign   Independent; a state able to make its own decisions.

System-Wide Tendencies   Generalized behavior of states (such as the balance of power).

Tension Level   The degree of expectation of conflict.

Third-Party Influences   One of four cardinal principles. It calls attention to the fact that problems and issues cannot be bilaterally resolved in a multilateral world; that neighbors are important.

PART ONE

The Intellectual Framework and the Cultural Background

1

Foreign Policy and the International Environment

We, too, born to freedom, and believing in freedom, are willing to fight to maintain freedom. We . . . would rather die on our feet than live on our knees.

Franklin D. Roosevelt
June 19, 1941

All knowledge resolves itself into probability.

David Hume
A Treatise of Human Nature
1739

The foreign policy of the United States is designed to preserve the Republic; to preserve its values, its way of life, its material prosperity, and—above all—its security. Security "above all" because without security nothing else is assured.

On the evening of October 22, 1962, when President John F. Kennedy addressed the nation on television, the issue of national security was very much at stake. The curtain was rising on the Cuban missile crisis—the nearest approach yet to the unleashing of nuclear war.

Kennedy began, "Good evening, my fellow citizens. This Government, as promised, has maintained the closest surveillance of the Soviet military buildup on the island of Cuba." Now "unmistakable evidence has established the fact that a series of offensive missile sites is now in preparation. . . . The purpose of these bases can be none other than to provide a nuclear strike capacity against the Western Hemisphere." This "sudden, clandestine decision to station strategic weapons for the first time outside of Soviet soil is a deliberately provocative and unjustified change in the status quo which cannot be accepted by this country, if our courage and our commitments are ever to be trusted again by either friend or foe."

The American response would center initially on a naval "quarantine" (blockade) to prevent the further shipment of "offensive weapons."

Kennedy's decision came after a prolonged, closely held debate *within* the American government over the probable future effects if nothing—or something—were done to meet what was clearly thought to be a deliberate provocation from the Soviets to test American nerves.

3

DIAGRAM 1 Policy: Three Parts, Two Phases

① Concept	② Content	③ Implementation
Weighs alternatives	Establishes specific interests pursued	Carries out policy with means available

Phase 1: Design

① Concept	② Content
	(Deciding content)

Phase 2: Implementation

② Content	③ Implementation
	(Achieving content/goals)

The Intellectual Framework and the Cultural Background

Kennedy spoke specifically about these visualized future consequences, about what he foresaw as occurring if no action were taken. Kennedy's views were strongly influenced by his assumptions about Soviet motives. Part of the reason the United States must react promptly and decisively was because the Soviet action was seen as a challenge. *So a decision on action,* as in this case, *is preceded by an analysis of the nature of the problem* and what could or should be done about it. This conceptual analysis will next lead, via a definition of the *issues* faced (i.e., questions to be decided) to the decision to do certain things and to do them in a certain way: to pursue certain alternatives, interests, or goals in a certain way. Policymaking is thus *a three-step process,* moving (first) from problem analysis and issue definition, to (second) a choice of interests and goals, and then (finally) to a choice of means to achieve those goals. Concept leads to content, and content choice leads to implementing action. This three-step policymaking process can also be thought of conveniently in terms of *its two phases: design and implementation.* Design highlights what is to be done by defining the specific content of the policy, whereas implementation highlights how the content of policy will be pursued. To say it another way, phase 1's job is to choose content; phase 2's job is to carry it out. Three steps require only two phases because the two phases share the middle step of content or interests or goals—all these words meaning, as we shall see, approximately the same thing in practice.

Both phases of policy are critically important and in both phases the policymakers had to take into account not only the probable American internal reaction to the Cuban problem but also the likely (external) reaction by the Soviet Union and among America's friends and allies (particularly the Latin members of the Organization of American States). If the American people did not agree that the Soviet move was "deliberately provocative" and could not "be accepted," difficulties would accumulate fast since the President, then and there, was proposing to commit the nation to a course of action whose outcome or result could be estimated but not guaranteed. If America's allies in the OAS failed to back the United States, there would also be serious difficulties. And, ultimately, so much depended on the Soviet reaction. We can see that the internal (i.e., domestic) and external (i.e., world state system) considerations could not ultimately be addressed separately in phase 1 (design).

Then the modalities in phase 2, the methods of implementation for the operation, would have an important effect, too. By stationing a line of intercepting U. S. destroyers some distance in front of the Soviet freighters with their deadly cargo of new missiles, time would be granted to the Soviets to think before reacting to the American challenge. A blockade, here called a "quarantine" since a blockade raised questions of international law, represented a tactic, a step in commitment that was quite different from a threat to bomb Soviet installations after some specific deadline had passed. A blockade was also a gambit in which the members of the OAS could cooperate with their ships. Tactically, the blockade made for an avoidable or postponable confrontation, for the Soviet ships could always slow down or stop. That is what actually happened. Later, the Soviet ships turned back. The American people and the Congress and the OAS stood solidly behind Kennedy all the way: judging that his analysis of the problem was correct and his response appropriate.

There is one further lesson in this example, to which we return in this chapter when we consider the nature of the state system to which policy must be addressed. That lesson is simple: once policy is decided in a crisis a process is set in motion that no single nation controls. In a crisis it is as though the players were on stage reciting their opening speeches but the rest of the play is not yet written and there is no playwright in position to assure the players or the audience that the third act will end with some satisfactory result.

The foreign policy of any single nation, therefore, is *designed* to achieve certain goals. There is no assurance in an uncertain world that the policy will actually achieve the purposes for which it is made. Policymakers, peering out at the world outside their frontiers must make judgments as to what will succeed and what, if attempted, will not. But if these things are attempted they may still fail, because the policymakers have misjudged the external universe or environment to which that policy is directed. Or the policy may fail because the policymakers have misjudged the mood, the values, and the views of their people whom they represent in office and whose power is needed to support them and sustain the policies they create. If foreign policy wears two faces, one directed inward, the other outward, it is the policymaker who must reconcile these faces.

1.

There Are Many Policymakers

As Part Two of this book makes amply clear, a policymaker is no inert barometer on which the pressures from outside or inside register themselves. The policymaker has views and prejudices, as well as ideas about what will work and what will not, about what is desirable and what is not. This is certainly and obviously true of any President, whether it is Carter warning about violations of human rights abroad or Reagan alarmed about Communist inroads in the Caribbean basin. It is also true of the bureaucrats who make the "machinery" of government work and who often, in the process of refining or amplifying the policy, alter it as well. The alteration may be carried to the point where a Henry Kissinger complains that his main problem with arms-control policy was not with the Soviets but with other Americans in the United States bureaucracy.

When we turn to the Congress the image of the barometer registering pressures is perhaps more appropriate in explaining the internal "face." A congressman, with a mere two-year term in office, cannot survive politically by repeatedly departing from the views, prejudices, and wishes of his electorate. But even the congressman's reactions and role should not be thought of too simply. Remember that he or she gets elected to Congress in the first place because he or she is "representative"—representative of the mainstream views of the leaders of the congressional district whose self-assumed task it is to pass the word that "Congressman Billy" is or is not doing a fine job in Washington. Senators, with six-year terms, may have a greater degree of independence, but the principle is the same.

So it would be wrong at the outset to think of President, bureaucrat, congressmen, and electorate as closed boxes on a flow chart who have no idea what anyone else in any other box feels or thinks or fears about foreign policy questions. They share a common national background because they all are Americans and that fact of nationality assures that they also share many important assumptions about the world outside their borders and what would be good or bad for America.

There are many policymakers and they share a basic national frame of reference.

2.

Consensus versus Debate: Successive Periods of Policy

Yet the fact that all the policymakers are cast in the same American mold does not preclude a separation between the government (the administration in office) and the people at large. We saw that happen in Lyndon Johnson's term as President during 1965 to 1968 when he pushed stubbornly ahead with the Vietnam War despite growing public skepticism about the war's utility or its morality or about its prospects. We saw that happen again in Richard Nixon's term in office when the growing shadow of Watergate separated him and the American people. And when President Reagan convened and addressed a special joint session of Congress in April 1983 to argue for support for his program on Central America—a matter on which public indifference was pronounced—he was trying to head off a similar split. Since a President may initiate policies that the American people will not ultimately endorse, such possibility of separation is always implicit in the American political process. But it is likely to happen, so far as foreign policy in particular is concerned, only when that policy is clearly not successful and a reappraisal is necessary. Where the inertia of the bureaucratic process (carrying the same policy forward) or the reluctance of an administration to confess a mistake (ensuring persistence despite growing doubts) conspires against change, the American public, growing restive, may force a reappraisal. The public will exert pressures on congressmen who substantially share the same doubts. The long debate in the United States between 1935 and 1939 over neutrality legislation, illustrates this. Similarly, between 1945 and 1949 a new debate focused on Soviet actions and behavior, and the Tet offensive in 1968 triggered a debate over containment that led to the liquidation of the Vietnam War in 1973. (We examine these debates in detail in later chapters.)

Such debates pit opposing views about the problem faced, of where and when to be involved and where and when not to be, against one another. These debates eventually result in victory for one concept over another.

As these three examples imply, times of debate reflecting disarray or doubt are by no means common, but we live in one such time now—ever since the end of the Vietnam War. That is why, in this book, we so often use the Vietnam War as a watershed, speaking about before and after Vietnam. The United States is currently in a period, after three decades of agreement, when the earlier consensus over policy has broken down and a new consensus has not yet been found and agreed. It is an argument with different dimensions but its two main focuses are on how global and vigorous a world role to play, and how to deal with the Soviets.

Partly that consensus broke down because the American policy was proving counterproductive (i.e., Vietnam in particular was obviously of questionable utility in advancing the interests of the United States, at least in the way the war was being carried on if not also in principle). Partly that consensus broke down because what was done in the name of the American people in Vietnam was morally abhorrent or unsatisfactory to growing numbers of U.S. citizens.

Such *periods of dissension* are of great interest intellectually even if they are very troublesome for those who hold office and must cope. Such periods alternate with *periods of consensus* whose hallmark is that "everybody knows" what the problem is and what ought to be done about it. Even when consensus reigns, we do not literally mean that everyone is agreed on the policy followed. What we mean is that any minority views are ineffective politically in swaying the leadership to alter course or even seriously consider doing so. In Part Three of this book we trace the history of the foreign policy of the United States from George Washington's time to the Vietnam War, especially from this point of view of the forming, maintenance, and dissolution of successive consensus views on how to deal with the world outside the American homeland. We shall see that, in periods of consensus, foreign policy, to use an income tax analogy, is designed by short form. It is as though there were agreed code words causing conditioned responses. Use code words, such as "unprovoked, premeditated Communist aggression," and "everybody knows" what to do about it. The preliminary analysis of the problem faced becomes telescoped intellectually while the focus of attention shifts away from phase 1, away from what is worth doing. ("Everybody" already knows what that is.) Instead, attention centers on phase 2, on how best to do it. When consensus reigns, attention shifts from *design* to *implementation*. When dissension reigns, the argument is over appropriate *design*.

3.

Reconciling Foreign Policy Goals: The Priority of Security

We have said that foreign policy is designed to preserve the Republic—its values, way of life, material prosperity, and above all its security. So policy must meet and pass a series of difficult tests. It must command popular support, as we have just illustrated. It must be realistic in coping with the exterior environment outside U.S. frontiers. And it must reconcile the divergent demands placed upon it by the very range and spread of its goals. It is by no means self-evident, even if an American popular consensus prevails on what is to be attempted, and even if those goals are each reasonably realistic, that the goals themselves will prove compatible. What assures material prosperity does not automatically provide security, or vice versa.

The Reagan administration, convinced in 1982 and 1983 that the signing or ratification of the new Law of the Sea Convention, although it assured immediate rights of transit of straits to U.S. Navy vessels (an important consideration), would ultimately subject American deepsea mining companies to rules to which the United States did not necessarily agree and could not veto (thereby infringing national sovereignty), decided to remain aloof from the treaty. This Reagan decision reflected the administration view that the United States could still continue to insist upon maritime transit rights on the basis of customary international law, whereas to sign or ratify the treaty would ensure one goal at the expense of another.

When such goal conflicts arise, the argument is rarely settled at the expense of security. That is to say, although there are many goals, not all of which are easily compatible, there is also *a hierarchy of goals,* with national security preeminent and leading the list.

Many people find the idea that security is the preeminent goal very uncongenial. They would like to deny it; they would like to change it. Yet the truth of its preeminence is difficult to deny, whether we like it or not. In 1984 the argument over the national budget, and whether to cut domestic programs or raise defense spending, did not turn on whether defense had a lesser *priority.* What was questioned was whether an MX system was worth buying, whether the United States had enough missiles, whether Americans were or were not "vulnerable" because of the increased accuracy of heavier Soviet weapons. No voices were raised in Congress asserting that defense was a second priority item; except perhaps in the limited and tactical sense that it might be argued that the strength of the nation rested in the first instance on sound fiscal procedures fundamental to being able to purchase an adequate defense.

4.

The Implications of Security's Preeminence

But if the preeminence of security in the list of concerns of the American people is a fact, certain consequences also logically follow. Policy is not in the first instance directed toward improving conditions of life throughout Planet Earth.

This inescapable conclusion is, as we said, uncongenial to many people. They point out that pollution knows no national bounds; like fallout, it is carried across frontiers by the winds. Or they point out that the problem the world confronts in feeding a constantly and even rapidly expanding population is probably not solvable through the actions of the nations most directly concerned. They point to the effects of international trade and finance, to the futility of "beggarmy-neighbor" policies through high tariffs or competitive and recurrent currency devaluations. They point to multinational corporations who have to do business in many countries. They argue that "peace is indivisible" (although the world at any one time is the scene of a number of separate wars).

In one form or another all of these arguments address the futility of a really narrow and shortsighted national policy that assumes that one area of the world can isolate itself from the difficulties of the rest. Most of these arguments are correct. The world from a technological point of view is shrinking. National boundaries do not deter pollution from abroad; the world probably cannot endure a situation indefinitely in which large numbers of foreign people are condemned to starve to death. (Nor are the American people in the least indifferent to their cries, both in terms of public policies on surplus foods and in terms of many private charities such as Foster Parents or Save the Children Federation.)

But to argue that security necessarily takes priority is not the same as saying that a single nation can hope to draw its frontiers up around it and shelter itself from the miseries and dangers outside. We are arguing only that the priorities of American policy cannot be understood by beginning with worldwide problems such as pollution or hunger. For better or worse, American security is the first concern of the United States and pollution, hunger, and the rest follow later down the list. Even the Roman Catholic bishops of the American church, in their letter on arms control in 1983, considered security issues as its focus, not arguing that it was wrong to defend oneself but arguing that the use of nuclear weapons in that defense would be morally wrong.

Some Americans refuse to accept the priority of security, arguing that the United States has a wrong sense of what counts. They would go beyond the bishops' letter to argue that money spent on missiles ought to be spent instead on schools and welfare or health. (A certain number of tax protesters in the United States regularly deduct the "defense percentage" before paying their taxes.) Some of those who dispute the funds going to defense are moved by a vague sentimentalism based on a sense of guilt that the American nation enjoys so high a standard of living. They point out that nations like the United States consume more than their "share" of the world's goods and they cry out for "justice" and "equity" in "dividing" the world's material resources. They too want their problems approached from some assumed universal point of view, as though the peoples of the world were agreed on what is just or equitable.

These are not unworthy concerns. But we have used quotation marks for "justice" and "equity" in order to underline the point that there are assumptions being made behind statements like "a proper share" of resources. Who is to decide what is fair? The United Nations, perhaps? Do the nations there assembled convey the image of impartiality? And what *is* fairness? Is the issue really one of fairness? If the great industrial output of nations such as the United States came to a halt because foreign materials were no longer used, there would be great dismay around a world which depends on and consumes that production. Japanese production depends almost exclusively upon imports and Japanese exports would cease if these imports first stopped.

Different nations make different contributions to world affairs, some for good, some for evil, some for better, some for worse. Some nations have contributed more than their share of war. Some have contributed more than their share of techniques to improve agricultural production. There are no international control devices that can authoritatively allocate roles and goals to the nation-states of the world. Multinational corporations (MNCs) cannot fill that role, even if they were sufficiently altruistic, for when the chips are down they are under state control. The United Nations cannot fulfill that role for it is a forum of nations that expresses their weaknesses along with their strengths.

The United States is not unique in setting national goals from its own (parochial) perspective. States are the implementors of policy and they simply do not take "moon views" of problems, aloof and impartial. What they do when they look out on pollution or hunger or war is decide in the first instance how it affects their own people. States may and sometimes do adopt very enlightened policies that will bring benefits on a much wider scale than only narrowly and directly to their own people. Persistent Swedish aid to underdeveloped nations is a case in point. Or they may (less often) try to preserve their own prosperity while others starve. The *variety* of state behavior in policy is one of the most obvious features of the international system.

It is well and good and a useful thing to point out the serious problems confronting all of mankind today—including the possibility of nuclear annihilation. It is misleading and mischievous to arouse hopes that, in a world where each state decides its own foreign policy, an avowedly universal problem will necessarily command an effective multilateral response. Policy is designed by states. Policy design results in the choice by states of national interests to pursue. Security will always bulk high or first on that list of *national interests*.

5.

The Role of National Interests

The term *national interests* recurs throughout this book. Although it is indispensable, this term can be confusing. What, beyond telling us that states act in their own interest as they see it and not in the interest of mankind as a whole, does the term national interest signify?

Earlier, in Chapter 1, we linked it loosely to "goals" and to the middle step of policy, to *content*. This raises a first difficulty, for how can the same term mean such apparently different things? To make matters worse, everyday we hear all sorts of contradictory things being advocated as "in our national interest." For years, those people for and against the diplomatic recognition of Communist China each labeled its view as in the national interest. Again, fierce arguments were heard in 1983 as to whether the national interest would be better served by a "made-in-America" parts content requirement for Japanese automobiles sold in America, or by continued free trade. This raises a second difficulty, for how can opposite courses of action both be in the national interest?

Taking the second difficulty first, what has to be understood from the outset is that when such opposing arguments are being advanced they are set forth as *claims on policy*. They are arguments that occur in phase 1, during policy design. Advocates are saying that it will be better for the American nation if tariffs were raised (lowered), recognition extended (denied). They mean that the benefits that will subsequently result from doing what they advocate will be greater than from some other course of action. Or perhaps they will even argue that their proposition, if accepted, will result in a positive value while their opponents' proposition will have only negative effects.

Their advocacy or claim does not prove that their argument has merit or that things will indeed work out the way they project. That is for the future (phase 2) to show. Unfortunately, however, the decision has to be made before the results can be observed. The choice between conflicting or alternative claims has to be made in the present, in the here and now. So policy is designed by states that choose between "interests" whose future value or advantage may be conjectural.

Not all claims on policy (i.e., items described as being "in the national interest") are matters of controversy. Sometimes it is quite obvious what is or is not in the national interest. There was never any real doubt, for example, through the whole period in the Carter administration during which the Iranians held American diplomatic personnel captive, that the United States could *not* buy the Iranians off by turning over the ailing Shah to them. There was much argument about the earlier question of whether the Shah should have been admitted to the United States for medical treatment in the first place, but little argument that he should be taken from his sick bed and used as ransom. The idea was simply incompatible with prevailing American values.

By contrast, the serious problems in making policy choices by resolving the opposed claims one way or the other occur where there are no strong national values at stake or where the future effect of present choice is not self-evident or agreed. For example, at the end of World War II, within the United States there was a lively debate over whether the Soviet Union could be "trusted" or not, whether it wanted peace or world hegemony, whether it felt threatened and needed reassurance, or instead was looking for opportunities for expansion. Obviously, which claim was correct, and what was in the "national interest" of the United States in dealing with the Soviet Union, could not be established apart from deciding, at least for the time being, how the objects of the policy—the Soviets—were to be categorized. (Again, the analysis of the problem had to precede a choice of what course of action to pursue, and how.)

A second illustration may help to drive home the point. During the Vietnam War, as the decade of the 1970s began, the argument in the United States was intense over the question of whether or not that war, and "winning" it, was or was not consistent with the national interests of the United States. To augment troops or withdraw troops are inconsistent actions and in this case also opposed courses of action, but that is how the issue was finally posed. Either choice might in the abstract have enhanced or undermined the future of the nation (i.e., served its national interests). Which claim, and therefore which choice, was correct?

To design or formulate a policy some official or organ of government must decide between these conflicting or alternative claims. *The claims chosen will form the content of the policy.* The alternatives, rejected or "shelved" at least for the moment, may find favor at a later time, especially if the expectations behind the choice between the alternatives are not realized as time goes on. In Chapter 4 we come back to this point and introduce the term *counterbalancing interests* for alternatives whose choice or rejection has important effects on the enmity confronted from other states.

If we do not use the term *national interests* to describe foreign policy choice making, we shall shortly find ourselves needing to invent a new vocabulary to cover the same thing—and one further away from actual usage.

Returning now to the first difficulty (that the term can mean apparently different things) let us take concrete examples to show why interests as policy content also inevitably imply goals. A choice to establish diplomatic relations with Communist China is not only a specific decision needing implementation; it also implies a new sense of direction, toward more friendly relations, and thus the choice not only establishes a particular content for policy but also implies the reason for the decision. Reciprocal tariff agreements, similarly, not only lower tariffs; they imply a wish for increased trade. A NATO treaty is not only a specific defense link; it implies what it is designed to achieve, a better defense against possible Soviet aggression. Thus the choices made articulate the goals sought and vice-versa.

Thus, to sum up, we can speak properly of national interests as claims on policy before some choice between alternatives is made. Or we can speak of those national interests that, included now in the policy, form the policy's content and imply (if not state) the goals or objectives of policy; interests first as claims, or interests later as content. As we use the term *national interests* from now on we shall specify which is meant if the meaning is not otherwise obvious.

National interests will hardly be selected, or, if selected, retained as policy, when they are clearly incompatible with national values. By definition, through surviving the political process of debate, they must represent national values. There is therefore no implication of cynical or unworthy or dishonorable purposes connected with the term national interests. The term may sound "selfish" or introverted, but that is merely the reflection of the fact that, as we insisted previously, policies are made by states and represent national (rather than universal) perspectives, however broad or narrow these may be.

Decision Making, Bureaucracies, and Rationality:
Some Distinctions

Although a public debate over policy may be aired over television and in the press, once the alternatives for choice become clear, at some point actual decisions have to be made by officials in government. The President will personally make the key decisions; the rest will be made by the bureaucracy, presumably acting under presidential guidance. How the American bureaucracy handles this decision process is considered in detail in Part Two of this book.

Analysts of that decision process are by no means agreed on exactly how it occurs, exactly how the bureaucracy makes choices. For example, some studies of bureaucracy, using computer-type language, stress that decisions are "outputs" of organizations made up of individuals with divergent interests to protect within the government, or with individual political "nests" to feather. Bureaucracies are described as "programmed" to produce certain results. (The implication is that if you know who produced the "output," you know logically what that "output" will be.) An obvious illustration is a defense budget too small to accommodate the desires of all the services, or a missile system that gives a strategic role to one service but denies it to another. Decisions and choices that emerge from such a context supposedly reflect the balance of power or influence within the bureaucratic organization rather than a thoughtful and adequate response to the problem faced by the nation.

There is truth in this suggestion, but one must be careful not to take it too far. It would be more exact to say that it is only natural that any part of a bureaucracy thinks first of the contribution *it* can make to the solution of a problem. These bureaucrats would be delighted to be called upon to make the chief contribution, thus proving their value. Additionally, it is only natural that any part of a bureaucracy prefers solutions to problems which do not require it to cease functioning. But it is surely farfetched to stretch this effect to argue that a portion of the bureaucracy will insist on having its way to the acknowledged harm of the nation. And, after all, since foreign policy content normally results from conflicting claims, there is no reason why bureaucrats should be expected to refrain from the contest or feel bashful in advancing the view that their part of the bureaucracy has the ideal solution. They are part of the public, too.

It is surely farfetched, on the other hand, if studies of bureaucracy promote the image that bureaucratic "outputs" represent merely the resolving of divergent views within the organizational apparatus—a resolution that may accidentally relate effectively to the problem faced, or not at all. Or promote the idea that individuals heading a given department of government will advocate views chosen primarily to be consistent with the special interests of their organization, even when their country faces a crisis. A look at a real crisis shows how far that conclusion would be from the truth. In the Cuban missile crisis it was the Secretary of Defense who initially tended to dismiss the Soviet move as requiring any drastic military response. During the Vietnam War, it was Secretary of Defense Laird who pushed for faster troop withdrawals while his own generals had the exact opposite view. (Laird, a former congressman, adept at judging public opinions and loyal to his President, knew that the public would not stand for foot dragging.) It would be far more accurate to say that bureaucratic special interests tend to show up when the gravity of an issue is less—and vice-versa.

Perhaps the greatest utility of these bureaucratic studies is to remind us that a state, designing a foreign policy, is not a single ("unitary") actor but a collective, with many, many people having a part in the decision and often with great arguments with one another. But that thought, in turn, has to be carefully qualified in another respect.

Policy may be *designed* by blending many voices into a single tune. Once designed, however, everyone inside the government who has a hand in its *implementation* is expected to sing the same notes. An ambassador is *not* expected to convey the policy of his government to a foreign regime and then add that he thinks it is tommyrot! (It has happened, though.) A general is not expected to refuse to attack an enemy because he thinks we should fight some other enemy instead! There may be rear-guard bureaucratic skirmishes over "what the decision really intends," and there may be calculated leaks after a decision is made, but, strictly speaking, none of this is forgivable if detected. The principle that applies has changed at this point. President Truman during the Korean War (1950–1953) relieved General MacArthur for these reasons, as President Carter later reprimanded General Singlaub, for publicly differing with him over the troop withdrawal issue in Korea. None of this means that covert opposition to policy ceases or that bureaucratic interests magically align in the postdecision phase. The significant difference between design and implementation is simply this: in designing policy many voices must and should be heard; in implementing policy, a nation in principle can only go with one policy at a time. In principle, it *is* then a "unitary actor," speaking with one voice, voting *either* yes *or* no in the United Nations, and so on. We shall see in Part Two how embarrassing it is when the machinery sometimes does not mesh and a government inadvertently speaks with two voices.[1]

Still other studies of decision making focus on whether policy decisions are "rational." This point is trickier than it looks, and we must be clear about its implications before we can profitably proceed. Those who raise this question of rationality really raise it to deal with another: whether decisions are or are not *predictable*.

Defenders of the predictability thesis tend to describe sets of decision makers, scattered about the world, as though they were observing identical problems and reacting to them according to an implied set of rules. The figure of speech that pops up when this is discussed is usually a chess game. In a chess game each piece has a clear, established value and "weight," with its own agreed functions and defined moves. Players of a chess game, by definition, necessarily are playing the same game, with identical features about which no arguments are possible regardless of *who* sits at the chess board and makes the move and regardless of *where* that decision maker sits at the chess board. A Chinese, a Russian, and an American all have to play chess the same way.

The chess image is a very powerful one, with great appeal, because the problems that nations face do have a great deal in common. Nations do to a large extent have to react in fairly standardized ways to standardized problems. Problems of diplomatic immunity in foreign countries, although an issue faced by the United States in the hostage case in Iran very acutely, are problems any nation may have to react to, for all nations send diplomats abroad. Problems of policy for the use of the high seas are problems all users of the seas must confront, for example, to determine who has jurisdiction over crime on the broad oceans. These problems and issues do not vary greatly depending on the identity of the nation facing the problem. Later in this chapter, when we turn our attention to *the system of nation-states,* we shall see much common behavior, much common reaction to common problems.

It would be helpful to a nation if it could, by a process of analysis, be sure that a second or third nation would arrive at identical dispassionate conclusions from identical evidence about an identical common problem (such as chess moves). The ability to count on this happening would, for example, eliminate unwanted wars arising from mishandled crisis.[2] Then also, all possessors of nuclear stockpiles would reciprocally and effectively be deterred once some dispassionate, scientifically established ratios of weapons were produced for both sides. No mistakes would occur by human error, by one state thinking it could utilize some imagined vulnerability of the other. Cuban missile crises would lose their terror.

---

[1]We shall also come across Henry Kissinger using "back channels" to negotiate outside regular channels—a procedure that sometimes *did* have the U.S. government speaking with contradictory voices.

[2]Careful studies have shown that, in a crisis, decisionmakers in two opposed nations may have dramatically different notions of what is at stake. See Richard N. Lebow, *Between Peace and War: The Nature of International Crisis* (Baltimore: Johns Hopkins University Press, 1981).

Unfortunately, this kind of precise prediction is impossible for a number of reasons that become clear in Chapter 4. Neither does our preceding discussion of the decision-making process offer any great encouragement that decisions are reliably predictable in the case of any individual nation-state and with particular attention to the United States.

The decision-making process described in this chapter is not rational if rational means predictable *content*. But it is certainly "rational" if by that word we mean that it follows a logical and predictable sequence. Nor is the process we have described rational if by that word we mean "unemotional." Emotions can and do play a part in decision making. Personality has some effect. But the process *is* entirely rational in the very important sense that an observer can see the causal connections between the analysis of the problem made by the decision makers and the actions they then embark on. The process is rational (and predictable) in the sense that *some* analysis of the problem, however perfunctory, must precede the choice of policy, and in the sense that phase 1, for instance, *has* to come before phase 2, simply because of the logic of the thing. Almost anyone with any real experience with the American government knows that this description is accurate.

We must not confuse the issue by assuming that states can only be acting rationally if they act in identical ways. Nations vary from each other in important respects, and not only in their size or power or the tragedy or fortune of their historical experiences. It is the particular nature of those national historical experiences and the divergent circumstances in which nations find themselves that, as we shall see, account for much of the fact that nations (and their decision makers) often perceive their neighbors and problems in very different ways.

Nations are often unable to define a "common" problem in identical terms. What the United States in 1950 saw as China's gratuitous aid to North Korean aggresssion through sending in "volunteer" troops was just as clearly perceived by the Chinese leaders as a minimum prudential role in the light of American hostility to Chinese communism. When the United States and China subsequently sat down at Panmunjom in Korea to negotiate an armistice and began to discuss whether Chinese prisoners of war should be sent home forcibly, the issue was only the same issue to both parties in a surface sense. To the United States, the issue might have been one of freedom for the prisoners to live the life they perferred, going to Taiwan if they liked. To the Chinese Communists, the issue distinctly involved national humiliation, since large numbers of Chinese did not wish to go home.

Individual state behavior is, then, extraordinarily various and in many ways very unpredictable. States vary immensely in the role they visualize as worth playing in world affairs. It would be quite false to assume that great nations always play large roles on the world stage or that "nations with limited interests," as small powers were called in the days of the Congress of Vienna (1815), confine themselves to these modest roles. States also, over time, vary considerably in how tempted they are to pursue the will-of-the-wisp of national grandeur. Neither are we able to predict kinds of actions from forms of government or geographical location or size of gross national product (GNP), or from the ideology espoused. Nations do not pursue uniform or consistently predictable roles in dealing with problems, nor do they always define those problems in some uniform manner.

7.

The Nature of the State System and Its Implications

We now shift our field of vision, to change lenses and look at the international system of states to which foreign policy is addressed. So far we have stressed the "internal" side of policy, how it represents a set of choices that form the content of policy, how the individuals in government, sharing national values, attempt to tidy the conflicting claims on policy into decisions that can

The Intellectual Framework and the Cultural Background

be implemented. We have also stressed how a consensus, once formed, may endure a long time; how prolonged debates occur only when the stereotyped responses to policy issues begin to lose their validity and the problem has to be thought through afresh by an American people with certain values and assumptions about themselves and the world in which they live; and how those assumptions may or may not diverge from external reality. It is time now to speculate on the nature of the external reality to which policy is addressed. What is the nature of the state system and what implications flow from that nature, whether Americans think so or not?

When we change to a wide-angle lens and stand off far enough from any individual state deciding policy, what we see as meaningful changes rather radically. Individuality and individual idiosyncracies vanish. We are no longer looking at the American political process or at President Reagan. Rather than observing the different styles, fears, and hopes of individual nations, we are looking at a whole system of states.

When we look at behavior using such a sample of one hundred sixty sovereign nation-states (the world today), quite definite uniformities begin to emerge. These uniformities are like insurance statistics that do not say who specifically will die, but assert that a certain number will. Applying the notion to nation-states, we do not know who may embark on expansion at whose expense, or who will create an incident. But we do know from experience that every year some will, somewhere. Using a wide-angle, world-view lens, *certain uniformities in behavior emerge clearly,* regardless of the state concerned, its past history, or its role preferences.

These behavioral uniformities arise from the very nature of the world state system. Consider the implications of the fact of *sovereignty* itself. Here we immediately confront a paradox. Sovereign denotes "independent." A sovereign state is one that rules itself, using whatever governmental form "it" wishes. To use a legal definition, such a state has a population, a government, and a specific territory over which it has full and exclusive control. Stated in reverse, no sovereign state has *any* direct control over the actions of a people (or government) of another sovereign state. And therein lies the paradox, for the price of full control over "one's own affairs" is no control over the affair of others. But that means that others are free to take actions which may severely interfere with *your* affairs. The paradox is that Americans can decide most of the conditions under which American life will be lived, but the Russians have the decision over whether that life in a real sense will be terminated by a nuclear attack, and vice versa.

Here we encounter the fundamental clue, from a systems perspective, as to why security is such a priority item in policy. It is the basic organizational anarchy of the state system that ensures early and continued preoccupation by every state with the security problem. Every nation-state can with certainty only count on its own military resources to ensure its survival in the event it is attacked. The nation-state may take out additional "insurance" through a system of alliances, and it may devote additional material and personnel assets to preparedness. But nothing it can do can free it with any assurance from the danger of attack so long as there are other states in a position to make policy independently. In a world of over one hundred sixty sovereign nation-states, each designing foreign policy according to its own preferences, no nation is truly secure. Each lives in the shadow of the possible use of power against it and every state knows that certain other states may attack it, if opportunity presents. Each state therefore has a *power problem.* Where a state is located will have much to do with detailing its specific power problem (determining which states are potential enemies). But every nation, as the implicit price of existence in the system, acquires anxieties arising from the possible policies of certain other states.

To stress the ubiquitous nature of the power problem at the outset is, again, not to downplay the importance of other considerations, such as access to food, raw materials, and energy resources. But no action by any state in the system will likely or for long be conducted in forgetfulness of that overarching fact of international life, the power problem. The unwary may not survive.

The most fundamental and inescapable role of a foreign policy is, therefore, "to preserve the Republic" in the light of what military men call "the threat," and which we have called the power problem.

The term *power,* which is used a great deal in political science, has no universally agreed meaning. We have already used it as a measure of threat. In a foreign policy-international affairs context, power is also applied as a measure of the *resources available* to a state for national purposes. It is a measure of strengths (and weaknesses), stemming from the economic and material base of an economy, the population to man a nation's factories or planes or tanks, its dependence (or lack) on critical raw materials imported from abroad, the up-to-dateness of its scientific and technological progress, and any number of such considerations. But national power, which is explained further in Chapter 5, is emphatically not composed of a series of strengths all translatable as effective pressures on opponents to bend their will to one's own. Under some circumstances, the elements described can be converted into effective pressures on another nation. Under conditions of mobilization and the deliberate use of military power, the case becomes more clear-cut. But even then "power" includes elements of weakness as well as strength. Thus the role of power, seen as "backing" to national policy, is not standardized but situational. Much of its effect, short at least of use of overt force, will depend on the opponent's assessment of the problem. Consequently, although power definitely affects outcomes, *how* it does so is invariably situational. It is impossible to say that a given amount of a certain kind of national power can be depended upon to deliver certain kinds of results in all situations (or even in all similar situations). And it is just at that point that the temptation arises to dismiss power from one's calculations about policy—which is always a grave mistake. It is important to recognize that a particular form of national strength may have highly effective results in certain cases. Power, consequently, is important to our analysis throughout this book in two connected senses: as a measure of threat (the power problem) and as a measure of relative strength and weakness (which the military call "net assessment").

8. The Systems Effects of Policy Choices

We next consider the systems effects of the foreign policy process itself. While within a nation opposing claims are weighed and some accepted as policy content, the same process is occurring in all the states. Each state will find its own policy more or less congenial to others. Stated another way, any two states having dealings with one another will evolve a set of relations, because of their policies, which can be ranked or scaled in terms of a friendship-hostility spectrum. The national interests chosen by two states will produce a pattern of common and opposed relations between them. If the policymakers on either side perceive a need to improve the bilateral relationship, they can substitute other national interests in their policy that then reduce the mutual friction. Since the system is multilateral, the two states, if they become convinced of mutual and irreconcilable friction, may resort instead to reducing hostility with third states in order to reduce the risks stemming from the bilateral antagonism.

It would be more exact to assume that bilateral antagonisms are tempered or influenced from the very beginning by multilateral considerations. A nation such as Russia, with China as an immediate neighbor, usually cannot confine its attention to the United States as though China's existence and Chinese policy did not count. But for most of three decades after the Communists took power in Beijing, Sino-American relations were so poor that that in effect happened. To express the general point another way, every nation is "surrounded" by other nations, and every nation, turning to another at its "front," has to bear in mind that it also has flanks and a back to protect. One of the reasons why war is in many ways an unpredictable gamble is because third parties may take part, for or against. From this, again, a systems observation arises: states generally conduct themselves with a great deal of prudence, and bilateral relations are influenced by their multilateral setting. States do not normally behave with brashness or in the assumption that risks can clearly and accurately be tabulated.

One reason why military establishments the world around are prone to "worst case" analyses is the danger of risks exceeding calculations. In a system in which every independent nation, because it is sovereign and independent, disposes of its own resources for or against others as it wishes, and has armed forces at its disposal, the dangers are obvious. Less obvious is whether help by others in such circumstances will be forthcoming. What a nation can count on, in most cases, is that other nations who are equally or substantially threatened by the same menace have a realistic basis and incentive for cooperation. By sharing the same power problem these nations have a strong incentive to work together and minimize friction with each other. These thoughts lead us back to the earlier point about flanks and rear. Nations confronted by strong antagonisms or serious threats have good reason to attempt to maximize their potential enemies' concern about flanks and rear as well as improve their own "frontal" defenses. If they are small, confronted by aggressive great powers, and cast in the role of potential victims, they have only the much looser assurance of ultimate support by powers if there are other powers who feel threatened as the map changes, as the status quo collapses on a wider scale.

Such assurance of support is "looser" in the sense that each nation threatened has to make its own decision to act or not to act. Critical support for someone in particular may not be forthcoming in time. But the assurance of support is far less "loose" in a systems sense, as a general proposition. Note how many would-be conquerors have appeared in the history of the world: from Ghengis Khan to Napoleon and Hitler, to give only an incomplete list. Not one has ever succeeded in unifying the world by force, primarily because enough power has eventually been concentrated against the aggressor by those who are the intended victims to frustrate the aggressor's designs. The recurrence of such phenomena is the central theme of what is discussed under the very ambiguous phrase, "the balance of power." It refers essentially to the tendency in the system for nations confronted with a disturbed set of power relations to seek to restore equilibrium.

So, depending on the lens we use for viewing, we can look at a single nation such as the United States weighing whether it should enter World War I or World War II, with important consequences for itself and particular other nations (such as Great Britain, which, in 1940, stood alone against Hitler). Or, using a systems lens, we can note how nations do tend in such circumstances to act to restore a disturbed balance. There is no assurance that a given nation will act, that a particular victim is saved, or even that the system will restore equilibrium. We can only say on the last point that it has happened so far for three thousand years.

We are now in a better position to appreciate why certain uniformities of behavior emerge in the system as well as why every nation, in designing a foreign policy, has a first concern with its potential vulnerability to attack.

Much of what we have said so far could be summed up with the remark that individual nations face common problems and common dangers, that their reactions to these problems and dangers are in a general sense predictable (i.e., they will raise and equip armies, they will frequently enter into security arrangements, and so on) but that their specific reactions in every case demonstrate much individual variation. Everyone must eat but not the same diet. Before dismissing that statement as nothing but the obvious, reflect on its real meaning: that certain characteristics of the foreign policy process are "givens" and cannot be altered by the wishes or preferences of any single state, no matter how large and powerful. But, on the other hand, each state is free to make its own decisions as it sees fit. The decision itself is free; it is the results of the decision that can become costly.

This is why national *perception* of the problem confronted is so critical. A nation can perceive hostility where none is really intended. It may misjudge the degree of common policy objectives on the part of other states, and it may mistake the priorities of other nations.

Because decisions are "free," decisionmakers can react to the world outside their doors with a very realistic understanding or on the basis of quite false ideas. It is their option. A lot depends then on how a nation's decision makers think the system is operating. For example, if Nation A believes that a common ideology, shared by two or more nations, *ensures* that they share overall common goals with each other, friends to friends and enemies to enemies, and if Nation A also perceives that ideology to be antagonistic, it will assume that it is confronted by an enemy in each case where that ideology prevails. It may also assume that all such states operate under common direction. Whether there is in this sense "a Communist bloc," or whether it ever existed in this sense, if a nation such as the United States *believes* that there is one, and if it believes that if one of the members of the bloc commits an aggression all are involved, the United States will react convinced that it faces a collective challenge.

When we look at the outbreak of the Korean War, in Chapter 3, we shall see that President Truman thought exactly that. He saw the North Korean attack as a probe by the whole bloc, which was searching for an effective point of attack in a worldwide struggle. The United States also was substantially convinced that the Communist attack might have been specifically designed to lure the United States into involvement in Asia as a means of lowering its resistance to attack in Europe. In addition, President Truman was firmly convinced that one successful aggression encouraged others to do the same, so that stopping a particular assault in Korea had ultimately much wider and quite predictable ramifications.

On the other hand, as we now know,[3] Stalin, who Truman assumed ordered the North Korean attack as part of a concerted and orchestrated Communist plot, saw that attack as urged on him by the North Korean leaders in much more limited terms, and as much more an ad hoc adventure. Stalin could hardly have assumed that the U.S. reaction would likely take the form it did—unless he had paid more heed to the kinds of theories held by American policymakers about "the march of aggression" and "collective security" and the "need for a world ruled by law, not by force."

Whereas a correct weighing of external threat is thus vital to a nation's present well-being and future existence, such national judgments will not be taken against universally agreed standards. They will not necessarily be correct judgments, either, even in a factual sense. Moreover, the reactions they provoke may be quite unexpected since those reactions reflect other peoples' foreign ways of perceiving cause and effect. But whether antagonism growing bilaterally is deliberate or accidental, whether resting on sound factual grounds or simply the result of divergent ways of assessing cause and effect, it will ripple out to have effects on third parties. And the generalized behavior of all of those third parties, which make up the rules and tendencies in the system, will equally certainly have a good deal to do with whether the policies followed by the antagonists bring them profit or distress.

9.

Qualifications to the Argument

Several qualifications are needed to the thrust of the argument so far.

First, we have pointed to the basic and overriding concern of any state with security and its power problem. This argument is correct but it should not be taken to mean that national secu-

---

[3]Khrushchev, in his memoirs, says: "I must stress that the war wasn't Stalin's idea but Kim Il-sung's. Kim [of North Korea] was the initiator. Stalin, of course, didn't try to dissuade him." Strobe Talbott, ed. and trans., *Khrushchev Remembers* (Boston: Little, Brown, 1979), p. 368.

rity concerns are always monopolizing policy attention. There are certainly other important aspects to world affairs and foreign policy: energy, resources, trade, finances, food, pollution, to name a few. Such problems take up much attention, as we shall see in later chapters. At times, especially when the danger of war appears small, these problems may be pushed to front stage center and preoccupy the nations. When the international tension level is low it is even possible to forget the fundamentally precarious basis on which peace and security rest. It may then be argued—hazardously—that war and the threat of war is no longer a meaningful approach to international problems. Conversely, in the shadow of approaching conflict, as in the 1930s, attention can shrink to an understandable but too narrow focus on national power, especially military power. To express the same point another way, because the *tension level* in the system varies (i.e., the expectation of conflict), and war seems at one time remote and at another time imminent or probable, the power-security equation seems likewise of varying importance. In fact, however, it remains always a vital part of any foreign policy.

Two further qualifications need to be made about this initial approach, the first of which is that world affairs do not consist exclusively of the relations of sovereign states. Private parties also play a part, for example, nongovernmental actors such as multinational corporations. Yet the role which such private groups play must be kept in perspective. MNCs are described sometimes as though they were always superinfluences on the affairs of states, completely overshadowing the independence of weaker or smaller developing nations with their great assets. The picture portrayed is similar to the old United Fruit Company dealing with any small Central American state circa the 1930s. In that portrayal or comparison lies some truth. But behind the giant, U.S.-run United Fruit Company in the first decades of the twentieth century stood the U.S. Marine Corps and presidents such as Teddy Roosevelt freely deployed the marines into a number of Central American states as they saw fit. In that day, presidents saw nothing wrong with using troops for economic purposes, even assisting private business as such. Today, such freewheeling use of troops is much harder to justify. President Reagan took great care in 1983, when ordering U.S. troops into Grenada, to stress the potential hostage issue. And governments tend to utilize business concerns for national purposes, when and if they do, in subtler ways.

It *is* governments that usually control businesses if they feel it necessary—not the other way around. Consider OPEC (Organization of Petroleum Exporting Countries) from this perspective, linking it to the MNCs. These militarily weak OPEC nations have had little difficulty forcing large MNCs to do their bidding. Such huge congolomerations as Exxon and Shell have yielded to the regulations of these OPEC nations.[4]

Or consider what happened in the natural gas pipeline controversy of 1982, when Western Europe cooperated with the Soviets in the extension of Soviet gas via the pipeline into Western Europe while the Reagan administration opposed. In the sequel, the United States prevented the U.S.-based Dresser Corporation from exporting parts for the pipeline but Dresser-France, a French subsidiary, was successfully pressured by the French government to honor the supply contracts. In both cases the corporations had to bow to the wishes of the governments, even to the extent of following different policies for two parts of the same corporation.

Perhaps the most significant aspect of MNCs, when all is weighed, is that they are the outgrowth of industrial development in large powers and, therefore, under certain circumstances can be an extension of the nation's power to exert influence abroad. In any event, the examples show how important it is not to arrive at too far-reaching conclusions that MNCs have made the power of national governments obsolete.

[4]One of the authors still retains a vivid memory of talking with the executive vice-president of one of America's largest corporations. He had just landed in the company jet and was fresh from Washington. He was both angry and dejected as, for a half hour, he detailed exactly how the corporation could *not* have its views accepted by the administration.

The last qualification is that everything said, although we think it is true, acquires slightly different practical implications as technology changes. For example, take the Teddy Roosevelt and OPEC illustrations. In a nuclear age, nations will likely think twice before deploying troops as they did in the 1930s. In an economically interdependent world, nations are less confident of extreme courses of action since so many variables need to be taken into account. Prices of raw materials fluctuate drastically, as do the comparative values of national currencies. Technological breakthroughs transform little-needed materials into avidly sought supplies—such as uranium, or later, cobalt. Whereas nations in the seventeenth century were hardly interested in military adventures in distant places, it is now practical to devastate a nation from positions a continent apart.

The definition of a power problem, the scope of a foreign policy, will reflect these ongoing technological changes. So a power-security focus is not the whole of policy. It is simply that, being most fundamental, it is a first (and last) consideration and runs like a red thread through the fabric of everything attempted or contemplated.

10.

Summing Up

This chapter has shown how much must be taken into account when foreign policy is discussed. Two major themes run throughout this chapter.

First, we contrasted the "internal" and "external" spheres to which policy must be addressed. On the internal side we must consider the national values of a nation such as the United States, the assumptions with which the American people collectively approach the making of policy, how they determine their goals and how they see their alternatives. On the external side we must understand the international environment to which U.S. policy is addressed, how the international system functions and therefore how policy's results are influenced by what happens there.

By looking at both sides we come to appreciate why both uniformities and divergencies occur in state behavior. Among the uniformities forced on states by the nature of the system is the priority given to the power problem; the stark necessity for making allowance for unpredictable reactions, especially on the part of third parties who may unexpectedly intervene; the pressing requirement to shape bilateral relations in the light of the existence of third parties; the urgent need to weigh any particular bilateral antagonisms in the light of the total antagonism encountered; and the continuing need to review policy for possible changes in content in order to restrict those antagonisms to acceptable limits. Nor can any state afford to ignore the implications for itself and for others of serious changes in the status quo. If these are not universal problems inducing fairly common behavior patterns regardless of the nation involved, they come close to it. It is to such familiar systems-induced behavior that we refer when we speak of the "rules" of the system. We do not mean anything literally binding, but we do mean customary behavior.

The divergencies in national behavior are equally significant. We start with the fact of different national historical experiences and cultural emphases, different value systems, and different expectations about life. Caught in a common problem, nations who are opponents may therefore visualize the dimensions of the problem very differently. They will make assumptions about motives that diverge. They will anticipate different results from the same actions and events, and they will have different ideas about how the system functions. They will contrast in their ambitions, and their decision-making arrangements will vary as will the power they can muster in pursuit of goals. In addition, their people may not be of a single mind or predominantly agreed over what to do about the outside world. The nation may at times be virtually paralyzed by dissension or preoccupied with internal affairs—even civil war. The range of variations in individual state approaches to foreign policy problems, despite the common behavior patterns, is very great. The problems nations face are fairly much the same by category, but their special solutions to problems differ a great deal by unit.

Second, as a major emphasis, we have focused attention on the two phases of policy, design and implementation, and the role of policy debate in phase 1. The purpose of debate is to decide between opposing claims that something is or is not in the national interest. It is a debate in which bureaucracies take part, from a perhaps more concerned and informed point of view; it takes place in public, by means of the media and congressional debate as well as in the local civic club. It occurs constantly over smaller issues, but it is most significant and persistent when a foreign policy consensus has broken down and a new one is needed.

The debate may focus initially on past mistakes, but it will soon turn to future opportunities, looking at present decisions or choices weighed against their presumed future effects. Such debates, while nominally focused on deciding the present content of policy, necessarily reflect expectations about where a policy will lead. Consequently, foreign policy debates (except over minor issues) inevitably *involve conceptual arguments:* about what causes what in the system, and about how a particular course of action will or will not work out. From these observations we can see why we began this chapter speaking about the *design* of policy.

We stress the importance of recognizing that there are two sequential phases to policy—for planning will be followed by doing. If the policy *design* (the concept or plan conceived in phase 1) proves faulty, the policy is not likely to work out very well when *implemented* (phase 2). If the people will not continue to back what is then attempted, or the path chosen is not feasible because it encounters too much opposition in the system, the policy will have to be rethought. A new design will lead to a new implementation—and, at some later point, also to a new cycle of design and implementation.

Almost everything of importance in the rest of this book reflects one of these two major themes. We are concerned with either the American approach to foreign policy as compared to the general problems and behavior in the system or with the design as compared to the implementation of policy.

In Chapters 2 and 3, to which we now turn, we explore the first of these major themes: how the American national experience in many important respects departed from the common experience of nations, giving rise to a distinctly American conceptual approach to foreign policy problems.

The Unique
American Experience

From the very beginning our people have markedly combined practical capacity for affairs with power of devotion to an ideal. The lack of either quality would have rendered the possession of the other of small value.

Theodore Roosevelt
Speech in Philadelphia,
November 22, 1902

Compared to the experience of any other contemporary great power, the total "mix" of American environmental conditions was highly unusual, if not unique. This highly unusual background experience furnishes important clues as to why the United States has conducted its foreign policy as it has. Let us begin with the effects of geographic isolation upon American security problems.

1.
The Effects of Geographic Isolation

The fact of *where* the American nation is physically located has had a profound and continuing effect, for the United States is the sole great power in the world without great power neighbors nearby. True, Soviet and American frontiers are close in the northern Pacific, but this particular proximity has very limited effects.

This freedom from close neighbors possessing sufficiently significant military power to challenge the United States was not true in America's initial decades (when the British, for instance, held Canada), but it was an accomplished fact before the time of the Civil War. Even in those early decades, logistics difficulties greatly limited the effective threat. For the rest of its history until recent times the American people gave little thought to dangers arising close to home. When the United States, beginning in 1898 (the Spanish-American War), first sent large forces overseas, it did not have to worry about exposing the continental land mass to attack by doing so. It was the same in World War I when millions of troops were sent to Europe, and again in World War II. Even after World War II, only at the time of the Korean War (1950–1953) did the U.S. Joint Chiefs of Staff worry about depleting the home-based reserve, and that was because American total forces at that point were small, following the World War II demobilization. The sending of 500,000 troops to Vietnam in the late 1960s (plus an estimated 250,000 support echelons at sea or nearby) was not weighed against an enhanced danger of attack from adjacent continental neighbors of the United States. But this kind of freedom, geopolitically induced by the absence of large military forces directly across American frontiers, is a very unusual experience. What other great power could say the same (or think in the same fashion about its vulnerability?)

In a nuclear missile age, this factor of distance does not imply the same degree of absolute security benefits as it frequently has in the past; but even today the effect of America's distance from other powers confers distinct benefits lacking for the rest. Without entering fully into the complex questions of what course a major nuclear war might follow and whether a missile exchange would both begin and end a war without the former need for an ensuing conventional occupation of the loser's territory, it is still clear that a grievously wounded America—unwilling to surrender—would be difficult to subdue merely because of the distance factor. By contrast, if Germany were devastated by nuclear attack, it would be more vulnerable to final defeat, merely because of the proximity of Soviet forces confronted by no formidable geographic obstacles. In a Soviet-American conflict, if the seas were highways of invasion, they also would offer secure hiding places for the harassment of those who would invade. Assuming an American defensive role, it would be a task of enormous dimensions for the Soviet Union (even with its expanding naval capability) to bring its power to bear upon the American continental land mass other than via the air.

If a missile exchange might be both the beginning and the end of a war, distance may no longer play a significant role—but such an assumption is very doubtful. If we assume both an initial rough parity in power and a fair degree of mutual destruction in such a war, the inability of the one nation to rouse itself to parry a further attack may be roughly counterbalanced by the inability of the attacker to readily mount its assault. This factor would be of greatest importance if the would-be attacker must proceed by sea. Although relatively formidable land forces might still proceed under fairly primitive logistical conditions to invade against a weaker opponent, an overseas movement is infinitely more sophisticated and technically complicated. The United States, which has twice deployed great forces across the Atlantic, has done so each time with friendly bases on the European end of the operation.[1] In its deployments in the Pacific to theaters of large-scale land fighting the United States has consistently enjoyed friendly bases at the far end—as in Korea and South Vietnam.[2]

Distance—especially sea distance—still seems likely to confer some degree of security from physical invasion. It is by no means obvious that nations would consciously choose to fight a missile war predicated upon the assumption that a nuclear exchange would be the sole significant military activity. To do so might well repeat Hitler's great error after Dunkirk, when he assumed that no invasion of the United Kingdom would be necessary to force the British to acknowledge defeat. Distance cannot confer immunity from physical destruction. It may well confer some immunity from the likelihood of a decision to engage in a nuclear exchange that cannot easily be followed up by a more conventional assault—if such an assault proves necessary to achieve a surrender. Such political-psychological imponderables, directly related to the effects of distance, are today still quite uncertain parts of the total strategic equation.

---

[1] In the North African invasion a part of the U.S. forces was deployed directly from the continental United States. The very comparison of this case with the use of Britain as an advance base in the Normandy invasion illustrates the point. North Africa was a comparatively small operation; the Normandy assault was on a grand scale.

[2] The Pacific island war (1942–1945) by its seeming exception proves the point, for these island invasions were relatively small scale and against enemy land forces that could not be substantially reinforced.

We have deliberately begun with one extreme of this question, where the security advantages today of distance may be most validly questioned. At the opposite extreme is the effect of distance in the prenuclear age, especially before the first great military-technological revolution, which began around 1855.

A comparison of two early wars, in both of which America fought England, is instructive: the American Revolution and the War of 1812. In the first the fighting extended over eight years. The British occupied Boston, New York, Charleston, and other American seaports virtually at will, launching land forces from these bases in marches calculated to destroy rebel resistance. At first glance the British military operations in the American Revolution seem to show the reverse of the point made that distance conferred a certain immunity on America. However, these British forces were not only small in size; they were consistently augmented by American Loyalist volunteers and drew much logistical support from native American sources. Without the indispensable Loyalist support of food, shelter and supplies—let alone men—the British war effort in America would have been much more difficult. The Battle of King's Mountain, to cite one illustration, was largely an American battle on both sides, even though British troops also participated. If all the Americans there had fought together against the British, the British would have been overwhelmed.

King's Mountain may not be typical, but consider the small size of the British forces. When the American Revolution reached a climax in 1781, with the crucial surrender of General Cornwallis to Washington, only 7,000 British troops were involved. This is an eloquent testimonial to the conditions of the day. Even though the French contribution to Cornwallis's defeat—in the form of a naval blockade and troops on shore—was an essential element in the American victory, the reason that France's assistance was so crucial was not because of Britain's ability to muster overwhelming military power in the American colonies three thousand miles from London, but because the Loyalist support in the colonies gave the British such important local resources.

Contrast this first American civil war, the American Revolution, with the course of the War of 1812. In the second war most of the important actions were at sea. The land campaign initiated on the American side involved a little-remembered attack against Ontario, Canada, which soon was frustrated by British forces. For their part, the British landed in Chesapeake Bay, marched on Washington, and burned the White House. That completed, they left to bombard Fort McHenry—an event that inspired Francis Scott key to write "The Star Spangled Banner," but which did the British no good. Landing later at New Orleans, they assaulted Jackson's troops, who from behind their cotton bales decimated the orderly British ranks—ironically with the war already over, although the news had not yet reached the United States. Altogether, even allowing for British distractions with the situation in Europe (then at a pause in the Napoleonic Wars), the War of 1812 illustrates the military futility of the British attempt to exercise power under hostile circumstances and at a distance. This time, since the Loyalists had left the colonies or were largely reconciled to an independent America, the British efforts were fruitless—with one very important exception, the thinly populated areas near Canada (the Northwest Territories and eastern Maine.) Frustration of the British in the populated areas was accomplished by a weak American army, this time unsupported by any French forces.

In this early period the military story elsewhere is again and again the same. Large-scale movement of forces to battle at distant points was frustrated by mere distance and its ensuing complications. Napoleon's campaign in Egypt and Syria (1798–1799) with 35,000 men proves the same point. The difficulties that defeated him there were sanitary and logistical, not military. Nor was Clive's conquest of India the accomplishment of large British forces but the result of Indian princes fighting one another to British benefit. The average army in Frederick the Great's time was 47,000 men; in Napoleon's wars the average size was still only 84,000 (but not for overseas campaigns). British victory over China in the First Opium War (1841–1842) was accomplished by the seizure of several coastal ports and was a testimony to China's weakness rather than to British war-making power far from home. Even in 1860, when the technological innovations in warfare were beginning, the British and French expedition that seized Beijing numbered only 17,000 troops. Today we chiefly remember the Crimean War (which broke out in 1854), for the charge of the Light Brigade, the introduction of systematic battle area hospital care, and the fact that the British and French transported large combat forces by sea and maintained them relatively effectively at a significant distance from home. The last two points broke new ground.

Distance in the first half of the nineteenth century in itself conferred substantial military security. Of all the nations who were subsequently to play a great role upon the international stage, the United States was most fortunately endowed by geography in this respect. It was not only far removed physically from the great powers, but as it grew in strength after the initial decades of independence, it also became the only significant power in all this part of the world. The corollary of Europe's limited ability to bring the United States readily to heel via military coercion became America's own ultimate ability to dominate affairs in the Americas. There were two real but opposite dangers in the first years: one was that Europe's powers might fight each other and draw America into the conflict, as had happened often enough. More remote was the possibility that they might unite to divide up the United States. In later decades, after technological progress made it possible to exert real force at a distance, the great powers of Europe and Asia were no longer sufficiently secure in their home areas to entertain thoughts of adventures in the Americas. Throughout, as America's power expanded, distance from danger was an important ingredient in the ability to act as an ultimately decisive, untouched, and reserve force on the world balance of power. This was the role the United States played successfully in two world wars.

Today, the linkage between distance and security is no longer so simple; yet the fact that the United States remains the sole great power in the world without cheek-by-jowl, indigenous great power neighbors continues to permit it a wider range of strategic choice on foreign policy problems—as we shall see in later chapters.

2.

The Effects of Historical Experience

Next for consideration is the fact of *when* the United States came to exist as a sovereign nation. The character of international relations in America's formative years was very significant in its effects. The United States is the sole great power in the world whose historical experience occurred so predominantly in the rather unusual—even peculiar—century between 1815 and 1914. Compare other powers in this respect. Whether one takes Prussia-Germany, England, France, Russia, China, Japan, or India, each had lengthy experience before 1815—as America did not.

The people of the United States did not begin their corporate background with the coming into force of the American Constitution (June 1788), or with George Washington's inauguration as first President (April 30, 1789). The American Revolution had already taught important lessons in diplomacy, on the significance of allies, on the need to pay prudent heed to how the affairs of nations greater in power could affect the destiny of the United States. These lessons were reflected in Washington's Farewell Address, in Jefferson's advice, and in the general outlook of the Founding Fathers. Even earlier, in colonial days, lessons were learned when the colonies were outposts of the British Empire and took limited part in the American branch wars of Europe's powers. Yet since colonial concern at that time was primarily oriented toward the twofold problem of hostile Indians and white foes, these lessons were not quite so meaningful as those from the Revolution.

The early period of American national existence has frequently and correctly been characterized as one of realism. A relatively weak United States had of necessity to brush aside illusion, to see the problems candidly. Very revealing is the action of Jefferson in acquiring the Louisiana Territory (April 30, 1803), doubling the area of the United States fourteen years to the day after Washington was sworn in as President. Despite Jefferson's principles about a modest and proper role for the federal government, the opportunity was too good to be missed. The rollcall of continental expansion continued with its notable landmarks: the area west of Lake Superior (1818), Florida from Spain (1819), the Maine boundary and Lake of the Woods area (1842), Texas (1845), Oregon (1846), California and the Mexican cession (1848), the Gadsden Purchase (1853); all in all a remarkable expansion from coast to coast in just sixty-four years. This expansion had the additional merit of removing foreign troops from those territories.

U.S. foreign policy was concentrated essentially on things close to home and well understood. The first of a number of foreign policy "doctrines" was announced by President Monroe (December 2, 1823) after the British foreign secretary, Canning, had suggested a joint warning against European intervention in the Western Hemisphere to restore Spain's possessions. The Monroe Doctrine, although rather grandiose for the small American nation if one forgets the large British fleet ready to enforce it by closing the exits from European waters, was nonetheless realistic in addressing a pressing American concern: to expand continentally while seeking freedom from effective European power bases in the Americas. Accordingly, the Monroe Doctrine addressed both ends of the problem, claiming a special role for the United States and denying it for Europe's powers. Although Britain's continued presence in Canada was unwelcome, the effects of that presence were counterbalanced by Britain's de facto underwriting of the basic Monroe policy and the fledgling development in Canada of separatist sentiments.

Gradually, one by one, European possessions in the New World began to disappear. Once literally encircled by European powers (1789), the United States broke out of its "containment." Only during the American Civil War (1861–1865) was new European military power introduced into the Western Hemisphere on any significant scale; Maximilian tried to conquer Mexico with the backing of French troops. When American unity was restored (1865), the French efforts were quickly abandoned, for it was clear that the United States both would and could expel the French expeditionary force.

The American Civil War represented a watershed in U.S. affairs and circumstances in several significant ways. First, as we shall see, the European balance of power changed at this time, although not to America's disadvantage. Second, the great military-technological revolution was begun, making it possible for large-scale military efforts, such as Napoleon III's Mexican adventure, to be carried out if the balance of power permitted—which fortunately for the United States was *not* the case. Third, the virtual insulation of the United States from military danger led to a lessened concern with and involvement in world affairs. Since Europe now largely remained aloof from New World commitments, U.S. foreign policy in turn became of modest dimensions and lessened importance. The very success of the Monroe Doctrine policy and continental acquisition turned much of America's attention and energies to domestic tasks: settlement of the West and industrialization in the East. It is not that American foreign policy became less realistic but rather that Americans attempted less because they felt less need. It was simpler than in Washington's day, less daring, and involved fewer risks. Outside the Americas it amounted to the proposition: Stay out of others' affairs.

The distinct change in American politics and foreign policy even before Lincoln's time can be seen in terms of the background experience deemed desirable in a President. In the early history of the United States, being Secretary of State was considered an important way station on the road to the presidency. Such active experience in foreign affairs, at first considered fairly essential for presidential prospects, later became relatively unimportant. The trend is quite clear from Table 1.

TABLE 1 Secretaries of State Who Became President

SECRETARY OF STATE	YEARS	UNDER PRESIDENT	BECAME PRESIDENT
Thomas Jefferson	1790–93	Washington	1801–09
James Madison	1801–09	Jefferson	1809–17
James Monroe	1811–14	Madison	1817–25
John Q. Adams	1817–25	Monroe	1825–29
Martin Van Buren	1829–31	A. Jackson	1837–41
James Buchanan	1845–49	Polk	1857–61

The tendency, and its gradual falling off, is unmistakable. Moreover, after the American Civil War the reverse was uniformly true: No Secretary of State *ever* became President.[3] One might argue that the increased complexity of the American political process after the early decades brought with it a further division of political labor, but it still seems significant that by Lincoln's time the presidential aspirant was cultivating other fields than foreign affairs. William H. Seward, our twenty-fourth Secretary of State, a member of Lincoln's cabinet, once remarked on how American senior diplomats and ambassadors were chosen: "Sir, some persons are sent abroad because they are needed abroad, and some are sent because they are not wanted at home."[4] Even allowing for the temptation to utter a *bon mot* for its own sake, it is unquestionably true that by Seward's day it was not Benjamin Franklin or John Jay who was representing this country abroad. The practice of choosing ambassadors primarily for their party fidelity and financial generosity, so notorious until well into the twentieth century, had already taken root. Able American diplomats were few and far between in major posts abroad until the 1930s or 1940s. It is difficult to avoid concluding that relatively small importance was attached to the job from the standpoint of the national security. If we tackle the point from another direction, the conclusion is reinforced. Consider how few important international relations or great power crises involved the United States outside the Caribbean area between the Civil War and World War I, aside from the Spanish-American War and the annexation of Hawaii.

Although U. S. foreign policy was realistic enough in this period in confining itself largely to the affairs of this hemisphere, the inevitable corollary was that Americans paid less attention to what was occurring elsewhere. Gradually, judgments of affairs abroad became somewhat abstract—it was all very far away and involved America only slightly. The exciting things were happening right here at home.

The unparalleled security of the United States was sustained by Britain's role and the balance of power after technological change no longer conferred almost automatic security, and was naturally reflected in the size and condition of U.S. armed forces. No one today can look at the figures for the size of the United States Army (regular forces) between 1817 and 1902 without a sense of awe or shock. They are given in Table 2.

In the last decade before World War I the picture does not change significantly. At a time when European standing armies were on the order of 600,000 (in 1914), the U.S. Army was 97,760. The utter neglect in which the U.S. Navy existed for most of the same period tells the

---

[3]One might argue that the reason that the Secretary of State tended to become President is that in early decades he was also the chief party organizer. One is still left with the observation that the chief party organizer was given the foreign affairs seat in the cabinet. Unless one wants to argue that the Secretary of State had so little to do in foreign affairs that this title was essentially a sinecure to support him in his party work, this combination can only mean that it had the significance here attributed to it.

[4]Quoted by Roy R. Rubottom, Jr., Assistant Secretary of State for Inter-American Affairs, Department of State *Bulletin*, May 12, 1958.

TABLE 2 Regular Army Strength: 1817–1901

1817	8,220	1847	21,686	1874	30,520
1820	8,942	1850	10,763	1877	24,854
1823	5,949	1853	10,417	1880	26,509
1826	5,809	1856	15,562	1883	25,547
1829	6,169	1859	16,435	1886	26,254
1832	6,102	1862	25,480	1889	27,544
1835	7,151	1865	22,310	1892	26,900
1838	8,653	1868	50,916	1895	27,172
1841	11,169	1871	28,953	1898	47,867
1844	8,573	1872	29,214	1901	81,586

SOURCES: House of Representatives, 57th Congress, 2nd Session, Volume 97, Document 446; Heitman, Francis B., *Historical Register and Dictionary of the United States Army* (Washington: Government Printing Office, 1903), p. 626.

same story. Although improvement came sooner in the sea forces, the long gap between the era of the U.S.S. *Constitution* (end of the eighteenth century) and the renewed forces of the Spanish-American War (end of the nineteenth) is an eloquent reminder of long decades when there was no fleet at all but only a gunboat navy, parceled out for porkbarrel purposes to the various naval yards which dotted the Eastern seaboard of the United States.

Indeed, the instruments of national power, from the nonexistent career diplomatic service to the virtually nonexistent armed forces (especially in view of the persistent use of the army for fighting Indians in the Far West) eloquently testify to a nation not actively concerned for its national security. The picture is completed if we add the fact that neither army nor navy was organized for effective fighting against foreign foes, either at the level of fleets and armies or in the Washington organization, and that no attention was paid at all to intelligence operations. The departments of the government dealing with the armed forces had no general staff or other such devices and were organized exclusively for routine administrative purposes.

These highly nominal gestures in the field of national security were not unrealistic; in all of this period the United States was confronted with no formidable military or foreign affairs threat. It is time to consider why not.

3.

The Hundred Years' Peace (1815–1914)

In all of modern history since the nation-state system emerged, there has never been so prolonged a period of general peace as between 1815 and 1914. Before 1815 Europe's great powers were repeatedly embroiled in conflict. The savage Thirty Years's War (1618–1648) is one illustration; the Peace of Westphalia that ended it did not usher in a period of prolonged general peace. New fighting broke out over the Lowlands; the Treaties of Nimwegen (1678–1679) were unable to bring a permanent settlement. The War of the League of Augsburg (1688–1697) was the third war in a series that began in 1667. Close after it came the War of the Spanish Succession (1701–1714). The Treaties of Utrecht (1713) and Rastadt and Baden (1714) did not entirely end the widespread conflict. Next came the War of the Austrian Succession (1740–1748) and the Seven Years' War (1756–1763). Relative peace was then restored until the French Revolution (1789) was followed by a series of European wars lasting to 1815.

After 1815 the picture was substantially, even radically, different. From 1815 until 1848, while there were a number of revolutions in Europe, there were no great power wars at all—not even bilateral ones. In this curious era the monarchs of Europe were far too busy attempting to stay on their thrones and retain their heads (literally) on their shoulders to afford the luxury of war. Between 1848 and 1870 there was a series of limited wars, but these each involved only two or—at the most—three great powers. The six wars that occurred during this period, with the exception of the Crimean War, were concerned with Italian and German unification. Next, after 1871, came a period when wars between great powers again ceased. Of the six great powers in 1871 (Germany, Austria, Russia, France, Italy, and England), not one fought a war with another in Europe until the actual outbreak of World War I in 1914. This cessation of war is a highly remarkable fact.

Minor wars—especially colonial wars—continued to occur; but the great powers did not fight one another. The single exception was in Asia—the Russo-Japanese War (1904–1905), marking the emergence of Japan into great power status. Although sometimes bloody enough, the colonial wars did not bring the wholesale destruction that comes when two or more powers, each well armed and modernly equipped, fight.

In this perspective, the twentieth century, even taking into account only World War I and World War II, stands in great contrast. The second to fifth decades of the twentieth century, so far as great power conflicts go, resembles far more the period before 1815, with the important change that today's mechanization of warfare and harnessing of scientific knowledge to weapon improvements has resulted in a completely new magnitude of bloodshed in whatever conflicts occur.

The unusually peaceful hundred years between 1815 and 1914, with its lack of general war, was a great but unearned boon to the United States. Although Americans accepted it with little thought, what actually caused so long a period of peace?

We have indicated one important clue for the initial phase (1815–1848), when Europe's monarchs cooperated internationally to preserve their thrones domestically. After 1848, especially during the next phase involving Italian and German unification, how was general war avoided? Unifying these nations represented a far more fundamental alteration in the map of Europe than even the Napoleonic Wars produced.

Two answers may be advanced. On the philosophical level, the first is that the unification of these states was not contrary to the long-run historical tendencies of the age. Even though the creation of a united Italy and a united Germany radically altered the map of Europe, the process involved an amalgamation of states predisposed toward union. The effects were not directed outward in the form of designs on the territories of non-Italian and non-German states. As such the amalgamations could be tolerated. Of course, in the process, neighboring great powers such as France and Austria had to be persuaded (by force) to relinquish special claims and positions in these territories. That is why the unifications did involve (limited) war.

The second answer to why the wars were limited involves observing the principle used by Otto von Bismarck, then Chancellor of Prussia, and the prime mover in what happened. His essential technique was to proceed against one foe at a time, ensuring through clever and patient diplomacy that that foe for the moment had no military allies. When Bismarck fought Austria, Austria stood alone. And when he fought France, France in its turn was isolated.[5]

Once Germany was successfully unified, Bismarck focused his attention on maintaining a stable peace in Europe—because German unity, while now formally achieved, had to grow real roots. Since France was the prime dissatisfied great power in Europe, the one nation who was disposed to challenge the new status quo, Bismarck proceeded to use the same technique in peace that he had already used so well in war. He isolated his primary potential enemy by an intricate alliance system centering on Germany, with intimate ties to Austria and looser ties to Russia

[5]The detail of these maneuvers can be found in Frederick H. Hartmann, *The Relations of Nations*, 6th ed. (New York: Macmillan Publishing Company, 1983), pp. 327–328.

(France's most important potential ally). Since Austria-Hungary was at odds with Russia and the temptation was strong, given Germany's alliance with Austria, for Russia to seek an alliance with France, the result Bismarck attained was not the most likely if he had simply allowed the situation to drift.

Bismarck avoided the "natural" expectation by a clear but complicated policy. Even while allying with Austria, whose "natural" enemy was Russia, he refused to support any and all Austrian interests. He remained determined to serve certain Russian interests which the Russians could not achieve by a policy of treating Germany as an enemy. (Russia, for example, also feared and distrusted the British Empire.) Since Bismarck knew well that Germany had "counterbalancing interests" his concept was to protect Austria from Russian attack while "reinsuring" Russia against Austrian attack. He guaranteed Austria help if Russia attacked Austria, but guaranteed Russia his neutrality if Austria attacked Russia. This protection was what Russia needed if it was not to ally with France. Russia's desire for a French alliance was motivated solely by a need to feel secure against a combined Austro-German assault.

Bismarck, taking into account the entire range of interests and concerns of France's potential allies, thus utilized the counterbalancing interests implicit in the system for Germany's benefit. His goal was not alliance of all those other states *with* Germany, but to prevent their allying *against* Germany. If he had instead attempted as impressive an alliance group as possible, he would have driven other nations into France's arms as a counterweight to German power. Although Britain was not an integral part of Bismarck's elaborate network, the persistent and perennial friction between Britain and France (who were colonial rivals) banished any serious likelihood of an Anglo-French entente, provided Germany did not arouse British concern by challenging important British interests. A significant stabilization of Europe's relations was the result.

When Kaiser Wilhelm retired Bismarck (1890), this intricate system was dismantled. Wilhelm foolishly refused Russian offers to continue the Bismarckian arrangements. The consequence was that by 1894 Russia had made a firm military alliance with France. In building a large German Navy Wilhelm next aroused serious concern in Britain—so much so that by 1904 Britain felt it only prudent to agree with France to settle outstanding colonial rivalries. By 1907 the British had reached a similar understanding with Russia (with whom colonial antagonisms had previously kept relations tense). By 1914, after a series of crises, war came and Germany found itself fighting not only France but Britain and Russia as well.

Consider the meaning of all of this maneuvering to the United States, for it is what made possible the small military forces and the inadequate diplomatic and security organization maintained by America. While the United States was concerned with acquiring coast-to-coast continental territories (until 1853), the American policy benefited from two important circumstances: (1) the technological difficulties of Europe's mounting an effective expedition to the New World; (2) the determination of Great Britain to prevent any important alteration in the status quo in the Americas. After 1853, on the other hand, although the technological difficulties in European expeditions to the New World were rapidly overcome, the British policy remained substantially as before. The invasion of Mexico by French troops under Maximilian (1861–1867) revealed the importance of both of these effects. It showed that European troops could be sent and maintained, and that this deviation from British policy (for Britain had originally sent troops, too, to collect debts from Mexico) was a vital part of making such expeditions feasible.[6] In this later period a new circumstance was added that had not existed before 1853: the Germans appropriated control of the European balance of power. It was Bismarck's actions as much as American hostility that led Napoleon III to abandon the Mexican venture. After 1871, when

---

[6]Becoming belatedly aware of the unlimited aims of Napoleon III in Mexico, Britain soon terminated its intervention. Maximilian was subsequently deserted by Napoleon III because of Napoleon's need for troops at home.

Bismarck encouraged France to new imperialism overseas, the British barred the way across the Atlantic. As a consequence Africa and Asia became the theaters of Europe's new imperialism.

It is startling to note that in the thirty years after 1873, in this new era of colonial imperialism, England alone added more than three million square miles to its empire (all but one-half million in Africa) and that France took an additional four million square miles (mostly in Africa too). Between 1884 and 1890, Germany acquired nearly a million square miles in Africa plus scattered areas in the Pacific (including a large part of New Guinea). Italy took Eritrea, Italian Somaliland, and Libya in Africa; Belgium took the nearly million square miles of the Congo. Japan took Korea from China; and in 1898 Britain, Germany, Russia, and France forced spheres-of-interest concessions from China which, if they had endured, would have destroyed China's independent future.[7] Even Chinese customs money was collected under British supervision.

These tremendous overseas activities of the European powers are remarkable in that they essentially did *not* involve the Americas. Whereas German-maintained stability in the European balance between 1870 and 1890 permitted and encouraged imperialism abroad, the British prescribed the areas in which it would be allowed. After 1890 and until 1914, as the European theater became increasingly tense, the European powers became steadily more inclined to concentrate their attention close to home. In addition, with so much of the colonial world now appropriated, significant gains began to be possible only at each other's expense: namely, one colonial power would have to take what another had already claimed.

4.

U.S. Policy (1815–1914)

Viewing American foreign policy during this same period, one is struck by the paucity of developments of much significance, especially if one excludes such strictly inter-American conflicts as the Mexican War (1846–1848). There was the Clayton-Bulwer Treaty (1850) with Great Britain over Central America, in which Britain retained ambitions bound up with a future interoceanic canal. There was the isolated incident of Commodore Perry's visit to Japan (1854), which was designed primarily to open up commercial relations with Japan. There was the Ostend Manifesto (1854), in which the American ministers to England, France, and Spain proclaimed that the United States would be justified in acquiring Cuba by force, if Spain refused to sell. There was the purchase of Alaska from Russia (1867). There was the Treaty of Washington (1871), by which the United States and Great Britain agreed to settle peacefully all outstanding issues. In 1889 came the first Pan-American Conference, followed by the Bering Sea Seal Fisheries Treaty with Great Britain (1892). The Venezuelan boundary dispute erupted between the U.S. and Britain (1895), but serious trouble was avoided. In 1898 Hawaii was annexed and the Spanish-American War broke out. The acquisition of part of Samoa came in 1899, and the Philippine insurrection (1899–1902). The Open Door Note (1899) asked for equal U.S. commercial access to China. In 1901 came the Hay-Pauncefote Treaty with Great Britain, which abrogated the Clayton-Bulwer Treaty and permitted U.S. construction of a Central American Canal, and which was soon followed by U.S. intervention in the Panama revolt against Colombia. The Alaska boundary question was settled (1903). In 1904 came the Roosevelt corollary to the Monroe Doctrine, justifying intervention in Santo Domingo. Other Caribbean issues arose between 1909 and 1912 and in 1914 new trouble came with Mexico.

When one considers that this listing is virtually a complete catalogue of important U.S.

---

[7]All of these "leases" were for ninety-nine years except for Russia's lease on the southern Liaotung Peninsula, which was for twenty-five years.

foreign involvements for two-thirds of a century, one is amazed from today's perspective at the modest dimensions of U.S. foreign affairs and the fairly complete absence of issues having no roots in the Americas. If one excludes issues connected with U.S. acquisitions of territories outside the Americas, there is almost nothing left. At a time when the political complexion of most of the world was being radically altered, American foreign policy, the Philippine involvement aside, was limited to issues in the immediate area and to minor overseas acquisitions.

A cataloguing of American military involvements is also revealing. After the War of 1812, United States troops did not fight the troops of a major power for over a hundred years. There were a number of minor military involvements such as the Undeclared War with France (1798–1800), the naval expedition against the Barbary Pirates (1801–1805), and a later expedition against Vera Cruz and pursuit of the Mexican bandit Pancho Villa (1916–1917) by General Pershing. Otherwise, the entire list of American wars during this whole time comprised two: the Mexican War (1846–1848) and the Spanish-American War (1898). Each of these wars was against a second-rate power, compared even to the then limited power of the United States. The United States won each war with comparative ease. Each, for that matter, could have been avoided if the United States had not chosen in favor of a larger sphere of interest and/or territorial expansion. The United States engaged in very little war, in a century distinguished by its world-wide great power peacefulness, and what little Americans chose to fight they won hands down. These experiences were to have distinct and important effects on subsequent American attitudes. Largely, the ability of the United States to "choose" its wars was intimately related both to the self-limits of American foreign policy and to the operation of the nineteenth-century balance of power, already described.

In 1917 when President Woodrow Wilson led the American nation into the "war to end all war," he was responding with perhaps pardonable naiveté to a very unusual hundred years' experience of general peace. World War I burst like a thunderclap on a psychologically unprepared world. Americans, even more than Europeans, had accustomed themselves with a certain smugness to the assumption that technological progress had overcome and made obsolete older "power politics." The mechanisms of statecraft were not understood; the significance was missed of the pre-Wilhelmian balance of power that had preserved the peace and the role of British seapower in underwriting American security. Little overt attention was paid by American officials (and even less by the American people) to how and why peace had been so long preserved. When American attention did finally focus on the recurrent crises that preoccupied the European great powers between 1905 and 1914, the reaction was essentially one of distaste and a spirit of thankfulness that America was above this sordid game. As crisis followed crisis without actual war, there was also a feeling that each would somehow be resolved—an expectation fulfilled until the aftermath of the assassination of Austrian Archduke Franz Ferdinand. The bottom fell out with sickening suddenness. Yet even then the whole truth of what lay ahead was not perceived. Europe's conscript armies mobilized with a pervasive air of enthusiasm—shortly to evaporate before the grim reality of trench warfare and the implacable machine gun.

When Wilson spoke of a "war to end all war," he meant putting an end to what he thought had caused World War I and of providing a new alternative. He variously described the cause of conflict as "Germanism" and "entangling alliances." In a speech in South Dakota (September 9, 1919), he declared: "Your choice is between the League of Nations and Germanism. I have told you what I mean by Germanism—taking care of yourselves, being armed and ready, having a chip on your shoulder, thinking of nothing but your own rights. . . ."[8] Speaking earlier to the U.S. Senate (January 22, 1917), he explained his remedy to avoid new war in different terms: "I am proposing that all nations henceforth avoid entangling alliances which would draw them into competition of power, catch them in a net of intrigue and selfish rivalry, and disturb their

[8]For text see *Addresses of President Wilson,* Senate Document No. 120, 66th Congress, 1st Session, pp. 83–88.

own affairs with influences intruded from without."[9] Instead Wilson wanted "a concert of power," a League of Nations.

The point is that Wilson (and the American people generally) became aware of balance-of-power alliances and their effects really only in the final phase of a balance that on the whole had worked well for a long time. In this last or declining phase of recurrent crises, the balance mechanism indeed came to look like entanglements permeated by "selfish rivalry." Such a judgment did not do justice to the role of the balance of power taken as a whole; Wilson's views help to explain the rather remarkable persistent antipathy with which American leaders for the ensuing three decades regarded the device of balance-of-power alliances. (Even the North Atlantic Pact in its early years was described by Americans not under the frank and accurate label of a balance-of-power alliance but under the euphemism of "regional collective security.")

Woodrow Wilson, presiding over the end of a century of American historical innocence, called himself an idealist. In many ways he was, particularly in his attempt to replace power politics with a new kind of international system. But at least in one sense he was a realist: he knew that the tried and true remedy of simple American abstinence from any important involvements in European affairs would no longer assure American security. At least one American leader (and there were others) had concluded by 1918 that the era of security without real effort that America enjoyed for so long was now gone. But the analysis of the cause-and-effect relationships that had brought on World War I left much to be desired. Later experiences affected American thinking on international affairs and will concern us at length in the chapter ahead. There can be little question, though, that the American experience between 1815 and 1914 was poor preparation for understanding the problems that lay ahead.

5.

The Effects of the Domestic Environment: From Immigration

The fact of *how* the American nation was formed, with cultural diversity interacting with unparalleled economic opportunity, had important effects. The United States is the sole great power in the world whose population came from across the seas by immigration and occupied a large, rich, and sparsely settled continent.

Many other nations have been settled in large measure by overseas immigration. Latin America, Australia, New Zealand, Canada, South Africa all come readily to mind. However, in few Latin American nations did the Europeans essentially displace or eliminate the natives. In most Latin American nations the opposite was true: intermarriage produced a new part-native, part-European culture, as in Brazil. At the opposite extreme, in South Africa, the Boers and their descendants drew a rigid color line; in later years they attempted a degree of physical separation the world today knows as *apartheid*. In Canada, in Australia, in New Zealand, the natives were relatively few in number and as in the United States were essentially displaced by the European immigrants; frequently they were placed on reservations or in areas isolated for their use. Neither in Australia, New Zealand, nor Canada were there simultaneously the rich abundance and enormous territorial areas that the American people came to control. Although large, Australia is comparatively poor, contrasted with the United States. New Zealand is comparatively rich like the United States but is much smaller in area. Canada's large size is even further exaggerated by the conventional Mercator map, and it has important sources of wealth but has a small population compared to the United States. Unlike Australia and New Zealand,

[9]*Congressional Record,* 64th Congress, 2nd Session, vol. 54, p. 1743.

Canada is the only one of these three nations that presently has a large non-British population (although Australia is now changing somewhat).[10]

If one surveys all the larger nations of the world it is difficult to find an exact parallel to the American mix in these respects: a large nation with a large population primarily originating overseas, which has duplicated the American experience of blending many people from many cultures into one nation enjoying vast economic resources and a very high standard of living. If, then, America's experience represents a unique blend of these factors, we ought reasonably to expect that their product will be a distinctive national flavor in approaching problems.

From the very beginning the American nation represented a cultural blending. New Sweden (Delaware) had been founded by the Swedish West India Company (1638). The people who settled it were not only Swedes but Finns. It was annexed (1655) by Peter Stuyvesant, governor of Dutch New Netherland (New York). New Netherland in turn became New York (1664) when a British expedition took control. These earlier events were to have later repetitions as parts of New France became the Northwest Territories of the United States, as the French of New Orleans and the Spanish of Florida, New Mexico, Texas, and California passed under the American flag. Even in the earlier period, Pennsylvania was largely settled by the Germans and Welsh, just as the Scots and Irish took over the Carolinas. As the area of the original thirteen colonies passed into British hands, a system of government familiar to Englishmen became the predominant political form. The largest cultural group in the infant United States was English. However, since these colonies possessed large non-English groups, the American people collectively were never simply English people overseas. The Scots and Irish were as un-English in outlook as any Dutchman, Swede, or German. Colonial population grew "from about 85,000 in 1670, to 360,000 in 1713. By 1754 it had quadrupled again to about 1,500,000. This increase owed much to heavy migration of non-English people—Irish and Scots, Germans, and French— favored by a liberal naturalization act of the British Parliament in 1740."[11]

Great waves of immigration continued to swell the numbers of the American people in the nineteenth century and into the twentieth these trends continued. To quote Morison: "During the decade of the 1820s, only 129,000 'alien passengers' entered the United States from foreign countries; in the 1830s the number swelled to 540,000, of whom 44 percent were Irish, 30 per cent German, and 15 per cent English; this figure was almost tripled for the 1840s, and rose to 2,814,554 for the 1850s. Roughly half of the immigrants from 1840 were Irish, with Germans a close second."[12] The census figures for the later decades of the nineteenth century for certain midwestern states show what this meant concretely as new settlers poured from Europe into that area. For example, the 1880 census figures for Minnesota show 72 per cent foreign born or with at least one foreign-born parent. Even California's figure was 60 per cent. The 1900 figures are 74.9 and 54.9 respectively.

It is not only that America from the beginning was culturally diverse, with important effects, as we shall soon see, on the character of American nationalism. What was also important was that the continental area into which these European millions poured was only lightly populated by Indians, who were relatively easily subdued or expelled. Not that life for the early pioneers on the Eastern seaboard was secure and unthreatened, but the threats were overcome. Symbolic of what was to come of this was the sale of Manhattan Island for $24 worth of beads and trinkets. An immensely rich land was there for the taking.

---

[10]In March 1966, Australian law was changed to permit some nonwhite immigration.

[11]Samuel Eliot Morison, *The Oxford History of the American People* (New York: Oxford University Press, 1965), p. 140.

[12]*Ibid.*, pp. 479–480. Compare against total populations of 9.6 million in 1820, 12.9 in 1830, 17 in 1840, 23.2 in 1850, and 31.5 in 1860. The first restrictive immigration act was the Johnson Act (1921), which set up quotas based on "national origins."

In the early colonies for a time economic constraints were in operation (e.g., the use of indentured servants on the great estates of the Hudson Valley); soon ended were systems of land tenure artificially limiting the acquisition of wealth by the many, despite their own willingness to work. "Go West, young man!" was advice being followed by droves of people long before Horace Greeley. This abundant and inexhaustible bounty of land stood in tremendous contrast with Europe's formal land tenure system, in which all was already owned; for those who reaped its bounty it was an entirely new psychological experience. Marx later dreamed of the destruction of property barriers, which he saw as the origin of classes, foreseeing the erection of a new society in which everyone could contribute according to his abilities and receive according to his needs. Something not far from the first part of that dream was a reality in the United States, even as Marx wrote. The hand of government had a light touch in this America, and taxes were few and far between. In Chapter 3 we look at how the effects of this experience profoundly influenced the American character, and how it imbued that character with an all-pervasive fundamental optimism. There we shall also see what other fundamental attitudes arose from the unusual historical experience we have already examined.

First, however, we must discuss the important effects that cultural diversity had on American nationalism and the American political process.

6.

The Effects of the Domestic Environment: On the American Political Process

In the United States people of many cultures worked side by side on free and abundant land, in an environment characterized from the beginning by a virtually classless society, in a setting in which (slaves apart, and even that only for a time) man was not subordinated into a permanently inferior position by the accident of birth. In such a land only certain kinds of political institutions were ultimately practical. Only certain kinds of political arrangements could be compatible with the nature of the new American nationalism, to undergird and reinforce it.

Consider the logical consequences of the great mixture of cultures in a largely unfenced, unformed land, in which many of the problems to be resolved had no traditional or customary answer. Captain John Smith's experiences in the founding of Jamestown (1607), the first permanent English colony in the Americas, set the pattern. Plagued by a scarcity of food and shelter in a physical environment that had yet to be mastered, and with an overabundance of "gentlemen" not accustomed to manual labor, Smith hit upon the well-remembered formula: "He who does not work, neither shall he eat"—a formula followed fairly faithfully ever since in the United States, even down to the present, when sons of well-to-do parents sometimes deliver newspapers for the "experience."

Two facts about this environment were fundamental: first, it involved strange new problems for which European ways contained no fully useful or transferable solutions; and, second, peoples from different European cultures had their own different preconceived solutions to problems. The effects of these two facts on the American character were lasting. Not so obvious were the effects that produced the new system of government, which permitted the United States to prosper.

If we consider the immediate prelude and aftermath of the Philadelphia Convention that produced the American Constitution (1787), we gain a first important insight. The federal Convention was called by the Congress of the Confederation "for the sole and express purpose of revising the Articles of Confederation" and exceeded its mandate, indeed set it aside, and instead produced a blueprint for a much different Federal Union. This document was filled with ingenious compromises. One of these permitted each former colony equality in the Senate, while retaining a separate population formula for the House (and even here slaves were counted on yet another compromise basis). The double break with European (especially English) tradition is apparent, for the dual chambers of the British Parliament had other origins and operated quite differently, then and later. Presidential elections constituted still another area for compromise. It was here that the complicated and indirect election by means of an Electoral College was born.

One could continue the illustrations, but the point is that the new American Constitution represented many adroit compromises for which European precedent and tradition offered little preparation. When this Constitution was offered for approval, a second significant development occurred: it was immediately amended (a stipulation that was made by a variety of the states when they agreed to ratification). The first ten amendments are known today as the Bill of Rights; they were and are collectively powerful brakes upon any tendency that the federal government might develop toward overbearing tyranny. Thomas Paine's formula, "That government is best which governs least," found a ready reception in the hearts and minds of the people.

These latter developments are often interpreted (correctly) as signifying suspicion on the part of the states that they would lose their individual identities if no safeguards were added to the Constitution. It goes deeper than that. Unless one wants to ascribe the depths of this so prevalent feeling merely to a parochial local patriotism that insisted that "Virginia shall remain Virginia," one is forced to probe beyond and ask why this viewpoint commanded such substantial support.

Two observations can be made. First, the variation in circumstances and problems from one former colony to the next was not unknown or hidden from view. Popular opinion rightly held that given that diversity, much local and individual autonomy was absolutely necessary. This answer does not really explain why the Bill of Rights per se was added. One could argue that *state* diversity was already amply protected by the compromises built into the original unamended Constitution. We come to the second observation. Whether altogether consciously or in part unconsciously the American people realized that in a land where unforeseen kinds of problems had been experienced and where novel solutions were frequently needed, the individual right to dissent would have great practical importance, especially in view of the mingling of many cultures already to be observed in the United States. If English cultural responses to problems would need substantial alteration when applied to American circumstances, it was even truer that the answers given to problems by a multitude of foreign cultures would be even more diverse. All would be in need of both integration with different views and modification to fit American circumstances. To accomplish this task with all possible viewpoints expressed, the habit of wide and free discussion had to be set upon the solid rock of Constitutional provision guaranteeing individual rights and freedoms. Even today in New England the Town Financial Meeting is a perfect illustration of this principle in operation.

Consequently, although it is possible to examine the Bill of Rights from the standpoint of pride and moral approval, as a way station toward democracy, it does not do the provisions full justice. Although "idealistic," they were (and remain) eminently practical political arrangements for a nation confronting unusual circumstances both in physical environment and cultural diversity. How else could the United States have succeeded so well as a political entity?

What happened in the United States is that a fixed and sacrosanct *method* was evolved for a people of many backgrounds to use in resolving problems as they appeared, in virtually any way they saw fit. The *solutions* to problems have varied with the times, but the *method* has remained the same, thus cementing a happy marriage between idealism and practicality. The free debate and compromise method has been used throughout American history to supply an endless variety of answers and solutions—most of them peacefully and ultimately accepted, with the exception of the slavery issue and Prohibition. After the original constitutional compromise, the slavery issue led to a whole series of later compromises and ultimately brought on the Civil War, which led to a further series of compromises. In more recent times segregated schools that could be "separate but equal" became illegal on the grounds that separate is *not* equal. The struggle and revision and new compromises over these racial issues is well known. When one looks back upon this illustration, one can speak of an evolving conscience. In political terms one can speak even more meaningfully of an endless revision of what was previously agreed toward some new compromise. Except for the resort to arms in 1861 to 1865, this method of problem solving has remained constant even while the solutions have varied in endless succession.

Illustrations from such other areas as taxation and medical insurance are not hard to find. If one wants to describe with some precision that ambiguous phrase, "the American way of life," one must recognize that it really has no fixed content, only a fixed method for problem solving. This fact describes above all else the essential character of the American domestic political environment and also tells us something about how Americans approach foreign policy problems.

How the American nation was formed thus directly influenced the political system Americans have evolved. At one and the same time it has made the American people remarkably open-minded about what policy they may choose to attempt and has—fortunately—equipped them with the means for its reexamination.

Today as before, that political process continues. It has not been frictionless and was never designed to be. What one can say about it is that it has survived "Know-Nothing" movements, hysterical "ban German from the schools" movements (World War I era), the Joseph McCarthy era (Korean War time), the Vietnam War, and the Watergate scandal. Indeed, the events of the Nixon administration showed the continuing strength of the American political process: it ended a war whose wisdom seemed increasingly doubtful and removed from office a President who had lost the confidence of the country. These experiences also initiated a continuing foreign policy debate—not about the desirability of remaining a major actor in world affairs but about the modalities of doing so and the limits of a necessary and prudent involvement.

7.

Summing Up

In this chapter we have shown that America's experience has been fundamentally unusual (and even, in its mix, unique) in three important areas of experience. First, the effects of America's geographic isolation have been profound. The United States is the sole great power in the world without great power neighbors nearby. Second, the effects of historical experience have been enormous. The United States is the sole great power in the world whose major period of historical experience as a nation was in the rather peaceful century between 1815 and 1914. Third, the effects of the domestic environment have been pronounced. The United States is the sole great power in the world whose population came from across the seas by immigration and occupied a large, rich, and sparsely settled continent, using a fixed method to approach novel problems and doing so with outstanding political and economic success.

The facts of *where* the United States came to exist, *when* it happened, and *how* the American nation was formed have had and continue to have extremely important consequences. These facts of where, when, and how are intimately related to both American successes and American difficulties in dealing with world affairs. In Chapter 3 we shall see how these experiences translated into specific attitudes about foreign policy. We shall see how America's separation from the larger tragedies of world affairs encouraged a certain moral sentimentalism after Americans began active participation in world affairs after World War II.

The American
Approach to Problems

Every idea is an incitement. It offers itself for belief and if believed it is acted on unless some other belief outweighs it or some failure of energy stifles the movement at its birth.

Oliver Wendell Holmes

If you want war, nourish a doctrine. Doctrines are the most frightful tyrants to which men ever are subject, because doctrines get inside of a man's own reason and betray him against himself. . . . Doctrines are always vague; it would ruin a good doctrine to define it, because then it could be analyzed, tested, criticized, and verified. . . . Somebody asks you with astonishment and horror whether you do not believe in the Monroe Doctrine. . . . Now when any doctrine arrives at that degree of authority, the name of it is a club which any demagogue may swing over you at any time and apropos of anything.

William Graham Sumner
War, 1903[1]

No nation is immune to its experiences and environment; on the contrary, the national attitudes and traits and the national character as a whole reflect the history of a people. To the extent that those experiences and the environment combine certain unusual features, the mix of attitudes will also have unusual aspects. What is striking in the American approach to problems is the strong emphasis on ability to make progress and resolve difficulties—an emphasis not at all unknown elsewhere, but certainly measurably stronger in the United States. This action-oriented approach is reinforced in its effects by a certain optimism and impatience that is not much tempered by the sobering experience of having many unpleasant things happen over many centuries.

Speaking of a whole nation in terms of behavior traits involves large-scale generalizing with

[1]Reprinted as the lead to the *New York Times* editorial, July 24, 1983, about the growing involvement militarily of the United States in Central American affairs.

fairly obvious limitations. "Typical Americans" and "typical American attitudes" are myths at close quarters; these generalizations lose firmness as descriptions of any flesh-and-blood individual person or particular issue. Two hundred and forty million people do not speak or respond or feel with one voice, action, or heart.[2] But if there are no distinctive national traits, neither can there be a nationalism. If there is no *national* character, no real differences in outlook can distinguish people from nation to nation. The frontiers that divide nations would be only arbitrary administrative lines. We know this is not true; differences are real and do exist.

Two sets of important American attitudes that affect foreign affairs trace fairly directly to our unusual national experience. The first of these attitudes is about politics and government generally and the second is about the American tendency to look forward, seeing problems devoid of their roots.

1.
Attitudes About Government and Politics: Americans Know the Way

The first attitude shows itself in the view that America represents an example in government in how to do it right, even to the ouster of a President as Nixon after Watergate. The very success of the American experiment established the basic soil in which this attitude takes root and there can be little dispute that the experience of Americans with government has been highly successful. As we said in Chapter 2, the key is that Americans evolved a fixed *method* for finding solutions, but the *content* of the solutions could vary greatly. What this means is that *American idealism* and *American pragmatism* found a happy marriage in the domestic instruments of government. The idealism spoke to a "government of laws, not of men." The pragmatism spoke to an open and evolving mind as to what ought to be done about civil rights or other issues.

Americans, formed by compact out of many diverse cultures, necessarily placed great stress on the contractual nature of government as a substitute means of cementing unity. Government in the United States was seen as "holding the ring" procedurally, while program preferences were argued out in free debate. Their domestic experience with government taught Americans to cling conservatively to constitutional ground rules for working out new solutions to new problems but to be very liberal about the practical merits of various alternative solutions to problems. In effect, the United States stumbled into a happy solution to the difficulties faced by a multicultural society that required flexible compromises. These compromises were made possible, in turn, by the lack of tradition and structure.

As a spinoff of such experience, Americans assumed that their methods for handling political problems at home, since they have worked so well for a nation whose people trace their origins to all areas of the earth, are suitable models for export. We can see how such views arose. As we saw in Chapter 2, the United States is the *only* large nation-state of first-class power in the world whose population is almost exclusively composed of immigrants and their descendants. Many of its settlers came to the New World to realize goals and dreams whose fruition was denied them in the political-economic system they had left behind. Americans often even take satisfaction in this thought. But if the latest generations in these older societies are now to achieve there what their own forefathers could not, on what grounds will it be done? Essentially only on the grounds of observing and learning from the American example, of seeing the "right-

---

[2]This point is further explored in Part Two when we look at public opinion and interest groups.

ness" of these dreams and aspirations. Then the old barriers in the older nations will fall and they too will follow the American-blazed path.[3]

Americans who believe that in the management of their own internal affairs they have conducted a living laboratory experiment directly relevant to the hopes and fears of all other peoples also shy away from the notion that an active American foreign policy may well create hostility and friendship in fairly equal degree. They repudiate this thought on the grounds that America's policy *must* win a net friendship as long as it remains faithful to "humanity's goals." In turn they argue that American faithfulness to universal goals is amply demonstrated by the recurrent American pronouncements in favor of self-determination of nations, human rights, the rule of law, and a high standard of living for all, plus the many concrete moves the United States has unquestionably made toward the implementation of such principles.

The assumption that other nations could do as well as the United States economically if they would only follow the American example defies simple arithmetic, which tells us that it is not possible for more than a minor part of the world to have the material abundance that the United States enjoys, since America does so by consuming more than a per capita share of the world's raw materials. Even assuming abundant technological advance and the achievement of a much greater degree of universal political stability, like most dreams, this particular dream is unreal. Not only can the greater part of the world not realize the American dream in the discernible future but even today there is relatively little equivalence outside U.S. frontiers to what exists inside them.

Much of the world is emphatically *unlike* the United States. If the political stability of the American system is not quite as unusual as United States material abundance, it too finds only relatively few equivalencies abroad. Although the American Constitution dates back only to 1788, it is already something of a world record. Few documents have lasted as long as popularly supported basic descriptions of the allocation of political power. Some stable political systems are older (such as the English have enjoyed), but most are much newer, and the majority of the older nation-states have experienced far more instability than the United States. The patterns revealed by French and Chinese experiences are much more typical.

Very few people in the world have lived, do live, or can live in the material and political environment that the American nation takes more or less for granted. Yet to many Americans this observation simply means that the other peoples have not yet been successful in finding their way to the right formulas. Foreign peoples are thought to be attempting to follow the same general path of development with less success. They are thought to be innately disposed to acknowledge American leadership and example in the pursuit of the "common" goals except where they are tempted by the false allures of communism.

This American attitude about politics and government leads also to many unwarranted assumptions about the newer nations. The people of the United States greeted the formation of the many new African states with unalloyed optimism, which testifies to the strength of these assumptions. The launching in Latin America of President Kennedy's Alliance for Progress was accompanied with the same sort of acclaim and expectations. The point is not whether the new African states can eventually accommodate themselves to life in the contemporary state system

---

[3]The popular attitude goes back well before contemporary times in the United States. Herman Melville, in his autobiographical novel, *White-Jacket,* which was published in 1850, remarks: "In our [American] youth is our strength; in our inexperience, our wisdom. At a period when other nations have but lisped, our deep voice is heard afar. Long enough have we been skeptics with regard to ourselves, and doubted whether, indeed, the political Messiah had come. But he has come in *us,* if we would but give utterance to his promptings. And let us always remember that with ourselves, almost for the first time in the history of earth, national selfishness is unbounded philanthropy; for we cannot do a good to America but we give alms to the world." Quoted from the Library of America edition, *Redburn, White-Jacket, Moby-Dick* (New York: Literary Classics of the United States, Inc., 1983), p. 506. Try topping that one as an expression of the view that what is good for the United States is good for everyone, everywhere.

on a basis far short of the initial euphoria or whether needed reforms in Latin America can be accomplished short of social revolution. Nor is it the point that the United States is wrong to encourage progress and reform. The point is rather that developments in these other lands too frequently are seen in terms of American experience. Actually it would be astonishing if the American experience were relevant elsewhere, since conditions in the United States have so little parallel to conditions abroad. These nations are aware of this difference, or are coming to suspect it, even if Americans do not. Other nations may welcome good wishes on their behalf, they may welcome certain tangible projects for development; but they cannot help but resent any assumption on the part of the United States that it has a patented solution for the cure of the world's ills.

This self-image of the American people as pioneers along humanity's preferred paths to progress is in fact a handicap to an effective foreign policy; it encourages a distorted conception of the value goals in a multitude of foreign societies. It is a handicap when it leads to judgments that another people's concern is to become more like America in fundamental ways. It is a handicap when it leads to assumptions that others will follow American leadership because they want to achieve the same objectives in the same way. It is a handicap when it tempts Americans to look out on the world and visualize each nation as occupying a position along a single spectrum of development, with some of them nearer the American lead position, some of them still far behind, and some of them wandering off the main road into the dead end of socialism-communism. It is a handicap when it leads to unrealistic expectations of what others can achieve and thus an underestimation of the problems to be confronted. And it is a handicap when it leads to the conclusion that the only reason others do not succeed is that they do not do things the American way. Far more useful is a very different assumption: that the world is quite diverse and will remain so, although each part of it will constantly be changing into something else which may resemble the United States or may not.

Even so, Americans believe they know the way.

2.

Attitudes About Government and Politics: Idealism Should Be Practical

Closely connected to the feeling of Americans that they are pioneers along a path that sooner or later will be followed by the rest is the view that what seems to work at home as a *method* ought also to work in foreign affairs. This second spinoff of the general American attitude toward government and politics assumes that idealism and practical, useful results ought to go hand in hand in U.S. foreign policy just as they have done so successfully at home. Consequently this habit and expectation are reflected in much of U.S. foreign policy programs and in American attempts to find suitable ways of participating in international relations.

From this perspective, one understands why the American people were initial strong supporters of the United Nations. Inarticulate as it often may be, an instinctive feeling is common to most Americans that the UN can prove useful and workable because it, too, blends the essential elements of a fixed constitutional method for handling international affairs with an open-mindedness about solutions to international problems. This instinct in the first decades after World War II led Americans sometimes to elevate UN decisions and their potential efficacy above what was justified. If there has been a falling-off in this faith, it represents a disillusionment with the actual workings of the UN rather than a rejection in principle of the thought that the organization should ultimately work. The United States *believes* in the possibility of effective compromises between diverse national cultures because its own way of life and American national experience seem to show that this approach is feasible.

Americans may be idealists, but they believe that idealism should be practical. They are also optimistic, thinking that all problems are ultimately solvable. This attitude is by no means restricted to application in the realm of politics and government, or foreign affairs. Its roots go deep into the general American experience with life.

Thus the contemporary American attitude about government and politics is distinguished by idealism in approach, pragmatism in content, expectations of relatively rapid progress in the solution of problems, and a general willingness to attempt to exert U.S. influence abroad.

3.

Attitudes Toward the "Lessons of the Past"

The second set of attitudes worth stressing is the rather cavalier American approach toward "the lessons of the past," the tendency to see all problems as new and tractable. As we saw in Chapter 2, because the American scene was not set in its outlines by centuries of class relationships, because it had no traditional feudal past that laid its restraining hand upon change, the solutions that could be reached for problems were remarkably open to the arguments of logic and the shifting pressures of political forces. This distinctive political experience is not duplicated in, or is at least not widespread in, the world arena. There the roots of some contemporary problems literally go back for thousands of years. The great Jewish exodus in Roman times has a direct relationship to the present tensions between Arabs and Jews. The antagonism and conflict between Teuton and Slav has a thousand years of active history behind it. The gradual and growing mutual impingement of Chinese and Russian has very long roots in the spread of these two cultures toward one another. These are not problems to which new solutions are applicable merely on the basis of logic, common sense, goodwill, or good intention.

Their weak sense of history equips Americans poorly to understand the dimensions of such problems. It is not just that the American national experience barely tops the two-century mark; temperamentally Americans live in the present or future tense. Change has been the American hallmark, and change is quickly accepted. Americans take pride in adjusting, in refusing to cling to the "outmoded" past, even in welcoming with recurrent but weakening optimism the "advances" dutifully and regularly incorporated in each new model year of each new television set, automobile, or gadget. Americans tend noticeably to believe that change is progress, and vice versa. So they look steadily forward as they move past the checkpoints of progress: the advent of television, the elimination of polio, the manned trip to the moon. It is a matter of "common sense" that they are better off now than they were then.

This outlook, however, leaves Americans short of an appreciation for the perennial aspects of the human predicament. Since change is progress and the present is better (and the future even better), Americans do not incline to look backward and consequently frequently fail to gain an appreciation of the long roots of things.

4.

Effects of These Attitudes on Foreign Affairs

These two sets of American attitudes, focused on foreign affairs, produced quite different results from their effects in the domestic arena. Paradoxically, where flexibility was assured domestically by an open-mindedness about solutions (using the fixed method for handling problems at home), that flexibility eroded drastically when the nation in the twentieth century became heavily involved in problems abroad. Then, as we shall see, America's lack of a long history, the American tendency to see old problems as new because they were new to Americans, encouraged the nation toward "doctrines" incorporating formula remedies regardless of the environmental or historical context. (William Graham Sumner, in the headnote, tells what is wrong with that.)

America's inward preoccupation during much of the nineteenth century in effect shortened the historical experience further. Since Americans did not concern themselves much with what was going on far from U.S. shores, the perception of these events was often inaccurate. Later, when the United States became very much involved in world affairs, Americans were to this extent poorly prepared to handle them. Lacking substantive knowledge, they frequently did not know the background of what they faced or the real historical sequence of cause and effect.[4] They were, in short, unprepared for the complexities of the real world. They overemphasized the importance of their own choices; they underestimated the effects of the system.

Many Americans tended to ascribe their nineteenth century immunity from invasion to a prudent regard to Jefferson's counsel to stay out of Europe's problems, plus the timely pronunciation of the Monroe Doctrine. Americans gave little thought to the intricate balance of power on the Continent contrived by Bismarck or to Britain's general refusal to see any alteration in the status quo of the New World. In the twentieth century, when the United States at last began to play a key role in world affairs, the American President or Secretary of State frequently spoke fervently of ending the very balance of power and the very rivalries and "power politics" that had played such an important role in buttressing America's own security.

One reason why the lack of historical depth in appraising problems did not betray the United States into fatal mistakes in policy in its first decades was that the issues faced were unmistakably clear. The controversies as a consensus was sought were over simple and immediately understandable problems. They were policy disputes over alternatives aimed at ensuring the security of a new weak nation surrounded by territories under European great power control. These great powers bounded the United States on all four sides and they included every great power in the world except for Austria. Even Russia had Alaska and the territory down to just north of San Francisco, and nearer to hand were the British in Canada and the Caribbean, the French in the Louisiana Territory and the Caribbean, and the Spanish in Florida and elsewhere—a total surrounding of the American territory. In these strategic circumstances the necessary, overriding objective of American policy was not in dispute: to extend the national frontiers by maneuvering the Europeans out of positions in the New World. It was obvious enough what *goals* were in the national interest. The arguments, such as they were, were over tactics.

Once the policies were chosen and achieved their strategic goals, American ventures in foreign affairs until the end of the nineteenth century could be—and were—of modest dimensions. Although Americans did not assign appropriate credit to the actions of other powers in contriving the beneficial state of affairs between 1815 and 1914 by which the United States profited, there was in this period no substantial outcry for a vigorous program of involvements abroad. In these decades public sentiment went in one direction, public policy in another. While Americans cheered the Polish revolt against the Czars; or financially supported Hungary's popular revolutionist, Louis Kossuth, in 1848; or aided the Irish in their struggle against the English; the official policy was unsentimental and uninvolved. In a word, American idealistic sentiment found an outlet abroad, but American pragmatism held the United States officially aloof in its actual policy. Idealism and pragmatism, the happy combination that worked so well at home by its innate natural harmony in meeting American needs, were made compatible in U.S. foreign policy by the simple device of compartmentalizing them into private and public sectors.

But, if the United States once entered on an *active* foreign policy, given this now ingrained

---

[4]Former Secretary of State Dean Rusk at the outset of World War II served as an army officer in intelligence. He tells the story that the total background data he found in the files for his new section, covering from Afghanistan through Southeast Asia and Australia, was a tourist handbook on India and Ceylon, a 1924 military attaché's report from London on the Indian army, and a drawer full of old *New York Times* clippings.

habit of popular idealist and sentimental interest in events abroad, the most likely result would be to attempt to incorporate idealist precepts into an actual policy. This is exactly what occurred in 1917 for a short period (and again, as we shall see, after 1945). American idealism was translated into a series of moral abstract principles to be applied to foreign policy problems. These principles included freedom of the seas, majority rule and the elimination of autocracy, a peace without annexations, and the establishment of a "parliament of mankind" (the League of Nations). Wilson announced these views in his famous Fourteen Points speech before Congress of January 8, 1918.

Wilson's attempt to establish collective security under the League of Nations in 1919 represented not only an idealistic but a drastic solution to the age-old problem of the balance of power's periodic disintegration into war. Wilson thought that collective responsibility for the peace could be formalized under such a League, prepared to act against aggression regardless of who posed the threat. Partly because Wilson's solution was so drastic and required nations to act against aggression even before they felt directly threatened, partly because the radical nature of these obligations in the end caused the United States itself to stay out of the League, the League proved impractical from a collective security viewpoint. Wilson's belief that the League would do the job illustrates his lack of acquaintance with the more pervasive forces at work in international affairs. He really had not thought much about what really caused nations to act together against a threat, for example. He had not thought much about why the balance of power periodically ended in war. (He thought it was because of the alliances the nations of Europe had made, thus confusing the symptom for the disease, for nations make alliances because they feel threatened and activate them in war in order to field common forces, whereas Wilson thought that the alliances dragged the nations into unwanted conflict.)

Yet in a way Wilson was right. It was not unrealistic for the United States, as a strategic goal, to seek better ways of maintaining the peace. The United States stood only to benefit from a durable peace. What was unrealistic about Wilson's proposals was not the idealism of his goal but the weaknesses of his remedy. He had not studied the external environment, the system of nation-states he was proposing to "reform."

In any event, disappointed by the results of World War I and skeptical about the wisdom of continued involvement in European affairs, the United States rejected the Versailles settlement (the Versailles Treaty of peace with Germany, and the League of Nations that went with it). The United States made a separate peace with Germany and in the 1920s retreated into "isolationism."

The consequences of both American policy decisions were ultimately to have far-reaching effects on the way Americans viewed world affairs. The United States more than anyone else had founded the League of Nations. Yet the League failed, and that failure coincided with the advent of World War II. The American people, drawn willy-nilly into World War II, concluded that the retreat into isolationism had been wrong and that a strong United States must play a responsible role in world affairs.

The subsequent vigorous policy of full participation (later dubbed "globalism") represented a complete reversal of earlier actions. Because what was done from 1919 to 1939 was considered essentially wrong, it was assumed that doing the *reverse* after 1945 would be essentially right.

If in 1919 to 1939 the United States refrained from membership in the League, from making alliances, from sending troops outside the hemisphere, from offering elaborate and continuing foreign and military aid to other nations far from American shores, after 1945 America did all those things. American moral abstract principles *became* American policy.

The United States became a founding member of the United Nations. The very Charter of the United Nations was adopted in a conference at San Francisco on the American West Coast. Thus called into existence, the organization was then established on the American East Coast, at New York. From the beginning the United States played a great role in UN affairs. Quite contrary to the suspicious attitude toward the League of Nations followed by the American government in the 1920s, the United States determined to make the UN a principal part of its foreign policy. When outright aggression in Korea challenged the UN in 1950, it was the United States that furnished the greatest single armed support to the UN effort (in contrast to American actions during Mussolini's assault on Ethiopia in 1935–1936 when the United States permitted augmented supplies of oil and war material to be shipped to Italian Africa even while the League groped to institute economic sanctions against Italy). At the height of the U.S. involvement in Korea, there were 250,000 American troops fighting on that battlefield. Not content with the limited ability of the veto-ridden UN Security Council to cope with such problems as the Korean aggression, the United States also led the way toward an enlarged security role for the UN General Assembly.

Not content even with these moves, the United States also created alliance commitments linking America to dozens of "Free World" states in defensive arrangements. Not only were such major commitments accepted—the Rio Pact with Latin America, the North Atlantic alliance (Senate vote, 82 to 13), and SEATO in Asia[5] but these obligations were supplemented by bilateral commitments to such nations as Australia, New Zealand, Nationalist China, and Japan. Less formal links were made by means of the military assistance program to many other nations. Curiously enough—or perhaps for understandable reasons—the close links to Israel were never converted into a formal alliance. The same was true for the Shah's Iran. Although the United States did not formally join CENTO,[6] it furnished the money and arms without which the organization would have had no significance.

5.

The Conceptual Basis of the American Involvement in the Cold War

In the period (1945–1955) of increasingly indiscriminate involvement, which came to be known as the beginnings of the "cold war," relations between the United States and the Soviet Union achieved a frozen rigidity. These developments are discussed in more detail in Part Three. Here our interest is not in the events themselves but in the conceptual basis from which the United States approached them. (Our concern is not really "external" but "internal.") The roots of this conceptual basis are found in two events or series of events during the post–World War I era that made a lasting impression on the American people. Each, like the explosion of some delayed timebomb, led to widely and strongly held ideas about the proper American foreign policy after World War II.

The first of these two events was the failure of the League of Nations to oppose what is commonly called Japan's aggression in Manchuria in 1931. In retrospect this complicated case, in which Japan had certain rights in China that confused the issue and led to League caution in indicting Japan, was seen as a precedent which then undermined the League's ability to deal with Mussolini's assault on Ethiopia in 1935 and 1936. This weakness in turn was supposed to have both encouraged Hitler's aggression and led to the failure of the Western democracies to restrain him. So a series of causally linked aggressions was now understood to have followed one another.

---

[5]The Rio Pact of 1947 linked the United States to Latin America. The NATO treaty came in 1949 and allied Western Europe (and Canada) to the United States, with other nations added later such as West Germany, Greece and Turkey, and Spain. SEATO, formed in 1954 for Southeast Asia, was a very loose arrangement. It included Pakistan and Thailand, two Asian onshore nations. All of these treaties are discussed further in Part Three.

[6]Originally formed in 1955 as the Baghdad Pact, after Iraq withdrew in 1959 the pact was renamed CENTO.

The second event was the aftermath of the Munich Agreement (1938), when Neville Chamberlain, British prime minister, returned to his people with the triumphant but fatuous conviction that by making a "deal" with Hitler (giving him German-speaking areas of Czechoslovakia), he had achieved "peace in our time." What Chamberlain had actually achieved by giving in to the aggressor was, of course, the weakening of the coalition against Hitler, the sacrifice of Czechoslovakian defenses, and the loss of the large Czech armaments industry to Hitler's use. Truly, that last year of peace (1938–1939) was dearly bought.

Leaving aside the complexity of these historical issues, the point here is that many Americans already had guilt feelings that their nonsupport had undermined the League. The simple lesson they then distilled from these events was that unrestrained aggression leads to further aggressions. As a result Americans enthusiastically endorsed the UN and unhesitantly backed going to war over Korea (1950). The belief that appeasement did not pay (as Munich showed), reformulated after World War II as the "domino theory," was translated for them into a general axiom of American foreign policy.

In fact, the real importance of the Munich episode stemmed from Czechoslovakia's strategic location. But it came to be identified in the United States with the abstract proposition that *any* aggression anywhere could have disastrous results. This simplification was widely shared by policymakers and led the United States not only to the Korean intervention but also to a whole philosophy on how to handle Communist bids for expansion, fairly indiscriminately applied. This approach led ultimately to American involvement in Vietnam. Jolted out of its unparalleled security, the United States suddenly became aware of the world and its danger. In the League and Munich experiences the United States saw object lessons in how not to do things. After 1945 the United States more or less literally began to apply these new prescriptions, under circumstances that, from a shallow perspective, they seemed to fit.

6.

The Three Postwar Formulas of U.S. Policy

The policy guidance summed up in these reactions consisted of three moral, abstract formulas: oppose aggression (since it is right to do so and failure to resist simply leads to even bigger wars), oppose communism (since Communists were seen as bent on committing aggression), and defend freedom (since free people deserve to be free and are on America's side). These three moral and abstract formulas actually came in the period from 1945 until the Vietnam War in the late 1960s to constitute the central intellectual thrust of American foreign policy—fundamental factors in its design. An inclusive name for the idea or concept behind all three formulas is *containment* (or, more exactly, [Soviet] bloc containment).

In the Truman Doctrine of 1947 all three formulas first appear together in a foreign policy statement, although it was not clear initially how widely or actively such a moral, abstract concept might be applied in practice.

President Truman's March 12, 1947, speech, which announced his doctrine, was in immediate terms about support for Greece and Turkey against Communist pressures. But President Truman also used phrases such as, "the creation of conditions in which we and other nations will be able to work out a way of life free from coercion"; "a frank recognition that totalitarian regimes imposed on free peoples, by direct or indirect aggression, undermine the foundations of international peace and hence the security of the United States." He also spoke about "two ways of life."[7]

---

[7]For Truman's speech see *Congressional Record,* 80th Congress, 1st Session, vol. 93, pp. 1980*ff.*

So Truman's speech, although about a specific threat in a specific corner of Europe, was also couched in rather farreaching terms that might be applied around the world if the United States so chose. To believe in such formulas passively or on some restricted geographical basis was one thing. To apply these formulas vigorously and on a global basis would be quite another.

What must be understood is that two things occurred simultaneously after World War II that actually have no necessary physical or logical connection. This Truman Doctrine-containment concept was accepted as a summation of the problem faced and the solution needed, both in moral and practical terms. Then this doctrine's statement of the issue was implemented through a very vigorous worldwide American policy. A nation with a quieter temperament than Americans possessed might have been content to adopt containment as a conceptual policy guide without feeling a compulsion to play a vigorous role in world affairs.

7.

Applying the Containment Concept

The *initial* application of the concept of containment was in Europe. It was a remarkably effective program in its content (regardless of the verbiage used in its concept) because the Soviets *did* need to be contained and Europe *did* need to be rebuilt. The Marshall Plan (the economic pump-priming for the European joint effort) and the North Atlantic Pact (which provided security) were, in tandem, a highly practical way of achieving the more loosely expressed goals of the Truman Doctrine.

The European program was a success because the American people supported it and there were willing laborers available in Europe once the pumps were primed. Helping these nations obviously contributed to the creation of a stronger, more secure world for the United States. America's friends were helped generously, their strength was restored and Western Europe was shored up against Soviet pressures, thereby doing the United States good as well. Idealism and pragmatism were at this point as happily married in foreign affairs as they had been domestically.

In retrospect, the fact that the containment concept was first applied so successfully to Europe may have encouraged the failure to assess its accuracy in terms of worldwide conditions. Who could quarrel with the need to call a halt to Russian expansionism in Europe, with the need to prime Western Europe's industrial pumps, to organize a defense structure against the heavily armed and apparently sullenly uncooperative Russian Bear? An older concept's precepts would have expressed the same goals in different words: restoring some semblance of a balance of power.

If one called this policy containing communism, defending free nations, and establishing an ability to thwart aggression, was it not the same thing in the end? Either choice of phrase meant that more or less the same policy actions would be taken—in Europe. The implementation of either of these two conceptual propositions (containment or the balance of power) would come down to very similar responses in the specific case, even if not distinguishing one concept from another encouraged imprecision.

But calling it one thing rather than another *outside* Europe was to bring tragic results in the 1960s. Even inside Europe it blurred the way to count Eastern Europe—victim or co-conspirator?

The tale after 1950 becomes more blurred as the United States involvement in the Far East deepened. Events in China in 1949 (as Chiang Kai-shek's Nationalists were overthrown by the Chinese Communists) and in 1950 (when the Korean War broke out and in November Chinese Communist "volunteers" began fighting Americans in Korea) soon produced a temporary flurry

MAP 1

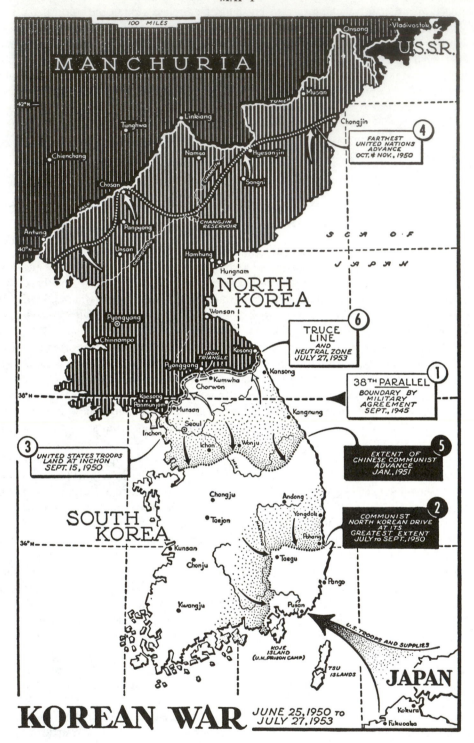

KOREAN WAR JUNE 25, 1950 to JULY 27, 1953

of dissension in Congress, coupled with the export of the concept of containment to Asia. But increasingly, the strategic rationale behind the success in Europe (aiding the recovery of those who could become viable and whose viability contributed meaningfully to the security of the United States) was less coherently followed. The words used about policy in Asia were much the same as those used for policy in Europe—but the *situation* was not the same.

The "loss" of China in 1949 (attributed by the Republicans to Democratic error) was followed very abruptly by the Korean War in June 1950. The initial reaction of the United States in deploying troops in Korea to defend the UN Charter had virtually unanimous support in the United States.[8] But the war dragged on and a debate began in the United States, not on the commitment but over how best to discharge it—a substantial minority arguing for a more aggressive military policy to punish China for its intervention with "volunteers." Whereas the nation had cheered Truman's decision to intervene against the North Korean aggression by force, it did not tolerate patiently the seesaw stalemate that ensued in Korea on the battlefield once the Chinese entered the fray. The United States was not "winning" the war, so what should be done? The solution of the electorate was to sweep Dwight D. Eisenhower into the presidency in 1952. Eisenhower, as a military man, was believed to have the answer. But "Ike's" election was not a repudiation of the containment strategy pioneered by Truman; rather, it was a judgment by the electorate that Truman had not followed the strategy consistently and successfully in the Far East where the Communist Chinese seemed to be in the forefront of the Communist world challenge.

Symbolic of the emotional upset of the time was Senator Joe McCarthy's rise to political power. He jumped opportunistically into the middle of the Korean War controversy with his famous charge of numerous (although always fluctuating-in-number with each repetition of the charge) Communists in the State Department. With great energy McCarthy began to sow loose charges right and left. Tolerated by his colleagues in Congress, undenounced by President Eisenhower even when he impugned General George Marshall's patriotic integrity, McCarthy destroyed careers and disrupted government, spreading fears of subversive infiltration into sensitive areas within the American government. McCarthy's approach, although simple, was convincing to many Americans. If the greatest, strongest nation in the world was not being 100 per cent successful in its policies, the trouble had to stem from sabotage from within rather than from American faulty ideas about policy in dealing with the world outside.

Meanwhile, General Douglas MacArthur was arguing that a relatively small military effort in Asia could defeat Communist China—a threat, that might better be met, he thought, sooner than later. The way to win the war in Korea was to fight a war with China, in China, or at least in the air above China, ending the Chinese "privileged sanctuary" of Manchuria from which they launched planes to Korea.

Yet, although both McCarthy's and MacArthur's simplistic solutions drew support predominantly from far right-wing Republican elements, the issues never became party vs. party. When Eisenhower made peace in Korea, the Democrats did not oppose him. When Eisenhower extended defense arrangements into the Asian theater by signing pacts with South Korea and Nationalist China, and then created SEATO (Southeast Asia Treaty Organization), the "opposition" party in Congress accepted these new arrangements with as little real debate or dissension as the "opposition" had to Truman's proposal on Europe. In turn, when Eisenhower gave way to Kennedy, these arrangements were not questioned.

---

[8]The reason was that the U.S. armed response to the North Korean aggression could plausibly be described variously as the United States honoring its pledged word (defending its ward, South Korea), or accepting the security burden agreed to by UN members (implementing collective security), or frustrating aggressive communism (containment), or acting on behalf of America's ally (Japan), or maintaining the balance of power. Since the action could be justified on multiple grounds, it postponed the problem of whether the rhetoric of containment provided firm enough ground on which to rest the Asian policy of the United States.

Consequently, what happened to U.S. policy in Asia in the 1950s was almost an accident: because China was "lost" and "turned Communist" and war broke out in Korea, Americans exported the readymade containment doctrine to Asia. There was no serious questioning either of its *applicability* to the strategic problem confronting the United States in the world, or of its *suitability* as a cost-effective way to handle the problem.

Since the Chinese had by their own admission added themselves to the Communist bloc, in the 1950s Americans simply extended the logic and perimeter of the containment strategy to thwart their anticipated aggressions in Asia. This strategy produced a very simplified map of the world. It did so without any prolonged and vigorous debate in the Senate of the United States. When President Johnson, in the 1960s, applied the next logical step in the sequence, by extending American armed involvement to Southeast Asia through the Senate-approved Gulf of Tonkin Resolution, the Senate's debate was, as usual, perfunctory, and only two votes were cast against the Resolution. This was the last real occasion when the U.S. Senate might have headed off the Vietnam War.

8.

The Formulas Lead to Vietnam

So the nation came by 1965–1966, when the United States assumed a combat role in Vietnam, to the logical end of where it began in 1947. If Congress did not probe more critically then and before, it was because Americans generally had become mesmerized by the power of the formulas that made up the containment concept. They were haunted by the conviction that *one* American failure to halt aggression would inevitably produce World War III—an absolutely horrifying possibility in the age of nuclear weapons. They believed this because that whole generation of American leaders "knew" that World War II began from seeds planted by U.S. rejection of its proper role in world affairs. This had much to do with Japan's leading the "march of the aggressors" in 1931 in China, which triggered Italy's assault against Ethiopia in 1935, which, in turn, was thought to have inspired Hitler to seize large slices of Europe. American leaders believed, oversimplifying history, that one event *caused* another, each failure making the next one worse and more inevitable, with the will of the keepers of the peace progressively paralyzed. To that generation of leaders the capstone of the whole tragic, helpless slide toward a war fought under adverse conditions culminated with the Munich Conference of 1938 when Czechoslovakia was betrayed by its own friends and allies, in the process undermining the embryonic anti-Hitler coalition.

Those who argued for more complex explanations of a great and involved tragedy made little impact. Just as sophisticated men once were substantially in agreement that the earth was the center of the universe, or that the world was flat, who could deny that turning away from an unchecked aggression anywhere in the world was not only cowardly but tragically shortsighted?

It is in this sense that Lyndon B. Johnson, when he was criticized so heavily for his Vietnam War involvement, complained that he was only continuing the policy of his predecessors. We can see that in a way he was right. Certainly Truman's bold action in Korea was a precedent. Certainly Eisenhower got very excited at one point about developments in Cambodia, and Kennedy allowed the number of American advisers in Vietnam to climb to sixteen thousand or more. But Kennedy never authorized a combat role; Johnson did.

Townsend Hoopes says of Johnson: "In matters of war and peace he seemed too much the sentimental patriot, lacking Truman's practical horse sense, Eisenhower's experienced caution, Kennedy's cool grasp of reality."[9] But anyone who remembers Kennedy's inaugural address,

[9]Townsend Hoopes, *The Limits of Intervention,* rev. ed. (New York: David McKay, 1973), p. 8.

with its grand moral and abstract promises to aid *any* friend and oppose *any* foe, indeed to "pay *any* price," will realize that what it really comes down to is that Truman was lucky not to have the issue posed in a swamp, that Eisenhower's military sense made him aware that Vietnam was a swamp, and that Kennedy was pragmatic and cautious when he sensed a swamp. Kennedy had had the sobering experience of the Bay of Pigs (the abortive invasion of Cuba) just after he delivered his inaugural address. Johnson, because he could not resist a challenge, went right in—up to his hips.

We can see that the range of presidential actions and inactions recounted reflected variations in temperament, not of conviction, and that little of it shows any real appreciation for the intractability of events, the tragic element in human affairs, or a sober view of the long sweep of history. Without any exception, *every* post-World War II Secretary of State and/or President held the same simple, general view of the role America should play in the world, and what would happen if "America failed to live up to its responsibilities." Indeed, Eisenhower invented, or at least popularized, the definitive phrase for the most fundamental formula in their general outlook, the "domino" effect, warning that a successful aggression would cause the remaining potential victims to fall over "like a row of dominoes." The same Ike who held the United States back from a combat role in Vietnam was ideologically just as committed to the concept as any of them. And *his* chief foreign affairs adviser was Secretary of State John Foster Dulles, who branded "containment" (or just holding the line, as he characterized it), not good enough. Until the Hungarian uprising of 1956 made the gulf between words and deeds too embarrassing, Dulles used to speak of "liberating" captive nations. Eisenhower then made Dulles tone down the verbiage. He did not like the military price tag. (Dulles's talk of "liberation" was understood by the American electorate for what it really was: a statement of moral outrage, because if anyone gained in the contest between the "Free World" and the "Communist bloc," it should have been the side of freedom—the American side.)

Truman was lucky in the place where he saw these moral, abstract principles at stake (for Korea *was* strategic). Eisenhower understood military price tags and was cautious. And President Kennedy, when he took office, was chastened and humiliated by his first politico-military venture—the Cuban Bay of Pigs. That induced caution, too, as Kennedy's handling of the Cuban missile crisis shows. But President Johnson had the disadvantage of intervening in the Dominican Republic crisis in 1965 and having it go well indeed. The ease with which that operation went forward and the sense of successful use of military power that it gave Johnson reinforced his temperamental predisposition to react to a challenge—a challenge Johnson saw in Vietnam.

In that decision to intervene Johnson had the enthusiastic support of Secretary of State Dean Rusk. Townsend Hoopes, who saw Dean Rusk close up, said that he

> seemed the very embodiment of the embattled Cold Warrior with convictions rooted in the Stalinist period. . . . He was, moreover, possessed of a special mania about China and of a knack for arguing by dubious analogy. Not only in public, but in private conversations with colleagues and with President Johnson, Rusk expounded his thesis that Communist China was actively promoting and supporting aggression in Vietnam, that aggression in Vietnam was not different from Hitler's aggression in Europe, that appeasement in Vietnam could have the same consequences as appeasement at Munich.[10]

Dean Rusk certainly did make that argument, to hundreds of audiences and to vigorous applause. His audiences almost invariably agreed with him during the first years of the Vietnam War, whether Democrat or Republican.

After the Communist Vietnamese Tet offensive in 1968, this was to change. But until then, what typified the whole period from 1947 to 1967 or so, with the exception of the arguments

[10]Ibid., pp. 16–17.

stirred up by the loss of China and the stalemate in Korea, was bipartisanship (i.e., agreement by both American political parties on the containment concept). This bipartisanship was never the product of an agreement to shelve serious conceptual differences on policy; bipartisanship came about as the natural result of a lack of serious differences on foreign policy in the largest sense.

The Vietnam War destroyed that consensus and initiated an intense and continued debate over every aspect of policy. The shortcomings of the three formulas of containment were drastically revealed. Whereas the formulas spoke clearly to the presumed need to fight in Vietnam, they also furnished little but negative guidance, telling Americans about the dangers of *not* doing something. They explained only the penalties of inaction rather than the rewards for involvement. They told what could be lost, rather than what could be gained by an involvement.

Secretary of Defense Clark Clifford grasped this point. As the Vietnam War continued without success, U.S. generals proposed ever larger numbers of troops. It was Clifford who finally said no. He could remember sitting in earlier in the war, as a member of the intelligence advisory board, listening to General Wheeler, Chairman of the Joint Chiefs, as he briefed President Johnson. After hearing a figure of seven hundred fifty thousand men mentioned, and a five- or six-year war, Clifford irritated the President by asking Wheeler what the United States, using such manpower and resources, would gain if it *won* the Vietnam War.

> Wheeler looked a little puzzled. "I don't understand the question." So Clifford repeated it: if we won, after all that time, with all that investment, "What do we do? Are we still involved? Do we still have to stay there?" And Wheeler answered yes, we would have to keep a major force there, for perhaps as long as twenty or thirty years.[11]

As a prize for winning, it did not seem all that appealing. The containment concept, already undermined by the growing realization of the Sino-Soviet split, began to lose its hold on the American public and American decision makers.

9.
The Paucity of American Strategic Thought and Its Penalties

We have argued that the willingness to rely on such simple abstractions as the basis for foreign policy may well trace back to the American domestic success in relying on abstractions such as freedom of speech and freedom of the press. Certainly only a nation combining small but reasonably satisfactory historical experience with great power would have likely embarked upon such costly involvements without more serious examination of the validity of the assumptions behind the policy. The American predilection for action encouraged the nation to go far with rather simplistic, morally formulated, abstract policy guidance.

A people will reflect its own experience. Americans have not predominated in the roster of the world's strategic thinkers, for the nation has been unusually isolated from serious threat until quite lately. Nor have Americans brought forth any great number of professionals dedicated to serious abstract thought, such as philosophers or theoreticians, because the need has been elsewhere. On almost any American campus the engineering building (applied physics) is much bigger than the physics (theoretical engineering) building. Americans have been doers rather than thinkers and are especially good at "practical" things such as production lines. Americans made good weapons, houses, kitchen equipment, and (until lately?) automobiles. And even

[11]David Halberstam, *The Best and the Brightest* (New York: Random House, 1969), pp. 596–597.

The Intellectual Framework and the Cultural Background

today, Americans know lots more about settling a wilderness, or increasing farm production, or designing new equipment, than they do about planning war, strategy, and foreign and defense policy. Neither are the youth and brains of the country stimulated easily to the choice of a career in government service. They prefer instead medicine, the law, banking, and business. Most Americans think politics much more corrupt and corrupting than other careers open to talent.

When Americans do turn to politics and strategic questions, they are likely therefore to approach them either as problems in mechanics or problems in ethics. If asked how food shortages in India can be ended or whether the United States can justify consuming so much of the world's food supplies, Americans rarely pause to make a detailed historical analysis of such a problem. Instead they simply start in the here and now and assume some reasonable norm from which the present problem must be a deviation. Americans like to *solve* problems, but not to study them, and are impatient when they persist. For most of the two hundred-year history of the United States, it also, as we have pointed out, enjoyed the luxury of being largely immune from the normal threat in this world of serious armed attack—a condition not conducive to in-depth strategic thinking.

Confronted with what is conceived to be a threat, Americans are likely to try to solve it by the mechanics of amassing arms and equipment, by signing up allies, and by sending economic and military aid missions. Large American standing forces are sent abroad to deal with and contain the enemy. Americans are not likely to sit down first in seclusion to consider such esoteric philosophical questions as "Is the enemy bloc larger than we feel comfortable in confronting?," to ponder whether common ideology really does bind nation to nation (rather than providing them a language for their arguments), or to ask whether the domino theory may be missing the point: that a potential coalition against aggression may first need a horrible example before it is willing to put away differences and unite against a now very obvious threat?

A people's ideas about foreign policy will reflect how it thinks the state system functions. But in America's hurry to solve problems it tends to rush past the conceptual phase of reflecting on cause and effect in the system, of visualizing alternative outcomes as the consequence of different policy choices. In Truman's time, and even in Eisenhower's time, the natural disinclination to first think thoroughly about the problem was compounded by the general assumption that Americans already had, and had reached perfectly sound conclusions. There were the Communists, expanding where they could; they needed stopping. The only remaining important questions were where and how.

Containment as a concept guiding U.S. policy was not the product of a careful consideration of the basic forces at work in the world; it generalized from one experience at one moment in recent history. As a consequence, containment failed by teaching the wrong lesson from the Munich experience. It had the additional very serious defect of surrendering entirely into the hands of foreign states the prerogative of deciding in principle where the United States would be compelled to deploy troops and expend blood, money, and weapons.

We consider the second point first. The Truman Doctrine, stripped to its essentials, implied or said that the United States would deploy against any aggressor, anywhere in the world. The Munich experience explained why this was morally and practically necessary: because once aggression occurred successfully, containing it became progressively more difficult. Again, the domino theory explained why it had to be stopped right away: because otherwise the potential coalition of resisters to aggression became demoralized and resistance became progressively less effective. Naturally, under those conditions, immediate resistance to an aggression, anybody's aggression, made sense. (Which meant in practice, after World War II, any Communist aggression.)

Anything more than a cursory glance at these events would, however, have led to more qualified conclusions. Although the Anglo-French appeasement of Hitler at the Munich Conference of 1938 was indeed the curtain raiser to World War II, and Hitler's unopposed aggression in March 1939 against the rest of Czechoslovakia did convince the Soviets to cooperate with Hitler in August 1939 in carving up Poland, the overall resistance to German aggression *increased* in the second phase of the war. Ultimately, the list of Hitler's enemies grew until he was overwhelmed and died a suicide in Berlin. If the domino theory was a solid strategic theory, then Adolf Hitler remained alive and well, and Germany won World War II!

Now consider the first point: drawing the wrong lesson from Munich. In 1938, when Hitler capitalized on English and French moral weakness, and they appeased him at Munich, Hitler gained tactical advantages. He destroyed the ability of the Czech army on his eastern flank to resist Germany, by taking the Sudeten fortress line. By taking the rest of Czechoslovakia in March 1939, Hitler achieved the ability to deploy troops on the southern flank of Poland (his next victim) while he already could jump off in the north from East Prussia. Simultaneously he motivated the Soviet Union (who had not been invited to Munich) to attempt its own appeasement of Hitler. If, to Russia, Munich seemed an attempt by the British and French to divert Hitler's attack eastward, then the Soviets felt justified in making a deal to avoid it.

The lesson of Munich is not that every successful act of aggression is a disaster; the lesson of Munich is that, if you are imprudent enough to dismantle your ally's strategic fortress and hand that key location over to the enemy, at the same time alienating a third great power whose help you clearly need, you can expect that the ensuing war will begin badly for you. Why not— you have given up what you obviously need. Czechoslovakia was of tremendous strategic value because of its location, and the Soviet reaction was critical to forming a common front. The "aggression" was the least important part of what happened, except as a trigger to the other adverse consequences.

Only a nation such as the United States, where the study of geography is more tolerated than honored on the nation's campuses, would miss the significant points of the Munich experience, applying the "lesson" even in Southeast Asia's least strategic areas. A "happening," such as being aggressed-upon, cannot convert a nonstrategic area into a strategic area, for the simple reason that strategic importance is far more the byproduct of geographic location than it is of a historic event. *Where it is* is fundamental in determining its importance; much less so, what evils befall it. To say it another way, important events tend to occur in important places.

As one rule of thumb, looking at on-shore relationships, a small nation becomes strategic in direct relationship to the number of large nations that share its frontiers.[12] A small nation adjacent to three (or sometimes even two) such powers is invariably highly strategic in its location. This is why Korea, at the focus of China, Russia, and Japan, has played a key role in Asia. It is why Switzerland (surrounded by France, Germany, Italy, and Austria) has played an equally key role in Europe. Similarly, the Low Countries (Belgium and Holland) are at the intersection of Britain, France, and Germany; just as Czechoslovakia offers access both to the Balkans and as a corridor between Germany and Russia, particularly during periods when Poland has existed between them as a buffer.

The containment doctrine, reflecting American attitudes, attached strategic significance to geographic location only in the limited sense that the line of deployment to contain expansive communism was to be held on the outer extremity of what was already in Communist hands, to prevent their taking any more.

It further assumed, on the basis of little real evidence, that communism represented a monolithic bloc, centrally controlled from Moscow. So all aggressions, if they occurred, would be Moscow-ordered. Naturally, they would represent probes of the weak points in American defenses. If Vietnam did not look like strategic real estate, Americans should not be misled. By attacking there, the cunning Communists were simply trying to delude the United States into

---

[12]Looked at in terms of maritime strategy we would want to add that nations lying athwart "choke points" or straits which the ships of large nations must pass or utilize, have a high strategic rating, too.

The Intellectual Framework and the Cultural Background

making judgments that ignored the potency of the domino theory to operate with disastrous effects *anywhere* in the world.

We have seen that, in 1950, when outright aggression occurred in Korea, Truman moved to stop the Communist aggression. Since that aggression had in fact occurred in a strategic area, the effort in principle was worthwhile, because it prevented a radical disturbance of the Asian balance of power such as would have resulted from South Korea's passing into the Communist orbit. But American leaders tended to justify the action on other grounds than the balance of power: that they were opposing and repulsing world communism rather than preventing what was probably the initiative of North Korea to unify the country. When China intervened after the United States had in its turn advanced into North Korea, and the Soviet Union underwrote the military effort with arms and supplies, Americans saw it all as confirmation of their assessment rather than as a reaction to their efforts.

Believing Communist China to be the puppet or client of the Soviet Union, the United States never paused long thereafter to consider China's view of its national interests, or the threat China saw in the American advance towards its frontiers while the United States simultaneously supported a rival claimant to power in China—Chiang Kai-shek. Americans saw the People's Republic of China with two-dimensional cardboard flatness, only as a part of a bloc.

The whole history of the dissensions in the worldwide Communist movement was ignored, even the well-known disagreements between the Soviets and the Chinese in the 1920s. So China became in American eyes the Asian flank of the Communist menace, irrevocably tied to the Soviet Union. That menace had to be contained.

Summarizing the operational (implementation) consequences of the main features of the containment concept, we can see that it (1) defines the enemy, (2) defines where the battle must be joined, and (3) defines when the battle must be fought.

The enemy is any Communist state, large or small; the battle must be fought anywhere the challenge is made through an aggression; and it must be fought anytime they wish (i.e., commit an aggression). About the only thing left open for Americans to decide is or was the choice of weapons for U.S. troops! To express the point differently, the United States, by embracing these views, had given up control over when and where and with whom it would make war. In its pursuit of a set of moral abstract principles, the United States had surrendered unwittingly its own essential moral responsibility for its own actions. It was this mindlessness of the Vietnam killing as a consequence of this mechanical application of morality that finally led to a reassessment of the whole approach.

One of Oscar Wilde's characters in *The Picture of Dorian Gray* remarks that "A man cannot be too careful in the choice of his enemies." The United States, guided and mesmerized by its containment strategy, gave up that discretion after 1947. It is no wonder that so many Americans felt helpless to control their own government. Their own government had abdicated control over its most important actions in foreign affairs. The United States had become involved both globally in scope and automatically by type of "happening."

10.

Summing Up

In this chapter we have sought to make clear what distinctive attitudes toward foreign policy have been produced by the unusual experience of the American people and what the strengths and weaknesses implicit in those attitudes have to do with the conduct and degree of success of U.S. foreign policy. Of all that has been said, one clear warning arises: the United States, temperamentally, is likely to err on the side of attempting too much once it begins to go outside the framework of traditional or clearly understood national interests. Partly this happens because of the relatively secure frontiers the United States enjoys at home, which encourages the thought of taking action abroad. Partly this happens because the "super" power of the United States sets no self-evident limits to what might be attempted. Partly this happens because it is consistent with the American temperament and character to "think big." Partly this happens because Americans have not really grasped how to make the system deliver acceptable results with conservative expenditures of money and blood.

But, if this is so, Americans need to understand more about the state system and how it really functions so that they can conceptualize policy more efficiently. In Chapter 1 we made a beginning by describing some of the elementary features of that system. In Chapter 4 we focus further on the intellectual links between the foreign policy process and the "rules" of the system. This focus prepares us for later judgments about the most basic question that policy must answer: where and when and how to be involved, and where and when and how not to be.

4

Phase 1: Designing Policy (The Cardinal Principles)

One of the curious omissions ... was what instructions should be given Mac-Arthur in event the Chinese Communists intervened in North Korea. This occurred, I believe, because of our view that North Korea was a Moscow-inspired operation and hence a Russian problem, not a Chinese Communist problem. Thus we believed Soviet intervention in North Korea was far more likely than Chinese intervention.

General Omar N. Bradley
Chairman, U.S. Joint
Chiefs of Staff[1]

We ended Chapter 1 by pointing out how two themes ran throughout. The first theme emphasized that explanations of policy decisions tended to be oriented in two different directions, which we called "internal" and "external." The internal explanations looked at such things as the bureaucratic process, the relations between the executive and the Congress or the role of the press and popular attitudes and assumptions, in order to explain what decisions were made, and why. (Chapters 2 and 3 elaborated the point about American attitudes and assumptions.) "External" explanations, on the other hand, put stress on the problem that a nation confronts, and the logical alternatives available to deal with it, regardless of the kind of nation facing the problem. External explanations stress the multilateral state system environment in which all nation-states exist and the logical conditions the system imposes on decision making. It would be foolish, of course, to try to explain decisions on the basis of only internal or only external considerations. Policymakers must and do take both "environments" into account and must function successfully in both. Decision making (policymaking), like the mythical Janus, has two *faces*.

The second theme emphasized that policy, in addition to its two faces, has two *phases*. It must be looked at sequentially, first as design, then as implementation.

[1]Omar N. Bradley and Clay Blair, *A General's Life: An Autobiography* (New York: Simon & Schuster, 1983), pp. 563–564.

Phase 1 (design) of the policy process is concerned with working out what could be tried, focusing on what any prudent nation will have to take into account in attempting such a course of action or such a set of goals. Phase 1 is directed toward the *intellectual appraisal* of policy from the point of view of what must be assessed by decision makers as they design policy or speculate about the likelihood of that policy achieving intended results. We saw in Chapter 3 that the decision makers in the United States have often approached this task with very nation-particular attitudes about the world.

Phase 2 (implementation), by contrast, is the realm of *doing it*. It is focused on the specific and sequential steps through which policy proceeds once it is implemented and becomes operational (passes from the drawing board to the operations room). Phase 2 is also influenced by national "style," but less so than phase 1.[2] Both phases are equally important because a good design will not prevail over a faulty implementation any more than an effective implementation can repair the defects of a poor concept or design. And the way in which both phases are accomplished will be somewhat different nation by nation even though the logic of the process is everywhere more or less the same.

To these two themes of the nature of policy and how it works we need now to add a two-part yardstick. If, as we intend in the rest of this book, we are to make judgments about the efficacy of past U.S. policy or to make suggestions and recommendations about future policy, we ought to have an explicit basis and set of standards against which to make those judgments. We ought, in fairness and for the sake of clarity, to provide a two-part yardstick or checklist against which design and implementation can be judged as U.S. policymakers attempt to reconcile internal demands with external constraints. Chapters 4 and 5 present such explicit standards. In them, we are looking to see what policymakers *should* take into account, or, in reverse terms, what most particularly, apart from lack of public support, will cause a policy to fall short of intended goals. Chapter 4, devoted to the "cardinal principles," makes explicit our major standards for judging phase 1: policy design. Chapter 5, devoted to the "operational steps," makes equally explicit our major standards for judging phase 2: policy implementation.

In presenting these standards we are asserting that adherence to them is important to success. We are far from arguing that these standards are always and everywhere rigorously adhered to in actual policymaking. (But, if that *were* so, we would have no need to criticize. And without any standards, we would criticize in a vacuum.)

1.

The Policy Process

Before we introduce the cardinal principles as a checklist for phase 1, it will help to recapitulate some of the key statements about design already introduced in Chapter 1, in order to expand them. It is necessary now that we think more exactly about what we mean by the policy process, particularly its design phase, and more exactly about how it proceeds.

First, to recapitulate the main thought, in Chapter 1 we said that a debate over national interests is a debate over claims to be included in the content of policy. The concepts or ideas that prevail in the debate will decide that issue, decide which national interest claims are to be accepted, decide then the content of the policy to be attempted. So there is (first) ideas or design or concept, which (secondly) give rise to a content, which (thirdly) is implemented.

Add now to this triad that the power backing for the policy will bear on its success, and

---

[2]This is not an off-the-cuff observation. One of the authors has taught senior foreign decision makers from about three dozen nations for almost twenty years.

that the process will, when implemented, produce some kind of results or outcomes, and we have a five-part expanded policy process which would look like Diagram 2.

Diagram 2 enlarges our consideration also in a second way. Whereas in Diagram 1, under each of the three parts of concept, content, and implementation, we used a relatively short description of the function of each part, here in Diagram 2 we have elaborated the meaning of that description. What, for example, would the phrase "weigh alternatives," used in Diagram 1 under content, really involve from an intellectual viewpoint? How does policy design proceed as an actual thought process? Consider four points.

First, the really critical job in policy design is to consider alternatives against expectations. But formulating these alternatives is itself difficult because doing that presupposes one has already *identified the problem* and is ready to proceed next to identifying what can be done about it.

How things can be made to turn out depends importantly on the nature of the problem confronted. For example, deciding what alternatives are available to deal with Nicaragua in 1984 and 1985 and what might be done about it to achieve a better situation entails first deciding what kind of a problem Nicaragua represents for the United States. Is it primarily a source of subversion in Central America? Do Nicaragua's policies stem from past resentments or from present hunger and deprivation? Are Nicaragua's neighbors such as Honduras or Guatemala vulnerable because they have inequities in distribution of wealth or because of cheap or free arms distributed there by foreign or native Communists, using Cuba and Nicaragua as way stations? Or a bit of both? Answering those questions is fundamental to framing the alternatives for dealing with them. (Diagnosing the illness must precede prescribing the medicine.)

Second, the alternatives, once formulated, must be considered against the power resources they would take to be implemented. Capability becomes important, whether in the form of food and economic assistance (or pressures), or in the form of military aid (or pressures). If one alternative for U.S. policy in the Caribbean is military, are the means potentially available given the likelihood of other problems occurring simultaneously? How high would the Caribbean rank in priority compared to elsewhere? Such considerations are important in the planning stages of policy. (We may have a clear idea of the illness and what to treat it with but we have either no penicillin or not enough.)

There is a third consideration. We may identify the problem or situation incorrectly, particularly as to who is the opponent. We may think we are dealing with Communist subversion in the Caribbean or somewhere else and decide to use military capability to deal with it, only to find that our *results* are not what we expected because the problem really was human rights or economic stultification or class divisions between rich and poor.

Even the briefest study of accounts of how the United States decided to fight the Vietnam War will show the uncertainty and vacillation that prevailed among the American policymakers. Who was the enemy? World communism? The whole Communist "bloc," with Russia at the controls? Or Russia using China and China using North Vietnam as frontman? Or North Vietnam, using the Viet Cong in South Vietnam as frontman? Deciding this question was fundamental to fighting the war effectively. It was hardly tenable to assume that one would fight the same war in the same way regardless of the answer given to this fundamental question.

Secretary of State Dean Rusk, testifying before the Senate Committee on Foreign Relations on February 18, 1966, said:

> South Vietnam is a long way from the United States, and the issues posed may seem remote from our daily experience and our immediate interests. . . .
> Why are we in Vietnam? . . . [B]ecause the issues posed there are deeply intertwined with our security. . . . what we are seeking to achieve in South Vietnam is part of a process . . .

DIAGRAM 2 The Policy Process

Power		Policy			Outcomes
Capability	X	**Concept**	**Content**	**Implementation**	= **Results**
		• Defines the problem • States the issues • Weighs' alternative courses of action against presumed future effects • Decides on most likely advantageous alternative, given nature of problem and power available	• Establishes one set of claims (alternatives) as policy • Defines therefore "the national interests" • Shelves the other alternatives for possible later use	• Tasks appropriate parts of the government • Coordinates plans for action • Carries out the policy using political, military, economic, etc., means	

of preventing the expansion and extension of Communist domination by the use of force against the weaker nations on the perimeter of Communist power.[3]

How clear was this guidance? Apparently the United States was fighting on behalf of some "issues" and against Communist expansion. But who was the real enemy? Look back at the headnote of this chapter, taken from General Bradley's later memoirs. He says the United States was prepared for Russian but not Chinese intervention in the Korean War. All these examples illustrate that our *perception* can be inaccurate as we design policy. (We have what might be the right medicine but for the wrong disease.)

There is a fourth point. We may not understand the significance of fundamental developments in the system. Since the design of a foreign policy also reveals national attitudes toward the world, it inevitably is also a statement of *how that world appears to the national policymakers to function*—in the U.S. case, of what makes the system better or worse from an American viewpoint. If the policymakers made different conceptual assumptions about the operation of the system, they would weigh different alternatives. They would include or exclude different contents to their policies. A China that was presumed to be essentially hostile to the United States because of Chinese ideological preferences would be seen in a different light if the American policymakers think ideology is a lesser factor in setting friend-enemy relationships. Again, if one country conquers another country, Americans can see it as the beginning of an irreversible trend (as dominoes fall), or as an isolated event with no discernible consequences. That event could, of course, also be the necessary catalyst for shocking indifferent neighbors into the creation of a common front against the aggressor. The event is the same event, but its perceived meaning alters and leads to a different concept of what Americans should do about it. (We may think we are seriously ill when we only have a minor cold or think we are healthy and are not.)

In both illustrations (to which we return shortly), the rules of the game by which the system functions can be interpreted very differently, depending upon the conceptual perspective shared by national decision makers. The history of U.S. policy shows some distinct tendencies in conceptual preferences. It also shows some (at times) serious departures from the real way in which the system operates.

Summing up the policy process in phase 1, we can see that in the design phase the argument over proposed policy contents (i.e., which particular national interests to pursue) will reflect conceptual perspectives. Within a nation some sort of political debate about values and means and ends will be triggered, leading sooner or later to a consensus. Within the government some compromise of divergent (or converging) bureaucratic interests (plus some influences from standard bureaucratic procedures) will occur as the issues become sharper. The debate itself, both in the public and bureaucracy, will turn on projections as to the consequences of what is to be attempted or ignored by any proposed policy and what is most or least dangerous. Such a debate may be informed or uninformed, highly public or very private. It may involve painful attempts at new thinking to meet new situations, or it may be a debate simply between rival clichés and generalizations of a very imprecise sort. But, in some form, it will occur.

In military or game terms, the debate will hold various "scenarios" up for scrutiny, involving assumptions as to the motivations and behavior of opponents or enemies, the prospective or probable reaction of third parties, and the consequent likely results (at some presumed cost). Consider the arms debate that began in 1983 over whether it is wise to match Soviet arms efforts missile for missile. Which conclusion one reaches turns on assumptions, including the motivation for the Soviet arms build-up and the alternative dangers of (1) keeping up with them (at the

---

[3]Dean Rusk, "The United States Commitment in Vietnam: Fundamental Issues." Testimony Before the U.S. Senate Committee on Foreign Relations, February 18, 1966. Department of State *Bulletin,* March 7, 1966. Department of State Publication 8054.

DIAGRAM 3 Policy Design

STEPS IN ANALYSIS

For Each Concept	For Each Content
1. What is the problem? 2. What could (should) be done about the issues thus raised? 3. Who would help? 4. Who would hinder? 5. What would it cost compared to anticipated results?	1. What kind of common and opposed interests will a given choice of interest produce bilaterally? Multilaterally? 2. What would occur in the system if a "swap" were made, substituting a presently "shelved" or rejected alternative? 3. What would happen if another state or other states made such substitutions in *their* policies?

The Intellectual Framework and the Cultural Background

cost of increased tension) versus (2) lowering tensions by falling behind (at the cost of increased potential vulnerability). The effects of each scenario, if implemented, have to be thought through in advance, tracing each alternative to its conclusion.

In diagrammatic terms we can now expand and elaborate the policy design portion of Diagram 2, showing more specifically how the thought process works. We have this time, in Diagram 3, set out specific questions that need to be addressed, some of them already discussed, the rest to be discussed. Bear in mind that Diagram 3 represents not a single thought process but a series of iterations looking at various possible combinations of goals and costs.

When the debate is over and some consensus is reached it means that one scenario has prevailed. Phase 1 is over until the consensus fails and a new debate ensues.

Now that we are clear on the stages of the process in phase 1, let us look behind the debate at the principles which will determine, from a system point of view, whether the policy will likely prove feasible as to design. We turn to the cardinal principles.

2.

The Cardinal Principles

Like the four major points of the compass, four cardinal principles serve as a handy checklist of the most important points about policy design. These four principles do not exhaust the list of relevant points any more than north, south, east, or west are the only relevant directions on the compass. But these four are what we consider the most important when policy design is at issue. We use these four principles as a "model" for appraising the "strategic" direction of a policy considered or attempted. By model we merely mean the essential bare-bones points and how they relate to each other. By strategic we do not mean military; we mean "by way of a sense of direction," or "the big picture," the overall conception. Therefore, a strategic model such as the cardinal principles is judging a policy in the large but only from the special point of view of how likely it is to succeed or work or not. And by "succeed," we mean acceptable results at acceptable costs.

All four principles have to do with what foreign policy makers should take into account, but the first two remind policymakers of the specific *national* context of each of the foreign "players" or "actors" (the states), whereas the second two remind policymakers of the *multilateral systems* context in which policy is pursued, regardless of national characteristics. These four principles are *past-future linkages, third-party influences, counterbalancing national interests,* and *the conservation of enemies.* We define and illustrate each one in turn.

3.

Past-Future Linkages

Past-future linkages as a principle directs attention to how the perception of what will happen in the future is linked to one's understanding of what has happened in the past, a point brought out in Chapters 2 and 3 for the United States.

Events themselves rarely contain convincing clues to their consequences. Greek tragedy is powerful drama because it uses the theatrical convention that the event itself has predictable (and tragic) results, inevitable and unavoidable. But in real life we puzzle as to the implications of what we see and then try to pierce the veil of the future. What we do in practice is to apply what we think are "the lessons of the past."

In June 1950, U.S. Secretary of State Dean Acheson phoned President Harry S. Truman at his home in Missouri and said: "Mr. President, I have very serious news. The North Koreans have invaded South Korea."[4]

Truman reacted both immediately and decisively, and despite the fact that U.S. military plans did not envisage sending troops to conduct land warfare in Korea, Truman ordered that it be done. He explained his reasons in his memoirs:

> In my generation, this was not the first occasion when the strong had attacked the weak. I recalled some earlier instances: Manchuria, Ethiopia, Austria. I remembered how each time that the democracies failed to act it had encouraged the aggressors to keep going ahead. Communism was acting in Korea just as Hitler, Mussolini, and the Japanese had acted ten, fifteen, and twenty years earlier. I felt certain that if South Korea was allowed to fall Communist leaders would be emboldened to override nations closer to our own shores [and] no small nation would have the courage to resist threats and aggression by stronger Communist neighbors. If this was allowed to go unchallenged it would mean a third world war, just as similar incidents had brought on the second world war.[5]

Decisions in foreign policy, then, reflect future expectations.

We see this same process at work on June 10, 1940, after the collapse of the French resistance in World War II, when it appeared that Hitler's chance of winning the war was very good indeed. President Franklin D. Roosevelt argued *his* view of the world and where Americans would end up, depending on the choices they made. Given Hitler's triumph on the European mainland, FDR said that it was a "delusion" that the United States could remain an island of peace in a world at war: "Such an island represents to me and to the overwhelming majority of Americans today a helpless nightmare of a people without freedom—the nightmare of a people lodged in prison, handcuffed, hungry, and fed through the bars from day to day by the contemptuous, unpitying masters of other continents."[6] FDR was laying out a progression of events and the outcomes of policy choice as he foresaw them, a vision necessarily reflecting his own view of how the system would reward or punish alternative courses of action.

As we see in Chapter 11, at this very time another influential group in the United States, the "America First" movement, thought that Hitler had the strength to win, that Britain could not hold out, and that the United States was virtually unassailable in the Western Hemisphere. In contrast, FDR thought Britain's survival likely, with support, and essential to keeping the war from America's very shores. This was a view congenial to the "interventionists" who at an earlier stage of the debate had argued that the United States must use its strength to support the League of Nations and end the "march of aggression." The isolationists, pacifists, and the America First members thought that the United States, with its geographical location far from the cockpits of conflict, could effectively choose to remain aloof from war—war that they saw as always an evil and never with right and wrong clearly parceled out among belligerents.

This debate, nominally over the content of the policy and argued predominantly in moral terms, was really centered on different visions of the future for the United States if one alternative was chosen over the other, different views of the issues drawn from different views of the operation of the system. Each side drew on a divergent set of background experiences to make its point. Roosevelt, more cosmopolitan, was pointing to the world's experience with a Napoleon, and to the sequence of events during 1914 to 1917 that convinced Woodrow Wilson that the United States must participate in "the war to end all wars" (World War I). On both occasions America found itself unable to stay aloof from Europe's turmoil, almost fighting both Britain

---

[4]Harry S. Truman, *Memoirs,* vol. 2, *Years of Trial and Hope* (Garden City, N.Y.: Doubleday, 1956), p. 332.
[5]Ibid., pp. 332–333.
[6]Robert A. Divine, *Roosevelt and World War II* (Baltimore: Johns Hopkins Press, 1969), p. 31.

and France in 1812, and declaring war on Germany in 1917. The America Firsters, more parochial, were pointing to the long period in American history between Napoleon and World War I when the United States was virtually immune to European invasion and "had the good sense to stay out of Europe's affairs."

Thus future (although contrasting) expectations are weighed against past experiences to yield present guidance to choice and decision. We can see that, regardless of how the debate terminates, once it does and decisions are made, certain claims (potential national interests) will be rejected or "shelved" (for possible use at a later time) and their alternatives pursued. So the interests chosen (and rejected) are direct reflections of assumptions made about future results in a system presumed to operate in a particular way. These assumptions and expectations will change as experience accumulates, usually becoming more realistic.[7]

A third illustration of the principle is the whole American approach to the Vietnam War, on which we earlier quoted Secretary Rusk. The conceptual design that ultimately led to the deployment of more than a half million men in a rather obscure area of Southeast Asia, and to the fighting of America's longest and most unsuccessful war, was made much more specific even if no less debatable in the policy statement of January 27, 1962, of the U.S. Joint Chiefs of Staff:

> It is recognized that the military and political effort of Communist China in South Vietnam. . . is part of a major campaign to extend Communist control beyond the periphery of the Sino-Soviet bloc and overseas to both island and continental areas in the Free World. . . . It is, in fact, a planned phase in the Communist time-table for world domination.[8]

By saying these things the Joint Chiefs were reflecting what they thought was true. Although they said Vietnam was "in fact" a part of a Communist plan for "world domination," they really did not know that factually. The question here is why the Joint Chiefs (followed by most Americans at the time) were so sure of their "facts," why they were so certain that common ideology means common friends and common enemies, that they were willing (by implication and later in fact) to spend lavishly of American blood and treasure to honor this statement. Because the truth is that everything that has happened since 1965 shows that this analysis was much too facile and basically wrong in assuming the continued existence of cordial Sino-Soviet cooperation. Everything since 1965 shows that the relationship between the People's Republic of China and the Soviet Union is fundamentally one of antagonism— a "natural" result of their border disputes; their contrasting cultures; the anxieties implicit in a long mutual frontier; and dissimilar strategic circumstances, problems, and capabilities. Poland, in Europe, in 1980 to 1982, was an even more direct indication of the feebleness of a common ideology as a means of overcoming nationalism, cultural differences or fear. Even so, this idea may not be entirely discarded in the United States. Indeed, President Reagan in the early 1980s showed a tendency to revive this kind of thinking.

The exceptional importance that American policymakers attached to ideology after World War II reflects the observations in Chapters 2 and 3, on a mirror-image basis. Since the United States built its own cohesion in a multicultured society to a great extent on abstract but unifying propositions (beginning with the Declaration of Independence), it did not find it difficult to think of communism unifying nations with different cultures abroad. The strength of such a view led to a discounting of the significance of the Sino-Soviet dispute, which was already quite public in 1963. Two years *after* the 1963 public exchange of acidic and unfraternal charges between Russia and China, the United States landed combat troops in Southeast Asia to contain what it still

---

[7]Auguste Comte argued that knowledge passed through three stages: fictitious, abstract, and scientific or "positive." *Cours de philosophie positive*, I, 1830.

[8]*Pentagon Papers* (Gravel edition), vol. 2, p. 664. Italics added.

thought of as a Communist bloc aggression. Although the pronouncements of American policymakers in these years showed frequent vacillation over *who* in the Communist camp was in operational control of the aggression (China, Russia, North Vietnam), from a strategic point of view the Vietnam War was consistently seen during President Johnson's administration as a test between a united "Communist bloc" and the "Free World," to which the United States had to commit enormous resources.

The American view of containment conferred on ideology an exaggerated value in deciding friend-enemy relationships. It superimposed on that the special power theory of a first aggression's critical consequences, known as the domino effect.

We saw in Chapter 3 that the domino theory or effect traces back in its modern form at least to President Eisenhower. In a news conference on April 7, 1954, he expressed the idea in the following words: "You have a row of dominoes set up, you knock over the first one, and what will happen to the last one is that it will go over very quickly. So you have a beginning of a disintegration that would have the most profound influences."[9]

President Kennedy, asked his views some years later, said of the domino theory, "I believe it. I believe it." President Johnson also indicated on many occasions that he subscribed fully to the domino logic.

There is little question, as we argued earlier, that the domino effect these American presidents were discussing as though it were a general law of politics originated in one specific event: the Munich Conference of 1938 at which Britain and France agreed to Czechoslovakia's dismantling and the cession to Germany of the Czech Sudetenland. That event proved to be only the initial stage in Hitler's complete takeover of Czechoslovakia in March 1939. These were critical events, soon followed by world war. So it is not surprising that many analysts (including Winston Churchill in his history of World War II) later emphasized the view that early opposition to Hitler would have been both effective and comparatively inexpensive compared to what did happen. They argued in effect that world war had to be fought *because* of the appeasement, *because* the confrontation was repeatedly postponed. (Notice the parallel here to Woodrow Wilson's thinking about the need for a League of Nations to confront and repulse any outright aggression as soon as it occurs.)

Churchill, though, was arguing about one specific historical occasion. The American presidents, speaking for a nation newly anxious about national security and with a limited international experience, were applying what they thought was a general rule of international politics.

No one can argue with the view that the domino effect often occurs in the early stages of an aggressor's expansion. But it is far from clear that *any* aggression by *any* aggressor leads to the drastic effects it did with Germany under Hitler. In some cases aggressors *do* have only limited objectives. Nor can it be taken for granted that the cost of stopping a first aggression is always cheaper than it will be later. (Consider a nuclear-armed Russia and Afghanistan.)

Modern American thinking has been generally hostile to ideas about "power politics" or any concepts implying the ultimate impossibility of universal harmony. The American distaste for balance of power theory (which is a prime example of power-political views) has led Americans to ignore the theory's teachings. Balance of power theory points out that the domino effect is a typical early stage development in the disintegration of any balance of power. But after that initial systems stage comes a later stage. The rest of the threatened, convinced they cannot hide from the threat, make common cause in a coalition to restrain the expanding conqueror, thus "balancing" the aggressor or aggressor bloc. This coalition effect indeed happened to Napoleon and Hitler alike when they overstepped themselves.

Interestingly, both the extraordinary value Americans impute to ideology as a determinant

[9]Dwight D. Eisenhower, news conference, April 7, 1954. *Public Papers of the Presidents: Dwight D. Eisenhower, 1954* (Washington, D.C.: U.S. Government Printing Office, 1960), p. 383.

of foreign policy and the stress American policymakers have placed on the domino theory are views not universally shared around the globe. Both of these views, although not exclusively American, are almost so—itself a warning that they are likely to lead to difficulties when they are applied universally. Consequently, what these ideas contribute (or have contributed) to American foreign policy is a tendency to early actions designed theoretically to abort more serious later threats, especially where the aggression can be clearly linked to communism. Such ideas reinforce the American temperamental tendency toward quick, automatic, and reflexive actions.

The cardinal principle of past-future linkages reminds us that problems are not perceived in identical terms by the parties to a dispute, negotiation, or crisis. Instead, each will assess the problem and weigh its policy alternatives and their projected future consequences in light of its own special past experience. The resulting paradox is that neither "the problem" nor "the solution" are seen as identical by the different parties involved.

4.

Third-Party Influences

The second cardinal principle, third-party influences, is a reminder both that the state system is multilateral and that the world is round. It is extraordinarily easy to forget this very obvious point, particularly for a nation such as the United States with its unusual location.

The most pressing consequence of a multilateral world is that states have more than one frontier. Every state, dealing with any other state, is doing so within a real environment that consists of many states. Two states may become preoccupied with one another, and to that extent oblivious to the rest, but such preoccupation is always dangerous. In a frontal preoccupation, to change the figure of speech, the flanks and rear are left unguarded. Such preoccupation necessarily is an abstraction from and a distortion of the real world. The United States, with oceans on either side and weak neighbors above and below (who, in turn, are insulated from much fear of attack across their other frontiers), is particularly likely to minimize the effects of more usual frontier-neighbor relationships. Most states know they cannot afford to look in one direction too exclusively. The Soviet Union, which borders on eleven other states, is a good example. One might argue that only one threat—the American threat—is really preeminent for the Soviets. But they hardly think so. They fear much more a revanchist Germany backed by American power, or a revanchist China aided by Japanese and American resources. The Soviet Union, in contrast to the United States, has only one compass direction it can feel is fairly safe from land attack—the polar ice cap. And, ironically, that polar ice cap is the main route of U.S. missiles targeted against Russia.

Many maxims originating in antiquity reflect the effects of geographical location, that "my neighbor's neighbor is my friend." One of the oldest of all dates back to before Christ and is found in Kautilya's *Arthasastra* in which the advice is given in this form: "The third and fifth states from a Madhyama (mediatory) king are states friendly to him; while the second, the fourth, and the sixth are unfriendly."[10] Although it is expressed somewhat mechanically, the idea of how the system effects work is clear enough.

To express the same proposition in more modern language, neighboring states are normally feared much more than remote states who would not find it convenient to invade. But neighboring states have to consider what would happen at *their* back if they did attack you at their front. Consider Imperial Japan in the summer of 1941 from this viewpoint. Japan had, for a number of years, been subjugating China—seriously since 1937. Although incomplete, Japan's conquest

---

[10]Quoted in Paul Seabury, ed., *Balance of Power* (San Francisco: Chandler, 1965), p. 15.

of China removed China as a serious threat if Japan became preoccupied elsewhere. In June 1941, Nazi Germany's assault on the Soviet Union removed Japan's second (and last) major power continental neighbor from Japan's strategic calculations. For the first and only time in modern history Japan could seriously entertain the idea of striking at the United States without being vulnerable from behind. Alternatively, Japan had the option of striking at Russia while the Soviets were preoccupied with the Germans. That option was tempting, but the first alternative was better from a Japanese perspective, for not only would the United States be free in the Japanese rear if Japan attacked Russia. A Japanese attack on Russia could not deliver the access to oil and raw materials that a war with the United States to dominate East Asia could bring. Also, a war with the United States could utilize Japan's large and virtually unused navy to national advantage. If the United States had been thinking in terms of third-party influences it would never have been caught napping at Pearl Harbor.

Many may be tempted to think today, given the enormous technological change that has affected weapons since World War II, that this example has been overtaken by events. A war between the United States and the Soviet Union might well be fought directly by ICBMs, from one continent to the other, with that missile exchange not directly influenced by the identity or sympathies of *anybody's* neighbors.

How accurate is this assessment, which implies that third parties today are really essentially irrelevant?

At its most fundamental, this question is asking what goes into a decision to wage war. Does the decision turn predominantly or exclusively upon a conviction that one has the military power to destroy an enemy? Granted such an assumption is often a prime prerequisite to ordering an attack, is it sufficient in and of itself? How much store should one place on a presumed "window of vulnerability?"[11] How much confidence should one place in the assumption that because one leads in weapons, no surprises are in store? At the opposite extreme, how much should one assume that an attack may be deterred through the potentially unpredictable actions of third parties? A war is inherently a gamble since not only is the respective power of the two sides not known in advance but neither are the sides ultimately predictable. How much does having an unfriendly China at its back influence Soviet willingness to face the United States in confrontation to begin with—or to end with?

Regardless of the pronounced tendency in much of contemporary strategic theory to simplify antagonistic relationships down to opposed weapons piles, there is no good reason to suppose that third parties can be dismissed as irrelevant today to two-party confrontations. If West Germany (a third party to U.S.–Soviet antagonism) were to join Russia against NATO, or Poland were to join NATO, the ramifications would extend far beyond adding and subtracting military units to each side's totals. Nuclear weapons have changed the ways in which wars may be fought tactically. They have changed the significance of deciding for war in the first place. But they have not changed the role of third parties in affecting the behavior of two parties caught up in an opposed and antagonistic relationship. A Soviet Union armed to the teeth but without a real ally in the world would act far differently from a Soviet Union also armed to the teeth but secure in the freely given support of a dozen or more allies.

Brezhnev, as ruler of the Soviet Union, obviously agreed with that assessment in 1973, when he visited with President Nixon at Camp David and San Clemente, after the United States, by opening relations with Communist China, had "played the China card." Brezhnev at San Clem-

---

[11]This term refers to the supposed opportunity of the Soviets, with their heavier yield weapons now linked to much greater missile accuracy, and with their supposed willingness to strike first, to take advantage of U.S. fixed silo vulnerability and attack before the United States can "harden" missiles or disperse or hide them. See also Chapter 16.

ente anxiously inquired of Nixon whether the United States contemplated a military alliance with China.[12] Brezhnev obviously thought that a China in his rear as he "faced" America (or an America in his rear as he faced China) was a less favorable strategic situation for his country—as indeed it was.

In 1982 the decision of Argentina to take the Falkland Islands (Malvinas, as the Argentinians name them) rested on a false appraisal of the likely policy of a crucial third power, the United States. Argentina assumed the United States would in no way aid Britain and that Britain, unaided, could not effectively retaliate.

The second cardinal principle of third-party influences reminds us that no bilateral relationship, whether political or military (or economic), is ever exactly that. When two nations "face" each other in negotiations, other nations are there too, in effect, even if not physically. The paradox here is that any "bilateral" problem is always also multilateral.

5.

Relating the First Two Cardinal Principles

The linking of third-party influences to the first cardinal principle yields the interesting proposition that in a multilateral system decisions will be made by "actors" from different bases in past experience and with different expectations about the behavior of various third parties. Cultural factors will reinforce the effects of diverse locations, both helping to ensure that a "common problem"will therefore quite frequently be perceived by different nations as not the same problem at all. Even the time sense of a nation with a long history will contrast with that of a new nation and influence how they each define an issue. Many consequences follow from these observations. For example, in the field of strategic thought, deterrence theory is heavily imbued with the assumption that a crisis or a weapons relationship will appear in identical or essentially similar terms to all parties involved. The cultural identity of the "player" or the identity of its neighbors is given little attention. How valid then is the assumption made that Chinese, Russian, and American thinking will be identical or similar about the "same" problem? Can we really assume that reaction under stress or willingness to compromise will reflect the logic of a situation rather than the cultural-temperamental characteristics of the players? And is the "logic" the same for any two players if a third is not exactly equal in friendship or hostility to both?

Because certain tendencies toward uniform behavior within the system exist, it is tempting to extend the sphere of uniformity beyond where it quite clearly exists. But the tendencies toward uniformity are largely of the type noted in Chapter 1. Each nation perceives a power problem. Each nation conceives a foreign policy. Each nation chooses interests to pursue. Each nation must consider the possible policies of all its neighbors. The uniformities do *not* extend to the point where the fears of nations are identical, where the type of policy is always exactly as ambitious (or modest), where the content of policy is standard, where the neighbors and third-party influences are identical.

It should hardly be necessary to argue that varying geographical locations, coupled with diverse historical experiences and different cultural habits will yield divergent assessments of "common" problems. It should not be necessary, but it is, especially for Americans with specifically American cultural biases that discount these differences and overstate the uniformities. Pollution or energy or the resources of the sea may all be "common problems" in one sense, but the actual significance attached to any one of them by a group of nations may cover quite a range. World hunger from some universal viewpoint may imply sharing. But a surplus of food

---

[12] *RN: The Memoirs of Richard Nixon,* vol. 2 (New York: Warner Books, 1979), p. 426.

in one area and a shortage in another will not necessarily lead to a transfer of resources, to the concerting of policy, or even to a more or less similar sense of priority among the nations on handling the problem. Such lack of uniformity is the "natural" result of divergencies in location, history, and culture.

6.

Counterbalancing National Interests

The third cardinal principle is *counterbalancing national interests,* and it is the connecting link between the public debate over policy at home and the system effect of policy abroad. The principle refers to the alternatives that confront decision makers as claims are advanced in public debate that various things are "in the national interest" and ought to be included (excluded) from present policy. Not every decision on policy that officials make involves such counterbalancing interests, only important decisions, especially choices that set policy in a new direction or influence the spectrum of opposition a nation faces from outside its frontiers.

It is not necessary to think of such choices as always and inevitably between two alternatives, although that is the usual and natural condition. Sometimes the number of alternatives may appear (or even be) more than two. It would not alter the point. What is much more critical is to understand that these choices are not mirror images, with the positive value of one alternative necessarily equal to the negative value of the other. If, for instance, a decision is made to no longer regard Communist China as an enemy, that change does not mean China becomes or must become an American ally. A policy of sanctions against South Africa does not guarantee black African support for the United States to the same extent as a refusal of sanctions may induce black African hostility. Neither of these examples, of course, is complete—the point here is only that the opposing values are not reciprocals.

The reason that that is so lies in the nature of the system. Although the actions of one toward another impinge on the rest, the effect of the action is not uniform. The initial and direct bilateral effect of a Sino-American rapprochement is a lessening of friction between those two states. Freeing China from undue anxiety about U.S. actions then impacts on Russia in a quite different and unwelcome fashion, leaving Russia no longer able to discount China. Russia's increased difficulties may, thirdly, influence the behavior of NATO allies. They may become less ready to assume Soviet readiness or willingness to attack in the West with its back to China. Because the world is round and the system is multilateral, such choices have a ripple effect.

Thus the "leverage" of any given policy change is asymmetrical. A bilateral change never affects each party in exactly the same way, primarily because both have different neighbors. Looking at the "China card" from this perspective we can see quite different effects of the same action for each of the three main actors involved. Compare Diagrams 4 and 5.[13] Until the card was "played," China was worst off (and had the most to gain from altering course), for China was at odds with both superpowers, each of whom in the 1960s was deploying significant armed forces on China's periphery. It was more useful to China to attempt to lessen the American on-continent presence (withdrawal from Vietnam) than to move directly against the Soviets, since Russia, sharing a frontier with China, cannot meaningfully "withdraw" and therefore is the more meaningful threat. The United States benefited almost as much by the China card, since

---

[13]A pentagonal diagram of this sort "seals in" the enmity in the system so that the effect of policy choices in recirculating the enmity can be seen clearly. It is not important for this purpose whether enmity stays constant in reality, since we are using an analytical construct for analytical purposes. But these diagrams do show where the term *conservation of enemies* came from. The conservation of *energy* argues that energy can be changed in form or allocation, but not in total amount, which is the root here of our approach.

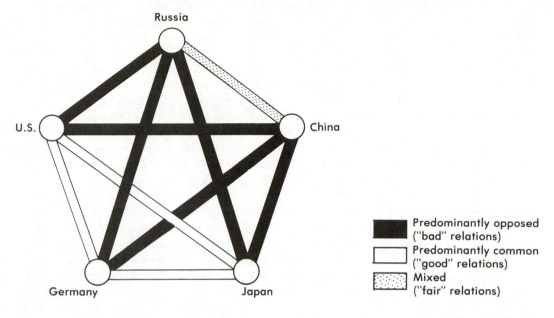

DIAGRAM 4 During U.S. Involvement in Vietnam War (Before "China Card")

Predominantly opposed
("bad" relations)

Predominantly common
("good" relations)

Mixed
("fair" relations)

it made Russia more cautious and more accommodating—as the events that followed, like the successful SALT I agreement, indicated. For Russia, the China card, although implicit in the system as a potential "game move," was highly unwelcome and had no advantages, only disadvantages.

As a second illustration, consider the implications for the Soviet Union of an American proposal, after the China card, of equal numbers of missiles or warheads for each of the two parties. Would their power problem or their targeting priorities be "equal" or the same?

A very important thing to notice about counterbalancing national interests is that, from a

DIAGRAM 5 After the Vietnam War (And After the "China Card")

Predominantly opposed
("bad" relations)

Predominantly common
("good" relations)

Mixed
("Fair" relations)

system point of view, the possible game moves open to each actor are fairly obvious—like the China card. These moves consist of taking what we earlier called a "shelved" or for-the-moment rejected alternative (see Diagram 3) off the discard pile, then inserting it as content to policy in place of the alternative chosen earlier. Such changes in choice of counterbalancing interests impart enormous momentum to the system as a whole. By observing the *rejected* or "shelved" choices and visualizing system effects if an actor reverses its choice and substitutes the alternative, one can see whole patterns of constraints added to or removed from the behavior of particular nations, as Diagrams 4 and 5 indicate for the system, comparing 1970 and 1980.

The third cardinal principle of counterbalancing national interests reminds us of the importance of remembering that national choices between courses of action are often rather narrowly balanced and that the "surprise" possibilities in the system, the dynamic elements as it were, find their source in what is *not* being done, but could be if the "shelved" interest is used. Such shelved interests are fairly obvious, so surprises need not be surprises.

One final point. There is a second sense (a system sense) in which interests may be counterbalancing. For example, in Chapter 2 we said that Bismarck in 1887 entered into a "Reinsurance Treaty" with Russia which guaranteed that Germany would not aid its Austrian ally if Austria *attacked* Russia, but would aid Austria if Russia did the attacking. In return, Bismarck got Russia's guarantee that Russia would not aid France in a war in which France had attacked Germany. In this example, neither Germany nor Russia wanted war, so they chose policies designed to decrease the danger. Their individual but common *interest* was to lower tensions. The *system effects* of their choices was to create a more stable (i.e., counterbalanced) equilibrium.

7.

The Conservation of Enemies

The logic of our observations about past-future linkages, third-party influences, and counterbalancing interests leads us naturally to the fourth cardinal principle, *the conservation of enemies*. This fourth principle asserts that a prime normal concern of any state is not to accumulate more enemies than is obviously prudent. No automatic or uniform assertion about behavior is implied here. States may indeed encourage by their own actions the formation of an overwhelming coalition against them, as Napoleon did in his time and Hitler did in his. Most states, however, most of the time, seek ways to avoid confronting dangerous levels of opposition or enmity. They seek to avoid clusters of enemies sufficient in strength to assure or make likely defeat in warfare. They seek, by proper policy choices, to influence and control the threat they confront, either in number of enemies, the virulence of the antagonism (enmity), or both.

It would not be worth pointing out this principle at all except for the obvious fact that some nations court danger recurrently in exactly this way, by accumulating too many enemies. *How* they do so is even more revealing. Consider, for example, the American policy of bloc containment of Communist aggression mentioned earlier. Such a concept permits enemies to multiply themselves, by the mere act of turning Communist. If instead of this blanket approach, the United States had been convinced of the need to prioritize power problems (or threats), it would never have drifted into a condition of fighting a third-class Communist nation in Vietnam while also potentially being ready to take on both Communist giants, China and Russia. Much this same mistake, of failing to prioritize, led both Napoleon and Hitler to their defeats.

The cardinal principle of the conservation of enemies reminds us of the importance of controlling the amount of enmity confronted, through necessary adjustments in policy, thereby keeping danger to a safer level.

Relating the Second Two Cardinal Principles and Linking Them to the First Two

The statement just made, "controlling the amount of enmity confronted," is not a very American thought. It is more in the American style to concentrate on how to defeat whatever enemies show up. Nevertheless, it is a definite American weakness not to approach the world determined to manage as best as possible the antagonisms resulting as by-products from our policies. Consider again Diagram 3 as it reflects on Diagrams 4 and 5. What made Diagram 4 into Diagram 5 if not a U.S. policy decision by President Nixon, concurred in by China, to manage and control the amount of enmity confronted?

We are not talking here then of the performance of miracles: how to invoke some form of words or charm so that immediately all America's problems vanish. We are speaking instead of a habit of analytical approach, of the way Americans perceive and relate to the state system.

It is not possible, if the analysis of the power problem in Chapter 1 is correct, for any state to escape having actual or potential enemies in varying numbers and intensities. Such antagonistic relations arise rather naturally among states who are both in a position to do one harm and are apparently so disposed. A famous statement, by Sir Eyre Crowe, dating from before World War I (January 1, 1907), makes the same point in quite different language:

> History shows that the danger threatening the independence of this or that nation has generally arisen, at least in part, out of the momentary predominance of a neighboring State at once militarily powerful, economically efficient, and ambitious to extend its frontiers or spread its influence.[14]

Crowe rather specifically had Germany in mind.

So states make judgments on this basis and translate these judgments into decisions based on expectations of behavior as they perceive them. Such judgments will reflect national biases and past experience, but they will, if prudent, include some sense of priorities. In terms of threat, they will specify or imply who is most threatening, and who is the greatest threat. In terms of interests, they will indicate with whom opposed interests are most pronounced, and who next, and so on. In terms of potential change, they will show what kind of shift in policy content might induce a more marginal opponent to be neutral or even friendly. This kind of approach was in British Foreign Secretary Sir Edward Grey's mind in 1895 as British relations with Imperial Germany worsened. Grey noted "a general tendency to vote us a nuisance and to combine against us," and he thought that "a bold and skillful Foreign Secretary *might detach Russia* from the number of our active enemies without sacrificing any very material British interests."[15] About this time U.S. Secretary of State Richard Olney's bombastic note of July 20, 1895, was arriving to cause Britain even more worries over the Venezuela boundary issue. Olney said that "the United States is practically sovereign on this [American] continent, and its fiat is law. . . ."[16] This American insistence on having its way created a potentially serious but nonetheless marginal concern for the British who responded ultimately by defusing the issue.

---

[14]G. P. Gooch and H. Temperley, eds., *British Documents on the Origins of the [First World] War, 1898–1914* (London: His Britannic Majesty's Stationery Office, 1926–1938) 11 vols. in 13, vol. 3, app. A, p. 403.

[15]Quoted in Zara S. Steiner, *Britain and the Origins of the First World War* (New York: St. Martin's Press, 1977), p. 40. Italics added.

[16]Ruhl J. Bartlett, ed., *The Record of American Diplomacy* (New York: Alfred A. Knopf, 1948), p. 344, reprinted from *House Ex. Doc.* (3368), 54th Congress, 1st Session, no. 1, pt. 1.

Obviously, the British were looking at the *entire* system and judging every bilateral move against the multilateral effect. As Imperial Germany became an ever more serious threat, forging ahead with a navy to challenge British control of the oceans, the British moved into (1) an alliance with Japan (1902), (2) an agreement with their oldest enemy, France (1904), and (3) an entente also with newer enemy Russia (1907), meanwhile (4) damping down frictions with the United States.

So the British were looking at the entire system, eliminating now marginal enmities in view of the emerging new and serious threat. The specific device they used to thus "conserve enemies" was a substitution of the "shelved alternatives" of their counterbalancing national interests from their previous policy. Instead of competing with France over African territories, which had led to the serious Fashoda crisis of 1898 in the Sudan, the British agreement with France of 1904 gave Britain a green light in Egypt and France the same freedom in Morocco, while allowing both former enemies to face Germany. In nautical terms, they both upped their helms and went over to the opposite tack. There was nothing magical about it. What it entailed, though, was *prioritization* rather than a mindless, automatic accumulation of enemies.

We can see now how and why the third and fourth principles are closely related. If a state wishes to reduce the effective enmity it confronts and reduce the number of its enemies, it must begin by determining their rank order of threat. Enemies will have to be prioritized and ranked, from the most significant to the least. To reduce the list and "conserve" enemies, the policymaker must focus on those nations lower on the list whose friendship toward those higher on the list produces an alliance or unity of policy dangerous to one's own nation. These are the critical third nations.

The intellectual process then continues by asking whether such third nations might change their orientation. Suppose one rearranged the problem that such third nations confront, either through an alteration in one's own policy or in the policy of some other friendly state. Foreign policies are never single-issue oriented. Since any choice of orientation is always at the expense of other issues, this is where the lever can be inserted.

This last point is absolutely crucial. *Any* policy choices by *any* state always have important disadvantages. When Italy (out of anger that France had taken Tunisia before Italy could) joined Austria-Hungary and Germany in the Triple Alliance before World War I, it did so at the expense of postponing its claim to the Austrian-held Tyrol. And when World War I broke out, the British and French, by promising Italy colonial gains, persuaded Italy first to stay neutral and then actually to fight against Austria (and Germany). Russia, in the nineteenth century, although always wanting control of the Straits into the Black Sea, was never able to accomplish that control because its ambition there could not be squared with the protection of even more significant Russian interests. We have already mentioned how England and France gave up mutual colonial competition in order to achieve a common front against a newly emerging mutual threat.

These frustrations, these disadvantages, are bound up with any choice already made. They can only be overcome by turning to the shelved counterbalancing interests and implementing the alternative to what previously was done, by revamping policy. So the problem of any state that wants to trigger this process in third states in order to deal more effectively with a second state is to change the valuation these third states had previously put on the alternatives. The calculus of advantage/disadvantage must be shifted so that the disadvantages of the policy followed seem now greater than before, and vice versa.

Thus the intellectual process, by concentrating on the reserved or shelved counterbalancing interests, aims to set in train a change in orientation by substituting alternative interests in one's own policy and in the policies of third states one can influence. In this way one's major enemies may be deprived of support from lesser enemies, and the lesser enemies may be converted to neutrals or even, in extreme cases, allies.

The Intellectual Framework and the Cultural Background

9.

Summing Up

Phase 1 of the policy process is concerned with working out intellectually what could be tried in policy, foreseeing where various choices of policy content will probably lead, given the likely reactions of other nations to what may be attempted.

As a yardstick to be used in making such judgments we have provided the cardinal principles. These four principles are reminders of the most important points to consider in designing policy. Each is a specific warning to avoid a serious common error. Past-future linkages as a principle points to the danger of assuming a common frame of reference among the nations addressing a "common" problem. Third-party influences points to the danger of forgetting, in a bilateral relationship, that each of the two parties has flanks and a rear in addition to a "front," and that third parties may be crucial to how the bilateral confrontation or negotiation turns out. Counterbalancing national interests points to the danger of neglecting the dynamic element in the system through forgetting what the effect would be (and being prepared for it) if any of the important actors "plays" its "shelved" interest. Conservation of enemies points to the danger of accumulating enemies or opposition gratuitously, without plan, or automatically as the result of certain actions (like joining the Communist world).

A model such as the cardinal principles has universal application (i.e., it can be used to good purpose as a checklist by any foreign office as well as by the U.S. Department of State). But it has special relevance to United States foreign policy because of the American tendency to forget exactly these four points in designing policy.

We have already seen some of this in Chapter 3 in the discussion of bloc containment— that set of ideas which for long after World War II dominated the U.S. approach to policy. Containment's thrust in designing or judging policy was to ignore the effects of geographical location and historical background, emphasizing ideology unduly as a factor ensuring loyalties across state frontiers. The thrust of containment was to portray a world rather rigidly divided into blocs, with little emphasis on the flexibility that the cardinal principle of counterbalancing interests, in pointing to the "shelved" interests, reminds us is inherent in the state system. The ultimate thrust of containment was to collect enemies by category rather than priority, and containment's incorporation of the domino theory committed it to automatic reactions rather than the cardinal principles' emphasis on prudence and the selection of commitments.

Where containment believed that certain objective occurrences required automatic reaction, even commitment, the cardinal principles assert the need to examine both the balance of forces and the balance of interests before choosing some response. Containment was prepared to pay whatever the price turned out to be, but the cardinal principles suggest that the price is an important part of the whole transaction. We consider these points in more detail in Part Three.

In Chapter 4 we introduced these four cardinal principles as a reminder of those features of the state system that policy design must take into account if the policy is to be cost-effective. Before concluding Part One and turning to how the government functions in the foreign policy area, we have one more task. In Chapter 5 we turn to phase 2 of policy, its implementation. There we detail the specific operational steps by which policy, ideally, is implemented. We pass from planning to operations.

5

Phase 2: Implementing Policy (The Operational Context)

On many occasions . . . I have been struck by the congenital aversion of Americans to taking specific decisions on specific problems. . . . We obviously dislike to discriminate.

George Kennan
Memoirs 1925–1950

Thus far in our search for direction and perspective, we have looked at a large picture, laying down fairly broad principles and approaches. That approach has emphasized the intellectual factors inherent in phase 1: problems in visualizing goals and outcomes. We have seen the importance of concept in determining policy content, and we have offered the cardinal principles as a convenient check of the most important points affecting that process in its design phase.

With this analysis as background, we now shorten our vision in phase 2 to focus on operational and implementation considerations. In phase 2 we must visualize policy from a more down-to-earth and practical standpoint. Once policy is designed, four steps are required to implement it effectively. Although various constraints, pressures, and time limitations may sometimes shorten the appraisal from the optimum, all four steps are unavoidable in fleshing out policy toward specific situations or problems.[1] These four operational steps (phase 2) are: identifying the actors, determining their objectives, analyzing the net capability available for the particular situation, and choosing an orientation (the degree and kind of involvement or commitment required). Roughly, these four steps must be sequential, as Diagram 6 indicates. More exactly, step 1 must begin the operational part of the policy process and step 4 must end it. Steps 2 and 3 are likely to go forward simultaneously.

1.

Identify Actors: Who Is Involved?

However careful the planning in phase 1, it cannot foresee the specific operational context, in all its important detail, in which policy will in fact be implemented. When a crisis occurs or a specific development must be addressed, the first and unavoidable operational step is to deter-

---

[1] The following analysis is based in part on Robert L. Wendzel, *International Politics: Policymakers and Policymaking* (New York: John Wiley, 1981), Chaps. 3–5.

76

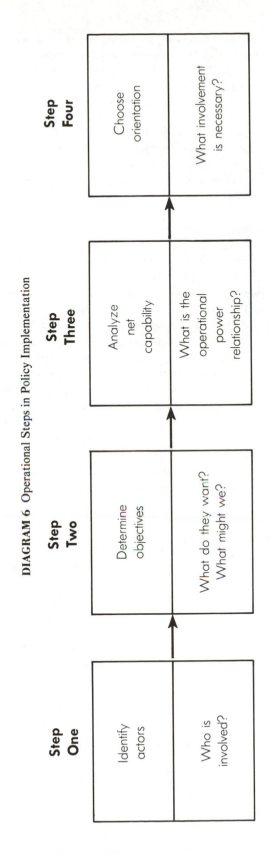

DIAGRAM 6 Operational Steps in Policy Implementation

Step One

Identify actors

Who is involved?

Step Two

Determine objectives

What do they want?
What might we?

Step Three

Analyze net capability

What is the operational power relationship?

Step Four

Choose orientation

What involvement is necessary?

mine the identity, nature, role, and importance to that situation of the various actors: How many parties are seriously involved with the issue? What is the nature and role of each? What are their relationships? And who is likely to wield decisive influence?

If policymakers do not answer these questions correctly, they will not know how to target their policy or whom to concentrate on. Obviously, if possible, these things need to be determined prior to undertaking *any* action. That is why this first step has prior claim.

Answering these questions is not easy. In the Vietnam War, for example, there were different views in Washington, and much resultant policy confusion and inconsistency, over who was in control of enemy forces. Was it the Viet Cong? Or was it really Hanoi, the VC being only a puppet? Were both Hanoi and the VC essentially controlled by the People's Republic of China? Was the United States facing a monolithic Communist bloc directed by Moscow? Who *was* the enemy?

Problems of identifying the actors surface with respect to many issues and areas today. Who really holds the key to Arab-Israeli peace? Who on the Arab side is more important, for example, the Saudis, Egyptians, or Palestinians? Indeed, is there an "Arab side?" Is that Arab "side" the same when evacuation of Lebanon is being discussed as when the West Bank issue is on the agenda? Switch to the European theater. Do the Soviets hold the key to the problems of divided Europe? Or do the opposing alliances hold that key? What of the states of Central Europe, themselves—what part do they play? Who are the key parties in the disturbances in Central America? Is it certain local actors, is it regional powers, or are the superpowers crucial? Or, in any or all of the foregoing, is it some combination of these actors, and if so, who?

Complicating all this is the fact that the list of the participants and the identity of who holds the key can change. Since change is the hallmark of the international system, as states alter their views and substitute one counterbalancing interest for another, they necessarily also produce an altered set of relationships. Any change in bilateral relationships also alters the multilateral context. When Communist China entered the Korean War, it replaced North Korea as Washington's primary adversary; it also enabled Russia to feel more secure with Washington tied down and Beijing diverted. Most changes are neither so sudden nor obvious, though. Consequently, policymakers need to monitor developments carefully and constantly to be alert to the total effects of the changes that occur.

Policymakers confronting a crisis must also think of *who might become involved* in that crisis and who might hold the key under altered circumstances. In the 1970 Jordan Civil War, Israel was not an active belligerent. It was apparent, though, that if the forces of King Hussein had been about to be defeated and his regime replaced by one controlled by Palestinian guerrillas or Syria, Israeli Defense Forces would have intervened.

The first operational step required in any crisis or problem situation then, *before* deciding the specific action required, is to identify the actors. Who is involved? What are their natures and roles? What interrelationships exist? And who holds the key to the outcome? Included in this step is a requirement for a careful monitoring of developments to detect possible changes, and the imaginative assessment of the evolving multilateral context.

2.

Determine Objectives: What Do They Want? What Might We?

Once step 1 is completed, a decision maker faces a second operational step: the determination, as nearly as possible, of immediate objectives. This determination has two facets. First, it requires an analysis of each of the *other* parties to see what they may hope to achieve in a given situation. Second, the decision maker must make a provisional reassessment of his own range of objectives by deciding whether the situational outcomes most beneficial to his country are prospectively realizable and, therefore, whether the planned national interests can be pursued. Objectives in this sense have a relativistic aspect. Objectives can vary widely, differing in terms of their importance, breadth, the time frame allotted for their achievement, the intensity with which they are sought, the resources a nation may be willing to employ to achieve them, and even the degree to which the nation really anticipates or requires success. But in one kind of situation objectives show far less variability—situations that involve vital interests. Survival, then, may be at risk; territorial integrity may be endangered; or belief, political, or economic systems seriously threatened by external forces or their agents. In these cases, there is far less flexibility as to what can be accepted, for it will be a fundamental objective of policy to counter or control the adversary. If the interest is truly vital, a maximum effort will be expended, including going to war if necessary. Determining whether this situation exists is a critically important initial decision.

In most situations in which the interests involved are less critical and the desirability of objectives much more relative, objectives can be considered within a far more elastic range, encompassing many political, economic, ideological, or prestige considerations. And since prestige, if it is fully enough involved, escalates the stakes toward "vital," it is critical that prestige not be gratuitously involved in otherwise less significant affairs.

It is very important here not to blur the distinction between the immediate action or objective and those goals of a more middle range or even fundamental nature that the initial action is designed to help achieve or protect. If this distinction is not maintained, what ought merely to be instrumental may take on a value wholly disproportionate to its real worth. One must go on because one has begun. This can lead to an inefficient use of resources, or even to following policies that are counterproductive to one's vital interests. The immediate objective of not losing the Vietnam War led the United States to undertake actions that hindered the full flowering of the Sino-Soviet rift.

Other factors must be kept in mind as action in a given situation is considered. Obviously, the objectives must mesh with and take into account the cardinal principles. Then, also, they must be formulated and implemented within a realistic assessment of capability relationships. Thus, until that assessment is made (the third step, discussed later), any determination must be provisional. Finally, it must be recognized that all actions produce differential effects. Whereas achieving every objective will entail both costs and benefits to all concerned, no matter what course is followed, all the parties affected will each be affected in a different way.

Further elaboration is needed here on this matter of costs and risks. As we saw in Chapter 4, in setting the framework for choosing between counterbalancing interests to pursue, it is essential that a state assess accurately the risks entailed and the costs involved in the achievement of any interest. But to make such an analysis first requires remembering that one always is acting in a multilateral context (third-party influences). Any interests chosen, setting some objective, and the efforts to achieve such goals impact on a number of actors. In the operational context we are considering here, each actor will be involved in several situations simultaneously. Because no state has unlimited resources, judgments need to be reviewed or made about each party's relative priorities, given developments to this point. Nation A's choice of an interest or objective in situation X will in part reflect its judgment of the importance of that objective compared to those pertinent to situation Y, and the obvious need to devote energy and resources to each since they have occurred simultaneously. Complicating this still further is the possibility that an action in situation X will be undertaken by one of the parties primarily to influence a third (external) party. United States Vietnam policy in the Nixon/Kissinger years often was conceived primarily in terms of its anticipated impact on the Soviets.

There is another point here, perhaps an obvious one: the interests chosen, the actions taken, or the objectives sought will be influenced greatly by what the other parties are thought to be attempting, especially in the specific context as it has developed. The extent to which the United States seeks to shore up NATO's defenses depends in part on how much it believes Soviet armed expansion is a real possibility at any particular time. Formulating (and reformulating) objectives, therefore, requires a careful assessment (reassessment) of the interests and objectives of all other involved parties. Such assessments (reassessments) are directed to analyzing the goals they are presumably seeking and whether such goals are vital, of middle-range importance, or of relatively minor significance to the opponent and to oneself.

In making this tactical assessment, it is vital to remember the background sources from which the interests and objectives of the other parties arise, and the influences they exert. High on the list of such influences is ideology. The Soviet view of the inevitability of change and the contradictions between systems until communism's final triumph excludes, in theory, the thought of negotiating agreements to eliminate conflict permanently. Ethical factors provide another general source of influences. President Carter's human rights campaign, arising out of American traditions, is a case in point. Other historical traditions and attitudes also can be significant. Russia's long-standing efforts to obtain warm-water ports and create a buffer around its periphery for defense in depth are examples. Of course, none of these three general sources of influence on policy is wholly or universally determinative. They are, however, all significant, they affect perspective, and any analysis that focuses primarily on current events and specific data to their exclusion is likely to lose the forest for the trees. Another way of making the same point is that one should not forget what the cardinal principles have to say about policy problems once one gets caught up in a moving problem. It is important to keep perspective.

Internal factors may also generate specific pressures in a given situation. The dependence of the United States on foreign nations for high percentages of its supplies of critical strategic materials is a case in point.[2] Even a leadership's need for domestic support may have an effect on how policy is implemented. Achieving a foreign policy success often is an effective means of enhancing popularity. Also, in some nations the fragmentary or primitive nature of the policy-making machinery may ensure that there really is no single "decision" as such but a continuous flow of decisional bits and pieces. In such a case, the source of the decision is really the decision process itself—something that would not be true, of course, of any sophisticated or mature nation-state.

Finally, any tactical assessment and reassessment of policy objectives must take place against the perceived threat to national security. Given the decentralized anarchy of international politics and the power problems that states face, there is no shortage of threats to be dealt with (conservation of enemies). As we have argued throughout, policymakers act on the basis of their perceptions, whether those perceptions are objectively accurate or not. The forward-deployment, bloc-containment stance of the United States in the post–World War II period reflected a perceived threat of Communist expansion. Similarly, if the Israelis believe an independent Palestinian state would constitute a major security threat, they will act on that basis, whether such a state would in fact constitute a major threat or not.

Discussing conflict situations may lead us to forget that objectives need not always be opposed, regardless of the divergent sources of policy in two states. They may share the need to handle a common problem in a common way. In the late 1960s the United States and the Soviet Union each perceived a growing instability, unpredictability, and unreliability in the "balance of terror"—in central strategic systems—with the attendant tension, increased risk, and barrier

[2]See Chapter 20.

to détente that they produced. This led to the common approach of strategic arms control talks and the SALT I agreements.[3]

In seeking to identify the interests and objectives of the various actors at any point in either phase 1 or phase 2, two rather common intellectual mistakes must be avoided. One is the failure to empathize and the other is the distortion caused by rigid preconceptions. To discover what others are seeking, it is imperative to empathize—to put oneself in the other person's shoes. Empathizing does not imply that agreement or cooperation will be likely. It only means that one cannot really understand what another actor is seeking, and design the optimum policy accordingly, unless one analyzes the situation in terms of *that* party's history, strategic circumstances, ideology, and so on. If one empathizes effectively, on the other hand, the chances of success are enhanced significantly. Russian policy in the Middle East provides a useful illustration. The Soviets' ability to enhance their influence with many Arab states is closely tied to the lack of a permanent peace in the Arab-Israeli dispute and Russian identification with the Arab perception that the United States is one-sidedly supporting Israel. The second common mental error, rigid preconception, is equally troublesome. Rigid preconceptions strongly distort reality, precluding careful analysis. If ideas are set in granite and images are fixed, the facts become irrelevant. Either information that does not fit will be ignored or "interpreted" to make it fit, or no analysis at all will occur. We saw this tendency in U.S. policy toward China, when the Sino-Soviet split was discounted long after it should have been. The purpose of analysis must be to discover the answer, not to confirm or negate preformed conclusions about "what they are *really* after."

These complexities illustrate the formidable problems encountered in the concrete implementation of policy in trying to be accurate about the interests and objectives of others. Two other points confuse the picture further. First, states are always seeking to achieve or protect a number of interests or objectives simultaneously. One cannot look at just a single interest or for *the* objective, because there will be many. Priorities will need to be established. But the other party may not in fact have determined real priorities; it may be simply testing the water or "playing it by ear." The other party may then show itself to be confused and inconsistent. In such cases, it will be very difficult to discover what the other party's objectives and priorities are. Of course, if the other party does not have any clear idea of its own objectives, even knowing or suspecting that can be important.

The final point to remember about determining the objectives of opponents or other parties is that it is always specific human beings who make decisions. No matter what the system or circumstances, it is still flesh and blood people who make the choices. Therefore, in a specific situation when seeking to discover an actor's objectives, the key persons in the decision-making apparatus and their characteristic behavior must be identified. What is their personality structure, previous experience, role concept, conceptual framework, knowledge level, understanding of international principles, tactical skill, and so on?

Having carefully reviewed what the specific interests and objectives of the other parties are in the crisis or problem that has developed, the policymaker now provisionally formulates his own. Taking their objectives into account, operating within an assessment framework that provides inputs on multilateral factors and the costs and benefits various alternatives entail, bearing in mind the cardinal principles, the policymaker decides what his interests and objectives are to be in the particular situation. By this process provisional priorities are established, linkages among them are determined, and to the extent possible incompatibilities and inconsistencies are eliminated. At this point every effort must be made to be careful, precise, and specific. Ideally, the interests and objectives then sought will be those that will produce the best cost-benefit ratio in terms of the expected net impact on all the parties in the situation confronted.

[3]See Chapter 16.

Despite all this effort, however, the formulation at this stage must remain provisional until a full-fledged capability analysis is undertaken.

3.

Analyze Capability: What Is the Operational Power Relationship?

The third operational step is capability analysis, the assessment of the various actors' "power." Capability analysis is a complex, demanding task fraught with uncertainty. It is imperative that it be done though, and done well. Errors in assessing power can be disastrous.

Capability analysis involves several operations. First, it involves an assessment and measurement of key elements that together provide the foundation for the exercise of influence.

Some power elements are tangible in nature. Geography is one. A state's location, size, shape, topography, and climate all affect its capability. Demographic features such as population size, age structure, educational and skills levels, density and distribution, and the trends in these categories also are significant. Obviously, a state's natural resource position is important. Its resource mix in terms of quantity, quality, variety, and flexibility, its needs, its dependence on others, the extent of that dependence, whether it can obtain substitutes—are all critical issues.

Economic strength is a prime tangible element. What is the country's agricultural capacity? Can it produce enough food to keep its population fed, or must it rely on foreign sources? If it can produce enough, can it do so only through the inefficient overutilization of resources in the agricultural sector? To what extent is the economy modernized or developed? What is its GNP, GNP per capita, energy production and consumption, steel production, and so on? What are the trends? What percentage of the labor force is employed in nonagricultural pursuits? What sectors of the economy are emphasized, what are the country's priorities, and how are economic resources allocated? These and other matters need to be investigated.

The last of the tangible factors is military strength. Quantitative considerations, such as how many Backfire bombers the Soviets have, are important. Also significant are distributive concerns such as how strong is the air force relative to the navy. Because states face different threats, have different equipment, structures, and procedures, and operate from different perspectives and assumptions, developing useful categories for comparison is difficult. But it is necessary. Qualitative factors such as personnel morale, leadership, strategy, training, readiness, sustainability, and mobility also must be evaluated. A key qualitative issue in the Central European theater today is the reliability or lack thereof of various Warsaw Pact forces. The level of technological development and sophistication, and command, control, communications, and intelligence efficiency and security also are highly significant.

Intangible elements must also be evaluated. More elusive and less easy to measure than tangible elements, they affect very significantly the degree to which, and how, the tangible elements can be employed effectively.

One intangible element is the degree of societal unity. Are there significant religious, ethnic, tribal, or racial cleavages? If so, to what extent do they divert attention and resources from productive pursuits, weaken the regime, or provide opportunity for outside exploitation? To what extent do the public and key interest factions support the regime and/or its policies, and what difference does this make?

The forms, structures, and processes of government are a second intangible element. It is through governmental action that potential power becomes actual power. Does the government operate in such a manner as to bring the country's capability to bear with efficiency and dispatch? Are the formal and informal processes such as to promote effective policy design and implementation, or are they a hindrance? And, of course, as noted earlier, here too one must analyze the impact of specific individuals, both those who propose actions and those who must carry them out. The end result may depend on who are the key players, what their ideas, role concepts, and personality traits are, and the extent of their knowledge and skill levels.

The final intangible factor is of enormous importance: cultural divergences. Every actor is a distinctive blend of features, a composite that is different from every other. Each state differs in its endowment of the power elements described previously. Each party's history and culture are different from every other, and the past-future linkages it perceives are unique. Each party's strategic circumstances are different, and it faces different power problems. The fact that each party's blend of power elements is unique implies also that each will make the decision of when, where, how much, and how to use power in its own fashion. Any analysis of the elements of power *must* take national variations and peculiarities into account. They are important in the design of policy; they are critically important to its implementation.

When assessing these power elements it is necessary to keep four points firmly in mind. First, the elements are interrelated. Where people live will affect what they possess, for example. Therefore, not only must each separate element be assessed but their effect on one another must be evaluated. Second, the elements are difficult to measure accurately. This is true even with respect to some aspects of tangible features, such as military leadership. It is much more so for the intangible factors. Third, states each day change in both potential and realized power. This is true in both absolute and relative terms. Because of this, any power estimate is obsolescent even as it is finished. Fourth, the intangible elements are crucial not only in their own right but also because it is through them that potential is (or is not) converted into actual power.

Assessing the elements is the first step in any capability analysis. But it is only a first step and to stop at this juncture would give a very distorted and inaccurate picture. Exercisable capability cannot be ascertained solely by assessing a list of components, although that must be done. One also needs to analyze the *context* in which power would be used, and its potential effectiveness at a reasonable cost.

Capability is exercised relationally, as parties interact one with another, so that party W overcomes party X, or influences X's behavior at least partially in the way that it wants to and in a direction that X would not have gone. Or party W persuades party X to do what it would not have done or not do what it would have done, or to alter partially its stance, intensity, or timing. Since capability is exercised in relation to another party, assessments of any given party's power must always ask, "Compared to whom, against what enemy or set of enemies?" In analyzing China's power, it makes a vital difference whether the potential adversary is Taiwan or the Soviet Union.

Even if, in gross terms, sufficient power is present, it is extremely important to address the question of pertinence, to ask if the quantity, quality, and type of power available can actually be employed effectively in the particular situation. For example, how useful is American military force in dealing with domestic instability in the Third World? Can American military force produce the desired policy modifications, can it solve the problem? Obviously, the answer is "it depends," but that is just the point. It *does* depend on the situation. What kinds of capability are effective in dealing with one's allies? How could the United States have compelled South Vietnam to reform without further weakening an already precarious power base? How could power have been exercised effectively in that situation?

Also critical to the utilization of capability are the relative costs and risks of the use of power. Perhaps one has the requisite capability to achieve objectives in the situation, but the costs and risks of doing so would be excessive. It is not only whether one *has* the type, quantity, and quality of power that would allow the production of the desired outcome; it is also a matter of whether it can be done at an acceptable cost.

In capability relationships, the pertinence of one's power may also depend on the characteristics of the party one wants to influence. Important is whether these characteristics are susceptible to the kind and amount of power one can bring to bear. How vulnerable is the target? Obviously, a state that is a net oil exporter is much less vulnerable to an oil embargo than one whose economy depends on oil, and who imports most of that oil. The link between Japan's import of more than 90 per cent of its oil needs and its views on the Arab-Israeli dispute is not unimportant. Again, after the Soviets invaded Afghanistan in December 1979, President Carter warned of serious consequences if the Soviets did not withdraw their forces. When this did not happen, Washington recalled its ambassador from Moscow, asked the Senate to postpone consideration of the SALT II treaty, instituted a grain embargo against the Soviet Union, sharply reduced the sale of advanced technology, and eventually instituted a boycott of the Moscow Olympics. But the Soviets refused to withdraw; they were not "responsive."

Being susceptible and responsive to the use of power is not always predictable. One could argue that in the Afghanistan case insufficient power was applied by the United States (and perhaps it was). But there are circumstances in which considerable power is utilized and in which it seems that the target surely would change its policy in the desired manner, but it does not. "Rational" or not, in effect the target just says "No!" In the mid-1960s the United States believed that through a carefully orchestrated program of systematically escalated bombing, North Vietnam could be brought to the bargaining table on Washington's terms, but this did not happen. As he left office in 1969, Assistant Secretary of Defense Warnke said that the trouble with America's Vietnam policy was "that we guessed wrong with respect to what the North Vietnamese reaction would be. We anticipated that they would respond like reasonable people."[4]

Determining the target's responsiveness is crucial but very difficult. A number of variables must be assessed, three critical ones being the balance of tangible power elements between the parties, the multilateral strategic circumstances each is facing, and the nature and type of objective being sought. Intangible elements in the target such as societal cohesiveness and support, government efficiency, and the quality of political leadership also will be important. Though it is difficult, determining the target's responsiveness is essential.

The last step is assessing the capability relationship is to connect it to the analysis we spoke of earlier of the various actors' intentions and their willingness actually to employ whatever power they have. There is a quite natural tendency sometimes to focus too heavily on the elements of power, not paying enough attention to an actor's intentions. When analyzing one's power problem, it is important not to succumb to the notion that if a party has a certain degree of power it intends to employ it. It may or may not. The United States has military strength far superior to that of Mexico, but it has no intention of using it against its southern neighbor.

Intentions, although an extremely important part of any capability assessment, are difficult to assess accurately because people do not always do what they had intended before they confront an actual situation in all its complexity. The real question is, will the state actually be *willing* to exercise its power when the time comes? In January 1980 President Carter declared that any attempt by an outside power "to gain control of the Persian Gulf region" would be regarded as an "assault on the vital interests of the United States" and would be repelled "by use of any means necessary, including military force." Given the disparities in American and Soviet theater capabilities, would the United States actually be willing to send combat units onshore against the Soviets in the Gulf?

Clearly, determining whether, to what degree, and how an actor will seek to exercise power in a given situation is an extremely important but difficult task. It is crucial to understand that this decision does not rest solely on an analysis of tangible power factors. To illustrate, wars frequently have been launched when the comparative order of battle (forces available to the two

---

[4]Quoted in Leslie H. Gelb, with Richard K. Betts, *The Irony of Vietnam: The System Worked* (Washington, D.C.: The Brookings Institution, 1979), p. 139.

sides) has not been the most favorable, and not been launched when it was. A number of additional factors may enter the decision, including ethical, legal or ideological concerns, prestige considerations, domestic pressures, the availability of policy alternatives, national peculiarities, geographical relationships, historical linkages, the views of specific leaders, and more. And, obviously, a state's overall strategic circumstances are important; third-party influences count. Whether a party will choose actively to employ its power will be strongly affected by its strategic circumstances, and these in large part are determined multilaterally.

Capability analysis is a complex, uncertain, never-ending task. Key tangible and intangible power elements must be assessed and measured, factors of relativity and pertinence examined, target susceptibility investigated, and intentions and willingness to use power analyzed. With this task completed, the policymaker can determine more definitively how much to attempt at a given time, thus avoiding seeking any goals for which capability is lacking or which have a value that is insufficient to justify the cost and risk their achievement would require, given the circumachievement would require, given the circumstances of the problem faced.

Having determined the operational power relationship, one is ready for the fourth and final operational step: choosing the orientation.

4.

Choose Orientation: What Involvement Is Necessary?

The final operational step is to choose one's policy orientation, to decide on the appropriate nature and level of initial involvement.[5] Here a distinction is necessary. We can visualize three separate kinds of situations facing the United States: (1) ones in which the outcomes are not important to the United States, (2) ones in which the outcomes are important to the United States but only in terms of stability, and (3) those in which the issues themselves are important to the United States.

Beginning with situations in which the outcomes are not important to the United States, we can see that three basic orientations exist: avoidance, minimal nonalignment, and participatory nonalignment.

The first policy orientation is avoidance: just do not get involved. A rational choice of avoidance could occur in a number of situations; perhaps the issue is irrelevant or unimportant. Despite the United States' global interests, things happen overseas that really do not affect the United States very much. Or, maybe the situation is such that whatever one does will be harmful, so it is better to do nothing. When Syria seceded from the United Arab Republic in 1961, Washington wisely decided not to make any public comment. Anything the United States said would have infuriated someone. Maybe, too, one really has no leverage. Such was Washington's position vis-à-vis the Iran-Iraq war in 1980. Or, maybe noninvolvement will compel other parties, acting in their own interest, to adopt policies that are beneficial. If the United States is not always deployed "in front" of those it presumably is seeking to support, they perforce will have to act more vigorously to defend themselves.

One will not always have the opportunity of deciding whether to choose avoidance. Previous commitments, the claims of allies and clients, domestic pressures, and a myriad of other factors may not allow it. And avoidance frequently would be unwise. It is evident that there are any number of situations in which direct, vigorous involvement is necessary. But this does not gainsay the point that sometimes it is not, and deep involvement in some situations may prove to be both unproductive and costly. To be as cost-effective as possible, therefore, one should always ask, *before* becoming involved: What will happen and how will it affect our interests if we do not do anything? Will anticipated developments be adverse? Will they be seriously adverse?

[5]This is developed more fully in Wendzel, *International Politics,* Chapter 5.

It is here that minimal nonalignment and participatory nonalignment, the other two basic orientations in this category, may be utilized, where one really does not care about the outcome but still feels some involvement is necessary.

Minimal nonalignment is low-level participation without taking sides on the issues. Such an orientation may be required because of alliance or client-state pressures, or domestic concerns. It can be useful if the issues are relatively unimportant, if operational capability is lacking, or if any deviation from neutrality would cost more than it would gain. Early in the Falklands (Malvinas) crisis in the summer of 1982, because the crisis involved two of its friends, the United States found minimal involvement unavoidable, but because of the obvious drawbacks to choosing, it sought initially to avoid taking sides. This orientation allows maximum flexibility at minimum risk but entails minimal influence. Again, the Falklands crisis provides a case in point.

Participatory nonalignment, on the other hand, involves participating vigorously in a situation but without taking sides in order to protect one's own interests irrespective of what other parties perceive to be at stake. Many LDCs (Less Developed Countries) employ participatory nonalignment to good effect in extracting military and economic aid from Washington and Moscow.

In the second and third kinds of situations in which an orientation must be chosen, the outcomes are important to the United States.

The need for stability is the key to the second kind of situation. One may feel required to act as a balancer, adding power to the weaker side. For such an orientation to be effective, though, one must have the capability to influence the outcome and be willing to use it, and the object of the restraint must decide that it is not worth the new level of cost and risk that confronting the balancer entails. Obviously, achieving a balance is neither a simple matter nor a guarantee of stability. A state confronted by equivalent power may instead strike. The situation becomes quite unstable if each side thinks it can win and that the attacker can obtain substantial advantage. Thus the potential balancer must ask two questions: (1) Can a balance be achieved? (2) Will that balance produce stability?

Stability may also be achieved through mediation. Choosing mediation as an orientation involves an effort to aid the parties in resolving their dispute via negotiations. One provides good offices, communicating between the parties to establish a constructive dialogue. If the disputants so desire, active mediation may be tried, the mediator acting to clarify positions, understand the other party's point of view, and make suggestions as to possible compromises—all in all demonstrating the benefits that would flow from a fair agreement. Because the mediator is a third party, suggestions may be accepted from it that could not be accepted directly from one of the disputants, for reasons of prestige.

If mediation is successful, not only will stability be maintained or enhanced but some advantage will likely accrue to the successful mediator. But mediation also carries with it some risk. If success is not achieved, the parties may conclude that this "proves" that the other side is not willing to resolve the dispute peacefully, thus decreasing stability. Moreover, an inept handling of the task could alienate parties from the mediator. Henry Kissinger, in his Mideast "shuttle diplomacy," showed great awareness of these risks, as we see in Chapter 19. A mediator cannot forget that he has no binding authority to impose a settlement. For success to be achieved, the parties must agree.

In the third kind of situation, the issues clearly *are* pertinent to American interests, what happens *does* make a difference, operational capability *does* exist, and direct involvement *is* necessary. It is still necessary to decide the orientation question. Is it more useful to cooperate in a particular case, or is opposition called for? If opposition is required, should it be indirect and low key, direct but moderate, or is a full-fledged confrontation required? If support of an ally is required, should it be relatively limited or be as full and complete as possible? These are the kinds of orientation questions one must ask in deciding on an active and partisan involvement

The Intellectual Framework and the Cultural Background

orientation. It is useful here, if somewhat arbitrary, to think in terms of the basic differences between quite limited and relatively heavy involvement orientations.

Suppose one believes that certain parties and/or positions should be supported. An orientation choice still needs to be made concerning the degree and intensity of that support. If the issue involves mutual relationships, an orientation choice needs to be made concerning the extent and scope of cooperation.

If one chooses an orientation at or near the full support/cooperation end of the continuum, certain consequences flow rather naturally. The resultant policy almost always will involve a major expenditure of resources and one's prestige will be on the line. Usually there will be little doubt among allies or adversaries about one's course of action so that once one is committed it will be extremely difficult for one to reduce participation or to disengage. And, obviously, whether one succeeds or not will matter greatly. The stakes are very high in this kind of game, and this orientation should not be chosen unless vital interests are involved.

An orientation of limited support or cooperation reduces some of these costs and risks. Fewer resources are required to execute policy and less prestige is involved. Because of its restricted nature, limited support tends to be less provocative than complete support or cooperation, and it thus entails less possibility of creating a crisis. Because of its low level, flexibility is enhanced, allowing a much wider choice of tactics and changes in levels of support.

Avoiding automatic commitment was a key reason for the Nixon Doctrine. Concerned about what was perceived to be an overextension of commitments and a loss of choice about when and where to become involved in a multipolar world, President Nixon declared that the United States would provide military and economic assistance to nonallied states when requested and appropriate, but he indicated that *they* would bear primary responsibility for providing the manpower for their own defense.[6] The United States *could* provide manpower if it chose, but the decision would be Washington's.

The limited support/cooperation choice is a low-cost, low-risk orientation that maximizes flexibility while minimizing the danger of provoking an assault on one's vital interests. But it also has a number of drawbacks. In some contingencies the very flexibility of this approach can be harmful. Adversaries may mistake one's resolve and be unduly encouraged, while nonaligned parties may be confused at the uncertainty or "indecisiveness." One's allies may resent the fact that support or cooperation is so limited, and/or begin to doubt one's reliability. Because all states have counterbalancing interests and some nonalliance objectives exist, providing only limited support may cause allies to alter their cost-benefit calculus toward giving nonalliance concerns more weight. A decrease in alliance cohesiveness may result.

The other major disadvantage of a limited support/cooperation orientation is that whereas costs and risks are relatively small, one's opportunities for gain may be also. The limitations imposed may also limit one's leverage. Still, in some instances one is benefited by not playing a major role because of the policies others must pursue to further their own interests. Limited leverage may mean limited gain, but it also may not. Others acting in their own interests may help us achieve our objective if we "allow" them to do so.

A third variation of an active and partisan involvement may seem desirable in some situations. It may be advantageous to have one's opposition secret, or at least disguised. Perhaps third parties would react (more) vigorously if opposition were open or at least acknowledged, or domestic pressures may increase. Even if the true character of an operation were known, maintaining the fiction of not being involved can lower the likelihood of a total confrontation. China's use of "volunteers" in the Korean War is an excellent case in point.

Indirect, covert methods have long been commonplace in international relations, and there

---

[6]See Richard Nixon, *U.S. Foreign Policy for the 1970's: Building for Peace, A Report to the Congress, February 25, 1971* (Washington, D.C.: U.S. Government Printing Office, 1971), pp. 11–21.

is no reason to think that such orientations will become less frequent. Indeed, given the dynamic uncertainty of the world of the 1980s, perhaps this policy orientation will become more popular than ever. Difficult to detect and prove, relatively low in cost and risk, hard to prevent, usually not prestige endangering, "indirect" opposition is within the reach of almost anyone.

Examining orientations only for the United States, as we have done thus far, would be very misleading. In international affairs the interest of states in a stable situation is by no means universal. As a state that frequently has been interested in maintaining the status quo, the United States often has attributed a number of positive meanings to the term *stability*. But whether, in fact, stability is "good" or not depends at least in part on the nature of the current situation as each of the parties sees it. If each party sees the situation as adverse, stability may not seem beneficial; instability may be more useful. In this situation such states may find it beneficial to choose the orientation of exacerbater. They may choose to exacerbate difficulties, to prevent the resolution of conflict, and to increase instability. Chaos, strife, and enmity sometimes provide fertile grounds for those seeking to bring about change. To illustrate, to what extent would the Soviets be needed by anyone in the Middle East if the Arab-Israeli conflict were once settled?

Choosing as an orientation to exacerbate difficulties is a risky business. Clearly, those parties who want problems solved will react negatively if they believe that one is only trying to keep the pot boiling. An exacerbater without sufficient circumspection can alienate everyone concerned, perhaps even giving them reason to combine against the exacerbater. And the situation may ultimately escape everyone's control to the benefit of none.

In deciding on the level of active involvement, an actor must weigh the important difference between an orientation of confronting enemies in support of one's friends and confronting enemies on one's own behalf, supported or not. Both require a willingness to take risks and to place one's prestige on the line, both produce antagonism, and both should be employed only when vital interests are threatened. But there are two basic differences: (1) whereas the support of allies assumes some commonality of approach with one's friends, confrontation is adopted as a result of calculations about the impact on one's own vital interests whether one's friends agree or not; (2) support of allies focuses originally and perhaps primarily on the security of one's friends, whereas confrontation is directly and specifically concerned with the actor's own security first.

These differences in orientation, reflecting differences in focus and priority, are important. If one's interest is essentially the support of another party, one may not be willing to exercise capability in an essentially bilateral situation. The objective may gain much of its value because of one's friend's policies, and might not have much value in their absence. Sometimes in a multilateral situation the same policy would be indicated by either orientation, but even here it is important to know which is the root. The reason is that the intensity of activity, one's persistence and tenacity, and the willingness to "go to the mat" are more likely to be at a maximum if one is confronting enemies on one's own behalf—especially in a nuclear world. Surely the Soviets will attempt to decide if American policy regarding the defense of Western Europe results primarily from a determination to help the Europeans as long as they help themselves, or instead springs from the view that a free Western Europe is a vital American interest "regardless," and must be defended whether the Europeans "do their share" or not.

5.

Summing Up

Our discussion has shown how critical the fourth step, choosing an orientation, really is. Our discussion has also shown how naturally the choice of an orientation grows out of the preceding three steps. Let us sum up this chapter with one comprehensive illustration.

Suppose Israel and Syria each have armed forces deployed in Lebanon, and each declares it is willing to withdraw from Lebanon but wants assurances that the other one will also. Assume further that, under murky circumstances, an incident occurs and as a result major fighting breaks out (which is always a distinct possibility). Hostilities quickly intensify, and within a few days Israeli F-15s and F-16s have shot down more than thirty Syrian MIGs while suffering the loss of only one plane in return. Using highly sophisticated electronic countermeasures, the Israelis also have inflicted serious damage on Syrian SAM sites in the Bekaa Valley, but the SAMs too have been effective, knocking eight Israeli aircraft out of the skies, and Syria has threatened to use the new long-range SAMs deployed around Damascus (and operated by the Russians) if the Israelis do not pull back. On the ground, to this point only small skirmishes have occurred and casualties have been low, but each side is reinforcing its front-line divisions, especially with tanks, and the possibility of a major escalation is high. Syria's Arab brothers, though denouncing the Israelis with varying degrees of enthusiasm (except for Egypt, which is saying nothing), are giving no indication they intend to intervene. The Soviets, meanwhile, have announced that they will come to Syria's aid according to the terms of their mutual friendship treaty unless the "Zionists" halt their "aggression."

In the United States the National Security Council Senior Interagency Group for Foreign Policy has gone through the first three operational steps and has reached these conclusions: (1) the primary actors, at least at this stage, are Israel and Syria; (2) the immediate objective of each is to make limited military gains in order to enhance its bargaining leverage on the issue of withdrawal of foreign forces; (3) the immediate American objective should be to bring an end to the fighting as soon as possible and to restore regional stability before either an escalation or third-party involvement occurs; (4) looking at the capability relationships, if hostilities persist the Israelis will be victorious if they wish and no one else becomes involved; (5) if the Israelis endanger Syrian security, however, the Russians *will* intervene; (6) U.S. situationally pertinent power that it is *willing* to employ at this point is relatively minimal.

Confronted with this situation, United States senior policymakers need to make a choice concerning the nature and level of American involvement, i.e., they need to choose an orientation. First, though, they must decide whether the outcome is or is not important to the United States, and if it is, is it primarily because of the perceived impact on stability or because the issues themselves are important. The President quickly decides that the outcome is important, so those options that would be relevant only when the outcome is not important—avoidance, minimal nonalignment, and participatory nonalignment—are rejected. A second decision is that (at least at this stage) restoring stability is the primary interest. What the bilateral situational issues are, who the United States would like to see prevail, is secondary. This being so, orientations in the third category are rejected also.

Having decided that the second situation (stability concern) prevails, the President and his aides must now survey their three basic stability-related choices. First, they could choose the exacerbater orientation, but that would run directly counter to the objective of restoring stability, so that approach is rejected. Second, they could choose to have the United States try to act as a balancer. In this specific situation though, acting as a balancer would require providing aid to Syria (because Syria is weaker) against Israel, and because of long-standing American friendship toward Israel and the belief that ultimately cooperation with Israel is essential if regional stability is to be achieved, this too is rejected. This leaves the third orientation option: mediation. The United States will offer its services to the parties to the dispute and seek to help achieve a negotiated resolution. The United States will appoint a special ambassador who will be authorized to make suggestions as to reasonable compromises, try to help the parties empathize, seek to clarify issues and the consequences of various outcomes, and so on. Of course, ultimately whether a settlement will be achieved will be up to the parties.

The foregoing example illustrates how one might actually implement the fourth operational step and choose an orientation. But two important caveats must be entered here to flesh out the picture fully. First, our example is greatly oversimplified. In the real world a party is not involved in just one situation but in several situations simultaneously, and third-party factors will influence (and be influenced by) policymakers' choices far more than we have indicated. Second, our example resembles a still photograph, focusing on the policymaking process only at one particular time. But the world is dynamic, change and diversity being its hallmarks, the policymaking process is ongoing, and the choice that is appropriate at one time may not be at another. Suppose in the example given the Israelis break out of the Golan Heights and roar toward Damascus, and in response a small number of Soviet MIGs and airborne units enter the hostilities. Clearly, the situation will have changed drastically and American policymakers will have to run through the operational steps again; most likely in this situation a different orientation will be chosen. And this will go on and on and on and. . . .

Timing is important in another sense. In many situations there is a certain point at which the circumstances are arranged in just the right constellation and a particular orientation will work, and it may not work as well, if at all, at any other time. In our example, mediation might well be successful only when both Israel and Syria can claim some success, domestic pressures do not force hostilities to continue, important third parties such as the Soviet Union and the United States are anxious for a cease-fire, positive consequences can be projected for both Damascus and Jerusalem if an agreement is achieved, and suitable terms can be worked out. Before such conditions exist it is too early to try mediation, and once they have come and gone it may well be too late. Timing can be crucial.

Although all four operational steps in phase 2 are important, we can see why the fourth step in the process, choosing orientation, is especially critical. The first three—identifying and examining key actors and relationships, assessing and determining interests and objectives, and analyzing capability—are essentially tasks that provide the context of the commitment. But when one chooses an orientation, it goes beyond that. With the choice of an orientation option, a nation definitely crosses the bridge to the commitment itself. Once the orientation is chosen, the policy is launched and cannot be recalled to start again. The chosen policy acquires an initial thrust and focus that eliminates or makes more costly certain alternatives. The probability of achieving some interests or objectives increases, the likelihood of obtaining certain others decreases, and the possibility of some outcomes is eliminated entirely. The orientation in important measure "locks the policy in."

In Chapters 4 and 5 we have set forth in some depth the concepts we use in analyzing United States foreign policy, especially in Part Four in which the focus is on the post-Vietnam era. Before we undertake that task, however, we must have a clearer idea of how policy is made. We now turn to Part Two, to see how Washington makes policy.

PART TWO

How Washington Makes Foreign Policy

The President and Congress

There is one person in this Nation who's responsible for the establishment of and the carrying out of American foreign policy, and that's the President of the United States.

Jimmy Carter
Public Papers of the Presidents, Jimmy Carter, 1980–1981

When a President does not have a fight or two with Congress, you know there is something wrong.

Harry S. Truman
Mr. Citizen

United States foreign policy is designed and implemented via policymaking machinery that is perhaps the most fragmented of any modern state. The President is the chief policymaker, but he is far from the only one. Members of the White House staff, the Assistant for National Security Affairs, the National Security Council, the Department of State, the Department of Defense, the intelligence community, and the Joint Chiefs of Staff also often play major roles. Even this list, because it is concentrated solely on the executive branch, understates the complexity that exists. Obviously the Congress exerts significant influence on policymaking, especially in reacting to or interacting with presidential initiatives or imposing limits on the President's freedom of action. As even a single reading of the Constitution shows, the Founding Fathers deliberately conferred significant powers on *both* the President and Congress, so that neither could absolutely dominate in making foreign policy.

In modern times the President's power in the foreign policy process has grown far beyond what it was considered to be in George Washington's time. To specific constitutional grants have been added the broadening influences of judicial interpretation, tradition, a much expanded role in world affairs, and what for most of the post–World War II era was a strategic consensus (bringing widespread support to presidential initiatives), culminating in a common view of what "makes sense." This combination, along with vigorous presidential initiatives and the demands of recurrent international crises, resulted in contemporary times in the President's gaining a significant preeminence in the policymaking process with the implicit concurrence of Congress on major issues.

Yet the constitutional provisions behind that presidential preeminence are mostly brief and vague, little specific detail being provided. Stripped to essentials, the American system of government enshrined in the Constitution creates separate organs with vague lines of demarcation and much overlapping authority. Thus tension and even conflict are to be anticipated whenever U.S. policy goes into high gear at a time when foreign policy consensus is not present. Congress will "reassert" itself, as people tend to express it.

The President stands at the center of this confusing process, as the following case in a postconsensus period illustrates.

It was early March 1978, and President Carter was worried. The preceding fall he and Panama's leader, General Omar Torrijos, had signed two treaties concerning the Panama Canal: the Neutrality Treaty, which guaranteed the neutrality of the Canal after the year 2000 and allowed the United States the right to use military force to protect that neutrality; and a Panama Canal Treaty, which relinquished American control over the Panama Canal Zone and worked out steps for the gradual turnover of operational control of the Canal to Panama by the year 2000.[1] But to Carter's chagrin the majority of the American public opposed the treaties, as did a number of U.S. senators. The Senate vote on the first (Neutrality) treaty was scheduled for mid-March, and Carter simply did not have the votes for ratification. Although an accord had been reached with Panama, none had been reached with the U.S. Senate.

Carter was only too aware of his problem, and he already had mounted a major attack. Among the maneuvers he had undertaken were an elaborate campaign of personal briefings (some by himself, and some by top Pentagon or State Department officials), public appearances throughout the nation by top State Department policymakers to explain the treaties to local community groups and thus influence public opinion, and the provision of trips to Panama for undecided senators so they could meet the Panamanian leadership and see the situation for themselves.[2] Throughout the struggle President Carter kept a private notebook on his desk with a section for each senator where the President would enter all reports and rumors about which way the undecideds were leaning, and note what might be done next. Sometimes direct efforts were made to convert the nonbelievers. On other occasions the tactics were indirect, the objective being to convince key state leaders and local opinion elites to give the senators room to make their choice unfettered by local concerns. Simultaneously, there was a massive public relations campaign to "educate" the mass media and the general public. But despite his efforts, as of early March the President still did not have the votes for ratification.

One of the undecideds was freshman Senator Dennis DeConcini of Arizona. Concerned about what would happen to American interests after the year 2000, DeConcini introduced a reservation to the Neutrality Treaty that would allow the United States "to use military force *in* Panama" [our emphasis] or take such other steps as it deemed necessary to keep the Canal open after the Panamanians took over. Though a number of U.S. senators favored the reservation, there was outrage in Panama; Panamanians thought the reservation implied an American right to intervene in Panama's internal affairs, the very thing Panama was seeking to eliminate; it resurrected fears of a not-too-distant Yanqui "imperialism."

Carter, angry, concerned that the reservation would be a violation of understandings he had reached with Torrijos, vigorously sought to persuade DeConcini to change the wording. But the senator refused; for all his vaunted power, the President of the United States could not get the freshman senator from Arizona to alter his course. Other senators told Carter that their votes,

---

[1] For more on the treaties, see Chapter 20.

[2] The general analysis is drawn from several sources, but the specific examples and quotes are all taken from Jimmy Carter, *Keeping Faith: Memoirs of a President* (New York: Bantam, 1982), pp. 162–178.

too, were contingent on the language in the reservation being retained. To save the treaty the President reluctantly gave in. With the language included, by the narrowest of margins the vote on the treaty was favorable.

But presidential-congressional relations are never static, and the battle goes on. The anger in Panama over the DeConcini reservation continued to grow, and Torrijos indicated he might renounce the treaties unless the language was modified. The President ordered further consultation, and hasty and somewhat frenetic bargaining now ensued between the Panamanian ambassador to Washington, U.S. Deputy Secretary of State Warren Christopher, Senate leaders, and Senator DeConcini. Finally a compromise was developed in the form of adding to the *second* treaty (before it was voted on) language stressing that the United States could not intervene in Panama's *internal* affairs. DeConcini, Torrijos, the Senate leadership, and Carter all found this acceptable.

But the battle for ratification of the treaties still was not over and the struggle continued. Some of the senators who had voted for the first treaty now were threatening to vote "no" on the second, mostly for reasons unrelated to the treaty itself. It was time for the President to do some good old-fashioned "politicin." Jim Sasser of Tennessee, who could not vote yes because of differences with the President on some home-state issues, was invited to the White House for a Country Music Association celebration; "Tom T. Hall, Loretta Lynn . . . and Charlie Daniels proved to be a lot of help to me [Carter] and Panama that evening!" Howard Cannon of Nevada was concerned about the attitude of the Mormon Church and powerful newspapers in Nevada; Carter found out the Church had no official position on the treaties and so informed Cannon, and he obtained a pledge from the editor of the Las Vegas *Review–Journal* to at least acknowledge the political courage of Cannon if the senator voted for the treaties, even if the newspaper itself held a different position. Senator Hayakawa of California earlier had been insisting that the President needed his advice on foreign and defense matters, and had brought Mr. Carter a book he had written on semantics. With push now coming to shove, Carter handled relations with Hayakawa this way:

> At the last minute, I received a call from some of the Senate leaders, who were closeted with Senator Hayakawa. I knew he was listening when they asked me if I needed to meet occasionally with the California semanticist to get his advice on African affairs. I gulped, thought for a few seconds, and replied, "Yes, I really do!", hoping God would forgive me.[3]

The second treaty, too, passed very narrowly.

Presidential-congressional relations in the Panama Canal Treaties example were characterized by tension and conflict, each side struggling to influence the other and to shape policy content significantly. In Chapter 6, as we examine the powers, roles, and relationships of the President and Congress in the design and implementation of United States foreign policy, it will become clear that today such tension, struggle, and conflict are commonplace.

We divide our analysis into two parts:

1. the effect of formal factors, such as the constitutional powers of the President and Congress, and
2. the reasons for the recent growth of congressional assertiveness in five areas (international agreements, intelligence operations, the use of military force, the nuclear nonproliferation issue, and foreign aid).

[3]Ibid., p. 177.

1.

Formal Factors: The President

We note six specific formal sources of presidential power.

First, the President is Commander in Chief. The Constitution provides that the President "shall be Commander in Chief of the Army and Navy of the United States" (today this also includes the Air Force). Authorities have disagreed vigorously about what the framers meant by this language, but throughout history presidents (usually) have interpreted this provision broadly and it has become a major pillar of presidential power.

Although constitutionally only Congress has the power to "declare war," and only five "wars" have ever been declared (the War of 1812, the Mexican War, the Spanish-American War, World War I, and World War II), the United States has been involved in some form of hostilities at least one hundred thirty times and nearly so in a myriad of others. As Commander in Chief, Thomas Jefferson employed the navy in the Mediterranean to protect American trade against the Barbary pirates. In 1846 President Polk ordered troops to occupy disputed territory along the Rio Grande River, a maneuver that (quite intentionally) led to the Mexican War. President McKinley sent troops to China to join in an international effort to crush the Boxer Rebellion. President Wilson ordered the marines into a number of Caribbean countries. Before the United States was officially in World War II, President Roosevelt ordered the navy to shoot on sight within a defined geographical area. President Truman ordered armed resistance in the Korean War, President Eisenhower landed U.S. marines in Lebanon in 1958, President Johnson ordered the marines into the Dominican Republic, in 1975 President Ford employed force in the *Mayaguez* affair, in early 1980 President Carter ordered what proved to be an abortive effort to rescue American hostages in Iran, and in 1983 President Reagan sent forces to Grenada. And successive presidents increased American involvement in Vietnam in the 1950s and 1960s.

It is not only in the decision to deploy forces in undeclared war situations in which hostilities exist or are imminent that the Commander in Chief power has been operative, however, although these have been the most controversial. Presidents also have utilized this power in three other ways. First, presidents have made policy decisions that could produce circumstances in which hostilities might erupt. President Kennedy's ordering of a blockade to halt Soviet shipments of additional offensive missiles into Cuba in the 1962 missile crisis is a case in point. Second, once the United States has been engaged in hostilities the President has been the chief strategist. In World War II it was Franklin Roosevelt who decided that the Allies should open a second front by landing in France, rejecting Churchill's plea for an assault against Europe's "soft underbelly" in the Balkans. President Truman ordered a significant strategy shift in an attempt to unify Korea during that "police action," and President Johnson controlled the major outlines of strategy from 1964 to 1968 in the Vietnam conflict. Third, it has been the President's decision when and whether to terminate hostilities, and he has been the one to decide when and if negotiations for peace should ensue.

Clearly, on the basis of his authority as Commander in Chief the President traditionally has exercised considerable power. Seldom until Vietnam was this authority seriously questioned.

Second, the President has unique powers in treatymaking. The Constitution provides that the President has the power "by and with the Advice and Consent of the Senate to make treaties, provided two thirds of the Senators present concur." It is not evident whether the Founding Fathers thought treaty making ought to occur in sequential stages, the President negotiating agreements and the Senate providing "advice" only afterward in connection with debate over concurrence, or if it was expected that senatorial advice and consent also would extend to the negotiation phase. In the event, except for some experimentation in the Republic's early years, presidents have generally adhered to the view that the negotiations are the prerogative of the

President, the Senate having the authority only to advise and consent at the concurrence or disapproval stage.

Although most presidents have viewed the division of legal authority in this manner, owing to needs for senatorial concurrence and domestic political support often they have *invited* advice earlier. Only too well do recent presidents remember President Wilson's failure to include any member of the Senate in the American delegation to the Peace Conference after World War I. Although there were many reasons for the Senate's subsequent rejection of the Versailles Treaty, Wilson's tactical errors certainly played a major role. Indeed, today presidents often engage in extensive consultation with the Senate prior to the signature of a treaty; in effect, the administration is "negotiating" with the Senate at the same time that it is negotiating with a foreign government. During the final phase of the negotiations of the Panama Canal Treaties President Carter's co-negotiators "consulted with at least 70 Senators."[4] On some occasions this goes even further. Not only was there a detailed and continuous series of briefings of the Senate by the Carter administration during the SALT II talks but twenty-six senators and forty-six members of the House sat in on the negotiations in Geneva.[5]

There is considerable confusion in the public mind about the stages in the treaty-making process, and perhaps we should speak to the point before going on. First, there is the negotiating process and the signature by duly authorized representatives of the parties. Then the agreement is submitted to the Senate for its advice and consent. The Senate may approve the treaty as it stands by casting the required two-thirds majority, approve with the requisite vote but attach reservations and understandings specifying the U.S. interpretation of various provisions, approve but attach amendments that require the treaty's renegotiation, or reject by failing to give the requisite vote. Although people speak of Senate "ratification" of treaties, the word is a misnomer; the Senate either concurs or rejects. If it concurs another step is required for ratification to occur. The treaty then must be signed by the President.

Throughout this process the President retains a degree of initiative. He may withdraw the treaty from consideration at any point prior to his signature. In 1884 American negotiators signed a treaty with Nicaragua for a canal linking the Pacific Ocean to the Gulf of Mexico. Before it could be acted on in the Senate a new President, Grover Cleveland, took office, and he quickly withdrew the treaty from consideration. The President may also refuse to sign a treaty that the Senate has approved. Or, as President Wilson did with references to the Versailles Treaty, he may make it clear he will not sign a treaty that is amended in a certain manner, thereby forcing a showdown on the agreement as it stands.

Third, the President may negotiate executive agreements with foreign states. Executive agreements are binding agreements between heads of state that, unless they are made pursuant to statutory or treaty authority so stipulating, do not require Senate approval. Even when concurrence is required, it is not two thirds but only a simple majority. Occasionally such agreements are informal, and sometimes they even may be oral, but in most instances they so resemble a treaty in form and impact that no difference is evident.

The exact boundary between treaties and executive agreements is not clear. Logically one might assume it would be possible to distinguish on the basis of relative importance, treaties being used for matters of fundamental significance, executive agreements for matters of secondary interest. But this is not so. Executive agreements may be just as significant as treaties. Among the myriad of highly important executive agreements have been the momentous Yalta and Potsdam agreements that provided the foundation for post–World War II developments in

[4]I. M. Destler, "Treaty Troubles: Versailles in Reverse," *Foreign Policy* (Winter 1978–79), 50.
[5]Hedrick Smith, in *New York Times*, April 14, 1979.

both Europe and Asia, the SALT I Interim Agreement limiting numbers of missile launchers for a five-year initial period, and the 1978 Camp David Middle East Peace Frameworks.

The major difference between treaties and executive agreements lies not in the level of importance but in the level of presidential power. Put simply, the President has much more flexibility in, and control of, policy in an executive agreement than he does in a treaty. The extensive use of such agreements produced a congressional backlash, however, and as we shall see later, Congress in the last decade has become more assertive in this sphere.

Fourth, the President has power to nominate and appoint policymaking officials. The President has the power to appoint, with the advice and consent of the Senate, the nation's highest ranking diplomatic, military, and intelligence officials. Although senatorial concurrence is required and thus could prove to be a major obstacle, in practice it is unusual (though not unheard of) to refuse it. Generally, the belief is that the President is entitled to a team of his own choosing. Even in most instances where a large number of senators oppose a particular nominee, he or she usually will not be rejected. The Senate may give the individual a rough time in the confirmation hearings and opposition senators use the occasion to advocate their own policy views, but when the vote is taken the nominee will usually be confirmed. Such was the case in 1983 with President Reagan's nomination of Kenneth Adelman to head the Arms Control and Disarmament Agency.

Although not as controversial as some of the President's other prerogatives, the capacity to determine who will fill key policymaking positions surely is a matter of great import. One only has to think of individuals such as Henry Kissinger, Robert McNamara, John Foster Dulles, and Dean Acheson to realize how different things might have been if different people had held certain positions at certain times.

It is important to note in this connection that the President can make a number of appointments that do not require senatorial approval. Key members of the White House staff, for example, are appointed (and removed) as the President desires. In the past two decades the President's personal (special) Assistant for National Security Affairs has been extremely influential, at times being more powerful than any of the Senate-approved cabinet officers holding the State or Defense portfolios. His appointment does not require senatorial concurrence.

Fifth, the President alone has the power to grant or withhold diplomatic recognition to foreign states. The Constitution provides that the President "shall receive Ambassadors and other public Ministers." From this grant the President derives the power to extend, withhold, or withdraw recognition of foreign governments. Because the President is head of state, diplomats of foreign governments are accredited to him personally. His is the choice as to whether or not to receive them.

Most states grant diplomatic recognition to a foreign government if that entity is in *de facto* control of its country. For more than a century after it was founded, the United States did likewise. Beginning with President Wilson, however, American presidents began to utilize recognition or nonrecognition as a tool of foreign policy, the criterion being whether the government in question met certain ethical standards. Used in this manner, recognition is conceived of as reward or stamp of approval, and policymakers assume a refusal to grant recognition demonstrates disapproval and provides a degree of leverage. Although the government of the People's Republic of China was in firm control of the mainland by the end of 1949, President Truman refused to grant it recognition. For a considerable time succeeding presidents followed the same course, and recognition of China was not extended until 1979.[6]

Sixth, the President, because of his position, has certain "inherent powers." Because the President *is* head of state, he is the individual with whom foreign governments have official

---

[6]See Chapter 18 for further discussion.

contact. Indeed, the President is the only official voice of the United States in foreign policy (although in practice, much of his authority is delegated to subordinates). In a landmark case the Supreme Court stated that in the realm of external relations the President "alone has the power to speak or listen as a representative of the nation." Indeed, the Court continued, the President is the "sole organ of the federal government in the field of international relations" and is able to operate with "a degree of discretion and freedom from statutory restriction which would not be admissable" in domestic affairs. There is a "marked difference between foreign and domestic affairs in this respect."[7]

2.

Formal Factors: The Congress

While the formal powers of the President are substantial, those of Congress are no less so. Although the precise intentions of the Founding Fathers cannot be determined, it is clear that they expected Congress to play a major role in foreign policy. We examine five formal aspects of that role.

The first power, over the military forces, actually has two aspects: declaring war and maintaining forces.

The Constitution provides that Congress shall have the power "to declare war," to "raise and support Armies," and to "provide and maintain a Navy." The authority and responsibility to maintain forces involve Congress not only in extensive annual budget making but also permit it to allocate funds among the services as it sees fit and as the President agrees. We comment further on this process as it becomes germane to our discussion.

The specific power to declare war, as discussed earlier, has only been exercised by Congress on five occasions. In all the other instances involving hostilities no declaration of war was made (nor was it requested). Although there were occasional exceptions, as a rule until the Vietnam War there was little constitutional controversy over decisions concerning the use and deployment of American military forces in combat, quasi-combat, and near combat situations; the President, it was believed, had the authority to act unilaterally in defense of the national interest.

One reason for the lack of concern was the fact that often the concept and the constitutional language were irrelevant to the facts of the situation. The Constitution refers only to a declaration of "war." Because of this, it does not deal with the innumerable potential conflict situations that arise, nor does it relate readily to the myriad of actual uses of the military policy instrument in situations short of "war." Policymakers and observers alike long tended to feel that the President had the power to act in such contingencies in whatever ways he deemed essential. Also pertinent here is the fact that states in modern times seldom issue formal declarations of war. Usually hostilities are commenced first, and only then, if at all, is a formal declaration issued. Once the United States is attacked, any declaration of war would acknowledge a state of belligerency, but an attack would hardly initiate abstract discussion of whether one ought to engage in hostilities.

Until very recently, even when the constitutional language was or might have been pertinent, there seldom was much dispute. If the President asked for a declaration of war Congress provided it; if he did not ask for it, war was not declared. Often when the President ordered the deployment and use of the armed forces Congress agreed with the substance of his actions and gave him support. Even if it disagreed with the President, Congress nearly always adopted the position that the President nevertheless had the *authority* to act as he did. And it usually did

[7]*United States* v. *Curtiss-Wright*, 299 U.S. 304 (1936).

not publicly object, feeling that to do so would weaken the President and thus be harmful to national security. The Vietnam War changed Congress's attitudes enormously, and led in 1973 to the passage over President Nixon's veto of the War Powers Resolution (discussed in more detail later).

The second power is to advise and consent on treaties.

The vast majority of treaties the Senate has considered have been approved. Traditionally, even when the Senate did not want a treaty, it hesitated to refuse consent because it knew that if consent were refused, the impact on relations with the other signatories was bound to be adverse. After negotiations have been completed and a treaty has been signed, the parties believe that an understanding has been reached and quasi-commitments made. To refuse consent at this point cannot help but antagonize the other signatories, add an element of concern over the United States' reliability, and by repudiating the President weaken his ability to deal vigorously and persuasively with foreign leaders. In recent years, such thinking has carried less weight than it used to, however, and Congress has become more assertive in exercising its prerogatives.

The third power is the power of the purse.

American foreign policy requires the expenditure of enormous amounts of money, and no monies can be drawn from the Treasury unless appropriated by Congress. Funds for military programs and personnel, foreign aid programs, the Department of State's activities, and so on all must be authorized and appropriated by Congress. Congress may decide to provide the funds for existing or planned programs, provide less than requested, or appropriate more than was sought.

Despite its potential utility, until recently Congress only rarely sought to influence significantly the course of general foreign policy through its control of the purse. Lacking the staff and expertise fully to evaluate administration requests, encumbered by an internal structure that treated budgetary matters in an episodic and fragmented fashion, and generally sharing the various administrations' strategic conceptions, Congress usually reacted more or less favorably to the executive's initiatives.

This is not to say that Congress played no role whatsoever. Occasionally it did try to modify or set some limits on foreign policy by saying "no." A particular weapons system might be less than fully funded, a foreign aid appropriation be smaller than requested, or the like. But these were much the exception, not the rule. And when such actions were taken, it almost always was because of concern over a specific narrowly defined policy issue. It was not the result of fundamental differences over long-term objectives and strategy, because on these matters Congress and the President usually agreed. And it was not the result of any concern with the executive-legislative balance in the policymaking process, because until the Vietnam War this usually was not much of an issue.

The fourth power of Congress is to legislate.

Many (though not all) foreign policies require legislation for their implementation. Until recent years Congress usually exercised its legislative function rather generally, seeking to set outer limits, provide broad guidelines, and help establish the overall policy thrust. Given the necessity for executive discretion and flexibility, it was believed unwise to try to legislate specific detail.

There were occasional exceptions to these rules, and some of them were quite important. One need only recall the Neutrality Acts of the 1930s, prohibiting arms shipments to all belligerents. When World War II broke out President Roosevelt proclaimed an embargo, as required by law. The result was to eliminate or curtail effective aid to states with whom America had common interests, Britain and France. Clearly Congress's efforts had unwisely limited presidential discretion. On those other few occasions when Congress legislated in detail, more often than not the result was similarly unproductive.

The fifth power of Congress is oversight.

Although the Constitution does not provide for it in so many words, supervising and monitoring the executive branch's conduct of foreign policy has become one of Congress's most influential functions. Detailed provisions in appropriations statutes instruct the administration on how to spend certain funds, and reports must be made on compliance; legislation is passed affecting the structure and staffing of the executive branch; hearings for presidential appointments are used to examine the execution of previous policies.

Investigation is a major oversight tool. Although Congress's right of inquiry is limited to subjects on which it can validly legislate, in practice this presents no obstacle to a determined desire to proceed; if Congress wants to investigate, a suitable justification can be found. Through its investigations Congress can bring maximum publicity to bear on various issues and individuals, and can examine the historical record in depth and detail.

Congressional investigations often have had considerable impact. In the mid and late 1960s the Senate Committee on Foreign Relations held a number of influential hearings on America's Vietnam policy that both affected and in some ways reflected the public's view of the administration's actions. In 1973 and 1974, House and Senate subcommittees investigated the role of the CIA in Chilean politics, and these investigations resulted in the passage of the Hughes-Ryan Amendment tightening control over covert action. Further investigations of the intelligence community surfaced revelations that led to the establishment of permanent intelligence oversight committees.

3.

The Growth of Congressional Assertiveness

The events of World War II and its aftermath impelled the United States to a greatly expanded role in world affairs. For a number of reasons, the President played the preeminent part in that expanded role. Policymakers and observers alike believed that the President had the authority to do whatever was necessary to protect the national interest, and that he was in the best position to determine what that interest was. Given the nature of the international political world and the intrinsic differences between the branches, the President was thought to be the only one able to act with the speed and decisiveness necessary. Moreover, there was a clear consensus on the nature of the problems confronting the United States; given that consensus, most Americans thought it was essential to give the President full and firm support.

By the late 1960s though, many Americans were questioning the President's dominance, and Congress was greatly expanding its role in the policymaking process. The factor most responsible for these changes, of course, was the Vietnam War. The strategic consensus that had undergirded United States policy for two decades was completely shattered by this conflict. It no longer seemed obvious that it made sense to leave policy initiatives to the President, and few positive expectations remained.

Although Vietnam was the catalyst and prime mover, other developments also helped fuel the disenchantment. The Soviets were engaged in a massive military build-up and were very active in the Third World, violating what many congressmen felt were the requisites of "real" détente. A number of improprieties and deceptions was revealed about the conduct of American intelligence activities, and at home the Watergate scandals surfaced.

Another reason for the expanding role of Congress in the late 1960s was that Congress was becoming better equipped in analytical capability. The Congressional Research Service (formerly the Legislative Reference Service) was created in 1970, and became an effective tool for policy research. The auditing surveys of the General Accounting Office provided more effective potential supervision. The Congressional Budget Office, created in 1974, was a giant step forward, permitting Congress to rival the executive branch in considering budget initiatives. Moreover, congressional staffs increased by leaps and bounds. From less than 500 committee staffers in 1947, by the 1980s the number exceeded 3,000. Personal staffs in Congress increased from about 2,000 to over 10,000 in the same period.

The result of the growth in support agencies and staff assistance is clear. Congress today has available to it independent sources of expertise and information that have reduced significantly its dependence on the executive for meaningful information.[8]

The third major cause of Congress's expanding role has been changes in the Congress itself. For one thing, the membership is different. There has been a considerable turnover. Congress as a whole is getting younger, and fewer of the new members are willing to "serve a proper apprenticeship." The post–World War II generation that shared a policy consensus with the presidents from Truman on, and tended to acquiesce in executive initiative, is largely gone. Second, congressional operations have become more democratized and the influence of seniority has lessened. This, in combination with the turnover mentioned earlier, has led to an even greater diffusion of power than that which had previously existed. The individual legislator today has more impact than at any time within memory.

For all these reasons, Congress is no longer willing to sit back and allow the executive to play the dominant role it once tolerated. This change in attitude expressed itself in five particular areas, most of them security related, which we shall now examine.

4.

Congress and International Agreements

The first area in which the changed attitude of Congress shows itself is in the treaty-making process. Although the Senate never believed that consent to a signed treaty was obligatory, usually such consent was quickly forthcoming. And although Congress was never favorably disposed toward various presidents' considerable use of executive agreements, it seldom raised much fuss. And although Congress always would have liked to have participated meaningfully during the negotiation stage, it never really expected to. In one way or another all of these things have changed. Because the Senate is not willing automatically to defer to presidential wishes, more than ever now the President must carry on two sets of negotiations; one with foreign countries who may become or are signatories, and one with the Senate. On March 13 and 14, 1978, in the midst of the struggle over the Panama Canal Treaties, President Carter's diary reveals these comments:

> It's hard to concentrate on anything except Panama. . . . I asked Cy [Vance] to go and spend full time on the Hill, and also to ask Henry Kissinger to do the same thing. I then asked Harold Brown and the Joint Chiefs to join them there, and Fritz [Mondale] will be spending full time—all working personally with members of the Senate. . . . I had lunch with Senator Stennis to try to get his vote on the treaties, but failed. . . . President Ford promised to use his influence with Heinz, Bellmon, Brooke, and Schweiker. . . .[9]

It is not only at the approval/disapproval stage that the Senate has become more assertive. Individual senators now are becoming involved in the negotiations phase. As mentioned earlier, congressmen are frequently appointed by the President to be official or unofficial members of the negotiating team. This is not entirely new. What is different, and startlingly so, is that on

---

[8]Because of their role in providing information and expertise, these sources, especially congressional staffers, have become important in their own right.

[9]Jimmy Carter, *Keeping Faith: Memoirs of a President* (New York: Bantam Books, 1982), p. 171.

several occasions in recent years *individual* senators have taken it upon themselves to enter into unauthorized *direct* negotiations with foreign officials.

Interestingly, it is not only the Senate that has become more assertive in the treaty process; the House has, too. Although it does not participate *directly* in the approval/disapproval process, sometimes in recent years the House, through debate and hearings, has sought to influence the negotiators nonetheless. Committees antagonistic to the Panama Canal Treaty were holding public hearings before the negotiations even were completed. And most treaties require considerable legislation for effective implementation. On this score, too, the House may prove obstreperous.

Another major and connected area of change has involved Congress's increasing unwillingness to acquiesce in the use of executive agreements instead of treaties. In the post–World War II era executive agreements have far outnumbered treaties, perhaps by as much as ten to one. But such a quantitative comparison gives a distorted picture of reality, because many of these agreements were made pursuant to congressional legislation or treaty provisions. Also, although it is evident that presidents frequently bypassed the Senate through such compacts, because of the underlying strategic consensus that existed for the first two decades after World War II, Congress usually would have agreed if it had been consulted. Disagreement was largely latent; it was not over the substance of policy but only over procedure. In the pre-Vietnam era, only once did Congress raise major objections, which came in the shadow of the Korean War, in 1954. The Bricker Amendment, which stipulated that Congress would have the power to regulate all executive agreements and that all treaties and executive agreements could become effective domestically only by congressional legislation, failed Senate approval by only one vote.

It was the Vietnam trauma that again fanned the smoke of discontent, turning it into the flames of sharp executive-legislative disagreements. In June 1969 the Senate overwhelmingly passed a sense-of-the-Senate National Commitments Resolution providing that no future foreign commitments could be made without congressional approval. Although this was nonbinding, it clearly signaled that the Senate did not plan to acquiesce passively to commitments unilaterally made by the President. Shortly thereafter, a Senate Foreign Relations subcommittee discovered that a large number of secret executive agreements existed, some with provisions that amounted to security commitments.

As a result, in 1972 Congress passed what is popularly known as the Case Act, which requires that all international agreements other than treaties be submitted to Congress within sixty days of coming into force. Such agreements may be provided under an injunction of secrecy to the Senate Foreign Relations and House Foreign Affairs Committees, however, if the President determines that public disclosure would be harmful to national security.

Whereas the Case Act demonstrates Congress's determination not to acquiesce passively to presidential initiative, it really does little to alter the executive-legislative balance. All it does is require that executive agreements not be kept from Congress. But Congress still has no role in the making of such agreements, nor any approval/disapproval function. And, apparently, most members of Congress do not want any. All efforts in recent years to legislate a larger role in such matters have been defeated.

5.

Congress and Intelligence Operations

The second area in which Congress also has become more assertive is in the exercise of its legislation and oversight prerogatives in matters concerning the intelligence community.

For most of the post–World War II era, Congress paid little attention to the intelligence community. It was believed that the Cold War dictated that an effective intelligence apparatus exist, and there was a general agreement that covert operations were necessary. Indeed, there was an extreme reluctance to question the substance of policy or the President's right to control it. About the only time much interest was shown was when some kind of policy debacle came to the public's attention, such as in the abortive Bay of Pigs invasion in 1961.[10]

The general aura of congressional disenchantment in the late 1960s provided a propitious context for a greater role for Congress in intelligence matters, however, and a series of specific developments in the early and mid-1970s brought this about.[11] Congressional investigations revealed that the CIA had covertly sought to prevent the election of Marxist Salvador Allende in Chile. Clear evidence of other covert activities was disclosed in these hearings also, surfacing developments that shocked many legislators (and their constituents). About the same time, the improprieties of the Watergate scandals were revealed. It also became evident that the executive's command and control arrangements concerning covert activities were far from clear and precise, and that sometimes the President himself was not wholly aware of what was going on.

In 1974, Congress required stricter controls on covert activities, through the Hughes-Ryan Amendment. Before a covert operation could be launched, now the President had to determine specifically that it was important to national security. Hughes-Ryan also required that all covert actions be reported by the President to the appropriate committees of Congress in a "timely" manner, and that the report include a description of the activity.[12] In late 1975 and early 1976 Congress went beyond simply requiring that it be informed. The CIA had been providing aid to the FNLA/UNITA coalition in its war against the Soviet-backed MPLA in Angola. Unhappy with this state of affairs, Congress cut off the Agency's funding.

About this same time broad-ranging investigations of the entire intelligence community were undertaken. More revelations were forthcoming about covert actions and some evidence and many allegations of domestic spying surfaced. In consequence, Congress voted to establish permanent select committees on intelligence in both the House and Senate. These committees were given broad oversight mandates and financial power. All authorizations for intelligence activities now were to be made by the committees and they were given authority to consider the budget on a line item basis. Previously, jurisdiction over authorizations had rested with the respective armed services committees, committees that had tended to be favorably disposed toward CIA activities.

Congressional activism continued with the passage of the Intelligence Authorization Act for Fiscal 1981 (IAA). The IAA made major changes. First, whereas Hughes-Ryan had applied only to the CIA, the new legislation placed limits on all elements of the intelligence community.[13] Second, under the IAA the appropriate committees must be informed not only of existing operations but also of "significant anticipated" activity. Prior notification can be limited if the President determines it is essential "to meet extraordinary circumstances affecting vital interests of the United States," or to protect sources and methods. But even in these cases he must give notice to the chairman and ranking members of the intelligence committees and to the party leadership of both houses. Whereas under Hughes-Ryan notice often was given, it was not required; now it is.

The IAA included provisions that *limited* Congress's role. The reason was clear. Although it wanted a major voice in policy formulation, Congress did not want to so restrict the President that all flexibility and room to maneuver were eliminated. It, therefore, carefully avoided defin-

---

[10]See Chapter 20.

[11]Much of the discussion in Chapter 10 is relevant here also.

[12]The "appropriate committees" at this juncture were those on foreign relations or affairs, armed services, appropriations, and intelligence in each house. In most instances the committees were contacted within twenty-four hours of the President's approval.

[13]The intelligence community is discussed in Chapter 10.

ing "significant" anticipated activities (although it did stipulate that, for funding purposes, non-intelligence-gathering covert activities were significant), thus allowing the President some discretion. Of equal importance, *the law reduced the number of committees that had to be informed from eight to the two intelligence committees.* Now it is the responsibility of these committees to call to the attention of other committees or their parent chamber intelligence matters meriting such attention. Reducing the number of committees to be notified came about for two reasons. First, trying to inform so many people was a considerable burden to the executive. Second, and more importantly, many of the covert projects about which the committees had been briefed since Hughes-Ryan had been leaked (which severely damaged the "covert" aspects of covert action).[14]

Note that Congress has not required that it have *prior approval authority* for covert projects. One also must remember that the intelligence committees are only involved in the authorization and not the appropriation of funds for such activities (although authorization is needed before appropriations can be made). In practice, Congress has steered a line between extremes. For instance, in 1982 it authorized covert actions in Nicaragua to interdict arms shipments to rebels in El Salvador, but prohibited funds to overthrow the Nicaraguan government.

During the early years of the Reagan administration relations between Congress and the intelligence community, if not cordial, at least were correct. But in April 1984 a bitter dispute arose. Lawmakers charged that they had not been adequately informed about the CIA's role in the mining of three Nicaraguan harbors, part of the administration's ongoing "covert" campaign against the Sandinista regime. Intelligence officials hotly denied the allegations, insisting Congress *had* been fully and currently informed as the law required. Regardless of whose version was more accurate, the upshot was that the two sides again were angry and suspicious. As had been the case so often previously, in mid-1984 relations between Congress and the intelligence community were poor.

How all this will be resolved only time will tell. But for perspective one key point should be remembered: Congress had considerable power in intelligence matters prior to the 1970s but chose not to use it. Because of the conceptual consensus that had existed Congress usually had agreed with the President. Then, as now, the key to presidential-congressional relations on intelligence matters lay more in policy views than in structural factors. Although it is unlikely that Congress in the near future ever will be entirely passive, whether or not it becomes vigorously assertive most likely will depend on policy concerns, not concern about the proper executive-legislative balance.

6.

Congress and Military Force

A third area with which Congress has become much less willing simply to follow executive leadership in recent years is decisions concerning the deployment and employment of military force. Again the primary catalyst was disenchantment over the Vietnam War and retrospective disillusionment with the decision making that led to the American involvement and escalation there. But while general frustration was already considerable by 1970, it was the Cambodian incursion that brought direct action. By the spring of 1970 the United States already had begun its policy of Vietnamization, gradually withdrawing American forces and turning combat responsibilities over to the South Vietnamese. But in neighboring Cambodia North Vietnam's military sanctuaries were growing rapidly, and President Nixon and Henry Kissinger were convinced that these

---

[14]See William Colby and Peter Forbath, *Honorable Men: My Life in the CIA* (New York: Simon & Schuster, 1978), p. 423, and Ray S. Cline, *Secrets, Spies and Scholars* (Washington, D.C.: Acropolis Books, 1976), p. 256.

sanctuaries constituted a serious threat to the Vietnamization program. Consequently, in April the American leaders ordered American and South Vietnamese troops into Cambodia to clean out the sanctuaries in the border areas. Domestic reaction in the United States was wildly bitter, both in government and out. In a demonstration at Kent State University, four students were shot to death by the Ohio National Guard. In Congress, immediately after the attack, legislators began work on legislation to restrict the President's power in such contingencies and to enhance that of Congress. The process culminated in 1973 with the passage over President Nixon's veto of the War Powers Resolution.

The War Powers Resolution was designed to ensure that the "collective judgment" of Congress and the President would apply to decisions concerning the introduction of American forces into hostilities or into situations in which hostilities appeared imminent, and to the continued use of military forces in such contingencies as well. It stipulated that as Commander in Chief the President could employ American forces only pursuant to "(1) a declaration of war, (2) specific statutory authorization, or (3) a national emergency created by attack upon the United States, its territories or possessions, or its armed forces." Once the President had exercised his powers, except in the case of a declaration of war, he had to report fully to Congress within forty-eight hours concerning the situation or circumstances, his authority for acting, and the estimated scope and duration of involvement. If Congress disapproved it could order the forces withdrawn by concurrent resolution. Even if Congress did not so act, troops had to be withdrawn within sixty days of the report—ninety days if "unavoidable military necessity" so required—unless Congress declared war, extended the sixty-day period, or was unable to meet. In all events, both prior to the introduction of forces and after, the President was to consult with Congress "in every possible instance." By its actions Congress thus asserted that the President could not unilaterally wage war.

Because of the War Powers provisions the President presumably was less free than previously to deploy unilaterally American forces or to order them into combat. Presumably, Congress would be consulted more frequently than before prior to such actions, and would be informed once they were undertaken. If Congress disapproved, according to the law it could by various means terminate American involvement. But suppose it so stipulated and the President refused to comply. What then? Presidents from Truman through Nixon inclusive believed that as Commander in Chief their authority to employ American armed forces did not depend on Congress, and thus they could not be constrained by that body. Would a President who thought that America's vital interests were in jeopardy act in ways he felt prejudicial to those interests just because Congress said he should? That seems most unlikely. The consultation requirement was another complicating factor. With whom should the President consult? The party leadership? Foreign Relations and Affairs Committees in each House? All committees that deal with foreign issues? All of Congress? The more individuals involved the more time would be taken, the greater would be the involvement of less informed individuals, the greater the likelihood of leaks, and the less likely that a consensus would be established. But if only a few members were consulted, Congress's views as a whole would not be accurately ascertained or represented. And *when* should consultation occur? And what happens afterwards? Did Congress have the right to veto the President's decision if it disagreed? If Congress did not disagree with the President, did it share the responsibility for the policy that followed? None of this was clear.

The historical record since the resolution's passage has done little to clarify matters. There have been some cases, such as the transferring of refugees from DaNang, Vietnam, in 1975 and American participation in the multinational force in Beirut in the fall of 1982, when Presidents Ford and Reagan both adhered quite closely to the resolution's requirements. But these were instances in which such action was convenient. In certain other cases, when presidents would have found consulting to be a problem and the resolution's provisions too restrictive, different presidents have found ways to take vigorous action *anyway*. In 1975, when President Ford decided to undertake military operations in response to Cambodia's seizure of the freighter *May-aguez,* he informed only a small number of congressmen, and did that only *after* orders to initiate operations had been given. In April 1980, as President Carter and his aides were planning a mission to rescue American hostages held in Iran, Carter had to decide how to handle Congress.

> On April 18, I had quite a discussion with my closest advisers about how to deal with the congressional leadership on the Iran decisions. . . . One or two key members of Congress might be consulted when our final plans were under way, but I would notify a larger group of the leadership . . . only after the rescue operation had reached the point of no return. . . . It was absolutely imperative that there be no leaks.[15]

So much for consultation and "collective judgment."

To this point in time presidents who have believed that action was essential but were convinced that the resolution's provisions were an unacceptable hindrance have found ways to bypass the resolution and to take action anyway. But it has only been a few years, and the jury is still out on this one. The history of congressional action in war making situations, at least in their early stages, has been one of almost wholehearted *support* for decisive presidential action. Appropriations and resolutions usually have been forthcoming if requested. If the War Powers Act had been in existence in the early stages of the Vietnam War, it would *not* alone have prevented the deepening of the American commitment. Only if over time the President's policy has proven *unsuccessful* has Congress withheld or withdrawn support. As has been true so often before, if the President is successful Congress tends to be supportive no matter what the legislative requirements. Americans want problems solved; it is lack of success that makes the critics howl.

This was the rather uncertain situation in June 1983 when the U.S. Supreme Court confused things even more by issuing a broad-ranging ruling that declared that legislative vetoes were unconstitutional. All valid acts of legislation must not only pass both houses of Congress, the Court said, but also must be "presented" to the President for approval. At first blush this seemed to indicate, at the very least, that the provisions in the War Powers legislation authorizing Congress by concurrent resolution to order the withdrawal of American forces overseas were invalid. Maybe the whole resolution was invalid, or, perhaps because it was presented to President Nixon in the first place, before he vetoed it and it in turn was passed over his veto, it *met* the "presentment" test.

Immediately after the Supreme Court decision, Congress began to examine the damage to its position to determine what should be done next, but no "remedial" legislation was immediately forthcoming. Despite the confusion, in the fall Congress again showed its determination to play a major role. U.S. marine members of the multinational peacekeeping force in Lebanon (see Chapter 19) began suffering casualties but President Reagan refused to apply the War Powers Act, saying "hostilities" did not exist and were not imminent. Congress supported the President's *policy,* but it wanted the act applied nonetheless. After intensive negotiations a compromise was reached. Congress passed legislation declaring that the act applied, but it also authorized deployment for eighteen more months, thus *deepening* the American commitment in Lebanon. Because only Congress, not the President, declared that the act was applicable (although Reagan did sign the legislation), and because instead of establishing significant limits the legislation authorized a deeper commitment, the long-term implications of these developments were unclear. When combined with the confusion resulting from the Supreme Court's decision, the uncertainty was compounded.

---

[15]Carter, *Keeping Faith,* p. 511.

7.

Congress, Nuclear Nonproliferation, and Foreign Aid

The fourth and fifth areas in which Congress has become more assertive are nuclear nonproliferation and foreign aid.

Nuclear nonproliferation was not a significant issue with Congress until 1974, when France announced plans to extend nuclear cooperation to Pakistan and South Korea, and Germany announced a broad nuclear cooperation program with Brazil. Then, in May, India exploded a nuclear device fueled by reprocessed plutonium. Congress responded in 1976 with the Symington Amendment, providing for the termination of economic and military aid to any country that received nuclear fuel reprocessing or enrichment facilities not under multilateral auspices and international safeguards, unless the President declared the assistance essential to national security. In 1977, the Glenn Amendment tightened requirements further, and in 1979 the Symington Amendment was used to cut off aid to Pakistan.

The Nuclear Non-Proliferation Act of 1978 (NNPA) codified the determination of Congress to play a larger role, requiring the President to negotiate all new agreements on nuclear cooperation (and to renegotiate all existing agreements) within strict guidelines. It also permitted Congress by concurrent resolution to overrule presidential decisions in specific cases.

President Carter was largely of the same mind as Congress on nonproliferation issues, but the Reagan administration's views were quite different. Reagan was much more tolerant of reprocessing facilities and the utilization of breeder reactors in an energy-hungry world, and was much less restrictive in dealing with friendly nations on such matters. An adversarial Congress responded in 1981 by adding a *congressional veto* to the President's authority to give nuclear assistance. (The Supreme Court's action in 1983, striking down the legislative veto, leaves this situation unclear.)

The fifth area in which Congress has become more assertive is foreign aid. Where earlier Congress had merely questioned specific items or the proposed overall amounts of such programs, now it went further, especially on arms transfers. Congress flatly prohibited aid to any state that "engages in a consistent pattern of gross violations of internationally recognized human rights," is "dominated or controlled by the international Communist movement," or discriminates against "United States person(s)" in its programs. Congress has forbidden all aid to particular states: in 1978, to Cuba, Angola, Chile, Argentina, Uganda, Cambodia, Laos, Vietnam, Mozambique, Ethiopia, and Uruguay. Restrictions also have been applied to states giving terrorists sanctuary, defaulting on a loan for more than one year, or failing to make adequate compensation after nationalization (although the President can make exceptions if it is *essential* to American security).

Congress has also ventured into actual policy direction: cutting off CIA funds to Angola and banning all military aid to Turkey after the Turkish landings in Cyprus in 1974—to which Turkey responded by closing U.S. bases in Turkey.

Congress has taken a number of other initiatives. Late in the Vietnam War, Congress sought to cut off funds to U.S. troops or advisers in Cambodia (but President Nixon withdrew the forces before the cuts took effect). It refused emergency aid for South Vietnam in 1975 as that regime collapsed. In the mid-1970s it amended the Arms Control Export Act to require reports of offers to sell articles or services of $25 million or more. Congress then had thirty days in which to consider the sale, during which time it could veto the sale by concurrent resolution. In fact, more than one hundred resolutions of *disapproval* have been introduced under this requirement, but none has passed. But Congress has intervened in the arms-transfer process in other ways, requiring President Ford, for example, to guarantee that Hawk missiles sold to Jordan would be nonmobile and defensive. Similarly, President Carter in 1978 proposed selling F-

15s to the Saudis, but first he had to assure Congress that they would not be configured to make major bombing raids and would not be based at Tabuk (the Saudi base nearest Israel). And sometimes the threat of disapproval has forced the President to withdraw an offer of aid. In March 1984 congressional opposition compelled President Reagan to withdraw an offer to sell anti-aircraft missiles to Jordan and Saudi Arabia.[16]

These actions certainly demonstrate a distinct congressional unwillingness simply to "go along" with presidential requests.

8.

Summing Up

With all the changes in recent years it is easy to lose perspective. Although Congress has enhanced its role in many areas, the President remains the central figure in policymaking. Despite the various congressional activities in the 1970s, for example, it was the President or his representatives who negotiated SALT I and the Paris Peace Agreements, normalized relations with the People's Republic of China, mediated the Camp David Accords and the Egyptian-Israeli Peace Treaty, ordered U.S. forces into action in the *Mayaguez* affair, encouraged NATO to adopt a Long Term Defense Program, cancelled production of the B-1 bomber, and so on. Still, things *are* different. Because of Congress's assertiveness, even when the President grasps the initiative he cannot do so without one eye on Capitol Hill. And in some areas the President just is not able to act unilaterally.

But though Congress today is more assertive, its inherent weaknesses remain. Congress's analytical and information-processing staff and support capabilities, though much improved, pale beside the President's; it is more decentralized than ever; it is necessarily slow moving, and is equipped not so much to initiate and direct as to react and limit. The President, as before, must play the dominant role.

What Congress *can* and *should* do more of is effectively *debate the major policy alternatives* at the turns in the road when major choices face the United States. It may be too late later. Through such a debate Congress could help assess likely costs and benefits of various specific options, as well as participate in the design of broad policy guidelines. But Congress in modern times has not done this essential job. To illustrate: Congress did not, as it should have, fully address the implications of either the Truman Doctrine or the Gulf of Tonkin Resolution, two of the most far-reaching policy developments of the postwar era. In the first case, in March 1947 President Truman, responding to a perceived Communist threat to Greece and Turkey, went beyond the specific case to state that it should be the policy of the United States "to support free peoples who are resisting attempted subjugation by armed minorities or by outside pressures." Scarcely a broader mandate for global involvement can be imagined, but although the Greek-Turkish Aid Act was debated for several weeks, the long-term implications of the Truman Doctrine's concepts and language were not thoroughly questioned. The act passed the House, 287–107, and the Senate, 67–23. In the second case, the Gulf of Tonkin Resolution, passed in August 1964 after apparent attacks by North Vietnamese torpedo boats on American destroyers in the Tonkin Gulf, authorized the President to take vigorous measures to protect American forces in Vietnam. The resolution was adopted unanimously by the House and by an 88–2 vote in the Senate after total estimated committee and Senate floor consideration of eight hours and

---

[16]Even though the Supreme Court had declared legislative vetoes unconstitutional, since no action had been taken on *this* statute both the President and Congress continued to observe its provisions, apparently proceeding as if Congress's veto power remained valid.

twenty-two minutes! Later the Gulf of Tonkin Resolution would be used by President Johnson as what amounted to a functional equivalent of a declaration of war, but at the time of passage the debate was largely perfunctory and the nature of the choice being made was left obscure.

Partially through the exercise of effective debate, and in part through careful but vigorous investigation, Congress also can give great attention to selected specific issues. Here, too, it may pose alternatives for presidential consideration. It also can help keep the executive accountable through the exercise of effective oversight. Past performance can be monitored and evaluated through careful scrutiny of the historical record. Whether commitments were or were not made; whether policy was or was not appropriate; whether new policies, legislation, or guidelines are needed; insights into all this and more can result from careful congressional investigation.

If Congress exercises its functions of debate and investigation effectively, there will be other benefits. Because in many ways Congress is a microcosm of informed public opinion, it can act as a vital link between the people and their government. As Congress represents America's diverse peoples, it gives governmental policies a stamp of legitimacy, surely a crucial matter in a democratic system. If Congress participates effectively, it ensures at least a modicum of domestic support for whatever the policy adopted; without this, at some point, the policy will fail. And effective debate ultimately is bound to have a positive effect on national morale; without it, in circumstances such as Vietnam in which public opinion is drastically split, national morale will be seriously affected.

With the pre-Vietnam policy consensus thoroughly shattered, the United States is groping for a new overall conception of the dimensions of its role in foreign affairs. No matter what organizational alterations one makes, unless there is an underlying consensus over that role, the level of tension and struggle between Congress and the President will be enormous. Although establishing a new consensus will not be easy, or may even be impossible, because of the importance of the task the effort must be made. Surely Congress should participate strongly in that effort.

The President must remain the central figure in policymaking. Whereas Congress can and should participate in the general design of policy—debating major alternatives, setting outer limits, helping establish direction—it is not equipped to be productively involved in phase 2, in day-to-day operations. And although neither end of Pennsylvania Avenue has a monopoly on wisdom, it is evident that in general Congress needs to allow policy initiative to reside in the executive. Given the nature of the American political system, though, it is apparent that presidential-congressional tension will be with us for a long time to come.

Bureaucratic Politics

I made it clear . . . that I would be President. . . . I left them in no doubt that all final policy decisions would be mine.

Harry S. Truman
Memoirs: Year of Decisions

I quickly learned what every policy-level official who has come to Washington soon learns—that for every hour he spends on dramatic policy-making he must spend at least ten on . . . making the bureaucracy function and moving it in the direction he believes important.

William Colby
Honorable Men: My Life in the CIA

Although the President is the central figure in the design and implementation of policy, the job is far too large and complex for one person to handle alone. On a single day the President may have to deal with problems in negotiations with the Soviet Union on the deployment of Theater Nuclear Forces in Europe, formulate possible alternatives for dealing with a guerrilla war in Central America, cope with growing dissension in the NATO alliance, prepare for upcoming talks with Japan over restrictions on auto imports, work on the defense budget, react to a crisis in Lebanon that threatens to erupt into full-scale war, as well as tackle a host of domestic problems, deal with Congress, and dispose of mountains of paperwork. And this is just an ordinary day; sometimes he is "really" busy. Obviously, the President must have assistance.

The presumed purpose of the bureaucracy is to help provide that assistance. Ideally, the various agencies work smoothly and efficiently in coordination with the President and are immediately and sensitively responsive to his direction. As much as is possible the machinery is designed to reflect the need for specialized expertise and information. When functioning effectively, the apparatus facilitates the identification and study of various options with their attendant projected costs and benefits, and provides the President with both ideas and recommendations on both the design and implementation of policy. The bureaucracy is charged with providing vast quantities of high-quality information, and routing it to the correct people in a timely fashion. The apparatus is supposed to provide accurate records of past performance so that senior policymakers have a historical base as a foundation for intelligent judgments about the future. By providing such records (presumably), it adds a degree of policy stability and reliability. On the implementation side the bureaucracy is supposed to have the capability to monitor carefully and evaluate performance, to provide the managerial tools essential to ensuring a cost-effective policy, and to assist the President in the crucial task of policy coordination.

It is clear that this ideal has not been (and cannot ever be) totally realized. In Chapters 9 and 10 we discuss the specific components of the policymaking apparatus in depth and detail. Here our analysis is more general, an examination of the role, importance, and nature of bureaucratic politics in the foreign policymaking process. The key questions in this regard are (1) What impact do the standard operating procedures that are followed in most large organizations have on policy? (2) How do personal judgments affect the processing of information? (3) What is the significance of the fact that the American policymaking machinery is extremely fragmented? (4) What are the effects of bureaucratic competition? (5) What generalizations, if any, can one make about the bureaucratic process as a whole? (6) What is the role of small decision groups in policymaking? and (7) Finally, and crucially, what is the relationship of the President to the bureaucracy? To what extent is the President central, and to what degree is he "just another participant" in an ongoing bureaucratic process?

1.

The Role of Standard Operating Procedures

Let us start with the impact of procedures. Because the United States is a large country with an enormous number of international relationships, standardized policy and procedural frameworks have had to be established. These standard operating policies and procedures (or SOPs) are designed to anticipate a wide range of contingencies. They program policy and procedural responses according to particular routines. To a considerable extent low- and mid-level bureaucrats today act within such established frameworks.

There are very few exceptions to this rule. Procedurally, all government agencies have a wide array of regulations that determine how things are to be done. If one works at the Department of State certain procedures simply must be followed; there is a "State Department way" of doing things. This is true also in the Department of Defense, CIA, and so on. And in policy terms, once the fundamental thrust has been determined and guidelines established, it is "SOP" both that the policy is right and that it must be supported and implemented faithfully. Once President Johnson decided to escalate the military effort in Vietnam, the bureaucracy was expected to reinforce and give support to his policies "SOP," without question. And generally it did. In fact, most of the time, as Gelb has pointed out, it did so with relish: "The bureaucracy became like a cement block in the trunk of a car—it added tremendous momentum. . . . by 1965 almost all career professionals became holier than the Pope on the subject of U.S. interests in Vietnam."[1]

SOPs are influential most noticeably in the routine conduct of noncrisis, program-oriented policy, the everyday activity that absorbs most of the bureaucrat's time. But the more a problem is unanticipated or does not fit the preexisting policy or procedural frameworks, and/or the more complex and important it is, the less likely it is that it will be decided on the basis of SOPs or be impacted significantly at the low or mid levels. Decisions on these kinds of problems, unless a mistake occurs, will be made at the top and will be determined on the basis of senior policymakers' conceptions of the national interest (a point we return to later).

---

[1]Leslie H. Gelb, with Richard K. Betts, *The Irony of Vietnam: The System Worked* (Washington D. C.: The Brookings Institution, 1979), p. 239.

Although it is essential that many matters be handled via SOPs, and it is inevitable that many will, there are at least three major difficulties as a consequence.

The first difficulty implicit in policymaking by means of SOPs is that the vast majority of "decisions" made occur without the President's specific knowledge. This is not automatically detrimental since the decisions might be wise, but naturally this is not always so. On numerous occasions presidents have been confronted with very unpleasant *faits accompli*. Early in 1948, on the advice of his advisers, President Truman decided to alter U.S. policy from a position supporting the partition of Palestine into separate Jewish and Arab states to a stance recommending the creation of a temporary UN trusteeship for the area. U.S. Ambassador to the UN Warren Austin was informed of this and on March 16, 1948, he was instructed to give a speech so indicating as soon as the time was appropriate. Before the ambassador could implement these instructions and give the speech though, unbeknownst to Austin the President changed his mind, choosing again the counterbalancing interest of supporting partition. On March 19, Austin, acting in accord with the previously accepted guidelines, gave his speech advocating the abandonment of the partition plan and the creation of a trusteeship. The President had been unaware of the precise timing, and did not find out about Austin's address until the next day. Thus the President was pursuing one line of policy, his UN ambassador quite another. Many other examples could be cited. From 1949 to 1955, covert activities of the CIA did not require specific presidential approval; although sometimes in fact approval was obtained, occasionally operations were undertaken that the President did not know about until later. Another illustration occurred in 1960, when a U-2 spy plane was dispatched over the Soviet Union by the CIA, according to customary procedures. But this one was shot down. Although President Eisenhower had not given specific clearance for the overflight, this was not required by the existing guidelines. The resulting incident provided the rationale for the Russians to torpedo the Paris Summit Conference. And the list could be extended. Because so much must be done via SOPs, where this is done presidents are always somewhat removed from the details of policy. The few cases in which this is not so are truly exceptional.

A second difficulty, perhaps even more pervasive than the first, is that the policies that are produced through the use of SOPs usually are status quo-oriented. Standard operating procedures tend to stifle innovation and initiative. Established on the basis of the results of past policy, these procedures generally produce decisions that involve few radical departures from that policy. Individuals in the bureaucracy are expected to conform to existing procedures, and to act on the basis of the instructions they receive. Usually they are given a particular task, told what is wanted, and generally instructed as to how it should be done. This reduces innovation. Another caution-inducing factor is the understandable disinclination of subordinates to "rock the boat." In most large organizations it is simply prudent to avoid proposing alternatives that depart significantly from established guidelines. As Richard Betts put it in his discussion of the pressures faced by intelligence analysts: "Integrity untinged by political sensitivity courts professional suicide."[2] In 1964, the CIA was asked by President Johnson if the rest of Southeast Asia was likely to fall (like a row of dominoes) if South Vietnam and Laos came under North Vietnamese control. The CIA's answer, essentially, was "no." Johnson did not ask for the Agency's opinion again.[3] To a considerable extent the combination of subordinates' concerns, the very nature of their job, and the character of the procedures themselves means that new ideas or innovations may not even get considered.

There are still other reasons why innovation gets stifled. Issues in which low- and midlevel bureaucrats are involved must ascend several horizontal layers within an organization before

---

[2]Richard K. Betts, "Analysis, War, and Decision: Why Intelligence Failures are Inevitable," *World Politics* (October 1978), 82.

[3]Gelb, *The Irony of Vietnam*, p. 230.

action can be taken. At each level there is a tendency to weed out the more extreme ideas (for the reasons mentioned previously). There is pressure toward a cautious policy also because, at each level, a variety of perspectives and views must be reconciled in what is a constant effort to develop policy consensus. This means that there is some tendency toward eliminating new or unusual ideas. By the time a proposal gets up to an action level, it often is the lowest common denominator, the most compromised, safest policy possible.

It is important to understand what we are and are not saying. We are not saying that conservative, status-quo oriented policies are always unwise. Quite clearly, there are situations in which such are very much in the national interest. But it is equally evident that there are times when this is not the case, when policy alterations, sometimes radical alterations, are required. Further, because one can never be wholly sure what the future holds it always is important to develop a variety of options so adaptability and choice can be maximized. When facing the fluid world of international politics, it is essential that one be able to continually reappraise and flexibly substitute one counterbalancing interest for another as the situation requires. The difficulty in the bureaucracy is that standard operating procedures frequently preclude so many alternatives and restrict flexibility to such an extent that high-level policymakers do not even get the chance to consider new ideas.[4]

A third major difficulty with standard operating procedures is that they are terribly time consuming. So many bases must be touched, so many individuals and agencies consulted, so many clearances obtained, that it takes "forever and a day" for anything to happen. This is not always unproductive; time for study and thought is important. President Eisenhower structured the National Security Council system very formally to ensure that careful, orderly, well-staffed deliberations would occur at all times.[5] Lengthy papers were produced analyzing all major policy problems, and comprehensive documents were developed providing general guidelines for almost all policy issues. But the problem was, unfortunately, that so many papers had to be drafted and cleared that the process became clogged with paper, a "papermill" which could not effectively respond to or deal with the dynamic forces that are always at work in the international system.

Not all presidents have sought a highly structured apparatus; indeed, some, such as John Kennedy, have done their best to avoid it. But the line departments such as State and Defense have to run through certain operating procedures no matter who is in the White House. Some of the specific procedures can be changed, but the fact that a multitude of rules, regulations, and guidelines must be utilized can not; a bureaucracy has to work in a deliberate, orderly way, and this takes time. The inexorable result is, to the chagrin of many, that there always will be some degree of built-in inertia.

2.

Problems in Information Processing

Standard operating procedures also are very important with respect to the information/communication system, but they can only decide things to a certain point. For the President and his key advisers to design and implement the policy that produces the best net cost–benefit ratio, large quantities of high-quality information obviously must be obtained. Data must be interpreted quickly and accurately, and sent to the *appropriate* people in a timely manner. Because there is so much information, far too much for any one person to digest, systematic routines need

---

[4]This statement applies only to those issues handled primarily via the bureaucratic process. This distinction is discussed in depth later.

[5]Carefully and succinctly analyzed in I. M. Destler, "National Security Advice to U.S. Presidents," *World Politics* (January 1977).

to be established to filter and select, to synthesize and summarize. Routing systems need to be established to make sure the people who need the data in fact get it. Specific criteria need to be established to enable officials at various levels to know what should go to whom.

But, in the nature of things, such criteria can only decide the level of attention in gross terms. For this reason midlevel bureaucrats must play key roles fine-tuning the information-distribution process. Except for crisis situations, they are the ones through whom most information is funneled and the ones who usually make the judgments concerning the importance, immediacy, and relevance of information communicated.

In national security matters NSC staffers often perform this function. Robert Hunter, a member of the NSC staff in the Carter administration, describes it this way:

> The key task for the NSC staff at this point . . . was to make a critical judgment about the level at which a decision should be taken. Should this memo go straight to the president . . .? Could it be shortstopped at the level of the national security adviser, without wasting the president's time—but with a short note sent into the Oval Office so that the president would know what was being done? Was a meeting required and, if so, at what level? And what did the other agencies think? If it was a State memo, did Defense have to have a say?[6]

Although systematic criteria and procedures exist, it is evident that they do not cover all contingencies. Personal judgments still play a major role. Though it is the exception rather than the rule, occasionally in the bureaucracy such judgments have distinctly negative effects. Sometimes information may not be passed up the line because a subordinate is concerned about a negative reaction from his or her superior. Or, the information may be forwarded but interpreted and phrased in a manner one knows will be favorably received. Any number of times during the Vietnam War, for example, bureaucrats told their superiors what they thought they wanted to hear.[7]

At higher levels, too, personal judgments are important. Ever since the position of (special) Assistant for National Security Affairs was held by McGeorge Bundy in the Kennedy administration, individuals occupying that post have coordinated and managed the flow of information, intelligence, and decision papers to the President.[8] Daily intelligence briefings inevitably require synthesis and judgment, and much of what the President sees and hears bears the imprint of the particular style and views of his assistant. In fact, when Henry Kissinger held this position under Presidents Nixon and Ford, no item could even be discussed at an NSC meeting without his approval.

A specific instance demonstrating the importance of personal judgments occurred in the spring of 1970. President Nixon and his aides were considering a military incursion into Cambodia with the objective of destroying North Vietnam's sanctuaries and bases. Thirteen days before the attack CIA Director Richard Helms received an Office of National Estimates memorandum that included a pessimistic evaluation of the results such an incursion would produce. Within the existing procedural framework, Helms had the discretion to decide whether the study should be forwarded or not. It was not. The attack went on as scheduled, but its objectives were not achieved.

Although personal judgments must be used in the interpretation of the procedures and there are occasional "foul-ups" in the machinery, as a rule the information/communication apparatus functions quite efficiently. Indeed, there is a veritable flood of data, so much that it threatens to

---

[6]Robert E. Hunter, *Presidential Control of Foreign Policy: Management or Mishap?*, The Washington Papers, no. 91, the Center for Strategic and International Studies, Georgetown University (New York: Praeger, 1982), p. 24.
[7]Gelb, *The Irony of Vietnam* (Washington, D.C.: The Brookings Institution, 1979), Ch. 11.
[8]Except for a brief period early in the Reagan administration.

inundate those at the top. The major problems are not mechanical; they are analytical. There are enormous difficulties in interpretation. What does it all mean? Sometimes the facts, themselves, are clear. The nature and magnitude of the Soviet military build-up in the late 1970s and early 1980s, for example, was apparent. From a host of sources American analysts were able to detail accurately the growth in Soviet capabilities, right down to specific weapon system numbers, performance characteristics, and deployments. The facts were not in dispute. The problem was, what did the build-up signify? Did it result inevitably from the nature of the Soviet system and ideology, did it reflect aggressive intentions? Or was it instead an essentially defensive reaction to a declining geopolitical position around the Soviet periphery and the lack of political cards to play because of American-Chinese rapprochement, thus reflecting increasing Soviet frustration and heightened concern with vulnerability? The data could support either view. (We return to this important point in Chapter 16.)

Although the facts sometimes are clear and the problem is "only" one of interpretation, it much more often is the case that the facts too are in dispute and policymakers are faced with ambiguous and partially conflicting information. In early 1979, for example, as the Iranian crisis became increasingly chaotic, President Carter was confronted with diametrically opposed indicators. With the Shah's days numbered the United States was throwing its support to the newly appointed government of Shahpour Bakhtiar. A key question was the degree of support Bakhtiar would receive from the Iranian military. Another question, obviously, was whether the people would support him. The American ambassador in Teheran consistently indicated to President Carter that popular support for Bakhtiar was very thin, Ayatollah Khomeini's support was growing, and the military might well not back Bakhtiar in a showdown. General Robert Huyser, a special presidential emissary dispatched to the scene in early January, reported that the military was holding together well and Bakhtiar had good public support. It was reminiscent of the problem faced by President Kennedy in 1963 when, seeking to assess the situation in Vietnam as accurately as possible to determine whether or not to continue to support the regime of Ngo Dinh Diem, he had dispatched the Krulak-Mendenhall mission to the scene to get a first-hand look. On the mission's return General Krulak said things were going well and current policies should be continued. Mendenhall said the situation was dismal and would get worse unless major changes were made.

Most of the time the alternatives are not posed so starkly, though. The world is dynamic and uncertain, and usually the indicators that analysts discover are partial, somewhat contradictory, and only partly verifiable. In most cases there is some evidence to support nearly any interpretation (and if there is not, it is not an information problem). Therefore, if analysts are to be honest in these situations their reports *must* reflect their uncertainty. Given the nature of the world being faced, usually the President and his key advisers have no choice but to decide on the basis of incomplete, ambiguous, and partly contradictory information. And even *that* information is absorbed (or rejected) in accordance with national biases or attitudes such as those discussed in Chapters 2 and 3. Concept influences content.

3.

Fragmentation

As noted earlier, the United States policymaking apparatus is extremely fragmented. This can present substantial obstacles to the effective design and implementation of policy.

One major problem area involves policy coordination, both coordination of and among the agencies and the coordination of presidential and bureaucratic efforts. With the machinery so fragmented, frequently the right hand does not know what the left is doing (a problem made even worse by the bureaucracy's enormous size). This can lead to a situation involving overlapping jurisdictions with resultant duplication, waste, and interagency friction bound to be engendered. Or, maybe the reverse will occur. Each unit will assume that a particular task is someone else's responsibility, and no one will do it. This was one of Secretary McNamara's most effective criticisms of the Defense establishment—with every service emphasizing its own missions, who would ensure that their plans meshed without strong central controls? Would the air force buy enough transports to carry the army to combat? Or, a number of agencies will develop their own approaches to a given problem or be so involved with their own programs that a coordinated approach is impossible. During the Vietnam War in April 1967 a diplomatic initiative was underway to expand and again demilitarize the (previously) demilitarized zone along the seventeenth parallel. To the chagrin of American diplomats, a bombing raid was scheduled against power plants in Haiphong at precisely the time they felt restraint was in order, but nothing could be done. "There was just no interest or effort expended in orchestrating military and diplomatic moves; everyone was doing his own thing."[9]

Another thing that frequently happens because the policymaking machinery is so fragmented is that one unit acts in such a way as to undercut the effectiveness of another. Often this occurs between agencies, as one pursues a course of action that pulls the rug out from under another. This also can be a problem between the President and the bureaucracy although, when it comes about deliberately, the bureaucrat is running quite a risk. In March 1978, President Carter gave a major address on defense policy. One of his objectives was to signal the Soviets that a continued military buildup could imperil détente. Shortly before the speech was given, however, an official in the State Department contacted the Soviet embassy and urged that the entire text of the speech be transmitted to Moscow so Kremlin leaders could see that there also were a number of conciliatory passages. Another example occurred in early 1971. The Department of State was not aware of the secret efforts of President Nixon and Henry Kissinger to prepare for a normalization of relations between the United States and the People's Republic of China. Shortly after Beijing had issued a private invitation for a high-level meeting on its soil, the department publicly began laying the ground work for possibly admitting the PRC to the United Nations while at the same time retaining a seat in the General Assembly for Taiwan. This view was wholly in conflict with Beijing's position. Soon thereafter, Secretary of State Rogers indicated that a purported PRC invitation reported in *Life* magazine was not "serious."[10] These activities, fully in line with existing policies, reflected the fragmentation in the policymaking apparatus and complicated matters enormously. Feverishly Kissinger and the President (who in this case themselves had created the problem by their use of "back channels") worked to assure the Chinese that the administration certainly was serious. They were successful, but their success was made more difficult by this deliberate lack of effective presidential-bureaucratic coordination.

The presumed remedy for most such difficulties is to establish clear lines of authority with no overlapping jurisdictions and to give the appropriate officials a degree of "authority" to match their "responsibility." But in the real world things are not that simple. Problems are multifaceted, complex, and interrelated. I. M. Destler provides us with a useful example:

> More generally, who in the broader government should have "authority" on the issue of possible U.S. troop withdrawals from Europe? The Secretary of State and his European Affairs Bureau? His Politico-Military Affairs Bureau? The Secretary of Defense? The Secretary of the Treasury, given his role as protector of the balance of payments? The Director of the Arms Control and Disarmament Agency, given the relation of troop withdrawals to the military

---

[9]Chester L. Cooper, *The Lost Crusade: America in Vietnam* (New York: Dodd, Mead, 1970), pp. 373–374.
[10]This example is based on Henry Kissinger, *White House Years* (Boston: Little, Brown, 1979), p. 720.

balance? For each of them, "responsibility" on this issue far outruns the "authority" to deal with it.[11]

4.

Bureaucratic Competition

Other difficulties arise from the fact that often there is a great deal of bureaucratic competition. Instead of working together in a coordinated and harmonious fashion, departmental and sub-departmental units compete with one another.

Although there are a number of causal factors behind bureaucratic competition, they can be conveniently synthesized into two major categories. First, organizations tend to have interests of their own, and their leaders and members seek to develop the capabilities necessary to achieve or protect those interests. Every bureaucratic unit has a certain "territory" and its members want to exert maximum influence over that bureaucratic turf. Each agency has a structural, personnel, and financial base; some degree of policymaking autonomy; and some amount of external influence. At a minimum these must be protected, and if possible, they should be extended. If successful, organization and individual prosper accordingly; if not, the converse is true.

Second, different organizations deal with different aspects of problems, operate from different perspectives, and have different responsibilities. The Joint Chiefs of Staff, ACDA, the State Department, and the intelligence community all view the issue of verification of strategic arms limitations agreements differently. Indeed, because they operate from different perspectives, and focus on and emphasize different aspects of the problem, they do not even see the same "reality." It is essential to remember that the various agencies have different jobs to do, that their members have training and expertise that is different, and that they operate on the basis of differing instructions and assignments. It would be only natural in such circumstances to expect different units to produce different recommendations, and they often do. Because each agency wishes to have its policy views prevail, each seeks to maximize its influence.

To a considerable extent as a result of these facts, bureaucratic agencies engage in an ongoing process of competitive bargaining. Each unit seeks to maximize its intrabureaucratic position and to exert as much policy influence as possible. When this occurs the effect sometimes is that the "policy" which emerges is simply a product, the result of bureaucratic interactions.[12] Such a policy might be effective, but there is no reason to assume that it would be. It might well be a "nonpolicy," or one that is ineffective, or even one that is detrimental.

A lot also depends on the nature of the problem faced, particularly its urgency and its obviousness. Most of the time during the competitive bargaining process the participants, even while advocating policies that will redound to the benefit of their organization, sincerely believe that these policies also will best serve the national interest. For example, while officials of the Arms Control and Disarmament Agency generally advocate stronger efforts to obtain strategic arms limitation agreements, which if achieved presumably would result in increased influence for their agency, they also firmly believe that such agreements are in America's national interests. Similarly, whereas the Joint Chiefs of Staff often strongly advocate a higher defense budget, which presumably would enhance the chiefs' prestige and power, they also genuinely believe that this is necessary to accomplish the country's defense policy objectives and to protect national security. It is important to recognize that in most instances what occurs is *not* a cynical manip-

---

[11]I. M. Destler, *Presidents, Bureaucrats, and Foreign Policy* (Princeton, N. J.: Princeton University Press, 1974), p. 24.

[12]The degree to which policy is simply a eunuch, a neutered output of the bargaining process, is often exaggerated, however, as our later discussion makes clear.

ulation in the interest of personal and/or organizational gain at the expense of the state. Usually the various policies that are advocated are believed to be in the national interest.

The preceding comment provides a significant interpretive qualification to the oft-heard charge "where you stand depends on where you sit." Although it is surely true that organizational infighting does exist, and such infighting sometimes is based primarily on intrabureaucratic and/or personal career concerns, there is a tendency today to give this charge more credence than it deserves and to view organizational activities in a too narrow, too "selfish" perspective. A second explanatory qualification must be noted also: bureaucrats operate within the framework of established SOPs and in accordance with the instructions of their superiors. Subordinate units are not expected to deal with the entire problem or to advance all-embracing recommendations. Their task is to do something with a particular aspect of the issue in accordance with certain procedures and within a certain policy framework. Quite evidently, the nature of the assignment will shape the nature of the finished product. In 1961 President Kennedy sent General Maxwell Taylor to Vietnam. On his return the general indicated that the United States needed to escalate its military contribution. Critics have concluded that this was a good example of "where you stand depends on where you sit." What they do not realize is that Taylor's instructions from the President were to recommend measures to strengthen South Vietnam. He did what he was told to do. In 1977 the Carter administration issued a Presidential Review Memorandum (PRM) ordering a study of various options related to withdrawing American forces from South Korea. The final report offered a series of different withdrawal rates and recommended slower, more cautious ones. The option of not withdrawing was not mentioned, because the instructions for formulating the proposal specifically stated that not withdrawing could not be considered.[13]

And there are other difficulties with this idea. One is that there are many situations in which the competition that "should" occur simply does not. In the conduct of American policy during the Conference on Security and Cooperation in Europe in the early and mid 1970s, for example, there was little organizational bargaining and maneuvering. Second, as anyone with personal familiarity with the various agencies in the policymaking apparatus knows, they are far from monolithic. Indeed, a wide range of opinions exist, and these are only partially pressed into conformity by SOPs. The consequence of this for our topic is that during the policy design and implementation process, when these agencies or departments supposedly are bargaining and competing, there frequently is not anything one could accurately call an agency or department position to advocate or defend. There is fragmentation within units, and often what one sees is an intricate web of informal interagency relationships and coalitions.

5.

Characteristics of Bureaucratic Policymaking

In addition to the utilization and impact of standard operating procedures, the results produced by the fragmentation of the policymaking machinery, and by bureaucratic competition, other features are characteristic of the bureaucratic policymaking process. We consider four.

The first of these is that most of the policies which emerge are the product of a flow of decisional fragments rather than the result of self-contained individual choices. Instead of the policymaking process consisting of specific, discrete decisions, it is a stream of interacting bits and pieces. Ideas and information flow into the process from a wide range of official and unofficial sources, papers and proposals are transmitted both vertically and horizontally, and incre-

---

[13]Cyrus Vance, *Hard Choices: Critical Years in America's Foreign Policy* (New York: Simon & Schuster, 1983), p. 128.

mental alterations and modifications are made by a whole host of people in various positions. Each portion is but a bit or piece of a long and complex chain, the result of many interacting factors. Each then incrementally shapes and influences others. Policy continuously evolves at a number of levels and to some degree is simply a product of the decisional flow.

In 1977, the Soviet Union began the deployment of multiple-warhead SS-20 medium-range missiles, targeted on Western Europe. The United States and its NATO allies immediately began to explore potential responses, and in December 1979 announced a two-track approach—plans to deploy U.S. Theater Nuclear Forces in Europe and a simultaneous attempt to negotiate mutual limits on Theater Nucs. Within the American foreign policy bureaucracy during this period a whirlwind of activity took place as a host of different agencies and individuals worked on the problem. Gradually, over time, a "decision" was reached, the decision announced in December 1979. Clearly it was the product of a number of bits and fragments from many sources. Hunter describes the process that took place this way:

> The NSC commissioned a PRM [Presidential Review Memorandum] and managed a complex of working groups, mini-SCCs [Special Coordination Committee], full SCCs, VBBs (Vance-Brzezinski-Brown lunch meetings], Friday Breakfasts [Carter-Mondale-Vance-Brzezinski] , informal meetings with the president, and full NSCs, plus discussion in the cabinet. By the time the work was done, hundreds of trips to European capitals had been logged by middle and high level State, Defense, and NSC officials; . . . thousands of cables had been dispatched and received; reams of paper had been produced; and several hundred if not thousands of people in the administration had become engaged.[14]

A second characteristic of bureaucratic policymaking is that the participants enmeshed in the process frequently operate under considerable time pressure. Bureaucrats in the foreign policy apparatus have no more time in their days than we do, and their job demands are enormous. To a much greater degree than outsiders expect, their priorities and daily activities are determined by external demands.

Given the enormous quantity of complicated and dynamic interrelationships that constitute the world of international politics, and the fact that the United States is a global power with worldwide interests, it is evident why these time pressures exist. Unfortunately, such pressures produce a number of negative consequences.

First, because there is just too much to do and not enough time to do it, standard operating procedures must be utilized extensively, with all that their use entails; to a great extent officials simply have to use the preprogrammed routines as quickly as possible and move on. Second, officials lack adequate time to evaluate fully and think about all the data pertinent to a particular issue. Because of their preoccupation with the Iran hostage crisis and problems with the Soviets, senior officials in the Carter administration were unable to give accumulating intelligence about possible Soviet actions in Afghanistan the attention it deserved. And as the subsequent invasion showed, events will not wait. Consequently, decisions often have to be made on the basis of incomplete information. Also, as we said in Part One, events do not, simply by happening, indicate their future implication. This is a very important way that information is "incomplete." Third, it is clear that with so little time available for careful thought and analysis the policy product at best will be mixed; overall it clearly will be lower grade than if more time were available. We have said that because time *is* needed for optimum policymaking and presidents need to reserve their energies for issues of major significance, in a number of areas they rely on senior officials and experts in the bureaucracy for much of the routine and/or preliminary work. While freeing up the President as designed, such procedures increase the time demands on high-level bureaucrats, leaving them with even less time for thought and analysis. Finally, there is

[14]Hunter, *Presidential Control of Foreign Policy,* pp. 47–48.

How Washington Makes Foreign Policy

not adequate time for the bureaucracy to reflect on the past and draw whatever lessons are appropriate, nor is there time to design carefully a coherent plan for the future. The necessities of day-to-day operations inexorably take precedence.

A third characteristic of bureaucratic policymaking is the effort by nearly all involved to fashion a consensus, to achieve an accommodation or compromise of views and language that all can support. If the case is one in which the President is actively participating, he wants to build a policy and bureaucratic consensus to enhance both domestic support and international credibility. If it is a matter of primary interest to a part of the bureaucracy, the various agencies and officials want a bureaucratic consensus so they can maximize their leverage when dealing with others. And when all the units of the apparatus are involved, some type of compromise may be sought in order to obtain maximum support, coordination, and efficiency in implementation. (Here is the other face of the bureaucratic competition. It is the same effect that leads to agreements among firms in the same business to divide the available customers but set a uniform price).

A consensus, if achieved, may produce the positive results mentioned previously, but it also may yield certain negative consequences. For one thing, as noted earlier, the policy most likely will not be radically new or innovative, especially if it is to avoid treading on bureaucratic "turf." Typically in such instances the most extreme views are weeded out (especially if it is a consensus of various compromises that have come up through several levels). This is not inherently detrimental, but it does mean that major policy changes will not be considered, whether they should be or not. Second, the policy consensus bears no automatic relationship to what would be optimum. Agreement merely as the product of the process is not the same as a carefully formulated plan. (As we discuss later, however, one should not draw this contrast too starkly.) Third, once a consensus has been reached as to the "big picture," people may come to believe it is the appropriate policy. Once an overall policy consensus is established conceptually, and actions are undertaken to implement that design, a degree of momentum sets in. Right or wrong, that *is* the policy and only infrequently (if at all) are its basic assumptions questioned or alternatives seriously considered until real difficulties appear. Once the United States adopted the anti-Communist, bloc-containment, forward deployment strategy, its conceptual underpinnings and implications went unquestioned for two decades—until the Vietnam War raised doubts about it.

Some issues cannot wait for a consensus. If the issue has been raised to the top level and is sufficiently important, the President may act anyway. After all, as President Truman put it, "the buck stops here." In late 1982, President Reagan had to decide whether to recommend the dense-pack MX missile-basing system (he did). The fact that there was no consensus, that his advisers were divided, with three members of the Joint Chiefs of Staff against and two for, with the Secretary of Defense tying the count, did not relieve the President of the responsibility of decision. Very infrequently, the President may even go against the will of his senior advisers, against a consensus less the President. The story is told that Lincoln asked his cabinet to vote and all voted nay. Holding a different view, the President voted aye, then announced "the ayes have it."

Early in 1978 President Carter was consulting with his advisers about the stalemate in the Middle East. Although Anwar Sadat had made a historic trip to Jerusalem the preceding November in an effort to break the diplomatic and psychological logjam, little progress had resulted and the negotiating prospects seemed bleak. The immediate issue in Washington was whether the United States should take the initiative and develop an "American plan" to be sold to Sadat and Israeli Prime Minister Menachem Begin. In his diary entry of February 3, 1978, Carter wrote:

We had quite an argument at breakfast, with me on one side and Fritz [Mondale], Cy [Vance], Zbig [Brzezinski], and Ham [Jordan] on the other. I think we ought to move much more aggressively on the Middle East question than any of them seem to, by evolving a clear plan. . . . I don't know how much support I have [with the public], but we'll go through with this effort.[15]

But going against a contrary consensus is unusual. And sometimes if counsel is divided, the President will make just a "minimum decision," deciding, but deciding as little as possible. When a consensus could not be achieved with respect to the development of the H-Bomb in 1950, President Truman did not terminate the program, but he ordered only continued research and the development of a few prototypes. President Carter followed a similar course with respect to the Enhanced Radiation Weapon ("neutron bomb") in 1978. After the proposed deployment of the neutron bomb produced enormous controversy both at home and abroad, the President announced a decision to postpone production, later indicating that some components would be produced (but not assembled). In both of these examples, presidents, dealing with highly controversial and sensitive issues and unable to obtain a strong policy consensus, made minimal decisions that "decided" very little and kept future options open.

A fourth characteristic of bureaucratic policymaking, one that has been implicit in much that has already been said, is the pervasiveness of bargaining. Much of the time, what can appear from a distance as an orderly, rational process of policy design and implementation, appears to those taking part as a gigantic and continuing negotiating contest. Since people are involved, discussions must occur, and discussions almost inevitably involve some aspects of bargaining. This bargaining occurs among individuals within organizations, between organizations, and even between the President and all the other individual and organizational participants. The stakes in this discussion or bargaining "game" are influence, and the "policy" that emerges in some cases will reflect the talents of the bargainers at the expense of the objective needs of the situation.

One has to be careful here. What, after all, is "objective"? A first caveat is that a too narrow reading of the point just made gives a false and too mechanistic picture of what actually happens. Just as policymaking organizations are made up of people with diverse skills, specializations, responsibilities, and policy views, so too the organizations, as organizations, differ on such matters. Dissension, discussion, and bargaining all are normal procedures, and we must never forget either that *the argument that occurs takes place within a framework of concern over the policy that results.* As we said about fragmentation, the participants generally are advocating policy positions that they believe are in the national interest, even if such recommendations frequently are also somewhat self-serving.

Second, and of considerable significance, *at each level some degree of thought and policy planning* has been involved. The bargaining that characterizes policymaking is not some haphazard process in which homogeneous inputs produce policy outputs in a wholly random manner. Policy may not be formulated in a wholly "rational" fashion (if there is such a thing), but neither is it simply the product of individuals and organizations with no policy concerns cynically bargaining with only their own self-interest in mind. Thought and analysis do play a role at each level of bureaucratic consideration.

The third caveat ties into what we just said: *policies perceived to have a major near-term impact on a state's vital interests and fundamental objectives are not determined at the low- and midlevels of the policymaking apparatus, the levels at which bureaucratic politics are dominant.* The most important foreign policy decisions are made at the top level by a relatively small number of individuals. Therefore, bureaucratic politics is not of major significance with respect to designing policy for the most important issues confronting the United States. Decisions regarding those matters are not made in the lower or middle levels of the bureaucratic maze.

[15]Carter, *Keeping Faith: Memoirs of a President* (New York: Bantam, 1982), p. 306.

6.

Higher-Level Decisions and Small Groups

At the upper levels of decision making, small groups (either of a formal or an informal kind) play a highly important role in the policy process.

There are a number of reasons why small groups are very significant in the design and implementation of United States foreign policy. One is simply that operating procedures often provide for their utilization. Under President Carter, for example, it was SOP to have the long-term studies designated as Presidential Review Memoranda in the NSC system sent to an NSC subcommittee, and it in turn assigned them to a small interagency task force for the development of alternatives. Within the bureaucracy itself, it is SOP for the most important and unanticipated issues to move up through channels to smaller groups composed of senior policymakers. Another factor is that in recent years presidents and other senior officials have been extremely frustrated by the problems associated with bureaucratic policymaking. Believing small groups to have a number of advantages (a point to which we return), they frequently have utilized such entities and consciously bypassed the established organizational machinery. Finally, small groups usually are a more suitable vehicle than the bureaucracy for the exercise of presidential influence in crisis situations. In matters perceived to impact strongly on the country's ability to achieve or protect vital interests and fundamental objectives, the President wants to be deeply involved and highly influential in policy determination. He can do this better in a small group than when dealing with the bureaucracy as a whole.

There are three major types of small groups.[16] *First, is the informal group without a permanent institutional base.* Such a unit is held together by various professional and personal ties, and its membership crosses department and agency lines. Usually, at least originally, it is both *ad hoc* and informal (although if there is sufficient need and the unit develops a degree of capability it may take on a greater degree of permanence and structure). In 1942, the Joint Chiefs of Staff came into being without a formal charter or executive order of any kind, and it began regular meetings solely on an *ad hoc* basis. This continued throughout the war. During Lyndon Johnson's presidency the majority of the most important decisions were made by the "Tuesday Lunch Bunch," an inner circle of senior officials composed of the President, Secretaries McNamara (Defense) and Rusk (State), the Special Assistant for National Security Affairs, the Director of the CIA, and the Chairman of the Joint Chiefs of Staff.

Many informal groups develop more or less spontaneously. Because of the enormous amount of interagency interaction and communication that occurs in the ordinary conduct of business, informal communication networks and personal relationships develop as a matter of course. And because of the nature of the social scene in Washington, individuals from different agencies are thrown together at all kinds of functions, and these, too, lead to the formation of informal groups. It can happen that bureaucrats at the lower and middle levels mingle with those at the top, and individuals at lower levels may achieve considerable influence because of such high level contacts. An NSC staff member may be close friends with the State Department's country director for Egypt, a congressional staffer from the House Foreign Affairs Committee, and Colonel X from the joint staff of the Joint Chiefs of Staff, and when issues of common interest arise, unless prohibited by orders from above or SOPs from doing so, they will share and exchange ideas. Informal cross-agency networks exist throughout the bureaucracy.

The second type of group is one created specifically to deal with a given crisis or short-term problem. Issue oriented, this group is (usually) disbanded when the issue is resolved, and like the first kind of group this one also has no firm institutional base. During the Korean War a

---

[16]For further analysis see Wendzel, *International Politics*, pp. 438–439.

group of twelve to fourteen members met four times during the first week of hostilities, and on some highly critical issues a smaller group of six senior officials was convened.[17] Perhaps the most famous group of this sort was the Ex Comm, a group of about fifteen trusted friends and advisers appointed by President Kennedy during the Cuban missile crisis. Key decisions were made here, not in or by the formal bureaucratic apparatus.

Third, are a number of transdepartmental entities that in effect become a part of the institutionalized machinery, interagency units whose existence is presumed to be (somewhat) enduring. These groups may be the result of considerable advance planning. Upon taking office President Nixon sought to enhance the role of the National Security Council in the policymaking process. To facilitate this, since that body could not alone handle the quantity of detail work essential to effective decision making, a series of small interagency subcommittees was established. Sometimes such transdepartmental groups are formed in response to particular events, and only later take on a degree of permanence. In April 1969, North Korean MIGs shot down a U.S. Navy EC-121, an unarmed propeller-driven reconnaissance plane. In response, National Security Assistant Henry Kissinger assembled a special crisis management group composed of himself and midlevel representatives of the State and Defense Departments, the CIA, and the Joint Chiefs of Staff. This was the genesis of what became the Washington Special Action Group, an NSC subcommittee that handled nearly all the major crises from that time through the *Mayaguez* incident in 1975.

As mentioned previously, one reason small groups have been utilized so frequently is that they are believed to have a number of advantages over the bureaucracy. Because they are small, other things being equal there will be relatively few viewpoints to reconcile. Because of this and because there are no established procedural barriers to overcome, decisions often can be reached quickly by small groups. Being outside the formal apparatus the group has no organizational interest to protect and is free to concentrate on the problem at hand. Because standard operating procedures do not come into play, the barriers to communication and the pressures toward conformity that such procedures tend to produce do not exist. And if secrecy is required it is much more likely to be maintained in a small group than if the bureaucracy as a whole is involved. Not all of these characteristics exist with respect to every group, and the extent that they do varies with time, circumstance, personality, and issue. For example, as Henry Kissinger observed concerning the WSAG's reactions to the shooting down of the EC-121, small groups, too, can seem to move in slow motion.[18] But generally these positive characteristics do obtain, and they give small group decision making a certain attraction.

One question that arises with respect to small groups is the degree to which the phrase "where you stand depends on where you sit" applies. In our earlier discussion of bureaucratic fragmentation we demonstrated how oversimplified and partially inaccurate this concept was in that setting, both as to positions taken and with respect to the reasons why. There is no reason to repeat our previous comments. Suffice it to say that with regard to routine, long-term program-oriented issues considered in small groups, everything said earlier applies here as well.

With respect to policy issues involving fundamental objectives, the phrase has even less applicability; despite its obvious appeal, one researching the point finds little evidence to confirm its validity. Indeed, what is apparent is that it usually is not valid! Although individuals from various organizations occasionally advocate the "expected" view, this often is not the case. In the Ex Comm deliberations during the Cuban missile crisis, for example, as we said in passing in Chapter 1, Secretary McNamara strayed far from defense issues per se, and Dean Rusk acted more as a "devil's advocate" than as a representative of the State Department. In these delib-

[17]See Glenn D. Paige, *The Korean Decision, June 24–30, 1950* (New York: The Free Press, 1968).
[18]Kissinger, *White House Years*, pp. 315–317.

erations several options were discussed. Although the input of various officials was essentially a *response to queries* in their area of expertise, many of those involved changed positions and recommendations, some more than once. Some parties, because of their knowledge and training, were inclined toward certain kinds of policy solutions and actions, but they were so primarily on the basis of their concern for policy. There is little to support the view that the discussions were a reflection of bureaucratic interests. *Importantly, what was true in the Ex Comm case is the norm with respect to the deliberations of top-level policymakers on important issues. Senior policymakers weigh policy alternatives primarily with respect to their (anticipated) probable outcomes, i.e., in terms of their anticipated benefit/cost results.*

Although small decision groups do possess a number of positive attributes, as we have made clear, they have a number of potentially negative characteristics as well. It is evident that the ability to act secretly could as easily be detrimental as advantageous, for example. Again, the fact that small decision groups are largely devoid of bureaucratic rules and regulations is not always an advantage. After all, SOPs have certain beneficial effects, and the constructive as well as the harmful effects have been removed. With no organizational memory to rely on, without the stored, interpreted, and coded data that exists in the institutions' memory banks, people have to rely primarily on personal recollection and perception. But personal memory is to some extent unsystematic, and often it is incomplete and partially inaccurate. Without organizational checks and challenges, specific personal views that are highly distorted can become accepted as "truth." Another difficulty is that the wide spectrum of specialized expertise that exists in the bureaucracy may not exist in any small group. Without the organizational guidelines and pressures that help bring such expertise to bear, decisions may well be made without expert guidance. Although small groups could bring in outside staffers, analysts, and others in this regard, and sometimes do, frequently they do not. Also, in the absence of regularized procedures, the rules for conducting the group's meetings are established by the group itself. Perhaps they will facilitate effective analysis and thoughtful choice, but perhaps not. Indeed, the rules established by the group could prove very detrimental.

Furthermore, in small groups personal factors are extremely important. In a large bureaucracy one may have a degree of anonymity, but in small groups individuals with unorthodox and/or unpopular views will be highly visible. Unless in a position of dominance, they may opt for silence, fearing rejection or retaliation. In the meetings analyzing the India-Pakistan-Bangladesh crisis, for example, a number of Kissinger's subordinates seemingly felt intimidated and thus remained silent.[19] In small groups one or two people can become dominant, and the policy recommendations or decisions that are produced are, in effect, the recommendation or decisions of just those particular individuals. As we discuss in more depth in Chapter 10, the Nixon-Ford-Kissinger NSC system was almost wholly dependent on Kissinger. The various committees and subcommittees were almost entirely dominated by this one man.

7.

The President and the Bureaucratic Process

After examining the impact of standard operating procedures, problems in information processing, the fragmented nature of the policymaking machinery, the effects of bureaucratic competition, the characteristics of the bureaucratic policymaking process, and the importance of small

---

[19]Some analysts have concluded that those who might have dissented remained silent for fear of being fired. See Dan Haendel, *The Process of Priority Formulation: U.S. Foreign Policy in the Indo-Pakistani War of 1971* (Boulder, Col.: Westview Press, 1977).

decision groups, one might conclude that the President is no more important than anyone else, that he is "just another participant" in an ongoing process. This conclusion would not be wholly absurd. In many situations the President finds that his power is essentially one of persuasion, that he is not in a position to "command." And the President, as others participating in the policymaking process, often must engage in bargaining. He is, to some extent, the prisoner of the advice and information he receives. Furthermore, there are times when the President gets no results at all when he gives orders—nothing happens. For example, in the spring of 1962 President Kennedy ordered the removal of U.S. Jupiter missiles from Turkey. The missiles were not removed, as Kennedy found out to his chagrin in the Cuban missile crisis when the Soviets offered to withdraw their missiles from Cuba if Washington would withdraw its missiles from Turkey. There are even occasions when actions are undertaken that are quite contrary to the President's desires. In February 1969 the new Nixon administration was wrestling with the touchy Arab-Israeli problem. The President was unsure as to what precisely should be done, and he did not wish to undertake precipitate action that might, on reflection, prove unwise. Thus, caution was the order of the day. The State Department, however, wanted to launch an American negotiating initiative, and quite in contrast to the President's wishes began to do so.[20]

Despite the foregoing, it would be erroneous to conclude that the President is no more important than anyone else, that he is just a cog in a gigantic bureaucratic machine. As we saw in Chapter 6, the President is the one who is ultimately responsible, the one who makes the ultimate decisions. He is the one to whom critical information is funneled (and most of it is timely and accurate) and he is the one to whom the key experts report. Moreover, as we saw, he has a wide range of powers that enable him to take action, to initiate and sustain policy. No one else can do this. And if action is perceived to be necessary, he is the one who must act.

It is essential when evaluating this matter to keep the issue in perspective, and to make certain important distinctions. Most assuredly the President is not directly involved in much of phase 2, in the tactical day-to-day operations of the bureaucracy. There is far too much for him to do. Authority and responsibility to a considerable extent must be delegated. But these operations involve issues that usually are not perceived to be of fundamental importance. They usually are routine policy concerns of a long-term programmatic nature, or immediate matters that fall within the established policy and procedural frameworks. In such situations the bureaucratic process *is* important and the President is not wholly determinative. But even in these situations the President is more than just another participant, for two reasons. First, the President and his senior advisers are the ones who carry dominant weight in determining the overall policy thrust for bureaucrats to follow in the first place. Second, they play a key role in establishing the specific guidelines within which the lower level daily decisions must be made.

When we turn to issues of major significance, the President is even less just another participant. In these areas he is central. Presidents differ in terms of individual decision-making style, so one cannot say with precision exactly *how* the important decisions will be made. President Kennedy was actively involved with the minutest of details, President Johnson sought to achieve a consensus, whereas President Eisenhower had a highly developed and orderly staff system. But these are not the crucial factors. *Irrespective of mechanics and structure, almost always, within whatever the machinery that is devised, it is the President who will make the critical choices in crises, and he is the one who will determine the essential direction and nature of policy. When vital interests are at stake and one is considering alternatives directly related to achieving or protecting fundamental objectives, the bureaucratic process is relatively unimportant. In matters of vital interest the President is far more than just another participant; he is preeminent.*

[20]See Kissinger, *White House Years*, pp. 350–358.

8.

Summing Up

We have looked systematically at bureaucratic politics in this chapter, beginning with a discussion of the effects of standard operating procedures on policymaking, then examining information processing and noting where such procedures necessarily have to be supplemented or supplanted by personal judgments. Noting the effects of fragmentation in the decision process and the inescapable bureaucratic competition inherent in it, we then turned to the significant characteristics of bureaucratic policymaking, taking care to point out how what we think of as "turf protecting" tendencies are most typical of lower-level decisions where the most desirable decision from the point of view of the nation's interests is most clearly debatable. We then looked at higher-level decisions made (typically) in small groups and ended by underlining the preeminent role of the President in the whole process.

We turn next to the role of public opinion and interest groups in affecting foreign policy.

Public Opinion, Interest Groups, and Policymakers

In the State Department we used to discuss how much time that mythical "average American citizen" put in each day listening, reading, and arguing about the world outside his own country. Assuming a man or woman with a fair education, a family, and a job in or out of the house, it seemed to us that ten minutes a day would be a high average.

Dean Acheson
Present at the Creation

Policymakers not only operate in a bureaucratic but also in a political context. There are large and small "interest groups" who have special axes to grind, who want to shape policies in specific directions. There is also the (generally amorphous but dangerous-to-ignore) "force" of public opinion. Public opinion, as we shall see, resembles what George Kennan once said about American democracy as a whole: it resembles a prehistoric monster lying in its primeval mud and hard to arouse, but once it is aroused it begins to flail about strongly in every direction. Both public opinion and interest groups can have a serious influence on policymakers but, as our analysis will show, that influence often is less than one might suspect.

We proceed as follows. First, we examine public opinion's major characteristics, looking especially at how those characteristics affect the potency of opinion. Second, because it is so prominent in our consciousness, we look at the mass media and how it affects public opinion. Third, since the media is so frequently, almost by nature, critical of policy (which policymakers resent), we examine the questions of adequacy and fair treatment. Fourth, we bring our conclusions to bear on the linkage we see between public opinion and the policymaker. Fifth, in the light of this examination, we turn to the specific role of interest groups. Sixth, we analyze special cases in which it is often alleged that the influence of interest groups does not conform to the usual rule.

1. ————————————————————————————————————

Five Characteristics of Public Opinion

What are the main characteristics of public opinion, and why does its effect on policy and policymakers vary so much? *The first characteristic, and one of prime significance, is that to a considerable extent the general public is uninformed.* Obviously, therefore, in most instances the public cannot give the policymaker effective direction.

The average citizen lacks even elementary knowledge of how the international political system works, and seldom has more than a slight awareness of even the most basic facts. To illustrate, in 1964 a Gallup poll indicated that less than 60 per cent of the population knew that the United States was a member of NATO. Indeed, only 38 per cent knew that the Soviet Union was *not* a member, and 28 per cent said they had never even heard of the organization.[1] In 1978, with attention focused on the energy situation because of events in Iran, only 60 per cent of the American people thought the United States really had to import oil, at a time when almost half of its oil needs had to be met by imports.[2] A year later, after the Shah's fall, things were even worse; only 46 per cent of Americans realized that oil imports were necessary.[3] Even these figures overestimate the degree of knowledge. Of the 60 per cent in 1978 who knew that some oil had to be imported, only about one third of those had even the roughest approximation of the percentage of America's consumption being met by imports.[4] Perhaps even more incredibly, in 1979 only 23 per cent of the public knew which countries were involved in the SALT talks.[5]

A second characteristic is that the public generally is not very interested in foreign policy matters. Not only do most people not know very much about foreign policy issues, most of the time they do not really care. There are exceptions, of course; at times particular issues or crises become the focal point of public concern. But those occasions are the exception, not the rule. Most of the time the public is not very interested in foreign policy matters.

To some extent this lack of interest is understandable. People are involved with the practical concerns of everyday living. Whether Johnny makes the basketball team or the plumber came to fix the sink, are their immediate concerns. Indeed, if people are interested in any kind of public affairs matter, it usually is only with issues believed to be of direct personal concern, and these usually involve domestic problems such as inflation, unemployment, crime, and so on. For most Americans such domestic concerns far outweigh foreign policy matters. The United States has no recent history of foreign invasion, no great power neighbors, and the dangers confronting it originate in areas remote from U.S. territory. To much of the American public many of the foreign policy problems being dealt with are neither sufficiently proximate nor personally impacting to seem very "real."

A third characteristic is that most of the time the public does not hold a single, coherent view. On the contrary, usually the public's views are highly fragmented, incomplete, and inconsistent. No precise signal can be transmitted from the public to policymakers because there is no precise, consistent, and clear signal to transmit. In 1967 and early 1968 the majority of the American people saw the original decision to enter the Vietnam war as an error, but opinion was

---

[1]Lloyd Free and Hadley Cantril, *The Political Beliefs of Americans* (New York: Simon & Schuster, 1968), p. 60.

[2]George H. Gallup, *The Gallup Poll: Public Opinion 1978* (Wilmington, Del.: Scholarly Resources Inc., 1979), p. 138.

[3]George H. Gallup, *The Gallup Poll: Public Opinion 1979* (Wilmington, Del.: Scholarly Resources, 1980), p. 168.

[4]Gallup, *Public Opinion 1978,* p. 139.

[5]Robert Erikson, Norman Luttbeg, and Kent L. Tedin, *American Public Opinion,* 2d ed. (New York: John Wiley, 1980), p. 19.

TABLE 3 Opinion on U.S. Policy in El Salvador

U.S. should stay out	29%
U.S. should help the government	27%
No opinion	6%
Uninformed	38%

Source: George H. Gallup, *The Gallup Poll: Public Opinion 1981* (Wilmington, Delaware: Scholarly Resources, Inc., 1982), p. 69.

severely divided on what to do next. A significant minority wanted a complete withdrawal, but a majority wanted to end the war by escalating, even to the extent of invading North Vietnam.[6] In early 1981 public views on the situation in El Salvador were similarly fragmented (see Table 3). What was "the public will?"

A fourth characteristic is that on most issues the public tends to be relatively acquiescent and at least mildly supportive of the President. Rather than significantly influencing presidential policy choices, in most situations the public looks to him for guidance and (usually) supports the actions he undertakes. Characteristically, the public is more of a follower than a leader. On a number of occasions the public even has done an immediate reversal, approving policies undertaken that, before their initiation, it had opposed. In 1968 only 40 per cent of the public favored a reduction in the bombing of North Vietnam, but as soon as that reduction occurred 64 per cent were in favor.[7]

The fact that the public tends to be supportive is of great importance in crisis situations, and often at such times that support is pronounced. Whereas in noncrisis times people are involved in the joys and frustrations of daily living and interest in foreign policy events is minimal, in a crisis the public tends to pay close attention and rally around the flag. But there are exceptions to this rule. *If a crisis is long lasting and if the objective is perceived to be out of proportion to the time, resources, and effort required, public support may decrease. Indeed, over time public support may disappear altogether and even be turned into opposition.* In the early stages of both the Korean and Vietnam wars the President received strong public backing, but as stalemates developed and it became clear that the wars were not being "won," the public mood changed drastically. This characteristic means that in the short run presidents usually have considerable flexibility and can assume that public support will be forthcoming. But if a crisis is not resolved swiftly, or if the public cannot be convinced that considerable progress is being made, it may withdraw its support and even become antagonistic. This puts great pressure on the President to act quickly, to try to resolve issues decisively, and at least give an appearance of success. As we noted in Chapter 3, Americans are a very impatient people who want results. If the desired results are not forthcoming, the public tends to withdraw its support and move on. World War II was an exception in that support was maintained over a long period of time, but there it was entirely obvious that national survival was at stake. If the threat is not perceived to be so clear and present, the public's patience wears thin.

An interesting aspect of this characteristic is that when the President takes strong action he tends to be supported almost without regard to circumstances; it is taking action that matters. It is evident why President Kennedy's actions were strongly supported in the Cuban missile crisis. What is less clear though, at least on the face of it, is why President Kennedy's popularity

---

[6]Leslie H. Gelb, with Richard K. Betts, *The Irony of Vietnam: The System Worked* (Washington, D.C.: The Brookings Institution, 1979), p. 172.

[7]Thomas L. Brewer, *American Foreign Policy* (Englewood Cliffs, N.J.: Prentice-Hall, 1980), p. 80.

TABLE 4 Opinion on Defense Spending

CURRENTLY SPENDING	TOO LITTLE	TOO MUCH
1980	49	14
1979	34	21
1977	27	23
1976	22	36

Source: George H. Gallup, *The Gallup Poll: Public Opinion 1981* (Wilmington, Delaware: Scholarly Resources, Inc., 1982), p. 97.

rose enormously after the Bay of Pigs debacle. Or why, with domestic dissent being so strong, the desire to get out of Vietnam completely clear, and the troop withdrawal well underway, nearly 60 per cent of those polled supported the 1972 mining of Haiphong Harbor. The answer seems to be that strong actions are almost reflexively supported. Apparently there is some truth to the saying that Americans believe one should "do something, even if it is wrong." Though there was some skepticism over the degree to which the action really was necessary, puzzlement over the precise nature of the objectives being sought, and uncertainty whether the operation was either ethical or legal, the public nonetheless strongly supported President Reagan's October 1983 decision to invade Grenada (discussed further in Chapter 20).

There is a second caveat to the notion that the public generally is supportive of the President: the degree to which support is automatic and wholehearted is considerably less now than it was prior to the Vietnam War and Watergate. A significant decline of confidence in all levels and branches of government has been gathering momentum for more than two decades. Vietnam and Watergate, though major contributing elements, at the same time were but parts of a more comprehensive trend. People are more skeptical and cynical than at any time within memory, and are no longer willing to assume automatically that the President knows best.[8] In 1982 *Washington Post*/ABC News Polls, for example, a 57 per cent majority indicated it did not believe that the government could make the "right decision" about a nuclear freeze without being guided by public opinion.

The fifth characteristic is that although fundamental images and views are relatively stable, opinions about particular issues and policy choices are extremely volatile. In 1976, still reeling from the effects of Watergate and the war in Vietnam, the American public was anxious for détente, concerned about the level of defense spending and alleged excesses in the intelligence community, and determined to avoid "more Vietnams." It wanted reduced commitments and involvements, less emphasis on defense, a generally more "moral" approach to international relationships, and a relaxation of tensions with the Soviets. By the end of 1980 a remarkable turnabout had occurred. Its pride deeply wounded and American strength and honor seemingly being challenged by the Soviet invasion of Afghanistan, the fall of the Shah of Iran and the seizure of the hostages, Soviet-Cuban activity in Africa, and the Soviet military build-up, the public was in an aggressive mood, supporting a significant increase in defense spending (see Table 4) and a "tougher" stance in dealing with the Russians, and generally showing much less "squeamishness" about the use of military force or having the CIA engage in covert operations. This, in only four years.

The total effect of the main characteristics thus is not a constant. Generally the public is uninformed and relatively uninterested in foreign policy matters and its views are fragmented and inconsistent, allowing senior policymakers great leeway; and usually it strongly supports

[8]Useful Is Daniel Yankelovich, "Farewell to President Knows Best," *Foreign Affairs*, 57, no. 3 (1979), 670–693.

decisive presidential initiatives. But on some issues if positive results are not forthcoming quickly, public support will erode drastically, and in some areas the public's views are highly volatile. Today, senior policymakers cannot take public opinion for granted.

2. The Role of the Mass Media

The mass media are so prominent in our consciousness that we need to ask how they affect the main characteristics of public opinion we have just discussed. How *are* the attitudes, images, and characteristics of American public opinion affected by the mass media?

On the surface it seems that the press and the national television and radio networks are enormously influential since they are the major vehicles for transmitting information to the public. But is this really the case? Have the images and attitudes that Americans derived from their unique historical experience been significantly changed by the mass media? Have the particular characteristics of public opinion discussed earlier been altered significantly by the press, radio, and television?

The general answer, despite widespread misconceptions to the contrary, is no. Deeply ingrained attitudes and images produced by fundamental historical and societal factors are highly resistant to change. Information tends to be selectively interpreted, incorporated, or rejected in a manner consistent with one's preconceptions; existing attitudes tend to be reinforced, whether they be negative or positive. The people's general lack of interest in foreign policy is not the result of the media, and seldom is seriously affected by it. And the media's fragmentary reporting of the most spectacular current developments to an apathetic public does little to enhance the quantity, quality, or coherence of the public's foreign policy-relevant knowledge.

Although the foregoing is accurate, one must keep these points in perspective. The media surely do have an impact. Before we can discuss that impact directly though, it is necessary to distinguish between the "general" public, the "attentive" public, and opinion "elites".[9] The term "general" public refers to the public as a whole. The "attentive" public is a considerably smaller group (approximately 15–25 per cent of the population); it consists of those well-informed individuals who constitute the primary nongovernmental audience for foreign policy discussions. Opinion "elites" are the articulate, concerned "core" who give some kind of structure to policymaking discussions and provide the means of access to those in authority.

Whereas the mass media have not altered significantly the basic characteristics of the opinion of the general public, is the same true with respect to their impact on opinion elites and the attentive public? These groups have a higher interest level than the general public and their views are more coherent and defined. *Nevertheless, the media's impact on these groups is essentially the same as it is on the public as a whole.* Although it provides much of their current information, in like manner that information is evaluated and interpreted within broader preexisting attitudinal and conceptual lenses. The characteristic attitudes and views of the American people resulting from their unique experiences and setting are not limited to the general public but in large part are shared by opinion elites and the attentive public. In consequence, as is true with respect to the general public, the media function for opinion elites and the attentive public far more as a fact provider than as an agency that significantly influences broad choices.

But this does not mean the media are unimportant. Although the media do not directly determine fundamental images and attitudes, they often *are* important in determining what the

[9]This is based on, though not wholly identical with, the distinctions in Gabriel Almond, *The American People and Foreign Policy* (New York: Praeger, 1960).

public will think about, in "setting the agenda" for public consideration. Although the media seldom can make something an issue if the people are wholly uninterested, they can greatly stimulate and intensify interest if a degree of concern already exists. Clearly, for example, by focusing the public's attention and stimulating its interest, the media significantly intensified the public's disenchantment with American policy in Vietnam. In early 1982, the fact that the press kept asking President Reagan whether he was planning to send troops to El Salvador greatly intensified public concern over that possibility, despite the President's repeated statements that he had no such plans. The "nuclear freeze" issue of the early 1980s emerged as a major issue in large part because of media attention. Perhaps equally important is the fact that if issues are *not* highlighted the public may not appreciate their significance (or in some cases even know of their existence). In early March 1977, President Carter held a news conference at which, among other things, he proposed a withdrawal of American forces from South Korea, proposed a compromise on the Arab-Israeli dispute, and offered a series of compromises on arms control. The media were preoccupied with the seizure of three buildings and holding of 134 hostages in Washington, D.C. by elements of the Black Muslims, however, and gave the President's far-reaching statements little coverage.[10]

3.

The Adequacy and Fairness Problem and Policymaker-Media Tensions

Policymakers inevitably complain, sooner or later, that the media are treating them unfairly. To what extent do ·print and electronic journalism present coherent, accurate, and objective accounts? To what degree do they inform the public in a manner that allows the formation of evidence-supported opinions? And what is the media's role vis-à-vis the President and other senior policymakers?

Taking the last point first, President Nixon firmly believed that much of the media was almost entirely hostile, that the media were an "enemy" of his administration. President Kennedy was so incensed at his treatment by the *New York Herald Tribune* that he ordered the White House subscription cancelled. Angered over what he believed was biased reporting on the Vietnam War, President Kennedy (unsuccessfully) tried to have the *New York Times* transfer reporter David Halberstam to another post. President Truman once wrote to a reporter "I wish you'd do a little soul searching and see if at *great* intervals, the President may be right."[11] Jimmy Carter was "disgusted" by the "negative" treatment his efforts in bringing about the Egyptian-Israeli Peace Treaty received,[12] and Ronald Reagan was thoroughly exasperated with journalists who compared the American invasion of Grenada with Soviet actions in Afghanistan.

To some extent a clash between the President and the media is inevitable. The media, in addition to reporting what the government is doing, act as a watchdog and check on those in power. Investigative reporting quite naturally on occasion leads to questions and criticisms of the government. Those on the receiving end may feel that all the media do is criticize.

There is another side to this story. Although there is a considerable amount of conflict between the media and the government there also is much cooperation. During wartime the press generally has accepted government requests that it refrain from releasing sensitive information, and that it not write certain stories deemed potentially harmful to national security. In the early

---

[10]Useful are the comments of James Reston in the *New York Times,* March 11, 1977, p. A27.

[11]Quoted in Roger Hilsman, *To Govern America* (New York: Harper & Row, 1979), p. 307.

[12]Jimmy Carter, *Keeping Faith: Memoirs of a President* (New York: Bantam, 1982), p. 426.

stages of the Cuban missile crisis, *New York Times* reporter James Reston "knew something was up," but at the urging of top policymakers he agreed not to print what he knew. Of course, such cooperation is not always in evidence. Verbatim transcripts of a secret meeting of the National Security Council's Washington Special Action Group during the 1971 India-Pakistan-Bangladesh conflict were published by columnist Jack Anderson.

The intrinsic tension between government and media often is exacerbated by two other factors. One is the effort by presidents to "manage" the news. The White House naturally seeks to project an image of competence and honesty. Many techniques are utilized to aid in achieving this image, including the careful timing of information releases, provision of selective access for cooperative reporters, social flattery, restrictions on the flow of detrimental data, and the selective leak of favorable information. On occasion, as in the Nixon years, some not too subtle efforts have been made to influence the content of news programming, and even to threaten freedom of communication. Though such openly coercive measures are unusual, careful news management is not.

The other factor that has exacerbated policymaker-media tension has been the development of what some call the "new journalism." Although many journalists still adhere to the traditional concept of factual reporting with personal opinion confined to the editorial segments of the medium, in some areas today such views have been replaced. In their stead the "new" journalists seek to discover "truth," not just "facts," and frequently one finds that the journalists' own viewpoints control both the scope and content of their work. Indeed, it is evident that some journalists, both print and electronic, believe that the media form a social unit or agency which is best equipped to give the nation direction. To the extent that the new journalists consider themselves the nation's preeminent political and social critics, no administration, regardless of what it does, will prove satisfactory.

Regardlesss of how the President or the media may see the problem, what can one say about the degree to which the media provide the public with information of a sufficiently high quality to satisfy those who desire to have the basis for an informed opinion? Two sub-issues must be dealt with in answering this question: capability and bias.

The mass media are severely hindered in any effort to inform the public adequately because of quantity, access, space, and time constraints. First, there is far too much occurring in the world for more than a small fraction of it to be observed and reported. Judgments must be made about what to include and exclude. Since most Americans obtain most of their information from the media, that which the media do not report remains largely unknown (to the public). In addition to material excluded for quantity reasons, there are situations to which the media do not have access. Few Americans were in Kampuchea (Cambodia) to report on the holocaust perpetrated by the Pol Pot regime in the mid-1970s, so for a long time most Americans were wholly unaware of it. In closed societies, such as the Soviet Union and East Germany, nearly all information about public affairs is treated as a state secret. The media just cannot obtain adequate access and many of the most significant developments thus cannot be reported.

Newspapers have space limitations. Being businesses, they must make a profit to survive, and decisions concerning how much and what to print must be based in part on their anticipated impact on profits. Given this imperative, the managing editor must decide how much space to allocate to news vis-à-vis sports, the society page, amusements, and so on. Within the news category, further allocations must be made between local, state, national, and international features. Even "prestige" newspapers such as the *New York Times* seldom give as much as 25 per cent of their news coverage to foreign stories, and most papers give much less. Foreign policy-relevant news thus usually is but a small part of a small part.

The national television networks, which today are the principal source of foreign policy information for the general public, suffer from severe time constraints. No matter what happens on a given day, in a half-hour telecast the news must be compressed into about twenty-one or twenty-two minutes of airtime. Some of the time will be lost in the mechanics of introducing and terminating stories, and the majority of hard news time usually is devoted to nonforeign policy issues. Maybe half a dozen or so thirty-second to two-minute spots will focus on different events at various points in the program, and usually that will be the extent of the foreign policy-relevant information. Obviously, very little of what has happened on a given day can be covered, and that which is is can be covered only superficially.

The result is that the media can provide only a partial, superficial, and largely fragmented picture, a picture which highlights those matters that are exciting and dramatic but ignores the remainder. But it is not just a matter of coverage. There also are serious problems of quality. Although there are occasional exceptions in the elite press and in some television documentaries, seldom are issues presented in context or analytical/historical perspective. The average citizen learns almost nothing about the basic causes of events or the underlying factors at work. Everything becomes simple and personalized; intellectual depth is almost nonexistent.

In March 1981 President Reagan created a senior-level crisis-management team to be chaired by Vice-President Bush. Rather than discussing in detail the impact this might have on the policy process and/or policy substance, the media focused on the unhidden anger and frustration of Secretary of State Haig over what he felt was a downgrading of his power, and the dramatic political-personal conflicts that resulted.

What about media bias? We earlier saw that many presidents have felt that the media treated them in a biased manner, but that to some extent at least this perception is inevitable. Does the evidence indicate a degree of systematic distortion by the media, either generally or in particular cases? There is no single answer to this question that is satisfactory. Although a majority of leading journalists describe themselves as liberals,[13] the elite newspapers such as the *New York Times,* the *Washington Post,* and the *Wall Street Journal* usually provide reasonably accurate and balanced factual reports (although they hold differing editorial views). Local newspapers, however, are far less even in their coverage, and they often are far from neutral or balanced. Because they usually buy their foreign news stories from one of the two major wire services (AP or UPI), they are quite dependent on those sources and their "objectivity." Additionally, there is considerable freedom to select or reject particular pieces. The result often is a very one-sided view.

The electronic media have not been studied as systematically and extensively as the print media, but what work has been done does not demonstrate any clearly observable general bias. One of the better studies of national television evening news programs indicated that perhaps there was a very slight "liberal" tendency, but the tendency was so slight as to be of marginal importance.[14] Furthermore, the result could well have been altered by a slightly different definition of liberal and conservative. And this inconclusive result is typical. The conclusions one must draw are that on the national level there is no demonstrated general and systematic media bias, although on the local level in some instances there may be.

These conclusions concerning the lack of any general national media bias also usually hold up with respect to the national media's treatment of particular cases. Here too, both print and electronic journalism usually are fairly well balanced and neutral. But there have been some significant exceptions (especially in cases involving the "new journalism") in which journalists have assiduously sought sources supporting one position while downplaying their opposite, or

[13]See S. Robert Lichter and Stanley Rothman, "Media and Business Elites," *Public Opinion* (October/November 1981), 43.

[14]See Robert S. Frank, *Message Dimensions of Television News* (Lexington, Mass.: D. C. Heath, 1973).

taken it upon themselves to interpret events according to their particular views.[15] Still, the number of such instances is quite small.

More frequent than cases of the deliberate selecting and shaping of information are instances in which the presentation is unintentionally distorted, the result either of a lack of adequate perspective or of premature judgments that filter out competing views. In Chapter 13 we point out how the Tet offensive of January/March 1968 proved to be a turning point for America's Vietnam War policy. The psychological and symbolic efforts of the North Vietnamese-Viet Cong attacks were considerable, increasing war-weariness among the American people and accelerating the beginning of the Paris peace talks. The media accurately portrayed these facts. What the media did *not* do, however, was give comparable coverage and emphasis to the fact that after some early successes the North Vietnamese/Viet Cong forces suffered severe losses and failed to hold any of their major military objectives.[16] On the ground the United States and South Vietnamese forces rather quickly scored a considerable military victory, but this received less "play" than the psychological and symbolic effects of the Tet offensive. Ultimately the psychological impact of the Tet offensive did far outweigh the military impact. Given the state of American public opinion at the time, perhaps that was inevitable; but perhaps not. A key question is, what would the impact have been in the absence of the powerful but incomplete image conveyed by the press and television?

Our earlier conclusion (that most of the time for most people the media are not determinative of basic views) stands, but as we have seen it is not the whole story. The media are the source of most of the current factual information for most Americans, including opinion elites and the attentive public. To some extent the media have an agenda-setting function, and often an intensity-altering impact. Because of their nature and function, the print and electronic media almost inevitably are perceived by presidents to be somewhat hostile. With respect to those whom they do influence, because of quantity, access, time, and space constraints the media can provide only a partial and superficial picture. Reality thus inevitably is somewhat distorted and lacking in perspective. Deliberate systematic bias on the national level does not appear to exist although in individual cases a highly distorted image may be conveyed.

4.

The Influence of Public Opinion

Let us now attempt to bring our conclusions thus far to bear on the linkages we have sketched between public opinion, the mass media, and the policymaker. This is, after all, the key issue. To what extent, and in what ways, does public opinion influence the President and other senior policymakers?

Because of the general characteristics of public opinion discussed earlier—lack of interest and knowledge, more of a follower than a leader, inconsistent, incomplete, and contradictory views, a tendency toward acquiescence and support—in most situations senior policymakers get little useful guidance. The public's views are too broad and amorphous, too uninformed, inchoate, and abstract, to provide much assistance in specific situations. Generally, in fact, senior policymakers pay little attention to the public on specific issues and questions of detail, and there

---

[15]Such appears to have occurred with respect to the 1972 bombing of Hanoi. See Martin F. Herz, with Leslie Rider, *The Prestige Press and the Christmas Bombing, 1972* (Washington, D.C.: Ethics and Public Policy Center, 1980).

[16]See the massive, well-documented work by Peter Braestrup, *Big Story: How the American Press and Television Reported and Interpreted the Crisis of Tet-1968 in Vietnam and Washington* (Boulder, Col.: Westview Press, 1977).

simply is not any direct linkage between public opinion and policy decisions. During the Berlin blockade, for example, the fluidity, lack of expertise, and apathy of the public gave Truman almost carte blanche in dealing with the Kremlin.[17]

In fact, the public's dependence, permissiveness, and tendency to follow along often is such as to allow policymakers to manipulate it to suit their purposes. Indeed, many times there is so much room for maneuver that decisions can be taken which actually run counter to the public's views. The majority of adult Americans opposed the conclusion and the subsequent ratification of the Panama Canal Treaties, but the agreements were negotiated and ratified. But one must not carry this concept too far—it is also true that Jimmy Carter was not reelected. As pointed our earlier, although the American public tends to be supportive and malleable, it is not willing to acquiesce passively in any and all circumstances. It never has been that permissive historically, and it surely is not today.

Although there is no direct public opinion/policy decision linkage in most concrete situations, public opinion *does* have two important effects on policymaker choices. Public images, attitudes and opinions may be vague, incomplete, and perhaps in part irrational, but the public *has* images, attitudes and opinions. In some situations these become highly significant. *One major function of public opinion is the provision of a set of boundaries, the establishment of some range of permissible actions.* The public usually has some (sometimes latent) notions about what policies, methods, and objectives it will tolerate and these will be transgressed only at considerable risk. The general public simply would not permit the American government to follow a course of (in)action that would allow the destruction of Israel. Once the withdrawal of American forces from Vietnam began, there were certain limits established beyond which governmental action would not be tolerated (e.g., a massive escalation). Public opinion set some limits here, precluding certain options and narrowing the range of policy choice.

Sometimes policymakers are influenced not by existing boundaries but rather by what, correctly or not, they anticipate the public's reaction would be. The effect here, too, is to eliminate certain policy alternatives. During the 1945 Yalta Conference, President Roosevelt, Winston Churchill, and Joseph Stalin were discussing plans for the postwar occupation of Germany. Roosevelt's position was strongly influenced by his expectation of strong public and congressional pressure to withdraw from the European continent. He believed that the American public would not permit American forces to remain for more than two years after hostilities terminated.

The boundaries establishing policy limits are not immutable, though. Although deeply ingrained images and attitudes are resistant to change, they can be altered gradually. Over time such incremental changes can result in a complete change of opinion, and this in turn can result in a complete change in policy limits. As we discuss in depth in Chapter 12, in the mid-1930s the United States was doing everything it could to avoid becoming involved in European crises. As war clouds gathered over Europe, however, more and more individuals began to doubt the wisdom of existing policies. Gradually the policy limits began to alter as the evidence supporting the need for a policy shift accumulated. Incrementally, as the limits changed so did the policy, the government at each step asking for as much as it felt feasible. What ultimately became a complete change in policy reflected a complete change in public opinion.

The other distinctive role for public opinion lies in positively marking out at least the general direction that policy should take. Because of its supportive and follow-rather-than-lead characteristics, and the general lack of knowledge and interest, more often than not this function is *not* performed. But sometimes it is, and in those cases it is very important. Once public opinion had coalesced around the essential idea of withdrawing from Vietnam, for example, it strongly and

[17]Morton Berkowitz, P. G. Bock, and Vincent J. Fuccillo, *The Politics of American Foreign Policy* (Englewood Cliffs, N.J.: Prentice-Hall, 1977), p. 51.

rather consistently influenced the government's course of action. Room remained for tactical variations, given the lack of agreement within the public on specific detail, but the strategic course was determined. As we saw earlier, in the late 1970s and early 1980s the American public, angered and frustrated by events in Iran and Afghanistan and convinced the United States was becoming "weaker" than the Soviet Union, strongly endorsed a "tougher" stance in dealing with Moscow. Ronald Reagan was elected with a mandate to restore American honor and to undertake initiatives that would reverse America's "decline." As in the Vietnam example there was much latitude in terms of specifics, but the general thrust was clear.

In the cases described, the principles that the public applied were limited and somewhat vague, but they were sufficiently clear to mark out a general direction. This is significant. Although there are many cases in which such direction is not given, when it is, it is a matter of great importance. Maintaining public support was critical to the success of U.S. policy in Vietnam. Once public opinion decisively turned, it was just a matter of time. Ultimately, in a democratic system, a policy cannot succeed without public acceptance of that policy.

5.
Interest Groups: The General Rule

Interest groups represent particular slices of often highly focused opinion. An interest group is an association of individuals, external to major policymaking positions, who share a more or less common set of attitudes and interests, and one of whose primary objectives is to influence governmental processes and policies in ways beneficial to itself. There are literally thousands of groups in the United States seeking to advance their cause by influencing government. It has been estimated that about three hundred such organizations even have their own foreign policy informational and educational programs.[18]

Given the myriad of interest groups that exist, it is easy to get the impression that policymakers are at their mercy and to conclude that policy is just a product of interest group interaction and bargaining. Individuals of a cynical mind especially find it easy to attribute policy in general and in particular cases to the secret conspiracies or machinations of "special interests."

Although interest groups do play a role in the policymaking process, it is far smaller than these suspicions would indicate. *In most situations, in fact, interest groups are relatively insignificant. One reason is that much of the time many of the groups simply do not attempt to exert much influence.* Several factors are at work here. First, in contrast to their activities with respect to domestic issues, interest group efforts in foreign policy matters are "internal" only in a limited sense. Although they occur within the territory of the United States, they do not occur without reference to developments outside that territory. To some extent at least, interest group decision makers formulate positions and make demands in light of their conceptualization of the nature of the external environment and the constraints it imposes. Thus government policymakers only seldom are confronted with absurd demands for foreign policies that have little or no chance of success. Second, although interest groups (usually) vigorously assert their views on matters of a technical nature that can be narrowly defined and shown to have a direct impact on their welfare, on most issues perceived to have a clear relationship to national security, groups tend to temper their efforts and sublimate their needs to the national good. In these matters "politics stops at the water's edge."

A third reason why groups often do not seek to influence policy is that they just are not concerned with many of the issues confronting the government. Although business groups are

---

[18]William O. Chittick, *State Department, Press and Pressure Groups* (New York: John Wiley, 1970), p. 222.

very concerned with foreign trade matters, human rights issues are of less relevance (unless they affect economic relationships); the National Council of Churches is concerned with the plight of Soviet dissidents but is not directly interested in whether tariffs should be increased on imports of footwear from Korea.

Of course, there are many cases in which interest groups do seek to exercise influence. *But even when they do make a strenuous effort they usually are unsuccessful.* This includes groups that are believed by some to have an enormous and nearly continuous impact. For example, as was noted in a study of United States policy in the 1967 Middle East war, "noteworthy by their unimportance during the crisis were the allegedly powerful pro-Israeli interest groups and the oil lobby."[19]

One reason interest groups often have less influence than their membership numbers imply is that most major groups such as the AFL-CIO or Chamber of Commerce, especially because they are large organizations, have members who also are members of several other groups. With this overlapping membership individuals often have multiple interests and competing loyalties. As a result, their allegiance to any one of the groups normally is qualified by their other interests. In fact, quite frequently by virtue of multiple affiliations and interests a citizen belongs on both sides of a question. Because of these facts an interest group's leaders often cannot influence the members sufficiently to have them act as a cohesive body. Indeed, often the leadership itself is divided. The result is that on many issues there simply is no group position (or if there is one it is so vague and unenthusiastically advocated that its practical impact is nil).

A second reason for interest groups' lack of impact is that on most issues many groups are involved and a number of positions are advocated. If a trade bill is under consideration some elements will demand generally higher tariffs, others will want only selective increases, and some will advocate fewer restraints in the hope that there will be a reciprocal diminution in other countries. In the 1973 Trade Reform Bill, a proposal to reduce tariffs was supported by such varied groups as the U.S. Council of the International Chamber of Commerce, the League of Women Voters, the National Feed and Grain Association, and the Aerospace Industries Association of North America. Groups that wanted to maintain the existing structure or increase duties included the American Iron and Steel Institute; the United Rubber, Cork, Linoleum and Plastic Workers of America; the Liberty Lobby; the Nationwide Committee on Import-Export Policy; and the AFL-CIO.[20] Such a situation is typical. *Counterbalancing coalitions occur with respect to almost all the specific issues that concern interest groups,* including military spending and defense programs, arms control measures, and economic aid. Often the result is that the coalitions balance or neutralize each other, allowing policymakers great flexibility. Quite in contrast to the idea that their policy choices are determined by interest group pressures, policymakers can pick and choose.

A third point concerns the difference between most interest groups' domestic and foreign policy knowledge. On domestic issues interest groups often are in a position to provide decision makers with needed specialized expertise and information. With respect to foreign policy and defense matters the situation is usually quite different. The government's foreign policy apparatus provides more than enough information and there are vast numbers of highly trained specialists to interpret its meaning and assess its significance. With only rare exceptions, interest groups are markedly inferior in such matters, *having neither the specific policy-relevant information nor the specialists to assess its meaning.*

[19]William B. Quandt, *Decade of Decisions: American Policy Toward the Arab-Israeli Conflict, 1967–1976* (Berkeley and Los Angeles, Calif.: University of California Press, 1977), p. 70.

[20]David H. Blake and Robert S. Walters, *The Politics of Global Economic Relations,* 2d. ed. (Englewood Cliffs, N.J.: Prentice-Hall, 1983), p. 219.

Fourth, and crucially, on major security issues involving vital interests and fundamental objectives interest groups simply do not have access to senior policymakers. Occasionally this is a matter of time. When the United States finds itself in a crisis situation, such as at the beginning of the Korean War, decisions must be made very quickly and there is no time for groups to obtain access. Sometimes it is a matter of lack of access because of official secrecy. During both the early stages of the Cuban missile crisis and the negotiations preceding President Nixon's trip to China, interest groups simply were not aware of what was happening.

Finally, the very importance of the issue may make access essentially irrelevant because of the simple determination of senior policymakers to act in terms of their own perception of the national interest regardless. Just as we pointed out in Chapter 7 that bureaucratic politics are essentially irrelevant to most policy decisions on vital security issues, with very rare exceptions interest groups are equally insignificant. *Interest groups almost always are unimportant in foreign policy matters perceived by senior policymakers to significantly affect America's vital interests and fundamental objectives.*

6.

Interest Groups: Exceptions to the Rule?

There are occasional exceptions to the rule we have just observed, that interest groups have much less influence than often is supposed. The first such "occasional exception" involves situations in which the focus is on certain kinds of political-economic issues that have a major domestic impact. Energy policy is an example. The evidence is not all in yet and the precise degree and type of impact is not yet entirely clear, but it is apparent that sometimes both Congress and the President are caught in a maelstrom of conflicting internal and external pressures in such matters. Second, although, as mentioned previously, interest groups seldom are able to exercise much influence with respect to important strategic issues, even those requiring considerable congressional involvement, in a specific isolated case they *can* play a major role. Usually only a few individuals can be swayed, but a few may be enough. Following the Turkish invasion of Cyprus in the 1974 crisis a well-organized Greek lobby, led by the American Hellenic Institute Public Affairs Committee, was crucial in convincing the Congress to suspend military aid to Turkey, for example.

A few special groups are alleged to have far more influence than our previous analysis would indicate. Two of the more famous have been the Committee of One Million (the China lobby) and various Jewish organizations. The Committee of One Million became active in 1949 and for two decades fought against the extension of diplomatic recognition to the People's Republic of China and its admission to the United Nations. Jewish organizations prior to 1948 mounted a well-organized campaign to convince United States policymakers to support the creation of a Jewish state in Palestine, and since its establishment they have sought to maximize pro-Israeli sentiments and policies.

It is factually true that American policy, following the introduction of Communist Chinese "volunteers" in the Korean War, was strongly anti-Beijing for nearly two decades. It is equally true that the United States supported the creation of Israel, and has had very cooperative relations with that country for much of its existence. But the fact that policy and interest group views in both cases were similar proves nothing other than that they were similar; no cause-and-effect relationship is demonstrated by this simple correlation. It is very important to remember that the President, other senior policymakers, most of Congress, and much of the general public shared these particular policy views. In other words, the interest groups in question were in the mainstream of the views held by nearly all Americans.

The significance of this point cannot be overstressed. *When policymakers later began to reassess their basic positions and for strategic reasons undertook policy alterations, and when large segments of the public altered their attitudes correspondingly, these same interest groups discovered that they had little policy-influencing impact.* When the Nixon administration moved toward the normalization of relations with Beijing, the China lobby objected but could do nothing about it. When during and after the 1973 Middle East war the United States adopted a much more evenhanded stance in the Arab-Israeli dispute, the Jewish lobby was unable to do anything to stop it.

Two other groups or groupings alleged to have influence far in excess of the norm are the military-industrial "complex" (MIC) and American-owned multinational corporations (MNCs). In his farewell address to the nation of January 17, 1961, President Eisenhower warned of the acquisition of unwarranted influence in the councils of government by a military-industrial complex. The potential for the "disastrous use of misplaced power by this complex," he said, "exists and will persist."

With the annual defense budget of the United States over $250 billion it is evident why the conglomeration of industries, bureaucratic agencies, labor unions, congressmen, states, cities, and military personnel composing the military-industrial "complex" are interested in influencing matters in ways beneficial to their interests. Large sectors of the economy are geared to defense and defense-related activities, with perhaps 15 per cent of the work force directly or indirectly dependent on defense spending. Although only a relatively small percentage of total United States industry is dependent for its livelihood on defense-related activities, several key industries are heavily reliant and for many others it is the difference between breaking even and making substantial profits. Much basic research and development work today, too, is related to defense requirements and possibilities.

Policymakers expect to be the targets of influence efforts by such groups, and frequently they are. Occasionally the pressures are considerable, and once in a while a decision is crucially altered. But this is very much the exception to the rule, despite popular misconceptions to the contrary. Although the volume of activity is great, usually the policy-influencing impact is minimal.

Why is this so? A major reason is that the military-industrial "complex" (MIC) is not a "complex" at all; most of the time it is rent with strife and competition. On some issues the various interest groups, industrial representatives, contractors, and community leaders align themselves with whichever armed service they believe will be most useful to them. The services often are in competition with one another, and the adding of these factional demands and pressures intensifies the natural interservice rivalries that already exist. In such cases, as a result, pressures offset pressures and senior policymakers can pick and choose.

This effect is even more pronounced in other cases where fragile, fluid, issue-based coalitions struggle for advantage within and across industry, service, and politico-community lines, in effect forming an unstable subsystem of conflicting and self-neutralizing "minicomplexes."

Even where substantial "internal" consensus reigns the complex often loses. In the late 1970s much of the military, especially the air force, plus a number of industrial and politico-community groups, wanted full production and deployment of the B-1 bomber. President Carter labeled the B-1 lobby "one of the most formidable ever evolved in the military-industrial community."[21] But Carter opposed production, and the B-1 was not produced. Add that, in this case, a strong countercoalition of three dozen groups as diverse as the Federation of American Scientists, Clergy and Laity Concerned, and the National Taxpayers Union opposed production, and you have another reason why the MIC frequently is unsuccessful. There is no reason to

[21]Carter, *Keeping Faith,* p. 81.

assume that the MIC will be determinative any more than any other influencer will, and the evidence does not indicate that it is; there is nothing that guarantees the superiority of the MIC.

Although the MIC thus is neither universally nor automatically influential, it sometimes does play an important role in at least one area, the area of weapons development and procurement. This role is complicated and not easy to describe. Perhaps the best way to put it is that rather than the MIC simply *influencing* policymakers, what exists is a very complex maze of interactions involving various elements of the MIC working and bargaining with the government from the beginning of the research process all the way through production and deployment. But even here the MIC is subject to many of the constraints discussed earlier. Moreover, although diverse parts of the MIC may marginally affect incremental choices at various points in the process, the fundamental decisions about defense strategy, force planning, procurement, and deployment are made by the President and his senior advisers in a much broader national security context, and in these the MIC seldom plays *any* role.

The last type of interest group many feel is an exception to the rule is the multinational corporation (MNC), which was mentioned briefly in Part One. Since World War II the growth of United States-based MNCs has been striking, and their economic magnitude today is immense. Although the majority of MNCs are relatively small, the giants have annual sales figures that exceed the GNP of more than half the countries in the world. In 1976, for example, Exxon's sales were larger than the GNP of all but twenty-two states.[22] Given their enormous economic strength and tightly controlled organizational structure, it is easy to understand why so many people assume that the MNCs are very successful.

Interestingly, however, and quite contrary to the common perception, generally MNCs do *not* have all that much influence. There are several reasons for this. First, many issues are simply outside their realm of concern. Most issues of peace and security, for example, matters of vital interest to the President and other senior policymakers, unless directly related to the MNC's profit potential, are outside its major area of interest. Second, even where the MNCs are directly concerned their influence usually is quite limited because they are subject to the same difficulties that non-MNC interest groups are: they are confronted with strong countervailing pressures and they often line up on opposing sides of an issue. In 1968, Exxon sought to have the U.S. government threaten to withdraw foreign aid from Peru unless Peru paid more compensation for Exxon properties it had expropriated, but several other MNCs opposed such a move out of concern that it would jeopardize their investments in Peru. Third, sometimes MNCs are countered by essentially domestic groups. The large multinational oil companies with significant operations in the Arab world constantly find themselves on the opposite side of the Jewish lobby, for example. And sometimes the larger MNCs face another problem: internal splits. In 1954 eight departments of General Electric opposed freer trade whereas the chairman of the board testified before a House committee in its favor.[23] Within a number of the major oil companies, divisions involved primarily in domestic work are much more "protectionist" than divisions in those same companies whose responsibility is essentially foreign.

That the influence of MNCs on policymaking is far more limited than some have believed does not mean that MNCs can be simply dismissed. The United States desires economic development, believes in capitalism and free enterprise, and needs access to strategic resources and raw materials. In these spheres the interests of MNCs often converge with official perceptions of the national interest, and the result many times is a highly cooperative relationship. Government subsidies through the Overseas Private Investment Corporation insuring against expropri-

[22]Joan Spero, *The Politics of International Economic Relations,* 2d. ed. (New York: St. Martin's Press, 1981), p. 103.

[23]Barry B. Hughes, *The Domestic Context of American Foreign Policy* (San Francisco: W. H. Freeman, 1978), p. 159.

ation and other risks, low-interest loans to foreign customers through the Export-Import Bank, special tax breaks, and the Hickenlooper Amendment, which directs the President to cut off aid to any country that nationalizes U.S.-owned property without adequate compensation, are just some of the more obvious evidences of this relationship. But the subject here is influence in the design and implementation of policy, and there are very few cases on the record that show compelling evidence that MNCs influenced policymakers to make choices *they would not have made anyway*. Much, much more typical is the type of thing we saw in Chapter 1. The government not only told the MNC (the Dresser Corporation) what to do, it took action that was adverse to the MNC's interest and made it stick.

The foregoing should not be read to mean that MNCs never, under any circumstances, play a significant role in the policy process. Occasionally they do. Sometimes they are able to supply a useful bit of information, especially concerning long-term programmatic issues that require congressional action. In matters with a combined internal-external, political-economic impact they sometimes help identify issues; raise the interest level of the public, the bureaucracy, and senior policymakers; and alter the emphasis various aspects of the issues may receive. Sometimes domestic political stakes, too, are affected by their activities, and surely the agenda for governmental action and the context within which it occurs are affected.

These are not insignificant matters. But elements in the military-industrial complex do the same things. Indeed, so do all interest groups to some extent. And that is exactly the point! *Although differing somewhat in size and wealth from other kinds of interest groups, both MNCs and the MIC are not special cases in terms of their influence on major policy issues.* They have essentially the same strengths and weaknesses on these matters as other groups.

7.

Summing Up

How, then, shall we sum up our findings? Looking first at the main characteristics of public opinion, our analysis showed clearly that the public generally is both uninformed and uninterested in foreign policy matters. Moreover, the "public will" most often is filled with contradictions, incomplete, and fragmented. The practical result of all this is that usually public opinion cannot provide policymakers with much effective explicit guidance. At the same time, public opinion sometimes can set the outer limits for policy choice and mark at least the general direction policy should take.

Policymakers have discovered that public opinion is a highly volatile phenomenon, sometimes fluctuating greatly even in a very short period of time. Usually the public supports major policy initiatives, especially in their early stages. But if positive results are not forthcoming as quickly as the public would like that support may erode drastically. Clearly this puts pressure on policymakers to choose strong action orientations and to seek quick, clear-cut solutions.

What influence do the mass media have? Though they provide much of the public's current information, contrary to what is often assumed the media do not decisively affect the public's most fundamental views. But the media are still important though, because they set much of the agenda that the public considers, and affect the intensity with which views are held. Unfortunately, because of inherent limitations the mass media can at best present only a partial and rather superficial picture, and cannot really inform the public sufficiently to allow solidly based judgments to be made. On the plus side, it does not appear that there have been many systematic attempts to present information in a biased manner. Nevertheless, presidents often have believed that the media treated them unfairly. Because the media seek to act as a watchdog and check on government and because presidents quite naturally want to project the most favorable image possible, there seems to be an intrinsic tension in their relationship. In recent years tensions with the media have been exacerbated even further by the development of the "new" journalism in which the journalists' personal views strongly influence both the scope and the content of their work.

Turning to those highly focused slices of public opinion known as interest groups, it is evident that "special interests" sometimes have an important influence on policymakers, but this occurs far less often than is generally assumed. Interest groups usually do *not* significantly influence policy choice. Not that they are entirely irrelevant. On certain kinds of political-economic issues with a major domestic impact special-interest groups sometimes are quite important, and in rare isolated cases they may even play a major role. And even when they do not significantly influence the choice of alternatives they can raise the salience of certain problems, compel policymakers to pay more attention to certain aspects of issues than they otherwise might, provide information to the public and raise its interest level, and on occasion increase the domestic political stakes in policy choices. But the general rule still holds: on matters of fundamental importance interest groups seldom are significant. One is hard put to find an example of interest groups influencing senior policymakers to the extent that they adopted a policy other than that which they would have adopted for other reasons anyway. This is true even of "special interests" like multinational corporations, the military-industrial complex, and the Jewish lobby, interests which often are alleged to be exceptions to the rule.

The conclusions in this chapter may come as a surprise because they conflict with so much that is generally assumed. Yet each point made is well documented. They add up to permitting the President much initial latitude in decision-making, with an initial bias in his favor if he acts. Later, when the results begin to show up, if they are negative, the restrictive effects of public opinion may become substantial. The effect of interest groups on most major policy choices is, however, as the analysis showed, usually minimal.

In Chapters 6–8 we have seen that the President is the central figure in the policymaking process. Although Congress has certain powers and performs certain functions, and bureaucratic factors, public opinion, and interest groups have a role to play, it is still the President who is crucial. But no one person can do the job alone. Because of this an elaborate and rather sophisticated apparatus has been developed; its purpose is to help the President. We examine this apparatus in Chapters 9 and 10, beginning with the Department of State.

The Department of State

The Secretary of State is my principal foreign policy advisor. As such, he is responsible for the formulation of foreign policy and for the execution of approved policy.

Ronald Reagan
Statement by the President
January 12, 1982

All presidents I have known have had uneasy doubts about the State Department.

Dean Acheson
Present at the Creation

The Department of State, founded in 1789, is the senior component of the foreign policy apparatus. It has primary responsibility for advising the President in the design and implementation of foreign policy, and because of this it is presumed to be at the operational edge of the policy-making process.

The reality frequently has been different. Many presidents, in fact, have been dissatisfied with the State Department's performance and have relied on it as little as possible. President Nixon frequently kept his Secretary of State uninformed about important initiatives as did President Franklin Roosevelt. President Kennedy believed that the department had a sort of built-in inertia, automatically deadening innovation. Most recent presidents have ultimately found a sameness in the department's recommendations no matter what the problem: an advocacy of minimizing risks, avoiding quick action, and allowing patient diplomacy a chance to work.

What does the record show about State Department performance? How is the department organized to do business, and how does this affect its performance? How does the personality of the Secretary of State (or of the President) affect what happens? We shall look first at departmental organization and structure and then at the key role of the Secretary of State. Next we examine the second and third echelons, the bureaus and associated agencies, and the overseas missions, paying particular attention to their impact on policy design and implementation. Then we look concretely at departmental operations and decision making. We then have the basis for a balanced assessment.

1.

Departmental Organization and Structure

Formal factors such as organization and structure never tell the whole story but in the case of the Department of State formal factors are of exceptional significance.

The home office of the Department of State is organized in a classical bureaucratic pyramid (see Diagram 7). The Secretary of State is at the top, and beneath, in descending order of importance, are a number of lesser officers and units. Reflecting the need for both area and subject expertise, State's fourteen bureaus are set up on the basis of functional and geographic criteria, five geographic, and nine functional. Throughout the department structured superior-subordinate relations exist, and standard operating procedures cover most of the daily operations.

Generally, authority and responsibility within the State Department correspond closely to the hierarchical pattern designated on the organization chart. The key policymakers are the individuals at the top of the pyramid, occupying (literally) the seventh floor of the Department's Washington offices. They are the Secretary of State, his alter ego and stand-in the Deputy Secretary, and four (as of September 1982) undersecretaries: the Undersecretaries for Political Affairs; Economic Affairs; Management; and Security Assistance, Science and Technology. Also at this level are a Counselor (an officer with a purposely vague mandate to allow him considerable subject matter flexibility as an adviser to the Secretary), several special assistants, the head of the Policy Planning Council, a Deputy Undersecretary of Management, and a few others of lesser rank. Decisions of major importance are made on the seventh floor. In carrying out their functions, seventh-floor principals receive considerable support and assistance from the Executive Secretariat, a command and control staff for the Secretary located adjacent to his office.

2.

The Secretary of State

Although the seventh floor is the locus of departmental decision-making authority, not all seventh-floor principals are equal. The Secretary sets the department's tone, and it is he more than anyone else who determines its influence and the way it is perceived by other agencies and the President. The Secretary officially is the principal foreign policy adviser to the President. Subject to the President's direction, he is charged with major responsibilities for the overall guidance, supervision, and coordination of America's foreign relations. Generally his foreign policy interests, though not his authority, are comparable to the President's although the President, of course, has additional concerns.

The Secretary of State has a number of duties to perform and plays several roles: department administrator, advocate, negotiator, policy spokesman, policy implementor, presidential representative, and, in some administrations, policy adviser. Because there are so many duties, the job (in some senses) is almost impossible.

Because of his many roles, all

> sorts of demands impinge on the life of the secretary of state and restrict his ability to set his own agenda: the exigency of events overseas, over which we have little . . . control; time spent with the president and the Congress; weeks of foreign travel; and meetings with the press. The hours a secretary spends with the president . . . take precedence. Also important is the time spent with individual members of Congress and in testifying on Capitol Hill. . . . I estimate that close to a quarter of my time was spent on congressional matters.[1]

[1]Cyrus Vance, *Hard Choices: Critical Years in America's Foreign Policy* (New York: Simon & Schuster, 1983), p. 14.

DIAGRAM 7 Organization of the Department of State (Source: *The United States Government Manual,* 1982–1983, p. 812)

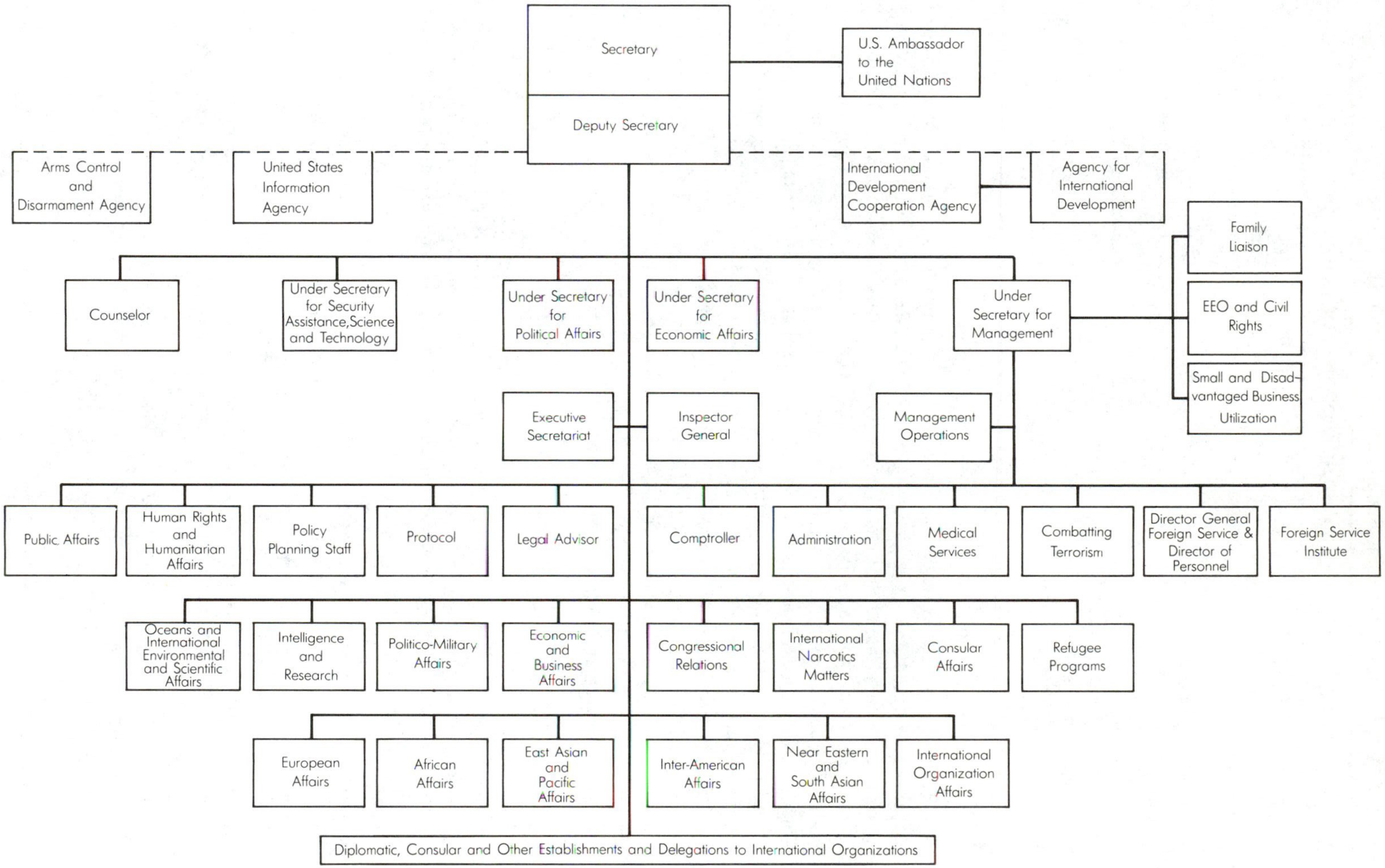

TABLE 5 Secretaries of State Since World War II

NAME	HELD OFFICE IN	PRESIDENT SERVED UNDER
James Byrnes	1945–1947	Truman
George Marshall	1947–1949	Truman
Dean Acheson	1949–1952	Truman
John Foster Dulles	1953–1959	Eisenhower
Christian Herter	1959–1960	Eisenhower
Dean Rusk	1961–1968	Kennedy and Johnson
William Rogers	1969–1973	Nixon
Henry Kissinger	1973–1976	Nixon and Ford
Cyrus Vance	1977–1980	Carter
Edmund Muskie	1980	Carter
Alexander Haig	1981–1982	Reagan
George Shultz	1982–	Reagan

Different personalities react differently to these strains and stresses. Different backgrounds may produce different role expectations. General Alexander Haig, President Reagan's first Secretary of State, had gained diplomatic and national security experience by serving as a deputy to Henry Kissinger and later becoming NATO's commander in chief (Supreme Allied Commander, Europe). Haig was a person with a very strong personality, and he made it known during his confirmation hearings that, within the President's team, he expected to have "clear" responsibility for foreign policy design and implementation. President Nixon's first Secretary, William Rogers, was quite a different story, bringing neither diplomatic experience nor a determination to be preeminent to the position. Dean Acheson, President Truman's Secretary of State from 1949 to 1952, presented yet a third blend of features, more near the middle of the spectrum. Acheson previously had served both as Assistant Secretary and Undersecretary of State. And during his years in the department he had developed strong policy views. But quite in contrast to Haig, and secretaries such as Henry Kissinger and John Foster Dulles who saw the job primarily in terms of influencing policy and sometimes acted as if they were the President's alter ego on policy matters, Acheson:

> saw his own role as Chief of Staff to the President in foreign affairs, directing and controlling the Department, keeping the President abreast of incipient situations that might call for decisions or action, acting as a principal assistant in making the decisions and assuring action upon them.[2]

The point here is simple but important: who the Secretary is makes a difference. Each Secretary being a unique blend of features and having his own distinctive view of what the Secretary's role should be, reacts to and works with, influences and is influenced by, the bureaucracy in his own singular fashion.

Whatever the Secretary's personality and expectations though, if he is to be effective there is one role is *must* fill: he must retain the President's trust and confidence. John Foster Dulles, Secretary under Eisenhower from 1953 to 1959, and Henry Kissinger, when he held the post in the Nixon-Ford years, provided us with excellent examples of secretaries in whom the President had great confidence, secretaries who had major roles in both policy design and implementation. These secretaries transcended contextual restraints.

[2]Dean Acheson, *Present at the Creation: My Years in the State Department* (New York: Signet Edition, 1970), p. 933.

How Washington Makes Foreign Policy

If a Secretary of State acts contrary to the President's desires, sooner or later it will lead to his downfall. In Secretary Haig's case, he from the first was determined to play a major role in designing policy. By the end of his first year in office though, that determination had resulted in a number of evident and sometimes open disagreements with the President (as well as bitter internecine warfare with many members of the White House staff and Secretary of Defense Caspar Weinberger). In the first half of 1982 a series of developments brought Haig's relations with the President to the breaking point. Three developments in particular stand out: (1) in the Argentine-British war over the Falkland Islands (discussed in Chapter 20) the Secretary thrust himself into the middle of the dispute in an unsuccessful attempt to mediate a peaceful settlement, a move undertaken with the President's acquiescence but without his wholehearted support; (2) after Israel invaded Lebanon on June 6 (see Chapter 19), it was an open secret that Haig and Reagan viewed Israel's drive to expel the PLO very differently; and (3) and very critically, Haig opposed Reagan's decision to extend retroactive sanctions to the European subsidiaries of American companies and to European companies operating under U.S. license that were cooperating in the construction of the Soviet-West European natural gas pipeline (see Chapter 17), a decision which was taken at a meeting held while Haig was out of town. Shortly thereafter Haig offered his resignation, and the President accepted. A Secretary of State at odds with the President simply cannot perform effectively on a sustained basis. To be effective, a reasonably cooperative relationship is essential.

Finally, presidents appoint individuals to the position of Secretary of State for various reasons. Although the President may desire to have the Secretary participate extensively and influentially in policymaking, he may prefer "to be his own Secretary of State" and make major decisions without the Secretary's assistance. Franklin Roosevelt did not even invite Secretary Hull to attend the important Teheran Conference in World War II. Secretaries play many roles, and sometimes an individual is appointed for his expertise in a nonpolicy area. Perhaps the President wants someone whose talent lies primarily in administration or in dealing with Congress and the public. There even have been times when policy knowledge (apparently) has been deemed a handicap. President Nixon considered William Rogers's unfamiliarity with foreign policy matters an asset "because it guaranteed that policy direction would remain in the White House."[3]

We begin to see why it is difficult to be a satisfactory Secretary of State.

3.

The Second and Third Echelons

The Deputy Secretary of State is the number-two man in the State Department. Working out of the Secretary's office, the Deputy is the Secretary's alter ego and is expected to work closely with him on all policy matters. When the Secretary is away from Washington the Deputy is in charge, and even when the "boss" is there the Deputy usually is responsible for most of the administrative tasks.

The four undersecretaries take primary responsibility for policy implementation in the functional areas that they serve, and provide key informational inputs both to the Secretary and across departmental lines in the various interagency groups in which they participate. They, like the Secretary, must keep themselves informed. Indeed, their knowledge must be deeper, more detailed, and more precise than the Secretary's in their particular sphere, for part of their charge is to inform him. They also have representational tasks vis-à-vis Congress, the public, and the

---

[3]Henry Kissinger, *White House Years* (Boston: Little, Brown and Company, 1979), p. 26.

media. Because so many actors participate in the design and implementation process, they must also spend a great deal of time in intra- and interagency conferences.

The Undersecretary for Political Affairs has another major responsibility: he is the ultimate clearance level for significant policy messages (other than those requiring the Secretary's attention) to be transmitted from Washington to the field. Messages of less importance can go out over the Assistant Secretary's initials, but cables dealing with significant issues, after being coordinated and cleared horizontally, must ascend to the Undersecretary. His initialing authorizes transmission, an action that commits the department and the country to a position.[4]

Before we leave the seventh floor, one other participant's function deserves brief discussion: the role of the Policy Planning Council (Staff). Established as the Policy Planning Staff in 1947 (and having undergone several incarnations since), the Council's mandate originally included developing proposals for long-range programs, preparing reports for senior policymakers on broad politico-military problems, examining and evaluating current policy, and coordinating planning activities within the department. But with very rare exceptions the promise in this mandate has been largely unfulfilled; generally the Policy Planning Council has been unimportant. Partly, this may have been the accidental result of timing. Almost immediately after its formation, a conceptual consensus developed around the containment, forward-deployment strategy. Since the fundamental issues of policy concept were now settled, the Council's efforts were siphoned off to a consideration of alternative orientations and means of implementation. Over time this thrust has continued, even now that the containment consensus has broken down. Even in the narrower sphere the Council has had little influence. To put it bluntly, the Foreign Service Officers manning the operational bureaus have paid little attention to the Council's activities, being both too busy with their daily responsibilities and convinced of their superior expertise. At the same time, typically there has been little support from the Secretary and his senior advisers. Though the Council today continues to prepare reports, work on long-range proposals, and examine and evaluate current policy, its impact is meager; the Policy Planning Council is not a major actor in the policy process.

The next key officials in the hierarchy are the assistant secretaries (or their equivalents). This represents the lowest policymaking level. Located on the sixth floor, each Assistant Secretary heads a minibureaucracy of his own—either a regional one like the Bureau of European Affairs, or a functional one like the Bureau of Politico-Military Affairs. They, like the seventh-floor principals, are presidential appointees. In recent administrations most have been career Foreign Service Officers.

Within the Department of State the regional bureaus generally are more important than the functional bureaus. In the last two decades any number of departmental and White House directives have stressed this importance and their key role in coordination and implementation. Because of this, the regional assistant secretaries tend to be first among equals.

An Assistant Secretary of State occupies a position of considerable significance. Although the Secretary can provide some degree of general policy thrust and guidance, and on a small number of selected issues can even provide rather detailed policy frameworks and procedures, there is far more to be done than any one person can accomplish. For this reason much responsibility must be delegated. This is especially true with respect to routine matters, where responsibility usually is delegated to the assistant secretaries.

If the Assistant Secretary normally does not play a continuous and major role in phase 1, policy design, or in crisis decision making because his sphere is limited, he is nevertheless important. Three factors explain this apparent paradox. First, most routine matters and tactical issues are first considered extensively within one of the bureaus. Such routine and tactical matters

[4]John H. Esterline and Robert B. Black, *Inside Foreign Policy: The Department of State Political System and Its Subsystems* (Palo Alto, Calif.: Mayfield, 1975), p. 46.

How Washington Makes Foreign Policy

constitute the vast majority of all policy concerns. As the head of the bureau, the Assistant Secretary has the power to "cause papers to be written, information to be amassed, and recommendations to be made."[5] Such power to table papers and help shape the agenda is of enormous significance in the bureaucratic context. Moreover, whatever is committed to writing in a bureau can be transmitted to the field only with the Assistant Secretary's concurrence.[6] Because of his expertise, and his responsibility for coordinating and balancing all policy recommendations for "his" region, the recommendations he makes generally are given careful consideration.

The second reason that assistant secretaries are so important is that they play a crucial role in phase 2 of the policy process, implementation. Once a decision has been made by seventh-floor principals (or the White House), it usually is the task of the bureau to interpret it, commit it to written form, and carry it out. As head of the bureau this becomes a major function and responsibility of the Assistant Secretary.[7]

The implementation function must not be underrated. Although less spectacular than the process of "making" the decision, it is enormously important. A decision is not worth much unless it is effectively implemented, and presidents need help in carrying out decisions, whatever they are, once the choices have been made. Much time and effort must be devoted to this task, and considerable negotiating skill, clear and persuasive communication, loyalty, and dogged persistence are necessary to achieve the objective. Relevant here is another thought: although it is realistic to separate policy design from policy implementation in an intellectual sense, from an operational perspective it is not that clear-cut. Assistant Secretaries frequently impact later decisions by the manner and extent that they carry out previous decisions. Also, policy in a micro and feedback sense can be the product of many bits and pieces of "decisions" accumulating from widely separated areas or problems. Allowed to be taken far enough, this process can undermine the conceptual rationality supposedly directing the policy.

The Assistant Secretary, then, has an important role to play. In position, he represents the lowest level of presidential appointment but one critical to effective implementation of presidential wishes. Sometimes, as under Nixon, he may even play an important role designing policy as did Joseph Sisco, Assistant Secretary for Near Eastern and South Asian Affairs at a time when Nixon was deliberately keeping Henry Kissinger's role limited in the Middle East and Secretary Rogers did not have the personal expertise necessary to do the job.

Finally, like all senior policymakers, assistant secretaries too lead busy lives. Consider this sample afternoon from the diary of a former Assistant Secretary for Educational and Cultural Affairs,[8] bearing in mind that this day's schedule began at 8:00 A.M.:

12:30 P.M. Lunch with Senator Fulbright.
2:00   Meeting with Bureau press officer: preparation of statement for newspapers concerning cultural exchanges with the Soviet Union. Clearances requested.
2:30   Conference with Counsel from the Kennedy Center for Performing Arts to discuss problems before the Board of Trustees.
3:00   Briefing by staff on a meeting the next day of the Government Advisory Committee on Books and Library Programs, concerning the need for U.S. textbooks overseas.
3:30   Meeting with the U.S. Ambassador to Ghana over problems with the head of state.

[5]See Roger Hilsman, *The Politics of Policy Making in Defense and Foreign Affairs* (New York: Harper & Row, 1971), pp. 35–37.
[6]As mentioned earlier, only relatively routine matters can be transmitted to the field over his initials, though. The Assistant Secretary quickly learns which decisions can be transmitted over his initials and which require review (and/or concurrence outside the department).
[7]Esterline and Black, *Inside Foreign Policy,* p. 49.
[8]Charles Frankel, *High on Foggy Bottom* (New York: Harper & Row, 1969), pp. 209–210.

4:00	Alternative statements on Soviet cultural exchanges received from the Bureaus of European Affairs and Public Affairs. Telephone calls to each bureau. Trouble-shooter assigned to work out or obscure the disagreements.
4:30	Meeting with the Assistant Secretary for International Organization to examine the U.S. position on a coming vote on who should be represented on the UNESCO Executive Board.
5:00	Meeting with representatives of the Bureaus of European and Public Affairs. One sentence and two commas deleted from the statement on cultural exchanges with the USSR. Clearances received.
5:30	Meeting with the President of a U.S. university in the Middle East, which needs money.
6:10	Call from the White House on the cultural exchange statement. Suggest that one sentence and two commas be added.
6:30	Reception at the Iraqi Embassy for the Iraqi Prime Minister and Foreign Minister.
8:00	Dinner at home with two colleagues from the bureau, an Undersecretary from HEW, an editorial writer from the *Washington Post,* and their wives.

An Assistant Secretary of State leads an exciting if somewhat frenetic life.

4.

The Bureaus and the Associated Agencies

The regional and functional bureaus are (mostly) on the sixth and fifth floors. They usually operate with three or four deputy assistant secretaries under the supervision of the Assistant Secretary or his equivalent.

To some extent the bureaus tend to take on the complexion of the particular Assistant Secretary who heads them, and therefore they tend to have tasks and influence in keeping with his special interests, abilities, and relationships with the seventh floor. But regardless of who the Assistant Secretary is and the particular functions that are performed, each bureau always executes two fundamental tasks. First, it acts as an information conduit, in Washington between American policymakers and foreign diplomats, and between the U.S. government and its diplomatic representatives abroad. Second, it is charged to provide data, ideas, policy analyses, and recommendations, to act as a resource for senior policymakers. The bureaus are to provide the information and preliminary suggestions on the basis of which (supposedly) major policy decisions will be made at higher levels.

As was mentioned earlier, the regional bureaus usually are preeminent. Organizationally, they are subdivided along country lines with major responsibilities residing in the various country directors.[9] The country directors have three major tasks: (1) coordination of all United States interests relating to "their" country; (2) acting as the major contact between foreign diplomats in Washington and the United States government; and (3) serving as the focal point for contact between American policymakers and United States diplomatic missions overseas.[10] In all these spheres the country director is expected to act according to SOPs within the policy and procedural guidelines established by his superiors. An interesting organizational fact is that many

[9]For a useful analysis of the country director's roles see William I. Bacchus, *Foreign Policy and the Bureaucratic Process: The State Department's Country Director System* (Princeton, N.J.: Princeton University Press, 1974).

[10]In reality, because of the plethora of agencies involved in matters relating to "his" country (in Washington and in the country), and the need for clearance of all significant messages by his superiors before transmission to the field, the country director is precluded from effectively carrying out his coordinating function.

How Washington Makes Foreign Policy

"country" directors are responsible for several countries simultaneously. In the Bureau of Near Eastern and South Asian Affairs, for example, though there is a country director for Egypt there also is a single country director for Lebanon, Jordan, Syria, and Iraq.

Although the foregoing is an accurate description of the country director's basic roles, it may mask the diversity of the subject matter with which the country director often must deal, thereby hiding the dynamic and variable nature of the job. Several years ago one of the authors spent one morning going over the cables country director X had received since the close of business the preceding day. Among the topics the cables covered on this very ordinary day (all of which required some response) were (1) warnings from the ambassador of a possible hijacking of a commercial airliner headed for the host country; (2) a report on the status of commercial negotiations for air routes to the country; (3) a preliminary report on the ambassador's negotiations with the head of state concerning a speedup in the delivery of nonlethal military equipment, and a request by the ambassador that the proposed deal be checked out with the Defense Department to see if it squared with existing SOPs; (4) a report that the host country was considering the covert provision of counterinsurgency forces to another government in the region, and a query from the host government concerning the probable American reaction; (5) a request from the host country's head of state that arrangements be made for the country's national band to perform at the halftime of a (Washington Redskins) professional football game; (6) a report that the host country was considering the purchase of U.S.-supplied military equipment from a third country, and a request from the ambassador to find out what the administration's reaction would be; (7) a report on personnel developments in the Embassy; and (8) the ambassador's assessments of a number of current problems in the region, and his request for the country director's views. The country director's job, like the Assistant Secretary's, is exciting, complex, and demanding.

Although the regional bureaus tend to be more important than the functional bureaus, two caveats must be entered if the picture is to be complete. First, this does not mean that the functional bureaus are *un*important or that they deal with matters that are insignificant. We are talking here in relative terms, not absolute. The Bureau of Politico-Military Affairs makes a considerable contribution in the area of arms transfer policy, for example, and the Bureau of International Organization Affairs often provides crucial information about activities at the UN. The fact that the functional bureaus are not preeminent does not mean that they are not listened to or that their role is insignificant. Second, there are occasional exceptions to the rule. In the Carter administration the Bureau of Human Rights carried considerable clout, often being backed by both the Secretary and the President. During the Iranian crisis (discussed in Chapter 19) the Bureau of Human Rights clashed repeatedly with the Bureau of Near Eastern and South Asian Affairs and held its own very well. But such prominence for a functional bureau *is* the exception, not the rule.

The fact that the State Department is organized into both regional and functional bureaus causes difficulties in coordination. Life would be much simpler if the basic units could be organized entirely one way or the other, but either alternative would raise even more problems. A purely functional approach would defy the facts that (1) each state is unique, with circumstances, problems and policies that are slightly or extravagantly different from those of every other, and (2) that each region has certain distinctive characteristics. A purely geographic approach obviously would be inappropriate for dealing with many of the functional problems that transcend state boundaries. So both are done; but an obvious problem of coordination results.

Another difficulty with the current structure is that functional or geographic bureaus, charged as they are with handling the daily business of foreign policy, can easily lose perspective on the total impact of what is developing. Individuals operating in highly specialized arenas tend to view situations from the perspective of their particular position. The further down the hierarchy, the more specialized and narrower the perspective becomes. Clearly, this is a problem. Somewhat balancing this consideration is the fact that the geographical bureaus and directorates can be manned by specialists who have been stationed in the country whose affairs they are now handling at home, providing an in-depth expertise. But here, too, there are trade-offs. The advantages accruing from the continuity of such expertise can be offset by an excessive sympathy for the country for which the official is responsible. There is not much that can be done to mitigate these dilemmas. Given the complex, interrelated nature of the international political system, separate geographic and functional bureaus are unavoidable and the problems this arrangement produces are inevitable.

The coordination problem highlighted by the division into geographic and functional bureaus has a number of other facets. First, several major units are involved in policymaking which are not integrated into or controlled by the Department of State. Certainly the military services, DOD, NSC, and the CIA fall into this category. It is evident that the Secretary's charge for the overall coordination of America's foreign relations vastly exceeds his capacity to achieve that objective. Second, State does not have under its administration all United States government personnel working abroad who are concerned with foreign affairs (more on this later). Third, three associated agencies with operational responsibilities in foreign policy areas have some linkage to State but also a considerable degree of independence. They are the United States Information Agency (USIA), the Agency for International Development (AID), the latest in a long list of bureaucratic units charged with handling foreign (economic) aid programs, and the Arms Control and Disarmament Agency (ACDA).[11] ACDA bears an especially curious relationship to State: it is a separate agency yet it reports to the Secretary. And although he "reports" to the Secretary, the Director of ACDA has considerable independence because he is designated the principal adviser to the President and the NSC (and the Secretary) on arms control matters, is given prime responsibility in the bureaucracy for arms control, and controls a separate personnel system.

USIA, AID, and ACDA are full-fledged participants in foreign affairs. How should they be properly related to State? One can argue that in light of the Secretary's primary responsibility for policy coordination these agencies either should be in the department or at least subject to its close supervision and control. From this perspective the loose relationship between State and ACDA and the relative autonomy of AID and USIA are negative features. But one can argue with equal logic that such specialized activities are best handled separate from the traditional State Department apparatus, that these agencies should be directly responsible to the President, and that the task of policy coordination can only be achieved by the White House. The checkered organizational past of these agencies indicates how hard it is to resolve this problem.

5.

The Overseas Missions

In 1981 the United States had diplomatic representation at 133 embassies and 149 other diplomatic posts throughout the world.[12] These overseas diplomatic missions serve as the official communication links between the United States and the foreign countries in which they are located. American diplomats abroad represent the United States at various ceremonial functions, implement policies according to the instructions they receive from the home office, and assess

---

[11]In 1979 AID became an agency within the International Development Cooperation Agency, but it still is charged with central direction of and responsibility for foreign economic assistance programs.

[12]*United States Government Organization Manual, 1981/1982*, p. 395.

situations and conditions in the states to which they are accredited, making reports and recommendations to Washington.

Diplomatic missions divide into various categories including: embassies to foreign nations, consular representatives to important cities, and permanent missions to international organizations. In many respects the most important unit is the embassy.[13] The embassy is headed by an ambassador, who is the personal representative of the President in the host country. As "chief of mission" the ambassador has responsibility for seeing to it that the United States is effectively represented abroad, that its policy is successfully implemented, and that it speaks with a single voice—things easier to say than to do. The ambassador also bears the ultimate responsibility for keeping the home office fully and accurately informed about events in the host country.

Before the modern era ambassadors had considerable autonomy. Because of the previous primitive state of communication and transportation systems, ambassadors often had no choice but to make vital decisions without consultation with their governments, designing a policy on the spot. Because of the contemporary revolution in communications and transportation, however, ambassadors today have less autonomy and discretion. Although sometimes they may advise their government of conditions they feel would make a policy change desirable (a not unimportant power), in many cases they must wait for instructions from home before they act. In parallel fashion, if things cannot be dealt with sufficiently via the communications channel and time permits, it is a simple matter for home officials to fly to the scene or for the ambassador to fly home for consultations.

The "eyes and ears" function of the overseas diplomat also has altered considerably in modern times. Although the ambassador continues to perform ceremonial functions (where he often obtains his most useful information), a wider net of contacts is required nowadays. To obtain the necessary understanding of conditions in the host country, today it is essential for diplomats to get away from the capital, to travel, and to acquire a penetrating first-hand knowledge of things political, economic, and social.

Much has also changed with respect to the implementation function. Here the ambassador usually operates under a fairly detailed set of instructions, and is expected to do as he has been bidden. If he has been instructed to negotiate, he is to do so to the best of his ability, but if the policy is to avoid negotiations while pretending to want them it is his function to carry out these instructions. Generally the ambassador (diplomat) "should be neither praised nor blamed for the policy of his government. What he deserves praise or blame for is how well he carries out the implementation of his country's policy."[14]

Although the foregoing is accurate, it may be misleading in one respect. It may give the impression that the ambassador has no impact at all on policy content. But as we have pointed out several times, policy design and implementation are not wholly separate. The ambassador, though technically executing rather than "making" policy, nevertheless has an impact on the direction and contours of policy content by the manner in which he carries out his instructions and the nature and substance of his reports. Occasionally this influence may be considerable. Reports from the embassy in Santo Domingo were a major factor in President Johnson's 1965 decision to land marines in the Dominican Republic, for example. Ambassador Tapley Bennett reported continually and consistently that there was a serious threat of a Communist takeover in the Dominican Republic and several times suggested that to stop it, to prevent "another Cuba" in the Caribbean, the United States might have to intervene militarily. As conditions deteriorated and Bennett's reports indicated "the Communists" might win, the President decided action was necessary and sent in the marines. Although technically the ambassador was only

---

[13]There are also, in descending order of importance, consulates general, consulates, and consular agencies.
[14]Frederick H. Hartmann, *The Relations of Nations*, 6th ed. (New York: Macmillan, 1983), p. 98.

reporting and not "making" policy, it is absolutely clear that his reports influenced Johnson's decision enormously.

The ambassador's "number two" is called the Deputy Chief of Mission or DCM. The role of the DCM varies widely according to the breadth and nature of United States operations in the particular country and the desires and needs of the ambassador. At some posts, the DCM becomes the ambassador's alter ego in policy matters and acts as a prime adviser and confidant as well. Procedurally, at all posts, the DCM takes over in the absence of the ambassador, and occasionally he substitutes at ceremonial functions. Still, in some missions the DCM's role is mostly administrative in nature, the ambassador's style precluding DCM policy influence. The ambassador's wishes and needs will be crucial in defining the DCM's role.

Because of the enormous disparities in mission size, not all missions are organized identically. They do, however, have a common core; whether large or small, each embassy has major sections for political affairs, economic/commercial affairs, consular matters, and administration. These "traditional" elements form the heart of most of the ordinary mission activities. Among the various subdivisions the political section is usually the most important. Its officers have the closest relations with the ambassador, work with him on key negotiating and reporting matters, and bear "coordinating and drafting responsibilities for formulation of mission-wide action and planning studies and reports."[15]

A diplomatic mission is a highly intricate and complex organization. It is apparent that to manage the mission efficiently and productively is a considerable task. But things are even more complicated than our discussion has indicated because the vast majority of United States government employees who work overseas *are not State Department personnel*. In 1964 other departments and agencies represented abroad included Defense; Treasury; Justice; Interior; Health, Education, and Welfare; Agriculture; the Atomic Energy Commission; and the Federal Aviation Agency.[16] The problem certainly has not diminished with the passage of time; the ratio of traditional embassy elements to nontraditional personnel almost never exceeds one to four.

As United States involvements expanded in the postwar period, mission staffs grew correspondingly and the problem of interagency coordination became severe. As a result, on May 29, 1961, President Kennedy sent a letter to all U.S. ambassadors strongly affirming the ambassador's authority over all mission personnel. All presidents since have taken the same position. Congress has echoed the same theme. The Foreign Service Act of 1980 provided that under the direction of the President the chief of mission "shall have full responsibility for the direction, coordination, and supervision of all Government employees in that country (except for employees under the command of a United States area military command)." Moreover, "any agency having employees in a foreign country shall keep the chief of mission fully informed" as to the activities of these employees, and shall "insure" that all of its employees (except those under military area command) "comply fully with all applicable directives of the chief of mission."[17]

Although the ambassador has the formal authority to control and coordinate the activities of the various mission elements, in many cases he does not have the real power to do so. The very scope, diversity, and technical requirements of the mission's operations would make it difficult to control even if organizational arrangements were ideal, and they are not. In the first place, many non-State personnel have the prerogative to communicate directly with their own Washington headquarters. Although all regular communications must be "cleared" with the

[15]Esterline and Black, *Inside Foreign Policy,* p. 92.

[16]Burton M. Sapin, *The Making of United States Foreign Policy* (Washington, D.C.: The Brookings Institution, 1966), p. 252.

[17]U.S., Public Law 96-465—October 17, 1980, Sec. 207.

chief of mission, this requirement does not extend to "official-informal" letters or messages transmitted electronically.

Second, career development for non-State personnel depends more on satisfying their home agencies than it does on satisfying the ambassador, and it is evident where one's allegiance would be if conflict occurred. In the event the ambassador makes decisions with which other agency personnel do not concur, the decision can be reviewed by higher authority in Washington. Another salient point is that in certain geographic areas or during certain historical periods the military services, DOD, or the CIA have possessed political clout with the President superior to that of State. In such contingencies the corresponding non-State mission elements have considerable influence and independence.

Yet one must not overstate the case either. Although *total* control seldom is achieved, most ambassadors do exercise *substantial* control. Traditional mission elements have no line of reporting except through the ambassador, and elements from the other agencies usually strive to effect a reasonable degree of harmony within the "country team" concept. And an individual who runs afoul of the ambassador with regularity usually will be in trouble professionally.

On balance, there is no gainsaying that a considerable amount of "bureaucratic" bargaining and negotiating will occur as various elements within an embassy strive for policy and organizational influence. The ambassador more often than not exercises preeminent control and coordination, but his influence is circumscribed in varying degrees by the relatively powerful subunits he "controls."

It is evident that the ambassador's job is difficult. Though there was a time in the history of the United States when appointment to an ambassadorial position was a typical means of rewarding an individual for political support, this happens much less frequently today. Recent presidents have made major efforts to appoint qualified people. Usually more than two out of three posts are filled by career Foreign Service personnel, individuals who have risen through the ranks of the diplomatic service and already demonstrated professional competence. Even when *new* ambassadorial appointments do not meet this standard, as was true of the Reagan selection process, because a number of career ambassadors remain at post, the overall ratio holds. Moreover, most of the noncareerists appointed qualify by virtue of an established expertise in, and long association with, foreign policy and security matters. The appointment by President Kennedy of the noted Asian scholar Edwin Reischauer as ambassador to Japan provides a useful example. To ensure that a degree of continuity and expertise is present, whenever an ambassador is not a career Foreign Service Officer (FSO), at such a mission the DCM is always an FSO.

6.

The Department in Operation

To this point we have discussed organizational and structural factors, analyzing how the features of the formal hierarchy affect policy design and implementation. We now turn to the State Department's operations, paying particular attention to the linkage between those operations and the policies they tend to produce.

Communications are a vital part of the operations of the State Department. Each of the 133 embassies and 149 other posts (1981) is in contact with State each day, and the message flow in each direction is enormous. Indeed, on the average day more than four thousand messages are processed. Each incoming message must be routed to all who should be informed. To accomplish this task, rules and indicators have been developed for classification, precedence, and distribution. Standard operating procedures are essential in this regard so that the selecting, filtering, and routing of information occurs in a relatively efficient manner. Outgoing traffic is handled in a similar fashion, each outgoing message being coordinated and cleared before the appropriate action officer authorizes transmission.

The combination of the sheer quantity of communications traffic and the need to inform those immediately or potentially affected by the message leads to a time problem: it seems to "take forever" to get things done. Department officials are well aware of the problem and there have been periodic efforts to reform and streamline the procedures. But to a great extent the problem is insoluble. Given the number of messages that must be transmitted (internal-external and vice versa, and within the organization) and the complex and interrelated nature of most foreign policy issues, there are few areas to cut.

Let's take a hypothetical example, looking only at a single, incoming message (recognizing that in reality there are thousands of criss-crossing messages). Suppose a cable comes in from the U.S. ambassador to Saudi Arabia stating that unless the United States supplies Saudi Arabia with weapons system X, the Saudis will significantly increase oil prices. Obviously this message is of sufficient import that seventh-floor principals must be informed, so the appropriate papers are moved. Clearly the information also must be transmitted to the Bureau of Near Eastern and South Asian Affairs and within that to the several concerned country directors. Because of the impact on the United States economy such an occurrence would have, the Bureau of Economic Affairs would have to be informed. Because the message involves arms transfers the Bureau of Politico-Military Affairs ought to be informed, and if there is any likelihood of the information being public or provoking a reaction from Congress, perhaps the Bureaus of Public Affairs and Congressional Relations (and the Office of Press Relations) should be advised. If there is any possibility of consultations or debate at the United Nations the International Organization Bureau should be alerted. Because of the importance of oil to the states of Western Europe and Japan, it might be necessary to alert the Bureaus of European Affairs and East Asian and Pacific Affairs. And the list could still be extended. Not all of these units are informed of every development of the type we have posited here, but most are and have to be. If some should not be, which ones? And what happens if they are not and future developments make it clear that they should have been?

Because the messages that go back and forth from State are a prime source of information, every effort is made to transmit them in secure codes and ciphers. In embassies located in states with which relations are not friendly, elaborate security measures are necessary. Some years ago in the American Embassy in Moscow it was discovered that a Soviet-presented Great Seal of the United States contained concealed transistors. Extraordinary care was taken in 1983, as the new American Embassy in Moscow was being built, to keep Soviet "bugs" out of the walls.

One more element of the communications system is worth comment: the Operations Center. The Defense Department has maintained "situation rooms" or "war rooms" for a long time. Equipped with elaborate communication and command facilities, these facilities are manned around the clock, ready to respond to an emergency. Curiously, until the early 1960s the State Department had no real equivalent. There was always a "duty watch" after most of the personnel ended their working day, but it was not organized for fast reaction. The experience of the Bay of Pigs crisis in 1961 led to the establishment of a full-scale 24-hour watch system, and following the Cuban missile crisis there developed the "task force" concept of handling crises from the Ops Center with a team working under the appropriate Assistant Secretary. Such a team was put together after the seizure of the American Embassy in Iran in November 1979, for example, another being formed in late April 1981 to monitor the increasing Syrian-Lebanese-Israeli fighting in central Lebanon.

The Ops Center is operated by teams working in three eight-hour shifts. Each team consists of a senior watch officer, a number of subordinates, and a senior military representative who provides close liaison with the Pentagon. It alerts officials to incoming cables, determines the distribution of messages of high sensitivity (EXDIS and NODIS), and is the clearance point for outgoing messages in those channels.[18] The Ops Center performs important functions in noncrisis situations also. It is the telephone center for most contact between the department and the overseas missions after normal working hours, is at the hub of the department's telephonic communications network, and it maintains direct links to and interchanges with the telegraphic communications center.

7.

Departmental Decision Making

How are decisions made in the State Department? As one might surmise there is no single answer to this question, but the process does exhibit certain characteristics and patterns that exist more often than not. Several of the factors have been alluded to in other connections and only need to be mentioned briefly here.

1. Within the department authority is essentially hierarchical and rank is very important. Decision making thus tends to be hierarchical in nature, with the key decisions being made on the seventh floor.
2. The process (often) is very time consuming. Rarely is there time to consider carefully issues concerning the crucial first phase of policymaking, policy design.
3. Low- and midlevel officers almost always operate within established SOPs.
4. There is an enormous flow of communications.
5. Much of the work involves either policy implementation or providing information to senior policymakers.

As the foregoing indicates, the State Department decision process tends to be carefully structured, incremental, and slow. There *is* sort of a built-in inertia. Several other factors contribute to these tendencies. Some of these flow naturally from the fact that the department is a large organization dealing with complex issues.[19] There is so much information, ideas flow in so many directions, so many individuals participate, and so many actions are taken that often it is more accurate to think of a flow of decisional fragments than in terms of discrete policy decisions. Because of the fragmentation, constraints, and time pressures, policy changes tend to be few and moderate; incremental change is much more prevalent than major policy alteration. And the enormous time pressure under which most FSOs operate adds to the tendency to operate within established SOPs.

Career concerns also have contributed to the difficulties, especially in inhibiting risk taking and innovation. A selection-out promotional system and a blockage at the top levels have helped produce a psychological environment resistant to change, one that stresses normal bureaucratic tendencies even further: conflict-avoidance and careful following of instructions. It is almost impossible for FSOs to acquire significant responsibility in the policymaking process until late in their careers, and prior to that time career advancement depends heavily on the favorable judgment of a long list of supervisors. These conditions

> inevitably move the Foreign Service officer to focus his attention on his immediate supervisors, to qualify present thinking and action with long-term career considerations, to think twice

---

[18]EXDIS ("exclusive" distribution) and NODIS ("no" distribution) are departmental designations or captions designed to ensure that the messages so designated are distributed only to those with a genuine need-to-know.

[19]Much of the discussion in Chapter 7 is relevant here.

before taking possibly disquieting initiatives, to interpret his responsibilities narrowly and develop a defensive reflex against obtrusive outsiders.[20]

The department's decision-making process also reflects the general views FSOs tend to share of the nature of international relations and the most appropriate ways of handling problems. Most FSOs share certain perspectives, viewing international politics as a dynamic mosaic of only partially controllable interacting forces. Within this complex system each unit is seen as acting in terms of its self-interest and its policy positions appear as the result of a long chain of historical developments produced by a host of interrelated causes. Granted that, careful thought and patient quiet diplomacy usually will be the most effective means of advancing or protecting national interests with minimum risk. Because the problems are so complex and numerous, and since they are interrelated, simple clear-cut answers frequently are not possible. Furthermore, every action one takes affects a large number of actors, and one needs to take the manifold ramifications into account. A constructive plus-minus balance is the best that one can hope for. Sudden efforts to solve complex problems seldom are effective (it is believed), and sometimes they can produce the very crisis one is trying to prevent. Nuances and subtleties must be explored, skillfully, cautiously, and painstakingly. Incrementalism in process and policy thus is in the national interest. (Compare these views with the cardinal principles.)

One must be careful, however, not to carry the idea of an "FSO belief system" too far. Anyone with the least familiarity with the State Department knows that on specific issues, FSOs may hold widely differing views. Partly this may be the result of the bureaucratic pressures resulting from the fragmentation and competition within the department, but for the most part it is simply the result of the fact that FSOs are highly intelligent, competent, and determined individuals, and quite naturally they do not all think alike. FSO variations in viewpoint were illustrated well in the early 1960s. Most FSOs, as one would expect, supported America's Vietnam policy strongly at the time, but a significant number raised some serious questions and suggested that alternative policies should be considered. To cite a specific instance, in the fall of 1964 one group of FSOs suggested that the United States should consider more carefully what degree of loss and risk it was prepared to take to hold South Vietnam, suggested that the South Vietnamese were not as interested as they should be in defending themselves, and argued that if South Vietnam were lost it would not automatically lead to consequences that were seriously adverse; the repercussions would depend on what Washington was willing to do in other countries.[21] Although it is fair to say that there are a number of rather widely shared beliefs and attitudes in the Foreign Service, FSOs are not faceless ciphers.

All of this being so, as more than one Secretary of State has found to his chagrin, it is extremely difficult for the Secretary to bend the department to his will. As Henry Kissinger writes:

> The procedures of the State Department are well designed to put a premium on bureaucratic self-will. Despite lip-service to planning, there is a strong bias in favor of making policy in response to cables and in the form of cables. The novice Secretary of State thus finds on his desk not policy analyses or options but stacks of dispatches which he is asked to initial and do so urgently. . . . Even if he asserts himself and rejects a particular draft, it is likely to come back to him with a modification so minor that only a legal scholar could tell the difference.

[20]U.S. Department of State, *Diplomacy for the 70s,* Department of State Publication 8551, December 1970, p. 381.

[21]Leslie H. Gelb, with Richard K. Betts, *The Irony of Vietnam: The System Worked* (Washington, D.C.: The Brookings Institution, 1979), p. 235.

> When I . . . became Secretary I discovered that it was a herculean effort even for someone who had made foreign policy his life's work to dominate the State Department's cable machine.[22]

Here is irony indeed! For if the President, as we saw, is frequently complaining about State's unresponsiveness, he is not the only one. When all is said and done, bureaucracies are hard to control.

Finally, just because the decision process in the State Department generally operates in rather ponderous bureaucratic style, that does not automatically make its operations unsatisfactory. *The ultimate question is, what is the impact of the process on policy and on decision making?* Generally the State Department acts slowly, recommends cautious policies that entail minimum risk, advises avoiding hasty decisions and confrontational orientations, and suggests tactics that emphasize the use of patient diplomacy. Reacting in a careful, thoughtful manner and recommending cautious policies are not necessarily bad; indeed, many times a gradual reaction is better than plunging in, and often cautious policies that minimize risk are exactly what the situation demands. And sometimes gradual diplomacy *is* the most appropriate means of implementation. The problem, of course, is that sometimes a rapid reaction is required, cautious policies are not always in the national interest, sometimes high risks must be taken, careful diplomacy is not always the best choice, and sometimes senior policymakers need fresh, vigorous, and innovative policy recommendations. In these areas the State Department often falls short.

8.

Summing Up

The State Department's organizational and operational features are close to our usual stereotype of how a large bureaucracy functions, with both the advantages and disadvantages that entails. The key issue is not how closely the State Department fits the stereotype, though. The key issue is, what can be done to improve the process? Since World War II, despite several commissions, several studies, a number of recommendations, and several organizational changes, the problem in large part remains. There is a lesson here. *Such efforts are only moderately valuable because the difficulties are not essentially the result of faulty structure or management.* Instead, they are largely the natural product of the complex nature of the world being confronted, the department's tasks and responsibilities in that world, the need to structure an organization to deal with that world, the typical functioning of a large carefully regulated institution, and the philosophies and beliefs of most of the personnel working within the organization. What can be done? The answer is, *not very much*. The characteristics of the department's performance that so many presidents have complained about are unlikely to be changed significantly no matter how things are restructured (or who is on the seventh floor, or in the Oval Office).

To keep things in proper perspective, another very important point must be remembered. As we explained in Chapter 7, decisions affecting vital interests and fundamental objectives usually are made by senior policymakers in small groups. Thus, the kind of decision-making process described in this chapter usually is not applicable to matters of top priority and sensitivity. *The State Department as an organization does not handle such concerns, dealing instead with the routine, noncrisis affairs that make up the bulk of everyday policy.* This not to say that State *never* deals with the most critical matters, but only that it does not do so at its own discretion and it does not handle such issues unilaterally through its internal decision-making processes. And when State does become involved in top priority issues it is through the utilization

---

[22]Kissinger, *White House Years*, pp. 27–28.

of some particular *sector* of the department, either as a support mechanism for the Secretary as he operates in one of the small decision groups, or through the department's interagency role in the National Security Council system.

We have examined in this chapter the State Department's role in the conduct of United States foreign policy. But State is not the only major agency involved in the policymaking process. The Defense Department, the intelligence community, the National Security Council among others also play important roles. For the design and implementation of a cost-effective policy that adequately protects United States national security, all agencies must provide high-quality advice to senior policymakers in a timely fashion, and the various parts of the policy-making machinery must be coordinated effectively. These issues of national security advice and coordination provide the focus of our discussion in Chapter 10.

10

The National Security System

*There is established a council to be known as the National Security Council. . . .
The function of the Council shall be to advise the President with respect to the
integration of domestic, foreign, and military policies relating to the national
security so as to enable the military services and the other departments and
agencies . . . to cooperate more effectively . . .*

National Security Act of 1947

*While the NSC is, . . . when correctly employed, a vitally important body, it is
only advisory in action.*

Dwight D. Eisenhower
The White House Years: Waging Peace, 1956–1961

Foreign policy, we said in Chapter 1, is always security oriented in very important features. Thus foreign policy issues must be effectively coordinated with the military, with intelligence, and with other organs of government. These coordinating devices are what we discuss as the national security system. Since the President, as we said in Chapter 6, is the prime decision maker for foreign policy, the national security system must serve his needs both in terms of making available expert advice across the government in policy design, and appropriate bureaucratic coordination in actual implementation.

The rather complex and sophisticated national security machinery of today emerged from primitive beginnings, and more recently than one might assume. In 1925 President Coolidge could state that "the business of America is business" and not be far off the mark; peace and security issues seldom were matters of concern. The content of U.S. foreign policy and the lack of sustained involvement in world affairs bore this out, as did Washington's meager foreign policy apparatus. Such national security "organization" as existed before World War II was highly primitive, to say the least. The State Department was small and rudimentary in nature, hardly capable of conducting the foreign policy of a major power. The situation was similar on the military side of the house (which was not connected to the diplomatic side, either). Two cabinet-level departments, War and Navy, had existed since the late eighteenth century, but the development of the forces was almost entirely separate and uncoordinated. Command relationships and defense organization for waging modern war were similarly primitive. Intelligence activity before World War II was also limited. Although the military intelligence services existed, they operated on a shoestring. Even then, their code-breaking activities, begun in World War I, were curbed. (In 1929, Secretary of State Henry L. Stimson ended State Department financing and participation in such efforts with an aloof, "Gentlemen do not read each other's mail.") Coordinating devices, such as the Office of Strategic Services (OSS) in World War II, were similarly slow in developing. Policy coordination, to the extent that it existed, rested almost solely on the President's making the effort.

All of this was to change as a result of World War II and the new global policy. New organizational relations for the components of the foreign policy system had to be evolved, to ensure that the design and implementation of policies impacting national security was efficient.

We have already discussed several of those components—the President, the Congress, and the State Department—and throughout this chapter we shall bring to bear points from our earlier analysis where they are relevant. But the focus in this chapter is on the advisory and coordination process and the political and military institutions and arrangements developed in the post-1945 period to handle national security problems.

First, we examine the landmark National Security Act of 1947, legislation that provided the framework for what really was a revolution in the handling of such problems and issues. Second, we describe the evolution of the Department of Defense into the elaborate and sophisticated apparatus that exists today, and examine as well the growing influence of the Secretary of Defense. Third, we analyze the intelligence community, discussing both the role of the CIA and that of non-CIA intelligence units. Fourth, we assess the specific problem of covert operations. Fifth, we discuss in some detail the national security policymaking system in operation, with special emphasis on the importance of presidential attitudes and styles. Sixth, we present a case study of the policymaking process during the first phase of the Iranian crisis, demonstrating how the process breaks down when the President fails to provide effective leadership. Finally, we sum up our findings and look ahead to Part Three, the foreign policy record.

1.

The National Security Act

During World War II a number of individuals, civilian and military, became convinced that major changes were necessary in the national security system. It was increasingly clear that a greater degree of unity among the military services, closer linkage of political and military moves, more sophisticated and regularized intelligence, and a more effective coordination of policies between units and between the President and subordinates were required. A number of plans surfaced, from both civilian and service sources. In late 1945 President Truman presented his proposals, calling for a stronger and more unified military organization and a merger of the services under a civilian Secretary of Defense. Shortly thereafter congressional hearings were begun.

At the end of the legislative gauntlet in July 1947, a remarkable piece of legislation emerged, the National Security Act. Though it contained many compromises and few of the conflicting forces were wholly satisfied, it provided a constructive basis for what really was a revolution in the American national security system. Its most controversial provisions were those affecting the armed services.

The act provided for three major changes. First, it created the National Security Council (NSC). The concept of a permanent organization to help the President coordinate national security policy and to advise him with respect to the integration of domestic, foreign, and military affairs had been well accepted by both the President and the Congress, so the disagreements during the congressional process had centered on details, not concept. The NSC was to be composed of the President (as chairman), Vice-President, Secretary of State, Secretary of Defense, the secretaries of each of the armed services (including the newly created air force), the chairman of the new National Security Resources Board and the Director for Mutual Security (both ultimately dropped), and others whom the President wished to add.

Second, the act created the Central Intelligence Agency directly under the NSC. The CIA was not designed to replace or supersede the existing service intelligence agencies, intelligence components of the State Department, or the FBI. Nor was the CIA established to set overall intelligence policy; that was to be the function of the President and the NSC. The CIA was created to advise the NSC on intelligence matters; make recommendations to the NSC for the coordination of the intelligence activities of other departments and agencies; and correlate, evaluate, and appropriately disseminate within the government intelligence related to national security. It also was to perform such other functions and duties related to national security intelligence as the NSC might from time to time direct.[1]

Third, the act created a National Military Establishment, which consisted of three executive level service departments (army, navy, and a separate air force) each headed by a civilian secretary. But these three service departments in turn were subordinate to the new Office of the Secretary of Defense (OSD), headed by a civilian with cabinet rank. (It was this provision that worried the U.S. Navy, which feared being moved progressively lower in the chain of command and being subordinated to a "land" view of strategic issues).

The act gave the Joint Chiefs of Staff (Army Chief of Staff, Chief of Naval Operations, and Air Force Chief of Staff) a formal legislative base, and provision was made for a modest joint staff. By the act the JCS were to serve, collectively and individually, as the primary military advisers to the President, the NSC, and the Secretary of Defense, and to act as the immediate military staff of the latter. Additionally, they were charged with ensuring coordination in defense planning, preparing strategic plans, and providing strategic and operational direction for forces in the field. Each of the Joint Chiefs wore two hats. Individually he was the senior military commander of his respective service arm and in that role he reported to the civilian secretary in the appropriate service department. Collectively, as the Joint Chiefs dealing with national defense and strategy, they had the right of direct access not only to the Secretary of Defense but also to Congress and the President.

Through the National Security Act a degree of military integration was achieved and the services were subordinated to some degree of centralized civilian coordination. But considerable independence and diversity (and uncertainty) remained. The Secretary's powers, in fact, were carefully limited, and he possessed virtually no subordinate apparatus or staff. In effect, the act created a kind of "federation" among the military services, and it left them substantial de facto autonomy within the new structure.[2] The act in particular did *not* do two things: it did not provide a unified service outlook on roles and missions (e.g., on budget allocations), and it did not avoid gaps in mission coverage or duplications of weapons systems.

---

[1] It was on the basis of this charge that covert operations later were conducted.

[2] Cecil V. Crabb, Jr., *American Foreign Policy in the Nuclear Age*, 3d ed. (New York: Harper & Row, 1972), p. 80.

2.

The Evolution of the Department of Defense

Experience with the new defense arrangements quickly led to some changes. In 1949 the act was amended, and the National Military Establishment was succeeded by the Department of Defense (DOD). The Secretary's (SecDef) powers were enlarged, the SecDef being designated as the "central figure" in coordinating the activities of the three services. New subcabinet positions were authorized including a Deputy Secretary and three assistant secretaries. The service departments were dropped from permanent seats on the NSC and placed in a second-level tier of DOD. The position of Comptroller was created giving the Secretary more control over the defense budget (and weakening that of the individual services), and more staff assistance was provided. The amendments also formally established the office of the Chairman of the JCS, the CJCS now having a permanent statutory base instead of being the President's ad hoc personal representative on the board, and the Joint Staff was more than doubled.

Meanwhile, severe interservice strife continued during 1949 and 1950, as an inadequate defense budget multiplied the effects of a deep disagreement focused on the air force B-36 versus navy attack carriers.[3] The Korean War interrupted this argument. It brought about rearmament, showed that an army and a navy were both still needed, and ended the most vociferous part of the defense debate.

More changes followed. In 1952 legislation authorized the Commandant of the Marine Corps to sit with the JCS as an equal when matters affecting the Marine Corps were on the agenda. In 1953 the Secretary's position was further enhanced by the creation of six additional Assistant Secretary positions. Steps were taken to emphasize the advice and planning tasks of the JCS while reducing their operational responsibilities. The President also made it plain that the service secretaries were to be the Secretary's operating managers, not defenders of separate service rights.

In 1958 a further major statutory reorganization occurred. The Secretary's position again was enhanced substantially, increasing significantly his authority to transfer, abolish, and consolidate military functions among the services. This new authority reflected the end of the primary service fight just noted and the beginning of a second argument—not over service *survival* but over the new missile systems. To control the problem, the Secretary of Defense was given firm authority over the key area of defense research, his role in this area being strengthened by the creation of the Office of Defense Research and Engineering. The size of the Secretary's support staff in OSD was also significantly increased, as was the JCS Joint Staff (to about 400). The trend toward functional unification also was increased. Provisions were made for establishing integrated agencies to carry out supply or service activities common to more than one military department, and unified and specified commands were authorized, sharply reducing the roles of the individual services.[4]

There have not been any large-scale reorganizations of DOD since 1958. However, a major innovation did occur in 1961 with the change in the Office of International Security Affairs (ISA). Called by some the "little State Department", ISA was tasked to orchestrate and coordinate DOD's approach to, and understanding of, the military *and political* aspects of foreign policy.

---

[3]Admiral Arthur W. Radford goes so far in his memoirs as to say that "the leaders of the Air Force had elected in 1949 to try to do away with the Navy's attack carriers . . ." Stephen Jurika, Jr., ed., *From Pearl Harbor to Vietnam: The Memoirs of Admiral Arthur W. Radford* (Stanford, Cal.: Hoover Institution Press, 1980), p. 163.

[4]A unified command consists of components from more than one service; a specified command, although assigned to a single service, has a global mission. An example of a specified command is the Strategic Air Command.

During Robert McNamara's tenure as Secretary of Defense in the Kennedy-Johnson years, ISA was very important. As McNamara and his "Whiz Kids" (young, intelligent, academically trained personnel) took control of the department and reformed its management procedures through the installation of the Planning-Programming-Budgeting-System (PPBS) and other techniques in the budget/weapons mixture/force level/contingency linkage, ISA became a major source of policy recommendations. During the Nixon-Ford-Kissinger years, it became less influential though, and although it is important today, it has not regained its former prominence.

The Carter administration did not introduce sweeping changes, but it did make a significant innovation with the establishment in 1977 of the position of Under Secretary of Defense for Policy.[5] It is this Under Secretary's task to integrate departmental plans and policies with overall national security objectives, and all the major subordinates with politico-military responsibilities report to him.[6] The emphasis given to politico-military concerns and the potential for departmental coordination achieved by the establishment of the Under Secretary's position were a step forward.

In addition to the organizational evolution of DOD into its present form, there has been a second thread running through the foregoing analysis: the immense growth in the power of the Secretary of Defense. That growth undoubtedly has been partially the result of the organizational changes we have described, but that is not the whole story. Specific Defense secretaries have left their imprints also.

Until Robert McNamara's tenure from 1961 to 1968, the Secretary's focus and influence had been relatively limited. The first Secretary of Defense, James Forrestal, was caught up in the birth pangs of the new National Military Establishment and spent most of his time in budget battles and trying to get the military to reduce interservice competition in favor of a more cooperative integrated approach. At best, he was only partly successful. Eisenhower's selections for Defense, Charles Wilson, Neil McElroy, and Thomas Gates, also were concerned primarily with budgetary issues and relations with and between the services. In these times the Secretary of Defense did not play a major role even in designing defense policy, let alone in broader national security matters.

McNamara changed all this. As was mentioned earlier, he centralized management within DOD by the installation of PPBS. A further centralizing move was his creation of an Office of Systems Analysis, a move that provided civilian decision makers with an analytical tool for judging cost comparisons of various options (and which reduced the leverage of the JCS and the military services correspondingly). Behind this expanded role, as indicated already, was the need to bring more efficiency into the nuclear and missile programs that, by their nature, could be approached on a more "joint" basis than other weapons programs. (There was no need for army and air force missiles, for example, with essentially the same strategic performance characteristics.)

This need gave McNamara entree into the problem. But McNamara's influence extended into far broader spheres. First, he had a significant impact on strategic nuclear strategy, in 1962 announcing the doctrine of counterforce, later emphasizing the need to have graduated deterrence and the capacity for flexible response, and finally playing a major role in the adoption of the doctrine of assured destruction, the doctrine that postulates that deterrence is best accomplished if the Soviet Union knows that the United States assuredly has the capacity, after absorbing a nuclear strike, to retaliate and destroy an unacceptably large portion of Russia's population and industrial capacity. But McNamara's influence extended still further, into the area of general national security policy. He was a key figure in both the Kennedy and Johnson administra-

[5]The position of Under Secretary of Defense for Research and Engineering was created at this time, also upgrading those functions.
[6]The Director of Net Assessment has a direct channel to the Secretary of Defense also.

tions' decisions concerning the Vietnam War, for example (until he began to oppose Johnson in the fall of 1967 and was asked to leave).

The trail blazed by McNamara has been followed in varying degrees by many of his successors. Melvin Laird, Nixon's first Secretary of Defense, although less influential in broad national security matters, had a significant role in the development of the policy of Vietnamization. He permitted much more latitude to the services, and controlled the Pentagon in a manner that was far less antagonistic to the military than that of his predecessor. (Partly this reflected his personal style, but it also was possible because duplication had been much reduced under McNamara.) James Schlesinger, Secretary of Defense from mid 1973 to late 1975, also was less influential than McNamara had been in broad policy matters, but Schlesinger played a critical role in the development of a new strategic doctrine. He was very influential in the development of the concept of "selective targeting options," a concept that advocated providing the capability for measured nuclear responses against a wide range of miltary targets. Carter's Secretary of Defense, Harold Brown, saw his role rather narrowly, more in train with the pre-McNamara days. Caspar Weinberger, Reagan's Secretary of Defense, became a major actor in both military and foreign policy design. Indeed, it was in part because Weinberger was so influential with the President that Secretary of State Haig resigned in June 1982.

The Secretary of Defense today has the potential to be a primary actor not only with respect to management matters within DOD and relations with and between the military services but also with respect to the design and implementation of both defense policy and foreign policy as a whole (assuming, as is true with respect to all the President's senior advisers, that this is what the President desires and the Secretary of Defense works in harmony with the team).

3.

The Intelligence Community

It is of incalculable value to policymakers to know the circumstances, intentions, and capabilities of the other parties with whom they are dealing; to be able to assess accurately the other party's concepts, content, and plans and capability for implementation. The intelligence community is supposed to provide this kind of knowledge.

Whereas before World War II the United States conducted little intelligence activity, since World War II the United States has evolved as elaborate a system as any nation except the Soviet Union. The best-known part is the Central Intelligence Agency (CIA), but as Diagram 8 shows, there are many other components to "the intelligence community." A glance at the diagram indicates that each military service maintains its own intelligence unit, to deal with specialized service needs. Yet there is also an overall Defense Intelligence Agency (established in 1961). DIA has not been very effective in controlling or coordinating the service units, though. They perceive themselves to have unique missions for which they alone are qualified.

The National Security Agency (NSA) is the second best-known intelligence unit. Created in 1952, it is occupied with communications, code making and code breaking (i.e., cryptanalysis). Added to NSA in 1972 was the Central Security Service to maximize service coordination in cryptological systems.

Diagram 8 shows the Director of Central Intelligence (DCI) at the center of the intelligence web. DCI and the Director, CIA, are one person with two functions. As Director, CIA, he is to head that agency's activities, and as DCI he is expected to coordinate the government-wide intelligence effort. In practice, different DCIs (see Table 6) have approached coordination differently. Even as Director, CIA, their styles have varied markedly, as well as their organization of CIA.

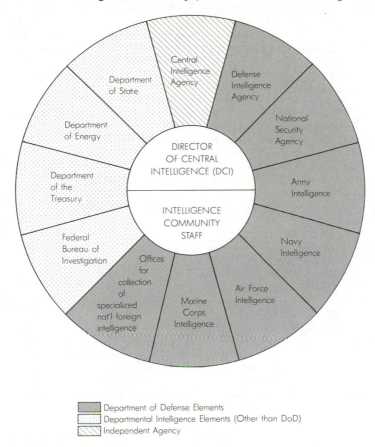

Until the advent of General Walter Bedell Smith as DCI, in late 1950, the CIA's intelligence product was of rather uneven quality. Smith made a significant change by setting up an Office of National Estimates to produce National Intelligence Estimates, or NIEs. NIEs went to the Board of National Estimates, "which reviewed the estimates, coordinated the judgments with other agencies, and negotiated their final form."[7] After being coordinated across the other agencies concerned by what for years was called the United States Intelligence Board (today the National Foreign Intelligence Board, or NFIB), the agreed NIEs would then be issued. William Colby, coming in as DCI in 1973, made the first significant change in Smith's system. Believing that the Board of National Estimates had an "ivory-tower mentality" and a certain "mind-set,"[8] he replaced the Office of National Estimates, creating instead National Intelligence Officers (NIOs) who had total individual responsibility to the DCI for particular geographical or functional assignments. NIOs then coordinated the NIEs.

The next significant change occurred under the Carter administration. Carter held the CIA in very low regard, being concerned more about the possible infringement of civil rights than in

[7]U.S., Congress, Senate, *Foreign and Military Intelligence: Book I: Final Report of the Select Committee to Study Governmental Operations with Respect to Intelligence Activities,* 94th Congress, 2nd Session, April 26, 1976, p. 104.

[8]William Colby and Peter Forbath, *Honorable Men: My Life in the CIA* (New York: Simon & Schuster, 1978), pp. 351–353.

TABLE 6 Leaders at DOD and the CIA

PRESIDENT	SECDEF		DCI	
Truman	James Forrestal	1947–1949	RADM Roscoe Hillenkoetter	1947–1950
	Louis Johnson	1949–1950		
	GEN George Marshall	1950–1951	GEN Walter Bedell Smith	1950–1952
	Robert Lovett	1951–1952		
Eisenhower	Charles Wilson	1953–1957	GEN Walter Bedell Smith	1953
	Neil McElroy	1957–1959	Allen Dulles	1953–1960
	Thomas Gates, Jr.	1959–1960		
Kennedy	Robert McNamara	1961–1963	Allen Dulles	1961
			John McCone	1961–1963
Johnson	Robert McNamara	1963–1968	John McCone	1963–1965
			VADM William Raborn (Ret)	1965–1966
	Clark Clifford	1968	Richard Helms	1966–1968
Nixon	Melvin Laird	1969–1973	Richard Helms	1969–1973
	Elliot Richardson	1973	James Schlesinger	1973
	James Schlesinger	1973–1974	William Colby	1973–1974
Ford	James Schlesinger	1974–1975	William Colby	1974–1976
	Donald Rumsfeld	1975–1976	George Bush	1976
Carter	Harold Brown	1977–1980	ADM Stansfield Turner	1977–1980
Reagan	Caspar Weinberger	1981–	William Casey	1981–

developing a high-quality intelligence product. CIA's Intelligence Directorate became a *community* asset, renamed in that role the National Foreign Assessment Center, or NFAC.[9] During Carter's regime, the CIA was the scene of much personnel turbulence. Congressional criticism of intelligence activities grew, and the U.S. intelligence product (as we shall see) suffered. The most positive development was the reconstitution of the NIO system into a corporate group, the National Intelligence Council, a move designed to upgrade the quality of NIEs.

President Reagan's DCI, OSS veteran William Casey, brought the estimates process directly under DCI supervision, separating it administratively from the rest of NFAC, and established a new coordinating body, the Intelligence Producers Council. Reagan was determined to "rebuild" U.S. intelligence capability, and this boded well for the quality of intelligence products, but whether a process in which the estimates were drafted under tight DCI control could produce an estimate that was sufficiently objective to be useful was not readily apparent.

As always in government reorganizations, we see here the endless quest for optimum organization. Diagram 9 shows arrangements as of 1984.

We have discussed how estimates are made but not yet the collection of the data on which such estimates are based. Data collection is either *overt* or *covert*. Much of CIA's intelligence collection—far more than the public assumes—is by overt methods, closely akin to procedures well known to anyone engaged in research: books, newspapers, atlases, timetables, government

[9]The discussion of organizational changes in the Carter and Reagan years relies heavily on Ray S. Cline, *The CIA Under Reagan, Bush & Casey: The Evolution of the Agency from Roosevelt to Reagan* (Washington, D.C.: Acropolis, 1981), Chaps. 6 and 7.

DIAGRAM 9 Director of Central Intelligence Command Responsibilities

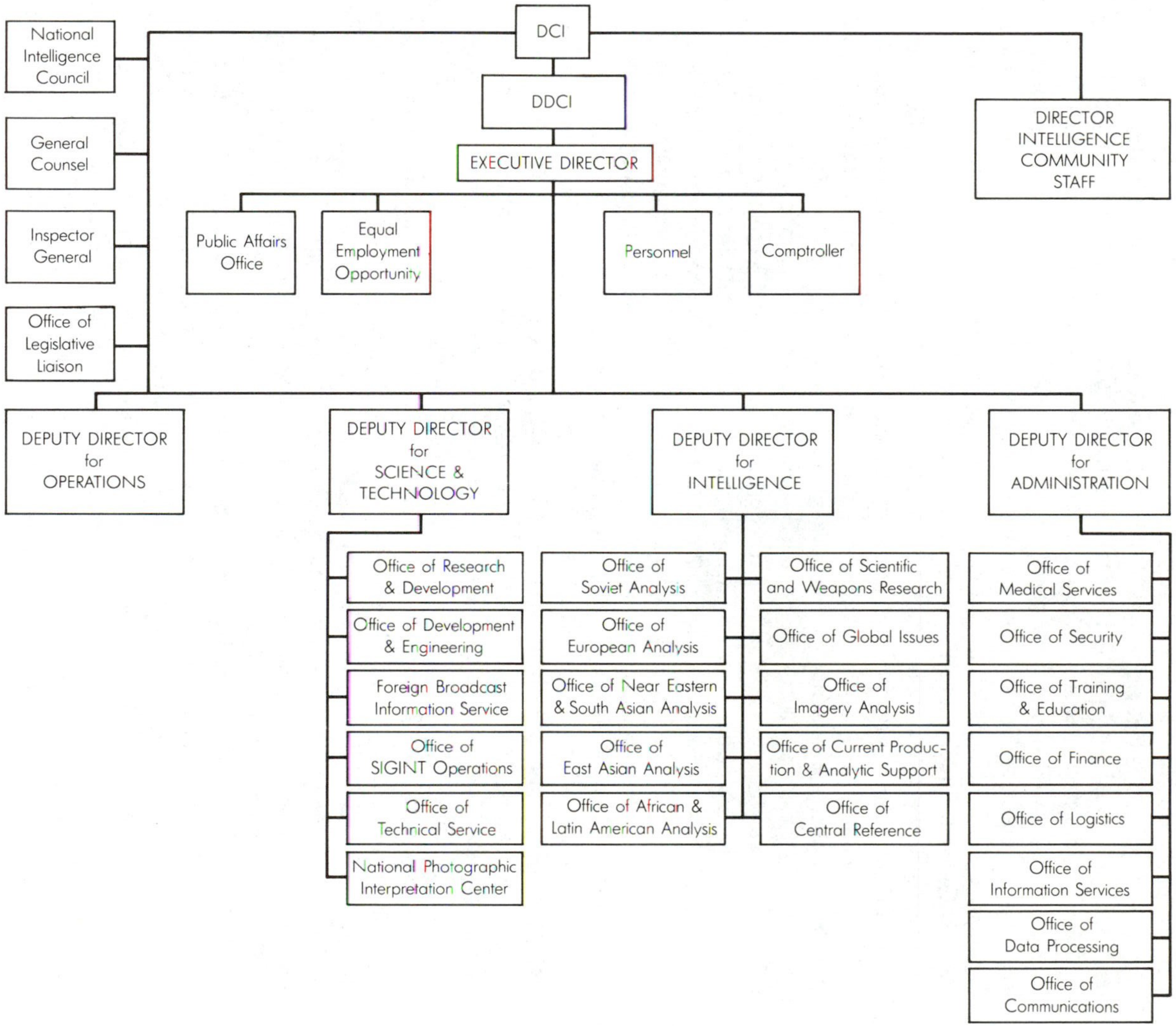

DCI

DDCI

DIRECTOR INTELLIGENCE COMMUNITY STAFF

National Intelligence Council

General Counsel

Inspector General

Office of Legislative Liaison

EXECUTIVE DIRECTOR

Public Affairs Office

Equal Employment Opportunity

Personnel

Comptroller

DEPUTY DIRECTOR for OPERATIONS

DEPUTY DIRECTOR for SCIENCE & TECHNOLOGY
- Office of Research & Development
- Office of Development & Engineering
- Foreign Broadcast Information Service
- Office of SIGINT Operations
- Office of Technical Service
- National Photographic Interpretation Center

DEPUTY DIRECTOR for INTELLIGENCE
- Office of Scientific and Weapons Research
- Office of Global Issues
- Office of Imagery Analysis
- Office of Current Production & Analytic Support
- Office of Central Reference
- Office of Soviet Analysis
- Office of European Analysis
- Office of Near Eastern & South Asian Analysis
- Office of East Asian Analysis
- Office of African & Latin American Analysis

DEPUTY DIRECTOR for ADMINISTRATION
- Office of Medical Services
- Office of Security
- Office of Training & Education
- Office of Finance
- Office of Logistics
- Office of Information Services
- Office of Data Processing
- Office of Communications

brochures, and the like, all are analyzed, and foreign broadcasts are recorded and translated. Nevertheless, what captures the public's imagination is covert collection, such as the CIA's coup in 1956 in obtaining almost immediately a copy of Khrushchev's sensational secret speech at the CPSU's 20th Party Congress, denouncing Stalinist tyranny and revamping significant ideological propositions.

A more sustained success in covert collection involved information obtained through the Berlin Tunnel, which the CIA in 1954 dug under the telephone exchange of the East German government and the Soviet army in East Berlin.[10] The details here are intriguing. The digging took four months and was "covered" by the construction taking place only a few yards away (in West Berlin) of a new U.S. Air Force radar station. Once the tunnel was finished, experts from the Bell Telephone Company were flown in to plug a CIA exchange into the East German/Soviet one. Eventually, all calls from Communist Berlin, from the Soviet Embassy, Red Army Headquarters in Pankow, the East German Ministries, and most of the private lines of key Soviet and East German leaders passed through the control of the CIA. The tunnel was staffed twenty-four hours a day with telephone tappers fluent in Russian, German, and the satellite countries' languages, and there always were maintenance men on duty. This operation produced enormous amounts of valuable military and political information, as well as yielding important insights into the character and personality of various officials. The tunnel operated very efficiently until 1956 when its presence was revealed to the Soviets by a British-Russian double agent.

Covert collection activities such as the Berlin Tunnel and the Khrushchev speech produce only a small portion of the data the CIA analyzes. As mentioned earlier, most intelligence collection activities are overt and quite prosaic. But that is not to underestimate the significance of covert collection. Certain kinds of information cannot be obtained by overt methods, and sometimes that information is extremely important. The CIA, like the KGB and other major intelligence organizations, must employ both overt and covert methods if it is to function optimally.

Between the collection of information and the production and dissemination of the finished intelligence product lie the critical functions of interpretation and assessment. These are the most agonizing problems, not collection. What does all the data mean? The intelligence community is awash in raw data; putting it together in a coherent, meaningful, and accurate manner is extremely difficult. Inevitably in this dynamic and confusing world there is a degree of ambiguity, inconsistency, and incompatibility among the indicators. Alternatively, important indicators of danger are submerged in repetitive events so that alertness is dulled. (This is what happened in Korea in 1950, and it is why North Korea's attack was a surprise.) As we have argued earlier, the meaning of any event rarely is clear. Any analyst is projecting patterns of fact and perception from the past and present into a very uncertain future, seeking to provide the basis for rational policy choices.

The CIA's record in collecting and producing useful policy-relevant intelligence has been quite good. Naturally there have been errors, some of which are well known: intelligence concluding that the Bay of Pigs landing would succeed and the misreading of the situation in Iran in 1978 and 1979 are two of the more glaring examples. But there also have been a number of notable successes, only a few of which are mentioned here.[11] We already have mentioned the Khrushchev speech and Berlin Tunnel episodes. In the early 1960s the CIA used Oleg Penkovskiy, a dissident senior Soviet military official, to obtain enormous quantities of information on Soviet military technology. This data was extremely valuable during the Cuban missile crisis.

---

[10]Information drawn from several sources. Perhaps most succinct is Leonard Mosely, *Dulles: A Biography of Eleanor, Allen, and John Foster Dulles and Their Family Network* (New York: The Dial Press, 1978), pp. 371–373.

[11]Because so much of the CIA's work is secret, the Agency does not advertise all its successes. The public record to some extent, therefore, is unbalanced, portraying the CIA in a disproportionately negative light.

Predictive estimates allowed the United States to anticipate the explosion of China's first nuclear weapon in 1964 and be ready with an appropriate statement. The CIA warned President Johnson that systematically escalated bombing against the North Vietnamese would *not* produce the results the President desired. And the list could be further extended.

Although the intelligence product generally has been quite good, three factors have prevented it from being as good as it could have been. First, there have been serious problems of coordination between the CIA and other units in the community ever since the Agency was established. Problems have been particularly acute with the units in DOD. Regrettably, the various interagency boards set up to achieve effective coordination often have been ineffective. Second, in the last decade or so there have been several major personnel disruptions. When he was DCI (see Table 6) James Schlesinger retired nearly two thousand CIA officers, many of whom were seasoned veterans. Under Stansfield Turner, President Carter's DCI, hundreds of key personnel resigned or were fired, including many at the most senior levels. Although presumably designed to eliminate "dead wood," such activities proved quite harmful to the Agency's capability and morale. It has been reported that at the time of the Iranian crisis there were at most two analysts working full time on Iran.[12] The other experts, apparently, had been fired, rotated, or "encouraged" to resign. Clearly the CIA's poor performance in the crisis was in part a result of personnel disruptions. Third, because of the shattering of the foreign policy consensus that had been widely shared for so long, the revelations about specific operations and intelligence abuses (discussed later), and the widespread public and congressional disenchantment with U.S. foreign policy in general and the intelligence community in particular, the reputation of the CIA and related agencies sank to an all-time low. Effective intelligence work, hard in the best of circumstances, becomes extremely difficult in such a situation.

4.

The Cloak-and-Dagger Issue: Covert Operations

Covert operations, naturally, are not only the most interesting to the public; they are also the most controversial part of CIA activity.

Covert operations began in 1947. When the Korean War broke out there was an expansion of covert activities worldwide, and with the advent of the Eisenhower administration covert operations expanded even further. Allen Dulles, Eisenhower's DCI, believed covert operations were an essential part of the "Free World" struggle against communism. Several "successes" were achieved, such the CIA-assisted coup against Premier Mohammed Mossadegh in Iran in 1953 (which paved the way for the restoration of the Shah) and the aid provided in 1954 in the overthrow of President Arbenz Guzman in Guatemala. (In each case, the CIA was acting under orders from higher authorities). In 1955, NSC directive 5412 stipulated that the DCI would consult with an NSC subcommittee and obtain its approval for all major covert operations. For the first time "designated representatives" of the President, Secretary of State, and Secretary of Defense were brought into the process. The Special Group, as the committee became known, now became the primary unit for approving covert activities. Importantly though, projects that were not major or politically sensitive, nor paramilitary in nature, or were low-cost and low-risk, did not have to be submitted. And of those that were submitted and approved, not all were brought to the President's attention.

---

[12]Michael Ledeen and William Lewis, *Debacle: The American Failure in Iran* (New York: Alfred A. Knopf, 1981), p. 132.

In the 1960s the number of covert operations increased again. Most were small-scale, such as channeling monies and information to non-Communist labor unions or political parties or encouraging leftist groups and individuals to find democratic alternatives to Communist organizations. A few were larger, and some, such as the Bay of Pigs, were colossal failures.[13] Under President Kennedy two new NSC subcommittees were created, their purposes being to oversee counterinsurgency work and to develop a program to overthrow Fidel Castro. These joined the Special Group that was already in operation. Soon after Lyndon Johnson became President the Special Group was renamed the 303 Committee and Kennedy's new subcommittees were disbanded. With the focus shifting to the Vietnam War, covert activities became concentrated on that conflict. Most major decisions now were made in the Tuesday Lunch Bunch, not the 303 Committee, however. Low-cost, low-risk operations continued to be carried out within SOPs, and were not submitted on a case-by-case basis.

In early 1970 the 40 Committee became the agency responsible for approving all major and/or politically sensitive covert operations proposals. Chaired by the Assistant for National Security Affairs, it also had as members the DCI, CJCS, and the number-two men in State and Defense. In 1972 the CIA's Directorate for Plans was renamed the Directorate for Operations. Large-scale covert activities continued, the more prominent involving the ongoing covert military campaign in Southeast Asia and (unsuccessful) efforts to influence elections in Chile.

A number of investigations of intelligence activities were launched in the early and mid 1970s, both in and out of government. The frequency, extent, and scope of covert activities revealed shocked the sensibilities of many and (as pointed out in Chapter 6) resulted in several actions by Congress to increase its oversight role. Occurring amid the widespread public, congressional, and media disenchantment and suspicion of the time, it produced another important effect: a significant decline in the number of covert operations.

The investigations also raised the issue of whether the CIA had strayed into illegal, domestic operations. It now seems that the widely publicized charges of "massive illegal" operations circulating at the time were exaggerated, but there is no doubt that some illegal activities had taken place. Many Americans were upset, too, over revelations of the extent to which private citizens, going abroad, were utilized for minor intelligence activities—such as "debriefings." The revelations also showed that the *President* was not always briefed. The Hughes-Ryan Amendment, discussed earlier, was the main consequence. Congress *required* that the President be notified of impending major covert actions approved by NSC committees. Political assassination also now was flatly ruled out, domestic surveillance was severely restricted, and mail intercepts were largely precluded.

As we have seen, reflecting the widespread conceptual consensus that existed for more than two decades, the CIA was extensively utilized by senior policymakers to help contain the Communist bloc, both through the collection and production of useful information and through covert operations. The shattering of that consensus, specific revelations, and the general disenchantment of the times led to changes that have somewhat restricted the community's operations and tightened command and control procedures. But the world goes on. Vast quantities of high-quality information are needed for effective policy, most modern states have elaborate intelligence services, a country without such is at a considerable disadvantage, and covert activities are still widely used in international relations. Although the exact nature of the structure and functions of the ideal intelligence community are matters of debate, the need for a strong intelligence capability is not.

---

[13]The Bay of Pigs was not just a *CIA* failure. *All* the President's advisers supported the operation, and the President himself gave the go-ahead.

How Washington Makes Foreign Policy

5.

National Security Decision Making and Presidential Styles

The President's preeminent role has been emphasized often in these pages. But presidents vary greatly in how they have played that role, in how they have utilized the national security machinery we have been discussing.

President Truman, as the first chief executive to work with the national security machinery, took an initially cautious role, making it clear that the NSC was advisory only. The Korean War produced a change. Previously, Truman had attended less than a fourth of NSC meetings; now all major recommendations came to him through the council, and he presided over all regularly held meetings. But Truman still stressed that *he* had ultimate authority.

President Eisenhower, with his army background, naturally thought in terms of staff work. His approach was structured, formal, and systematic. Clear lines of responsibility and authority were set up. The aim was a "staff solution," based on consensus, with the President not participating in the process until the staff work was completed. In 1953, President Eisenhower appointed Robert Cutler, a Boston banker, to the newly created post of Special Assistant for National Security Affairs—a post made famous later by Henry Kissinger. Cutler was the channel by which NSC business came to the President.

Although the President was satisfied, and policy recommendations were generally well coordinated and integrated, the Eisenhower system had the disadvantage that it often produced severely watered-down alternatives. It also created a vast "paper mill," churning out policies that often were obsolete. (And not all business, even so, went through regular NSC channels, for "special NSC meetings" were held to deal with current problems, and Secretary of State John Foster Dulles worked directly with the President, bypassing the NSC.)

President Kennedy, with a vastly different personality from "Ike's," and an activist in every sense, could not abide the cumbersome NSC machinery he inherited. He injected himself directly into the process at various stages instead of waiting for problems to be brought to him. Choosing McGeorge Bundy for the Cutler post, Kennedy opted for a "single, small, but strongly organized staff" that would "assist *me* in obtaining advice from, and coordinating operations of, the government agencies concerned with national security."[14] Kennedy also dismantled Eisenhower's NSC subunits (the Planning Board and the Operations Coordinating Board).

The Bay of Pigs fiasco of April 1961 strengthened Kennedy's distrust of formal NSC procedures. (From his point of view, the operation had been very formally approved, with all the appropriate officials present and no one opposing the plan. But in fact the plan had been so closely held that the lower-level staffing was inadequate. In any event, the failure increased his determination to exert personal control.) Disenchanted with the State Department, Kennedy turned more and more to his personal staff, with Special Assistant Bundy playing a key role. With the President's blessings, Bundy even established the principle that virtually all memoranda to the President from State would reach him only after preparation of a cover memo by the NSC staff. At the same time as State's role declined precipitously, DOD, under Secretary of Defense McNamara, achieved a degree of autonomy and policy influence that would not have been possible under Eisenhower. Of course, there were still formal NSC meetings, but they were not occasions of much import.

Kennedy also produced two other changes. First, he broadened the advisory process by obtaining inputs from individuals other than the usual foreign policy advisers. Midlevel special-

[14]Press Release, President-elect John F. Kennedy, January 1, 1961 (emphasis added).

ists at State or DOD often received a telephone call directly from the Oval Office. Old friends, relatives, and a number of academics also had a line to the White House. Second, he put together ad hoc crisis management groups, the best known being the "Ex Comm" of the Cuban missile crisis.[15]

President Johnson, like Kennedy, believed more in personal relations than in elaborate machinery. Key decisions in his time were made by the "Tuesday Lunch Bunch": the President, Secretary Rusk, Secretary McNamara, the Special Assistant, and (later) the presidential press secretary, the DCI, and the CJCS. This small group, unlike Kennedy's freewheeling type, was essentially permanent and closed.

But Johnson, like Eisenhower, sought staff consensus, and demanded teamwork and loyalty. He also revamped the formal NSC machinery. In March 1966, through National Security Action Memo 341, he created a two-tier committee system for the NSC. At the top was a permanent interagency committee called the Senior Interdepartmental Group or SIG. Chaired by the Under Secretary of State, in theory the SIG was to have the power of decision. To support the SIG a number of Interdepartmental Regional Groups (IRGs) were established, chaired by the appropriate Assistant Secretaries of State. In practice though, because of the role of the Lunch Bunch, Johnson's style, and the pressures produced by the Vietnam War, the SIG-IRG system never really got off the ground.

Johnson's approach to national security policymaking left much to be desired. The NSC was reduced to a shell, playing almost no role in either policy design or implementation. The closed nature of the Tuesday Lunch Bunch and its operations (and the widely shared strategic consensus prevailing therein) precluded the reception of information from "unfriendly" sources, prevented critical (re)examination of current assumptions and policies, and wholly eliminated the consideration of certain types of policy orientations. And the SIG-IRG system never functioned as designed, neither Johnson nor Rusk giving it much support.

President Nixon was determined to "restore the National Security Council to its preeminent role in national security planning." Nixon's experience in the Eisenhower administration had a significant impact on his approach. He believed that the apparatus should be highly structured, and a clear line of authority and responsibility should be established. But Nixon differed from Eisenhower in that instead of seeking policy consensus and agreed recommendations Nixon wanted "real options" from which he could choose. To accomplish Nixon's objectives, an elaborate network of interagency NSC support committees was created at two levels: NSC subcommittees at the Deputy Secretary level, and Interdepartmental Groups (IGs) at the Assistant Secretary level (see Diagram 10).

There were seven principal NSC subcommittees: the Senior Review Group (SRG), the Under Secretaries Committee (USC), the National Security Council Intelligence Committee (NSCIC), the 40 Committee, the Verification Panel, the Washington Special Actions Group (WSAG), and the Defense Program Review Committee. NSCIC provided guidance to the intelligence community; the 40 Committee handled covert operations; the WSAG dealt with crisis management; the Defense Program Review Committee assessed the impact of changes in the defense budget; and the Verification Panel monitored arms control agreements and provided advice on arms control negotiations.

The key policymaking committees were the SRG and USC. The process worked something like this. The President would order a National Security Study Memorandum (NSSM). The NSSM would identify the problem, set a deadline for completion of the project, call for various

[15]The "ExComm" membership was not drawn exclusively from NSC membership. For example, it included former Secretary of State Dean Acheson. And Acheson, in Truman's time, chaired a "Special Committee" of the NSC that included others such as President Dwight D. Eisenhower of Columbia University. Dean Acheson, *Present at the Creation* (New York: Norton, 1969), pp. 314–315.

DIAGRAM 10 Nixon National Security Council Structure

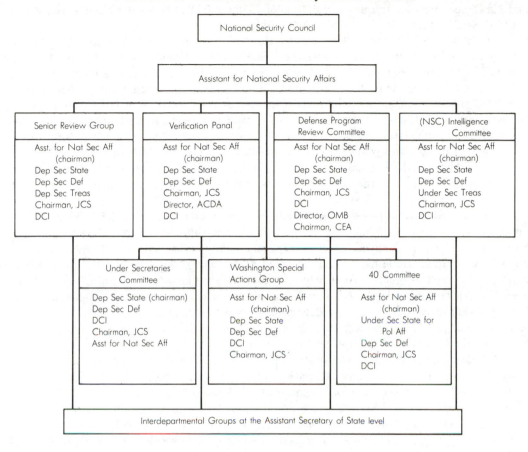

DIAGRAM 10 Nixon National Security Council Structure

options and their pros and cons, and assign the project to a specific IG. When the study was finished it was moved from the IG to the SRG for review. The SRG would determine whether the study met the President's requirements and fully considered the various options and their attendant costs and benefits. If it did not, it was redone. If it did it was forwarded for debate at a formal NSC meeting. After the debate ended the President would take time to reflect on the study, sometimes consulting with individual NSC members privately. When a presidential decision was made, it was published as a National Security Decision Memorandum (NSDM). Overseeing implementation of the NSDM was the responsibility of the USC or Under Secretaries Committee, although unless a problem surfaced it was assumed that the line agencies were executing appropriately.

The Nixon-Kissinger system (as originally conceived) was a distinct improvement over its predecessors, emphasizing as it did the systematic analysis of problems and the presentation of options for presidential choice. The SIG of the Johnson era reappeared as the SRG, but now it was an integral part of the NSC system, a major plus. The USC, chaired by the Deputy Secretary of State, brought the State Department into the coordination picture but did so within the parameters of the revitalized NSC.

But there were two serious deficiencies. First, the system depended far too much on one man: Henry Kissinger, the Assistant for National Security Affairs, was chairman of most of the NSC committees, and a member of the others. The system simply could not operate without Kissinger, and his influence soon became overwhelming. Second, in practice the NSC system quickly fell into disuse. Although a large number of NSSMs were ordered in Nixon's first year and NSC meetings were frequent, by the end of 1970 a policymaking inner circle of two existed and the NSC as such was relatively unimportant.

President Ford did not alter drastically the NSC system he had inherited from Nixon, although he did institute a few changes. The NSCIC was abolished and the 40 Committee was replaced by an upgraded Operations Advisory Group. The Defense Program Review Committee was renamed the Defense Review Panel, and the Secretary of Defense became its chairman. A new NSC subcommittee, the International Energy Review Group, was established, chaired by the Assistant for National Security Affairs. To provide a greater range of inputs and to obtain some critical perspective on his performance, every six or seven weeks President Ford met with seven long-term associates who were free to speak their minds. And in November 1975, Kissinger, who had been both National Security Adviser and Secretary of State since being named to the latter post by Nixon in the fall of 1973, was replaced as National Security Adviser by Lt. General Brent Scowcroft (USAF).

But the NSC system failed to function effectively under Ford as Henry Kissinger retained his preeminence in the policy process. Ford had little foreign affairs background before becoming President and stressed the need for continuity and stability amid the turmoil of Watergate and Nixon's resignation. Quite naturally Ford relied heavily on the in-place expert, Henry Kissinger,[16] and the replacement of Kissinger by General Scowcroft changed very little. Scowcroft had been Kissinger's deputy on the NSC staff, and was a "Kissinger man." Although Ford's style was somewhat more open than his predecessor's, the policymaking atmosphere was considerably less tense, and the NSC did meet more frequently than it had since the early years of Nixon's first term, the NSC's impact in this period was minimal.

President Carter tried to restore more authority to line departments and agencies, while still using the NSC "to integrate and facilitate foreign policy decisions."[17] He reduced the NSC committees to two: a Policy Review Committee (PRC) and a Special Coordination Committee (SCC). The PRC was for long-term projects and changed chairman with the topic assigned; the SCC was always chaired by the National Security Assistant. The scheme was for either of the two bodies, when tasked through a Presidential Review Memorandum or PRM, to establish working groups (such as an IG) to provide a paper to the parent body, and then, under National Security Adviser Zbigniew Brzezinski's direction, process the study up to the President who would issue a Presidential Directive or PD, to implement.

In crises this procedure was streamlined. Robert Hunter describes the operation of the SCC during the Iranian hostage crisis as follows:

> Throughout the hostage crisis, the SCC met at 9:00 a.m.—at first daily, later less frequently—with an agenda coordinated within the government by the NSC staff in the early hours of the morning. Discussion was brisk, options were presented . . . and recommendations were . . . formulated for presidential decision. . . . Soon after the SCC adjourned . . . an NSC-drafted synopsis of discussion with recommendations for action was sent to the president, and, with his concurrence or change, was promptly put into action. Subcommittees of the SCC worked on specialized parts of the problem. The State Department Iranian Working Group worked around the clock for all 444 days and fed information back and forth and coordinated the

---

[16]President Ford, in his memoirs, *A Time to Heal* (New York: Harper & Row, 1979), p. 30, records telephoning Kissinger: "Henry, I need you. The country needs you. I want you to stay. I'll do everything I can to work with you."

"There will be no problem," Kissinger responded. "Sir, it is my job to get along with you and not yours to get along with me."

[17]Presidential Directive/NSC-2 January 20, 1977, quoted in U.S., Congress, Senate, Committee on Foreign Relations, Hearing, *The National Security Adviser: Role and Accountability,* 96th Cong., 2nd sess., April 17, 1980, p. 81.

massive amount of regular diplomatic effort; the results of the day's labors were reported back; new wrinkles in the crisis were assessed; and the SCC was ready to act again the next morning.[18]

Things are never quite as simple as they appear on paper.

In many respects the Carter NSC system was not much different from its predecessor. True, the number of NSC committees had been reduced substantially. But, as under Kissinger, the committees had virtually identical membership, the name being changed according to the issue being considered. And although the names of the documents were different, the process itself was pretty much the same. And when a crisis developed, as before, the elaborately constructed procedural design bore little resemblance to what actually was done. But there was one positive change: the separation of the chairman of the PRC and the SCC, and its rotation in the PRC. This was important, since it prevented any one person from dominating the process, as Kissinger clearly had done, and it broadened the advisory process considerably.

The Carter system also exhibited some deficiencies. There was no interagency group whose prime responsibility was to make sure that the PDs actually were effectively implemented; in practice, clear distinctions were not always made between short- and long-range projects, causing jurisdictional problems between the PRC and SCC. Often the PDs that emerged did not provide clear guidance to the agencies responsible for implementation.

Like many of his predecessors, President Carter often operated through small decision groups outside the formal NSC structure. There were regular Friday morning planning breakfasts with Secretary of State Vance, National Security Adviser Zbigniew Brzezinski, Vice-President Mondale, and Secretary of Defense Harold Brown (with others being added if the issue being discussed called for it), and working lunches with Vance, Brzezinski, and Brown (who regularly lunched together on Thursdays without the President). And crises often were handled outside the NSC structure (often with members of the White House staff playing major roles).

Carter, like Lyndon Johnson, was handicapped by a lack of knowledge of foreign affairs. As a consequence, he relied heavily on National Security Assistant Brzezinski, who had frequent daily access to the President. In his memoirs Carter describes his contacts with Brzezinski this way:

> My first scheduled meeting in the Oval Office each day was with National Security Adviser Zbigniew Brzezinski, when he brought me the Presidential Daily Briefing . . . from the intelligence community. I would see him several times during the day at different hours, and in times of crisis he was either at my side or coordinating meetings with my Cabinet officers and other leaders in the Situation Room, the isolated and permanently secured compartment on the floor below the Oval Office.[19]

Originally Carter had hoped to restore the Secretary of State as primary foreign policy adviser and coordinator (subject to the President's authority, of course). The Assistant for National Security Affairs was to have a lower profile, providing confidential advice without regard to constituency and directing the NSC system. He was to act primarily as a facilitator and coordinator, not as a policy architect or advocate.

But this ideal seldom was realized. Very quickly, Brzezinski came to play a major role in both policy design and implementation. Because the President failed to exercise effective lead-

---

[18]Robert Hunter, *Presidential Control of Foreign Policy: Management or Mishap?*, The Washington Papers, no. 91, The Center for Strategic and International Studies, Georgetown University (New York: Praeger, 1982), pp. 45–46. As we will see later, although the SCC met regularly, because it received little presidential direction its effectiveness was limited.

[19]Jimmy Carter, *Keeping Faith: Memoirs of a President* (New York: Bantam, 1982), p. 51.

ership, many times a discordant cacophony of views was heard, the President going one way, Vance a second, and Brzezinski yet a third. Over time, Brzezinski's influence increased greatly, and on many occasions he rather than the Secretary of State spoke for the Carter administration. Vance, although maintaining a degree of policy impact in matters of secondary interest and chairing PRC studies on a number of long-range problems, found that on major issues his views only occasionally carried any weight with the President. His power declining more and more, in 1980 Vance resigned because of his disagreement with the President's decision, supported by Brzezinski, to use force to try to rescue the American hostages in Iran.[20] Vance's successor, Edmund Muskie, was no more influential.

President Reagan took office firmly convinced that the Carter foreign policy had been weak, ineffectual, and confused; strong leadership, Reagan believed, was necessary to reverse America's decline. Reagan was convinced that the policymaking process would have to be altered significantly if this objective was to be achieved. Like many others before him, President Reagan wanted the Secretary of State (General Haig) to be the President's principal foreign policy adviser, and upon taking office Reagan made an announcement to this effect (as we saw earlier, this also was what Haig wanted). Richard Allen was appointed Assistant for National Security Affairs. In contrast to the roles performed by his predecessors, Allen, in fact, did act primarily as a coordinator, leaving major policymaking functions to others.

In January 1982 Allen resigned, and was replaced by Deputy Secretary of State William P. Clark, a trusted friend and adviser of President Reagan since the President's political career began in California. The new National Security Adviser played a much more vigorous role in policy formulation. And whereas Allen had reported to the President through the Counselor to the President, Edwin Meese, Clark had direct access and briefed President Reagan daily. In his January 12, 1982, statement concerning the NSC structure, the President explained the new Assistant's role this way:

> The Assistant to the President for National Security Affairs, in consultation with the regular members of the NSC, shall be responsible for developing, coordinating, and implementing national security policy as approved by me. He shall determine and publish the agenda of NSC meetings. He shall ensure that the necessary papers are prepared and—except in unusual circumstances—distributed in advance to Council members. He shall staff and administer the National Security Council.
>
> Decision documents shall be prepared by the Assistant to the President for National Security Affairs, and disseminated by him after approval by the President.[21]

In October 1983, Reagan unexpectedly named Clark to succeed the controversial James Watt as Secretary of the Interior, replacing him with Deputy Security Adviser Robert McFarlane. McFarlane, who had previous military and NSC staff experience, immediately announced that he saw the National Security Adviser's primary function to be policy coordination. McFarlane intended to act as a facilitator; policy *design* was to be left to others. Whether over time he would be content with such a role, and whether that would remain the President's desire also, only time would tell.

Reagan also believed that the NSC committee system needed restructuring. The new system remained three-tiered as it had been since Lyndon Johnson's time, but the number of principal subcommittees was enlarged from two to three: the Senior Interagency Group–Foreign Policy (SIG-FP), the Senior Interagency Group–Defense Policy (SIG-DP), and the Senior Interagency Group–Intelligence (SIG-I). (See Diagram 11.) The SIGs were to ensure that

---

[20]The interested reader can compare the memoirs of Carter, Brzezinski, and Vance, all being now available.

[21]U.S., The White House, Office of the Press Secretary, *Statement by the President,* January 12, 1982.

DIAGRAM 11 Reagan National Security Council Structure

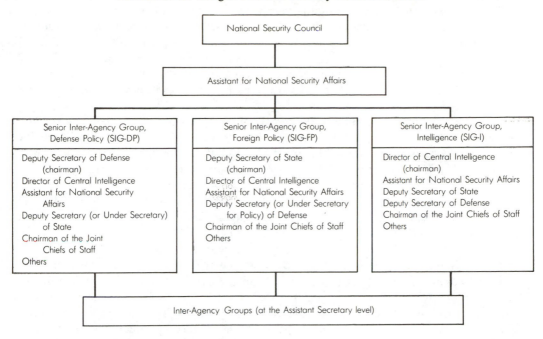

issues within their areas requiring interagency consideration received immediate careful attention. They were to establish objectives, develop options, and make recommendations to the NSC in their respective areas, and they were to monitor policy implementation.

The composition of and relationships within the SIGs reflected Reagan's view of the advantages and disadvantages of previous structures. Like Nixon and Ford but unlike Carter, Reagan did not include the Secretary of State or Secretary of Defense on the major subcommittees. Reagan wanted them free from such responsibilities to operate at a higher level or in other capacities. But unlike the Nixon-Ford period and similar to Carter, Reagan did not believe in a single chair. This was in part the result of his desire to short-circuit any possibility of dominance by one person, but it also had the objective of ensuring the influence of the functional experts. Thus SIG-FP was chaired by the Deputy Secretary of State (or Under Secretary), SIG-DP was chaired by the Deputy Secretary of Defense (or Under Secretary for Policy), and SIG-I was chaired by the DCI.

The third level in the Reagan NSC system consisted of regional or functional interagency groups established under the SIGs. Their functions were to prepare papers for SIG consideration and to prepare contingency plans pertaining to potential crises in their area of expertise. Membership and chair were to be determined by subject matter, but the appropriate Assistant Secretary or equivalent always would be in attendance.

The process was to work more or less as follows. Issues could be initiated either by the NSC staff or by the President. Once initiated the issue was worked through the IG/SIG process and then forwarded. When the issue reached the NSC agenda, discussions were held, minutes taken, and if advice was perceived necessary a Decision Memorandum was formulated for the President. Because he controlled the NSC staff and memorandum formulation, the NSA (Allen or Clark, or later McFarlane) held a key position in this process. Usually the President would make a decision after the formal NSC meeting, in consultation with his key advisers. If a formal decision statement was deemed necessary, a National Security Decision Directive (NSDD) was to be issued (replacing the PD of the Carter system).

There was one other major change: crisis management was removed from the direction of the NSA. But it was not controlled by the Secretary of State, as advocated by many who had objected to the influence of previous National Security assistants. In the Reagan administration, the crisis management group was chaired by Vice-President George Bush.

In the Reagan system the successor to the PRM was the National Security Study Directive (NSSD), but few actually were issued and the NSC committee system was used only sporadically. The NSC itself, however, met often, with frank interchanges occurring. On this level the system worked reasonably well.

Reagan's decision-making style bore some resemblance to some of his predecessors, but the composite was uniquely his own. Like Kennedy, Reagan was a confident, action-oriented President who tended toward an informal approach that would cut through red tape and minimize delay. But unlike Kennedy, Reagan did not want to be immersed in detail, believing that this would distract him from the more important matters. More in the pattern of Eisenhower, Reagan preferred to deal only with fundamental issues, leaving the detail to subordinates. Like Ike, Reagan delegated enormous amounts of authority to trusted advisers, especially to the "troika" of Counselor to the President, Edwin Meese, White House Chief of Staff James Baker, and Deputy Chief Michael Deaver. Most routine decisions were made by some combination of the Secretary of State, DCI, the Secretary of Defense, and the "troika." Operating at a slightly higher level was an informal National Security Planning Group consisting of the Vice-President, DCI, Defense and State secretaries, and the troika, the Vice-President's inclusion giving the group more clout. Only the most fundamental choices were made by President Reagan himself.

The Reagan administration, like many before it, was marked by a deterioration of relations between the President and the Secretary of State, as discussed at some length in Chapter 9. The replacement of Haig by George Schultz improved the climate somewhat, but competition for the President's ear remained vigorous. It was clear that the administration was having trouble settling on its priorities—as we shall see in Part Four.

6.

American Policy, the Shah, and Khomeini: A Study in Confusion.

Throughout our analysis of the American foreign policy system, in Chapters 6–9, as well as here in Chapter 10, we stressed that the President is the central figure in the policymaking process and must provide clear leadership if the machinery is to function efficiently and policy is to be optimum in both design and implementation. When such leadership is not provided, major problems develop. Few examples illustrate the point more vividly than United States policy in the first phase of the Iranian crisis.

As explained in more detail in Chapter 19, by the early 1970s United States policy toward the Persian Gulf rested on the so-called "twin pillars" of Iran and Saudi Arabia. With the direct commitment of American strength overseas less feasible than in earlier days because of the war in Vietnam, Teheran and Riyadh were viewed as surrogate keys to maintaining stability in the Persian Gulf.

The Carter administration, like its predecessors, believed that Iran was firmly under the Shah's control. If there was any concern in Washington it was that the Shah might be too powerful. Almost no one in Washington expected trouble to develop, as was illustrated by President Carter during his visit to Teheran at the end of 1977 when he expressed his pleasure at being on a "stable island" in a turbulent world sea.

Throughout 1977 and early 1978, although there were indications of discontent in Iran, Washington minimized their significance. The major components of the intelligence community were especially categorical in this opinion. The CIA in August made an assessment that was typical, stating that Iran "is not in a revolutionary or even a prerevolutionary situation."[22] The military was loyal to the Shah and the opposition did not have the power to be more than troublesome, it was said. But the intelligence community's assessments were wrong; the advisory process was not working. In September 1978 mass demonstrations occurred, and soon order threatened to disintegrate entirely. Warnings of the gravity of the situation from U.S. Ambassador to Iran William Sullivan, Israeli intelligence, and Anwar Sadat had not received the attention they deserved.

But the Carter administration remained confident. Earlier when the Shah had professed concern, Carter had assured him that America would "back him" all the way. This was still the President's position. But what this would mean in practice was unclear. Given Carter's moralistic inclinations it was extremely unlikely that the United States would intervene directly in Iran, and several times Carter had emphasized to the Shah the importance of improving the human-rights situation and the necessity of resolving the dispute peacefully.

There was another complicating factor: within the U.S. bureaucracy great divergencies soon developed, both in assessing the situation and in proposing what should be done. Led by the Bureau of Human Rights, many in the State Department were antagonistic toward the Shah on human rights grounds; these officials wanted U.S. support to be conditional upon changes in the Shah's domestic policies, and they would not have opposed his downfall. Others at State, less ideologically motivated, simply believed that the Shah's days were numbered so that some compromise with the opposition was only prudent. On the other side of the fence the NSC staff, led by National Security Assistant Brzezinski, believed that there was no palatable alternative to the Shah, United States credibility was on the line, and the Shah's downfall would send the wrong signals to both friends and allies of the United States. By the early fall of 1978 then, Iran was near revolution, Washington did not know it, the foreign policy apparatus was divided, and it was unclear how far the President's pledge to back the Shah would be implemented.

Throughout the fall the situation deteriorated further; each time major incidents occurred the Shah made concessions, but they were too little and too late. Gradually the opposition began to coalesce around the exiled religious leader, Ayatollah Khomeini. CIA analysts were tragically unfamiliar with Khomeini's views, not even possessing copies of his writings; the State Department was in no position to give competent advice either, seemingly determined to dismiss any evidence that the Shah's opposition could be antagonistic to American interests. UN Ambassador Andrew Young went so far as to call Khomeini "a saint."

The Shah was increasingly disturbed by the contradictory signals coming from Washington, and with good reason; he had as many opponents as allies there. To counter the negative views, on November 3 Brzezinski called the Shah directly, assuring him that Washington would back him to the hilt. Discovering with some asperity that the State Department was preparing a cable to the ambassador instructing him to advise the Shah to transfer considerable power to a coalition government, Brzezinski was able to have the cable cancelled.[23] But Vance, Sullivan, and most other key officials at State now believed that a major change was necessary; the Shah either had to be removed or have his power diminished greatly.

[22]Carter, *Keeping Faith,* p. 438. Remember that this was a CIA many of whose key personnel had recently been fired or "encouraged" to resign by DCI Stansfield Turner. Moreover, because of Carter's aversion to clandestine activities the agency's covert collection capabilities had declined precipitously. Before the Carter administration it had been common practice to penetrate dissident groups such as those opposing the Shah, but under Carter the practice had been cut back drastically.

[23]Ledeen and Lewis, *Debacle,* p. 159.

The NSC system at this time was operative in name only. Although SCC meetings were held, the President did not take an active role, and without any clear guidance from the Oval Office the committee floundered. As time went on the conflict between State and NSC became even more heated. To a considerable extent Brzezinski was able to prevent State participation in high-level consultations, but this led to a flood of leaks from State to the press. The President, meanwhile, seemed indecisive. At a press conference on December 7, when asked if he thought the Shah could remain on the throne, the best Carter could answer was "I don't know, I hope so." This was something, he said, that was in the hands of the Iranian people. At the Embassy Ambassador Sullivan was without instructions. Later he wrote: "During the weeks when I was meeting regularly with the Shah and reporting the results of our conversations to Washington, I received no specific political guidance about the attitude of the government of the United States."[24] But perhaps the incident that illustrated Washington's policy confusion most graphically was the dispatching on December 29 of the aircraft carrier *Constellation* and a small task force to the Indian Ocean, only to have it turn around five days later.

The confusion that was so evident in Washington had prompted Energy Secretary James Schlesinger earlier to recommend that the President dispatch a personal representative to the Shah to clear things up. Such a mission, Schlesinger felt, was necessary also to ensure that the Iranian military stayed in line. If the army stopped supporting the Shah, it was all over. Schlesinger thought that Brzezinski should be the special emissary. Brzezinski liked the idea but said send Schlesinger.

Carter recognized the military's importance in Iran but he was not the least interested in authorizing a mission that might imply U.S. intervention or support for a military solution. Full backing for the Shah did not mean that. So while accepting the idea of a special emissary, rather than choosing Brzezinski or Schlesinger, both of whom really wanted to back the Shah all the way, Carter chose General Robert Huyser. Huyser, unencumbered by any specialized knowledge of Iran or familiarity with the details of the crisis, and not being hampered by close contacts with anyone in the Iranian government, was charged to report what "really" was going on (Carter no longer trusted Sullivan's reports) and to demonstrate America's support for the Iranian military. At the same time, Huyser was to make it clear that the United States would not intervene directly.

The Shah by this point was thoroughly confused. About the only thing that was certain was that his American ally, despite its verbal support, had no intention of coming to his rescue. Taking this into account, with the loyalty of his army uncertain and unrest rampant, on January 16, 1979, the Shah left the country.

The situation now disintegrated rapidly. The government of Shahpour Bakhtiar, which the Shah had appointed at the first of the year, had little popular support, and more and more the masses were turning to Khomeini. Despite Huyser's constantly optimistic reports, which were based largely on (mis)information obtained almost exclusively from generals in the Iranian military, support for Bakhtiar was declining in the military also. Though Ambassador Sullivan's reports told a very different story, Carter paid them little heed, convinced they were shaped more by Sullivan's desire to reach a compromise with Khomeini than by a desire to report objectively.

But, in fact, Sullivan was close to the mark. Conditions continued to deteriorate and in February Huyser was recalled. Soon it was over. The President saw his worst fears realized as Khomeini returned to Iran and set up the Islamic Republic, determined to eliminate all vestiges of American influence in Iran.

We can see that the most basic failure of the United States in this crisis was its inability to settle on step 4 of policy implementation, which, in turn, traced back to conceptual (or design)

---

[24]William H. Sullivan, *Mission to Iran* (New York: Norton, 1981), p. 191.

difficulties. What to do about the problem turned on what the problem *was*. Were the Shah and his policies the problem? Or the unrest, to be put down?

Carter had four basic orientations from which to choose. First, offer complete support for the Shah. This was Brzezinski's choice. Of course, ultimately, this choice might have required massive involvement and/or support for a military solution. Second, help mediate a negotiated compromise involving some reduction in the Shah's power and the formation of some kind of coalition. For pragmatic reasons, Vance and several others felt this was the best outcome possible given the circumstances. Third, oppose the Shah indirectly and perhaps aid in his removal. This was favored by some in State's Bureau of Human Rights. Fourth, avoid taking a stand and just make the best of whatever happened. Given the American propensity for action, this was never seriously considered (though some observers think this was the actual effect of Carter's policies). Because the President never made up his mind entirely on the problem faced (and therefore which of these four orientations to pursue), the results were abysmal.

Our analysis has shown clearly that American policy in the first phase of the Iranian crisis (the second phase being the hostage crisis) was confusing and ineffectual. It was imperative in the circumstances confronted that the President provide effective leadership both in designing an appropriate policy and in settling on the best means for its implementation. He could do this only if he was guided by a coherent, valid, and appropriate concept. Regrettably, he was not. Carter had no clear idea of the fundamental forces at work, little conception of the problem he faced or recognition of what the best outcome could be in light of the circumstances, and he did not know what implementation steps would be most effective. Because the President did not provide effective guidance, the NSC machinery was poorly coordinated and ineffectual; the SCC met but contributed little. The confusion in the process as a whole was enormous. Coordination from the Oval Office was nearly nonexistent. Different individuals and agencies jockeyed with one another for influence, and sometimes everyone seemed to ride off in different directions simultaneously.

7.

Summing Up

Our examination of the national security policymaking system has shown a mixed performance in providing the President with high-quality advice. The same is true of the mechanisms for effective policy coordination. What judgment should we make?

It is clear that there is no single recipe for success, no magic elixir that guarantees the system will operate effectively. All of the arrangements tried have exhibited both strengths and weaknesses. The point that was strikingly evident in our discussion is that *the President's role is crucial*. Different presidential attitudes and styles have affected strongly the manner in which the various systems have operated, sometimes enhancing and sometimes diminishing their utility.

In broader perspective, our analysis in Part Two as a whole has demonstrated how difficult and cumbersome is the United States foreign policy process. It showed that regardless of the difficulties, or perhaps because of them, if policy is to be designed and implemented effectively the President must provide effective leadership. When he does not, as in the case study, the process is clearly ineffectual. There seems no way to guarantee the system in a mechanical sense against poor guidance from the top.

For the first two decades or so after World War II the disconnects and conflicts in the system and the need for presidential leadership were not so apparent because all the major participants—the President, Congress, the public, the intelligence community, State, NSC, and others—wholeheartedly embraced the containment/domino theory/forward deployment strategy. Because "everyone" shared a belief in the validity of these related concepts and their logical implications, an intellectual unity helped to fuse policy together. The institutional mechanisms designed to provide advice to senior policymakers and enable policy to be coordinated effectively could safely focus on implementation, there being no perceived need to examine the larger issues of policy design, issues concerning the appropriateness and validity of the fundamental concepts that provide guidance about whether, when, where, and how to become involved. But when that conceptual consensus was shattered by the war in Vietnam and nothing emerged to replace it, the mechanisms and the leadership guidance had to carry policy's full weight unassisted.

Our discussion in Part Two reveals how little the foreign policy machinery, both in the bowels of the bureaucracy and at the top, is geared to the consideration of basic concepts. It is not well equipped to help fashion and shape a new consensus. Though Congress today is much more assertive in certain areas than it was in earlier times, it too has little capacity (or inclination) to help build a new consensus. Its role is reactive, rather than initiatory. And the approach of the attentive public (and even that of opinion "elites") is uncoordinated and inchoate. Only the inspiration of a President or the slow wisdom brought by experience can move the nation to a new conceptual consensus.

There are really two related questions here: whether one knows where one wants to go, and whether it is in the right direction. The first is largely what we called an "internal" question; the answer to the second question depends largely on the nature of the external world and how it functions. The chapters in Part Two show that effective implementation is important, and that implementing policy content based on inappropriate concepts can lead a nation efficiently and rapidly in the wrong direction.

Having completed our analysis of how Washington makes foreign policy, we now turn in Part Three to an analysis of policy itself. We have two connected purposes in mind in Part Three: to give a résumé of American experience by looking at the foreign policy record from the viewpoint of its design and implementation, and evaluating that record through the use of the conceptual tools developed in Part One. Throughout we focus on the arguments that accompanied policy design, as the American people struggled repeatedly toward a policy consensus which could protect vital national interests and be implemented with minimum costs and risks.

PART THREE

Design and Implementation: The American Policy Record

11

Extending the Security Perimeter

If we remain one people, under an efficient government, the period is not far off when we may defy material injury from external annoyance.

George Washington
Farewell Address

. . . foreign policy must start with security.

Henry Kissinger
White House Years

In the chapters of Part Three, which trace the evolution of U.S. policy, the major focus is on the security issue. This emphasis reflects the facts, for it is only in the contemporary period that the United States began to pursue a really broad-gauged, multifaceted foreign policy. And even in the present time, as we shall see in Part Four, the security issue remains preeminent.

Given this focus, we are not attempting a complete history of all facets of U.S. foreign policy but one that is more conceptual and analytical. We are especially providing judgments made in the light of the basic framework described earlier in Chapters 4 and 5. How well has the United States designed and implemented policy? Has the United States effectively "conserved" enemies or has the nation paid more than it should have in the goals sought?

We shall see in Part Three that the United States for much of its recent policy history has been better at implementation than at design, better in phase 2 than in phase 1.

1.

The First Century

The United States of America, when George Washington was inaugurated as first President on April 30, 1789, was a weak, debt-ridden, almost friendless nation. Its one ally, France, had assisted it to independence for quite selfish motives; its aid and support remained uncertain. In any event, France very soon was caught up in revolution, civil war, and decades of bloodshed in

Europe—and therefore, in the crucial early years of United States' existence, France was either preoccupied at home or with its own aggrandizement. The problem facing U.S. foreign policy was survival and the odds were against the infant republic succeeding.

Years later, the witty Jules Jusserand, French ambassador to the United States from 1902 to 1925, would quip that the United States was blessed among the nations of the world in terms of its frontiers: a weak neighbor to the north, a weak neighbor to the south, fish to the east, and fish to the west.

But the situation that confronted George Washington and his immediate successors was much more grim. In its first decades, the United States had the British to the north (in Canada), the Spanish to the south (in Mexico, Florida, and Central and South America), the British and the French to the southeast (in the Indies), and the French to the west (dominating the Mississippi). Even further to the west were the Spanish (in southern California, New Mexico, and elsewhere), the Russians (in northern California and up into Alaska), and the British again (in the Oregon territory). The United States had as immediate or near neighbors *all* the great powers of the world except for Austria.

American territories were small compared to present United States frontiers. Of the 3,084,000 square miles that comprise the continental limits of the contemporary United States, George Washington presided over only 892,135 square miles of nominal territory. *Nominal* because the Maine boundary was unsettled and the British, despite the treaty of peace, remained in secure control of the forts in the Northwest Territory (i.e., the Great Lakes). U.S. shipping could use the oceans only, in effect, with British permission, and British ships continued their age-old custom of impressing American seamen at will. The Spanish, at New Orleans, were in a position to turn American shipping and trade on or off as they pleased. (Since the whole western area of the infant United States was served by a river system emptying into the Mississippi, and since the rivers were the roads of that day, this was a serious consideration. Before that problem was solved it almost tore the fragile union apart.)

We saw in Chapter 2 that the American armed forces were almost unbelievably small and feeble and how the weak United States tried to make up for its weakness in arms by utilizing men with foreign affairs experience as presidents in those early years. In a later time, in our own time, when colonial affairs have acquired the romantic patina of antiquity, it is extremely difficult to resurrect the fears and anxieties of these early, very uncertain days. Since the United States prospered and expanded, becoming successful and strong, we are tempted to discount the alternative possibility.

All the evidence shows that the "Founding Fathers," although daring gamblers for initial freedom, were not at all self-satisfied and relaxed with the nation's accomplishment in gaining independence. They understood the peril. Two of the weak republic's "neighbors," England and France, had fought each other seven times between 1689 and 1815: 60 years of warfare in a 126-year period. Most critical for the United States, every one of those wars in Europe had a colonial or American counterpart, as shown in Table 7.

Of this series, the French and Indian War and the American Revolution were the only ones that *began* in the New World, as a comparison of the dates indicates. But, whether the American counterpart was the first or second stage of conflict, the conclusion is inescapable. America had a war when England and France fought, and most such wars began in Europe over European issues. One might argue in 1789 that this would no longer continue to be true (although it did continue), because the United States was now independent. But the likelihood was the other way around. Especially since the United States was allied to France[1] and confronted with serious unsettled issues with England, peace and tranquility for the infant Republic could hardly be assumed or taken for granted.

---

[1]From February 6, 1778, until abrogated (after an undeclared war with France at sea) in 1800.

TABLE 7 European-American Wars

IN EUROPE	IN AMERICA
1688–1697 War of League of Augsburg	1689–1697 King William's War
1701–1713 War of Spanish Succession	1702–1713 Queen Anne's War
1740–1748 War of Austrian Succession	1744–1748 King George's War
1756–1763 Seven Years' War	1754–1763 French and Indian War
1778–1783 American Revolutionary War	1775–1783 American Revolution
1793–1802 French Revolutionary Wars	1798–1800 Undeclared French War
1803–1815 Napoleonic Wars	1812–1814 War of 1812

Not only was this infant Republic weak and surrounded by the territories of Europe's great powers; to make matters more difficult, the United States came to independence at a time when extraordinary turbulence prevailed in international affairs. Within a week of Washington's inauguration, the French Estates-General convened at Versailles. Their initial meeting, on May 5, 1789, was the opening act of the French Revolution and Napoleonic Wars. When the storming of the Bastille occurred on July 14, 1789, the United States was only six weeks into Washington's administration. Europe's peace and tranquility was ruptured now with war and violence, a condition that prevailed for the next twenty-six years. And, if Europe was at war, in view of the record, could the Americas remain at peace?

One thing could be said in favor of the drastic nature of the national security problem that the infant Republic faced. Like the fictional man about to be hanged, it wondrous cleared his mind. Tactical issues (such as whom to approach for support, in what order to address the problems) could be and were fiercely debated. What was clear beyond any dispute, however, was the strategic situation. For reasons not its fault, the United States had more potential enemies than it could handle. It had no reliable friends. It would survive, if it did, through good judgment in the conservation of enemies, plus luck. What had to be done, therefore, was to hold on; to avoid disastrous self-sought involvements; to parry aggressive initiatives from abroad; to avoid all-out confrontations until, with the passing of time, American strength increased. Where possible, avoidance was the orientation of the day.

Time was on the new nation's side. If it simply survived long enough, it would gain steadily in strength. By 1790, the population of the United States stood at 3,929,214. By 1800, it had reached 5,308,483, growing to 7,239,881 by 1810 and 12,866,020 by 1830. In 1840 there were 17,069,453 Americans, and, on the eve of the Civil War in 1860, the population stood at 31,443,321.

In Chapter 2 we saw how developments in the European balance of power after Napoleon generally favored U.S. security. As a generalization, the United States prospered in its first century from the actions of third states, but it also avoided serious errors of its own. Not that the Founding Fathers and their successors were always wise in their decision making. The War of 1812, fought only against Britain even though French behavior was almost as much of an irritant, almost ended poorly even against one opponent—the British being disposed to retain occupied areas near Canada. Yet the U.S. Senate only defeated the motion of declaring war *also* on France by the close vote of 18 to 14! Again, in December 1845, President Polk, losing patience with the British in the controversy over the division of the Oregon territory, claimed all of Oregon.[2] On January 13, 1846, with this issue still in doubt, Polk ordered General Taylor to

[2]The Oregon Territory lay between the 42nd parallel, which was the northern boundary of California, and parallel 54°40′, the latitude of the southern tip of Russian-controlled Alaska. It had been governed more or less as a U.S.-British condominium since 1818.

advance into the disputed Mexican territory up to the Rio Grande. A two-front war might have ensued had not the British compromised on Oregon. In another way, the Civil War was a time of extreme danger. The British, who were tempted to cultivate the South as a way of weakening the American state, went so far as actually to permit the building and outfitting of Confederate commerce raiders such as the *Alabama*. (The damage done by such raiders subsequently was arbitrated as "the *Alabama* claims.") In these same years the French had troops in Mexico under Maximilian. But threatening disaster was averted in each case.

May 1871, when the United States and England signed the Treaty of Washington that disposed of most outstanding issues between them, marked a real watershed. This treaty, with its rules for arbitration which ensured a judgment against England in the *Alabama* claims, showed more clearly than any other British action to that date that England wanted peace with the United States. Although things were still to get worse in later years for England, they were already complicated enough in Europe and elsewhere for the British to avoid needless struggles with an America too strong for it to fight with any hopes of a worthwhile outcome. From now until almost the Spanish-American War, foreign issues faded virtually from sight in the United States.

So ended the first century as America counts it: from the Declaration of Independence. The record shows a fairly gifted touch, marred by occasional bombast and questionable action; on the whole a policy that did not overreach itself. Except for the War of 1812 and the Oregon-Texas controversies, the prudent emphasis in American policy and the sense of priorities on enemies was very pronounced. Starting surrounded by Europe's great powers, the United States ended its first century powerful in population and industry, extended to continental dimensions in territory, and virtually invulnerable to invasion.

As General Sheridan said in his report as Commanding General of the U.S. Army in 1884:

> I do not think we should be much alarmed about the probability of wars with foreign powers, since it would require more than a million and a half of men to make a campaign upon land against us. To transport from beyond the ocean that number of soldiers [and their supplies] would demand a large part of the shipping of all Europe.[3]

2.

Toward a Larger Role

The no-longer vulnerable and weak nation had now to decide whether to settle for this ideal status quo arrangement (assuming it could continue), or attempt to play a role on the larger stage.

In the 1880s and 1890s signs could be found pointing in two opposite directions for U.S. foreign policy. Richard W. Leopold says that of "the four men who sat in the White House from 1889 to 1905, none had prior experience in diplomacy and none was elected because of his ideas on world affairs. Such was the rule, not the exception in those years."[4] Substantive issues in foreign affairs were few—consider the shortness of the list we gave in Chapter 2. The record and the leadership deserved each other. What is striking is that, if one removed from the list the issues with Great Britain and the Caribbean involvements, there would be little left. If one further removed all issues involving neighbors, the record would be almost bare. American interests outside the continental perimeter were still very limited.

---

[3] *Report of the Secretary of War, 1884,* p. 49. From John Bigelow, *The Principles of Strategy Illustrated Mainly from American Campaigns* (New York: Greenwood Press, 1968), p. 55.

[4] Richard W. Leopold, *The Growth of American Foreign Policy* (New York: Alfred A. Knopf, 1962), p. 106.

Yet that way of looking at these years would also be inadequate, for significant changes were underway in both attitudes and outlooks. In 1883, in the middle of no meaningful activity in foreign affairs at all, for example, the Congress voted appropriations for three light cruisers and a dispatch vessel, which became the famous "White Squadron." This marked the beginning of a new steam and steel navy after years of neglect.[5] Weigley remarks, "By the end of the decade, Congress added other cruisers and authorized two large armored cruisers or small battleships, *Maine* and *Texas*."[6] Coastal fortifications also began to be overhauled. The United States Naval Institute was established in 1873 and began publishing its *Proceedings*. The U.S. Army set up the advanced School of Application for Infantry and Cavalry at Fort Leavenworth in 1881.[7] Three years later, the Naval War College was established at Newport. All of this took place at a time when foreign affairs were stagnant; all were harbingers of a growing and wider American interest in strategic and military problems. This at a time when "No nation except Great Britain and possibly France possessed enough ships to carry 50,000 troops across an ocean. . . . An invasion of the United States by a European power was out of the question."[8]

The ideas being published by individuals such as Alfred Thayer Mahan, who preached the doctrine of seapower to an awakening American nation,[9] found an enthusiastic reception with influential individuals such as Senator Henry Cabot Lodge and Theodore Roosevelt,[10] but the transition to popular and congressional full support of those ideas was more attenuated. In the Naval Act of 1890, Congress compromised, providing for three "sea-going, *coast*line battleships,"[11] each with a cruising range no greater than 5,000 nautical miles. This deliberate restriction was far from an outright sponsoring of a more expansionist, imperial role. This 1890 program produced the *Indiana, Massachusetts,* and *Oregon,* each 10,288 tons, with four 13-inch guns. Even so, these were the ships that fought the Spanish-American War, and when the *Oregon* made its famous 13,000-mile transit, it had to be supplied with coal from a gunboat as it went! In later years, President Roosevelt got Congress to build four more battleships, and his successor, President William Howard Taft, had six more battleships constructed, the largest of which were 31,400 tons. In 1907–1909 this new American battle fleet toured the world.

It is as though the United States got ready to play a role on a larger stage, beyond the continental dimensions, even before the conscious decision had been made. As we shall soon see, the acquisition of the Philippines itself was not—or not totally—a conscious and premeditated event.

One must not ignore the spirit of the age. Imperialism was in full flower between about 1874 and 1907. Europe's powers were industriously carving up Africa and southern Asia, even beginning the giant process of cutting strips of coastal-oriented spheres of influence off the great

---

[5]John D. Long, Secretary of the Navy between 1897 and 1902, remarks in his memoirs that the Navy List of 1879 showed five "first-rates" twenty-five years old and "practically useless as men-of-war" plus twenty-seven "second-rates" of which only nine could really go to sea. Of the Navy's total of 142 ships in President Hayes's administration (1877–1881), says Long, 48 were immediately ready, and 69 more "capable" of being used. He adds: "In the entire navy there was not a single high-power, long-range, rifled gun!" Long says the new construction came from the need for secure communications across the Isthmus. See John D. Long, *The New American Navy* (London: Grant Richards, 1904), vol. 1, pp. 13–15.

[6]Russell F. Weigley, *The American Way of War* (New York: Macmillan, 1973), p. 169.

[7]Ibid, p. 171.

[8]Ibid, p. 169.

[9]Mahan's most famous book, published in 1890, was *The Influence of Seapower on History, 1660–1783*. Translated into German, it was placed on every German warship by order of the German emperor. Both Oxford and Cambridge universities honored Mahan with degrees in 1894, and Mahan became a world celebrity.

[10]Theodore Roosevelt was Assistant Secretary of the Navy under McKinley, organized the "Rough Riders" in the Spanish-American War (and led them up San Juan hill), and became Vice-President, then President in September 1901 (following McKinley's assassination). He was President until March 1909.

[11]Italics added.

carcass of the Chinese whale. Part of the American incentive to acquire Hawaii (and Samoa) was the fear that other nations would do so first.

In Chapter 2 we saw how the European situation became more threatening after Bismarck's "retirement." Britain, confronted by an unpleasantly dangerous trio of potential foes (France, Russia, and Germany), made a deliberate decision to keep relations with the United States on an even keel. Viewed in this light, the American intervention in the dispute over the boundary between Venezuela and British Guiana must have seemed to the British almost a deliberate provocation, as tensions mounted in 1895. U.S. Secretary of State Olney twisted the British lion's tail on July 20, 1895, with his brash (although accurate) claim that the United States was "practically sovereign on this continent" and "its fiat is law."

Exactly why the United States had become aroused is not clear in a rational sense from today's perspective. Lord Salisbury, the British Foreign Secretary, was quite correct in arguing on November 26, 1895, that "The disputed frontier of Venezuela [with adjoining British possessions] has nothing to do with any of the questions dealt with by President Monroe. It is not a question of the colonization by a European Power of any portion of America." It was "simply the determination of the frontier of a British possession which belonged to the Throne of England long before the Republic of Venezuela came into existence."[12]

Such assertions of fact merely increased American anger. Salisbury's note made President Cleveland, in his own words, "mad clear through." Cleveland asked Congress on September 17, 1895, to set up an American investigating commission to establish the boundary. Once that was done, he proposed that the United States would "resist by every means in its power" any British exercise of sovereign rights over territories unilaterally determined by the United States to belong to Venezuela. The House cheered; even the more dignified Senate applauded these bellicose words. Congress at once unanimously appropriated $100,000 for the expenses of the boundary commission. (Young Teddy Roosevelt cheered the development: "I rather hope that the fight will come soon . . . this country needs a war.") Relatively fewer sober voices were raised, although Joseph Pulitzer wrote in the *New York World*: " . . . it is not our frontier, it is none of our business. To make it such . . . is something more than a grave blunder. If persisted in, it will be a colossal crime."[13]

The British were rather astounded to find themselves moving toward the brink of war with America over some obscure jungle dispute. On January 3, 1896, the telegram of congratulation from Germany's Kaiser Wilhelm II to President Kruger of the South African Boer Republic for repulsing the Jameson raid called British attention forcibly to a more important problem for them. By this time, the British had already determined to try to find a peaceful way out from the American quarrel, but the Kaiser's action reinforced that determination. The British now cooperated, providing the American boundary commission with information. Eventually, with the United States assisting, a treaty between Venezuela and England was signed in February 1897 that provided for arbitration. The British clash with the French at Fashoda in 1898 made the British glad they had agreed, and the award in October 1899 was not too far from what Britain had earlier suggested as a settlement. So passed the threat—the last time in a serious vein—of a third American war with England. It is difficult to construe this whole episode other than as the action of a nation, conscious of its power and full of its importance, spoiling for a fight.

England, perhaps at some price to its pride, could divert the United States to another outlet for its energies—a policy consistently followed now. After the U.S. Congress in defiance of the terms of the Clayton-Bulwer Treaty in January 1900 took up a bill to permit American con-

[12] *Papers Relating to the Foreign Relations of the United States, 1895,* part 1, pp. 564–565.
[13] *New York World,* December 21, 1895.

struction and control of a canal through Nicaragua, British Ambassador Lord Pauncefote in February 1900 was empowered to conclude a new treaty with the United States.[14]

By the terms of the new treaty, the Clayton-Bulwer Treaty was set aside and the proposed American actions were legalized, except that the canal could not be fortified. When the Senate objected, Britain in November 1901 agreed to a *second* Hay-Pauncefote Treaty, this time including tacitly an American right to fortify the canal.

3.

A Watershed: The Spanish-American War

There could no longer be any reasonable doubt that, for better or worse, the United States was launched on expansion and a larger role. The American thunder and lightning of the last years of the nineteenth century, diverted from its popular and traditional English target, soon focused on the less adroit Spanish and the Cuban issue. Since 1895, a Cuban insurrection had been underway and the Spanish had responded with concentration camps and other oppressive measures. The so-called American "yellow" journals whipped up popular emotions, much like television in our own day. When the *Maine* blew up in Havana harbor with a loss of over 250 officers and men on February 15, 1898, the pressures for war with Spain grew overwhelming. Congress in March voted for war preparations and on April 11, 1898, two days after the Spanish authorities had indicated in principle a willingness to meet American demands, President McKinley decided to request authority to intervene with force in Cuba. On April 19, Congress passed such a joint resolution. Assistant Secretary of the Navy Theodore Roosevelt, having first prudently deployed American ships within attack distance of Manila, resigned to seek personal involvement by becoming Lieutenant-Colonel Roosevelt of the "Rough Riders." Admiral Dewey promptly destroyed the Spanish fleet in Manila Bay while their sister fleet, departing the shelter of Santiago harbor in Cuba, was similarly sunk.

President McKinley said once disarmingly: "When we received the cable from Admiral Dewey telling of the taking of the Philippines I looked up their location on the globe. I could not have told where those darned islands were within 2,000 miles!"[15] Now the dilemma arose: What to do? McKinley later made his famous statement to his fellow Methodists of how he had decided what to do by prayer:

> The truth is I didn't want the Philippines and . . . I did not know what to do about them. . . .
> I thought first we would take only Manila; then Luzon; then other islands, perhaps, also. I
> walked the floor of the White House night after night until midnight; and . . . I went down on
> my knees and prayed Almighty God for light and guidance.

And, finally things became clear:

> And one night it came to me . . . (1) that we could not give them back to Spain—that would
> be cowardly and dishonorable; (2) that we could not turn them over to France or Germany—
> our commercial rivals in the Orient [since] that would be bad business and discreditable; (3)
> that we could not leave them to themselves [since] they would soon have anarchy and misrule
> . . .; and (4) that there was nothing left for us to do but to take them all, and to educate the

[14]In the Clayton-Bulwer Treaty of 1850 the United States and Britain had agreed that any future canal would be jointly constructed and remain unfortified.

[15]H. H. Kohlsaat, *From McKinley to Harding* (New York: Scribners, 1923), p. 68. According to Kohlsaat, some months later McKinley added: "If old Dewey had just sailed away when he smashed that Spanish fleet, what a lot of trouble he would have saved us."

Filipinos, and uplift and civilize and Christianize them, and by God's grace do the very best we could by them, as our fellow-men for whom Christ also died. And then I went to bed . . . and slept soundly.[16]

Duly incorporated into a treaty with Spain, this line of reasoning was accepted (two-thirds vote required) by the very narrow margin of 57 to 27 in the Senate on February 6, 1899, two days after, ironically, the Filipinos rose up in revolt against their new masters. This is the same treaty which ceded Guam; it also provided for Cuba to be free and independent (under American protection) and for Puerto Rico to become an American territory. The Spanish were to be paid $20 million in exchange.

Shortly thereafter, in the first significant overseas deployment in American history, the United States moved 70,000 troops to the Philippines (or about four times the size of the forces used in Cuba). Not until July 1902 was order restored in the Philippines. In the meanwhile, with the Open Door Notes of 1899 and 1900 (discussed later), the United States capped a sequence of moves indicating a wider and more enduring Pacific interest. In a sense, the acquisition of Alaska from Russia by the treaty of March 30, 1867, and of Midway by occupation on August 28, 1867, established the bridge, but the Spanish-American War provided the fuel. In a short period now, Hawaii was added (joint resolution of Congress, July 7, 1898), then the Philippines and Guam (treaty signed on December 10, 1898), Wake Island (occupation, January 17, 1899), and Tutuila in American Samoa (by treaty with England and Germany, December 2, 1899). The later acquisition of the Panama Canal Zone (by treaty with Panama of November 18, 1903) and the purchase of the Virgin Islands from Denmark (by treaty of August 4, 1916), together with Puerto Rico, soon rounded out a much more modest Caribbean expansion.

These acquisitions represented a very substantial change in attitude for a nation whose presidential public papers show no mention of the word "China" until 1831 or of "Japan" until 1852.[17] The acquisitions led directly to an enhanced interest in the fate of China. The European colonial imperialism that began about 1874 had by 1898 succeeded in seizing vast areas in Africa and Asia. The largest prize left was China, whose huge size had thus far protected it from outside forces. But a de facto consortium of Britain, Germany, Russia, and France in 1898 forced China to grant 99-year leases (in Russia's case, a 25-year lease) covering a good part of China's sea-adjacent areas and a significant part of China's economic resources, including mines and railroads. Chinese customs were being collected by foreigners. Under these circumstances the most immediate American concern was the fear of being left out. In the Open Door Note of September 6, 1899, the United States demanded equal treatment in the British, German, and Russian spheres in China so far as harbor and railroad duties were concerned.

Sensational events now occurred in China as the "Boxers" (a fanatical Chinese patriotic society) rose up to exterminate the "foreign devils," and beseiged the foreign legations in Beijing. Included in the 18,000-man international rescue force sent in were 2,500 U.S. troops. This was another landmark, the first American fighting men on the Asian mainland, where many would follow in later years. China's political disintegration under the impact of these events encouraged Secretary of State Hay to send a new note, on July 3, 1900. It repeated the demand "for equal and impartial trade" with all parts of China but added the proposition that the "policy of the Government of the United States is to seek a solution [which would] preserve" China "as a territorial and administrative entity."[18] How much serious attention would have been given to

[16]New York *Christian Advocate,* January 22, 1903.

[17]T. A. Bailey, *A Diplomatic History of the American People,* 4th ed. (New York: Appleton-Century-Crofts, 1950), p. 301.

[18]*Papers Relating to the Foreign Relations of the United States, 1901, Appendix,* p. 12.

these words by the European powers is hard to say; since they could not yet agree on how to proceed farther in carving up China, the question remained moot. Soon Japan and Russia would fight over rights in Manchuria and Korea. Not until the 1930s would the United States have to ask itself how much it cared whether China really remained whole.

American attention was soon diverted nearer to home, to the Panama Canal question. Fascinating as a story of intrigue and semiserious comic opera, what concerns us here is the assumption by the United States, for better or worse, of an expanded security perimeter, rather than the complicated question of American connivance in the Panamanian revolt. The terms of the Hay-Bunau-Varilla Treaty of November 18, 1903, were in any case extremely generous to the United States. For $10 million plus $250,000 a year, the United States acquired a zone ten miles wide in which the United States was sovereign in every practical sense. On February 23, 1904, the Senate agreed to the treaty by a vote of 66 to 14. The United States acquired a canal across the Isthmus plus a greatly enhanced Latin American suspicion of American actions and power. Such suspicion increased in the next years as the Platt Amendment of 1901 increased American control over Cuban foreign relations, and the United States began to intervene more actively in Caribbean affairs.[19] As these unstable nations plunged themselves into debt beyond their ability to repay, Europe's heavy-handed collection methods brought on a crisis over Venezuela in December 1902 when Britain and Germany (plus Italy later) seized Venezuelan gunboats, and again in January 1903 when the Germans bombarded a Venezuelan village.

President Theodore Roosevelt was not the man to permit these "violations" of the Monroe Doctrine. His solution was announced to Congress in his annual message on December 6, 1904. After saying that the United States had no "land hunger" and only wanted its neighbors to be prosperous and orderly, he came to the crux of the issue: "Chronic wrongdoing [might] ultimately require intervention by some civilized nation, and in the Western Hemisphere the adherence of the United States to the Monroe Doctrine may force the United States, however reluctantly, in flagrant cases . . . to the exercise of an international police power."[20] Roosevelt repeated this theme in his annual message of December 5, 1905, almost word for word and certainly thought for thought. This "Roosevelt Corollary" was the stepping-stone to intervention in the Dominican Republic in 1905 and in Cuba in 1906.

Restless Teddy Roosevelt rounded out his term in office by having the United States take part in the Algeciras Conference—that first pre-World War I crisis over Morocco; and by mediating the practically stalemated Russo-Japanese War at Portsmouth, New Hampshire. For the first time the United States was willingly making itself a party—even if only in a peacemaker role—to the quarrels of both Europe and Asia.

Woodrow Wilson on entering office in 1912 was the first Democratic President in sixteen years. In his administration the United States was to mark another milestone: sending American troops to fight in Europe for the first time. Wilson, even today, is a study in contrasts. Pacific in inclination, he sent United States troops to seek combat in Mexico (under provocation, to be sure) and in Europe. "Liberal" in his thinking, Wilson expressed much of the narrow limits of his tolerance when he said, "I am going to teach the South American republics to elect good men!"[21] In the process he tore up the Jeffersonian doctrine of de facto recognition, and instituted moral judgments as substitutes. Reformist about international relations, he was to insist down to defeat on his own special version of the League of Nations.

---

[19]Agreed to in exchange for American evacuation, the Platt Amendment gave the United States the right to intervene in Cuba's domestic and foreign affairs in order to preserve Cuba's independence and maintain law and order.

[20]Congressional Record, 58th Congress, 3rd Session, vol. 39, p. 19.

[21]Ray Stannard Baker, Woodrow Wilson: Life and Letters (Garden City, N.Y.: Doubleday, Page, 1931), vol. 4, p. 289.

Throughout, Wilson remained a controversial figure. It is highly ironic that, as a specialist in congressional government, he admittedly knew very little about foreign affairs. Wilson had intended to be little involved with them; he ended up totally absorbed by them.

Wilson's first critical foreign affairs problem grew out of events in Mexico, where he refused to recognize the government of Victoriano Huerta. (Huerta had murdered Francisco Madero who had overthrown the more than thirty-year dictatorship of Porfirio Díaz.) With more than 50,000 Americans in Mexico and American investments—especially in oil—greater than all other of its foreign interests combined, events below the southern border were not a matter of indifference. Incidents at Vera Cruz combined with investor pressures pushed Wilson into requesting Congress on April 20, 1914, for authority to intervene by force of arms; soon more violence occurred at Vera Cruz. When Huerta gave way to General Carranza, Wilson, after more than a year, extended de facto recognition. But in January 1916 Pancho Villa's men massacred eighteen American mining engineers at Santa Ysabel. In a more pointed insult, Villa raided and sacked Columbus, New Mexico, on March 9, 1916. General Pershing was sent quickly in pursuit of Villa with a force of, ultimately, twelve thousand troops. With these frayed relations with its immediate southern neighbor, the United States faced the growing threat arising out of World War I.

4. World War I

World War I began in Europe in August 1914. President Wilson's initial reaction was that Americans should be neutral in thought and word and deed. Avoidance should be the orientation. This made a certain amount of sense in view of the dramatically polarized sympathies of significant portions of the American population, plus a tradition dating back to the Founding Fathers. Besides, it was not clear at the outset whether American strength would be needed to affect the outcome of the war in Europe.

The United States population in 1914 had moved even further toward diversity. Significant numbers of Irish and Germans continued to pour in to the United States from abroad, and other European groups followed: Russian, Italian, and Scandinavian. The United States census for 1900 shows that 74.9 per cent of the people in Minnesota were either foreign-born or had at least one foreign-born parent. For California, the figure was 54.9 per cent. These peoples, split in their sympathies between the warring groups, plus the many other millions of Americans who wanted no part in it on anyone's side, made a popular backing for a neutral stand in the war. Even so, three years after the war began, the United States entered the war on the side of the Allies.

From the beginning of that conflict the United States had to choose whether or not it would insist on neutral rights to continue to use the seas and conduct trade. Whether wisely or not, the United States took a strong stand, one that ultimately, because of circumstances, created far more friction with Germany than with Britain. The German proclamation of February 4, 1915, that the waters around Britain were a zone of war in which the security of neutral vessels could not be guaranteed, drew an American response on February 10 that the belligerent rights of Germany "in dealing with neutral vessels on the high seas is limited to visit and search, unless a blockade is proclaimed and effectively maintained, which this Government does not understand to be proposed in this case." To "attack and destroy any vessel entering a prescribed area of the high seas without first certainly determining its belligerent nationality and the contraband character of its cargo would be an act so unprecedented in naval warfare that this Government is reluctant to believe that the Imperial Government of Germany in this case contemplates it as possible."[22]

Germany's dilemma, for its part, arose from the fact that, although it did intend to maintain an effective blockade, it could only do it with the submarine weapon and there were no agreed rules for the conduct of such warfare. Since submarines had fragile hulls, prolonged surface discussions with merchant ships or taking passengers or crew aboard from ships sunk were equally unfeasible alternatives.

With the torpedoing and sinking of the British steamship *Lusitania* on May 7, 1915, by which over one hundred American citizens lost their lives, events reached a first climax. The U.S. note of May 13 was brusque, expressing American "growing concern, distress and amazement" and insisting on "strict accountability." The U.S. objection to the German "method of attack against the trade of their enemies lies in the practical impossibility of employing submarines in the destruction of commerce without disregarding those rules of fairness, reason, justice, and humanity, which all modern opinion regards as imperative." The United States would not "omit any word or any act necessary to the performance of its sacred duty of maintaining the rights of the United States and its citizens." In an earlier section of the note, those rights were specifically enumerated to include Americans "taking their ships and in traveling wherever their legitimate business calls them upon the high seas. . . ."[23]

Meanwhile, there was also friction with Britain. It began with the British Order in Council of August 20, 1914, which redefined contraband. Soon the British had also extended the traditional right of visit and search to a right to force suspected merchant ships to enter British ports for more extended searches. The British as excuse for these arbitrary diversions of shipping pointed to the opposite end of the U-boat warfare dilemma: both the warship and the merchant ship, stopped long at sea, became sitting-duck targets for submarines. British practice, in many cases, of paying for confiscated cargoes mitigated American anger at these interferences. And, in the last analysis, the Germans took both American lives and American goods by their actions at sea, whereas the British at most took only American goods.

As the British blockade tightened, the Germans lost anticipated imports drastically while British and Allied imports increased enormously. U.S. foreign trade with the Central Powers declined from $169,289,775 in 1914 to $1,159,653 in 1916, whereas trade with the Allies in those same years went from $824,860,237 to $3,214,480,547.[24] As these economic balances tilted, so too did official American sympathies (but not really for that reason). American protests against British actions continued to be lodged and British responses were ultimately made, but the game of protest notes was already being played with two sets of rules. Secretary of State Lansing, in his notes to the Germans, by his own admission, "did all that I could to prolong the disputes by preparing . . . long and detailed replies, and introducing technical and controversial matters in the hope that . . . something would happen to change the current of American public opinion or to make the American people perceive that German absolutism was a menace to their liberties and to democratic institutions everywhere."[25]

Consider, by contrast to the sharp-toned notes sent to Germany, the American protest note to Britain of October 21, 1915. It reads like a polite debater's brief: the United States could "not submit to the curtailment of its neutral rights" by these "illegal" measures. "The United States

---

[22] *Papers Relating to the Foreign Relations of the United States, 1915, Supplement,* p. 98–99.

[23] Ibid., pp. 393–396.

[24] Figures from T. A. Bailey, *The Policy of the United States Toward the Neutrals, 1917–1918* (Baltimore: Johns Hopkins Press, 1942), p. 481.

[25] *War Memoirs of Robert Lansing* (Indianapolis: Bobbs-Merrill Co., 1935), p. 112, as quoted in T. A. Bailey, *Diplomatic History,* 4th ed. (New York: Appleton-Century-Crofts, 1950), p. 621.

might not be in a position to object to them if its interests and the interests of all neutrals were unaffected by them [!], but, being affected, it can not *with complacence suffer further subordination of its rights* to the plea that the exceptional geographic position of the enemies of Great Britain require or justify oppressive and illegal practices."[26]

The notes of protest sent to the British—or, even more accurately, the notes deliberately *not* sent to the British—were never designed to fan the flames. William Jennings Bryan, Secretary of State in 1915 until he resigned, said plainly in his memoirs that "the administration was lacking in neutrality—not in commission, but in omission. . . ."[27]

Germany on June 6, 1915, secretly ordered U-boat commanders to avoid sinking enemy passenger liners. But on August 19, 1915, the British passenger ship *Arabic* was sunk and two Americans onboard were killed. This time the Germans gave reassurances and then, on October 5, 1915, Germany announced "stringent" orders to its submarine commanders to avoid such sinkings.

While Congress considered warning American citizens against traveling on armed belligerent passenger ships, the unarmed French ship *Sussex* was torpedoed by a U-boat that mistook it for a warship, and several Americans were injured. The U.S. note to Germany of April 18, 1916, was very blunt: "Unless the Imperial Government should now immediately declare and effect an abandonment of its present methods of submarine warfare . . ., the Government of the United States can have no choice but to sever diplomatic relations. . . ."[28]

In reply, on May 4, 1916, Germany declared that unresisting merchantships (including but going beyond only passenger liners) would not be sunk without warning or efforts to conserve life. But the Germans also drew attention to the other side of the coin: If Washington brought no pressure on the British to relax the starvation blockade, Germany would have to reconsider.

Wilson, running for reelection under the slogan, "He kept us out of war," was returned to office in 1916. He had, however, given sufficient public warning that he might not be able to continue this situation. In speeches in January 1916 at Pittsburgh, Cleveland, and Chicago, Wilson had, with varying words, said he had laid upon him "the double obligation of maintaining the honor of the United States and of maintaining the peace of the United States. Is it not conceivable that the two might become incompatible?"[29] In January 1917, he proposed to the Senate a "peace without victory." Germany on January 31, 1917, responded by proclaiming unrestricted submarine warfare. *Any* ship in designated waters would be sunk (except for *one* American ship a week to and from England). On February 3, 1917, Wilson announced the severance of diplomatic relations with Germany. Then, on March 1, 1917, came an authentic spy drama. The German "Zimmermann Note" (intercepted and deciphered by the British) was published in the American press. The American people were shocked to find that the Germans were secretly seeking an alliance with Mexico, with the promise of a return to Mexico of Texas, New Mexico, and Arizona. The rural South and West, lukewarm until now about Europe and its quarrels, and inclined to criticize Wilson for too active a policy, became positively excited.

American merchantships were now armed, the first one putting out to sea in March 1917, ready to fire on hostile submarines. Four unarmed American ships were soon sunk by German U-boats, with many casualties. On April 2, 1917, Wilson went before the Congress to ask that body to recognize "formally" that the United States was at war. Wilson said: "The present German submarine warfare against commerce is a warfare against mankind. . . . The challenge

---

[26] *Papers Relating to the Foreign Relations of the United States, 1915, Supplement,* pp. 578–589. Italics added.
[27] W. J. Bryan and M. B. Bryan, *The Memoirs of William Jennings Bryan* (Chicago: 1925), p. 404, quoted in Bailey, *Diplomatic History,* p. 577.
[28] *Papers Relating to the Foreign Relations of the United States, 1916, Supplement,* pp. 232–234.
[29] The quotation is from the speech in Chicago, January 31, 1916.

is to all mankind." The United States had "no quarrel with the German people," only with the "little groups of ambitious men who were accustomed to use their fellow men as pawns and tools. Self-governed nations do not fill their neighbor states with spies or set the course of intrigue [applause]. . . ."[30]

In none of this is the balance of power so much as mentioned by name by the Americans. Wilson's choice of words shows throughout his preference for moral language, his wish to clothe American national interest in the garments of universalism. Yet, underneath, one can sense that the reaction to the belligerents is not equal in part because their offenses against American interests (i.e., "the rights of all mankind") are never equal. Nor are the British seen as "auto-cratic" (i.e., dangerous). Then, ultimately, the Zimmerman Note is a threat to dismantle actual American territories, and the resort to unrestricted submarine warfare is an obvious threat to American prestige since the United States had throughout said such actions were not acceptable. Add all this together and Wilson is actually picturing a ruthless opponent bent on inflicting serious damages on the United States. Wilson could and did use moral terms to describe it all; but the Germans and their actions were perceived by the government of the United States as a tangible and realistic threat to concrete American interests, with an arbitrary manner of pro-ceeding that increased American alarm about what the future might hold. The vocabulary is not balance-of-power terminology, but the thrust of concern is. The old argument that the United States fought without understanding why has a certain truth in the sense that the vocabulary is less than precise. But the thought behind the action is clear.

The Senate agreed to war on April 4, 1917, by a vote of 82 to 6; the House agreed on April 6 by 373 to 50—most adverse votes coming from Midwest (i.e., German-inhabited) states.

In taking the action at sea, the Germans had been influenced by two calculations. First, the total number of U-boats at sea, in dock, or undergoing repairs had risen steadily from 27 in February 1915, to 74 in August 1916, with an anticipated total by February 1917 of 103. That was enough, by German calculations, to finish England by mid-1917.[31] Second, it was assumed by the Germans that U.S. forces could not be effective in time. The Germans could not believe that an American army of about 200,000 men on April 6, 1917, could grow to a force of over 3,600,000 by November 11, 1918,[32] of which over 2 million would actually go to France. (In Ludendorff's great 1918 offensive, after Russia left the war, the German army smashed within 40 miles of Paris by the end of May.) But American troops, arriving in France in 1918, increased steadily from a monthly total of 50,000 in January to 100,000 in April and 250,000 in May (when a half million were already in France). This fresh American strength altered the war, with 29 of the 42 divisions sent over (1,390,000 men) committed to combat. At a cost of 48,909 battlefield dead (112,432 from all causes), plus 230,074 wounded, and a direct war expenditure of about $22 billion, the United States finished the war and assured an Allied victory.

5.

The Aborted Peace Settlement

The national interest of the United States, once the war was over, was to create conditions for a lasting peace. Wilson accurately reflected this approach in his Fourteen Points of January 8, 1918, in which he proposed "open covenants of peace, openly arrived at," free use of the seas, equality of trading opportunity, reduction of arms, and adjustments of territories to correct old

---

[30]*Congressional Record*, 65th Congress, 1st Session, vol. 55, part 1, pp. 118–120.
[31]Leopold, *Growth of American Foreign Policy*, pp. 328–329.
[32]Ibid., p. 340.

wrongs (such as the establishment of an independent Polish state). His fourteenth point was the proposal for the League of Nations.[33]

Wilson's Fourteen Points were accepted by Germany as the basis for peace in October and by the Allies the following month, but the peace conference at Versailles was in no mood to coddle Germany. The peace treaty it produced was far more vindictive.

It is difficult to assess Wilson's program impartially today; so many opinions have been registered about it by writers often jaundiced by Wilson's love to preach. Yet the Fourteen Points, except for some allusions in the preface to a just peace and making "the world ... fit and safe to live in," is no mere set of moral platitudes. Many of its specific provisions made a good deal of sense if the object was to achieve a solid basis for an enduring new equilibrium, rather than to reap vengeance on Germany. But the policy, as designed, could not be effectively implemented because it did not square with the state of the exterior environment. World War I was such a disaster, such a bloodletting, that moderate programs of this kind were soon swallowed up by the emotional upheaval. The "dictated peace" of Versailles, as Adolf Hitler correctly called it, could sow only the seeds for a new war once sufficient time had passed for Germany to rearm.

Wilson's decision to link the Covenant of the League with the Treaty of Versailles (of which it became a part) was probably a mistake.

In the postwar settlements Germany was stripped of territories to which it had little valid claim but also of territories to which it had a quite good claim. Russia, although on the "winning side," lost even more significant territories, including most of what became Poland, while Austria-Hungary was dismantled into a group of small, weak states, including Hungary, Austria, and Czechoslovakia. No poorer basis for a proper peace than these "realistic" settlements can be easily imagined. The diplomats at the Congress of Vienna of 1815, who redrew the frontiers after Napoleon and who well understood that the defeated must not be despoiled, would have shuddered in horror. They would have recognized the dangers in creating two, in effect, "defeated" major powers (Germany and Russia) fundamentally dissatisfied with the status quo, separated only by a series of weak, small states, incapable of resistance if their major power neighbors acted against them. Wilson's hope that the injustices contrived at Versailles could be remedied later by the League of Nations at Geneva remained only a forlorn hope.

Watching Europe's quarrels at the Versailles Peace Conference did not improve Europe's image with the American people. The American public after the war was increasingly disenchanted by that war, more and more Americans coming to believe that it had been a mistake for the United States to have taken part at all. Even so, as has frequently been pointed out about the "Lodge" reservations to the Covenant and treaty (on which the Senate's ratification debate turned), Wilson could have achieved ratification of the Covenant if he had been more compromising toward the Senate. Whether the United States would then have stayed in the League, whether it would have played a prominent and positive role, cannot be known. Senator Warren G. Harding, speaking for the Lodge reservations on November 19, 1919, said plainly: "I have not liked this treaty; I think, as originally negotiated, it is the colossal blunder of all time. . . ." Later, Harding said "that in this covenant we have originally [i.e., unless altered] bartered American independence in order to create a league. We have traded away America's freedom of action in order to establish a supergovernment of the world, and it was never intended to be any less. I speak for one who is old-fashioned enough to believe that the Government of the United States of America is good enough for me."[34]

---

[33] *Congressional Record,* 65th Congress, 2nd Session, vol. 56, pp. 680–681.
[34] *Congressional Record,* 66th Congress, 1st Session, vol. 58, part 9, pp. 8791–8792.

Senator Harding was shortly to become President Harding.[35] In a rebuttal of such arguments, Wilson was expending his strength. At Indianapolis on September 4, 1919, Wilson argued strongly for the treaty, using an interesting mixture of arguments. He stressed that the League of Nations Council could only "advise" and that "there could be no advice of the council on any such subject without a unanimous vote," which must include the American affirmative vote. He stressed that, in the event of an obvious violation of the Covenant, "there ensues automatically . . . an absolute economic boycott." He argued then that "A nation that is boycotted is a nation that is in sight of surrender." These measures were needed "to protect the weak." (Wilson explained that "every one that I consulted with" at the Peace Conference had come "with the same idea, that wars had arisen in the past because the strong took advantage of the weak. . . ."). Moreover, American sacrifices should not be thrown away because,

> if Germany should ever attempt that again, whether we are in the League of Nations or not, we will join to prevent it. We do not stand off and see murder done. We do not profess to be the champions of liberty and then consent to see liberty destroyed. . . . If a power such as Germany was . . . were to do this thing upon the fields of Europe, then America would have to look to it that she did not do it also upon the fields of the Western Hemisphere, and we should at last be face to face with a power *which at the outset we could have crushed. . . .*[36]

Wilson is surely arguing a balance-of-power argument here amidst the moral hyperbole—although whether in traditional terms or domino terms is unclear.

Harding, now as presidential candidate, said the issue was whether Americans favored "the particular League proposed by President Wilson." The problem was not with clarifying those League stipulations: "I do not want to clarify these obligations; I want to turn my back on them [because] the present league strikes a deadly blow at our constitutional integrity and surrenders to a dangerous extent our independence of action. . . . [Candidate Cox] favors going into the Paris League and I favor staying out."[37]

The columnist Walter Lippmann may have said correctly in 1920 that Harding was "distinguished by the fact that nothing distinguishes" him, but as Leopold says, he was what was wanted that year and he won.[38]

6.

The 1920s and 1930s: Unilateralism

America now definitely turned its back on cooperation in Europe and at Geneva. To say, though, that America "retreated into isolationism" is to give a misleading impression. If H. G. Wells could say of American "isolationism" that "Every time Europe looks across the Atlantic to see the American eagle, it observes only the rear end of an ostrich,"[39] it was because the American eagle-ostrich had its neck craned toward Asia and Japan. In the 1920s and 1930s America did not turn away from world affairs. It simply reasserted its independence and its natural inclina-

---

[35]With, as Kohlsaat, *From McKinley to Harding,* points out (p. 228) a plurality of 7,000,000 in November 1920, "the largest ever received by any candidate, on any ticket, for any office."

[36]*Congressional Record,* 66th Congress, 1st Session, vol. 58, pp. 5000–5003. Italics added.

[37]Speech at Des Moines, October 7, 1920. *NYT,* October 8, 1920.

[38]Leopold, *Growth of American Foreign Policy,* p. 406.

[39]Bailey, *Diplomatic History,* p. 628.

tion to "go it alone," concentrating especially on the Pacific but also on Latin America. The American policy in the interwar period was not isolationist; it was *unilateralist*.[40]

But whether avoidance was the orientation, as for European affairs, or the more active involvement as in the Far East and Latin America, the United States, acting alone and having largely dismantled the military establishment, now largely lacked an adequate power basis for the conduct of its policy.

For much of the 1920s or 1930s, whether one looks at the American concern over Yap, or Secretary of State Hughes's warning to Japan about troops still in Siberia on May 31, 1921, or to the provisions of the Washington Naval Disarmament Conference treaties (discussed later), the American policy focus remains primarily on China and Japan. That much is easy to prove. More difficult is to assess how to characterize the U.S. stance: the United States hardly ignored events, but clearly did not intend to resort to war if it could help it. Americans, acting alone and without a power backing, and moreover ambivalent about how hard a line to embrace, were therefore left with the rather feeble option of commenting adversely on Japanese manners. Ignoring Machiavelli's sage advice about the folly of inflicting limited injuries by uttering gratuitous insults, the United States irritated the Japanese to little practical effect. Let us see how this came about.

Whereas Woodrow Wilson once said (perhaps correctly) that the United States did not covet one foot of foreign territory, he did not comment on the corollary problem of *others* coveting territories the United States preferred to have in third-party hands. The corollary of Japan fighting in World War I was that Japan had a perfect pretext to seize the German islands of the Central Pacific: the Marshalls, the Carolines, and the Marianas. Japan also dispossessed Germany of China's Shantung province. In the Twenty-one Demands of January 8, 1915, Japan made a bid to turn China into a Japanese protectorate. The demands included requiring all advisers to Chinese officials to be Japanese.

In a U.S. note to Japan on March 13, 1915, the United States said it "frankly recognizes that territorial contiguity creates special relations between Japan and [certain Chinese] districts." But the note went on to say that the United States "could not regard with indifference the assumption of political, military or economic domination over China by a foreign Power. . . ."[41] On May 11, 1915, a further U.S. note said simply that the United States would not "recognize any agreement . . . impairing [its own] treaty rights [or] the political or territorial integrity of the Republic of China. . . ."[42] In the Lansing-Ishii agreement of November 2, 1917, these differences were not really resolved. The phrase, "territorial propinquity creates special relations" was included for Japan but it was also stipulated that the "territorial sovereignty of China, nevertheless, remains unimpaired" and the United States acknowledged Japan's assurances that its "special interests" would not produce trade discrimination.[43]

These exchanges papered over disagreements. American suspicion of Japan remained very real, especially until Japan agreed to the full evacuation of its troops from Siberia in January 1922.

The mutual recognition that the United States and Japan were headed on a collision course played a role in making the Washington Conference on Naval Disarmament of 1921 successful. The conference postponed the confrontation for more than a decade. The limited cooperation orientation made good sense.

---

[40]See Frederick H. Hartmann, "Away with Unilateralism!" *The Antioch Review*, 11, no. 1 (Spring 1951), 3–9, which introduces the term.

[41]*Papers Relating to the Foreign Relations of the United States, 1915,* pp. 105–111.

[42]Ibid., p. 146.

[43]Ibid., *1917,* p. 264.

American motives in convening the conference were mixed. It seemed senseless for the United States to continue its large naval expansion program in competition primarily with Britain, now that the war was over. In addition, Americans wanted the Anglo-Japanese Alliance terminated and the British would not consider doing that unless the United States gave up its rush toward naval supremacy. There was also a genuine wish to come to some agreement with Japan. These diverse motives, shared with the other participants in major respects, account for the odd cluster of treaties that came out of the Washington Conference. In addition to a treaty regulating naval armaments, there was a Nine-Power Treaty that essentially reflected the U.S. position on China. There was also a Four-Power Treaty pledging consultation on any Pacific question that might arise and (Article IV) terminating the therefore no longer needed Anglo-Japanese Alliance.

The question immediately leaps to mind: Why did Japan agree to the Washington provisions? For one thing, Japan could hardly insist on a continued alliance with Britain if Britain did not want one. But a second and more important reason lies embedded in the naval limitations provisions. Capital ships, meaning battleships and battle cruisers—the cut-off line being 10,000 tons or above—were controlled by a tonnage ratio formula: the United States and Britain, 525,000 each, with 315,000 tons for Japan (and 175,000 tons for Italy and France). Aircraft carriers were also controlled by tonnage ratio: 135,000 for the United States and Britain, 81,000 for Japan (60,000 each for Italy and France). The popular form of the formula, 5:5:3, applies to either group. These formulas were coupled with provisions requiring the United States, Britain, and Japan to maintain the status quo "with regard to fortifications and naval bases" in the Pacific except for the Japanese home islands, Hawaii for the United States, and Singapore for Britain. That meant, for example, that Japanese bases in Formosa could not be improved, nor could British bases such as Hong Kong or American bases in Subic Bay in the Philippines. Given fleet operating conditions, with their inevitable erosion of efficiency over vast distances (plus the need to load more fuel and food at the expense of shells), this meant that each of the three nations was assured in principle of naval superiority *in its own corner of* the Pacific Ocean area. Since under the technological conditions of the day, war between Japan and the United States in the Pacific would be fought at sea (through naval assault) or not at all, the Washington agreements in theory insured each party against effective attack.[44]

When Secretary of State Hughes proposed the reduction and scrapping formula at the Washington Conference on November 12, 1921, he made a tremendous impact, for he proposed doing away with 30 American, 19 British, and 17 Japanese ships. Naturally the dramatic disarmament aspect continued to dominate the public reaction. Less obvious were the base restriction provisions inserted to gain Japanese agreement on December 15, 1921. The Navy understood what the agreements meant for American possessions in the Western Pacific. Admiral Sims said: "Anybody can spit on the Philippines and you can't stop them."[45] Rear Admiral Harry S. Knapp, USN, Ret., explained the point at greater length:

> In the unfortunate event of hostilities with Japan, our Philippines are 7000 miles from our home coast while only 1500 miles from her home islands; her outlying islands are at farthest about 1000 miles from her home island while 7500 miles from our continental coast. Japan's possibilities of attack upon our outlying islands, or of defense of her own outlying islands against attack by us, are immeasurably superior to those of similar action by the United States.

[44]Part of the reason the United States Navy was caught unprepared by the Japanese attack on Pearl Harbor was that, theoretically, the odds were so great against Japan as to give Japan little incentive for such a high-risk venture.

[45]Quoted in Bailey, *Diplomatic History,* p. 647.

Admiral Knapp went on to explain that "naval opinion," in "accepting" the 5:5:3 ratio, did so only in the (by now proved unfounded) belief that each nation would remain free to strengthen bases by unilateral sovereign decisions. "To surrender the right to go beyond the *status quo* is to make the defense of our western possessions—their retention—well-nigh hopeless in case of need."[46]

The United States exchanged military inferiority in the Western Pacific for a Japanese promise to behave in that region. But the Japanese did in fact behave for quite a few years. When Japan refused (as was its right) to extend the treaty, denouncing it effective as of December 31, 1936, and there were no longer restrictions on base extension or strengthening naval forces, the United States did not move in any substantial way to end its vulnerability in the area. It did not even keep up a significant naval construction program between 1922 and 1930 in categories that were *not* restricted. While the Japanese laid down or appropriated for 125 vessels in that period, and the British planned for an additional 74 vessels, the United States total was 11.[47] Weigley said that at the Naval War College in the 1920s and 1930s as the ORANGE war (with Japan) was examined and reexamined, "The idea of a rapid strike by the battle fleet westward across the Pacific, to avenge the expected initial loss of American possessions to the Japanese, became ever more plainly unacceptable."[48] Thus, the United States found itself ever more impaled on the horns of a dilemma. Unable to make itself felt off China, should it continue to say much about it if Japan expanded there?

Although the history of U.S. diplomacy in this period shows much activity in relation to Latin America, this dilemma did not exist there, where, because it *had* great operational power, Washington's word continued to be "fiat" (at the cost of strained relations). That period of unilateral dominance came to an end with Franklin D. Roosevelt, whose concept of the "good neighbor policy," first announced March 4, 1933, had by August 14, 1936, advanced in its implementation with the abrogation of the Platt Amendment and the withdrawal of American marines from Haiti. As Roosevelt said without great exaggeration: "Throughout the Americas the spirit of the good neighbor is a practical and living fact." In that same year of 1936, the United States signed a consultative pact to provide for mutual consultation by the American republics in the event of war. Such instruments of growing agreement continued to accumulate in 1937, and accelerated still further with the outbreak of World War II into (ultimately) a full-blown regional collective security arrangement. In dealing with Latin America, the United States in this period showed every sign of a realistic appreciation of its interests and its problems, coupled with an imaginative approach to hemispheric cooperation.

For the world at large, the American effort, such as it was, had far less precision and tended toward empty generalizations. Not that this was surprising; what *did* the United States want Europe to do except remain at peace? In any event, the Kellogg-Briand Pact adopted with enthusiasm in 1928 "outlawed" war. In the Senate debate over the treaty, Senator Hiram Johnson of California cross-examined Senator William E. Borah of Idaho. Borah stoutly maintained that the pact contained no obligation, expressed or implied, binding on the United States. Senator Johnson pushed the point to its extreme and Borah replied: "Exactly. In other words, when the treaty is broken the United States is absolutely free. It is just as free to choose its course as if the treaty had never been written. . . ."[49] Senator Claude Swanson of Virginia called the treaty "a mere gesture, yet it is a gesture of peace, not hostility. . . . It is a noble gesture . . . and as

---

[46]Rear Admiral Harry S. Knapp, "The Limitation of Armament at the Conference of Washington," *Proceedings of the American Society of International Law,* 1922, pp. 12–19.

[47]*Senate Document* no. 202, 78th Congress, 2nd Session.

[48]Weigley, *American Way of War,* p. 254.

[49]*Congressional Record,* 70th Congress, 2nd Session, vol. 70, p. 1066 (January 3, 1929).

such I shall support it. . . ."[50] On January 15, 1929, the Senate advised ratification of the Kellogg-Briand provisions and on January 24, 1929, the treaty was proclaimed.

In September 1931 an explosion occurred under somewhat murky circumstances near the Japanese-controlled South Manchurian Railway, not far from the Chinese city of Mukden. Claiming it was the work of Chinese troops, the Japanese overwhelmed the Chinese garrison and occupied Mukden. In the wake of the incident, the United States on January 7, 1932, sent Japan a note that in wording and spirit would be easy to confuse with those sent in 1915, so little had the issues and attitudes altered. The note repeated the old American refrain: The United States would not "admit the legality of any situation de facto nor does it intend to recognize any treaty or agreement" between China and Japan which impaired its treaty rights, the Open Door, or China's integrity.[51] (Thus was promulgated the so-called Stimson Doctrine.) Thereafter, the United States cooperated gingerly with the League of Nations (which was careful in its own Lytton Report not to place unqualified blame on Japanese shoulders).

The United States was still very far from willing to take a firm stand backed by threat or force—and especially not alone. Discussing the possibility of the United States joining in a League arms embargo against China and Japan if one were instituted, Secretary of State Cordell Hull, in a memorandum to the Senate Committee on Foreign Relations dated May 17, 1933, argued that an embargo "would not be an effective means of restoring peace" since Japan had a large munitions industry. What would likely happen would be "a Japanese blockade of Chinese ports," thus diminishing the arms in China's hands. The United States would be inclined not to go along with a League embargo and certainly not "unless we had secured substantial guarantees from the governments of all of the great powers which would ensure us against the effects of any retaliatory measures which the Japanese might undertake." The United States would act only "with a due and prudent regard for American interests and in particular for our *paramount interest of remaining free from any entanglements* which would involve this country *in a foreign war*."[52]

Was this really America's "paramount interest"—remaining "free" from "entanglements"? Once the United States actually found itself (at the end of 1941) at war with Japan, was that war, since the United States was then part of it, no longer "foreign" (and therefore acceptable)?

One cannot choose between counterbalancing national interests very well until one has established what the issues and alternatives really consist of. Were the crucial alternatives Hull confronted simply avoidance of entanglements and involvements in "foreign" wars on the one hand, or becoming entangled or involved on the other? Would deciding these points decide the real issues? If Japan's war with China was a foreign war and America's paramount interest was avoiding involvement, why then did the United States care what happened there? Or, if the United States did care, in what sense was the war "foreign?"

Certainly, suspicion of the maneuvers of foreigners to embroil the innocent United States in "their" quarrels was still very much a part of American official thinking. In that same memorandum, Hull went on to say that there was "danger that . . . certain European governments may find it to their interest to make it appear that this Government is responsible . . . for a failure on their part to proceed with the imposition of sanctions to which they are committed" as League members. One can almost hear Hull thinking: "and which we were wise enough to avoid."

[50] Ibid., pp. 1186–1189 (January 5, 1929).

[51] *Senate Document* no. 55, 72nd Congress, 1st Session, pp. 53–54.

[52] *Peace and War: United States Foreign Policy, 1931–1941*, Department of State Publication no. 1853 (Washington, D.C., 1943), pp. 183–186. Italics added.

The First Three Neutrality Acts

As the "gathering storm" of World War II drew clearly visible on the horizon, the issue sharpened as to whether the United States could "sit it out." The initial American reaction to Adolf Hitler and the "march of the aggressors" was to do exactly that. The disintegration of the world economic system known as the Great Depression also played a significant role in the American attitude. That Depression was triggered by the economic dislocations of World War I and, especially, the punitive reparations toward Germany. It led through inflation to the pauperizing of the German middle class—and to Hitler's coming to power. From 1932 onward at least until 1941 an important part of the energies of all the democracies was diverted inward—to the establishment of domestic economic health. It is important to keep this division of attention in mind, for it explains some of the poor decisions that were made. Pertinent also were the heavy European casualties, especially dead, in World War I, which sapped the energies of the West to deal with the rising threat of Nazi Germany.

In the middle 1930s, Congress began to enact precautionary legislation, collectively known as "the neutrality acts," that were designed to avoid U.S. involvement in war abroad by curtailing American activity abroad. The First Neutrality Act was a temporary measure. Adopted on August 31, 1935, and due to expire February 29, 1936, it provided for licensing trade in arms and made it unlawful to export such arms to belligerents or for U.S. citizens to travel on belligerent ships, once the President invoked these provisions.[53] The more permanent Second Neutrality Act of February 29, 1936, tightened restrictions on presidential discretion and added a prohibition of loans to belligerents.[54] The Third Neutrality Act of May 1, 1937, carrying these provisions forward and applying them also to areas having "civil strife," added a further constraint that any categories of goods not otherwise prohibited sent abroad to belligerents or areas having civil strife had to be paid for and title transferred first.[55] Considering the record of how the United States ended up as a belligerent in World War I, no clearer evidence of congressional desires to avoid a repetition could be assembled. Clearly, avoidance was the preferred orientation.

All of these acts, like Hull's memorandum, were reactions to increased militarism in Japan, to the rise of Hitler in Germany, and to Mussolini's irresponsible actions in Ethiopia. On July 7, 1937, the Marco Polo bridge incident near Beijing inaugurated the full-fledged Japanese assault on China proper. U.S. Ambassador to Japan Joseph C. Grew had certainly warned about what was coming. In a report of December 27, 1934, he had said the United States was faced with two main alternatives: oppose or withdraw. Grew claimed flatly that the militaristic faction in Japan was rising in power, especially encouraged by a lack of effective opposition. He urged building the U.S. Navy up to Washington Treaty levels and thereafter matching the Japanese effort. The best way to avoid war was to be prepared. "The Soviet Ambassador recently told me that a prominent Japanese had said to him that the most important factor in avoiding a Japanese attack on the Maritime Provinces was the intensive Soviet military preparations in Siberia and Vladivostok. I believe this to be true. . . ."[56] But about this time the inadequate U.S. Pacific Fleet was only beginning to emerge from the Depression restrictions that allowed it oil for steaming for only one or two weeks a year.

When Mussolini attacked Ethiopia in 1935, Adolf Hitler took advantage of the League crisis to remilitarize the Rhineland. League opposition to Mussolini, irritating but not effective,

[53] *Peace and War*, pp. 266–271.
[54] Ibid., pp. 313–314.
[55] Ibid., pp. 355–365.
[56] Ibid., pp. 247–248.

encouraged him to transform the Rome-Berlin Axis into a formal partnership and both Germany and Italy now intervened in the Spanish civil war. In March 1938, in a new coup, Hitler gathered Austria into the expanding Third Reich.

Cordell Hull, in a speech in New York on February 16, 1935, said:

> Seen from the distance of this hemisphere, the manifold boundary lines on the map of Europe become blurred and Europe emerges as an entity. We have no direct concern with the political and economic controversies of the European states. We have time and again expressly disassociated ourselves from these disputes. Nevertheless, we are deeply interested in the peace and stability of Europe as a whole. . . .[57]

By the late 1930s, if not before, the question could be put whether the United States could simply be against war in Europe, and not against some specific disturbers of the peace. What was the problem the United States confronted because of European developments? Who was the enemy? War—or Germany and Italy? In Asia the enemy tended to have a name, but the United States continually deferred paying the price (even by arming itself) to restrain that enemy while continuing to irritate that enemy by futile gestures of nonrecognition of accomplished acts. In Latin America, the abstract concerns of the United States to gather the "peace-loving" states of the hemisphere into a common front had somewhat more promise since most were threatened by the same potential enemies. Like a thread running through these events, and exemplified by the neutrality acts, was a strong American reluctance to rearm, a hope to avoid conflict, a shrinking from taking specific sides for and against specific friends and enemies. The United States obviously preferred to be "against war" instead. Pearl Harbor would ultimately put an end to that and provide some specific rather than abstract enemies to be opposed. The nature of the problem would be abruptly clarified.

8.

Summing Up

Our analysis shows clearly that the United States, in its search for national security, passed through distinct stages. First came weakness, a small nation surrounded by great power neighbors. Expansion at this stage equaled both growth in power and a receding of the immediate threat. Second came fulfillment, as these first goals once realized brought both opportunities for choice and a freedom from assault against the continental domain. Third came ambition and a larger sense of national purpose as the United States accepted the gospel of Alfred Thayer Mahan and fought the Spanish-American War. Fourth came involvement in World War I, disillusionment with Europe, and a unilateralism tinged with a frustrating ambiguity about how to deal with the rising power of Japan. Fifth, as we see in Chapter 12, came commitment as the balance of power deteriorated in Europe, and the growing threat of a new world war became reality for Americans on December 7, 1941. Through these later periods of increasing involvement, as the security perimeter was progressively extended, Americans struggled to perceive a proper role for the United States to play. No longer limited by power (except in the immediate sense of mobilized armed forces), they had to decide the proper limits of involvement through policy.

[57]Ibid., pp. 248–255.

12

In Pursuit of a Global Role

A common ground between the United States and the U.S.S.R., and one that will obtain for a long period of time, in my opinion, lies in the fact that both are sincere advocates of world peace. . . .

Communism holds no serious threat to the United States. Friendly relations in the future may be of great general value.

Ambassador Joseph E. Davies,
Final Report from Moscow, June 6, 1938[1]

The temptation to explain American world strategy after World War II purely in terms of countermoves to Soviet expansionism is almost as great as the temptation to explain the latter exclusively in terms of Marxist-Leninist ideology.

John G. Stoessinger,
Crusaders and Pragmatists[2]

Bernard Brodie once pointed to "the tendency of our national leaders to slip into expansive habits of interpretation concerning the real meaning of threats that are quite remote in space. . . ." That sentence, in the original, ends with the words: "and at least for the time being directed against others."

Here is that haunting and fundamental question back again: Where should one draw the policy line and where, if necessary, should one deploy forces? And when should a threat be seen as directed not solely against others but against oneself, whoever else may share the danger? How does one recognize a serious threat in the first place? To answer this fundamental set of questions on too niggardly a scale, or to respond too readily to the always present opportunities to be caught up in war, is a recipe for disaster. That is a prime reason why the way in which the problem is perceived is so crucial. It is not possible to approach such issues "with an open mind," resolved to do only that which is "necessary." What is defined as "necessary" is ultimately in

---

[1]Dispatch no. 1341 from Moscow, June 6, 1938, to the Secretary of State. Reprinted by Davies in his *Mission to Moscow* (New York: Simon & Schuster, 1941), pp. 377–425.

[2]John G. Stoessinger, *Crusaders and Pragmatists: Movers of Modern American Foreign Policy* (New York: Norton, 1979), p. 64.

the mind of the beholder. Put differently, the policy content that one deems "necessary" and believes must be implemented is largely governed by one's basic concepts.

In this chapter we see the United States struggling successively with two problems that, in each case, were ultimately perceived as a serious threat requiring a determined response. First came the final acts in the challenge of the Axis powers in the 1930s: Japan, Germany, and Italy. Second came the new threat of an expanding Russia.

1.

War Clouds Gather

As the war clouds gathered over Europe in the late 1930s, Americans struggled with the Axis problem. Counterbalancing interests of the United States offered a choice between withdrawal and participation. As usual when a war is in the offing, the behavior of those nations with whom the United States would probably make common cause if the United States participated in the looming struggle was far from edifying. England and France could not agree on a strategy for dealing with Hitler. Italy was adding an empire in Africa as prelude to its own undoing. Savagely suspicious Joseph Stalin interpreted English-French weakness and capitulation at Munich in 1938 as a deliberate opening for Hitler's Germany of a corridor to the East, a convenient route in aid of attacking Russia. Perhaps the serious structural problems embedded in the Peace of Versailles and the postwar vindictive settlements left little hope even initially that a firm stand for peace could be contrived. But if such a chance existed, it had surely been lost.

The American Congress and people assessed these developments with differences of opinion, to be sure, but with a strong bias toward staying out of this latest of "Europe's" quarrels—an attitude duly reflected in the passage and continual augmentation of restrictions in the three neutrality acts. Before the tide of opinion turned there was to be still a Fourth Neutrality Act, passed on November 4, 1939, after the war had begun in Europe.

Those in the executive branch and those whose professional concerns gave them more direct interest and knowledge of events abroad were the first to depart the avoidance (isolationist) consensus. For example, Henry L. Stimson in a letter to the *New York Times* on October 7, 1937, listed the bold Fascist "coups" in Ethiopia, the Rhineland, and Spain, comparing it to the dispirited reaction of the democracies still "absorbed with the work of recuperation from the depression. . . ." Stimson could find some excuse for Britain,

> faced . . . with an extremely perilous European condition within range of her home cities. But in America, occupying the most safe and defensible position in the world, there has been no excuse except faulty reasoning for the wave of ostrich-like isolationism which has swept over us and by its erroneous form of neutrality legislation has threatened to bring upon us in the future the very dangers of war which we now are seeking to avoid.

There was the perennial issue posed: Would the danger recede if one did nothing about it?

Such neutrality legislation, said Stimson, which "attempts to impose a dead level of neutral conduct . . . between right and wrong, between an aggressor and its victim, between a breaker of the law of nations" and law-abiding nations, "won't work." Not only was it "a policy of amoral drift" but it would "not save us from entanglement. It will even make entanglement more certain. History has already amply shown this last fact."[3]

---

[3]This is the same Stimson who in 1931, during the Manchurian crisis, rebuffed the mild League flirtations with the idea of sanctions with the remark that the United States Navy would "probably" not interfere with them if they were imposed. See T. A. Bailey, *A Diplomatic History of the American People,* 4th ed. (New York: Appleton-Century-Crofts, 1950), p. 695. Of course, Stimson was then reflecting official policy.

Other groups were equally sure that "history" proved something else. Soon the Committee to Defend America by Aiding the Allies formed the center bloc of the first opinion, whereas its opponents clustered together in the America First movement in which Colonel Charles A. Lindbergh played a prominent role. Both argued in the beginning that its policy would preserve the peace: the first, by helping the Allies so the United States would not have to fight; the second, by staying strictly neutral and avoiding danger. President Roosevelt, increasingly sure that the Stimson view was correct, found his hands tied. Although the Gallup Poll showed huge majorities opposed to Japan's renewed militarism on the mainland, Roosevelt's "Quarantine-the-Aggressors" speech of October 5, 1937, aroused sufficient adverse criticism to cause him to back off. Even the *Panay* incident of December 12, 1937, when Japanese planes bombed and sank an American gunboat in broad daylight on the Yangtze River, did not bring on full crisis, especially as the Japanese civilian government immediately apologized and paid reparations. Part of the explanation is also, as Stimson noted, the American profound preoccupation with the Depression, which made jobs still scarce as late as 1939.

The tragic events of 1938 began to make a belated impact on American opinion, but not enough to inspire a change of course. The proposed Ludlow Amendment to the Constitution, requiring a nationwide vote before going to war (except for actual invasion), was shelved in the House by the extremely close vote of 209 to 188 as late as January 10, 1938. In March, Hitler took Austria, and in September he arranged at Munich for Czechoslovakia's friends and allies (the British and the French) to put the pressure on Czechoslovakia to submit to its dismemberment. This event was described by the fatuous Neville Chamberlain as securing "peace in our time" after Adolf Hitler gave one of his usual assurances, in this case that the Czechoslovak, German-populated Sudentenland was "the last territorial claim which I have to make in Europe."

Cordell Hull, speaking on March 17, 1938, said that, in announcing America's intentions to protect its "rights and interests in the Far East," he had "stated clearly that we are fully determined to avoid the extremes either of internationalism or of isolationism. Internationalism would mean undesirable political involvements; isolationism would compel us to confine all activities of our people within our own frontiers. . . ." In his view, "steering a sound middle course" instead was what was required "to serve our national interest."[4] But what was the "national interest"? Hull explained that in the specific case at issue, since Congress hardly could have foreseen the undeclared war of Japan against China and could not therefore have intended the neutrality acts to be applied there, the President would not invoke them and embargo arms. At the same time, U.S. government-owned merchant ships would not be allowed to transport arms to China and Japan. Privately owned U.S. merchantmen could continue to transport arms "at their own risk." Hull called these Solomon-like divide-the-baby provisions "the essence of our foreign policy"!

In the summer of 1939, after Hitler in March had shamelessly taken the rest of Czechoslovakia, as Congress wrestled with a revision of the neutrality legislation, President Roosevelt forwarded to Congress a paper by Hull in which Hull argued that the American arms embargo provision "plays into the hands" of the aggressive powers and "works directly against the interests of the peace-loving nations." Congress was still contemplating this change of emphasis when Stalin made a sudden pact with Hitler (actually, to divide up Poland), and World War II began on September 3, 1939. Britain and France, pushed to the wall, had honored their pledge of support to Poland that a skeptical Stalin had assumed was a "sucker play" designed to involve Russia in supporting Poland against Hitler while the French and English hung back. (Stalin

[4]*Peace and War: United States Foreign Policy, 1931–1941,* Department of State Publication no. 1853 (Washington, D.C., 1943), pp. 407–419.

made it explicit in his speech of March 10, 1939, to the Eighteenth Communist Party Congress: "England and France have taken up a position of nonintervention [which] reveals an eagerness, a desire, not to hinder the aggressors in their nefarious work . . . not to hinder Germany . . . from embroiling itself in a war with the Soviet Union. . . .")

2.

The Final Pre—World War II Debates

Congress, contemplating a disintegrating international environment, and with the cash-and-carry provision of the Third Neutrality Act expired as of May 1939, finally enacted the Fourth Neutrality Act. This act made it unlawful for any American vessel to carry "any passengers or any articles or materials to any state" named by the President as being in "a state of war." No American citizen without special permission could travel into any "combat area" proclaimed by the President. After such a proclamation, no "American vessel, engaged in commerce with any foreign state" was "to be armed, except with small arms. . . ." Bonds of belligerents could not be sold, or credit extended to them. Arms dealers would be licensed and arms could be shipped to belligerents only with such licenses.

This was the new "middle course," designed for one thing to put an end to the situation brought about under the Third Neutrality Act when, on September 5, 1939, President Roosevelt, bound by the law, embargoed all arms shipments. Britain and France were thus cut off from some $80,000,000 worth of arms they had already ordered. The new neutrality act allowed the flow to resume provided the Allies paid cash and picked up the arms. The new act was a compromise between those Americans (50 per cent, according to Gallup) who wanted to supply the Allies (which would now be legal) and those Americans who wanted war zones from which Americans would be barred (84 per cent, according to Gallup). The compromise postponed the choice between counterbalancing interests.

President Roosevelt, in requesting the revised legislation, had said of the third act on September 21, 1939, that its continued existence was "most vitally dangerous to American neutrality, American security, and American peace," adding: "I regret that the Congress passed that act. I regret equally that I signed that act." The new act, although still very restrictive, at least allowed the obvious to be done: to quit aiding a Hitler victory.

The whole sequence of events just described, and the debate in Congress over the Fourth Neutrality Act, as well as the Gallup percentages quoted, show the extent of American confusion. The disagreements went deeper than the question posed by Brodie of where to draw the line. They involved the more fundamental points of agreeing on the problem, defining the issues, and formulating the alternatives. Bureaucratic interests or organizational processes were minor aspects of this decision making. What was most obviously lacking was a fundamental conceptual agreement in the United States about what the United States faced as the most serious threat to its security, what it wanted the trend of events to be, as to just who its friends were, as to which nations were a menace to its peace and security (and in what order of priority), and of what the best course of action was to achieve U.S. goals—whatever those were. Even Stimson spoke of peace-loving democracies and hovered between an argument based on moral (good guy vs. bad) considerations and practical questions as to whether the American policy would "work." Which was the critical variable: that it was morally wrong or right or that it would or would not work? Or, if nations are moral enough, can things be expected to work for them for that reason? Is that in its turn a convoluted and indirect way of arguing that a broad policy of support to nations with a common appreciation of the threat will pay off better than evenhandedness between friends and enemies? The imprecisions in these arguments accurately reflected the confusions and uncertainties in American thinking.

The public groups and congressional blocs debated what policy would preserve the peace when they meant what policy would preserve American security. Yet they clearly felt that the choice should not be expressed in this way. When President Roosevelt lumps together American neutrality, security, and peace as being threatened by the provisions of the 1937 neutrality act, shall we interpret his stand as deliberately misleading or as a sign of personal confusion about the nature of the problem? Obviously, being neutral was not threatened by that act (although the act voluntarily surrendered American rights and interests that had brought the United States to belligerency on earlier occasions). The United States could refuse *all* trade with anyone and still be and stay neutral. What that policy would do to American security was something else again. And whether peace was compatible or incompatible with any particular policy choice that might be made depended primarily on reactions abroad. It was not a condition of things that could be preserved or eroded simply as an American act of will. One can understand following generations, including revisionist historians, who are hardly able to visualize the problem at all as it seemed to Americans in the 1930s. It is natural for them to assume some kind of hypocritical and Machiavellian intent by Roosevelt to sneak the United States into the war.[5]

The United States, trying to deal with the problem of enmity and enemies in this period, had the initial difficulty that there was still little tendency to use such terms or think in them. Preferred were euphemisms such as "immoral" nations or "aggressive" nations, as compared to "peace-loving nations" who "believed in the rule of law." Just as a puritanical period in history is difficult for people in a sexually permissive period to understand, and vice versa, a people accustomed to think in contemporary security terms has difficulty taking in the debate of the 1930s. It becomes slightly clearer if one remembers the implicit baseline from which these judgments take off: that the United States, long at peace and prospering through peace, *can decide of its own will* (or at least through policy judgments) *whether to remain at peace*. There is no Greek tragedy element in this American thinking; outcomes will be good or bad depending upon the actions taken (or maybe even the goals sought). There is no real thought that things may grow more dangerous or worse regardless of which policy option is followed, and simply because the environment is moving that way as others respond with their choices. In this earlier age of innocence, the reality and decisiveness of free will are not questioned.

Most of all, one is struck by the *abstract* nature of the debate with its tendency to slide off from concrete observations about friends and enemies. Even when President Roosevelt extends much needed aid to "our" side by making the Destroyers-Bases Agreement with the British on September 3, 1940, after France has fallen and only the British stand between the United States and Nazi Germany, he gives the usual assurances that his actions are "not inconsistent in any sense with our status of peace. Still less is it a threat against any nation. It is an . . . act of preparation for continental defense in the face of grave danger."[6] How giving destroyers to the British to use against the Germans qualifies under any of these statements would take a magician or a metaphysician to establish. Preferably a metaphysician, who would understand that a people accustomed to one form of highly inappropriate and indirect security language are continuing to use it under circumstances highly awkward for the common meaning of words.

Only the continuing impact of events intruded more sense of reality. By January 6, 1941, when Roosevelt addressed the Congress with his call for America to become the "arsenal of

---

[5]One "revisionist" theme even argued that FDR left the U.S. fleet exposed at Pearl Harbor to lure a Japanese attack so that FDR could have "his" war, despite American popular reluctance.

[6]Message to Congress, September 3, 1940. *Peace and War*, pp. 564–565. The agreement provided for the transfer of 50 overage destroyers to the British in exchange for base rights in British Caribbean territories and Newfoundland.

democracy," a coherent concept is finally beginning to emerge. The tone has altered when Roosevelt says "that principles of morality and considerations for our own security will never permit us to acquiesce in a peace dictated by aggressors. . . . We know that enduring peace cannot be bought at the cost of other people's freedom." (At least the abstractions have assumed a rank order here, with peace becoming a variable rather than an absolute.) Roosevelt further said that "we will not be intimidated by the threats of dictators that they will regard as a breach of international law," or act of war, American "aid to the democracies." He then added a very sound and realistic proposition: "When the dictators are ready to make war on us, they will not wait for an act of war on our part."[7] Shortly afterwards, on March 11, 1941, Congress passed the "Lend-Lease" Act, whose official title was "An Act Further to Promote the Defense of the United States." Lend-Lease was designed to aid a Britain that soon would be unable to finance its purchases. It authorized the President to "sell . . . exchange, lease, lend . . . any defense article [to] any country whose defense the President deems vital," and permitted him to determine what if anything was required in exchange. Isolationist Senator Wheeler promptly proclaimed it a bill to "plow under every fourth American boy," but it passed by a vote of 60 to 31 in the Senate and by 317 to 71 in the House.

The public debate, too, became more concrete. In April 1941, Lindbergh, speaking in New York, argued that the United States militarily was in no position to fight in Europe but, conversely, "no foreign power is in a position to invade us today. If we concentrate on our own defenses . . . no foreign army will ever attempt to land on American shores."[8] The *New York Times* responded editorally: "It has been said, times without number, that if Hitler cannot cross the English Channel he cannot cross three thousand miles of sea. But there is only one reason why he has not crossed the English Channel. That is because forty-five million determined Britons in a heroic resistance" stand on alert. Hull's argument is quoted with approval: "It is not the water which bars the way. It is the resolute determination of British arms. Were the control of the seas by Britain lost, the Atlantic . . . would become a broad highway for a conqueror moving westward."[9]

That argument has some holes in it, too, but at least it has become a fairly tangible comparison of alternative outcomes dependent at least partially on the choice of interest pursued and the American initiatives taken or not taken. As 1941 continued, the concerns became ever more immediate and concrete. After Japan took control of Indochina, on July 25, 1941, FDR, who had already cut off war supplies to Japan, froze all Japanese assets in the United States. As the Japanese oil supplies fell, the die was cast since the Japanese would have to submit or attack. So little did U.S. congressional or public opinion reflect any real appreciation of these strategic issues, however, that the vote by which Selective Service was extended in the House on August 12 was 203 to 202. And the year 1941 ended with that very concrete Japanese attack known as "Pearl Harbor." On December 8, 1941, the Congress, by a Senate vote of 82 to 0 and a House vote of 388 to 1, acknowledged that the United States was at war with Japan.

It is even today difficult to say with assurance what would have happened if the Japanese had not attacked at Pearl Harbor, since antiwar sentiment remained very significant in the United States. Still, as Roosevelt had told Congress on December 8, "There is no blinking at the fact that our people, our territory, and our interests are in grave danger." The nearer and more obvious the threat, the more specifically it could be described.

[7]Ibid., pp. 608–611.
[8]*New York Times,* April 24, 1941.
[9]*New York Times,* April 30, 1941.

3.

World War II: Political versus Military Issues

The American entry into the war brought a new concreteness and specificity about the nature of the immediate problem and the issues to be decided. Since Hitler also declared war on the United States in the wake of the Japanese attack, the conflict was broadened for the United States to global dimensions. It was now clear who the enemy was; to the planners it was fairly clear which theater of war to emphasize first (Europe getting preference). For the longer run, it was less clear what the fighting was intended to procure the United States other than an end to Axis fighting capabilities and the displacement of the dictators from power. It was also less obvious what state of affairs and set of relationships the United States expected to achieve as a result of its victory. When the American government thought in *those* terms, it invariably came up with new moral slogans, such as FDR's "four freedoms." In FDR's formulation (January 6, 1941) these were freedom of speech and worship, and freedom from want and fear. (The second two were soon to be included in the first Anglo-American statement of "common principles" on which they "base their hopes for a better future for the world.") With peace aims so vague and immediate war aims so clear, it is not surprising that American generals were soon given their way over American diplomats, who got second billing and sometimes were forgotten altogether. This approach meant literally that the Secretary of State sometimes was not even invited to the important World War II conferences.

High-sounding declarations continued in vogue throughout the war. As George F. Kennan once wrote, in reference to the Open Door policy:

> The tendency to achieve our foreign policy objectives by inducing other governments to sign up to professions of high moral and legal principle appears to have a great and enduring vitality in our diplomatic practice. It is linked, certainly, with the strong American belief in the power of public opinion to overrule governments. It is also linked, no doubt, with the pronounced American tendency to transplant legal concepts from the domestic to the international field: to believe that international society could—and should—operate on the basis of general contractual obligation, and hence to lay stress on verbal undertaking rather than on the concrete manifestations of political interest.[10]

American diplomacy brought forth a number of such declarations. In August 1941, as the United States and United Kingdom moved closer to de facto alliance, Roosevelt got Churchill to agree to the eight points of the Atlantic Charter. The charter, in addition to including Roosevelt's third and fourth "freedoms," announced that "their countries seek no aggrandizement, territorial or other," and ended by expressing the Anglo-American belief "that all of the nations of the world . . . must come to the abandonment of the use of force." Other Wilsonian-type postulates were scattered in between. This Anglo-American statement of "common principles" formed, they said, the basis of "their hopes for a better future for the world."[11] In the Moscow Declarations of October 30, 1943, signed also by Russia and China, the two nations declared they would fight until "unconditional surrender" by the enemies. In the Cairo Conference declaration of November 1943, the Americans, British, and Chinese avowed their intention of "fighting this war to restrain and punish the aggression of Japan" and as punishment they intended to begin by stripping Japan of all territories seized, occupied, or "stolen" by Japan since 1914. At Teheran on December 1, 1943, the Americans, British, and Russians expressed their "determination that our nations shall work together in war and in the peace that will fol-

---

[10]George F. Kennan, *American Diplomacy, 1900–1950* (Chicago: University of Chicago Press, 1951), p. 46.
[11]*Peace and War*, pp. 717–720.

low." They would seek "the elimination of tyranny and slavery, oppression and intolerance."[12] And at Yalta on February 11, 1945, the Allies agreed to eliminate German militarism and to establish a United Nations.[13] The Potsdam Declaration of July 26, 1945, at the end of the war, was fairly concrete about objectives but managed also to say a few words in favor of "peace, security and justice" once "irresponsible militarism [was] driven from the world." The American influence in all these statements was not negligible.

But always included in these communiqués were concrete provisions for dealing with the enemy states—for example, in the case of Germany, dividing that nation (and Berlin) into occupation zones. These concrete proposals, however, were sometimes drawn rather haphazardly, or left out important details—a reflection of the American preoccupation with "winning the war" and the corollary assumption that those united against Hitler were destined to remain friends and allies *after* Hitler was defeated. The problems shortly encountered were therefore of two kinds. First, those that were the natural result of putting "military" considerations first, so as to win the war quickly and decisively, and second, those which stemmed from the unfounded assumption of postwar cooperation by the victors. Arrangements to deal with Germany illustrate both points.

Take the question of reaching Berlin. Churchill, in the spring of 1945, raised the question, urging its significance. Dwight D. Eisenhower's response as commanding general was to tell General Marshall:

> I am the first to admit that a war is waged in pursuance of political aims, and if the Combined Chiefs of Staff should decide that the Allied effort to take Berlin outweighs purely military considerations in this theater, I would cheerfully readjust my plans and my thinking so as to carry out such an operation.[14]

But the Washington political authorities did not want to do anything that could look like a sign of distrusting the Russians.[15] General Marshall's reaction was close to indignation that he should be asked to shed the blood of American soldiers for "political" purposes. That Eisenhower *really* thought himself that such a move on Berlin made little sense is apparent from his dispatch of March 30, 1945, to Washington in which he argued that "Berlin itself is no longer a particularly important objective. Its usefulness to the German has been largely destroyed and even his government is preparing to move to another area."[16] General Marshall replies on March 31, with FDR's approval: "The battle of Germany is now at a point where it is up to the field commander to judge the measures which should be taken. . . . The single objective should be quick and complete victory."[17]

---

[12]Demonstrating the predominance of military advisers, *Foreign Relations of the United States: Conferences at Cairo and Teheran, 1943* (Department of State, 1961) on p. 462 lists the *complete* American party as follows: the President, Harry Hopkins, Ambassador Winant (EAC), Ambassador Harriman, Charles Bohlen (interpreter), Russell W. Barnes (OWI), plus *thirteen* generals and admirals, *forty-four* "other ranks," and fourteen Secret Service.

[13]*Foreign Relations of the United States: The Conferences at Malta and Yalta, 1945* (Department of State, 1955), on p. 553 lists as present for the first formal meeting: the President, Secretary Stettinius, Ambassador Harriman, and six generals and admirals. In later meetings, with five more civilians present, the civilian-military balance finally changes.

[14]Alfred D. Chandler, Jr., ed., *The Papers of Dwight David Eisenhower: The War Years* (Baltimore: Johns Hopkins Press, 1970), volume IV, p. 2592. Cited in Russell F. Weigley, *The American Way of War* (New York: Macmillan, 1973), p. 353.

[15]Weigley, *American Way of War*, pp. 353–354; see also Stephen E. Ambrose, *Eisenhower and Berlin, 1945: The Decision to Halt at the Elbe* (New York: Norton, 1967).

[16]Dwight D. Eisenhower, *Crusade in Europe* (New York: Doubleday, 1948), p. 401.

[17]Ibid., p. 402. Also in Truman, *Memoirs*, vol. 1 (Garden City, N.Y.: Doubleday, 1955), p. 212. In *Crusade*, p. 396, Eisenhower says: "Military plans, I believe, should be devised with the single aim of speeding victory. . . ."

Later, Churchill, disturbed by the developments in Poland, as the Soviets showed no sign of being willing to share power and went ahead installing their own puppets instead, pleaded for the United States not to withdraw from the advanced positions in Germany occupied by American troops as German resistance crumbled. (These areas were slated to pass under Soviet control.) On May 4, 1945, Churchill told Truman: "The Polish problem may be easier to settle when set in relation to the now numerous outstanding questions of the utmost gravity which require urgent settlement with the Russians." A withdrawal of American troops "would mean the tide of Russian domination sweeping forward 120 miles on a front of 300 or 400 miles." This would be a "most melancholy" event, and "the Allies ought not to retreat from their present positions to the occupational line until we are satisfied about Poland, and also about the temporary character of the Russian occupation of Germany." But Truman, concluding that the United States had given its word, ordered the withdrawal and the British felt obliged to concur. The evils predicted by Churchill shortly came to pass.

These episodes at the very least show a lack of sensitivity to orchestrating military movements in terms of political values. Actually, more accurately, they show an odd basis of calculation by the American authorities. Eisenhower and Marshall think that Berlin is worth taking only if there is resistance there. Truman goes ahead with withdrawal to honor U.S. commitments even while the Soviets are way behind in honoring theirs. The purpose is to avoid offending the Soviets (even though the Soviets are offending *us*). There is no appreciation here for any of the more obvious axioms of balance of power thinking. One should ponder Admiral J. C. Wylie's remark that "War for a nonaggressor nation is actually a nearly complete collapse of policy."[18]

The story of how the occupation zones were fixed reads like fiction. It includes the fact that President Roosevelt, while en route to the Cairo Conference without having invited his own Secretary of State along, drew up a proposal for a possible division of Germany which the military kept and the diplomatic side of the house knew nothing about.[19] This is what lay behind George Kennan's remark that when he was attached to the European Advisory Commission (EAC) which drew up the zonal boundaries, and after the Soviets had accepted the zones put on the table by the British delegation, the U.S. delegation "still had no instructions [and were] puzzled by the Russian action. We were not officially informed as to what had taken place at the Teheran Conference (neither was the Department of State, for that matter)."[20]

Kennan says he learned many years later that the British proposals were given to the American military at the time Roosevelt departed for the Cairo Conference and were discussed (FDR and the military) en route and again within the Combined (Anglo-American) Chiefs of Staff at Cairo. "Of all this," says Kennan, "no one in the White House or in the military establishment gave to us, or apparently even to the State Department, at any time the slightest inkling of official information, despite the fact that we were now supposed to negotiate with the British and Soviet governments on precisely this subject."[21]

When Kennan was finally sent to Washington to unravel the confusion, he found FDR preoccupied with *the Anglo-American argument* over which country should have the more

[18]J. C. Wylie, *Military Strategy: A General Theory of Power Control* (New Brunswick, N.J.: Rutgers University Press, 1967), p. 80.

[19]See Frederick H. Hartmann, *Germany Between East and West;* and Robert E. Sherwood, *Roosevelt and Hopkins: An Intimate History* (New York: Harper, 1948). On p. 767 Sherwood lists FDR's entourage on the *Iowa:* Hopkins, five generals, and five admirals. On p. 777, Sherwood adds: " . . . it should be noted that throughout the Teheran Conference Hopkins acted, in effect, as Secretary of State in relationship to the two Foreign Ministers."

[20]Kennan, *Memoirs, 1925–1950* (Boston: Little, Brown, 1967), p. 167.

[21]Ibid., pp. 167–168.

important northern German zone of occupation. The orders subsequently sent to the EAC in London told them to accept the British-Soviet proposals. They contained nothing about *access* to Berlin.[22] It is worth thinking about this entire episode, here told in absolutely bare-boned terms, in relationship to the chapters in Part Two. When the President himself prevents coordination, bureaucratic oddities will certainly be the consequence.

Whether the zones themselves made sense is a more difficult question. Hitler's own maneuvers were determining. First, the Germans went all-out in the Battle of the Bulge to hold the American forces on the western frontier (which predictably permitted a slashing Soviet advance against weakened German forces). Alarmed, Hitler then shifted forces to hold the Russians (whereupon the Anglo-American armies sliced forward, ending further east than had earlier seemed likely). Arguable also is the wisdom of the war strategy itself, with the British urging a peripheral or Mediterranean strategy, while the Americans wanted a direct-assault, cross-channel invasion as soon as possible. For a variety of reasons, the actual choice favored both these approaches sequentially.

It is hard to argue that the North African campaign which Roosevelt forced upon his own staff in 1942 was not needed to give American troops some introduction to combat before the hazardous cross-channel invasion was attempted. But the Italian campaign, which was essentially an extension of the same military strategy, was a very costly choice. Even after that, the British continued to prefer a steady pursuit of invasion opportunities against the "soft underbelly" of Europe (Churchill's phrase). If that advice had been followed, the Allies probably would have found the Soviets already further west in Central Europe once the Allies had laboriously crossed the southern European mountains.

To return to the main issue, it is perfectly apparent from the evidence here presented that the United States was not thinking in coordinated national security terms during World War II. Clausewitz may have been read in the war colleges but, if so, the point he made was lost.[23] Eisenhower, after making a ritual bow toward Clausewitz in acknowledging that military events are only in the service of political aims, goes on to ignore the value of Berlin in any but military terms. Just so is General Patton's armored drive across Germany stopped at the point where he could easily have liberated Prague. Such decisions allowed the Soviets to occupy Berlin, Vienna, and Prague.

Article 10 of the United States Rules of Land Warfare of 1914 says that "the object of war is to bring about the complete submission of the enemy as soon as possible by means of regulated violence." That is certainly the way Marshall and Eisenhower looked at it. It was this kind of thinking, too, that caused much confusion in the American mind a little later in the Korean War.

As we see, part of the reason the military and political aspects of World War II were allowed (or even encouraged) to separate was the military's wish not to be hobbled by political considerations and the President's lack of faith in the State Department (a phenomenon that continues for many years after these events to the point of appearing a perennial feature of American bureaucracy). The other part came from the wish not to offend the Soviets.

---

[22]When General Clay, at the end of the war, described U.S. requirements to the Soviets he also avoided specific agreements. See Lucius D. Clay, *Decision in Germany* (Garden City, N.Y.: Doubleday, 1950), p. 26: "We did not wish to accept specific routes which might be interpreted as a denial of our right of access over all routes...."

[23]Carl von Clausewitz, a nineteenth-century Prussian military theoretician, is most remembered for his view that war is a political instrument, a continuation of political activity by other means. See Carl von Clausewitz, *On War,* edited and translated by Michael Howard and Peter Pavet (Princeton, N.J.: Princeton University Press, 1976), Chap. 1.

The Coming of the Cold War

Roosevelt was convinced he could work effectively with "Uncle Joe," as he sometimes called Stalin.[24] At the wartime conferences, FDR went out of his way to reassure "Uncle Joe" that the Americans and the British were not ganging up against the Russians.[25] He felt that Soviet distrust of Anglo-American motives and policies had a real basis in the allied intervention at the time of the Russian Revolution and in the long refusal of the United States even to establish diplomatic relations with the Soviet Union. Then the long-delayed Second Front meant that Russia was bled severely while the British and Americans appeared to saunter toward an invasion of the continent. This was one reason that FDR insisted on the North African landing (which turned out to be highly useful in revealing American military weaknesses). So in this rare case the military rationale was subordinated to the political. The aim was to encourage Russia to continue to resist Nazi Germany until victory was won. Roosevelt had very much in mind that Russia, after severe punishment, had quit fighting Imperial Germany in the first world war. And there was some fear that Russia and Germany might revive their 1939 cooperation if the Soviets were sufficiently motivated by suspicion of the motives of their allies.

The Potsdam Conference proceedings in the aftermath of Germany's defeat make almost pathetic reading today from this point of view, although now the American delegation is led by the new American President, Harry S. Truman. Like Wilson who gave up on many concrete issues at Versailles in return for support for his cherished League of Nations, Truman and Secretary of State Byrnes show themselves preoccupied with a host of secondary issues such as who will be admitted to the UN and when, and the size of reparations, while the Soviets blandly shift their demands successfully from the eastern Oder-Neisse to the western Oder-Neisse rivers as the frontier for Poland, the difference being the important territory of Silesia! Where Truman feels it dishonorable to delay withdrawal from the Soviet zone, Stalin blandly wins this point by giving the area in question to the Poles to occupy. The innocence of the Americans during these proceedings is hard to believe, especially if one reads the memoir accounts by President Truman and Secretary of State Byrnes that explain how "tough" they were![26]

---

[24]Roosevelt wrote, for instance, to Churchill on December 11, 1942: "Dear Winston: I have not had an answer to my second invitation to our Uncle Joe. . . ." *Foreign Relations of the United States: Conferences at Washington, 1941–1942, and Casablanca, 1943* (Department of State, 1968), p. 498. Sherwood, *Roosevelt and Hopkins*, pp. 785–786, tells of FDR's idea, presented to Stalin, of the "Four Policemen" to enforce the peace: "The President cited the Italian attack on Ethiopia in 1935 as an example of the failure of the League. . . . He said that had the Four Policemen existed at that time it would have been possible to close the Suez Canal and thereby prevent Mussolini from attacking Ethiopia."

[25]Sherwood, *Roosevelt and Hopkins*, pp. 798–799, records that at the end of the Teheran Conference "Roosevelt now felt sure that, to use his own term, Stalin was 'getable,' . . . and that when Russia could be convinced that her legitimate claims and requirements . . . were to be given full recognition, she would prove tractable and cooperative in maintaining the peace of the postwar world."

[26]For a quite contrary analysis see William Appleman Williams, *The Tragedy of American Diplomacy* (New York: Delta, 1972), 2d. ed., especially Chapter 6. Compare with *Foreign Relations of the United States: Conference of Berlin (Potsdam), 1945*, two volumes, Department of State, 1960. In volume I, p. 754, the State Department Briefing Paper recommends that the territory between the Oder and Lower Neisse rivers should remain part of Germany. In volume II, p. 472, at the Truman-Molotov meeting at noon on July 29, 1945, Byrnes explicitly links reparations and the Polish western frontier, handing Molotov Document No. 1151 (which provides for an *eastern* Oder-Neisse German frontier). On p. 480, it is reported that Byrnes (Monday, July 30, 4:30 P.M.) tabled Document No. 1152 (which provides for an *western* Oder-Neisse line) "as a concession to meet the Soviet desire." No other explanation is given for his vital change. Truman's memoirs are almost equally vague although he does imply a package deal combining reparations, Poland's western frontier, and Eastern European membership in the UN. Truman does say "that cession of territory was subject to the peace treaty" so only "the temporary administration of this area" was involved. See Truman *Memoirs*, vol. I, pp. 400–406.

American "revisionist" historians, reacting against the too simple assumption that the United States had *no* share of blame for postwar U.S.-Soviet tensions, have tried to build a case emphasizing that the Cold War which began soon afterward was essentially the fault of the United States in seeking "predominance" or failing to understand Russia's "real needs."

Without trying to be categorical, it should be evident already that the United States was completely unprepared at Potsdam and afterwards to find the Russians so uncooperative and difficult; that at first the Americans went to great lengths to be even more agreeable, and that gradually the lack of Soviet response irritated and finally angered the American authorities. One can observe this happening quite apart from the question of whether the Soviet or the American demands of each other were more "proper" or who deserved which concessions over what.

On the American side, naive assumptions about the Soviets were clearly followed by disillusionment. Simply compare Ambassador Davies' *Mission to Moscow,* either the film or the book, with the subsequent Truman Doctrine, and the progress of reactions is hardly arguable. Davies' point of view is accurately reflected in the headnote that opens this chapter. Truman's point of view began to harden about the time of Kennan's "long telegram" of February 22, 1946, from Moscow, which brought explanation and enlightenment to a very confused Washington officialdom wondering at the end of World War II why its problems with Russia kept increasing.[27] Kennan explained it was the result of the effects of communism as it shaped the Soviet Union's way of looking at problems and setting policy goals, that communism was expansionist and had to be "contained." Kennan's argument, which might have stressed the imbalance of power in Europe, chose instead to emphasize the "cause" of Russia's behavior—the cause rather than the *result*. Kennan's "containment" concept as we saw in Chapter 3, by defining the problem the United States faced, became the conceptual foundation for America's approach to the Cold War.

Whatever the merits of an argument over which of the two superpowers showed less toleration, each of the two nations obviously approached the other on a basis of perception that left too little common ground. (Even if one accepts the revisionist arguments that American intransigence was the result of capitalist profit or power motives, that would still be true.) There is no great law of the international system that asserts that any two nations *must* find a basis for common understanding.

But leaving aside such questions of attitude and perception and turning to concrete issues, there is no obvious reason why the United States should be blamed for attempting (at a very late date) to oppose Soviet hegemony in Europe, particularly in Central or Southern Europe. One can sympathize, for that matter, with the Soviet wish to dominate its western approaches after the experiences of this century without forgetting that the Poles may not feel that their own desires to lead an independent life have no standing whatsoever by comparison. If one wanted to argue for some abstract standard of "right" in the area it would have to rest on some arrangement "freely accepted" by both Poles and Russians—and in view of the disparity in power and the lack of Soviet bashfulness in using it on occasion, how does one contrive that miracle? But if settlements are to be made in terms of power rather than justice, why should the United States be blamed for wanting Soviet forces to extend less far into Central Europe than the Soviets might?

It is too simple to assume with the radical right that the entire shape of the ensuing Cold War followed from some Communist master plan in which, without any provocation or reason, the Soviets always pushed to take everything they could and deliberately maximized friction. But the reverse assumptions of the less cautious revisionists about American "hard hats" pushing Soviet "good guys" to the wall whenever possible is equally empty. And equally irrelevant!

[27]The famous article by "X" (Kennan), "The Sources of Soviet Conduct," *Foreign Affairs,* 25 (July 1947), 566–582, explains these views at some length.

Take a specific issue. Reparations at the Potsdam Conference and thereafter were important to the Soviets; it is possible (as authors such as Williams assert or imply) that the American failure to deliver fully on United States' promises according to Soviet ideas of those promises caused them to refuse to reciprocate by honoring their promises and that the United States stands at fault. But such a proposition fails to be very convincing for most of the concrete cases at issue. For instance, the United States permitted the Soviets to print German occupation marks from American plates. The Soviets printed money without restraint, draining German assets with those marks. So while Germans had no jobs, the United States shipped food to Germany. That policy made so little sense that no American government would have persisted in it, and it is hard to believe that any Soviet government would have expected it. As a final illustration, if one looks merely at the *sequence* of East-West moves as both moved to the creation of separate German governments, it is easy to come away with the impression that the Soviets kept reacting to Western moves. But Western moves took place against the backdrop of the clear Soviet intention to convert their occupation zone into a client state.[28] Such arguments over "who started the Cold War?" ultimately remain inconclusive, because the premises on which judgment of "fault" should be assessed are not agreed.

On a *micro* close-up (or tactical) level, resolving the question of fault for the Cold War for any one issue might be attempted: to do so entails examining who took what action and when.[29] This is really the level on which the revisionists argue. On their side is the fact that the American government frequently explained policy on this micro level, and the record shows it. The issue of Soviet troops remaining in Iran past their promised withdrawal date of March 2, 1946, is a good illustration. Truman, who initially (like Roosevelt) thought dealing with Stalin was primarily a case of establishing good personal relations, records that he changed his mind abruptly at that point. Earlier, Truman had said that "Stalin is as near like Tom Pendergast [the old Kansas City party boss for whom Truman retained great respect] as any man I know." But after the Soviets initially refused to withdraw from Iran, Truman said that he had "held Stalin to be a man of his word" but he was not. "They understand one language and that is the language they are going to get from me from this point."[30] This micro level of action and reaction to particular events is not only a level of approach of which American presidents in more modern times have been very fond, but one which lends itself well to moral judgments. As Chapter 11 indicated, Wilson saw the issue facing him in 1917 in the narrow terms of an amoral German government wantonly sinking ships and threatening American lives, and reacted accordingly. Roosevelt spoke of "the hand that held the dagger" having plunged it into the back of its neighbor, as though Italy's perfidy and unreliability were the important thing rather than the systems effect or strategic result of Italy's action. Again, FDR, by calling Stalin "Uncle Joe," personified the relationship, implying that the relations between two great nations could be visualized on a personal basis. Stalin could "be had"—i.e., he would react to a "good" deal, and we have just quoted Truman's reaction to Stalin.

We have already quoted from George Kennan's book, *American Diplomacy,* in which Kennan makes much of America's love to express issues in abstract and moral rather than strategic or system terms. Kennan's insight is helpful. If we add the American preference to understand issues on a personal and micro level, as just argued, we round out the picture further.

---

[28]The interested reader can follow the tactical moves in Frederick H. Hartmann, *Germany Between East and West* (Englewood Cliffs, N.J.: Prentice-Hall, 1965).

[29]See the thoughtful essay by J. David Singer, "The Level-of-Analysis Problem in International Relations," in Klaus Knorr and Sidney Verba, eds., *The International System* (Princeton, N.J.: Princeton University Press, 1961), pp. 77–92.

[30]Stoessinger, *Crusaders and Pragmatists,* p. 60.

Plutarch's tale about Phyrrus is instructive. Phyrrus is asked what he intends to do next and he sketches out some intended conquests. The questioner asks finally, "What then?" and Phyrrus says he will recline on a couch and eat fruit. The questioner points out that he is already doing just that. The point of that story is that Phyrrus could lie at his ease and eat fruit under either of two strategic circumstances: by not stirring up fears and anxieties through a series of conquests in the first place, or by conquering everything in sight and then taking his ease. He could maintain the status quo or overthrow it. If he chose the latter, he would inevitably encroach on the rights of other parties. Whether tactically he did it with good manners or bad, out of the blue and unprovoked or in "retaliation" for some real or supposed action by his opponent, would be essentially irrelevant from a strategic or systems point of view.

Revisionists see the issues as micro or tactical in part then because the American chief executives they study do so as well. So it seems fair to reach a judgment on that basis. But if Germany in World War I is well on its way to domination by 1917 unless the United States intervenes, if Germany under Hitler has set a standard of action and behavior that most clearly threatens all outside its orbit, or if Stalin stakes out positions in the center of Europe or in northern Iran whose maintenance will undermine the security of the rest, the issues are not fundamentally micro or tactical. They are *macro* or strategic, for they involve threatening rearrangements of the status quo or the balance of power.

Here we come to one of the great reasons *why* Kennan's containment concept took hold in Washington: The difficulties being encountered with the Soviets cried out for an explanation and the United States had no systematic concept of world affairs to turn to as a guide. Instinctively, the American leaders realized that short-range, micro improvisations were of limited utility and were not dealing adequately *with the situation confronted.* That situation was an imbalance in the European balance of power caused by the positioning of Soviet power in the middle of Europe, thus threatening a still weak Western Europe. This was no simple problem of *attitudes,* which might be dealt with tactically. It represented a situation for which a more fundamental appraisal and response was called for.

What was needed was a systems or macro view. Specifically, the United States badly needed guidelines for recognizing and responding appropriately to the threat that the overextension of the Soviet presence represented. For the first time in a period of peace the United States had to deal with serious frictions and tensions arising from a systems imbalance. What Kennan provided was a macro view, but one based on ideology and intentions rather than on power and its distribution.

The Cold War, although it "began" over the conversion of the Balkan states into Soviet satellites and pressures on Greece and Turkey, really heated up over the Czechoslovakian coup and the Berlin blockade. Czechoslovakia, attempting a middle course between East and West, fell victim to an internal (but Soviet-arranged) coup in February 1948. Considering the strategic importance of Czechoslovakia, this changed even more adversely the situation confronted by the West. Then in June 1948, the Russian full blockade of Berlin (and regardless, from a micro view, of who "started" it) shook the West profoundly. The blockade obviously aimed at making the imbalance even worse, by terminating the Western presence behind the Iron Curtain. When the United States, without secure and spelled-out written provisions for unimpeded land access to Berlin, responded with a great airlift, relations between the United States and Soviet Union grew tense. In the eleven months between June 1948 and May 1949, a total of 1,402,644 metric tons of food and supplies were flown by American and British planes into Berlin in 277,728 flights. Convinced that there was a threat, the West formulated defense plans, signing the North Atlantic Pact on April 4, 1949. The pact became effective on August 24, 1949, but until the Korean War raised world tension levels it was only as a set of pledges and promises and not as a functioning organization. The Soviets eventually "responded" with the Warsaw Pact of May

14, 1955 (which was really a multilateral overlay on the series of existing, Soviet-controlled, bilateral pacts).

In the perspective of the micro-macro argument just made, we can see that it was not *really* the fall of Czechoslovakia that shook the West, especially when Berlin was blockaded too. It was the growing but unarticulated realization that the Soviet overextension into Europe and its retention on an apparently semipermanent basis of such forward positions represented an unacceptable political situation and a potential military menace. The dimensions of this problem were simply dramatized further by the two specific Soviet moves against Prague and Berlin.

What the United States badly needed in 1949 was a set of concepts and a vocabulary that would allow more precise and pertinent descriptions of problems and issues and which encouraged a more exact prioritization of threats. Instead, the outbreak of the Korean War encouraged a further expansion of the containment concept to Asia and a proliferation of perceived threats (i.e., the Communist states in Asia were seen also as responding to Moscow's direction in a Soviet-run worldwide threat to the "Free World").

5.

Extending the Containment Perimeter

It is still a matter of debate how much the North Korean invasion of South Korea in June 1950, which led to the actual transformation of the North Atlantic Pact into the North Atlantic Treaty *Organization* (NATO), was undertaken at Soviet initiative. Khrushchev, in his memoirs, shows that Stalin was informed by the North Koreans and gives the impression (probably accurate) that Stalin was not greatly interested. Whether this is correct or not, certainly Western leaders tended to see the North Korean incursion into South Korea as a deliberate choice of a weak point on the perimeter of the "Free World," to which an adequate military response in both Korea and Europe was required. If there were differences of opinion among Western statesmen, they stemmed from a sense of priorities: The United States felt that the active military threat in Korea had first priority as the theater in which the Communist bloc had mounted an overt challenge; European leaders were more concerned that U.S. military preoccupation halfway around the world might tempt the Soviets to drop the other shoe and do something unpleasant in Europe. So, while the British and Turks sent troops to fight in Korea, the North Atlantic Treaty signers also set up a real organization outside Paris under General Eisenhower.

General Omar Bradley, in his later memoirs, describes President Truman's council of war as the chief American policymakers met to decide what the problem was and how it should be met. Bradley says that he said at the meeting: "We must draw the line somewhere" and Korea "offered as good an occasion for action in drawing the line as anywhere else."

Bradley went on:

> In those days we held the rather simplistic belief that *all* communist moves worldwide were dictated from Moscow by Stalin personally. The guessing that night was that Stalin had temporarily set aside his designs on Europe and the Middle East for an all-out push in the Far East conducted by his satellites. Korea might only be one phase of this push. Formosa could be another. Indochina might well be still another. The Philippines could also be a target. But we did not believe Stalin wanted all-out global war.[31]

---

[31]Omar Bradley and Clay Blair, *A General's Life: An Autobiography* (New York: Simon & Schuster, 1983), p. 535.

The Korean War, thus begun, destroyed certain myths and encouraged others in the minds of Americans.[32] Woodrow Wilson, it will be recalled, had explained that force might well be needed in the service of sanctions to suppress aggression. But the odds in favor of the peace-loving nations would also, presumably, be overwhelming. Nothing of the kind occurred in Korea. Many words were spoken in support, but only sixteen nations sent troops. Even so, the assault was halted at the Pusan perimeter and then, on September 15, 1950, General MacArthur, in a daring amphibious landing at Inchon, altered the whole course of the war. Significant North Korean forces were cut off. As MacArthur's troops plunged north toward the Yalu River, the whole war went into reverse, with the North Koreans now facing imminent military disaster. But Chinese military "volunteers," despite MacArthur's unfounded confidence that they would not, infiltrated and struck at the UN's divided columns, mauling them severely. Soon a full retreat was in progress. Then the line stabilized essentially again and a stalemate set in which was prolonged especially by an argument over the fate of the prisoners of war. Eventually, after much time, the armistice was signed at Panmunjon and the shooting stopped.

The Korean War was in many ways both a psychological and a policy watershed for the American people.

From a policy standpoint, as we showed in Chapter 3, it marked the beginning of an on-continent, U.S. military role in Asia. The Korean commitment was initially highly popular as different groups of Americans perceived different (but converging) issues at stake. Those who believed in the UN and collective security saw it as a clear-cut case of aggression to be punished. Those who now saw the war in terms of "Free World" vs. Communist bloc simply assumed that this was its latest episode. Even the few Americans who thought in balance-of-power terms approved because of the obvious strategic, geographical importance of "this dagger pointed at the heart of Japan."

But the war lingered on inconclusively, trying American patience. And China (with troops) and Russia (with supplies) weighed in on North Korea's side. Slowly, the hitherto unquestioning American faith in the quick and decisive victory supposed to follow collective security action began to evaporate.

Not only did the common action fail to go according to the script in these respects. It was also discovered late in the game that the collective security concept was strangely vague on what punishment would fit the crime: whether North Korea should merely lose its intended gains or be fined, say, ten per cent of its territory? After the armistice negotiations began, the complex-ities made everything even more unclear when, with hardly a precedent to be cited in favor of that course of action, the United States decided that POW's would be given a choice on whether to return home or not. This idea really opened Pandora's box, especially because so many Kore-ans and, particularly, Chinese most obviously did *not* want to go back. Whereas the United States might have clung to its position with success if it had "won" the war, this policy stance was hardly suitable for a stalemate. The stalemate itself came from the unwillingness of the United States to take on China totally (which led also, indirectly, to MacArthur's dismissal by Truman), plus the inability of the Chinese to broaden the war significantly. But there were limits to how much humiliation the Chinese would accept, and only when they ultimately figured a way around the problem did they end the fighting. (What they did was use the agreed "thirty

---

[32]Among other things it put an effective end to the then-existing political movement, spearheaded by Henry Wallace, which put the blame for the Cold War on American shoulders. After the war in Korea broke out, Henry Wallace said: "Undoubtedly the Russians could have prevented the attack and undoubtedly they could now stop the attack any time they wanted." And he concluded, "the time has passed for trying to find out who is to blame." Quoted in Norman D. Markowitz, *The Rise and Fall of the People's Century: Henry A. Wallace and American Liberalism, 1941–1948* (New York: Free Press, 1973), p. 311.

days" of POW interviews, which the Americans had intended to mean "one month," as a number of days to be used as they wished—one day a week, or whatever.)[33] The Korean War, which had cost over 54,000 American lives (and over 100,000 wounded or taken prisoner), ended on a very sour note.

A significant casualty of the Korean War was any American attempt to put U.S.-Chinese relations on a better footing. If the Soviets are to be given "credit" for the Korean War, then this should be marked up to their account, too. After all, the U.S. military action in Korea had precisely the same strategic effect as the later war in Vietnam: (1) It tied down U.S. troops, substantially circumscribing American ability to react elsewhere short of full mobilization; (2) it deployed the United States militarily on the Asian mainland, where landing is always easier than leaving; (3) it brought U.S. forces adjacent to Chinese frontiers, thus at the very least ensuring better Sino-Soviet relations unless the Chinese reacted completely irrationally; and (4) it created domestic disturbances within the American body politic over whether the war needed to be fought, how it should be fought, and how it should be ended. There is no question that Dwight D. Eisenhower's pledge, that if he were elected President he would go to Korea (to investigate and somehow end the war) played a significant role in his first election in 1952. But the war also resulted in an actual U.S. treaty of alliance with Taiwan (and a precautionary deployment of the U.S. Seventh Fleet off the Chinese mainland) where, earlier, the United States had opted for a nonaligned orientation in the Chinese civil war and was prepared to accept a Communist Chinese conquest of Taiwan (or Formosa, as it was then usually called).

This was quite a change from previous policy. As Acheson, in his memoirs, points out: "From October 1948 to the outbreak of the Korean war on June 25, 1950, [the] policy—that United States forces would not be used to defend Formosa—never wavered."[34] And, later:

> General Wedemeyer had suggested the preparation of a guidance paper for press and public-affairs officers [in American embassies] intended to minimize the significance and damage resulting from a quite possible fall of Formosa to the Chinese Communists. On December 23 [1949] such a paper was sent out to (among a great many other recipients) General MacArthur's headquarters in Tokyo. There someone—never discovered—put it in an outgoing box of press releases.[35]

After that, Truman still tried to cling to the nonaligned orientation. On January 5, 1950, in his State of the Union message, Truman rejected the notion that the United States desired military bases on Formosa. "Nor does it have any intention of utilizing its armed forces to interfere in the present situation. The United States Government will not pursue a course which will lead to involvement in the civil conflict in China."[36] But it did pursue such a course, after the Chinese intervention in Korea.

And so the Cold War containment perimeter became extended to Asia, the events just recorded feeding on themselves and extending the period of deep freeze in Sino-American relations—a state of affairs that contributed substantially to the security of the Soviet Union. To say that the Soviets gained does not mean that the American action was a mistake. Only in a world where the concept of tragedy does not exist would it be proper to reach that conclusion. It is to say that it had side effects which were not intended and quite unwelcome.

---

[33]For more detail about the negotiations, see Frederick H. Hartmann, *The Relations of Nations,* 6th ed. (New York: Macmillan, 1983), pp. 381–384. John W. Spanier, *The Truman-MacArthur Controversy and the Korean War* (New York: Norton, 1965) is the best single source for MacArthur's dismissal.

[34]Dean Acheson, *Present at the Creation* (New York: New American Library, 1970), p. 457. (Hardback edition is Norton, 1969).

[35]Ibid., p. 458.

[36]Ibid., p. 459.

A further contribution to Soviet security came from the actions of Great Britain and France in 1956 in the Middle East. Responding to Nasser's abrupt nationalization of the Suez Canal Company, Britain and France (in concert with Israel) resorted to force—Britain and France tardily and ineptly. The United States, whose tactical handling of the events leading up to Nasser's actions left much to be desired, supported—indeed, virtually led—the UN majority in condemnation of their NATO allies, bringing severe pressure on them precisely at a time when unrest in Poland and in Hungary confronted the Soviet Union with one of the first important consequences of its overextension into Europe and its domination of its neighbors. While the Red Army ruthlessly suppressed the Hungarians, the British and French gave up their venture in disarray. Whether one wants tactically to blame John Foster Dulles for his abrupt manner in refusing the Aswan Dam loan (which triggered the whole series of events), blame Nasser for his ultimately dangerous tactics of playing off the superpowers, blame the British and French for failing to understand that the age of colonialism was over and reacting with force, or blame Eisenhower for promising the UN that the United States would support any action the majority agreed on (and thus surrendering U.S. control over its own actions), the results for NATO were very poor and, for the Soviets, very good.

In the sequel, it led Dulles further in the direction of "pactomania"; where Dulles had created SEATO and alliances with South Korea and Taiwan in the Pacific, in the Middle East he built on the Baghdad Pact and created CENTO. The "Eisenhower Doctrine" was also issued to bolster up the Middle East. Then, in 1958, American marines landed in Lebanon, presumably to impress Nasser and the others that the United States, even if it had acted to curtail British and French influence there, had no idea of letting the whole area slide.

The net result of these Eisenhower years was to deepen the Cold War lines and increase American military commitment, while ending the Korean War and avoiding actual resort elsewhere to war. With the U.S. military budget heavily slanted toward nuclear arms and the Soviet strategic position enhanced overall by these developments, the United States, with John F. Kennedy's inauguration, faced a far from stable national security situation. For better or worse, though, a consensus prevailed about the problem faced. America's enemies were all Communist states. Because *all* Communist states were seen as part of a single bloc, those enemies could not readily be prioritized as to the significance of their threat to American interests. And since the containment concept now contained the domino corollary, which asserted that *any* aggression was a vital matter because of the chain of events it would produce, *any* Communist state, by committing an aggression, might initiate the next round. Since the problem the United States faced was defined in these terms, and the American consensus now envisaged more or less automatic reactions to "Communist aggressions," the stage was set for the Vietnam War.

6.

Summing Up

The period between 1935 and 1960 in some ways represents an enormous policy change, as the United States moved from isolationism (unilateralism) to global involvement. The United States moved from no alliances to many, from aloofness to the League of Nations to sponsorship of the United Nations and leadership in its first collective security venture. This "revolution" in American policy, as one scholar called it in the title of a best-selling text after World War II, represented an enormous change.[37] It settled (at least in the time surveyed) the choice between the counterbalancing interests of withdrawal and participation, choosing a clear orientation of taking part and carrying the burden.

[37]William G. Carleton, *The Revolution in American Foreign Policy,* 2d. ed. (New York: Random House, 1957).

But this same period, looked at from a different perspective, shows little meaningful change. The moral and abstract slogans in use in the mid-1930s are updated to other, more contemporary similar slogans. Events, however, continue to be assessed against an inadequate conceptual framework. The containment concept, like the arguments over peace and security that accompanied the debate over the neutrality acts, remained vague guidance as to the problems faced and the issues to be decided: as to where and when and why to dig in with firm opposition. Misdirecting attention from the real source of the trouble (the unstable balance of power) it directed attention toward arguments over Soviet (or Communist) *intentions*. Increasingly, after the innovative beginnings of the Truman years, as Western Europe's power was restored, the policy of the United States became reactive. Increasingly, both the sense of strategic direction and the priorities of the problems faced became confused. We see this development unfold in the next chapter.

13

Berlin, Cuba, and Vietnam

The problem of innovation and change ... tends to be subsumed in a rather abstract way in the concept of "the choice among alternatives". ... This is a gross evasion; for the very heart of the decision-making process is the posing of the alternatives.

Walt W. Rostow
The United States in the World Arena

[Le Duc Tho, the North Vietnamese negotiator] then asked me the question that was also tormenting me: "Before, there were over a million U.S. and puppet troops, and you failed. How can you succeed when you let the puppet troops do the fighting? Now, with only U.S. support, how can you win?"

Henry Kissinger
White House Years

Admiral "Cat" Brown, U.S. Sixth Fleet commander, shadowing the British fleet as it approached Suez in 1956, is said to have radioed Washington: "Have the British fleet in sight. *Who is the enemy?*" John F. Kennedy, in his inaugural address in 1961, said the United States would "defend *any* friend, oppose *any* foe," in the cause of liberty. Both statements suggest the opposite of a concrete preference on the part of the United States for some friends over others or a concrete wish to frustrate the actions of some enemies over others.

It would not be correct to say there was no feeling for the constraints forced upon American policy by the international system (or environment) and its "rules of procedure." The domino "effect" is such a presumed rule. It distinctly limits choice unless one wishes to court disaster. But the domino rule is impersonal. It really does not matter who attacks whom. Like collective security, the containment concept revels in its automaticity. The judgments needed are predominantly tactical rather than strategic. One does not choose among enemies; one takes them in the order in which they commit aggression. One does not try to establish the relative importance of areas where the enemy, by his aggression, offers combat (to whomever it may concern); one responds necessarily wherever the challenge. There is no concern for policy design; all that matters is implementation.

So it would not be correct to say that the United States, on the brink of serious commitment in Vietnam, had no sense of enmity and enemies, or had no sense of the presumed rules which the system imposed. All that can be said is that the rules assumed were questionable, that the whole approach tended to be both automatic and rather too easily inclusive, and that freedom of will (or foreign policy choice) was rather distinctly downgraded in the process, with the beliefs so prevalent in the 1930s, of staying uninvolved, now turned on their heads. Especially important now was the failure of the United States even to recognize the need to prioritize enemies or determine appropriate versus inappropriate lines for American deployments.

The departing President Eisenhower conveyed to the incoming President Kennedy his concern over Laos, which Kennedy took very seriously (although, apart from a containment framework and a domino theory, it would be difficult to say why). So Eisenhower, who had had the sense not to intervene in Vietnam during France's last agony there in 1954, by January 1961 was by way of changing his mind. Eisenhower left two other problems for the new President: an unresolved German issue over the fate of Berlin; and a planned invasion of Cuba, organized by the CIA and manned with Cuban refugees.

1.

The Berlin Crisis of 1958–1959

Eisenhower's handling of the second Berlin crisis had been sure-handed and quite adequate. In late 1958 Khrushchev had stated it was time for the Western powers to renounce their "occupation regime" in Berlin. The solution to the problem, he said, was to convert *West* Berlin into a "free" city (i.e., under Soviet domination whether swallowed up or not initially, with Allied troops withdrawn). The West was to have a six-months' grace period to accept the inevitable, following which, Khrushchev made clear, Western rights would "terminate" and the Allies would have to deal with the "sovereign" German Democratic Republic (with whom none of the West Berlin-occupying powers had diplomatic relations). Khrushchev had several gains in mind by this procedure: He wanted to stop the refugee flow to the West; he wanted to eliminate the Western salient 100 miles behind the Iron Curtain; he wanted to undermine West German morale; and he wanted to force the West to deal with the East German puppet regime (propped up by great numbers of Soviet bayonets). (If "puppet" sounds harsh, consider that in free Berlin, in the West, in late 1958, the Communists got 1.9 per cent of the vote.)

The refugee flow problem had the greatest tactical urgency because East Germany was literally bleeding to death from a manpower point of view—with most refugees slipping into East Berlin and then across the sector line into West Berlin. Consider that the one millionth *registered* refugee from the GDR arrived in West Berlin on September 20, 1956, and that the official GDR statistical yearbook shows the population falling by over a million between 1950 and 1958! Over half these people were young, under twenty-five. This for a regime with a total population under twenty million, with a large number of children and old people to support (the young and old were together estimated at 64.8 per cent of the total East German population).

When the subsequent Geneva Conference of 1959 failed to solve the Berlin issue, Khrushchev came to talk with Eisenhower at Camp David, and a "formula" was announced that in effect extended the six-months period indefinitely. In Khrushchev's words: "We agreed indeed that talks on the Berlin question should be resumed, that no time limit whatsoever is to be established for them, but that they also should not be dragged out for an indefinite time." A new summit conference was agreed for Paris in May 1960. But the Paris meeting was aborted as a result of the shooting down of an American U-2 spy plane deep in Soviet territory. An angry Khrushchev, balked of an apology from Eisenhower, left for home saying he would wait "until the dust had settled" and then negotiate with the new President.

By the time that meeting was held, though, at Vienna in June 1961, President Kennedy was laboring under the handicap of the Cuban "Bay of Pigs" fiasco. (Castro had easily frustrated

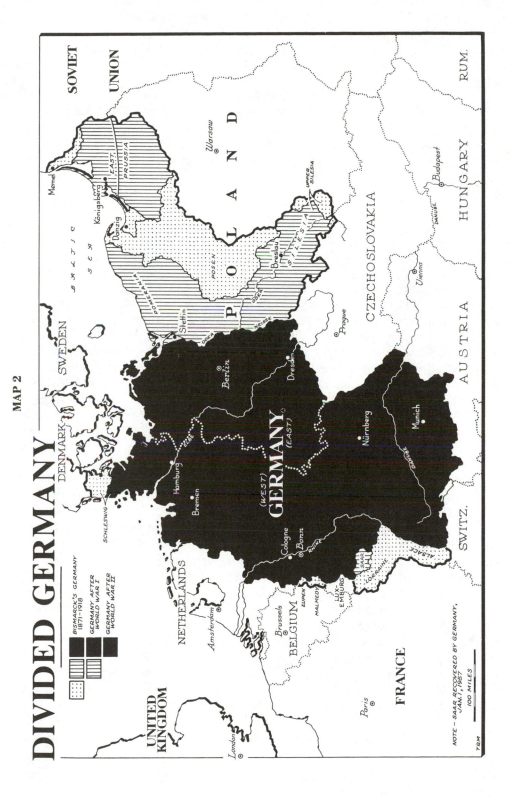

MAP 2

DIVIDED GERMANY

Legend:
- BISMARCK'S GERMANY 1871–1918
- GERMANY AFTER WORLD WAR I
- GERMANY AFTER WORLD WAR II

NOTE – SAAR RECOVERED BY GERMANY, JAN. 1, 1957

100 MILES

TRM

SOVIET UNION • Warsaw

RUM.

Memel

EAST PRUSSIA

Königsberg

Danzig

POMERANIA

POSEN

POLAND

Breslau

SILESIA

UPPER SILESIA

CZECHOSLOVAKIA

• Vienna

• Budapest

DANUBE

HUNGARY

Prague •

ODER

OSER

NEISSE

Stettin

Berlin •

Dresden •

GERMANY (EAST)

Nürnberg •

Munich •

AUSTRIA

DENMARK

SWEDEN

SCHLESWIG

Hamburg •

Bremen •

GERMANY (WEST)

Cologne •

Bonn •

RHINE

DANUBE

SWITZ.

NETHERLANDS

Amsterdam •

BELGIUM

Brussels •

EUPEN

MALMEDY

LUX-EMBURG

SAAR

LORRAINE

ALSACE

FRANCE

Paris •

UNITED KINGDOM

London •

the CIA-sponsored assault by Cuban refugees, and the whole episode had conveyed a clear impression of American ineptness.) Confronting this young and presumably immature new President, Khrushchev was rough. (Kennedy called it a "somber" experience.) Returning to Moscow, Khrushchev on television said: "We ask everyone to understand us correctly: the conclusion of a peace treaty with Germany [ending Western rights] cannot be postponed any longer. A peaceful settlement in Europe must be attained this year." Kennedy, on American television, responded: "The solemn vow each of us gave to West Berlin in time of peace will not be broken in time of danger. If we do not meet our commitments to Berlin, where will we later stand. . .?"

The renewed crisis doubled the monthly refugee flow and the totals for August went even higher. On August 13, 1961, the Berlin Wall went up. Although it was not immediately apparent, this was really the end of the second Berlin crisis. Half a measure—stopping the flow with this tourniquet—was better than none. (Later, as a consequence of Willy Brandt's *Ostpolitik,* the GDR was to gain diplomatic recognition, too—at the price of seeing West Germany received diplomatically all over Eastern Europe.)

2.

The Cuban Missile Crisis of 1962

Khrushchev had not intended to give up with the Berlin Wall; he had one more string to his bow and he used it in Cuba in 1962, causing the even more dangerous Cuban missile crisis.

As one might expect, the failure of the Cuban "Bay of Pigs" venture at the beginning of the Kennedy administration had led to much public soul-searching in Washington and in the nation's press. All were agreed that it was a fiasco, some because it had been tried at all, others because it failed. A vocal minority in Congress was outraged at communism's continued foothold in the Western Hemisphere and pressed for vigorous action against Castro's Cuba, up to and including the use of force. Fidel Castro announced himself publicly after the "Bay of Pigs" as a convinced Marxist-Leninist and in the summer of 1962 sent his brother Raúl, the Foreign Minister, and Ché Guevara, the Finance Minister, to Moscow to arrange for supplies of Soviet arms and Soviet technicians to service and instruct. On September 11, TASS announced that "defensive" arms were being sent, adding explicitly that Soviet nuclear weapons were so powerful in range that there was no need to send these to bases outside the Soviet Union. But in point of fact, 42 medium- and intermediate-range ballistic missiles were then already in or soon to be on their way to Cuba.

Roger Hilsman (who in the Kennedy administration first headed the State Department Bureau of Intelligence and Research and then, later, became Assistant Secretary of State for the Far East) ascribes the Soviet motive in large order to *their* understanding of *America's* understanding that they were not really ahead of the United States in intercontinental missiles.[1] This complicated proposition has to be understood against the background of the argument during the Kennedy-Nixon presidential campaign, at a time when U-2 flights over the Soviet Union had been suspended, as to whether or not there was a "missile gap." *Sputnik's* military meaning was that the Soviets were well ahead of the United States in thrust. Whether that meant they were equal or ahead or behind in numbers of missiles or in actual delivery capability was hotly argued. But by the summer and fall of 1961, says Hilsman, the American intelligence community had decided that the Soviets did not really have effective ICBMs, that in their attempt to move forward too fast in thrust, they had achieved "a behemoth . . . too bulky to serve as a

---

[1]See Roger Hilsman, *To Move a Nation* (Garden City, N.Y.: Doubleday, 1967), Chap. 13, especially pp. 161–165.

practical weapon." Hilsman says further that it was decided to tell the Soviets that the United States knew this; which was done in a speech by a senior official (November 1961) and by briefings of other nations. Hilsman claims that the Soviets suddenly realized that the "softness" of their system (other than in a first-strike situation) was now known to the United States, and that Castro's request for arms opened an opportunity to make good the defects in Soviet defenses by establishing shorter-range missiles on the American flank in Cuba. How the massive shipment of bulky equipment and technicians—Hilsman describes it as equal to a hundred shiploads and comprising several thousand vehicles including fueling trucks, radar vans and equipment, together with over 20,000 men—was to be kept secret is not explained.

Whatever these issues had to do with the Soviet decision, it is at least clear that the Soviet maneuver (if it actually succeeded) would be of major psychological importance. It would "outflank" American defenses (which were primarily oriented toward a missile attack from the Soviet Union), bring significant new U.S. targets under a very clear threat, and induce U.S. caution if and when a new Soviet squeeze on Berlin was mounted. South America would be within target range, and therefore it might induce at least dissensions there. Khrushchev apparently involved himself in Cuba with at least one eye on rewards in Germany. If one accepts Hilsman's argument, one must accept the proposition that even with (or especially because of) a "soft" ICBM system in the Soviet Union Khrushchev was gambling on checkmating Western resistance through the Cuban gambit. It is clear by any standards that Khrushchev was taking major risks in the hope of major gains. The difference in interpretations possible over Soviet motives runs in a narrow range between seeing it as a "defensive" move with "offensive" gains likely and seeing it as an "offensive" move, designed to yield "offensive" gains.

In early October 1962, no "hard intelligence" had yet revealed the Soviet move. Kennedy's response to domestic pressures to do something about Castro was to refrain from any new military moves but, as he said, "to watch what happens in Cuba with the closest attention." This meant especially U-2 flights over Cuba. On October 14, one such flight brought back pictures of a medium-range missile base in western Cuba, in the San Cristobal area. Later verifications gave a more complete picture of five other MRBM (1,100-mile) and three IRBM (2,200-mile) sites. The stage was now set for the most dramatic superpower confrontation in the postwar period.

An interview between President Kennedy and Soviet Foreign Minister Gromyko had been arranged before these developments were known, for October 18. At this meeting Gromyko repeated Khrushchev's statement that the Berlin question would not be reactivated until after the American elections on November 6. But after that—and Gromyko said it twice—the Soviets would be "compelled" to sign a separate peace treaty with East Germany, which would end Western rights in Berlin. Gromyko also said that such Soviet missiles as were in Cuban hands were purely defensive. Reflecting on this interview and the continuing photographic intelligence that showed the rate at which the Cuban missiles were becoming operational, Kennedy concluded that the apparent gesture of political friendliness in avoiding tension until after the election had more to do with when the missiles would be in "go" condition.

On October 22, over TV, Kennedy publicly unmasked the Soviet maneuvers in the speech quoted in Chapter 1.

America's initial response would be a naval "quarantine" [blockade] against the further shipment of "offensive weapons." Kennedy gave clear warning: "It shall be the policy of this nation to regard any nuclear missile launched from Cuba against any nation in the Western Hemisphere as an attack by the Soviet Union on the United States, requiring a full retaliatory response upon the Soviet Union."

Next afternoon, the Council of the Organization of American States backed the American stand by recommending that the member states "take all measures . . . including the use of armed force," to cut off the flow of offensive weapons into Cuba and prevent those already there from becoming "an active threat." That evening (October 23, 7 P.M.), Kennedy proclaimed the quarantine: " . . . the forces under my command are ordered, beginning at 2:00 P.M., Greenwich time, October 24, 1962, to interdict . . . the delivery of offensive weapons and associated matériel to Cuba." Force would be used "only to the extent necessary." To this proclamation "I have . . . set my hand and caused the seal of the United States of America to be affixed." There could be no doubt the United States was committed—and with unanimous hemispheric backing. Confrontation, with all its risks and opportunities, was the orientation chosen.

Wednesday the quarantine went into effect and the world held its breath. Eighteen Soviet dry cargo ships were known to be on courses toward the quarantine line. Reports of six Soviet submarines arriving for escort duty came in. Then the Soviet cargo ships nearest Cuba appeared to slow down.

Thursday, October 25, was another dramatic day of suspense. In the UN, U.S. Ambassador Adlai Stevenson—with U-2 photos in hand—cross-examined Soviet Ambassador Zorin in the Security Council. "Do you . . . deny that the USSR has placed and is placing medium- and intermediate-range missiles and sites in Cuba? Yes or no? Don't wait for the translation. Yes or no." Zorin's answer snapped back: "I am not in an American courtroom, sir." Stevenson replied, "You are in the court of world public opinion right now!" Zorin temporized, "In due course, sir, you will have your reply." To which Stevenson rejoined, "I am prepared to wait for my answer until Hell freezes over, if that's your decision. I am also prepared to present the evidence in this room."

UN Secretary-General U Thant had already proposed that the Soviets voluntarily stop arms shipments and that the Americans voluntarily suspend the quarantine for two to three weeks. Kennedy in his reply pointed to the other half of the equation, "the removal of such weapons" already there that were being rushed to readiness.

On Friday, October 26, came news that sixteen of the eighteen Soviet dry cargo ships, including all five with large hatches, had turned around. Khrushchev's answer to U Thant that day confirmed the Soviet decision: he had "ordered . . . Soviet vessels bound for Cuba but not yet within the area of the American warships' piratical activities to stay out of the interception area" temporarily. But U-2 flights showed that work on the missile sites for the missiles already in Cuba was still being pressed. The United States had half a loaf, but that was not enough.

Direct exchanges of letters (radiograms) had started between Kennedy and Khrushchev. Two Khrushchev letters came, one on Friday (October 26) at 9 P.M., the other the next day. The Friday night letter seemed to indicate that since Soviet missiles had been put into Cuba to frustrate any American invasion plans, they might be withdrawn if the United States gave a pledge to refrain from invasion. This letter had the genuine Khrushchev flavor, polemical and long. Saturday's letter was more carefully drafted and followed a harder line, demanding the withdrawal of Jupiter missiles from Turkey as the *quid pro quo*. (How ironical for Kennedy, who earlier had ordered the State Department to negotiate with Turkey the withdrawal of the Jupiters, but bureaucratic confusion and Turkish objections had frustrated action. To agree publicly to this move now would appear as giving way under pressure and might encourage other Soviet demands and delays.)

Kennedy decided on the bold but simple course of ignoring the Saturday letter and agreeing with Khrushchev's Friday "proposal."

> As I read your letter [of October 26], the key elements of your proposals—which seem generally acceptable as I understand them—are as follows:
> 1. You would agree to remove these weapons systems from Cuba under appropriate United Nations observation and supervision; and undertake, with suitable safeguards, to halt the further introduction of such weapons systems into Cuba.

2. We, on our part, would agree [assuming such effective UN agreements] (a) to remove promptly the quarantine measures now in effect and (b) to give assurances against an invasion of Cuba.

Robert Kennedy personally handed this note to the Soviet ambassador, adding verbally that unless the President "received immediate notice that the missiles would be withdrawn,"[2] other U.S. measures would have to be taken to see that it happened. Time was indeed running short, for the United States was determined to intervene with force to prevent the missiles in Cuba from becoming operational.

On Sunday morning, the Soviet answer came, first on Moscow radio and then with the delivery of a note: "In order to eliminate as rapidly as possible the conflict . . . the Soviet Government . . . has given a new order to dismantle the arms which you describe as offensive and to crate them and return them to the Soviet Union." The Soviets were "prepared to reach agreement to enable representatives to verify the dismantling. . . ."

The Soviet attempt to persuade Castro to allow verification by a UN team failed. Mikoyan, a senior member of the Soviet hierarchy, was sent by Khrushchev as his agent, and he argued with Castro for most of a month before giving up. Convinced of Soviet good faith on this point, the United States carried out its own inspection by air. Eventually, the complications involved in the withdrawal of Soviet bombers and some 23,000 Soviet troops were ironed out. The world could breathe again.

So failed with finality Khrushchev's bid to exploit the Western disarray following Suez and the great space leap forward of *sputnik*. When a chastened Khrushchev withdrew the missiles from Cuba and Kennedy proposed to make a beginning with arms control of nuclear weapons, Khrushchev accepted. These Soviet moves in turn further soured Soviet relations with the People's Republic of China. The Chinese, confronted with a hostile American presence, felt that the Soviets were "soft" and certainly unreliable as a source of support.

3.
The Road to the Vietnam War Commitment

In Chapters 3 and 4, as we looked at the evolution of the conceptual basis of American involvement in the Cold War, ideas that eventually led to Vietnam, our focus was on phase 1: the search for a policy consensus. Here our emphasis shifts to phase 2, as we see those ideas implemented.

With the resolution of the Cuban missile crisis, finally, events were taking a turn for the better (from the American viewpoint) by the time President Kennedy was assassinated and Lyndon B. Johnson assumed the presidency. The most important exception was in Vietnam where Diem's assassination shortly before with some American complicity had made a bad situation worse.

The question of what importance to attach to developments in Southeast Asia had been off and on the American policy agenda ever since World War II. We have seen that Eisenhower, although he turned back from a last-ditch assist to the French, impressed Kennedy with the possible need to intervene in Laos. When the supposedly unsophisticated Eisenhower was criticized for his "domino theory," the supposedly sophisticated Kennedy came to his support: "I believe it. I believe it."[3]

[2]Theodore C. Sorensen, *Kennedy* (New York: Harper & Row, 1965), p. 715.
[3]Quoted in May, *"Lessons" of the Past*, p. 93, from State Department *Bulletin*, vol. 49, September 30, 1963, p. 499.

Asked about the apparent Sino-Soviet rift, Kennedy said in 1963 that "hope must be tempered with caution. For the Soviet-Chinese disagreement is over means, not ends."[4]

Secretary of State Dean Rusk, installed in office by Kennedy and retained by Johnson, recommended as early as November 11, 1961 (as did the Secretary of Defense) that: "We now take the decision to commit ourselves to the objective of preventing the fall of South Vietnam to Communism and that, in doing so, we recognize that the introduction of United States . . . forces may be necessary to achieve this objective."[5] The Joint Chiefs of Staff, although initially skittish about another land war in Asia, concluded in a memorandum dated January 27, 1962, quoted in Chapter 4, but bearing repeating:

> It is recognized that the military and political effort of Communist China in South Vietnam . . . is part of a major campaign to extend communist control beyond the periphery of the Sino-Soviet bloc and overseas to both island and continental areas in the Free World. . . . It is, *in fact, a planned phase in the communist timetable for world domination.*[6]

When President Kennedy sent General Maxwell Taylor and Walt Rostow to Vietnam to investigate in October 1961, their report included the conclusion that "the Communists are pursuing a clear and systematic strategy in Southeast Asia."[7]

In a similar vein, the staff report issued by the Subcommittee on National Policy Machinery of the Senate Committee on Government Operations, of October 16, 1961, begins:

The Problem

> The struggle with world communism is broadening, deepening, and quickening.
> Our rivals are pledged to see their system triumph over the free way of life. They think, plan, and act in terms of the long haul.
> The task confronting us is harshly plain—to outthink, outplan, outperform, and outlast our foes.

Such quotations could be multiplied to the point of boredom. The Kennedy administration, with almost everyone agreed, opted for increasing the small group then there to substantial numbers (16,000) of American military advisers in Vietnam. It is these facts that make it difficult to judge whether Kennedy with certainty would have shrunk from the combat role which Johnson accepted in 1965. Although we know that Kennedy on the eve of his death was contemplating the possibility of pulling out entirely from Vietnam, he had certainly increased the Vietnam commitment to substantial dimensions. Johnson, somewhat defensively, was wont to say a little ruefully that he was only continuing the policy of his predecessors. That was not true in one special and important respect: no one previously had committed the United States to a combat role in Vietnam. But otherwise Johnson was quite right. One should also remember, as we brought out in Chapter 3, that Johnson, unlike Kennedy, had little feel for or knowledge of international affairs.

The shape of things to come was clearly foreshadowed by a NSAM (National Security Action Memorandum) that Johnson endorsed in March 1964:

> We seek an independent non-Communist South Vietnam. . . .

[4]May, *"Lessons,"* p. 96, from *The Public Papers of the Presidents: John F. Kennedy, 1963,* pp. 17–18.

[5]May *"Lessons,"* p. 94; *Pentagon Papers* (Boston: Beacon Press, four vols., 1971–1972), vol. 2, p. 113. Popularly known as the "Gravel Edition."

[6]*Pentagon Papers* (Gravel Edition), vol. 2, p. 664. Italics added.

[7]Ibid., p. 107.

MAP 3

THE VIETNAM WAR, 1965

☆ AMERICAN AIR BASES*

⚫★ COMMUNIST AIR BASES

- - - → COMMUNIST INFILTRATION ROUTES

AREAS OF VIET CONG CONTROL

AREAS OF VIET CONG INFLUENCE

AREAS OF PATHET LAO CONTROL

AMERICAN FORCES

Unless we can achieve this objective . . . almost all of Southeast Asia will probably fall under Communist dominance (all of Vietnam, Laos, and Cambodia), accommodate to Communism so as to remove effective U.S. and anti-Communist influence (Burma), or fall under the domination of forces not now explicitly Communist but likely to become so (Indonesia taking over Malaysia). Thailand might hold for a period without help, but would be under grave pressure. Even the Philippines would become shaky, and the threat to India on the West, Australia and New Zealand to the South, and Taiwan, Korea, and Japan to the North and East would be greatly increased.[8]

Even Adlai Stevenson in the summer of 1964 said: "The point is the same in Vietnam today as it was in Greece in 1947 and in Korea in 1950."[9] President Johnson said almost the same thing at about the same time: "The challenge that we face in southeast Asia today is the same challenge that we have faced with courage and that we have met with strength in Greece and Turkey, in Berlin and Korea."[10] And, long afterwards, in his memoirs, Johnson added: "A divisive debate about 'who lost Vietnam' would be even more destructive to our national life than the argument over China had been."[11]

Ernest May points out that Johnson's speeches justifying his 1965 decisions were full of containment-domino rhetoric. For example, Johnson argued that defeat in South Vietnam "would encourage and spur on those who seek to conquer all free nations within their reach. . . . This is the clearest lesson of our time. From Munich until today we have learned that to yield to aggression brings only greater threats."[12]

In his important "Patterns for Peace" speech at Johns Hopkins on April 7, 1965, Johnson said that the "first reality is that North Vietnam has attacked the independent nation of South Vietnam." Behind that reality was another reality: the deepening shadow of Communist China. "The rulers in Hanoi are urged on by Peiping. . . . *The contest in Vietnam is part of a wider pattern of aggressive purposes.*"[13]

When Secretary of State Dean Rusk testified before the Senate Foreign Relations Committee on February 18, 1966, his message did not vary from his views years earlier:

We must view the problem in perspective. We must recognize that what we are seeking to achieve in South Vietnam is part of a process that has continued for a long time, a process of preventing the expansion and extension of Communist domination by the use of force against the weaker nations on the perimeter of Communist power. . . . The Communist world has returned to its demand for what it calls a world revolution. . . . So what we face in Vietnam is what we have faced on many occasions before—the need to check the extension of Communist power in order to maintain a reasonable stability in a precarious world.[14]

So there was virtual unanimity—virtual continued unanimity across the years—as to what the policymakers were seeing, what its implications were as a threat to the United States, what would happen to the security of the United States if it failed to respond adequately. This is not to say that underneath this policy consensus there were no tactical differences of opinion over who in the Communist world was in operational control and giving the orders. Although most

[8]*Pentagon Papers,* (Gravel Edition), vol. 3, pp. 50–51.
[9]State Department *Bulletin,* vol. 50, June 8, 1964, p. 908.
[10]*Public Papers of the Presidents: Lyndon B. Johnson, 1963–1964,* vol. 2, p. 930.
[11]Lyndon B. Johnson, *The Vantage Point* (New York: Holt, Rinehart and Winston, 1971), p. 152.
[12]*Public Papers,* Johnson, 1965, vol. 1, p. 449.
[13]For the speech see Department of State *Bulletin,* April 26, 1965, pp. 606–610. Italics added.
[14]Ibid., March 7, 1966, pp. 1–17. State Department publications in these years had titles such as: *A Threat to Peace: North Vietnam's Effort to Conquer South Vietnam* (Publication 7308, 1961) and *Aggression from the North: The Record of North Vietnam's Campaign to Conquer South Vietnam* (Publication 7839, 1965).

of the time the adversary was described by officials as a monolithic bloc micro-managed by Moscow, sometimes Hanoi or the PRC was seen as the driving force. Secretary of State Rusk can be quoted on both sides of this line, for example. But in broad perspective these tactical differences did not mean much, because senior officials believed that, underneath, all Communists shared the same goals and aspirations. They would ultimately work in concert, *simply because they were Communists*. Strategically, a Communist was a Communist was a Communist. Therefore, all Communists automatically were members of "the bloc." Almost the only significant question left for discussion then was what steps in what order, and with what timing, to take to meet this ideologically inspired menace. How to *implement* policy most effectively? The *Pentagon Papers* is devoted primarily to this issue as a record of the government's deliberations.

How inflexible the new macro conceptual vision had become was not recognized. Few voices were raised at policy levels in questioning the assumptions and analysis just recorded. John Kenneth Galbraith and George Ball raised questions at an early date, and Clark Clifford raised questions at a later but vital point. Most everyone else at the senior level apparently agreed. After all, as should be clear from the discussion in Chapters 3 and 12, the problem as it had evolved to this point pandered simultaneously to three American traits that in this situation reinforced each other: the tendency and preference to think in ideological terms, the preference to use moral abstractions as a guide to policy, and great energy.[15]

Franz Schurmann, in his controversial but provocative book, *The Logic of World Power,* remarks quite accurately on this first point:

> Americans are generally unaccustomed to the idea that they are governed by ideologies, preferring to believe that ideologies are what foreigners have. It is accepted that ideas govern policies, but the conventional American view is that either these ideas are correct and true and action naturally flows from them or they are rhetorical lies designed to cover up sinister machinations.[16]

Thinking in terms of a "Communist bloc" came naturally to Americans as a consequence. Since the proposition was "true," it needed no real proof. The macro conceptual framework of containment found a ready-made receptivity.

The second preference (for moral abstractions) ensured (in view of the American energy and habit of "moving it forward") that the discussion *would* move quickly to the merits of alternative tactical implementations: to what orientation was most *practical,* to what to *do*. The discussion would shift from objectives to the mechanisms for achieving them.

General André Beaufre, an acute observer of American habits in approaching problems, once expressed somewhat similar thoughts in other language. He thought it was a parallel effect of these tendencies, that Americans tended to confuse logistics and tactics with strategy.

> The thought processes applicable to tactics or logistics are almost entirely methodistic, their object being the rational employment of the military resources available in order to produce a given result. [But] strategic thinking is a mental process, at once abstract and rational, which must be capable of synthesizing both psychological and material data . . . in order to produce from these data the diagnosis itself. . . .[17]

---

[15]It is these same traits in a different aspect that Theodore Roosevelt, in a speech at Philadelphia in 1902, pointed to with pride: "From the very beginning our people have markedly combined practical capacity for affairs with power of devotion to an ideal. The lack of either quality would have rendered the possession of the other of small value."

[16]Franz Schurmann, *The Logic of World Power* (New York: Pantheon Books, 1974), p. 101.

[17]André Beaufre, *An Introduction to Strategy* (New York: Praeger, 1965), p. 12.

But it is precisely the diagnosis itself that, once containment had become an accepted and congenial way of thinking, was passed over as essentially self-evident.

Certainly, Johnson was not the man to revise American *thinking*. He was preeminently a doer. Townsend Hoopes says that the "most exhaustive search of the Johnson record reveals no solid core of philosophical principle or considered approach to foreign policy—indeed no indication that he gave the subject much serious attention before 1964."[18] Hoopes quotes Philip Geyelin's characterization that:

> by political background, by temperament, by personal preference he was the riverboat man . . . a swashbuckling master of the political midstream—but only in the crowded, well-travelled familiar inland waterways of domestic politics. He had no taste and scant preparation for the deep waters of foreign policy, for the sudden storms and unpredictable winds. . . . He was king of the river and a stranger to the open sea.[19]

In late 1963, when President Kennedy was assassinated, the U.S. military presence in Vietnam, as we saw, consisted of about 16,000. Already, by the end of 1964, merely as a result of bureaucratic pressures, the size of the group had grown about a third, to 21,000.

4.

The Sino-Soviet Split—Disregarded

By the day of John F. Kennedy's death, November 22, 1963, it was clear beyond dispute that the Sino-Soviet disputes were real and were serious. The pending U.S.-Soviet Nuclear Test Ban Treaty seemed to the Chinese to be the last straw. The Chinese published an open letter, dated June 14, 1963, protesting a variety of Soviet actions, including a lack of revolutionary concern for China, and disclosing frontier incidents. A month later the Soviets responded with an open letter, refuting the Chinese claims and charging that the Chinese attitude toward nuclear arms was reckless and irresponsible: "We would like to ask the Chinese comrades, who offer to build a wonderful future on the ruins of the old world destroyed by a thermonuclear war, if they have consulted the working class of the countries where imperialism dominates on this matter?" On September 1, the Chinese resumed their public attack. On September 21, the Soviets responded: the Chinese statement was "no longer a comradely discussion between Communists but an action by people who are determined to discredit the C.P.S.U. and the Soviet Union at any cost. . . ." The Soviets, in this same note, accused the Chinese of "more than 5,000 violations of the Soviet frontier from the Chinese side" in 1962 alone. When the Soviets had offered talks, the Chinese had not responded. "This cannot but make us wary. . . ."[20] But the Chinese frontier fight with India in September 1962, which was an expression of their anger over the casual assumption that the Indian border line was known and agreed, continued the image of an aggressive China in American minds. (Even though the Chinese unilaterally and voluntarily withdrew their forces twenty kilometers "behind the lines of actual control" in November 1962.)

President Kennedy, in his last news conference, on November 14, 1963, said:

> We are not planning to trade with Red China in view of the policy that Red China pursues. When the Red Chinese indicate a desire to live at peace with the United States, with other

[18]Townsend Hoopes, *The Limits of Intervention*, rev. ed. (New York: David McKay, 1973), p. 8.

[19]Philip L. Geyelin, *Lyndon B. Johnson and the World* (New York: Praeger, 1966), p. 15.

[20]See, for texts, *Two Major Soviet Statements on China* (New York: Crosscurrents Press, 1963) and *Statement of the Soviet Government, September 21, 1963* (New York: Crosscurrents Press, 1963).

countries surrounding it, then quite obviously the United States would reappraise its policies. We are not wedded to a policy of hostility to Red China. It seems to me Red China's policies are what create the tension between not only the United States and Red China, but between Red China and India, between Red China and her immediate neighbors to the south, and even between Red China and other Communist countries.

If this is the presumably sophisticated appraisal by Kennedy, acting after the events just recorded, what could one expect from his successor? Here is no thought that India deserves little from the United States, all things considered. Here is no thought that a quarrel between two enemies should receive more response than a ritual denunciation of either or both. In the light of this, the statements quoted earlier make interesting reading: Are there *any* real differences in American condemnation of the "aggressive Communist bloc" *after* the Sino-Soviet split became obvious and public?

These events are worth having clearly in mind. They show that the decisive event in the broadening of U.S. involvement in Vietnam took place significantly *after* the Sino-Soviet split became public. Yet the rationale containment gave for opposing the "aggression" in Vietnam, *despite its intrinsic unimportance strategically* in affecting Asia's power balance in any significant way, was that it was the tip of the spear, the advanced action element of a coordinated Communist thrust. If this argument had not been seen as compelling, it would obviously have been useful at this point for American policymakers to have considered the gains and losses of a more committed policy in Vietnam against the larger issues of U.S. relations with both the Soviet Union and China. They would have considered very carefully whether a large deployment of American troops off China's other flank (the United States was still in Korea) really served the American national interest.

5.
The Tonkin Gulf Resolution and Commitment

The actual record makes dismal reading from this point of view, for no serious consideration of counterbalancing interests, of policy alternatives, was really attempted. The (later disputed) North Vietnamese attacks by their torpedo boats on U.S. destroyers in the Tonkin Gulf in August 1964—again, well after the public phase of the Sino-Soviet dispute—effectively aborted any real further thinking. President Johnson ordered a retaliatory air strike, and asked Congress for what became known as the Tonkin Gulf Resolution authorizing the President "to take all necessary measures to repel any armed attack against the forces of the United States and to prevent further aggression" in the area. We pointed out in Chapter 6 how very brief this debate was. Some doubting senators were quickly reassured by Senator Fulbright, who described the resolution as "quite consistent with our existing mission and our understanding of what we have been doing in South Vietnam for the last ten years." Senator Daniel Brewster of Maryland persisted: "I would look with great dismay on a situation involving the landing of large land armies on the continent of Asia. So my question is whether there is anything in the resolution which would authorize or recommend or approve the landing of large American armies in Vietnam or China. . . ."

Senator Fulbright responded: "There is nothing in the resolution, as I read it, that contemplates it. I agree with the Senator that it is the last thing we would want to do. However, the language of the resolution would not prevent it. . . ."

But when Senator John Sherman Cooper of Kentucky asked whether passage of the resolution could be interpreted as an implementation of Article IV of the SEATO Treaty, as "giving the President advance authority" to act in Vietnam, Fulbright also said: "I think that is correct."

Senator Wayne Morse of Oregon, one of the two senators to vote no on the resolution, bluntly called the resolution "a predated declaration of war," whereas Fulbright assured the Senate that "the President will consult with Congress in case a major change in present policy becomes necessary." But that never happened.[21]

On February 7, 1965, the Viet Cong attacked American installations at Pleiku, causing U.S. casualties. A retaliatory U.S. air strike followed. To safeguard the installations, two reinforced U.S. marine battalions were sent ashore on March 6 at Da Nang. They were, said Rusk and McNamara, assigned "defensive operations" as their mission. In April, Johnson's Johns Hopkins speech offer to negotiate with all governments concerned got no response.[22] By June some 50,000 American troops were already in Vietnam and the White House acknowledged that they were "authorized" to engage in combat under certain conditions. By the time the summer of 1965 was over, "there were 170,000 troops in Vietnam [and] U.S. air forces were bombing the North with mounting intensity. . . ."[23]

Halberstam remarks of this period when the United States was moving rapidly to a substantial commitment of unknown size:

> There were brief moments when the reality seemed to flash through. Once during the early June discussions the President turned to General Wheeler and said, "Bus, what do you think it will take to do the job?" And Wheeler answered, "It all depends on what your definition of the job is, Mr. President. If you intend to drive the last Vietcong out of Vietnam it will take seven hundred, eight hundred thousand, a million men and about seven years." He paused to see if anyone picked him up. "But if your definition of the job is to prevent the Communists from taking over the country, that is, stopping them from doing it, then you're talking about different gradations and different levels. So tell us what the job is and we'll answer it." But no one said anything . . . and they did not define the mission.[24]

At the end of January 1966, even as U.S. reinforcements continued to pour into Vietnam, the evidence of a continued Sino-Soviet split steadily accumulated. The official Beijing *People's Daily* said then, for example: "The Soviet Union is preparing the ground to strike a new deal with U.S. imperialism just as the Lyndon Johnson administration is quickening its pace toward a wider war of aggression against Vietnam." The United States continued to ignore the implications.

Hoopes remarks: "By October 1967, 40 per cent of our combat-ready divisions, half of our tactical airpower, and at least a third of our naval strength—the whole numbering some 480,000 men—were waging full-throated war on the Southeast Asian peninsula."[25] Casualties and costs were accumulating. Roger Hilsman, after cautioning, quite correctly, about the "slippery" nature of Vietnam statistics, gives some figures for the increase in Viet Cong strength. At the beginning of 1965, he gives 124,000. By the start of 1966, Hilsman shows the Viet Cong as numbering between 215,000 and 245,000.[26] Earlier, he gives figures (unfortunately only up through 1965) on Viet Cong terrorism against civilians. In 1960, Hilsman cites 1,400 assassinated, 700 kidnapped, and 2,100 total acts of terror. By 1963, the corresponding figures are 2,073, 7,262, and 9,335, and for 1965, Hilsman cites 1,895, 12,778, and 14,673 as the numbers of acts of terror committed by the Viet Cong.[27] Hilsman concludes that the smaller percentage

[21]For convenience, we have followed the Hoopes, *op. cit.,* account, pp. 25–26.
[22]By using the word *governments,* Johnson excluded the possibility of independent Viet Cong participation. Because of the prevalent strategic conception, the VC was perceived to be only a puppet.
[23]Hoopes, *Limits of Intervention,* pp. 31–32.
[24]David Halberstam, *The Best and the Brightest* (New York: Random House, 1969), p. 596.
[25]Hoopes, *Limits of Intervention,* p. 57.
[26]Roger Hilsman, *To Move a Nation* (Garden City, N.Y.: Doubleday, 1967), p. 529.
[27]Ibid., p. 525.

of killings within the larger total figure as time goes on suggests that the Viet Cong were winning on one important level; they had grown strong enough to "brainwash" and not just kill. That is one reason the United States resorted to a troop build-up. But, as Hilsman's first figures indicate, the Communists, being there, could always reinforce—and did, and troops deployed in battalion or divisional strength had limited utility for a struggle for control on a village level.

6.

Confusion at Three Levels

So the United States moved by increments into a war for which it had no clear, positive plans at all, either at the grand strategic or military strategic or tactical levels.

The confusion over grand strategic aims stemmed from faults in policy design, from the very nature of the containment concept, with its domino corollary. As we know, Munich-type appeasements, with aggression unopposed, were supposed to lead to a disintegration of the opposition as the dominoes fell. Therefore, the conceptual guidance emphasized the negative: do not fail to frustrate the aggression the first time it is attempted. (The positive guidance was simply: "Be there.") Like that other concept Americans have found congenial, collective security, the guidance ran out once appropriate blocking action had been taken. Aggressive episodes had to be terminated, but that termination in and of itself was seen as essentially sufficient. The objective was not to achieve some better and mutually acceptable rearrangement of affairs (the spirit of the Congress of Vienna). The objective was to punish the crime (the spirit of Versailles). But the post-hostilities phase, once crime was proved not to pay, remained vague.

In short, the grand strategic or macro-level analysis of the situation left much to be desired.

So far as the *military* strategy and tactics used in Vietnam are concerned, much argument about what went wrong continues. One three-star air force general, retired, shown a draft paper on Vietnam that described the Tet offensive as a "disaster" for the United States, insisted it was a "victory" because the United States had inflicted so many casualties on the Viet Cong—which about sums up the argument. Some military analysts thought the "hamlet" concept would have worked if it had not been sacrificed on the altar of the "search-and-destroy" tactics that were so much more suitable to the conventional army forces actually employed. Certainly, "search-and-destroy" on its face was not very suitable for "unconventional" warfare where, so the jargon has it, the intention is to win the hearts and minds of the people.

Robert L. Galucci argues that "The military strategy of the United States in South Vietnam from the spring of 1965 through the spring of 1968 was the strategy of 'search and destroy.' It did not become the American strategy as a result of a joint decision by civilians and military leaders; some of the latter and many of the former thought that it was a costly failure. And yet it prevailed."[28] Galucci shows that Westmoreland "pursued a course designed to involve as many American units as possible, quickly and actively, in combat." He was no innocent "boy scout" with no thoughts of his own. As Galucci says, "Search and destroy was the 'traditional attack mission of the infantry,' and General Westmoreland maneuvered, in the beginning of 1965, to get into a position that would enable him to pursue that mission."[29] The military's idea, predominantly (and understandably) was that they should be "turned loose" to do their job. Significant parts of the army distrusted the Green Beret budget-consuming notions foisted upon them by President Kennedy, although such "counterinsurgency" forces were also used. The air force and

[28]Robert L. Galucci, *Neither Peace Nor Honor: The Politics of American Military Policy in Viet-Nam* (Baltimore: Johns Hopkins Press, 1975), p. 106.
[29]Ibid., p. 115.

navy wanted less restrictions on missions and the army wanted freer fields of fire. Galucci quotes one Defense Department study as follows:

> In 1966, some 65 per cent of the total tonnage of bombs and artillery rounds used in Vietnam was expended against places where the enemy *might* be, but without reliable information that he *was* there. The purpose of these unobserved strikes was to harass, discourage, and drive off the enemy if he happened to be around.[30]

When, in 1968, after Tet, the International Security Affairs (ISA) civilian group in the Pentagon made an effort to shift the thrust of military activity, General Wheeler was "appalled at the apparent repudiation of American military policy" contained in the draft ISA recommendation that concern should be shifted from search-and-destroy to denying "the enemy access to the populated areas of the country and prevent him from achieving his objectives of controlling the population and destroying the GVN."[31] Wheeler won the argument and the civilians lost. As Wheeler explained the point on another occasion: "You must carry the fight to the enemy. . . . No one ever won a battle sitting on his ass."[32]

So it went with the military strategy and tactics—partly because of traditional military concepts, partly because of bureaucratic preferences, and perhaps partly for professional career reasons (you get promoted quicker for combat and how can you win if you do not fight?). There was also the academically inspired belief in game theory, sending "signals," and distinguishing "appropriately" between "levels of violence," especially coupled with the "limited war lessons" of the Korean War. These were at the other end of the spectrum from General Wheeler's point of view. The idea was to jab the enemy and wait to see his reaction. If he needed more, you "went up the ladder of escalation" a step. You bombed the enemy a while and then had a "pause" while the enemy considered whether he had had enough.

The combination of these new-fangled and overly sophisticated civilian ideas for how to fight a war with the traditional "blood-and-guts" ideas of most of the military produced the oddest half-house seen in contemporary warfare: a combination of power that was at the same time frequently extravagant, undirected, and intermittent.

But none of this is to say that the "enclave" theory or any other proposed approach would have worked if it had been consistently attempted. It simply was highly unlikely in the very nature of things that anything attempted by Americans under the circumstances would have averted the tragic ending in Vietnam. Although one can read General Westmoreland's memoirs without finding much feeling for the real problem he was confronting, that does not mean there was a good military or politico-military solution to the problem. From the point of view of the North Vietnamese or Viet Cong, it might take an entire generation to complete the expulsion of the Westerners (first the French, later the Americans). If it did, then it did. With an objective this fundamental, whatever was necessary would be done. Americans, serving their country and carrying out its policies far from American shores, could not feel the same urgency or dedication. It was quite remarkable that American professional military standards were so well maintained under the circumstances.

The military tactical level of discussion that we have just so lightly touched on is the third level down in terms of importance. The first level, the grand strategic or macro level, is the level at which one has to question whether policy actions were being guided by an *appropriate* con-

---

[30]Ibid., p. 118, quoted from Enthoven and Smith, *How Much Is Enough?* (New York: Harper & Row, 1971), p. 306.

[31]Galucci is quoting from the *Pentagon Papers,* vol. 4, p. 564.

[32]Galucci, *Neither Peace Nor Honor,* p. 126, from Henry F. Graff, *The Tuesday Cabinet* (Englewood Cliffs, N.J.: Prentice-Hall, 1970), p. 128.

cept: whether it made sense for the United States to fight the Vietnam War at all. It is difficult to avoid the conclusion that the war made little sense unless one somehow believed in the continued unity of a Communist bloc despite the public evidence. One might argue, as a variation, that *one* of the giant Communist powers—say China—was really backing the North Vietnamese so it was a war to restrain China's expansion (occurring, presumably, with Soviet tolerance). But then it hardly made sense to allow China to choose that location for a confrontation. And that is to beg the more fundamental question of whether it made sense to restrain Chinese peripheral expansion per se, even while China was showing antagonism toward the Soviet Union. Is it not necessary, for success if not survival, to have some rank-order of enemies? Is not the *prioritization* of enemies a first politico-military strategic essential?

On the second level, the theater (military strategic) level, there is a profound emptiness of content, as we said, because the containment theory stresses what cannot be allowed to happen rather than the circumstances under which it may not need to occur or how to transition from the one situation to the other. In game theory terms, it does not provide any detail about the end-game.

On the third level, that of tactics, there is little more to add on the nature of the problem. Certainly, even with the best tactics, the uncertainties of the second level could not really be resolved. Nor could superb tactics make the war useful to the United States unless it met the criteria of the first level. Not the least tragic and ironic feature of the Vietnam War was the sight of an America, faithfully trusting in mechanical/physical/practical solutions, trying to make politico-military sense of a very questionable choice for a war.

Confronted with problems for which his concepts were either inappropriate or unhelpful, President Johnson throughout chose half solutions to every major problem connected with the war. He did not mine Haiphong Harbor or invade neighboring Laos and Cambodia, or bomb close to China, because he did not want to widen the war. He did not call up the reserves because it would have meant using forces greater than the problem would seem to deserve and would also produce domestic uproar. He neither authorized really ruthless military tactics nor withdrew the forces. He let the military have its way without requiring a sound plan of procedure. He fought a war without having one declared. He spent large sums of money without asking for new taxes. In the end, bitter and isolated, Johnson announced he would not run for reelection.

7.

Nixon—and (Eventually) War's End

Johnson's successor, Richard Nixon, was elected to end the war without dishonor. (More exactly, some voted for him to end the war, some voted for him above all to sustain American honor, and some voted for him to achieve both objectives.) As it turned out, the task that Nixon faced was difficult. Nixon also appeared more interested in the honor part than in ending the war. It took until 1973 for the war to wind down. Of course, a significant aspect of this timing stemmed, too, from the policies of the enemy.

The Paris Peace Agreements ultimately resulted in the United States' withdrawal from Vietnam. Rather than beginning by examining the twists and turns in the Vietnam negotiations, it will be more productive for us to enumerate first the prime issues and see how these were handled in the *final* agreements. With that clearly in mind, we can then examine the major checkpoints as the negotiations were conducted.

The issues, once America surrendered the objective of "victory" and opted for a compromise peace, were: (1) whether an anti-Communist regime would continue to exist in South Vietnam after American withdrawal, (2) the modalities (timing and form) of such withdrawal, and (3) the return of American POWs.

The breakthrough came on October 8, 1972, when the North Vietnamese chief negotiator, Le Duc Tho, told Henry Kissinger that the two nations should (in Kissinger's words) "sign an agreement settling the military questions between them—withdrawal, prisoners, cease-fire. On the political problems of South Vietnam, 'we shall only agree on the main principles. After the signing of this agreement a cease-fire will immediately take place.'"[33] Kissinger comments that "After four years of implacable insistence that we dismantle the political structure of our ally and replace it with a coalition government, Hanoi had now essentially given up its political demands."[34] But, significantly, as Kissinger admits, Hanoi said "nothing about withdrawing its troops," not even admitting they were there.[35]

Le Duc Tho over and over repeated that "this new proposal is exactly what President Nixon has himself proposed: cease-fire, end of the war, release of the prisoners, and troop withdrawal. . . ."[36] And Kissinger agrees: "And so it was. Hanoi had finally separated the military and political questions, which I had urged nearly four years earlier as the best way to settle. It had accepted Nixon's May 8 proposal and conceded that the South Vietnamese government need not be overthrown as the price of a cease-fire. . . . The demand for a coalition government was dropped; the political structure of South Vietnam was left to the Vietnamese to settle."[37] Replacement of armament in the meantime was permitted, which, Kissinger comments, meant "we could continue to supply South Vietnam."[38] Infiltration into South Vietnam was to cease, supposedly. (But Hanoi's troops would remain in place.)

On January 23, 1973, essentially these terms of peace were initialed in Paris.[39]

Kissinger, in an earlier part of his memoirs, describes Nixon's May 8, 1972, proposals in detail. In that context he says:

> The terms were, in fact, the most forthcoming we had put forward: a standstill cease-fire, release of prisoners, and total American withdrawal within four months. The deadline for withdrawal was the shortest ever. The offer of a standstill cease-fire implied that American bombing would stop and that Hanoi could keep all the gains made in its offensive. We were pledged to withdraw totally in return for a cease-fire and return of our prisoners.[40]

What Kissinger does *not* emphasize is that, whereas Nixon's May 8, 1972, speech did include those elements, it began on a far different note: "There is only one way to stop the killing. That is to keep the weapons of war out of the hands of the international outlaws of North Vietnam." Nixon continued: "I have ordered the following measures. . . . All entrances to North Vietnamese ports will be mined. . . . Rail and all other communications will be cut off. . . ."

Nixon's specific words on terms on May 8, 1972, were:

> First, all American prisoners of war must be returned.
> Second, there must be an internationally supervised cease-fire throughout Indochina.
> Once prisoners of war are released, once the internationally supervised cease-fire has

---

[33]Henry Kissinger, *White House Years* (Boston: Little, Brown, 1979), p. 1343.
[34]Ibid., p. 1344.
[35]Ibid.
[36]Ibid., p. 1345.
[37]Ibid.
[38]Ibid., p. 1344.
[39]The agreement did not explicitly provide for a cease-fire in place throughout all Indochina, only South Vietnam, but the provisions of Chapter VII make it apparent that formal cease-fires were expected to follow soon in Laos and Cambodia.
[40]Kissinger, *White House Years*, p. 1189.

begun, we will stop all acts of force throughout Indo-China, and at that time we will proceed with a complete withdrawal of all American forces from Vietnam within four months.[41]

In the sequel, under heavy pressure and not buoyed up by any Soviet decision to suspend the planned summit, the North Vietnamese indicated their "acceptance."

However, even these May 8, 1972, terms were not incorporated into the final agreement of January 23, 1973, without further ups and downs following the October breakthrough. South Vietnamese President Thieu proved difficult; the North Vietnamese went through second thoughts that brought on American heavy bombing "using B-52s on a sustained basis for the first time over the northern part of North Vietnam."[42] But, finally, an agreement was reached between the parties.

The most useful way to assess this agreement is to go back and look at the *initial* terms proposed by each side *in 1968*.

On December 20, 1968, even before Nixon's inauguration, Kissinger arranged for a message to Hanoi suggesting peace talks. On December 31, the reply from Hanoi "stated brutally two fundamental demands: the total withdrawal of *all* American forces and the replacement of what Hanoi called the 'Thieu-Ky-Huong clique.'"[43] Kissinger remarks that Johnson's bombing halt, November 1, 1968, had clearly produced *no* change in Hanoi's position. Nixon tried a new tactic:

> On May 14, [1969] Nixon went on national television and elaborated for the first time the premises of his Vietnam policy....
>
> He proposed an eight-point program that represented a quantum advance in the American negotiating position over that of the Johnson Administration. Specifically, he abandoned the Manila formula (Hanoi's withdrawal six months before ours) and advocated simultaneous withdrawal.... The United States agreed to the participation of the NLF in the political life of South Vietnam; it committed itself to free elections under international supervision and to accept their outcome. The President offered to set a precise timetable for withdrawal, and he offered cease-fires under international supervision.[44]

Kissinger remarks that the "only conditions it did not meet turned out to be the Communist *sine qua non*: unconditional withdrawal of United States forces and collusive installation of a Communist-controlled government."[45]

Nixon, in the May 14 speech had proposed withdrawal of "the major portions" of U.S. forces within one year; in a later speech on November 3, 1969, he accepted a *total* withdrawal if it was agreed and mutual.[46] By May 1972 this position had eroded further. Now all American forces would leave in four months, and the North's troops could stay.

It is therefore reasonably clear that what happened after May 1972 was that Hanoi pulled back from its political demands (convinced they could be reached in other ways) and concentrated on a cease-fire which allowed North Vietnamese troops to remain in a position to resume the offensive after the American troops were withdrawn within the four months' agreed deadline. The supervisory features of the agreement and the reiterated "respect" for the DMZ were so much window-dressing.

---

[41] *RN: The Memoirs of Richard Nixon* (New York: Warner Books, 1978), vol. 2, pp. 83–84.
[42] Kissinger, *White House Years,* p. 1448.
[43] Ibid., p. 259.
[44] Ibid., p. 270.
[45] Ibid., p. 271.
[46] Ibid., p. 306.

The United States, which in October 1966 demanded Hanoi's withdrawal six months before American troops would *begin* pulling out, settled in January 1973 for Hanoi's troops staying in South Vietnam but the United States pulling out all troops in a four-months period after the cease-fire.

Over seven years of additional warfare, to settle for that! Kissinger, however, points out that Hanoi never until 1972 backed down from the demand that the United States help impose a coalition (i.e., Communist-infiltrated) government on Saigon. There was little chance that either Johnson or Nixon would ever accept that, since acceptance would have meant not only United States defeat but United States humiliation. Yet the longer the war continued the more POW's were in North Vietnamese hands, and the ultimate settlement really did nothing for the United States but three things: (1) it put an end to a wasteful war, (2) it allowed the United States to withdraw, and (3) it returned American POWs. South Vietnam itself subsequently collapsed.

The most interesting feature of this dismal story is why Hanoi for so long preferred to attempt to humiliate as well as defeat the United States. It may well be that the Communists were simply determined not to be caught twice ending hostilities with a promise—such as they got with the 1954 Geneva accords promising elections south of the 17th parallel, which they felt confident of winning but which were not held for them to win.

Whether this is so or not, it is apparent that the Vietnam War involvement of the United States represented an unhappy combination of policy adrift in the service of a containment concept that was vague about what happens after the initial commitment, of a military strategy and tactics adrift at the hands of standard operating procedures for a conventional war, of a limitation on fighting reflecting new and unproved ideas about warfare, and of a negotiating position which changed repeatedly in many of its essentials.

Where the policy left most to be desired was in its unwarranted assumption about who was the enemy, its lack of concern with prioritization of enemies, its vagueness on how enmity could be reduced (or, at least, controlled), and its lack of guidance on how some useful results could be extracted from the venture at some reasonable price.

8.

Summing Up

The Vietnam War committed the United States to expensive and prolonged military operations in an area of little strategic importance. As we saw, this commitment seemed worthwhile because of the conceptual lenses used: the containment of Moscow-run, bloc-communism, and the prevention of the domino effect.

Significantly, the commitment of *combat* forces (which automatically, in the course of time, led to the POW problem as Americans fell into enemy hands) occurred after clear evidence was available of a Sino-Soviet split. Yet that split, if acknowledged and accepted as more than temporary, undermined the basis on which the bloc-containment concept rested.

Some Americans responded to this dilemma by arguing that the split was neither real nor permanent. Others sought to exploit it. We see in Chapter 14 how this led to the playing of the "China card."

14

Détente and Afterwards

My view was that the bilateral issues were peripheral to the imperatives now driving the Chinese. Only extraordinary concern about Soviet purposes could explain the Chinese wish to sit down with the nation hitherto vilified as the arch-enemy. If I was correct, what the Chinese really wanted to discuss was the global balance of power. . . . the Peking invitation made sense only if the Chinese were seeking to reduce the number of their enemies.

Henry Kissinger,
White House Years[1]

1.

Nixon, Kissinger, and a New Approach

It is quite true, as Kissinger claims in his memoirs, that the Nixon administration could not proceed immediately to an integrated and coherent foreign policy that was designed to fit that policy more realistically to the world outside. Much debris had to be cleared away first; a new path had to be charted and the intellectual and diplomatic resources had to be assembled. In looking at this new path, once taken, it is possible to make two serious mistakes in evaluating the record.

The first mistake would be to overstate the degree of conceptual homogeneity among the decision makers in the later Nixon years, the period loosely called détente. The second mistake would be to see greater tactical consistency in procedure than any large bureaucracy is ever likely to yield. On the first point, the change in stance toward China and the subsequent movement to unfreeze the Middle East stalemate did not command full-scale and voluntary popular and official support and enthusiasm in the same sense, for example, as containment once did. In the 1950s, everyone more or less understood containment in theory, even if they were not sure how far it would or should be taken in the form of faraway commitments in fact. With détente, the label so loosely attached to the 1970s, there was always much disagreement on what it was supposed to mean and represent in theory terms, as well as continued argument over where it should lead to taking stands. The details of the policy were clearer than the appreciation of the thrust of the theory behind the policy.

---

[1] P. 690, italics in original.

Part of the reason was that the ideas and intellectual inclinations of both Richard Nixon and Henry Kissinger, besides including a very healthy respect for the fundamentals of balance of power thinking or the kind of approach represented by the cardinal principles, also contained a heavy admixture of ideological thinking. Kissinger was slow to appreciate the real nature of the Sino-Soviet break and could become significantly excited about Marxism's advances in Angola. Nixon, it can safely be assumed, never winced in the presence of that grand oversimplification which played for so many performances, the "Free World" versus the "Communist bloc." Nevertheless, both had almost an innate feel for *Realpolitik*. They understood instinctively, and better than any administration in a very long time, what the central rules of the game really were, including the conservation of enemies. They understood very well that accumulating more enemies than necessary, instead of yielding that pursuit to one's prime enemy, was a sucker's game. And beyond any doubt, they appreciated the idea of prioritizing enemies. This "realist" emphasis gave U.S. policy a much sharper conceptual edge.

2.

Rapprochement with China

President Nixon, less than two weeks after his January 20, 1969, inauguration, instructed Kissinger to begin *privately* exploring the possibilities of a rapprochement with the Chinese. In Nixon's first Foreign Policy Report to Congress (itself an important illustration of the new administration's emphasis on imparting conceptual coherence to U.S. policy), the section on China, as Nixon points out in his memoirs, began with the words:

> The Chinese are a great and vital people who should not remain isolated from the international community. . . .
> The principles underlying our relations with Communist China are similar to those governing our policies toward the U.S.S.R. United States policy is not likely soon to have much impact on China's behavior, let alone its ideological outlook. But it is certainly in our interest, and in the interest of peace and stability in Asia and the world, that we take what steps we can toward improved practical relations with Peking.[2]

It took until the middle of 1971 for this approach to yield real fruit. On July 15, 1971, though, Nixon was able to announce what he correctly calls "one of the greatest diplomatic surprises of the century": that Kissinger and Premier Zhou Enlai had held talks in Beijing from July 9 to 11, and that the next step would be for Nixon himself to visit China "at an appropriate date before May 1972." Nixon indicated he had accepted and would "seek the normalization of relations. . . ."[3]

So began the first stage of the new China policy. At long last, the United States was abandoning its confrontation orientation toward China.

The new policy was designed to end a negative condition: having Communist China automatically included in a list of prominent American enemies. It was not intended to make an ally of China. It rested upon appreciating that China had been immobilized by strained relations with both superpowers simultaneously, each with troops near or on the Chinese border. Looked at that way, the policy of Vietnamization, announced by the Nixon administration in the spring of 1969 and which by 1972 had already removed 480,500 troops from China's southern flank,

---

[2]Richard Nixon, *RN: The Memoirs of Richard Nixon,* vol. 2, p. 8.
[3]Ibid., pp. 7–8.

was restoring some degree of Chinese freedom of decision.[4] The events just recorded, including Nixon's Beijing visit, were a natural consequence. (To say "natural consequence" does not mean that any unimaginative American administration would have experienced the same result; only that the conditions in the system permitted those next steps to occur.)

The new policy, though much more reasonable and natural than the policy it replaced, was denounced by some Americans who construed this "playing the China card" gambit as an effort by the United States to *use* China for American purposes, quite apart from Chinese interests. (This argument, with its unconscious overtones of American omnipotence, reminds one of the "who lost China?" issue, only in reverse.)

That the Soviets were disturbed was just as natural. When Nixon explained that the United States wanted normal relations with China, the Soviets could hardly respond by denouncing it as an unfriendly act—even though it was. The point is that it was a "natural" unfriendly act. The United States had no need (and no intention) to enter into an alliance with China for the Soviets to pay full heed to this change and its significance.

Very wisely, the Shanghai communiqué issued at the end of Nixon's visit in February 1972 resorted, instead of papering over the Sino-American differences, to a parallel listing of points with each party choosing its own wording.[5] It was a highly appropriate format, for each government in that way was able to express its own views on Taiwan and other issues. (It should be remembered, too, that the breakthrough in the Vietnam peace talks was still months ahead so that China was still supplying arms to an active American opponent.)

3.

Impact of the China Card on Soviet-American Relations

As we pointed out in Chapter 4, when Brezhnev came for a visit to the United States in June 1973, says Nixon, he was "apparently still worried that we were contemplating some secret military arrangement, possibly a mutual defense treaty, with the Chinese." Nixon gave him a reassuring but indirect response and then said to Brezhnev that "it would be at least twenty years before the Chinese would acquire a sufficient nuclear capability to risk an aggressive action against the Soviet Union or any other major nuclear power." Brezhnev, according to Nixon, disagreed: "Ten, in ten years, they will have weapons equal to what we have now. We will be further advanced by then, but we must bring home to them that this cannot go on." Brezhnev related how Mao in 1963 had said: "Let 400 million Chinese die; 300 million will be left." Mao's death would change nothing. Brezhnev, says Nixon, "was certain that the entire Chinese leadership was instinctively aggressive."[6]

It was not necessary for the United States to take any action toward China other than to cease being actively antagonistic in order for very serious strategic reevaluations of counterbalancing interests to occur also in the Kremlin. The Kremlin was very sensitive to the nuances of how much China, under varying conditions, might act adversely against the Soviet Union. Perhaps that is what makes it such a curious feature of Kissinger's generally hardheaded memoirs that he apparently really thought Russia might be persuaded (short of some *in extremis* situation) to help end the Vietnam War—a development bound to curtail Soviet freedom of action

---

[4]Kissinger, *White House Years,* p. 1101 says 480,500 of the 545,000 troops there when Nixon took office.

[5]But, even then, negotiating the separate wording together.

[6]Nixon, *Memoirs,* vol. 2, pp. 426–427.

and assist in the settlement of Sino-American differences. For example, Kissinger in 1969 wanted to have Nixon send Cyrus Vance on a special mission to the Soviets: "The mission which I had in mind [was] nothing less than to enlist the Soviet Union in a rapid settlement of the Vietnam War." Kissinger continues: "In all my conversations with Dobrynin [the Soviet ambassador to the United States] I had stressed that a fundamental improvement in U.S.-Soviet relations presupposed Soviet cooperation in settling the war. Dobrynin had always evaded a reply by claiming that Soviet influence in Hanoi was extremely limited."[7] Kissinger was practicing "linkage," withholding (by his own listing) progress on SALT talks, Middle East talks, and expanded economic relations.

There were two problems with that approach. The less serious one was that mutually satisfactory agreements, when reached, necessarily reflect fairly equal advantages—meaning that the United States was not really going to accept progress on Vietnam in return for inferior terms in SALT and a bad agreement on the Middle East. The second problem was that the United States, having blundered into a hostile relationship with Communist China, begun by the civil war, solidified by the Korean War, and intensified by the Vietnam War, had thus presented the Soviet Union with a priceless but completely free strategic gift. Kissinger was asking the Soviets to give up this gift for very minor concessions, if any. No wonder the Soviets "evaded a reply." When the United States finally managed to free itself of this incubus, the burden was necessarily transferred to the Soviet Union for all the reasons that the cardinal principles make clear. The Soviets did not like that; they tried very hard to avoid it, but without success.

If the Sino-American decision to avoid unnecessary mutual antagonisms had rested on some ingeniously contrived, highly unstable policy stances, the Soviet Union might have counted on putting pressure on some fragile joint and collapsing the whole thing. But here were the Chinese and the Americans, in the name of the conservation of enemies, simply ending an active hostility that had little solid basis to it. Tactically, however, that strategic transformation could not occur fully until the Vietnam War ended. Then the strategic freedom sacrificed mutually by the United States and China could be restored, thus inevitably curtailing the strategic freedom that the Sino-American antagonism and the Vietnam War had for so many years conferred upon the Soviets.

Looking at the Soviets from this point of view, thinking now of their frontiers in a 360-degree frame of reference, what we see is a Soviet Union able to act more freely between 1949 and 1972 than it ought to have been able to act in Europe and the Middle East because its eastern flank remained secure without much Soviet effort. When this happy state of affairs ended, it produced a traumatic shock in the Kremlin. There was no good way for the Soviets either to derail the Sino-American venture in diminished tensions, or to do something somewhere else that would produce in Soviet-positive terms an equivalent strategic effect.

We do not have hard and detailed evidence of what happened in the Kremlin as a result, but it is possible to observe the alteration in Soviet behavior that followed. The Soviets' very first reaction was to tighten the screw; the problem was the availability of appropriate pressure points. They turned to the most obvious possibility first—one of China's less friendly neighbors. The Soviets, too, understood the cardinal principles; third-party influences could work both ways.

The nearest approximation to an offset for the U.S. "new China policy" was an intensification of relations with India. On August 7, 1971, three weeks after the announcement of Kissinger's first trip to Beijing, the Soviets unveiled their Soviet-Indian Friendship Treaty. This move, coupled with Pakistan's unimaginative and heavy-handed approach to the East Pakistan unrest, culminating in the establishment of Bangladesh and a new Indian-Pakistani War (November-December, 1971), raised U.S.-Soviet tensions to a high level. This is the period of the famous Nixon "tilt" (discussed further in Chapter 18).

[7]Kissinger, *White House Years*, p. 266.

Even according to Kissinger's own account, apparently he and Nixon almost alone wanted to support Pakistan against India. (Kissinger, incidentally, devotes seventy-six pages—about 5 per cent of his entire book—to this Indian-Pakistani development.) In a paper prepared for the Senior Review Group of the National Security Council, there was a recommendation, says Kissinger, "that if China intervened in an India-Pakistan war, the United States should extend military assistance to *India* and coordinate its actions with the *Soviet Union* and Great Britain. Nothing more contrary to the President's foreign policy could have been imagined."[8] Such an action, if taken, might have produced turmoil domestically. But, consider what the reaction would likely have been if the United States instead had announced plans to aid "dictatorial" Pakistan against "democratic" India! Yet, at the high point of the crisis, Kissinger actually called in the Soviet chargé and read to him an American aide-mémoire from November 5, 1962, in which, says Kissinger, "the United States promised assistance to Pakistan in case of *Indian* aggression. I warned him [on the morning of December 10, 1971] that we would honor this pledge."[9]

Kissinger's justification for this move is that the China initiative would have been aborted if the United States had permitted "the public humiliation of China's friend—and our ally."[10] The impression he gives is that the United States was required to take riskier actions than China actually offered to take in order that China would be convinced of American sincerity. This kind of recurrent sentimentality in American policy is usually—and quite rightly—condemned by Kissinger in other contexts. It is hard to avoid the impression that Kissinger has allowed his Beijing trip to involve him personally in this issue. He says that acquiescing "in such a power play, we would have sent a wrong signal to Moscow and unnerved all our allies" and China. He complains that his "essentially geopolitical point of view found no understanding among those who conducted the public discourse on foreign policy in our country" who, instead, wanted to look "on the merits of the issues that had produced the crisis."[11] Kissinger, even now, does not take in that what he was contemplating had no public backing and therefore, put simply, was not feasible no matter how geopolitical. (If these chapters show any one thing, they show that.)

The question of Pakistan's defense would rise again, after the Soviet invasion of Afghanistan at the end of 1979.

Whether India and Russia were impressed by these "signals" and turned to a more moderate program because of them (leaving West Pakistan intact) is not known. In any event, the Soviets had no other meaningful political cards to play immediately so they turned to a generally more restrained and cautious policy. The changed Soviet policy, in combination with the Nixon-Kissinger search for global equilibrium, produced a less tense relationship that became known as détente.

4.

The Advent of Détente

Most American senior military officers never saw détente in any other framework than as a ploy to lull the United States into treading water while the Soviets continued an arms build-up. Admiral Zumwalt, in his first venture into politics after retirement from his position as Chief of Naval Operations, made many such speeches. Zumwalt in his memoirs at one point even suggests that Kissinger was animated by a doomsday feeling that time was running against the West, and

---

[8]Kissinger, *White House Years*, p. 865. Italics in original.
[9]Ibid., p. 905. Italics in original.
[10]Ibid., p. 913.
[11]Ibid., p. 913–914.

that unsettled issues would be less tractable later as American strength declined—that détente was a reflection of American weakness. What gave this more "hard-line" kind of criticism a certain plausibility was the undoubted fact that the Soviets indeed *were* continuing with their massive arms build-up, then and later. Yet Soviet actions in the next years, though no more perfectly consistent than nations generally manage, were certainly less provocative and adventurous in areas vital to U.S. security.

What likely happened in the Kremlin after the new China policy of the United States was implemented was a reappraisal of counterbalancing interests, which concluded that, apart from the Indian situation, only very slim and transient *political* gains for the Soviets could be achieved anywhere in the world. Whether the Soviets then understood fully their problem in Third World interventions is not clear: the futile policy of going into Egypt with arms and aid, then being expelled; of assisting Somalia to fight Ethiopia, and then having to reverse its aid. But the Soviets must have seen that, with political opportunities in short supply, the declining balance of their national security status could only be restored by a greater emphasis on arms and the distribution of arms. After all, national security is basically an amalgam of the political and the military working in tandem. Cripple the political option and the burden will be thrown to the military to reverse the erosion of security. The logic of that situation was a continued upward trend in Soviet armaments complemented by a more forthcoming and accommodating political stance. Détente, for the Soviets, reflected essentially a lack of other viable alternatives.

To say this does not mean that the Soviets did not believe sincerely in peaceful coexistence. It is only to say that they would have welcomed greater opportunities to forge ahead with their programs.

5.

Effects of Détente on the Middle East

One can argue, without detracting from the brilliance of Kissinger's later Middle East "shuttle diplomacy," that the policy pursued there by the United States was made possible to a significant extent by the adversely changed Soviet strategic situation (and increased Soviet security problems) of the détente years.[12] For the Soviets, once conditions on their Asian flank worsened, had to consider long and carefully how reckless to be elsewhere, especially in areas that were not adjacent to Soviet frontiers.

United States policy in the Middle East, leaving aside a few tactical oddities, was remarkably consistent in a strategic sense from at least the time of the U.S. marines' Lebanon landing in 1958. Because Nasser had by his actions enmeshed both superpowers into an increasingly direct confrontation in the area, the tension level increased; but the determination of the United States to prevent any power from acquiring a hegemonic position in the area remained constant. Whether Nixon's comment to Secretary of State Rogers was precisely true or not it reflected the American view earlier and later: "The difference between our goal and the Soviet goal in the Middle East is very simple but fundamental. *We* want peace. *They* want the Middle East."[13] Nixon sent a memorandum to Kissinger in which he made much the same point. He wrote that American "interests are basically pro-freedom and not just pro-Israel because of the Jewish vote. We are *for* Israel because Israel in our view is the only state in the Mideast which is *pro*-freedom and an effective opponent to Soviet expansion."[14]

[12]Of course, altered conditions in the Middle East were also important, as pointed out in Chapter 19.
[13]Nixon, *Memoirs,* vol. 1, p. 591.
[14]Ibid., p. 596.

The difficulty with the American position for a number of years stemmed from the nature of the Arab approach. Since the Arabs were so bitterly anti-Israeli, it appeared that the United States was seeking *only* to support Israel. But the real thrust of American policy was to promote and support a stable equilibrium, thus preventing either Israeli, Arab, or Soviet domination of the region. In short, the United States was pursuing a balance of power policy in the Middle East that appeared to lack even-handedness because of extremism on the part of other parties.

A fundamental shift in the situation, however, began to emerge once Nasser had disappeared from the scene and Anwar Sadat had taken over in Egypt. In July 1972 Sadat, finding his dependent relationship unfruitful and intolerable, expelled Soviet civilian and military advisers from Egypt. Since the Soviets had 15,000 military personnel there at the time, this was a highly significant change. Yet, contrary to what seemed implied as a consequence of this move—increasing Egyptian military impotence—Sadat launched hostilities against Israel in October 1973 and, making effective use of advanced SAMs to inhibit Israeli air action, sent the Israeli armed forces into initial and unaccustomed disarray. When the Israelis did recover and launch a lightning probe across to the west bank of the canal, in the rear of an Egyptian army still moving eastward through the Sinai, the Egyptian victory began to turn into defeat. As the noose tightened around the Egyptian Third Army both superpowers (for different reasons) worked hard to achieve an effective cease-fire. Kissinger went to Moscow to confer with Brezhnev and on Sunday, October 21, they reached an agreement that the Israelis and Egyptians accepted on October 22.

Hardly was this achieved when both belligerents accused the other of violations. The Washington-Moscow hotline came alive as Brezhnev complained. Another cease-fire; another Brezhnev complaint (plus intelligence reports of alerts for seven Soviet airborne divisions.) Sadat's request for both superpowers to send a joint peacekeeping force to the Middle East increased tension. Soon Brezhnev was back on the hotline to endorse this idea. It was late that night that, in Nixon's words, "all American conventional and nuclear forces [were put] on military alert." Nixon then told Brezhnev "that we could in no event accept [Soviet] unilateral action" and rejected the joint dispatch of forces as well.[15] Early on October 25, the next morning, a message from Sadat informed the United States that Sadat would instead request a UN peacekeeping force. Brezhnev sent a message then that the Soviet Union would be sending seventy individual "observers." Nixon says: "This was completely different from the military contingent he had described in his earlier letter."[16]

Nixon ends his discussion of these events with a definition of the meaning of détente and a summary of the Soviet actions:

> The Soviet Union will always act in its own self-interest; and so will the United States. Détente cannot change that. All we can hope from détente is that it will minimize confrontation in marginal areas and provide, at least, alternative possibilities in the major ones.
>
> In 1973 the Soviets, with their presence in the Middle East already reduced, feared that they would lose what little foothold they had left. As our direct approaches to Egypt and the Arab countries had met with increasing success, the Soviets had undoubtedly compensated with increased anti-Israeli bravado.[17]

Whatever the Soviet role, says Nixon, for "the second time in six years the Arabs lost most of the Soviet equipment. . . . Moreover, for the first time in an Arab-Israeli conflict the United States conducted itself in a manner that not only preserved but greatly enhanced our relations

---

[15]Nixon, *Memoirs*, vol. 2, p. 499.
[16]Ibid., p. 500.
[17]Ibid., p. 501.

with the Arabs—even while we were massively resupplying the Israelis."[18] Nixon ends by saying that now "the Arab leaders had a place other than Moscow to turn."[19]

For his part, Sadat, with his personal prestige now much enhanced, began to cooperate in unfreezing the old hostile relationship with Israel—a process that was well on its way by the advent of the Carter administration and one which that administration carried forward to new and dramatic successes.

Behind the new Egyptian realism was a confrontation of a stark dilemma: either continued mortgaging of Egypt's economic future in return for new infusions of Soviet arms, or some settlement with Egypt's major enemy. With a population that was continually expanding and economic and industrial progress limited, Egypt had very little to gain other than emotional satisfaction by periodic wars with the Israelis. Without a major change in the military balance future wars would not end in victory. Thus better relations for Egypt were essential with the United States because only Washington could effectively influence the Israelis. Sadat made the choice for peace, progress, and the recovery of territory. That he went as far as he did had something also to do with his shrewd recognition that Nixon, under fire in the Watergate affair, might be removed from power if Sadat waited too long. In any event, the crucial and initial disengagement agreement in the Sinai was reached in January 1974 (and the follow-on Syrian-Israeli agreement was reached in May), comfortably before Nixon's resignation in August 1974.[20]

It is difficult to see these events in an assured perspective. For one thing, the leading memoir accounts (Nixon and Kissinger) quite understandably attach enormous significance to some events that may appear less earth-shattering to a third party. The Soviet "threat" in the October War may have been as really significant as Kissinger says. Nixon is cooler in his account. But if the Soviets were tempted toward military adventure then, they did not try it. From this point forward the two superpowers were, at least nominally, *jointly sponsoring peace moves* in the area. That is certainly a strategic role reversal for the Soviet Union.

Nixon records these events quite matter-of-factly:

> On December 21, 1973, UN Secretary-General Kurt Waldheim had opened the Geneva Peace Conference on the Middle East. Syria did not attend, but Egypt, Israel, Jordan, the United States, and the U.S.S.R. sent representatives. On December 22 the initial round of talks ended, with instructions to Egypt and Israel to begin immediate discussions on the disengagement of their forces along the Suez Canal.
>
> From January 10 through January 17, 1974, Kissinger began what came to be known as his "shuttle diplomacy."[21]

To put the point more bluntly, the United States succeeded in getting the Soviets to co-sponsor a peace session. Then, leaving the so-called Geneva Conference on the Middle East to sit in fairly indefinite intermission, the United States took on the "shuttle diplomacy" role while the Soviets occasionally complained correctly that they were being essentially excluded from the negotiations.

Kissinger's tactics no doubt found part of their motive in enjoying the new American ability to make progress with the U.S. policy. They also reflected his view that (1) it was important to exclude the Arab radical elements from the critical negotiations and that (2) Soviet diplomacy at its best was extremely tedious. Kissinger remarks at one point, in relating the Berlin negotiations, that "I have known no Soviet diplomat—including Gromyko—who would accept a new

[18]Ibid., pp. 501–502.
[19]Ibid., p. 502.
[20]The next agreement was in September 1975.
[21]Ibid., p. 552.

major proposal without referring it to Moscow."[22] That kind of foot-dragging would have been completely incompatible with Kissinger's fast-moving shuttle.

Kissinger explains the point further himself: "If after 1973 I sought to keep Moscow out of Middle East negotiations, the reason was partly geopolitical, partly the Soviet negotiating style. I was convinced that progress in Middle East diplomacy depended on fluidity. . . ." Gromyko's pedantic style, even if backed by Soviet goodwill, would have given "a veto to the most radical elements" unless movement permeated the negotiations.[23]

This, in overall terms, was the record of the Kissinger-Nixon-Ford period. It demonstrates a clear design to swing the pendulum inhibiting American flexibility and conferring freedom on the Soviets from the one extreme to the other. It shows that this design was implemented.

6.

The Carter Administration

The Carter administration, in its initial years, made a startling contrast. It deliberately set out to separate itself from the air of "secret diplomacy" still left over from the previous administration. Far from showing concern over enemies or their "conservation," Carter began pursuing a "human rights" program that quickly reaped a harvest of antagonism; the Soviets and others quite correctly took it as a criticism of their handling of their own internal affairs. Brezhnev, for example, in March 1977, condemned "direct attempts by official American bodies to interfere in the internal affairs of the Soviet Union." He went on: "Washington's claims to teach others how to live, I believe, cannot be accepted by any sovereign state. . . ."[24] The Carter policy did not succeed in improving human rights within the Soviet Union, but it did move the Soviets to put the SALT negotiations on ice for a time and destroyed the delicate progress that had been made in advancing United States-Soviet economic relations.

China at first was substantially neglected by the Carter administration, long enough for voices to be raised speculating on the meaning of this neglect. Luckily for the United States, the Sino-Soviet split had its own momentum. Brezhnev said as much at the Twenty-fifth Congress of the Communist Party of the Soviet Union in February 1976: "Peking's frantic attempts to torpedo détente, to obstruct disarmament, to breed suspicion and hostility between states, its efforts to provoke a world war and reap whatever advantages may accrue, present a great danger for all peaceloving peoples."

On the other hand, the emphasis on "human rights," coupled with the announced determination of the new administration to cut the export of American arms, especially to the developing nations, cost much goodwill abroad outside the Soviet bloc. Much of what used to be fondly known as the "Free World" is, after all, usually run by military governments who found this new dual emphasis equally uncongenial. The "preachy" attitude alienated without conferring any tangible benefits.

Candidate Carter had also made it clear that he advocated severe cuts in the Pentagon budget.

Thus, the total strategic posture initially conveyed was of a nation with a confused set of priorities.

President Carter, for example, in a speech in May 1977 at Notre Dame said: "I believe we can have a foreign policy that is democratic, that is based upon fundamental values, and that uses power and influence . . . for humane purposes. We can also have a foreign policy that the

[22]Kissinger, *White House Years,* p. 828.
[23]Ibid., p. 791.
[24]*New York Times,* March 22, 1977.

American people both support and, for a change, know about and understand."[25] Carter cited events in India, Portugal, Spain, and Greece as recent gains for democracy which, in turn, made the United States "now free of that inordinate fear of communism which once led us to embrace any dictator who joined us in that fear." It encouraged us at times to fight "fire with fire, never thinking that fire is better quenched with water." It led us to a policy "that Soviet expansion . . . must be contained," coupled with a strong "belief in the importance of an almost exclusive alliance among non-Communist nations on both sides of the Atlantic." There was merit in this part of Carter's approach. More questionable was his assertion that the "unifying threat of conflict with the Soviet Union has become less intensive. . . ." Carter saw the new policy as more third-world oriented, resting on human rights, creating closer links among the "industrial democracies," ending the arms race, ending Middle East tension, and controlling nuclear proliferation. But this is only a listing of desirable goals, not a concept for achieving them.

It was here that Carter had trouble. As one of his speechmakers once said: "Carter has not given us an *idea* to follow. The central idea of the Carter Administration is Jimmy Carter himself . . . since the only thing that gives coherence to the items of his creed is that he happens to believe them all."[26]

In any event, a year and a half later, President Carter's policies had changed in their priorities. Much more prominent now was the issue of national security. In his State of the Union address on January 23, 1979, Carter still said that "We have no desire to be the world's policeman. America does want to be the world's peacemaker." But the forthcoming visit of Chinese Vice-Premier Deng Xiaoping was noted as a positive step and Carter also took account of growing popular anxieties about the lagging U.S. defense program and SALT II, saying specifically that one Poseidon missile submarine, representing less than 2 per cent of the American strategic nuclear arsenal, "carries enough warheads to destroy every large and medium-sized city in the Soviet Union." When Carter finally turned to human rights, it was in an American *domestic* context.

By Christmas 1979, with the Soviet attack on Afghanistan (following the earlier Iranian "student" assault on the U.S. Embassy in Teheran), Carter's emphases had altered once more. Now he led the way to a very blunt condemnation of the Soviet move, asked for a greatly increased U.S. defense budget, and began to explore arms aid to Egypt and the use of bases in Somalia.[27] In his address to the nation on January 4, 1980, Carter said:

> The Soviets claim falsely that they were invited into Afghanistan to help protect that country from some unnamed outside threat. . . .
> This invasion is an extremely serious threat to peace—because of the threat of further Soviet expansion into neighboring countries in Southwest Asia and also because such an aggressive military policy is unsettling to other peoples, throughout the world.
> This is a callous violation of international law and the United Nations Charter.[28]

Asserting that "aggression unopposed becomes a contagious disease," Carter put the SALT II Treaty in abeyance in the Senate, sought and got a UN condemnation of the Soviet action,

[25]See *Weekly Compilation of Presidential Documents,* May 30, 1977.

[26]Quoted in Seyom Brown, *The Faces of Power: Constancy and Change in United States Foreign Policy from Truman to Reagan* (New York: Columbia University Press, 1983), p. 460.

[27]In the State Department release, Current Policy no. 102 of October 24, 1979, "U.S. Foreign Policy Achievements," the Counselor is quoted in a speech summarizing the achievements in the following order: national defense, the role of the United States in peacemaking, world economic issues, energy, SALT, and human rights. It noted with pride the MX system and the 3 per cent "real increase in defense spending."

[28]State Department release, Current Policy no. 123 of January 4, 1980, "President Carter: Soviet Invasion of Afghanistan."

cut off grain supplies to the Soviets, and in other ways showed the extreme U.S. displeasure with the Soviet invasion.

Writing a year earlier than these dramatic events, William J. Barnds had made a careful analysis of the Carter program to that date. He noted that the Carter stance seemed unclear, with uncertainty existing "about the focus of the administration's foreign policy," a vagueness about "the likely direction" of that policy. Carter, said Barnds, "was fortunate in that he faced no international crisis when he took office [or] during his first two years." Barnds notes how the tactical handling of the Soviet Union led to a "deterioration" of relations and the lack of effective consultation with "principal allies." He praises the Camp David summit on the Middle East, but adds that "in its first two years the administration made little progress in formulating and articulating an integrated strategy to guide its actions in world affairs." There was no overall guidance for setting priorities. That meant the policymakers could easily slip into "treating each issue on its merits . . . each in isolation."[29]

The further distinct shift in priorities between national security issues and human rights in the wake of the double-barreled crisis over Iran and Afghanistan continued for the rest of the Carter administration. So did the conceptual fragmentation of policy. In the opening months of 1980, people were talking of a Cold War II, and students were burning their prospective but nonexistent draft cards to protest the nonexistent draft. With the new sense of priorities surfacing in the administration, criticism began to be heard from precisely the opposite end of the political spectrum that initially questioned the Carter policies.

A grossly oversimplified polarization of American political opinion began to set in. On the Stanford University campus, at one extreme, student groups opposed registration of youth. Speakers argued that registration would lead to the draft, the draft would lead to armed forces sufficient to challenge the Russians, the challenge would lead to war, and the war would result in mutual nuclear destruction. Similar oversimplifications were heard on other campuses. At the other extreme, old Cold Warriors emerged to say that the United States, by its military weakness and gentle handling of the Iranian hostage issue, had encouraged the Soviets to go ahead and "test the waters" by taking Afghanistan. Next would be Pakistan, or Iran, or both; then the choking off of Middle East oil supplies.[30]

7.

Evaluation

Political pundits filled the pages of American publications with commentaries contradicting each other. George F. Kennan, in a thoughtful piece, pointed out that Afghanistan "was a move decidedly not in character for either Aleksei N. Kosygin or Leonid I. Brezhnev. Andrei A. Gromyko, too, is unlikely to have approved it. These reflections suggest the recent breakthrough, to positions of dominant influence [in Russia], of hard-line elements less concerned for world opinion, but also less experienced, than these older figures."[31]

---

[29]William J. Barnds, "Carter and the World: The First Two Years," *Worldview,* 22, no. 1–2 (January–February 1979).

[30]Edward Teller, the "father of the H-bomb," gave an interview to the *Peninsula Times Tribune* in February 1980, at the Hoover Institution at Stanford. It contained this question and answer:

"Q. You have made statements recently, with reference to the invasion of Afghanistan, that the Soviet Union might attempt to close off the Persian Gulf. What would this mean to us?

A. It is a real possibility. The Russians are beginning to close the pincers, and if they do, they will gain control of one third of the world's oil production."

[31]*New York Times,* February 1, 1980, p. 27; also *San Francisco Chronicle,* February 8, 1980, pp. 8–9.

Even so, Kennan thought that the move probably reflected "defensive rather than offensive impulses" even if "the American view [ran] overwhelmingly to the assumption that it was a prelude to aggressive military moves . . . farther afield." Kennan said: "Never since World War II has there been so far-reaching a militarization of thought and discourse" in Washington.

General "Davy" Jones, Chairman of the U.S. Joint Chiefs of Staff, pointed out on television that a Soviet invasion of Iran would probably be launched, if it came, from Soviet territory bordering Iran on the north, and not importantly from Afghanistan. But his view got little attention in the public debate.

There was a thread of continuity in all of this, if one goes back to the earlier point in this chapter that the Soviets, following the U.S. "new China policy," had far narrower political maneuvering room than before. Deprived by the American action of its cozy but unearned security status on one frontier, and confronting at best an unenthusiastic acquiescence by the nations forming its security belt in Eastern Europe, the Soviets could find no good political card to play. After the Indian-Pakistani War of 1971, that situation offered little gain. Kicked out of Egypt in 1972, the Soviets were reduced to little more than a weapons-supplying role in the Middle East in 1973. Even then, Kissinger put the Soviets into a holding pattern while he shuttled. The Soviets after that point had little opportunity to create crisis in the area, compounding the effects of their now lessened desire to create new problems there. With their own frontiers a problem or potential problem on both east and west (from China to Poland), there was too much danger for the Soviets in a really adventuresome policy elsewhere in any area of prime American concern.

But the less the political options the Soviets might pursue for profit, the more the national security position of the Soviet Union depended upon that other half of the national security equation—armaments.

At this point, consider the American side of the relationship. Jimmy Carter came to office without a crisis on the horizon, thanks to his predecessors' able efforts. It can be argued that he wasted time with unsynchronized and abortive efforts and dissipated much goodwill abroad with a strong human rights program. Simultaneously, American military might settled increasingly into the shadow of the Soviet military effort. Few Americans were grossly disturbed since the United States was still ahead on *total* national security points (political plus military). But soon the American political surplus was being indifferently handled in the first part of the Carter administration. Next, the military component was put essentially on hold with the veto of a new nuclear carrier, the decision not to produce B-1 bombers, the decision not to produce neutron weapons, and the decision to allow the trouble-laden voluntary military force system to limp along. Taken together, the total national security effect was noticeable and negative. Whether this played any role in the Soviet action in Afghanistan is hard to say, but it was at least plausible to argue that it did. More probably, it was really Soviet concern about the potential removal of a friendly regime from their sphere of influence and the possibility of a radical Muslim movement stirring up problems among the 20 per cent of the Soviet population who share the same cultural and religious heritage (and happen to live geographically adjacent to that ferment). Anyone who thought in terms of 360 degree frontiers would probably note that, once the Ayatollah Khomeini movement took hold to the south, the *only* really tranquil Soviet frontiers were the northern ice fields.

Kennan's comment on the "hard-liners" is probably correct although it probably ought to be expanded and extended more specifically. What may very well be occurring is that the internal Soviet policy debate has shifted to a second stage. Assume that the first stage of the debate did involve, as we argued, a side-by-side comparison of the political and military options for Soviet national security, with that debate won by 1972 or 1973 by the military side. If that is true, there is still a second, highly important question to settle: *Where* should any arms-troops-base options be implemented? Was it in the Soviet interest merely to stir up trouble by distributing arms and aid to *any* customer? Should the Soviets aid any professed friend and oppose any apparent enemy? Or should distinctions be drawn? For after Khrushchev in 1955 extended Soviet arms to the Middle East, to nations not even pretending to be "socialist" in the Communist sense, where was the ultimate line to be drawn?

Kissinger, in his memoirs, makes much of the line the Soviets crossed when they furnished pilots for Egyptian airplanes. But the larger question is the one just posed. After all, critics of Soviet "globalism" could point to enormous programs of aid to Indonesia, to Egypt, and to Somalia each of which had paid the Soviets a dismal return. They could point to the enormous Soviet investment in Cuba, in India, and in Angola and ask whether the spotty and uneven results were worth the sunk costs. These critics could very specifically ask whether the adventures far away from Russia were really worth the money, especially with the Soviet frontier areas increasingly sensitive, not to mention a lack of progress at home in areas such as grain where the Soviets were still dependent on occasional but massive imports. It is not known whether this is the real focus of the debate—one between the small-circle, frontier-oriented hard-liners and the large-circle, stir-the-pot "globalist" hard-liners—but it *could* be. There is no reason why the most fundamental national security issue of them all, in any nation able to export military power, should somehow not be a problem for the Soviets—especially in view of the record just cited.

In any event, continued popular concern in the United States with the prolonged, massive Soviet arms build-up played a key role in the election of Ronald Reagan in 1980. A form of Cold War fever continued in 1981. Indeed, the new emphasis on American armament increases, coupled with a postponement of serious arms negotiations with the Soviets, alarmed many Europeans. Reagan's choice of General Alexander Haig as Secretary of State, whatever its merits, added to the growing image of a war-minded United States. President Reagan himself, in October 1981, caused further alarm when he answered a newsman truthfully that there was no certainty that the use of a tactical nuclear weapon in Europe would lead to a full nuclear "exchange." The tactical handling of foreign policy was causing problems.

The conceptual basis of the Reagan approach also contained some difficulties because the old ideological emphasis was quite strong. Yet an alienation of Communist China could hardly be in the national interests of the United States. Somewhat reluctantly, Reagan played down his own obvious inclination to remain close to Taiwan. Confident in judgment of complex issues (although weak in knowledge of foreign policy substance), Reagan might be expected to increase the coherence of U.S. policy over time. Certainly he represented the opposite of Carter's uncertainty over the issues. Whether that coherence (if, indeed, it did occur) would be the result of an appropriate concept, or instead would flow from a resurrection of containment and the domino theory, was not evident.

8.

Summing Up

The Nixon-Kissinger years saw the nearest approach in recent American foreign policy to a conceptually consistent policy offering hopes of increased effectiveness at decreased costs. Unfortunately, the secrecy of the method, its staining by Vietnam, and the policy's ultimate sharing in a sense of corruption and unworthiness stemming from the Watergate affair limited the permanency of its foundations. The very dissatisfaction with its "deviousness" assisted Carter to his election victory. It testified to American popular reluctance to think and to act in power-interest terms. Carter, losing ground with his human rights emphasis, was next succeeded by Reagan with his renewed ideological emphasis. The net result by 1983–1984 was a new coolness in Sino-American relations and a new frigidity in Soviet-American relations, an indifferent record in the Middle East, a coolness with Argentina after the Falklands War, and an (as yet) minor American military role in Central America. Not all these adverse effects could be helped or avoided. But the increase in American problems after the short breathing space of détente suggested that, after more than two hundred years of foreign policy experience, we still cannot say with confidence that the American nation has an agreed conceptual way of arriving at a national security consensus. But, as this book amply demonstrates, it is ultimately not possible for a nation to pursue a meaningful policy without a concept that permits a foreign policy consensus. The search for that concept and consensus today must take place against the backdrop of a world gradually changing in some significant ways, as Parts Four and Five make very clear.

15

Postlude and Prelude

There must be, not a balance of power, but a community of power; not organized rivalries, but an organized common peace.

Woodrow Wilson
Address to the U.S. Senate,
January 22, 1917

The first three parts of this book are intended to introduce Part Four. For Part Four is where we turn to the important and substantive problems that face the United States, the problems which U.S. policy must address effectively. In Part Four we describe these problems, show how they frequently are interlinked, consider the issues arising from them that call for policy decision, define policy alternatives for dealing with them, weigh the merits of these alternatives, and suggest which alternatives on balance hold the most promise.

1.

What Parts One, Two, and Three Argue and Why

Before we turn to these problems it is important to have clearly in mind what we have done so far in Parts One, Two, and Three, for if these three parts are to fulfill their purpose of preparing us for Part Four's problems, we must be able to say of what that preparation consists, so that we can apply it.

In Part One our first objective was to describe the nature of the state system (or the environment) in which U.S. foreign policy is implemented. Our second objective was to show how unusual, even unique, the American experience has been in terms of geography, history, and the American domestic environment, and how this experience, in turn, has shaped American attitudes about foreign policy and the international environment in some special ways and even toward the creation of an unusual way of thinking about policy; how it has even created an unusual policy *style*. (American policy pronouncements tend to be general and abstract.)

These American attitudes critically influence how Americans approach phase 1 of policy: its design. These attitudes govern what is attempted and the goals sought. In the large sense

```
┌─────────────────────────────────────────────────────────────┐
│  Phase 1 of Policy                                            │
│                                                               │
│  CONCEPT    leads to    CONTENT                               │
├─────────────────────────────────────────────────────────────┤
│  Phase 2 of Policy                                            │
│                                                               │
│                CONTENT    leads to    IMPLEMENTATION          │
└─────────────────────────────────────────────────────────────┘
```

they control goals and objectives because in a more specific sense they control which national interests are included in the content of policy, to be implemented in phase 2.

Our third objective was to emphasize that policy is a two-phase, three-part process, with *content* both as the end product of phase 1 and the beginning substance of phase 2. In describing phase 1, *design,* we stressed the importance of the *concept* with which one begins the analysis. If we repeat the diagrams of Chapter 4 in slightly altered form, the point should be clear.

A concept is more complex than it at first appears. It necessarily has several subparts. It involves a view of the nature of the problem confronted and the issues it presents for decision, an expectation as to how the problem might develop or be eliminated through recourse to different policy alternatives (i.e., through the choice of one policy content over another), and therefore some expectation of how the state system will function in terms of that particular problem.

To show how these subparts of concept should be taken into account in addressing concept, we indicated a sequence of three questions to be asked when considering policy alternatives (i.e., alternative policy contents). These questions were (1) what kind of result did we want to see at the end of the evolution? (2) who would help and who would hinder? and (3) what then would be the expected cost for achieving that anticipated result? Answering these questions involves arriving at some distinct view of how the system functions. (And noting what appeal different views of the system have for different nations also tells much about their national experience and idiosyncrasies.)

Our fourth objective was to provide our own conceptual model for understanding how that state system functions. We called it the four cardinal principles, and we elaborated the nature of each in Chapter 4. Since perception of the system counts so heavily in formulating (designing) policy, the first two principles (past-future linkages and third-party influences) provide concise guidance on *how to approach the analysis of any foreign policy problem*. These two principles remind policymakers that nations hold quite diverse views about how the state system functions (or what a particular opponent is trying to achieve)—views which will be strongly influenced by the past experience of the nation making the decision. Past experience will directly affect future expectations, and any decision in the present will be made with the express intention of bringing about or avoiding specific imagined or foreseen future consequences. Prudent decision makers, estimating "Who will help and who will hinder?" in a given situation, will not forget this fact. In a word, history counts.

The second cardinal principle, third-party influences, particularly reminds decision makers when they consider policy alternatives toward a second state, that they must not forget the impact on each other, third states. A bilateral confrontation may be decisively affected by neighbors on the flanks or in the rear of either contender. *Where* you are in part accounts for the problems you feel required to respond to in the first place.

The third and fourth cardinal principles (counterbalancing national interests and the conservation of enemies) provide concise guidance *on what the point of pursuing policy is all about*. Where the first two principles remind policymakers how to understand the problem, the second two provide guidance to the prudent decision maker on how to respond to the problem effectively. The strategic intent of keeping active opposition limited (the conservation of enemies) can only be achieved through prudent choices (between counterbalancing national interests). Such choices require a sense of priority about the enmity stemming from the goals sought as well as a sense of tactics about how to induce marginal opponents, who might side with a major opponent, not to do so. The tactics therefore focus on satisfying the needs of marginal opponents who would otherwise turn to alliance with major opponents for the same or equivalent satisfactions. Carried to its fullest extent, the idea is to isolate the major opponent from support.

The cardinal principles tell how policy should actually be made for maximum effectiveness. They provide an ideal standard but one that can be readily utilized.

Our fifth objective was to enumerate four operational steps in Chapter 5 that show how the decision-making process applies to the implementation of policy in specific cases. These four steps provide a succinct and practical checklist for how phase 2 is carried out, as plans are implemented. These four steps involve first, identifying the actors really involved (and the degree of their involvement); second, determining objectives (of all the parties involved, in the context of the emerging problem); third, analyzing capability (what power each has that is pertinent and available); and fourth and most important, choosing an involvement posture or orientation (establishing how much the United States should be involved). These four operational steps of phase 2 also can be expressed in question form: (1) Who is involved? (2) What do they want? (3) What is the operational power relationship—what power can each bring to bear? and (4) What involvement appears necessary?

What is common to every point made so far is the continuing stress we have placed on the *expectation of outcomes*. In this sense every policy decision begins with its end, and the most important action in policymaking is always intellectual.

In Part Two our first objective was to show how difficult it is to make policy in the American system today. We argued that the President is the central figure in the policy process, and if the system is to function optimally it is he who must provide leadership in both policy design and implementation. For more than two decades after World War II the manifold conflicts and problems almost inherent in the American system and the crucial and fundamental role that presidential leadership plays, were not as apparent as they are today. The reason is clear: the participants substantially shared a conceptual consensus on how the international system worked, what the threat was, and what should be done about it; to counter the threat from the Communist monolith in a world where the domino effect was operative, a containment/forward deployment strategy was essential. Because this consensus was so pervasive the larger issues of policy design—the validity, appropriateness, and logical implications of the basic concept—were ignored, attention instead being focused on the efficiency of policy implementation. But with that consensus shattered by the Vietnam War it was essential that the major actors in the foreign policy system, led by the President and his senior advisers, go back to square one and address the crucial issues of concept and the policy content that different concepts produce. Otherwise, we argued, no matter how efficiently policy was implemented, no matter how well the President was advised and policy was coordinated, no matter what organizational changes might be made, as the United States confronted the problems of the post-Vietnam era it would not be able both to protect American interests adequately and minimize costs and risks.

In Part Three our objective was to examine the actual historical development of American policy, particularly as it focused on that central policy concern for all nations: security. In four chapters we stressed the transformation of the American commonwealth from a weak object of great power intrigue to a vital superpower in its own right. We watched the design and implementation of policy change accordingly, and we underlined the fundamental dilemma encountered by a power strong enough in contemporary times to attempt many, even most things; able to cross the oceans with significant forces. The crux of that dilemma consists in knowing what *not* to attempt. What, indeed, is worth doing, and *why?*

It is here in Part Three, against the background in Part Two of understanding how the government functions, that we applied the themes of Part One. For if the experience of the United States has been unusual and its attitudes about the system equally unusual, this will substantially affect American ideas about what is feasible to attempt in policy, about what is worth doing and why.

Here we come to the root point, for the American affection for such abstract propositions as collective security and bloc-containment shows one overriding habit, just as does American support for the domino theory and its fear of repeating a Munich-type appeasement. Every one of these propositions has the same feature: *it identifies responses required by categories of events,* rather than by the nature of the specific problem faced. Collective security, an American conceptual favorite, says that when X attacks Y, the United States should help Y. Bloc-containment says that when X (who this time is any Communist country) attacks Y (who this time is any member of the Free World) the United States should aid Y. The domino theory says that any aggression results in a steady decrease in opposition, as the dominoes fall, and therefore the United States must come to the aid of the first Y to be attacked, anywhere in the world, anytime. As President Kennedy put it, "defend *any* friend" and "oppose *any* foe." And the "lesson" of the Munich appeasement is that giving in—anywhere, anytime—to a threat inevitably leads to disaster.

These abstract propositions have in common mechanical responses to certain set occurrences that ignore the guidance of the four cardinal principles and turn the orientation step into a mere formality. As a design for policy these abstract propositions propose contents that, when implemented, can be very expensive indeed. They answer the questions of where and when and how to be involved on a rather open-ended basis—one almost certain to be rather expensive, compared to results obtained, especially if great power is available to use to serve the policy commitments.

In a word, American policy statements do not tend to a *direct and specific analysis* of the real point at issue in the context of a sober understanding of how the system functions. There is a parallel and pronounced reluctance to analyze the issue on its own merits, a marked preference to encase any issue in some framework of moral or general principle. We quoted the Truman Doctrine (containment, applied there to Greece and Turkey) and the Open Door notes (equal commercial trading opportunity—a "good" in itself—applied there to China). We could multiply the references almost indefinitely, including Secretary of State Cordell Hull's assertion that the United States would not continue to sell war goods to nations which bombed women and children from the air (he meant Japan). We have seen Wilson talk about freedom of the seas (he meant Germany).

To state the point negatively, there is relatively little discussion of power or national interest advantage as sufficient justification for action in American diplomacy or statecraft, at least after the period of the Founding Fathers. Americans may not notice how unusual this habit is, or the difference in the manner in which most great nations approach such problems, so we shall try to make the point clear by giving representative quotations from Americans and foreigners to show clearly the difference in style.

Before we do so, however, it should be recalled that the point we are making is not merely academic. The American habit of analysis affects how the United States designs policy, affects what the United States chooses to try to do. The price for mistakes here is one paid in blood and treasure—of which no nation can ever afford to be offhand or wasteful.

2.

American Style—Foreign Style

Our first pair of quotations is from the early history of the United States. Washington's Farewell Address (September 19, 1796) is like more modern American statements in its tendency to generalize, but it is not enmeshed in moral propositions and is refreshingly directed at American interests. Remember while reading Washington's Farewell Address, that the United States, allied to France during and after the American Revolution, had found the alliance highly profitable during hostilities. Afterwards France had threatened continually to enmesh the United States in European power politics. So Washington in his address is actually indicating his view— although not stated directly—that *any* alliance with *any* European power is a disadvantage to the weak United States, currently then surrounded by territories in the hands of all these foreign powers.

> Europe has a set of primary interests, which to us have none, or a very remote relation. Hence she must be engaged in frequent controversies, the causes of which are essentially foreign to our concerns. Hence, therefore, it must be unwise in us to implicate ourselves, by artificial ties, in the ordinary vicissitudes of her politics, or the ordinary combinations and collisions of her friendships, or enmities.
>
> Our detached and distant situation invites and enables us to pursue a different course. If we remain one people, under an efficient government, the period is not far off, when we may defy material injury from external annoyance; when we may take such an attitude as will cause the neutrality, we may at any time resolve upon, to be scrupulously respected; when belligerent nations, under the impossibility of making acquisitions upon us, will not lightly hazard the giving us provocation; when we may choose peace or war, as our interest, guided by justice, shall counsel.
>
> Why forego the advantages of so peculiar a situation? Why quit our own to stand upon foreign ground? Why, by interweaving our destiny with that of any part of Europe, entangle our peace and prosperity in the toils of European ambition, rivalship, interest, humour or caprice?[1]

Compare now the "other side" looking at the same problem, as French Minister Vergennes, before the American alliance is made, writes to the King of France on that crucial question of how to respond to the rebellion of England's colonies. Notice the much more direct and specific phrasing.

Vergennes begins from a fixed point:

> England is the natural enemy of France—and she is a rapacious, unjust and faithless enemy. The invariable object of her policy is the destruction of France, or at least her abasement, humiliation and ruin.

France therefore

> should seize every possible opportunity to enfeeble the might and power of England [and] it suffices to ascertain whether the present state of affairs and the actual situation of the Colonies are of a nature to conduce to this end: they are now in open war with their mother country;

---

[1]Washington's Farewell Address was originally printed in the *American Daily Advertiser*, September 17, 1796. Reprinted in Ruhl J. Bartlett, ed., *The Record of American Diplomacy* (New York: Alfred A. Knopf, 1948), pp. 86–88.

their aim is to free themselves from British dominion; they have solicited succor and assistance from us.

If France responded, certain advantages would accrue:

1. England's power will be diminished, and ours correspondingly increased.
2. Her commerce will suffer an irreparable loss while ours will flourish.
3. It is probable . . . that we shall be able to recover some of the possessions that the English have taken from us in America. . . .

Vergennes concluded with a summary:

Affairs in America present one with two hypotheses; the first: England will triumph over the Americans and they will submit; the second: Great Britain will be repulsed by them, and obliged to admit their independence. In either case, it is possible that England will decide to attack our colonies; in the former, to avenge herself for the aid which she will suspect we will have given her colonies (for she will take that view if she finds it exigent to do so, irrespective of our passivity); in the latter, to indemnify herself at our expense, or at the expense of Spain.

Because of these facts Vergennes felt that it was in France's interest "to assist the Colonies, and in case of need, to make common cause with them."[2]

For a second set of quotations we juxtapose President McKinley's war message of April 11, 1898, with British Prime Minister Balfour's December 29, 1903, analysis of whether or not Britain should aid Japan.

McKinley, calling upon Congress to declare war on Spain, first calls attention to the bitter war that has been going on in Cuba since the revolt against Spain. He then says that "The forcible intervention of the United States as a neutral to stop the war, according to the large dictates of humanity . . . is justifiable on rational grounds." Such action serves "the cause of humanity" and will "put an end to the barbarities, bloodshed, starvation, and horrible miseries. . . ." Then: "In the name of humanity, in the name of civilization, in behalf of endangered American interests which gave us the right and the duty to speak and to act, the war in Cuba must stop."[3] So Congress should declare war.

Notice that there is virtually no attempt to mention the tangible advantage to the United States of ousting Spain from Cuba and using it as an American base (which is what was actually done: Guantanamo). Notice the consistent use of moral propositions to clothe what is deemed practically necessary. Notice also the tendency to create categories of actions and responses— "in the cause of humanity"—rather than make a direct, interest-couched analysis.

Compare now from the same period the quite different tone of British Prime Minister Balfour's Cabinet Memorandum. True, Balfour is addressing the cabinet and McKinley is addressing Congress (and asking for war). Even allowing for that difference the whole style of analysis is in definite and obvious contrast. The question Balfour is discussing is whether Britain, an ally of Japan's, ought to intervene in a Russo-Japanese War, which soon breaks out. (Britain is *obligated* to intervene only if Russia is aided by an ally.)

1. Our moral obligations under the Anglo-Japanese Treaty do not exceed our legal obligations. The latter we are bound to fulfill at all cost, in the spirit as in the letter. Every demand

[2]Quoted from Samuel B. Griffith II, *In Defense of the Public Liberty* (Garden City, N.Y.: Doubleday, 1976), pp. 256–259.
[3]For whole text see *House Ex. Doc.* (3743), 55th Congress, 3rd Session, no. 1, pp. 750–760.

made on us beyond this should be considered solely in the light of British interests, present and future.

2. It is most dangerous to admit any other view. The Japanese would assuredly refuse to consider themselves bound to support us in any controversy which might arise in connection with the Indian frontier or Constantinople. If war with Russia suited them at such a moment, they will doubtless make it. If not, not. So it must be with us.

It has been suggested that if we take this view, and if, in consequence, Japan fights without an ally and is beaten, she will in revenge for our "abandonment" of her, throw in her lot with her former enemy and combine with Russia against us.

3. Such a course would be in the highest degree unreasonable. It is also, I venture to think, extremely improbable. Japan is divided from Russia by an antagonism of interests deep-rooted in the fundamental conditions of Far Eastern affairs. Her interests and ours, on the other hand, so far as can be foreseen, will continue to run on parallel lines. Harmony of interests, and that alone, gives stability to alliances: and so long as that harmony persists unchanged, an alliance once formed is not to be easily shattered by temporary misunderstandings, should such unhappily occur....[4]

There is more, but the contrast should be apparent.

We could multiply such comparisons almost indefinitely. But, in the interests of economy of space, let us end with President Jimmy Carter and Prussian Prince Otto von Bismarck, each quotation taken from their respective memoirs. It is a fair comparison, for each has written for history.

Carter says of his overall approach to policy problems:

I was familiar with the widely accepted arguments that we had to choose between idealism and realism, or between morality and the exertion of power; but I rejected those claims. To me, the demonstration of American idealism was a practical and realistic approach to foreign affairs, and moral principles were the best foundation for the exertion of American power and influence.... I was determined to combine support for our more authoritarian allies and friends with the effective promotion of human rights within their countries. By inducing them to change their repressive policies, we would be enhancing freedom and democracy, and helping to remove the reasons for revolutions that often erupt among those who suffer from persecution....

A human rights effort would also help strengthen our influence among some of the developing nations that were still in the process of forming their own governments and choosing their future friends and trading partners. And it was the right thing to do.[5]

Carter means *morally* right, of course.

Now compare the so-called "blood and iron" Bismarck who actually wants to restrain a potentially expansionist Austria to whom Germany is also allied, an alliance vital to German security.

I regarded it as no less enjoined upon us to cultivate neighbourly relations with Russia after, than before, our defensive alliance with Austria; for perfect security against the disruption of the chosen combination is not to be had by Germany, while it is possible for her to hold in check the anti-German fits and starts of Austro-Hungarian feeling so long as German policy maintains the bridge which leads to St. Petersburg [Russia's capital then], and allows no chasm to intervene between us and Russia which cannot be spanned. Given no such irreme-

---

[4]The whole memorandum is in Blanche E. C. Dugdale, *Arthur James Balfour* (New York: Putnam, 1937), pp. 284–285.

[5]Jimmy Carter, *Keeping Faith: Memoirs of a President* (New York: Bantam Books, 1982), p. 143.

diable breach Vienna will be able to bridle the forces hostile or alien to the German alliance. Suppose, however, that the breach with Russia is an accomplished fact, an irremediable estrangement. Austria would then certainly begin to enlarge her claims on the services of her German confederate. . . .

. . . The wants and plans of the inhabitants of the basin of the Danube naturally reach far beyond the present limits of the Austro-Hungarian monarchy. . . . It is, however, no part of the policy of the German Empire to lend her subjects, to expend her blood and treasure, for the purpose of realising [Austrian] designs. . . . In the interest of the European political equilibrium the maintenance of the Austro-Hungarian monarchy as a strong independent Great Power is for Germany an object for which she might in case of need stake her own peace with a good conscience. But Vienna should abstain from going outside this security, and deducing from the alliance claims which it was not concluded to support.[6]

And, a bit later:

We cannot abandon Austria, but neither can we lose sight of the possibility that the policy of Vienna may willy-nilly abandon us.[7]

Bismarck calmly recognizes his ally's feet of clay and stipulates that being allies does not automatically make all the interests of two states common. Bismarck does not apologize for that fact (which might make an American uncomfortable).

The comparison should be clear. American statements are consistently more general and, after Washington's time, wrapped in moral and abstract packaging. American statesmen preferred addressing a whole class of problems at a time, whether aggression, communism, human rights, or anything else, and doing so to the accompaniment of moral justifications. The habit of doing so is unusual, it tends to unfocus the issue and encourage debates peripheral to the real question, and it leads easily to trying to do too much or to policies peripheral to the precise issue at stake. Keep this point in mind as we approach the problems and issues facing the United States.

3.

Looking Ahead at Part Four

Part Four looks at the problems, issues, and choices confronting the United States in the major geographical areas of the world.

The most formidable problem is discussed first: the Soviet Union. The United States is not accustomed to a prolonged, peacetime antagonism, such as typifies its relationship to the Soviets. We have already seen in Part Three how troublesome an issue this was immediately after World War II, how the "explanation" that Russia's conduct could be understood in terms of aggressive communism was embraced and gradually extended to the entire Communist bloc until the Sino-Soviet split made a simple bloc view no longer tenable. In the aftermath, once the long consensus broke down, American opinion has stood divided between the two alternative explanations of Soviet behavior—one "offensive," the other "defensive"—to which we turn in Chapter 16. We examine there the implications of these alternative understandings of Soviet behavior as they have an impact on U.S. policy.

[6]Otto, Prince von Bismarck, *Bismarck, the Man and the Statesman: Reflections and Reminiscences* (New York: Harper, 1899), vol. 2, pp. 276–277.
[7]Ibid., p. 282.

Chapter 17 focuses on the security balance in Europe, considering three interlinked problems: (1) the arbitrary and unnatural division of Europe, (2) the implications of the now long-continued deployment of Soviet troops in Central Europe, and (3) the implications of the fact that European and American interests do not automatically align.

Chapter 18 turns to Asia, viewing it in the perspective of post-Vietnam War developments. The discussion centers on the lessened American direct military role and the interlinked relations between China, Japan, and India and Pakistan, as they impinge upon the prospects for a stable Asia in the post–Sino-Soviet split era.

Chapter 19 examines the Middle East, arguing that the thread of U.S. policy has been consistent in this area. Five interlinked problems confront the United States there, and the American concern has been and continues to be (1) resolving the Arab-Israeli conflict, (2) preventing control by a hostile power, (3) preventing regional disputes from leading to a superpower nuclear confrontation, (4) ensuring access to oil for U.S. allies, and (5) minimizing area instability.

Chapter 20, which deals with the developing nations, pairs Africa and Latin America, areas where U.S. security interests have not resulted in any substantial military commitments. We examine these areas in terms of three problems: (1) the widespread instability that exists and the opportunities it provides for foreign exploitation, (2) the growing U.S. deficiency in strategic materials and the importance of the developing nations as sources, and (3) the need to ensure the security of the vital sea lines of communication. All of this is done within the context of an examination of the general conditions and aspirations of the LDCs, in light of their particular histories and circumstances.

Part Four ends with Chapter 21, in which we examine four overarching problems that the United States faces, along with every other nation in the world, for these four problems have universal effects. We look at mushrooming technology and the changing global environment, beginning with the technological revolution itself, and then consider (1) quality-of-life issues such as pollution, food supplies, and raw material scarcities as these interact with one another and put pressures on living standards; (2) the development and effects of terrorism; (3) the hotly debated changing regime for the high seas; and (4) the exploration and uses of space and its relationship to weapons developments.

Part Five then, in Chapter 22, sums up the major policy conclusions reached in this book.

As we survey the geographical areas we shall see a very great range in U.S. military commitments that is only partially reflective of U.S. interests in each area. The point is that, in areas of great interest to the United States, in some cases other nations which could do more have chosen not to do so, with the United States then filling the gap. Although it is clearly an over-riding and strategic objective of the United States—one not shaken by the dissolution of the containment consensus—to prevent Soviet or third-party hegemony in any major geographical area of the earth, this objective need not be (and often should not be) oversimplified to mean direct U.S. military involvement everywhere. It was that tendency more than anything else which destroyed the post–World War II consensus.

We turn now to Soviet-American relations.

PART FOUR

Problems and Issues Facing the United States

16

United States–Soviet Relations

The Russians are not to be persuaded by eloquence or convinced by reasoned arguments. They rely on what Stalin used to call the proper basis of international policy, the calculation of forces . . . ; the only way of changing their purpose is to demonstrate that they have no advantageous alternative. . . .

Sir William Hayter[1]

The Soviet people and the Americans . . . have a common enemy, the threat of war. . . . It would seem that awareness of this common threat should become the common denominator inducing statesmen in the USSR and in the United States to display reciprocal restraint.

Unfortunately, we do not see the present American administration displaying such a responsible approach.

Yuri V. Andropov,
June 2, 1983[2]

In Part Four we come to the problems, issues, and choices concerning which way the United States should go in attempting to find solutions to problems whose lack of solution is dangerous to American security. (In Part Four, as earlier, we use "problems" to refer to situations confronting the United States, "issues" to mean what must be decided, and "alternatives" to describe the available choices. Problems are faced; issues are decided; alternatives frame the choices.)

The very way we have stated the focus of Part Four is a warning that not every problem needs to be solved, not every issue resolved. In one sense, because the United States is a global power with a wide range of interests, it is to some degree concerned with almost everything that happens. In this sense, whatever is a problem anywhere is a problem for the United States. But no state has unlimited power, and, as our earlier analysis of the Vietnam War showed, the effort of the United States was completely disproportionate to the results; for whatever reason might be given, it certainly was not a cost-effective approach. The critical lesson of Vietnam is that, although the United States may be interested in what happens everywhere, it does not auto-

---

[1]*London Observer,* October 2, 1960, as cited by Dean Acheson, *Present at the Creation* (New York: Norton, 1969), p. 275.
[2]*New York Times,* June 3, 1983.

matically follow that whatever happens is important or that an active involvement orientation is required.

For a cost-effective policy to be workable, priorities must be established, costs considered, and the principles developed in Chapters 4 and 5 systematically applied. Approaching serious problems and issues in these ways necessitates considering very early what other states may do, given U.S. action or inaction, and considering therefore how the whole episode is likely to end.

So, on the one hand a problem has to be graded for its importance; on the other hand, the utility or requirement for specific U.S. action has to be established. The latter requires visualizing interactions in the system, as the states affected weigh their counterbalancing national interests in the light of *their* priorities and design their policies. Then, in the implementation phase, the United States must decide concretely who is involved, to what degree, and with what effect. The whole policy process is complex, requiring both an accurate *perception* of the intrinsic importance of the problem in the design phase and an accurate *appraisal* of the likely policy choices of all the principal actors once they face the issues with which they are involved.

For these reasons, in each of the chapters of Part Four, we proceed with the analysis in four basic steps. First, we state the nature of the problem or problems that exist (and the issues these create) in the post-Vietnam period (i.e., after 1968), with special attention to those requiring some degree of American response. Second, we fill in the factual background, if not already covered earlier, so that the post-1968 form of the problem becomes clear.[3] Third, we analyze the main lines of the U.S. reaction to these problems since Vietnam. And fourth, we analyze the issues, using the four cardinal principles of phase 1 and the four-step operational sequence of phase 2 as guides to arrive at a preferred U.S. policy reaction (or, failing any clear choice, a weighing of the alternatives). We begin in this chapter with U.S.–Soviet relations.

1.

The Problem of U.S.–Soviet Relations

The relations of the superpowers with each other are matters of direct and obvious concern to each, since they represent reciprocally the gravest kind of potential military threat. Each superpower has targeted on the other quantities of nuclear warheads sufficient, according to most estimates, to devastate the other country.[4] Just this aspect of their relations alone would justify detailed and early treatment in these chapters on problems, issues, and alternatives.

But it is also true that there is hardly any other major problem confronting the United States on which the Soviet shadow does not somehow fall—and vice versa. The Soviets are a seen and unseen participant when the United States is addressing such diverse problems as relations with China, developments in Western or Eastern Europe, the Middle East, the less-developed countries, or even many aspects of the impact of technology in a changing world. (A glance at the contents pages of this book will show that that list is substantially a list of the problems to be examined in the rest of Part Four.)

So U.S.–Soviet relations are important to each superpower from a bilateral point of view. Each is especially concerned with their fundamentally and mutually threatening relationship. And the superpowers are also important third-party influences in many other relationships. Naturally, too, this process also works in reverse as superpower relations are themselves affected by third parties. Third parties both play a major role in contouring the "bilateral" relationship between Washington and Moscow, and are affected by it.

---

[3]The year 1968 was chosen as the dividing point because of its critical importance—immediately, in terms of a climax in the Vietnam War; ultimately, as marking the collapse of the post–World War II conceptual consensus.

[4]Chapter 17 will consider the military balance in some detail.

In stating the obvious military threat concern of each superpower over the other's capability to wreak destruction, we have attempted initially to avoid implying judgments about who, if anyone, is at "fault" for this circumstance. In an obvious sense, looking at the mere systems effect of the existence of two superpowers, each armed to the teeth, no one really has to do anything in particular or stand for anything threatening in order to create mutual fear and tension. The United States and the Soviet Union *are* each other's power problem by their very positioning and weight in the scales of the system. They alone can mutually bring any war home to the other on a vast, destructive scale.

So long as they are mutually so positioned and "weighted," the United States and the Soviet Union continue to represent major, mutual threats. *But the sense of immediacy or inevitability in that threat can vary (and has varied) considerably.* The tension level between them has not remained constant. That tension level is, in turn, substantially influenced by the impression prevailing in each at any one time as to the other's *intentions* or *motives*.

In considering American-Soviet relations, because an element of anxiety is present, objectivity is particularly difficult to achieve. As Einstein once said about scientific problems generally, the data do not arrange themselves before our eyes, independently of our input. So whatever the *real* Soviet-American relationship may be, it will almost certainly seem something different from that reality to Americans anxious about possible Soviet moves, or to Soviets anxious about possible American moves.

This observation has not only intellectual applicability (how difficult it is to arrive at the truth) but has policy implications as well. If the United States or the Soviet Union perceives itself actively threatened, behind in the arms race, or at a disadvantage in some other respect, no amount of objective citation of the "facts" will have any substantial influence on its attitude. That does not mean that facts or imbalances in weapons have no ultimate effects, especially if objective truth is put to the test in armed conflict. What we mean is that "facts" initially will weigh what decision makers think they weigh when it comes to adding those facts into an analysis. Facts have no automatic or intrinsic weight in any decision making balance sheet. Because this is so, we begin our analysis, not with any attempt at the objective truth about Soviet-American relations, but with their perceptions of each other. We examine American views first.

2.

Alternative American Strategic Concepts of Soviet Behavior

For much of the time since World War II, two views of Soviet behavior have competed for acceptance in the United States. Both views have much common ground, especially in recognizing the enormous and continuing Soviet arms build-up. But the views differ, especially on the causes and implications of that build-up. We call these two American views the "hard-line" or "offensive" view and the "soft-line" or "defensive" view of Soviet behavior—meaning that Soviet behavior is alternatively seen as *motivated* by aggressive or expansive ambitions or by anxiety and concern over vulnerability.

The hard-line or offensive view of Soviet behavior asserts that the Soviet Union from its beginnings has had the goal of communizing the world by guile or by force. In this view, Soviet tactics of "ebb and flow" call for advances against weakness and temporary retreat in the face of firmness. As Secretary of State Dean Acheson expressed it, the United States, dealing with the Soviet Union, had to do so from "a position of strength." Otherwise the Soviets would not be willing to negotiate and would press forward against weakness. George Kennan, the "father" of the containment concept, wrote in his famous article by "X" in *Foreign Affairs* that the Soviets assumed an "innate antagonism between capitalism and socialism." Any move apparently to the contrary must be seen "as a tactical maneuver permissible in dealing with the enemy (who is without honor) and should be taken in the spirit of *caveat emptor*."[5] Kennan said bluntly that the United States

> must continue to expect that Soviet policies will reflect no abstract love of peace and stability, no real faith in the possibility of a permanent happy coexistence of the socialist and capitalist worlds, but rather a cautious, persistent pressure toward the disruption and weakening of all rival influence and rival power.

Therefore, said Kennan, the United States must pursue "a policy of firm containment, designed to confront the Russians with unalterable counterforce at every point where they show signs of encroaching upon the interests of a peaceful and stable world." Such a policy would "promote tendencies which must eventually find their outlet in either the break-up or the gradual mellowing of Soviet power."

In this hard-line or offensive view of Soviet behavior, the internal dynamics of communism provide both the incentive for the Soviet masses to forego improved living standards in favor of weapons and the incentive to communize the world. In this view, the United States is dealing with zealots, with a group of fanatics set on an undeviating course. They can be stopped in their expansion, but they will never cease trying to expand. The Soviet leaders are seen as true to a Communist religion, serving it with all the fervor of fanatics. (A minority variant of this view of Soviet behavior holds that the Soviet leaders are merely cynical and power hungry. It makes little difference in explaining their behavior.)

Those who believe in the accuracy of this view of Soviet behavior accept as highly natural the Soviet arms build-up, and think of détente as the Soviet tactic to lull the United States while the Soviets gain the lead. The hard-line or offensive view, then, emphasizes Soviet *unrestrained ambition*.

The soft-line or defensive view of Soviet behavior, by contrast, sees the Soviets as reacting to what in Chapter 14 was referred to as the deterioration of the Soviet geopolitical position. As problems increase around the periphery of the Soviet Union, this view asserts, the Soviets have become increasingly concerned and alarmed. Confronted with a Communist China in *de facto* partnership with the United States, the Soviet Union has drawn closer to India and Vietnam as regional counterweights. Facing a losing situation in Afghanistan, the Soviets, afraid of a "domino effect," have moved troops into a highly unsatisfactory punitive expedition that has no easy ending. Nations astride the main corridor of Western invasion, Czechoslovakia in 1968, or Poland in 1981, have each shown active signs of the same restiveness that caused the Hungarian revolt of 1956 and the East German uprising of 1953. Such restiveness undermines the security of the Soviet Union in a most direct sense. How are the Soviets to cure this unrest without sacrificing the socialist facade they have fastened on these countries? The soft-line or defensive view, then, emphasizes Soviet *dilemmas*.

Looking at Soviet adventures or activities further afield, the offensive view asserts that the Soviets have been concentrating their subversive efforts in areas that would effectively "turn NATO's flank," as in the Caribbean basin or in Africa. The Russians have concentrated their effort in particular on gaining influence or control over maritime "choke points" such as Yemen or Aden (or Egypt and Indonesia, some years ago). The defensive view responds by admitting that the Soviets are stirring up trouble wherever they can but sees these tactics as a basic reflec-

---

[5]This and following quotations are from "X," "The Sources of Soviet Conduct," *Foreign Affairs*, vol. 25, no. 4 (July 1947), 571–582. Kennan was later to regret his use of the term "counterforce," especially the militarization of the U. S. approach he here encouraged. Kennan's later positions became much more "dovish."

tion of weakness. The Soviets are seen as simply opportunistic regardless of the real value of the target nations. Advocates of this view also tend to dismiss the success of these efforts, pointing out how the Soviets since World War II have made major efforts in Indonesia, Somalia, and Egypt (each accompanied by massive arms sales), only to be expelled unceremoniously in each case.

To those who believe in the defensive view, the increasing piles of Soviet weapons of every description are the recourse of despair. Given the lack of assured (and convinced) Soviet friends and allies, they point out, the Soviets are increasingly vulnerable and fearful. What else are they to do, confronted by an implacably hostile capitalist world, but to arm to the teeth? But to those who take the offensive view, the piles of weapons speak for themselves, their aggressive purpose being only too obvious.

From a historical perspective, the ongoing debate between these two points of view goes back after World War II to 1946–1947. The argument between Truman and Wallace was its first postwar focus. It pitted Truman's hard-line containment doctrine against Henry Wallace's Progressive party's plea for more concessions by the United States to overcome Soviet "suspicions." The offensive view won, reflected in Truman's reelection in 1948, and a containment policy was implemented. Eisenhower and Dulles were even more hard-line, Dulles calling for "liberation" rather than just containment until the Hungarian uprising of 1956 showed clearly the costs for the United States implied in any such action. Kennedy was too busy reacting to Soviet-induced crises to intellectualize much about policy. But in Nixon's time, an interesting initiative was taken in the launching of "détente."

The new approach fanned the flames of controversy once again, producing the dichotomy of views just surveyed. To those of the "offensive" persuasion, Henry Kissinger was a pessimist seeking to hold off the rising tide of communism by making temporary deals. As mentioned before, Admiral Elmo Zumwalt, then Chief of Naval Operations, is not untypical of this view. In his memoirs Zumwalt describes one session at the Pentagon (apparently in March 1974) at which Kissinger gave a briefing to Secretary of Defense James Schlesinger and the Joint Chiefs. He says that "Henry was at his most brilliant at that meeting. Chameleon that he is, he turned red, white, and blue for the occasion, arguing eloquently and at length that détente had increased the Defense budget, saved NATO, stabilized the Middle East and forced the USSR into a series of damaging concessions—all of which I couldn't have disagreed with more, of course."[6] Zumwalt then gives generous abstracts from his notes of what Kissinger said and the discussion which apparently followed after Kissinger left: "When it was all over, the Chiefs all felt that he had three times committed himself for full consultation now [about arms talks]. I said I felt much better. Admiral Moorer (Chairman, JCS) said, 'don't turn your back, Bud.'" Zumwalt apparently replied, "I think that is about right. But at least there were a lot of people in the room that heard him say it. It is going to be harder for him to go to Moscow and sell out again. . . ."[7]

By contrast, to those of the "defensive" persuasion, Kissinger was trying to lower dangerously high tensions and build mutual Soviet-American confidence. Those of the "offensive" persuasion thought Kissinger dangerous since he was supposed to be implicitly encouraging a lessened American arms defense alertness. Those of the "defensive" persuasion hailed the progress finally made on arms control as the first fruits of détente and thought that a reassured and relaxed Soviet Union might relax into increasingly more normal behavior as time went by.

Notice again that the primary facts—especially those relating to the Soviet build-up—are not really seriously in dispute in these two interpretations of Soviet motivation and intentions. Yet the choice of how to deal with the Soviet build-up, of what kind of U.S. policy to design toward the Soviet Union, could not be made effectively without some decision as to which view

[6]Elmo R. Zumwalt, Jr., *On Watch: A Memoir* (New York: Quadrangle, 1976), p. 482.
[7]Ibid., p. 485.

was the correct one. If the Soviet build-up reflected primarily Soviet fears, paralleling their build-up might make the Soviet leaders truly paranoic. Yet if the Soviets were moving toward a planned expansion, lagging behind them would give them a most dangerous temptation to proceed, once they had an assured advantage. This is why the focus of the debate in the United States came to turn so heavily on arms issues. This debate was in this sense a revival of the older debate of the 1920s and 1930s over whether arms races produced insecurity or were instead the inevitable reflection of insecurity. Which was cause and which was effect?

Before considering how correctly each of these two views may have encapsulated the truth, let us shift to a Soviet perspective.

3.

A Soviet Perspective

Two opposite errors are possible in sketching a Soviet perspective. The first mistake would be to attach more than a cautious confidence to specific portions of the appraisal, since so much about Soviet policymaking remains secret. The second mistake would be to believe that Soviet behavior is far too secret and mysterious to yield real clues.

Soviet publications abound with commentaries and explanations of Soviet views. Interviews are given by Soviet leaders on special occasions. Public posture statements are delivered to the Supreme Soviet. Radio commentaries fill the airwaves in many languages. So there is much material, some of it, particularly at first glance, contradictory. (For example, the radio transcripts tend toward harsher and simple judgments and may depart even obviously from the truth to make propaganda points—something the written material is more cautious about.) There is more than enough material to judge overall Soviet perspectives.

To begin with, communism, an ideological system that provides a framework for, purportedly, explaining all international activity, is very self-consciously removed from sentimentality. Communism's view is fixed on what Communists consider to be "objective" forces that in turn arise out of material conditions, and which can be "scientifically" analyzed. The ownership of the means of production in any state is considered the key clue to the politics that that state will attempt to follow. Even if, on a personal basis, capitalists show themselves to be "friendly," it means nothing serious, since policy is not personal and cannot in the end change "objective" conditions. Smiling Jimmy Carter or frowning Richard Nixon are all the same so far as fundamentals go. So the most the Soviets hope for in relations with the United States is to avert war until the tide of history "inevitably" turns in their favor.

The Soviet conviction that communism is "scientific" and permits accurate perception both of capitalism's innate hostility and the world's future is very deep-rooted. It traces back to the original formulations by Marx and Engels in the nineteenth century, as they analyzed capitalism within the perspective of world history as they understood it.

As seen through Communist eyes, the "class struggle" between the propertied class and the dispossessed began as soon as men settled on the land. That struggle initially focused on landowner versus serf or peasant. In early modern times feudal barons contested with kings over their respective rights of exploitation (King John was forced to grant the Magna Charta to his barons), but the exploited gained nothing. As industrialization commenced and farm laborers drifted to the cities, a new form of exploitation of labor began, as entrepreneurs gained their profits through suppressed wages, meanwhile contending with the landed aristocracy to control the state apparatus. The bourgeoisie won out (i.e., the rise of the middle class) but the plight of the worker (proletariat) got worse. But beginning with the risings of 1848 in Europe, when the Communist Manifesto first provided a rallying cry for the masses, workers began to resort to armed violence, even though they were as yet too weak to seize control of the state apparatus.

Capitalists, confronted by the inability of their own workers to buy enough of what they themselves had made (since their wages were too low), sought new markets and cheap raw materials abroad, thus exporting their domestic exploitation to foreigners, taking colonies. As this competition of monopoly capitalism intensified in the opening years of the twentieth century (as witness the Fashoda incident between Britain and France and the two Moroccan crises between Germany and France), the capitalists prepared to fight over the division of the spoils. Thus World War I came about.[8]

But that very war, by intensifying the class struggle and exposing the shallow roots of the autocratic rulers, caused the collapse of the czarist regime in Russia and began the era of communism, with the leadership of the movement now in the hands of the mature cadre of leaders of the working class, the "vanguard of the revolution," the elite Communist party.[9]

This process, successful first in Russia, would "inevitably" spread around the world everywhere that industrialization had occurred and brought the class struggle to its climax. Just as inevitably, its spread or even existence would be fiercely and forcibly opposed by capitalists whose property and even lives were ultimately at stake. This is why Lenin made the famous statement:

> We are living not merely in a State, but in a system of States, and the existence of the Soviet Republic side by side with imperialistic States for a long time is unthinkable. One or the other must triumph in the end. And before that end supervenes, a series of frightful collisions between the Soviet Republic and the bourgeois States will be inevitable.[10]

The Soviet view of the causes of international war was thus closely linked from the outset with its own historical experience, for in fact White Russian counterrevolutionary armies were supported on Soviet soil by the French and British at the end of World War I, while Japanese and American troops landed at Vladivostok. "Capitalist encirclement" and hostility seemed very real indeed. In the 1920s and 1930s the principal task of the Soviet Union was seen as avoiding major war and surviving until world conditions favored the expansion of the Soviet system and Soviet influence. This opportunity came about with the defeat of Hitler and the end of World War II.

That new opportunity, once Germany and Japan were powerless, also contained certain dilemmas and problems. There was first the United States with its nuclear monopoly and the future implications for communism if war (and in all probability, nuclear war) was inevitable. Communism might triumph for the few still left alive but the inevitability of history was now more threat than promise. Second, there was the problem of "rice communism" in China, as Stalin put it. Mao Zedong, an avowed Communist in a virtually unindustrialized land, had ousted Nationalist leader Chiang Kai-shek by 1949, leading peasants to victory. How was this strange twist of events to be explained within the confines of traditional Communist beliefs? And would Sino-Soviet relations prove (as theory insisted) harmonious? Third, there was the problem of the former colonial world, where much anti-Western feeling could be exploited but where there was no working class to do it with and where cooperation, if undertaken, would have to be with rulers such as Nasser in Egypt (who actually put his few Communists in jail).

Even this short list of problems sheds light on why the Soviet perspective had to be altered in certain respects after World War II, particularly as experience with the results of certain experiments began to accumulate.

[8]See Lenin, *Imperialism, the Highest Stage of Capitalism* (New York: International Publishers, 1939). The book was written in 1916.

[9]See Lenin, *What Is to Be Done?* (New York: International Publishers, 1929). The book was written in 1902.

[10]V. I. Lenin, "Report of Central Committee at Eighth Party Congress" of March 18, 1919, *Selected Works* (New York: International Publishers, 1943), vol. 8, p. 33.

Experience showed, for example, that the installation of Communist regimes in states did not necessarily or noticeably produce the changes in national attitudes that are supposed to follow such installation. China is the leading case, if not Yugoslavia, with Hungary and Poland not far behind. From a Soviet security point of view, the only assured and proven formula for safety in relation to such other states is a Communist regime plus a Russian army of occupation.

Despite such problems, Soviet subversive assistance to many foreign groups seeking power in their own states continued to have obvious utility. In the first place, such subversion could weaken the United States or NATO or the capitalist bloc in terms of security or logistics. In the second place, such action could then remove such areas from becoming breeding places for additional hostility to the Soviet Union.

Starting in 1955, we can see from the record that Soviet power obviously expanded from an initially conservative role of aiding only Communists to assistance to nations or rulers capable of and willing to take anti-American points of view, even if they themselves opposed communism. Nasser is an obvious example. Cuba has been an especially useful and durable ally in such ventures. At no time have the Soviets been willing to renounce such aid to "national liberation movements," as they call the type of development that Castro symbolized. "Peaceful coexistence" with the United States did not in their view rule out Soviet aid to such movements. As Leonid I. Brezhnev said, at the Twenty-fifth Congress in February 1976, "We make no secret of the fact that we see détente as the way to create more favorable conditions for peaceful socialist and Communist construction."[11]

What has given the Soviets the most to think about has been the events in nations around their own periphery where "Communist construction" had already taken place, such as Hungary and China. At the same Twenty-fifth Congress, Brezhnev also spoke to this point, saying, "Peking's frantic attempts to torpedo détente, to obstruct disarmament, to breed suspicion and hostility between states, its efforts to provoke a world war and reap whatever advantages may accrue, present a great danger for all peaceloving peoples."[12]

As we have seen, the extension of socialism (communism) to other lands is supposed in theory to have two effects. First, it changes forever the material basis of society. Once the ownership of the means of production has been placed in the hands of "the vanguard of the proletariat" (the Communist party), a nonreversible process is supposedly occurring. It comes as a great shock then when Hungarian workers, supported by elements of the Hungarian Red Army, combat Soviet Red Army troops, as in 1956. Somehow the vaccination did not work. Somehow, counterrevolutionary tendencies have not been successfully eliminated. If that can happen in Nation X after Y years of communism, when can the Soviets be confident that it is outside the realm of possibility in Nations A, B, C, and D, after G, H, or I years of Communist rule? Second, the coming of communism is supposed to entail the end of nationalism, at least in all but its folk festival connotations. A common affiliation with communism is supposed to eliminate "bourgeois" fixations on "meaningless" national frontiers. But China is not prepared to accept this proposition and continues to dispute the frontier with Russia.

As noted in Chapter 14, the Soviets, looking out at their periphery, cannot help but see a strategic position that has deteriorated in an objective sense from what it was when the Cold War began in the 1940s. Germany and Japan have regained their power, China has become a threat, unrest prevails in Eastern Europe, and militant Islam agitates to the south. Garrisons are still maintained in forward positions in Europe that, although a plus for the Soviets in one sense, also encourages close U.S.–European NATO relations. Although the Soviets may take comfort from some gains farther afield, such gains do not relieve the sense of discomfort around their immediate periphery.

[11] *New York Times*, February 25, 1976.
[12] Ibid.

Many of communism's most optimistic hopes about the outer world have failed too obviously to be ignored. Agricultural problems plague the Soviets and economic problems are increasing as productivity gains lag and the surplus is skimmed off into war material.[13]

4.
A Corrected View of Soviet Behavior

If these observations about Soviet perspectives are accepted as reasonably accurate, the debate in the United States between the "offensive" view and the "defensive" view can be seen from a different perspective. The United States is neither dealing with an anxious Soviet Union that will be reassured by tangible gestures of friendship (such as concessions on arms ratios in favor of the Soviet Union), nor with a Soviet Union looking forward to waging war against the United States once "the window of vulnerability" is opened wide enough. The Soviet Union will neither respond to smiles nor threats in the way many Americans assume they will. Smiles will be discounted and threats (direct, or implied by an arms race) will be countered by continuing arms expenditures.

What détente really meant to the Soviets, in the context in which it occurred during the Nixon administration, was that the Soviets were convinced that two simultaneous actions were required in the wake of the change in objective conditions produced by the "playing of the China card." First, Russia would have to take fewer risks, since the United States was no longer tied down in Southeast Asia, with its gratuitous and simultaneous deflection of Chinese attention away from Russia. Second, in view of the limited political options available to the Soviet Union to redress the adverse shift in the balance of power that accompanied the "China card," even more reliance would have to be placed on a continued Soviet arms build-up to deter capitalist attempts to exploit their newly favorable position.

The first Soviet conviction led to a much lower profile and far less troublemaking Soviet policy in the Middle East in the years after the "fourth round" of the Arab-Israeli Wars. The second Soviet conviction led them to actions that created a sense of alarm in the United States by the end of the decade of the 1970s, as Americans asked themselves what the purpose of the endless build-up could possibly be since it had already surpassed the limits of "legitimate" defensive requirements. So the playing of the "China card" in one sense led to the demise of SALT II (which ultimately foundered on a resurgence of mutual distrust fueled by Soviet armaments).

All of this adds up to a much more complicated analysis than either the offensive view or the defensive view in pure form suggests. Communism, as our analysis shows, *is* aggressive in the sense of assuming that the status quo can and should change in its favor. But communism, contrary to many assertions, has never contained a concept of aggressive war waged by the Soviet Union. The emphasis in Communist theory has always been on the danger of war waged *against* the Soviet Union. To note this fact is in no way to give assurances that the Soviet Union can necessarily be trusted not to initiate a conflict, even a nuclear conflict. But it does clear the decks of certain debris if we recognize that the major Communist theory on war, dating as we saw from Lenin, reaffirmed by Stalin, but set aside by Khrushchev in 1956, focused on whether capitalist aggressive behavior would or would not "inevitably" cause wars. Lenin and Stalin said war was inevitable; Khrushchev, contemplating the practical implications of this pessimistic theoretical conclusion, revised the theory (thereby substantially strengthening its political appeal).

---

[13]Moscow's 1982 wheat production *goal* was 237 million metric tons. Its best recent harvest was 237.4 million tons in 1978. In 1979 output was 179.2 million tons and the 1980 crop was a near-disaster. See *New York Times,* May 11, 1982. The 1983 crop was estimated by the Soviets at between 195.7 and 223.8 million metric tons. See *New York Times,* November 17, 1983.

At the Twentieth Congress of the Soviet Communist party in February 1956, Khrushchev proclaimed that world war was no longer inevitable, because "the Socialist [Communist] camp is invincible." Capitalists, observing Russia's "invincibility" as its arms build-up continued, might now sensibly decide against fighting.

The impetus for the revision of the theory is perfectly clear from the comment in *Kommunist* (September 1960), that

> the working class cannot conceive of the creation of a Communist civilization on the ruins of world centers of culture, on desolated land contaminated with thermonuclear fallout, which would be an inevitable consequence of such a war. . . . It is thus clear that a *present-day nuclear war in itself can in no way be a factor that would accelerate revolution and bring the victory of socialism closer.*[14]

Add the Soviet conviction that a war between the superpowers would tend to be nuclear, and the strands of thought and policy come even closer together. The Soviets are going to persist in policies that can provide them arms in sufficient quantity and quality as to leave no doubt in any potential enemy's mind that there is no rational advantage in attacking the Soviet Union. The policy question here for the United States is whether arms agreements reassuring each side on this point can be achieved. (We examine this issue in some detail in Section 6.)

One hopeful and optimistic note can be added. Khrushchev's doctrinal revisionism, never repudiated after his fall from power, has a significant influence today on how the Soviets view their American antagonist. Khrushchev made the revision because he otherwise was arguing that war was inevitable, that nuclear weapons in such a superpower war would inevitably be used, that such nuclear war would destroy civilization, and that the remnants would "enjoy" communism. But when Khrushchev made this revision he began an intellectual process affecting the Soviet perspective much more deeply and significantly than he had in mind. The reason Lenin insisted that war was inevitable was because he saw capitalists as doomed by "objective forces" to behave in certain patterns, always focused on the search for maximum profits. The very "inevitability" of the presumed final victory of socialism *derived* from this rigid anticipated capitalist behavior. But once it is assumed that capitalists have the wit to observe that the Soviets have become invincible, and as a result alter behavior and not attack, the door swings open wide to the notion that capitalists are rational beings *able to alter their behavior to cope with problems.* The traditional Communist view of capitalists rigidly marching to their own destruction is "inevitably" undermined. It means, at least in theory, that the Soviets become less rigid in their assumptions about capitalist behavior.

5.

Carter and Reagan Deal with the Soviets

If the foregoing analysis has merit, we can see that the post-Vietnam American administrations have overstated (Carter) and understated (Reagan) the possibilities for improved U.S.–Soviet relations.

President Carter came to power after the bloom was already off détente. Indeed, in the Ford administration, as the argument over Angola intensified, Secretary of State Kissinger began to charge that the Soviets had violated the understanding basic to détente by fostering armed changes in the status quo in the Third World. The Soviets immediately replied that their

[14]As cited in Zbigniew Brzezinski, "A Book the Russians Would Like to Forget," *The Reporter,* December 22, 1960. Italics in work cited.

agreement to cooperate toward "peaceful coexistence," as registered in the Nixon-Brezhnev summit meetings, did not extend to "national liberation movements" in the Third World. (Factually, the Soviet assertion was correct.) President Ford, fighting for reelection, actually banned the term détente from official descriptions of U.S. policy objectives, since the term had become a political albatross around the neck of the Republicans.

Carter, riding into power on a wave of popular indignation against Ford's pardon of Nixon, and a popular wish to "clean house" after Watergate, began his administration with a declaration that the U.S. policy emphasis on the Communists had been substantially overdone, and with it the associated view that the Soviets only understood power. He relegated defense to the lower half of his list of policy priorities and set out to emphasize "human rights." Seeking to broaden the arms-control understanding reached between Ford and Brezhnev at Vladivostok in 1974, Carter encountered a highly suspicious Soviet reaction, and arms-control negotiations received a severe setback. Now the human rights emphasis also began to plague U.S.–Soviet relations, as the United States began to pressure the Soviets to permit more freedoms for Soviet dissidents in Russia. Relations deteriorated further—and spectacularly—when Soviet troops invaded Afghanistan in December 1979. SALT II, negotiated with so much difficulty, was withdrawn from the Senate ratification process.

President Reagan made no secret of his views about the Soviets. In February 1981, for example, Reagan said that the Soviet leaders do not "believe in a god or a religion, and the only morality they recognize, therefore, is what will advance the world of socialism." *Pravda* responded in acid tones: "In contrast to the leaders of the United States, we do not pray to weaponry as though it were a holy icon and we reject the policy of force because we believe in the values, the creative potential and the justice of socialism.[15]

In both 1982 and 1983 the Reagan emphasis in policy was weapon-oriented. An enormous rearmament program was pushed, presumably as a prelude to serious arms-control negotiations—which were minimal until the United States felt securely buttressed by an ongoing MX weapon procurement program and a Pershing II-cruise missile deployment in NATO Europe. Reagan also tried hard (and unsuccessfully) to discourage Europe from dealing with the Soviets in building a natural gas pipeline to Western Europe—of which more later. Intermittently, too, Reagan reverted to his conviction that Soviet-inspired subversion was at the root of the unrest in Central America.

6.

Key Issues in U.S.–Soviet Relations

If we were to isolate major factors in these developments as they affected the perception of the overall problem of Soviet-American relations and therefore the definition of the issues that sum up the contemporary parts of that problem, we would have to underline (1) the Soviet invasion of Afghanistan, (2) the shelving of SALT II, unratified, and (3) the intensification of the U.S. effort to eliminate Central American insurgencies. Each of these three major developments posed a policy issue. (Each of these three issues is also addressed elsewhere since the significance of all three extends beyond their influence on Soviet-American relations.)

As we saw in Chapter 14, what disturbed Washington so much about the Afghanistan operation was that it seemed to represent a deliberate and overt extension of Soviet power by force of arms across existing lines of influence. If left unchallenged, it might lead to more such moves. In the Reagan administration the point was well expressed by Secretary of State Haig: "Soviet diplomacy is based on tests of will. Since Vietnam, the United States had largely failed

---

[15]*New York Times,* February 5, 1981.

these tests. . . . [T]he Russians would send out a probe. . . to test the strength of Western determination. Finding the line unmanned, or only thinly held, they would exploit the gap."[16]

Afghanistan itself was not seen as of overriding importance; its importance lay in its "signaling" of intent, resolve, and so on. Here, again, we see the U.S. tendency, brought out in Chapter 15, to approach an issue as representative of a category rather than on its own strategic or geopolitical merits or implications. The question put was: Did the Afghanistan operation represent Soviet expansionist, offensive intent (a first domino), or was it a "defensive" move undertaken to offset disturbing developments around the Soviet perimeter? In either case, it represented a change in the status quo and altered the existing distribution of power in the system, but the motivation behind the move was considered of even greater importance.

Historically, only a strong British presence in India (before its present subdivision into India, Pakistan, and Bangladesh) had prevented Russian hegemony in Afghanistan. The situation in Afghanistan was, for example, an important part of the negotiations leading to the momentous 1907 Anglo-Russian entente. Once the British withdrew from the Indian subcontinent after World War II, Pakistan broke off its link to India, and India moved closer to the Soviet Union in the wake of the U.S. playing of the China card, there was no indigenous or neighboring force of sufficient dimensions to *prevent* a Soviet occupation of Afghanistan. The United States under these circumstances had to decide on an appropriate orientation (step 4 of policy implementation). What involvement was necessary? The United States could (1) show its displeasure (which it did by imposing various economic sanctions), (2) use force unilaterally in the area to restore the status quo (which raised the question of how troops could be introduced without violations of the air space of other nations and also the question of how much sense that action would make), (3) organize a military or political coalition in the area against the Soviets (but with India obviously not willing), or (4) do nothing. There can be little argument that a United States so severely constrained in its orientation options chose the correct response, since option 4 would have appeared as an acceptance of the Soviet move and options 2 and 3 had great disadvantages. The Afghanistan problem also had a powerful influence in inducing the United States to place far more emphasis on the possible use of significant American forces in the area. In American official circles, talk of the "Southwest Asia theater" and the difficulties of deployments there became common. The creation of the new U.S. joint "Central Command" was a further result, a step specifically designed to increase U.S. capability in the area (step 3 of policy implementation) so that a wider range of options (step 4) would be available for the future.

The shelving of SALT II unratified was a very complicated issue. It was made even more complicated when the United States announced it would observe the treaty, even if not ratified, as long as the Soviets did.

We are not here primarily concerned about the technical aspects of the arms debate within the United States, which had already undermined the treaty's prospects for ratification before the Afghanistan invasion. The gist of that debate was the charge (and defense against it) that the treaty offered the Soviets advantages superior to those derived by the United States from the same treaty, because although it provided for equal numbers of missiles, Soviet missiles had greater throw-weight (were bigger). There is real irony here. The first SALT agreement was criticized heavily because it permitted *unequal* numbers of launchers, more for the Soviets. So in SALT II the agreement was for equal numbers of launchers (whereupon the criticism shifted as indicated).

If one examines the arms-control record of the superpowers since World War II, one quickly sees that years and years of negotiation achieved relatively modest results until the SALT agreements. Testing in the atmosphere, outer space, and under water was banned, and placing nuclear weapons on the ocean floor (other than in submarines) was prohibited. But no direct attack on

---

[16]Alexander M. Haig, Jr., *Caveat: Realism, Reagan, and Foreign Policy* (New York: Macmillan, 1984), p. 95.

DIAGRAM 13 1979 Plan: Salt II Limits. (Source: U.S., Department of State, *The Strategic Arms Limitation Talks*, Special Report 46 (Revised), May 1979, p. 7.)

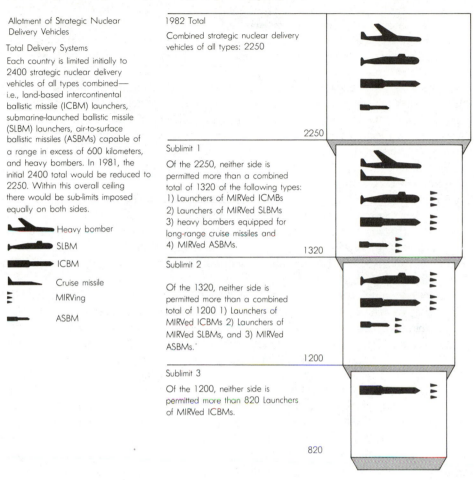

Allotment of Strategic Nuclear Delivery Vehicles

Total Delivery Systems

Each country is limited initially to 2400 strategic nuclear delivery vehicles of all types combined— i.e., land-based intercontinental ballistic missile (ICBM) launchers, submarine-launched ballistic missile (SLBM) launchers, air-to-surface ballistic missiles (ASBMs) capable of a range in excess of 600 kilometers, and heavy bombers. In 1981, the initial 2400 total would be reduced to 2250. Within this overall ceiling there would be sub-limits imposed equally on both sides.

Heavy bomber

SLBM

ICBM

Cruise missile

MIRVing

ASBM

1982 Total

Combined strategic nuclear delivery vehicles of all types: 2250

2250

Sublimit 1

Of the 2250, neither side is permitted more than a combined total of 1320 of the following types:
1) Launchers of MIRVed ICMBs
2) Launchers of MIRVed SLBMs
3) heavy bombers equipped for long-range cruise missiles and
4) MIRVed ASBMs.

1320

Sublimit 2

Of the 1320, neither side is permitted more than a combined total of 1200 1) Launchers of MIRVed ICBMs 2) Launchers of MIRVed SLBMs, and 3) MIRVed ASBMs.

1200

Sublimit 3

Of the 1200, neither side is permitted more than 820 Launchers of MIRVed ICBMs.

820

Source: U.S., Department of State, *The Strategic Arms Limitation Talks,* Special Report 46 (Revised), May 1979, p. 7.

the ICBM weapons bore fruit until SALT I and the (unratified) SALT II. These SALT agreements were only made possible because the superpowers finally decided that the most important variable to control was the launch vehicle. SALT II would have also imposed subrestrictions within a general restriction: an initial ceiling of 2,400 delivery vehicles (to be reduced later to 2,250), with no more than 1,320 MIRVed missile launchers and heavy bombers with long-range cruise missiles, no more than 1,200 of these to be MIRVed missile launchers, and no more than 820 within that second group to be MIRVed ICBM launchers (see Diagram 13).[17] (A second, three-year agreement was to cover cruise missile and mobile ICBM constraints, and a third agreement was on principles for negotiating a SALT III.)

This primary emphasis on launchers had a great deal of merit. Such launchers could be "counted" and verified by satellite. Suppose, for example, they had tried instead to base agreement on some combination of throw-weight, warhead size, and accuracy of delivery. Very sen-

[17]Warheads were carefully limited also. To avoid verification disputes, all types of launchers tested with MIRVs were to be counted as MIRVed, and in each case the maximum number of warheads tested assumed to be installed.

sitive information would have been involved, suspicions of evasion would easily have arisen, and doubts about the reliability of the agreement would continually have been heard.

However, already by SALT I, and even more by SALT II, the question was being raised whether an agreement that essentially focused on ICBM launchers made enough sense in view of the increasingly varied offensive nuclear arsenals available to both superpowers, such as bombers, cruise missiles, and even heavy attack planes from carriers, plus the proliferation in multi-warhead launchers.

Thus two arguments became superimposed. The first involved lingering doubts about the desirability of an arms agreement that equalized numbers of launchers (SALT II) but not the other characteristics, such as throw-weight and accuracy. The U.S. choice made years earlier to develop smaller warheads than the Soviets became now a self-imposed "disadvantage." The Soviet heavy missiles, with their accuracy improved, sparked a U.S. fear that a "window of vulnerability" had opened up. It was feared that heavy and accurate Soviet missiles could destroy even the hardened U.S. Minuteman III missile sites.

The answer the United States gave this first difficulty was the proposed MX. Since the MX would be "hidden," or the effects of a Soviet strike minimized by "fratricide," accuracy would not count.[18] But the tension would rise because of the "destabilizing" effect. When because of congressional opposition President Reagan abandoned the dense-pack basing concept and chose instead to emplace the MX in the already vulnerable Minuteman silos, fears of destabilization increased further.

The second argument was over the question of how to count the increasingly varied offensive systems in order to achieve "equality," particularly as the old distinction between tactical and strategic nuclear weapons became blurred. Tactical weapons were, in theory, short distance, battlefield oriented. Even if some battlefields were quite large, the idea was clear. These were relatively small-sized weapons, compared to the larger ICBM weapons. But weapons such as the new SS-20s, theater nuclear weapons, were capable of destroying all of Western Europe from firing sites within the Soviet Union, just as nuclear submarines, secreted in the oceans, could fire comparable distances. Conceivably the launcher approach would still work for theater nuclear and intercontinental weapons, as well as for submarines and aircraft carriers as platforms for units. But the many sets of weapons on carriers, tactical nuclear weapons, and cruise missiles, each of concealable size, could hardly be controlled using the launcher concept. After all, hundreds of cruise missiles could be hidden in just one nondescript-looking factory. Would it do to control one set (countable launchers) and not the other?

The United States at first had no clear response to this second difficulty. In 1982 the Reagan administration decided that, all in all, it would be better to respond to the issue by shifting in part to warhead count in seeking an agreement with the Soviets. The President proposed reducing to 5000 the number of warheads of both sides (on no more than 850 missiles), with no more than 2500 warheads on land-based ICBMs. (As we can see, that would be no cure-all for the whole extent of the problem.)

The two arguments thus superimposed were as responsible for the failure of SALT II as anything else. What it came down to was that there was no obvious way to control more than a certain share of offensive systems. Given enough residual attack ability in the uncontrolled systems, a meaningful attack might be pressed if a surprise attack were mounted.

This shelving of SALT II's ratification represented a classic case of the United States shooting itself in the foot. First, it was an act undertaken to "punish" the Soviets. Yet, *if* the treaty conferred equal benefits on the two parties, it hardly helped to punish Americans in order to punish the Russians. And if the critics were right and the treaty was unwise, it should have been

---

[18]The concept of "fratricide" involves the idea that the effects of the explosion of the first warheads would neutralize or destroy those following.

rejected on that ground. In that case, what sense was there in observing the treaty anyhow, even while it was unratified and allowed to remain so? Second, the action violated an old rule of politics, that something is usually better than nothing, because some agreement or progress often helps create the path to more. Putting the result of a prolonged and tedious arms-control negotiation into the dustbin or into a "holding pattern" implied that work on the problem could be resumed at any time. This assumption violated a second old rule of politics: you never begin later from where you were when you stopped, because much will change in the meantime. The *absence* of ratification of SALT II did not leave Soviet-American relations where they were; it made them worse. And when the next administration obviously relegated arms control to a low priority, it made things even worse. For quite apart from the deterioration in the political atmosphere, a third effect was the ongoing advance in military technology that was simultaneously complicating the problem still more. Why bother to control ballistic missile launchers (and count them) while uncounted (and uncountable?) cruise missiles proliferated? Such small, inexpensive, easily hidden cruise missiles represented a very difficult proposition to handle. It would have been so even if SALT II had been ratified. Without ratification it meant that the negotiations would be infinitely more complicated.

In the (mis)handling of this issue its real crux was forgotten by the United States: that the United States was manifestly threatened as well as protected by proliferating piles of armaments. It became important to find a new basis for an arms agreement.

The third issue, the intensification of the U.S. effort to eliminate Central American insurgencies, immediately revived fears of "a new Vietnam" among large segments of the American population.

It was certainly true that the largest part of the arms flowing to the Central American insurgents originated from Soviet sources. It was equally obvious that the Sandinista government in Nicaragua was a source of radical left encouragment. Nor was the hand of Cuba, stirring the pot, hard to discern. (Estimates of Soviet aid to Cuba in 1983 ran at the $3 billion mark. Obviously, portions of this aid both financed Cuban troops in Africa and Cuban subversive efforts nearer at home.) The basic U.S. reaction was to send advisers and train the "loyal" troops. There was little reason to expect that this response would, over the long haul, produce the expected results. More dramatic was the U.S. intervention in Grenada in 1983 as Cuban combat engineers pushed the completion of a 10,000-foot runway "to enhance tourism."

The United States meanwhile was remaining rather conspicuously aloof from the efforts of a number of the Latin American states (especially the "Contadora Group" led by Mexico and Venezuela) to mediate between the governments and the insurgents. Nor had the United States effectively utilized the mechanisms of the Organization of American States either.

These developments raised the question of whether it was at all likely that developing societies with such great gulfs between rich and poor could be stabilized by military forces or reorganized without extensive bloodshed. But the Reagan administration tended to categorize the problem as one *primarily* the result of deliberate and provocative Soviet subversion. There was little doubt that this approach to the problem helped create the coldest Soviet-American relations since the days of President Truman and the early crises over Berlin.

7.

Summing Up

The end of the Vietnam War and the playing of the China card by the United States put an end to the Soviet freedom to act to its own advantage while China and the United States deployed their forces each to deal with the other. As Soviet troops were moved then to the Chinese frontier, Soviet cooperation with the United States was accentuated. The Nixon-Ford administrations by and large handled these new opportunities to offset the natural tensions between two superpowers with agreements that benefited both—such as SALT I. The Carter administration, by insisting on the human rights theme, worsened relations with the Soviets but, since relations with China were not sacrificed, still retained pressures on the Soviets. That, plus its willingness to reach mutually advantageous arms-control agreements, ensured that U.S.–Soviet relations did not utterly disintegrate—at least until Afghanistan.

The Reagan administration, predisposed to see the Soviets as aggressive and expansionist because of communism, simultaneously in 1983 allowed relations with the Soviets to disintegrate, while recklessly permitting relations with China to worsen because of U.S. arms support for Taiwan. This classic disregard of the cardinal principle of third-party influences (not to mention conservation of enemies) brought the obvious result of increasing Soviet freedom of maneuver while making the relations themselves more and more negative. This was not an advantageous result for the United States.

All of this occurred against the background of the debate with which this chapter began, as to whether the Soviets were "offensively" or "defensively" motivated. By the time of the Reagan administration a government was in power in the United States that leaned decisively to the "offensive" explanation and which, in making policy accordingly (and producing Soviet reactions to it), made reality increasingly conform to its picture of reality—made Soviet behavior more "aggressive."

Yet, as we saw earlier, the Soviet arms build-up is a rational reaction either for a nation planning aggression or one fearing attack. The arms build-up in and of itself is no convincing clue either way.

What is most noticeable about Soviet policy generally is that it is fairly successful in causing trouble abroad (arms shipments at cheap prices, surrogate Cuban troops), but fairly unsuccessful in building any positive accomplishments. Where is there a Communist regime outside of Russia, grateful and loyal to the Soviet Union, and dependable even if the Red Army were withdrawn? The list would be small; perhaps Bulgaria. Where is there a positive and dependable change for the Soviets that has stemmed from their massive arms shipments abroad. Syria? (Certainly not Indonesia, or Somalia, or Egypt.)

The past successes of the Soviet Union would seem to have been the result, apart from the results of World War II militarily, more of a passing phase in world history, especially the end of colonial regimes. The Soviets' opportunities are fairly limited to nations with great disparities in the distribution of wealth—and such influence is likely to be passing, too. Their difficulties in holding a subject empire in Eastern Europe meanwhile increase (of which more in the next chapter). Is it worthwhile for the United States to deal with the Soviet Union entirely at arms length and substantially as though the advantages of any agreements would inevitably be one-sided, in Soviet favor? In arms control, the United States also has much to gain and this cannot be done while putting all the rest of the relationship with the Soviet Union in deep freeze. Afghanistan proves equally two possibilities: Soviet expansiveness or Soviet fears. Central American unrest proves less equally two possibilities: that the unrest is Soviet-inspired, or indigenous. On balance then, the case rests with swinging the relationship between the superpowers, so far as American policy affects it, away from complete negativism. Otherwise, once again the United States will encounter more enmity than it has to, and increase both costs and risks without the likelihood of corresponding gains. Otherwise, once again the United States will be implementing a policy whose design ignores the cardinal principles, a policy that runs directly counter to the natural tendencies in the system.

17

Europe — The Divided Continent

The numerical balance of forces has moved slowly but steadily in favor of the Warsaw Pact over the past two decades [and NATO has] lost much of the technological advantage which permitted NATO to rely on the view that quality could compensate for quantity.

Joseph M. A. H. Luns
Secretary-General of NATO, 1982

The world has now lived for about four decades with an unresolved problem. That problem is the division of Europe between East and West, with its accompanying tensions, including a semi-permanent deployment of large numbers of foreign troops on the soil of a divided Germany. It is a supreme irony of history that Europe, a handful of whose nations once literally ruled the world in the heyday of colonialism, is itself now reduced to this situation. The division thus enforced upon Europe (and upon Germany) is unnatural in the most basic sense of world politics. Even if it were not already known from other evidence, the history of the system would tell us that such an arrangement of Europe flies in the face of the wishes of the overwhelming majority of its inhabitants, on either side of the Iron Curtain line. Yet this division has endured—at a considerable human price, in the West in the sense of living in heightened tensions, and in the East in the sense of a substantial sacrifice of freedoms. That this situation will endure "forever" is quite another question. Some day this situation will end, and its potential and ultimate transformation is probably the single most important long-range problem confronting U.S. policy anywhere in the world.

In any condition, divided or united, Europe's importance to the United States can hardly be overstated. If Western Europe's power and resources, presently associated with NATO, were suddenly somehow transferred to the Warsaw Pact, that would completely and drastically alter the world balance of power. From a priority point of view, there is no other area of the world outside the American frontiers that is so obviously of critical importance to the United States. American history recognizes this fact. The United States intervened on the continent of Europe with armed force in two successive world wars to right and restore a threatened balance. The United States has maintained an army in Europe for four postwar decades to ensure that that same balance is not eroded in the face of Soviet pressures or European despair. The Soviets, too, recognize Europe's importance and have more than 65 per cent of their military manpower assigned to the European theater.

Because Europe is that important, it by definition is rich in the elements which make for national power, especially in its literate and skilled manpower and its possession of advanced technological abilities. These elements obviously translate into high economic and military potential. To point this out is not only to underline again that the United States cannot afford seeing Europe "lost." It is to add that Europe, precisely because it is a rich prize, is also a serious weight in the balance of power in its own right. Europe is no mere inert pile of gold to be carted off by some rich Red robber baron so much as a strongpoint of great utility to whoever possesses it. It is not just a prize but a prime player in the game.

1. _____

Europe: Its Unity in Diversity

Looking more closely at Europe, we realize again how tricky making any generalization always is. For Europe is no single entity, from any standpoint. To begin with, there is the arbitrary Iron Curtain line down its middle, bisecting Germany. Looked at politically, or militarily, or economically, Europe has different profiles, different faces. Even if we restrict our statement to Europe west of the Iron Curtain, the differences between European nations stand out clearly. In membership and makeup, Western democratic (political) Europe is not synonymous with NATO (military Europe), and NATO is not synonymous with the European Community (economic Europe). Even within NATO, there are members who are participants in the fully integrated command structure and other North Atlantic Pact members such as France who maintain liaison but command their forces independently. Some NATO members such as Greece and Turkey have significant disputes with each other—as over Cyprus, and both nations have at times limited their NATO relationship. Within the European Community there are those nations such as West Germany and Britain, who contributed more money to it than they received, and those who, like France (with heavily subsidized agriculture), received more than they contributed. Sweden, a significant European state, belongs to neither NATO nor to the European Community. Switzerland similarly remains an outsider to both organizations. Conversely, Spain, long ostracized under Franco, is gradually winning admission to these more integrated features of Western Europe. So the political, military, and economic faces of Western Europe actually need separate appraisal.

Speaking of the Iron Curtain dividing line itself is misleading because it creates the images we have already used of a Communist Europe opposed to democratic Europe. Yet the briefest acquaintance with the real situation tells us that the Soviet forces in Eastern Europe are as much stationed there to prevent free choice by the people of East Germany, Poland, Hungary, or Czechoslovakia as they are deployed there for purposes of either assaulting or repelling NATO. The eastern part of Europe is culturally much closer to the West than to Russia, which fact presents the Soviets with a great dilemma. Russia cannot permit Eastern Europe its political and economic development because Russia (with reason) does not trust the area enough to give it independence. As recently as World War II, Hitler found willing allies in the Balkans as he moved to attack Russia. The Hungarians and the Poles, in particular, have age-old hatreds toward Russia. But the imposition by Russia of an imposed way of life on the peoples east of the Iron Curtain line not only continues the strains inevitably associated with foreign occupation. It also prevents the German people from being reunited: literally walling up East Berlin from West Berlin and maintaining a fenced puppet German state as an advanced base. And by maintaining Soviet (that is, foreign) troops in Central Europe the Soviet presence upsets the tranquility of Europe.

Looking more closely within this Soviet-dominated area, we can also see differences, just as in Western Europe. Not all the members of the Warsaw Pact are equally happy or unhappy,

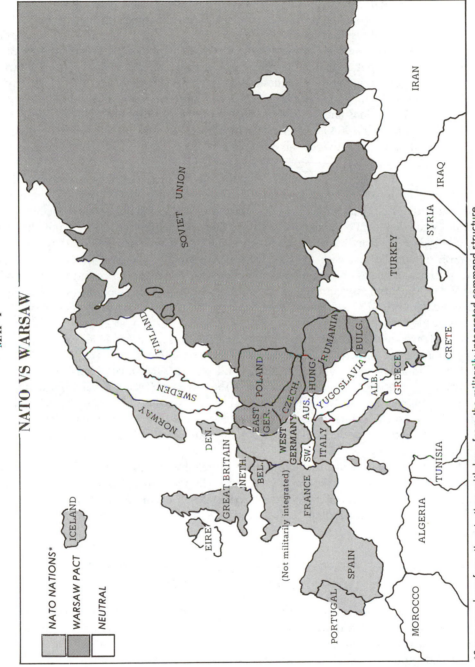

MAP 4

NATO VS WARSAW

NATO NATIONS*

WARSAW PACT

NEUTRAL

ICELAND

EIRE

GREAT BRITAIN

NETH.

BEL.

DEN.

NORWAY

SWEDEN

FINLAND

SOVIET UNION

(Not militarily integrated)

FRANCE

GERMANY
WEST

SW.

EAST
GER.

POLAND

CZECH.

AUS.

HUNG.

ITALY

YUGOSLAVIA

RUMANIA

BULG.

ALB.

GREECE

TURKEY

IRAN

IRAQ

SYRIA

CRETE

PORTUGAL

SPAIN

MOROCCO

ALGERIA

TUNISIA

*Some members from time to time withdraw from the militarily integrated command structure.

under the shadow of the Russian bear. Bulgaria has, as always, a close affinity to the Russians, sharing a similar Cyrillic alphabet and close, historically nurtured ties. Bulgarians remember Russia in the role of liberator from the Turks. Poland is at the other end of the extreme, forever exposed to and never willing to settle for Soviet control, its strong Catholic and national traditions always reemerging. Rumania goes its own way as much as possible in terms of the Warsaw Pact, but has preserved a strict and proper Communist stance at home in its internal institutions. Czechoslovakia, once well disposed toward the Russia that "liberated" it from Nazi occupation as the Soviet armies rolled west at the end of World War II, has since the Soviet military reoccupation of 1968 (which put an end to the democratic stirrings of the "Prague Spring") participated in the Soviet bloc reluctantly. Czechoslovakia is awaiting a chance to go its own way as Yugoslavia long ago did. Hungary, the victim of Russian military suppression in 1848 and again in 1956, has no viable options but the true feelings of the Hungarians are not very deeply submerged. The Hungarians in 1984 led the Eastern bloc in terms of prosperity, especially through allowing capitalist-oriented activities—a development watched by the Soviets with mixed feelings.

East Germany, the German Democratic Republic, is the most complicated member of the bloc to explain. The East Germans alone represent a Communist form of what is duplicated under free conditions right next to them. That is, there are two Germanies but only one Hungary, one Poland. Whatever the Poles would like to be, there is no other present Poland they can compare themselves to. They have to change the Poland they have to a Poland they visualize. This, however, is not the case with the East Germans. Some two thirds of East Germany can receive West German television programs. A direct comparison between two ways of life can be made every day; the alternative already exists and East Berlin's Alexanderplatz and West Berlin's Kurfürstendamm can be compared "live," even if the German people are not free to pass across from East to West.

Europe, then, though a natural geographical single entity, is not one in all things. It would be neither accurate nor sufficient to describe either bloc on either side of the Iron Curtain as homogeneous. Old antagonisms among neighbors still persist, subordinated beneath the major lines of East vs. West, just as Hungary still covets the return of Transylvania from Rumania. But Europe, *compared* to Russia, *is* a single cultural entity. A visitor from outer space, set down anywhere in Europe outside Bulgaria or Turkey or Russia would recognize the common features, despite every difference. It is this basic unity of values and outlook that threatens the Soviets more than any other thing.

But if generalizations about Europe have to be handled with care, and the issues posed are complex, the fate of this area of the world (and especially its western half) remains at the top of the list of foreign area concerns for the United States. An American commitment to the security of this area remains essential.

2.

Three Interlinked Problems

Europe's present situation gives rise to three important and interlinked problems. The first problem is the arbitrary and unnatural division of Europe we have already noted. We discuss the implications of this division further in Section 3.

The second problem stems from the first, in that Soviet troops are deployed in Central Europe. The issue for the United States is how to respond. There are two basic alternatives. One is to continue the precautionary, forward-deployed stance that has been basic American policy since the late 1940s. The strong, widely shared belief has been that the forward Soviet position, coupled with the great military strength at the Soviets' disposal, makes the U.S. forward deployment almost inevitable. The other option is to reduce the level of deployment and, if hostilities erupt, play a more supporting and reinforcing role. In a strictly military sense, unless there are offsetting increases in European troop levels, this alternative at first glance seems very dangerous. Even those who consider a Soviet military attack the least likely contingency have to accept the notion that the prize is great and the temptation strong if the West is grossly negligent in its defenses. But it is possible that reduced U.S. deployment *would* produce a greater European effort. After all, it is the Europeans' land which must be defended. And it is quite possible that a reduced U.S. deployment would not reduce U.S. influence significantly, either. Although American policymakers since World War II have linked a serious U.S. role in world affairs with an active forward deployment, deployments, commitments, and influence do not automatically go hand in hand.

The variety of possible responses to the advanced Soviet deployment triggered a NATO-wide debate in the early 1980s, focused on the rapidly growing deployment of Soviet mobile, three-warhead SS-20 missiles and the plan to counter them (beginning in late 1983) with ground-launched cruise missiles (GLCMs) and Pershing II IRBMs. We discuss this further in Sections 5 and 6.

The requirement for Western Europe and the United States to remain closely associated does not guarantee a frictionless relationship or even an identity of national interests inside or outside of NATO. This lack of uniformity of interests is the third problem.

Europe's weakness immediately after the end of World War II disguised these differences as the United States turned to rebuilding Europe's strength through the Marshall Plan and pump-priming with dollars. Encouraged by the United States and motivated by the conviction that a new beginning must be made, Western Europe turned to the building of the European Community. As progress was made and European cooperation increased, a European Common Market was established (with U.S. products outside). The renewed European economic strength inevitably resulted in a degree of competition by this new economic unit, which though capable of still absorbing significant trade with the United States was capable also of acting in direct competition in third markets. The corollary to this development was eventually to raise the policy issue of how much the United States should continue to encourage European unification or integration.

Turning to another aspect of this problem area, the fact that West Europe's prime security threat stemmed from the Soviet Union did not automatically produce complete agreement between the European states or between them and the United States as to how to handle that threat. Nor did it ensure an identity of interests or outlooks between West Europe and the United States on issues arising elsewhere in the world, such as the Middle East or Asia. There was also a notable difference between the dependence of Europe on Middle East oil (very great) and that of the United States (much less). NATO as a treaty had geographical limits, and those limits excluded the Middle East. These divergencies created strains.

In 1981 and 1982, the lack of uniformity in interests led directly to differences on how to deal with the Soviets, especially in terms of closer Eastern Europe–Western Europe economic relations. Western commercial banks by September 30, 1981, had loaned the Soviet Union and six of its Eastern European "allies" some $65.4 billion—an eightfold increase in Communist debt over 1970. We have already mentioned the specific disagreements between the United States and Western Europe that arose over the natural gas pipeline connecting Western Europe with the Soviet Union. Whereas the United States attempted to discourage the pipeline deal on the grounds that it increased Soviet abilities to blackmail Western Europe politically, the Europeans tended to be more impressed with their vulnerable dependence on oil from volatile Arab states whose ready recourse to violence could interrupt assured supplies of oil. The issues raised here by the differences between European and American interests were political, military, and economic. Was it feasible or necessary for West Europe and the United States to evolve a common policy toward third areas of the world, especially the Soviet Union and the Middle East?

To summarize, the shape of contemporary Europe poses three major problems for the United States, each problem raising one or more issues for U.S. decision. The fundamental and overarching problem is the arbitrary division of a Europe culturally a single unit but divided into two parts. This makes for continual dissatisfaction, especially in the eastern part. The issue here is whether Europe's division can be undone and, if so, whether any negative implications of such change will be compensated. The next most important problem derives from the first. It is that the advanced position of Soviet forces in Central Europe disturbs the balance of power. This makes for insecurity. The issue here is how best to coordinate U.S. and European resources to counter the Soviet military threat as it arises from that forward position. The third problem, a natural offshoot of the relations of any group of states, is that European and U.S. interests do not automatically align. This makes for dissension. The issues it raises are three: (1) How much the United States should encourage further European unification or integration? (2) How to deal with divergencies about events or situations inside Europe? (3) How to deal with divergencies about events or situations outside Europe?

3.

Problem One: Europe's Arbitrary Division

The most fundamental problem in Europe is Europe's division between East and West, now continuing into a fifth decade.

We saw in Chapter 12 how this came to be. Germany at the end of World War II was "temporarily" divided into occupation zones that, as it turned out, gave the Soviets more German territory to occupy than they took by force of arms. At the same time, the American government permitted the Soviets to occupy both Prague and Berlin, each within easy reach of American forces. The combination of these events gave the Soviets an advanced territorial presence in middle Europe. When the "temporary" arrangements, including the Soviet Union's grudging permission for Allied passage to and from Berlin, began to break down, the first Berlin crisis pitted a Soviet land passage denial against a Western airlift to Berlin in 1948. The crisis was terminated as a "draw," but the consolidation of the British, French, and American zones that precipitated the crisis created the basis for a single West German government, which the Soviets then paralleled in their own zone. There were now two German states. A President for the Federal Republic of Germany was elected on September 12, 1949, and a President for the German Democratic Republic was elected on October 11. Periodic East-West foreign ministers' conferences, as in 1954 and 1959, altered nothing fundamental.[1] Nor did a second Berlin crisis in 1958 and 1959, when Nikita Khrushchev tried to create a "free" West Berlin (without a Western presence)—and had at last to settle for the Berlin Wall of August 1961 to stop East Germans from fleeing.

Bilateral negotiations were more successful in normalizing Soviet-German relations. West Germany, which had established diplomatic relations with Moscow in September 1955, in August 1970 signed a German-Soviet treaty recognizing the "inviolability" of existing European frontiers. Bonn also then disavowed all territorial claims and renounced the use or threat of force in their mutual relations. A similar treaty was signed with Poland in December of 1970, and

---

[1]See Frederick H. Hartmann, *Germany Between East and West: The Reunification Problem* (New York: Prentice-Hall, 1965).

provisions of the same import were included in the Final Act of the Conference on Security and Cooperation in Europe (the 1975 Helsinki Agreements).[2]

Encouraged by these (early) West German successes, the Four Powers undertook negotiations on the Berlin problem. In September 1971 the Four Powers signed an agreement providing freer access to the city and freer movement and communication between the sectors. On November 6, 1972, West and East Germany initialed the Basic Treaty, an arrangement designed to somewhat enhance intra-German cooperation. In 1973 the treaty between West Germany and Czechoslovakia was ratified, with Bonn acknowledging that the 1938 Munich Agreement was invalid.

The formula by which West and East Germany could deal with one another and exchange representatives ("two German states within one German nation") aptly summed up the *de facto* situation.

All of these fruits of "Ostpolitik" can be variously interpreted either as concessions by West Germany (*de facto* acceptance of borders) or gains (in that they were accompanied by agreements over access to Berlin—which was guaranteed for the first time by the Soviets). What indisputably changed was that real progress was made toward enhancing the German position in Europe in the 1970s. Trade, capital flows, communication, and travel increased between East and West under the rubric of détente. West German capital became available to East Germany, while East Germany tried to balance such dependence on the West against clinging to communism. The reintroduction of a degree of West German political and economic influence in Eastern Europe provided a counterweight to Soviet domination that, although less than the effect of Soviet troops there, was still troublesome to the Soviets. Although Russia's vulnerable western approaches seemed fully secure against a military assault, continuing internal unrest in the Warsaw bloc showed that the apparent stability had a fragile base.

From the standpoint of Soviet behavior, the actions of the Soviet Union from the period when it first laid siege to Berlin in 1945 to the contemporary period represented almost a straight, undeviating line. So long as no great challenge appeared, the Russians had little interest in surrendering their control over East Germany. That control divided Germany and provided a convenient pretext for the continuing presence of Soviet troops in Poland (and Czechoslovakia). It kept NATO's front line further west.

The Soviet presence also imposed a highly unnatural situation on Europe that exploded into armed resistance in East Germany in June 1953, in armed resistance in Hungary in 1956, in a freedom movement in Czechoslovakia in 1968, and in a freedom movement in Poland of smaller dimensions in 1956 and of larger dimensions in 1981. These events raised the issue of whether the division of Europe, with its corollary of suppression of freedom, would continue or be undone, and what, if anything, the United States ought to do about it.

The answer one gives to the first part of the question is significantly related to how one assesses the strength of cultural attitudes as over against the efficacy of bayonets. The great Soviet weakness in East Europe is that the Russians are not loved; they are, in fact, thoroughly disliked, and they are not respected for much besides their ability to muster brute force. The peoples of East Europe are accustomed to look down in cultural terms on the Russians, creating in some sense the kind of problem the Jews in ancient Judea created for the Romans who occupied them, except that the East Europeans are far too numerous to be slaughtered or dispersed to compel their obedience.

Even more controversial is the issue of German reunification, for it is alleged correctly that there is sentiment on both sides of the Iron Curtain for the proposition that the Germans are

---

[2]Bonn made it clear in all these cases that these agreements would not be binding on a reunified German state. Furthermore, they would not substitute for the definitive delimitation a peace treaty would provide, which remained the responsibility of the Four Powers.

less dangerous when divided. There is also inertia within Germany, stemming from the problems bound up with any change from the status quo. The Soviet risk in remaining where they are may well seem to be less than the risk in withdrawing, regardless of the terms on which such withdrawal takes place. The ultimate judgment on this issue requires some confident assessment as to whether the extended stay of the Soviets in Central Europe increases the chances of the catastrophe of a third (and nuclear) world war—a part of the second problem, to which we turn shortly.

If Germany is to be reunited in peace one day, it is hardly likely to occur through a process of adding both Germanies as armed assets to either side. That is, it is hardly conceivable that the Soviets would withdraw from East Germany and then permit East Germany to become part of a united Germany in NATO. It is equally unlikely that the West would distance itself from a West Germany exposed to Soviet pressures along the Iron Curtain, or permit West Germany to hand itself over in desperation to Soviet control. So any solution of the German problem would seem to imply an evacuated, neutral Germany, not allied to either side. Such a solution obviously has its own risks. To be acceptable to all, a neutral unified Germany would need to be viable and stable rather than an invitation toward further (and unpredictable) change. These aspects of the problem are better addressed after sketching in the outlines of the second problem.

4.

Problem Two: The Advanced Soviet Position and Its Political-Military Implications

So long as the Soviets stay where they are the issues are focused on what to do about the military threat implied by that advanced presence, and how to compensate to create as stable a balance as possible under difficult conditions.

Here, too, the situation was not static. By the early 1980s it could no longer be denied that the Warsaw Pact was engaged in a major military build-up. By almost all indicators the East-West military balance in Europe was adverse to the West. Warsaw Pact forces held an edge in deployed manpower, a considerable margin in conventional artillery, a massive superiority in tanks, far greater standardization and interoperability of equipment, much superior near-term reinforcement capability, more secure logistical systems, an edge in theater nuclear forces, and so on down the line. In only a very few areas, such as tactical nuclear weapons, did the West appear to hold an edge. And it was not just a matter of the current balance; in nearly all spheres the *trends* were adverse.

For years the West had counted on three factors to offset the Warsaw Pact's quantitative advantages. First, NATO forces usually had been superior technologically. In the 1970s, however, the margin had eroded severely. Second, there always had been the backup provided by the United States nuclear umbrella, the nuclear superiority of the United States in central strategic systems. This was eliminated in the 1970s. The third factor was the unreliability of Moscow's East European allies. Since the ordinary people of the Warsaw Pact members such as Poland, Hungary, or East Germany were of doubtful loyalty to their Soviet-sponsored regimes or to their Soviet overlords, Soviet military planning had to take account of possible large-scale sabotage across their rear area. Only this third factor remained in the mid-1980s as a possible offset to the force disparities mentioned earlier.

Another problem existed, one not always given sufficient attention: as a result of France's expulsion of NATO forces and facilities from her soil, NATO's logistical tail had been shortened severely. NATO forces and equipment are now more temptingly concentrated in Germany and in the Low Countries. NATO supply lines run north and south, within easy range of the front;

as such, they are prone to disruption and confusion within a very short time after hostilities commence.

NATO's official strategy to handle this situation remained "flexible response." Forces are to have the capacity to respond appropriately at whatever the level of violence and with whatever the means necessary. The possession of a series of differentiated graduated responses, the theory goes, allows the punishment to fit the crime and prevents NATO from being faced with a choice of capitulation or a fight for survival on every issue. Flexible response is supposed to be both an effective deterrent and a sufficient combat strategy.

One can raise a number of logical questions with respect to flexible response even when forces operate under the most ideal of conditions. As just one example, in the midst of hostilities can matters be sufficiently controlled and can parties act with the rationality, precision, and calm that flexible response requires? And now, after the removal of NATO from French soil, conditions are far from ideal. By so severely altering NATO's geopolitical situation, France severely reduced whatever capability had previously existed for precise, limited actions. Moreover, it drastically shortened the time that will be available to policymakers to make the decision concerning whether or not to cross the nuclear threshhold. This is a matter that needs serious thought.

One major issue confronting the United States thus involved NATO's military strength and strategy. What was necessary to enhance the alliance's deterrence functions, and what had to be done to shore up its defense capabilities? Since different domestic factors, economic concerns, and views of the Soviet threat were held by various alliance members, it would be necessary to handle the fact that the different states were not uniformly willing to contribute to the common defense. Indeed, they made different assessments of the alliance's contemporary worth. And it was not at all self-evident what Washington should do, and what its military strategy should be. How much of the military burden should be borne by the Europeans? Was it reasonable for their defense expenditures for NATO to lag behind those of the United States? What did the changed and changing military and geopolitical conditions imply for U.S. policy?

A related part of the issue involved Washington's view of the nature of the alliance itself. Is the NATO of the contemporary world a coalition of equals in which the United States is a genuine partner, or should it be seen as an organization requiring American leadership? And what about political cohesion? Should NATO be expected to develop a consensus across a broad spectrum of both political and military issues in a wide range of geographical areas? Indeed, should such a range of problems even be raised in this forum? Or should NATO concentrate on politico-military issues in the alliance area alone? Or, somewhere in between? Given the counterbalancing national interests of alliance members, how much consensus is possible, and are efforts to achieve agreement likely to be counterproductive? None of these was an easy issue to resolve.

5.

Problem Three: Lack of Uniformity of U.S.–European Interests

The differences that emerged between the United States and its European allies were already evident in the 1960s when Charles de Gaulle raised the question of whether Washington was prepared to die *because of Paris*. In fact, De Gaulle at the time was ready to concede that the United States would risk or fight a war to defend Paris. What he really was raising was a different issue: whether France was to be permitted its own independent foreign policy or be subject in its every decision to an American veto justified by the enormous mutual risks if either party got into trouble. Since the United States at the time was well embarked upon policy ventures in both Asia and the Middle East that France did not automatically equate to its own interests, coordination could mean French compliance with American initiatives. De Gaulle, on French television in April 1965, put the point this way: "The fact that we have again taken up our faculty of judgment and action toward all problems seems sometimes to offend a state [the United States] which could, because of its power, think that it has a supreme and universal responsibility." De Gaulle's persistent skepticism about British overtures to join the European Common Market reflected his conviction that the British were not prepared to sever their "special relationship" with the United States. His March 6, 1966, announcement of France's withdrawal from NATO's integrated command structure was a further evidence of his belief.

At the time, American statesmen were inclined to dismiss De Gaulle's acidic comments as a special case of inflated ego. That was before even West Germany began its major initiatives toward the Eastern bloc, and well before Greece and Turkey went their separate paths over NATO issues and even came into conflict over Cyprus in 1974. But De Gaulle's statements and actions were more than individual idiosyncracies. They were early examples of differences in perceptions and interests, differences that later surfaced in many guises throughout the alliance. Behind these dissensions were deep fears and frustrations as well as significant variations in priorities and goals.

It is not surprising, for instance, that Europe became less docile in following the American lead about the time that the strenuous Soviet effort in armaments was finally bringing the Russians out of the obvious inferiority that had played its part in making them back down in the Cuban missile crisis of 1962. U.S. forces in 1964 and 1965 were two and a half million as compared to the Soviet's three million, but the United States held a significant nuclear lead. By 1976–1977, U.S. forces were 2.6 million, but Soviet forces had increased to 3.65 million, with Russia substantially closing the nuclear gap. In 1981 and 1982, total U.S. armed forces were 2,049,100, compared to total Soviet forces of 3,673,000.[3] By this time, the number of Soviet nuclear delivery vehicles exceeded that of the United States. Soviet throw-weight also exceeded the U.S. weights. Only in numbers of (smaller) warheads did the United States still maintain a lead over the Soviets.

According to NATO sources in 1982, NATO-Warsaw Pact forces in place in NATO Europe, leaving out France and including Warsaw Pact as far east as but excluding the three Soviet western military districts of Moscow, Volga, and Urals, compared as follows: total military, 2.6 million NATO versus 4.0 million for the Warsaw Pact; divisions, 84 NATO versus 173 Warsaw Pact; main battle tanks, 13,000 NATO versus 42,500 Warsaw Pact; antitank guided weapon launchers, 8,100 NATO versus 24,300 Warsaw Pact; large artillery and mortars, 10,750 NATO versus 31,500 Warsaw Pact; armored personnel carriers and infantry fighting vehicles, 30,000 NATO versus 78,800 Warsaw Pact; and helicopters, 2,200 NATO versus 1,700 Warsaw Pact.[4] The combat aircraft comparison is NATO fighter-bomber, 1,950 versus 1,920; interceptors, 740 versus 4,370; reconaissance planes, 285 versus 600; and bombers, none versus 350.[5]

As Soviet strength grew, so too did Europe's sense of skepticism about an automatic U.S. commitment to war to defend Europe. Two points more or less united NATO Europe on the official level in these circumstances: (1) the vital importance of a significant U.S. armed presence on NATO's frontline, and (2) a determination to ensure that any response to a deliberate Soviet assault across the Iron Curtain would be met, if necessary, by a nuclear response.

---

[3]Figures taken from appropriate annual volume of the International Institute for Strategic Studies, *The Military Balance.*

[4]Data from North Atlantic Treaty Organization, *NATO and the Warsaw Pact: Force Comparisons,* p. 11. No date, but reflects 1980 or 1981. The comparison *includes* the westernmost military districts of Leningrad, Baltic, Belorussia, Carpathian, Kiev, Odessa, and the Caucasus.

[5]Ibid, p. 15.

The reasoning behind the first point is more obvious than with the second. By insisting on a substantial U.S. front-line presence (a quarter-million or so), NATO was assuring itself that the United States would have no option but to fight, once Americans in large numbers were dying on European battlefields. The second point (if necessary, a nuclear response) is more obscure. How does it square with European uneasiness in 1981–1984 over President Reagan's apparent belligerency toward the Soviets? What about the popular rallies of hundreds of thousands of people in favor of a nuclear freeze all over free Europe in 1983? How should we explain this apparent inconsistency?

We must first distinguish between the reactions of the man-in-the-street, compared to the more elaborate calculations of official NATO European defense policymakers. The prevailing official viewpoint in NATO Europe, with some exceptions, went something like this. The Soviets are not really likely to attack anyhow (so why bother with as much diversion of real resources into conventional forces as the United States keeps urging?). But, if the Soviets do attack, it will only be because they see the possibility of a quick and easy steamroller forward plunge, at no great expense in destruction to the Soviet homeland. To oppose such a Soviet assault with Western conventional forces, *even if equal in strength,* would produce protracted warfare on NATO soil for the third time in the twentieth century. Since this prospect is intolerable and unacceptable, the Soviets must be deterred by the inescapable conviction that they will suffer nuclear destruction. That conviction can only come from a Soviet military assessment that they might well win in a purely conventional struggle but that NATO would then quickly be forced either to accept defeat or resort to nuclear weapons and would choose to go nuclear.

The by-now traditional official American view, to which a number of defense commentators on both continents also subscribe, is somewhat different. It argues instead that having the capability and determination to make a nuclear response to a Soviet attack is *forced* upon NATO because of the unwillingness of Western Europe to pay the political and economic price for fielding sufficiently strong conventional forces to deter the Soviets without the threat of the use of nuclear weapons. Implied is the proposition that Europe's leaders have missed that point and need to be made aware of it.

Whether NATO's implicit reliance on a nuclear defense comes about for one reason or the other, it is an old argument, often repeated in years past. What was new in 1983 was the reaction of the man-in-the-street to the prospect of new and substantial quantities of nuclear weapons (especially cruise missiles scattered around at a number of sites) being deployed in his homeland. In view of these developments, the argument for a nuclear freeze seemed to many people to make sense. Closely connected in time and in the popular mind but distinct in logic was the popular call for "no first use" of nuclear weapons. These were two entirely distinct issues, even if they tended to blur together in popular discussions. Those who argued for "no first use" had to say either (1) that no use of nuclear weapons is ever justified morally, or (2) that the Soviets could or would be deterred by sufficient conventional forces (which were, however, conspicuously not available), or (3) that the Soviets did not intend to attack.

The logic of such a popular argument swayed uneasily between assumptions and hopes, suspended between sets of fears: (1) that war, if it came, would be devastating in any form (one point for the official view), (2) that once nuclear weapons began to be used there would be no safe house for anyone (not incompatible necessarily with the public view), and (3) that acquiring more weapons and threatening first use raised tensions and decreased security (one point against the official view). Result: frustration.

If one understands that the logic of each of these counterbalancing arguments leads to choices by very narrow margins, one sees why Chancellor Helmut Schmidt of West Germany was able to withstand the assault of the left wing of his Social Democratic party (SPD) on his defense policies in April 1982 (only to fall over economic issues that same October and be replaced by Helmut Kohl of the CDU). And one can see with equal ease why later the SPD in

November 1983, at its party congress, finally came out against the new American missile deployments.

Compare the "official" European logic with U.S. interests. The United States, as indicated, wants Europe to provide a greater conventional defense effort in order to have options other than a nuclear response. In the United States nuclear weapons are most frequently referred to as "unusable" since their use would presumably destroy both the Soviet and American homelands. But since war with the Soviets is still feared, and it is assumed that both sides would have an initial incentive to stay with conventional weapons (once any opportunity for a preemptive nuclear strike had passed), that incentive is furthered if Europe could be made defensible conventionally. It was usually in this kind of framework in the United States that the argument was heard that NATO should announce a non-first use of nuclear weapons.[6]

Thus the 1983–1984 debate over the SS-20s and the Pershing IIs and GLCMs (ground-launched cruise missiles) not only touched deep emotions in Europe but underlined the contradictory nature of the European response to the problem. Once the Soviets began to deploy SS-20 missiles, on their own soil but with a range sufficient to target any point in Europe, this would create, as Helmut Schmidt pointed out originally, a *theater* imbalance. The Soviets would now be able to hurt Europe severely, but the NATO response, without the new weapons, would fall short of Russia in terms of range from their West European bases. We can see why in strategic logic the European governments then initially pressed for Pershing IIs and GLCMs as a counterbalance and why NATO decided in principle in 1979 to match the Soviets beginning in December 1983 unless arms agreements were reached in the meantime. However, even after the Soviet deployment of SS-20s had reached 315 by July 1982,[7] European leaders except for Helmut Schmidt and Margaret Thatcher of Great Britain did not press very vigorously for implementation of the NATO decision. In 1982, when Brezhnev, after Soviet deployments of SS-20s had begun but before NATO had acted to balance that move, made an unsatisfactory compromise offer, many European leaders toyed with agreeing with him. The reluctance by some NATO members to go ahead with deployment reflected the general European fear that the Reagan administration was more interested in an arms race than in arms control, although it is fair to add that the United States put no undue pressure on the Europeans.

There was the natural feeling in Europe that Europe would be even better off if Russia would dismantle its arms than if NATO added its own arms to restore the balance of destructive power—a point of view the United States did not dispute. Any arms race, by inevitably raising tensions, was bound to increase the danger of a European war—especially since that arms race was focused on the most destabilizing of weapons, offensive strategic missiles with very short flight time to their targets. Europeans, even more than the peoples of other areas of the world where freedom of assembly or freedom of the press permitted real debate, were fearful of the apparently endless proclivity of the nuclear powers for increasing their already bulging piles of warheads. The fear was growing that the problem was escaping human control. Europe, as a prime target, was also a prime center for the expression of this feeling.

These offsetting considerations explain Europe's slow and reluctant handling of the issue. Even after the number of Soviet SS-20s deployed reached 350 in March 1983, in June of that year, when NATO reaffirmed its intention to proceed, it was not a unanimous vote, although the votes on actual deployments in the fall of 1983 in Italy, Britain, and West Germany were all affirmative.

Other questions involving Europe and the United States were of a political or economic character, these being often intertwined.

---

[6]See the influential article by McGeorge Bundy, George F. Kennan, Robert S. McNamara, and Gerald Smith, "Nuclear Weapons and the Atlantic Alliance," *Foreign Affairs,* vol. 60, no. 4 (Spring 1982) 753–768.

[7]The Soviets also had 280 single-warhead SS-4s and SS-5s on station against NATO.

DIAGRAM 14 SS-20 Coverage from Soviet Bases (Source: U.S., Organization of the Joint Chiefs of Staff, *United States Military Posture for FY 1983*, p. 28.)

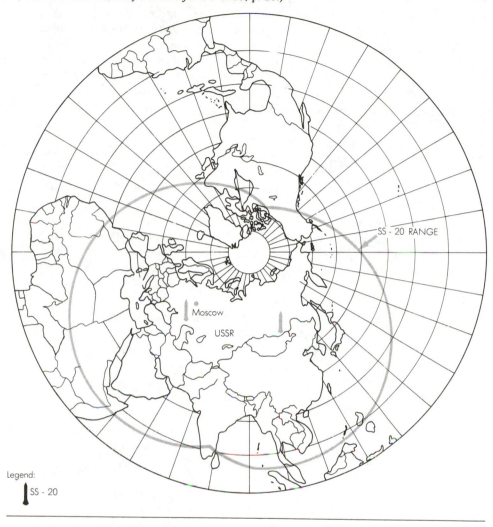

SS - 20 RANGE

Moscow

USSR

Legend:

SS - 20

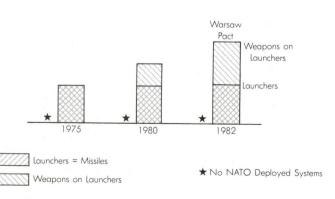

NATO — WARSAW PACT
Long - range TNF (Longer - range INF) Missiles
Land - based systems — worldwide

Warsaw
Pact
Weapons on
Launchers

Launchers

1975   1980   1982

Launchers = Missiles

Weapons on Launchers

★ No NATO Deployed Systems

Europe—The Divided Continent

Although the creation of the Common Market did establish a trading rival for the United States, it also established a greatly expanded market for American goods. Trade between the two entities increased to $13 billion in 1969, or to an amount three times the level of trade in 1958. As the 1980s began, both the United States and the Common Market found themselves more often than not in common accord that the real trade problem concerned Japan's inability or unwillingness to absorb imports in proportion as these entities accepted Japanese exports. This problem, which in part derived from unequal competitiveness, tempted both the United States and the European Community toward protectionism. But protectionism, if implemented in any direction, could soon lead to general economic warfare, including a direct clash between the United States and Western Europe.

Echoes of dissension were being heard in the early 1980s as Europe complained about American continued high interest rates, which the Europeans saw as discouraging widespread economic revival from the depressed conditions of 1981–1982. The Summit of the Industrialized Nations, meeting under President Reagan's chairmanship in June 1983, failed to make any progress on this issue.

Inside Europe, the British and the Germans kept to a tight money policy themselves (which tended to keep their own interest rates high, along with unemployment). The French, by contrast, had taken the initially easier route under Mitterand's Socialists, of producing cheap money. Internally, cheap money initially provides more purchasing power in advance of what often is its eventual corollary of inflation. Not surprisingly, the French franc soon had to be devalued.

The problem of inflation and the overextension of credit was one that reached far beyond either the United States or Europe. Already by 1981–1982 the economic crunch had become so severe that any default of Polish loans (as Poland was placed under martial law), or of Argentinian loans (as the British fleet advanced to retake the Falklands) could have triggered an economic chain-of-events comparable to that brought about by the collapse of the Kredit Anstalt in Vienna in 1931. That collapse made the overextended, short-term loan structure fall apart completely, spurring on the Great Depression.

Outside Europe, in the political field, the greatest differences in the 1980s were focused on the Middle East, as earlier they had been focused on mainland China (a nation that Europe on the whole "recognized" much sooner than did the United States). Beginning with the Arab oil embargo of 1973 (as a result of the October War with Israel), Europe felt its vulnerability. In contrast to the United States, which was then dependent on imports for 25 per cent of its oil, Europe imported a much greater percentage of its oil, and oil constituted the greatest part of Europe's energy consumption. For example, in 1977 U.S. oil production was 8,245,000 barrels per day (bpd), compared to a consumption of 17,925,000 bpd. Western Europe's figures for that year (including Yugoslavia) were 1,335,000 bpd production, compared to 13,885,000 bpd consumption. So Western Europe was far more dependent on oil imports than the United States. Taking 1973 figures, at the time of the Arab oil embargo, the Western European area imported 664,056,000 metric tons of crude oil, 488,924,000 metric tons of it from the Near and Middle East.

Europe's reaction after the embargo was primarily political. The Europeans calculated that the principal danger to their oil supplies arose as an offshoot of the Arab-Israeli question, and they sought to appease the Arabs who controlled the oil. The American reaction was primarily military—to establish a rapid deployment force for potential use in the area against what was seen as Soviet penetration and subversion in the region.

Europe also had far less feeling for the plight of Israel than did the United States. Europe had been through the horrors and destruction of World War II, of which Europe's Jews were only a more extreme case. In any event, in the postwar period, few Jews remained in continental

Europe to bring pressure on their governments. The British were relieved to be freed from their Palestine involvement (between World War I and World War II, as Mandatory power under the League of Nations) and did not want a new involvement. West Germany quite naturally approached the whole affair gingerly, in view of the horrible events of the Hitler era. In the United States, by contrast, a significant Jewish population existed which was able to focus the traditional American sympathy for an underdog on the plight of Israel, which fought off parts of the armies of five or six Arab states simultaneously in 1947–1949. The U.S. sympathy, expressed in a tangible sense by multimillion dollars of American private contributions to Israeli defense, continued through the decades. U.S. public funds were soon added to the flow of private aid, and in the fourth round of the Arab-Israeli conflict in 1973 it was only U.S. arms airlifted directly to Israel that saved the day for Israel after initial setbacks. For years the French also supplied significant arms to Israel—but for full price and for assured cash.

Such differences in interests and attitudes were the natural consequence of the different problems facing Europe and the United States. The problems would not go away and they had to be reckoned with as offsets to the significant interests that Europe and the United States continued to have in common.

6.

Issues in United States–European Relations: Europe's Division

The U.S. government, by the mid-1980s, was experiencing more than its usual sense of frustration in dealing with these crosscurrents. There was no question but that European popular fears were at a new high as the theater nuclear deployments began in late 1983. One main clue to this heightened fear was that the new deployments, especially since they had first been long debated, were seen by Europeans as making more West European areas into prime targets. The Soviet missiles were out of sight; the Western missiles were in their own "back yards."

Particularly acute was the West German reaction (with muted echoes in East Germany as well). It was unquestionably frustrating to Germans, already forced to accept the inconvenience if not humiliation of having their country divided, to see the consequences in terms of foreign troops and foreign-controlled weapons of mass destruction piled higher on both sides of the Iron Curtain line. The West German man-in-the-street found himself torn between wanting an American presence for protection and wanting the foreigners to go home and take their weapons with them, while feeling increasingly that the weapons would not protect them and that Germans could not be free of foreign troops. It was the peculiar nature of these frustrations and the German ambivalence that combined a new nationalist emphasis with a new neutralism, both in the SPD and the new Green party.

The French were also ambivalent although not quite to the same degree. They vigorously rejected the Soviet suggestion in 1983 that NATO's missile count should include British and French nuclear launchers as one offset against Soviet SS-20 numbers. The French government, in the person of President Mitterand, even spoke out vigorously against yielding to Soviet intimidation on the missile question. Even so, the French showed no willingness to return to an integrated defense role in NATO.

Soviet problems in Eastern Europe increased, too. Poland, subdued by martial law since December 13, 1981, under General Wojciech Jaruzelski, was reacting at the end of 1983, after the removal of restrictions, with sullen apathy mixed with gestures of defiance by Solidarity union leaders such as Lech Walesa. The Polish external debt remained huge and Polish worker productivity remained low.

The peoples of East Germany and Czechoslovakia, too, were frustrated by the Soviet intentions of putting SS-20 missiles on their soil.

One conclusion that might reasonably be drawn from all of this was that one way of handling Europe's division (by the deployment of rival armies and armaments along its center line) had been taken practically to its logical extreme without making any of the participants on either side feel more secure. That fact (if it was a fact) did not make any alternative more feasible.

Here we come to the first set of issues for U.S. policy: how to treat the problem arising from Europe's unnatural division.

The initial American reaction had been to prevent further deterioration in the status quo. The U.S. policy of containment, announced in the Truman Doctrine of March 12, 1947, in reference to the possible loss of Greece and Turkey to the Communist orbit, was followed by the economic "pump-priming" of the Marshall Plan and the military arrangement of NATO, all designed to rebuild Europe's war-shattered strength. The Marshall Plan aid offer, originally extended to all of Europe, was rejected by Stalin for Eastern Europe, even though Czechoslovakia and Poland in particular would gladly have taken part. The North Atlantic Pact, a simple treaty of alliance, was turned into a complex defense *organization* after the North Korean aggression incited fears of the same kind of attack occurring in Europe, especially once the United States was tied down fighting in Korea. All of these actions, though positive and effective, merely held the line where it was. They contained Soviet advances.

The Eisenhower administration criticized this approach. Eisenhower's Secretary of State, John Foster Dulles, was particularly vocal about "rollback" and "liberation," but the tragic Hungarian revolt of 1956 essentially ended such rhetoric as the realization sank in that forcing the Soviets to retreat from Hungary would mean war. It was in Eisenhower's administration that significant negotiations took place with the Soviets in the Berlin Conference of 1954, a summit at Geneva in 1955, and a new Geneva Foreign Ministers' Conference in 1959. This last event occurred in the shadow of Khrushchev's threat to close off West Berlin to Allied access—the second Berlin crisis. Khrushchev, as we saw, ultimately instead settled for sealing off captive Germany from its free counterpart by means of the Berlin Wall and land mines along the Iron Curtain. The deadlock otherwise continued. Nevertheless, the 1954 conference was notable for the "Eden Plan," which provided a plan for achieving a reunited Germany. But if that occurred, and the united Germany opted for a Western affiliation, it raised the spectre of NATO troops on the Polish frontier. The West Germans, in a note of October 27, 1955, to the Soviets, pointed out that this was not intended to happen: there would be a demilitarized zone (East Germany). But further discussions at the 1959 conference failed to convince the Soviets that the risk was worth taking. Throughout the negotiations the West never proposed a reunited and neutral Germany.

One result of the Berlin Wall and the Cuban missile crisis was to renew Western efforts merely to hold the line against further Soviet advances, and President Kennedy, apart from declaring, "Ich bin ein Berliner" and reasserting the U.S. intention to defend Berlin, had no opportunity to do much else about it.

The U.S. approach favoring free decisions for Soviet-occupied areas did not alter in subsequent administrations, but under President Nixon the emphasis shifted to an implied acceptance (or at least toleration) of the status quo under the rubric of "détente." Détente implied logically that the European status quo would not be altered without the free agreement of both sides. Kissinger was to complain later about Soviet actions in Africa, but President Nixon also altered the status quo in Asia rather drastically by finally terminating the Vietnam War and by sending Henry Kissinger to Beijing as the first step toward improved Sino-American relations.

With the Vietnam War, the "China card," and SALT, Nixon in effect never got around to dealing frontally or specifically with either the German problem or the division of Europe. What little attention the division of Europe got from Nixon was insignificant. However, as mentioned earlier, *Ostpolitik* and a more relaxed approach to the Berlin problem by then had been pushed by the West Germans. In short, once neither the Soviets nor the West Germans were making active efforts to upset the existing division, it would have been difficult for the United States to take the lead in altering a status quo that nobody (except in Eastern Europe) seemed actively interested in changing. This was the situation when President Carter took office and it was still the situation when President Reagan succeeded him in 1981.

At that point, with Poland full of ferment, the issue again was raised whether the continuance of the situation was really less dangerous than seeking some change, with Soviet consent. Yet that very idea had little appeal considering the deep freeze into which U.S.–Soviet relations fell in 1982–1983.

In advocating free institutions for all European states, U.S. policy has not in any way been in conflict with that of its European allies, including West Germany. Even on tactics, there have been no real differences over whether and how the Soviets can be induced to withdraw. None of the nations involved in the negotiations since World War II has really believed that the Soviets have any overwhelming or sustained interest in withdrawing from Central Europe. The most they have hoped for is that NATO guarantees to the Soviets that NATO's front line would not be advanced if Soviet troops withdrew to Poland or Russia might induce a change in Soviet policy. These nations have not really been prepared to see a complete and mutual American and Soviet withdrawal. The ambivalence of Europe over the prospect of German reunification is effectively concealed by the Soviet unresponsiveness—to which there has been just one, temporary exception. In February 1955, at a Warsaw, Soviet-controlled interparliamentary conference on the German question, 150 delegates, "including representatives from the Soviet Union," unanimously voted to offer negotiations "on free, controlled elections in Germany, such as were proposed by Sir Anthony Eden . . . a year ago at the Berlin Conference. . . ." Such negotiations would also assume "that the territorial integrity of a neutralized Germany should be guaranteed by the European states and the United States."[8] Before this news reached the United States, Malenkov, who had succeeded Stalin, was overthrown (February 8, 1955). His successor, the hardliner Khrushchev, later spoke (March 1963) of Malenkov's "provocative proposal to liquidate" the GDR. Unfortunately, that brief moment in February 1955 was the only time when Russia, even in passing, seriously considered withdrawal from Germany.

Considering these counterbalancing interests in which change threatens new dangers to replace ones now well known, there does not seem to be any real point in the United States trying to be more European than the Europeans in championing European freedoms and German unity. At the same time, it would be a serious mistake to assume that Soviet domination of Eastern Europe and its position in Central Europe can or will continue indefinitely without raising more significant strains and stresses than in the past. For one thing, economic prosperity in Europe until 1981 kept Europeans generally in a more optimistic frame of mind. It is not clear that this will continue. Then there is the additional prospect of more "Polish situations." And what if East Germany blows up in revolt? Just to mention these possibilities should deflate any belief that the situation cannot turn adverse.

Since all of the U.S. proposals for Soviet withdrawal have lacked the feature the Warsaw conference attached to the Eden Plan—that a reunified Germany must be neutral—it is apparent why the proposals have had little appeal to the Soviets. In Chapter 22 we return to this issue within the context of the overall United States–Soviet security balance.

---

[8] *New York Times,* Feb. 11, 1955, pp. 1 and 4.

Issues in United States–European Relations: The Soviet Threat

If, turning to the second problem, the Soviet armed forces remain in their advanced positions, what should be the American response?

We saw that under Truman the initial American response was to propose a North Atlantic Pact (1949) which included a solemn pledge of U.S. backing. After the North Atlantic Treaty Organization came into existence in 1951, no American administration gave any serious thought either to withdrawing U.S. forces from NATO Europe or to changing U.S. ties with NATO.

In the U.S. Senate, by contrast, for some years a fluctuating number of senators supported the "Mansfield Resolution" calling for withdrawal of U.S. troops from Europe. As with any resolution of this type, it appealed to supporters on diverse grounds, ranging from the conviction that the United States had no business maintaining a quasi-permanent force in Europe to those who felt that Europe should carry more of the load of its own defense. In fact, it was over the issue of the *form* and *share* of the U.S. contribution that the policy question kept being raised again and again after NATO came into being. We have already discussed the question of conventional versus nuclear defenses. Now we must look at the other aspects of the form and share question.

The United States has consistently discouraged Europe from developing its own national nuclear arsenals or even an integrated European nuclear force without any American finger on the trigger. American reasoning has been that European nuclear forces could not, in the nature of the resources available, achieve more than a severely limited capability—enough to persuade the Soviets to blanket those European forces with nuclear strikes but not enough to deter any Soviet assault. Worse, with several nuclear arsenals to face, the Soviets might feel compelled to strike at all as a preventive precaution when only one nation had taken what the Soviets might consider provocative action. Such U.S. arguments, when all was said and done, were hardly more than rationalizations for the American wish to control completely the nuclear option. This view reflected the U.S. conviction that the United States knew better than the rest when to consider resort to nuclear weapons. Britain, disagreeing, quietly proceeded to create and maintain a modest, submarine-based nuclear capability. France, more flamboyantly, proceeded to build a more capable *force de frappe*. Germany, heedful of the tremors that would shake all of Europe, refrained from any nuclear weapons actions—as it had promised on admission to NATO.

A variation on the U.S. attitude on the form and share question occurred under President Kennedy when the United States proposed a multilateral nuclear force of warships manned by crews drawn from various NATO nations. Behind this gambit was the scarcely disguised U.S. intent to retain ultimate control through its own national military command structure. De Gaulle quickly vetoed this proposal. It was never clear how this MLF, as it was called, would really solve the problem. If two or three nations share having fingers on a single nuclear trigger that particular weapon will not be fired until all these nations concur. But unless all nuclear weapons are so encumbered, individual action would remain possible. So would a conflict that began with an act of conventional force, which then escalated to a nuclear threshhold. In the end, there is no mechanical way that members of NATO can be assured in every case that one of them may not start a war which quickly engulfs the rest, whether they wanted it or not. The real remedy for this situation is to arrange for all foreign troops to withdraw behind their own frontiers. Short of that, the remedy is to seek progressively to reduce unnecessary tensions caused by unduly large troop and arms confrontations across the Iron Curtain.

This last proposition began to be explored in 1973, under the name of "Mutual and Balanced Force Reductions" (MBFR). Discussions quickly ran into problems as NATO proposed a reduction in the ground force manpower of both sides to equal levels and the withdrawal of a Soviet tank army, which certainly would have helped NATO's position, while the East sought to perpetuate its superiority by proposing that all forces in the area be reduced by equal percentages in three annual stages. By 1980 each side had modified its position somewhat, the Warsaw Pact even accepting the principle of common collective ceilings on manpower, but there still were major differences concerning rival order of battle data (which specified how many troops, weapons, and the like existed, and therefore provided the base for calculating reductions), timing and amounts of phasing, specific subceilings within the overall limits, what types of arms (and whose) should be limited, and a host of associated measures. Such differences prevented progress throughout the early 1980s.

On a different tack, the Reagan administration on November 18, 1981, proposed canceling the deployment of the GLCMs and Pershing IIs in exchange for the elimination of all Soviet SS-20s, SS-5s, and SS-4s (the so-called "zero option"). The Soviets rejected Reagan's offer, responding with a proposal that NATO and the Soviet Union each reduce to 300 medium-range missiles and aircraft "intended for use" in Europe. This plan, by including British and French nuclear forces and all forward-based aircraft on the NATO side, would have precluded entirely the American deployment of GLCMs and Pershing IIs. After Washington rejected this proposal Soviet Premier Andropov announced that the Soviet Union would agree to a subceiling on missiles within the 300 limitation, a subceiling equal to the amount of (and including) British and French forces. The United States countered that it would not seek to offset all SS-20s aimed at Europe if U.S.–Soviet agreement on equal numbers globally could be achieved, and in November 1983 suggested a global ceiling of 420 warheads for medium-range missiles. Because this still would exclude British and French forces, allow some U.S. deployment, and give the West more missiles (though not warheads) than the Soviets, Moscow turned it down immediately. When American missiles began arriving in Europe at the end of November, the Soviets, having failed in their efforts to prevent deployment via negotiations, walked out of the talks.

If clever devices for sharing the nuclear trigger had drawbacks, if some NATO nations besides the United States were creating nuclear arsenals, if MBFR and arms talks were stagnant, if negotiations for withdrawal behind national frontiers remained only an idea, if Soviet troops continued in place in the heart of Europe, and if the Soviets also pushed the SS-20 program, then Europe and NATO had to face the unpleasant issue of what to do in response.

It is in this context that the "nuclear freeze" ferment had to be addressed. On the one hand, it made little sense for an endless proliferation of arms to go on, yet it was difficult to establish what "parity" would consist of, especially when the line between "theater nuclear forces" (with "European" ranges) and strategic weapons proper (with greater ranges) kept blurring once one introduced the question of Backfire bombers, nuclear submarines, and cruise missiles. The problem here is no different from the oldest problem encountered in traditional balance of power thinking: that a margin of safety is needed to ensure against error. In short, "superiority" equals "equality." Only in *types* of weapons are parity agreements likely; once one tries to weigh a set of different weapons against another nation's set, the problem begins to be too difficult, especially since the opposed nations in one case may have additional possible enemies (Russia, with China). The cardinal principle of third-party influences applies very definitely to bilateral arms negotiations.

In the absence of East-West agreements restricting the deployment of ballistic missiles such as the SS-20 or Pershing II, the only feasible alternative for NATO, short of accepting theater nuclear inferiority plus conventional inferiority (as things are now) was to install the Pershing IIs and GLCMs. But, because those missiles had to be installed on West European soil it was wise for the United States, in choosing its policy orientation, to try to let Europe take the lead.

The initiative properly had to come from Europe, since the Europeans are the ones who are most directly involved. Once Europe took that initiative, it was also in the United States' interest to respond positively while working toward more positive approaches to the endless arms race.

8.

Issues in United States–European Relations: Diversity of Interests

The third problem, divergent interests, is the most far-reaching. On the issue of whether the United States should encourage further European integration, an avoidance orientation would seem advisable; it would seem advisable not to push integration but also not to oppose it. The issue was clear-cut in the 1940s and 1950s. Without a substantial unity of effort, Europe would remain too weak. That is not the problem now. Now Europe has come up against both quantitative and qualitative problems that it must solve itself and which the United States is in no position to solve. The European Economic Community has grown in numbers, and recent new members have introduced elements obviously difficult for older members to reconcile with their own interests. If, as projected, the Community grows further, this aspect will become more difficult. (Portugal and Spain will each be more difficult to digest.) The European Community already has seen the difficulty of keeping national currencies aligned in value while each nation goes its own way on tax policies and the rest. The hopes expressed in the 1970s to agree on a single EEC currency had largely been abandoned by the 1980s as the German mark increased steadily against the French franc (although both weakened against the dollar). And disagreements over proposed cuts in farm spending and "unfair" contributions (particularly Britain's demand for a $1 billion refund) surfaced again at the December 1983 summit meeting in Athens, producing almost total deadlock. On the qualitative side, there is no uniformity about desired political life styles: while Germany moved to the right (as did Britain), France moved to the left. Each might move again. Uniformity cannot be imposed. So the future of the EEC is really up to its own members. It is not clear that the United States has an interest to serve trying to persuade the European Community to do anything else. An avoidance orientation here, too, is desirable.

The issue of divergencies on weapons has already been addressed, so we now turn to divergencies outside Europe.

NATO as a military and political grouping is a response to a power problem shared by its members. Whatever any of them may have in mind for dealing with problems or issues outside Europe, it will not change what brought NATO into existence unless or until they no longer see the Soviet Union as a potential military threat. But, by the same token, there is no reason why facing a common threat in Europe makes their interests common or compatible throughout the world. The existence of both phenomena simultaneously may not be desirable, but it is to be expected. This situation is merely a parallel example of what we just said about the EEC: agreeing on certain things does not mean agreeing on everything. To put the point in traditional political terms, politics makes for strange coalitions, comparing everything to everything—which would miss the point, that the agreement in politics is on a program or objective, not on creating identical sets of values or life styles.

When the British and French in 1956 moved militarily against Nasser's Egypt, after Nasser nationalized the Suez Canal Company, the United States put extreme pressure, successfully, on those NATO allies to abort their operation. Whether the U.S. action was wise or not, and although it cooled relations for some time, it did not remove the common agreement of all three NATO members that they had to stand together against any Soviet threat to Europe. When the

U.S. diplomats were made hostage in Iran, world sympathy was with the United States. But U.S. allies were not anxious to see an American military involvement there as a consequence. When Russia in December 1979 invaded Afghanistan, U.S. allies were less willing to institute sanctions against the Soviet Union than the United States. And when Poland was placed under martial law after the ferment of 1981, NATO was more cautious about instituting sanctions. As already mentioned, Europe is recurrently more cautious on the Arab-Israeli issue. On the other hand, when Argentina seized the Falkland Islands in 1982, Britain's European allies quickly instituted limited economic sanctions against Argentina, whereas before the United States sided with Britain it first avoided involvement and then sought to be an "honest broker" between its OAS ally and its NATO ally. The point of this recital is that NATO continued intact as an alliance throughout, and that each member of NATO dealt with each successive issue according to the number and seriousness of its interests in it. That is quite natural and there is little the United States could do about it, even if it tried. It is not possible either to manufacture common interests artificially or to provide uniform interests even between or among old friends.

The greatest policy gulf between the United States and its European allies was in reference to Middle East issues. We have seen that there is even a fundamental difference on the root cause of the trouble there, the United States being far more inclined to blame the Soviets for the continued tension and bloodshed in the region—a point we consider further in Chapter 19. The greater U.S. willingness to defend the oil supply routes (especially from the Persian Gulf) from interference from any source contrasted oddly with the far lower-key responses from those Western European nations and Japan who were, in fact, much more dependent on these oil supplies.

9.

Summing Up

United States policy toward Europe was slow to recognize the military and security problem that even a democratic Russia (let alone a Communist Soviet Union) would pose if allowed to advance so far into the center of Europe and remain there. The United States was not inclined (because of its past-future linkages) to see the problem in balance of power terms, by reflecting that the destruction of the military capability of Russia's most dangerous neighbors, Germany and Japan, would (through changing third-party influences) permit and encourage Russian ambitions to control the approaches to Soviet soil, permanently if possible. Once the realization came, the United States organized an effective blocking action to further Soviet advances, although never seriously exploring what it might take to restore the fate of Europe into its own hands by inducing mutual superpower military withdrawal from European soil. Part of the explanation for this inaction was Western Europe's own ambivalence over the German reunification question, just as Germany's own ambivalence (previously detailed in the nuclear question) made it unwise for the United States to insist too strongly on taking the lead in pushing issues to resolution. As we have said more than once, given these ambivalences, in many cases a low-key or avoidance orientation was called for. Where the United States was least willing to play a minimal role was in reference to the Middle Eastern interests of its NATO allies. There the United States and NATO were far from fully agreed on how to assess and respond to Soviet influence and policy. A similar divergence was true between Europe and the United States when it came down to doing business with the Soviets, especially by contributing to Soviet technological advance. To those issues, too, there was no simple solution.

18

On Its Own—A Stable Asia?

We moved toward China not to expiate liberal guilt over our China policy of the late 1940s but to shape a global equilibrium. It was . . . to give us a balancing position to use for constructive ends.

Henry Kissinger
White House Years

Asia is a vast realm containing more than half the earth's people and resources. It also is an area of great diversity and turmoil where regional relationships have often been fluid and uncertain. For decades Asian politics have been shaped above all by the interacting interests and policies of three "local" great powers: China, Russia, and Japan—relations in which before World War II the United States seldom played a central role. By contrast, since 1945 America has been very deeply involved in Asian affairs. Indeed, all U.S. wars since 1945 have been fought on Asian soil. More than 100,000 Americans gave their lives in the "struggles against Communist aggression" in Korea and Vietnam. Although it is clear that the fundamental objective of contemporary U.S. Asian policy must be to prevent Asia from being dominated by a single hostile power, the forward-deployment, confrontation orientation that was employed by the United States between 1950 and 1970 was an exceedingly costly and controversial means of seeking that objective. In the post-Vietnam era, a new and sounder approach was obviously necessary, an approach that would protect American vital interests in a more effective, more prudent manner.

1.

The Strategic Problem: How to Ensure an Asian Security Balance

The fundamental problem, then, confronting the United States in Asia after Vietnam was to design a policy to maintain an appropriate Asian security balance without the recurrent commitment of U.S. troops. Crucial to an implementation here was step 1—determining who is involved. Because the Soviets by geography were and would remain an Asian power, they inevitably would be a major player. Also important would be China, Japan, and India as they regulated their relations with each other and with the two superpowers. Especially the Chinese.

312

And, of course, the United States would also be important. Out of the framework of this problem came many of the issues to which U.S. policy had to be responsive.

In the late 1960s, as the Vietnam War wound down, United States relations were excellent with Japan, fair with Pakistan, poor with India, and bad with China.

It was at this point that both Beijing and Washington began to reappraise their strategic positions with the mutual intent of conserving enemies and reducing the strategic freedom so gratuitously granted the Soviets over the years by Chinese-American hostility. But there were serious problems to be resolved. First, how far should and could Washington go in improving relations with Beijing? Was an alliance with Beijing possible or desirable? Second, what should Washington do about the Taiwan issue?

While attaining more cooperative relations with mainland China had great strategic merit for the United States, Beijing still continued to view Taiwan as an integral part of China. Existing American treaty relations and aid to Taiwan extending back for decades were serious obstacles to the prospect of normalization of relations. Even if the United States were to consider simply dropping Taiwan, it had to consider also what impact that would have on American credibility, both in Asia and elsewhere. How third parties such as Indonesia, Malaysia, Singapore, Thailand, and the Philippines (composing ASEAN, the Association of Southeast Asian Nations) would react to close American-Chinese ties would also weigh in making the choices. Although such third parties were leery of the Soviets, would they not be equally concerned over growing Chinese influence? After all, "Middle Kingdom" legacies and territorial concerns linger on.

These questions were not resolved merely by the establishment of diplomatic relations between the United States and the People's Republic of China on January 1, 1979, as later parts of this chapter indicate. Some loose talk of "playing the China card," which flourished after this event, implied a Chinese role as an American puppet, but how much could the United States control China? Would it, in fact, be within Washington's power to do so? Would not an attempt to do so simply alienate the proud Chinese rulers? There was a meaningful difference between trying to control China and taking advantage of the opportunities produced by the policies of the Asian nations as they sought their own objectives. Merely listing these shows how much easier it is to design the general policy course than to choose the most profitable nuance of orientation within it to implement.

In addition to fleshing out an appropriate China policy, if the United States hoped to maintain an Asian security balance while itself playing a more conservative role, it would have to take account of the growing importance of Japan.

Japan seemed destined to play a gradually larger role in regional affairs, in a politico-military sense as well as economically. But exactly how and when this would occur was far from clear, nor were all its effects predictable. Would it, for example, occur in such a way as to increase stability, or would changes in Japanese policies produce such a chaotic balance that the most likely disturber of the peace in Asia would be encouraged by the disorganization? What could the United States do to encourage stability in light of the anticipated changes? To what degree should the United States' political role also have a military component?

There were two specific issues with Japan: The first was whether the United States should encourage a greater military role for Tokyo. How much influence could Washington have in this regard? If the United States were to urge the Japanese to enhance their defense capabilities significantly, would the Japanese be likely to do so if they thought Washington would fill the breach if they did not? On the other hand, if Japan was *not* willing to play a larger military role, what should U.S. military policy be where Japanese interests were concerned?

The second issue posing serious decision choices was whether amicable relations between Japan and the United States could be maintained if Japan continued its enormous economic growth, the American trade deficit continued to grow, and Tokyo continued to be a prime com-

MAP 5

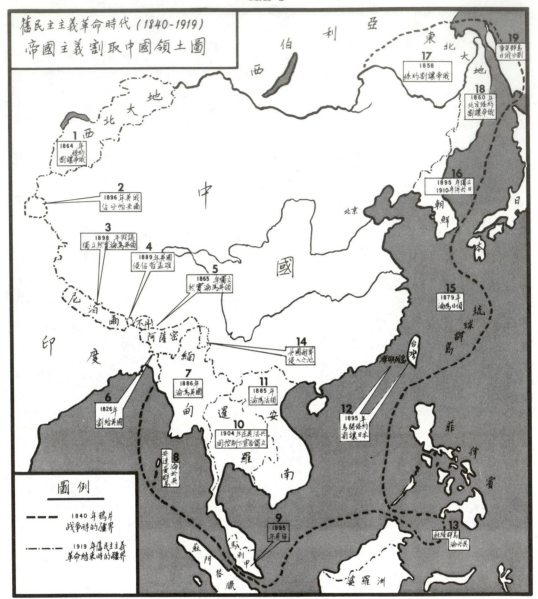

A CHINESE VIEW OF CHINA

The map is reprinted from a Chinese textbook entitled, *A Brief History of Modern China, 1954*. The legend in the bottom left in the map reads: *Dash Line:* Borders at the time of the Opium War, 1840; *Dash-and-Dot Line:* Borders on the conclusion of the era of the old Democratic Revolution, 1919. Basic translation of the text inside the map:

"1 The great North-West [covering huge segments of the present-day Soviet Republics of Kazakhstan, Kirghizia and Tajikistan] was seized by Imperialist Russia under the Treaty of Chuguchak, 1864.

2 The Pamirs was secretly divided between Britain and Russia in 1896.

3 Nepal went under the British after 'Independence' in 1898.

4 Che-Man-Hsiung [i.e., present-day Sikkim] was occupied by Britain in 1889.

5 Pu-tan [i.e., the whole of Bhutan] went under Britain after 'Independence' in 1865.

petitor for world markets as well as for the U.S. market (meanwhile keeping the United States effectively out of *Japanese* markets).

As the United States faced the post-Vietnam world, relations with Japan posed nearly as complicated a set of issues as did relations with China.

Finally, as the United States sought policies that would help establish and maintain a stable balance, it had to choose policy orientations that took account of other Asian nations such as India and Pakistan. In one sense, most of the states of Asia were "natural allies" of the United States, meaning they had no desire to be controlled by the Soviet Union and would strongly resist any such effort. But India in particular also feared a resurgent China, especially one linked to Pakistan, and the problem here for the United States was to preserve a suitable equilibrium on the subcontinent without severely alienating India.

But, first, some historical perspective.

2.

The Chinese Relationship

China is a great civilization stretching back thousands of years, a civilization that for untold centuries perceived itself the center of the civilized world (the "Middle Kingdom"). For many hundreds of years China exerted dominion over (much of) Asia, at one time or another controlling all or parts of Vietnam, Laos, Kampuchea, North and South Korea, Burma, Singapore, Nepal, Malaysia, Indonesia, Taiwan, many islands, and the over 500,000 square miles taken by Russia in 1858 and in 1860.

By the early nineteenth century though, the Manchu Empire had become weak and fragmented, incapable of responding effectively to external threats. Soon foreign encroachment began, and by the dawning of the twentieth century much of China was under foreign control (see Map 5 and commentary). These encroachments, along with internal pressures, sparked the "Boxer" rebellion (discussed in Chapter 11) and the dispatch of foreign military forces to protect the foreign legations and restore order. The Chinese government, which had been unable to oppose effectively either the Boxers or the foreigners, was thoroughly discredited. In 1911 the long-expected Chinese revolution began. China now was prey to rival warlord groups, and rival "central" governments existed at Beijing and Canton. In 1921 the Chinese Communist party (CCP) took its place among the competing factions. The CCP initially collaborated with Chiang

---

6 Ah-sa-mi [i.e., the whole of Assam, NEFA, and Nagaland] was given to Britain by Burma in 1826.

7 Burma became a part of British Empire in 1886.

8 The Andaman Islands went under Britain.

9 Ma-la-chia [i.e., Malaya and Singapore] went under Britain, 1895.

10 Hsien-Lo [i.e., the whole of Thailand] was declared 'Independent' under joint Anglo-French control in 1904.

11 Annam [covering the present-day North and South Vietnam, Laos and Cambodia] was captured by the French in 1885.

12 Taiwan and P'enghu Islands were relinquished to Japan in accordance with the Treaty of Shimonoseki, 1895.

13 Su-Lu Island was 'occupied by the British.'

14 The Region where the British crossed the border and committed aggression.

15 Liu-Chiu [i.e., Ryukyu Islands] went under Japan in 1879.

16 Ch'ao-hsien [i.e., Korea] 'independent' in 1895; to Japan, 1910.

17 and 18 The Great North-East [covering a huge area of the Soviet Far East] was given Russia under the Treaties of Aigun (1858) and Peking (1860).

19 K'u-Ye [i.e., Sakhalin] was 'divided between Japan and Russia.' "

Kai-shek's Nationalists (Kuomintang), but Chiang launched a military campaign to gain control of all China, and by 1928 he clearly was winning. The Communists, now Chiang's bitter enemies, fled under the leadership of Mao Zedong into the northwest provinces.

Japan, alarmed at China's progress toward unity, used the Mukden incident in 1931 as an excuse to absorb Manchuria. Following this, Tokyo began to encroach on China proper, and by 1933 Japan had advanced south of the Great Wall. Although a pause occurred at this time, the threat to Chinese sovereignty remained, and in 1937, after an agreement between Chiang and the Communists to make common cause against the Japanese, the Sino-Japanese war began in earnest. In the ensuing hostilities Japan occupied the cities, but the rural areas always remained Chinese.

When this war blended into the larger struggle of World War II, ending in Japanese defeat, the tenuous cooperation between the Nationalists and Communists broke down and China was plunged again into civil war. The United States attempted mediation, but the gulf between the parties was too great and by the end of 1949 Chiang and his remaining forces were defeated and forced to escape to Taiwan. Mao and the Communists had triumphed. Interestingly, the Soviet attitude toward Beijing was (privately) distinctly negative. Stalin never had much confidence in Communist regimes he did not control through Red Army occupation.

A Sino-Soviet alliance was concluded in early 1950, inaugurating a period when the peoples of the two very different Russian and Chinese cultures attempted collaboration. Then in mid-1950 the Korean War broke out. By November 1950, Chinese "volunteers" were fighting American units on the Yalu frontier, while the Soviets supplied war material to the North Koreans and Chinese. To Americans, it seemed natural to think of the struggle in Asia as "the Communist bloc versus the Free World," even though the degree of Sino-Soviet cooperation existing in the 1950s was in rather stark contrast to the usual state of Chinese-Russian relations.

Although Chinese intervention in Korea in the face of the UN advance toward the Yalu was hardly surprising, given Chinese interests and the state of relations and perceptions between Washington and Beijing, it did solidify Sino-American antagonisms. The Korean War brought the extension of the U.S. containment doctrine to Asia, and the inclusion of China as one of those to be contained. The war was followed by the formal American commitment to Chiang's government in a mutual security treaty (with similar arrangements made with South Korea). But this new alliance structure and the accompanying American forward deployments gave both China and Russia a strong common incentive to cooperate. Sino-American relations became worse as the termination of the Korean War allowed Mao to escalate his aid to the Viet Minh in their struggle against the French in Indochina. It moved Beijing again toward armed clash with the United States as Washington agonized over whether to intervene to save the French at Dienbienphu. It may be that the moderation the Chinese and Indochinese Communists displayed at the Geneva Conference (even then in session) flowed from a realization that Washington had been provoked almost past peaceful endurance.

As 1954 blended into 1955, the spotlight shifted to the Taiwan (Formosa) area. With Korea stabilized and Indochina also divided so that friendly forces controlled the area adjacent to China's southern frontier, Mao stepped up his campaign to "recover" Taiwan and the island groups still in Nationalist hands, shelling heavily the islands of Quemoy and Matsu. American policymakers indicated the United States would participate in the islands' defense, further extending America's commitments. With the initiation of direct conversations between China and the United States in Geneva, the pressure was deflated. But no settlement was achieved on this or on other issues.[1]

Meanwhile, in the middle and late 1950s, as the Chinese and Russians confronted different power problems and priorities their policies increasingly diverged, and this was reflected in sev-

[1] Indeed, in 1958 there was a second and even more severe offshore crisis.

eral areas of disagreement. Moscow did not carry through in assisting Beijing to develop its nuclear capacity. Russia did not back China sufficiently (in China's view) during the 1958 Quemoy-Matsu crisis with the United States. By 1962, Moscow was beginning seriously to negotiate arms-control agreements with the United States (such as the Nuclear Test Ban Treaty of 1963), agreements that were seriously to China's disadvantage. In 1962, during the Sino-Indian frontier war, Russia actually shipped arms to China's Indian foe. In these years, just prior to America's combat role in Vietnam, each of the Communist giants was coming to view the other as a serious threat.[2]

Ever concerned about recovering "Chinese" territory, border revision was (and remains) a fundamental objective of Chinese foreign policy. Tibet was "recovered" by force in 1950 and 1951, and, as we noted, military operations were undertaken on the Indian frontier. Meanwhile, an intensive internal struggle broke out in China as Mao attempted to reverse the increasing bureaucratization and "revisionism" of party and government officials.[3] Mao's purge, "the Great Proletarian Cultural Revolution," threw China into chaos and retarded both China's defense efforts and its economic modernization. Such continuing weakness was highly dangerous to a China with negative relations with two superpowers, one on the east (and north and south), the other on the west (and north). China, confronted by its drift into a situation completely contrary to the principle of the conservation of enemies, had to consider a reshuffling of counterbalancing national interests. The Chinese realization of their need coincided in time with the American realization that the Vietnam War was a very expensive and not very effective way of maintaining a stable Asian security balance. The path was cleared for America's "China card" (or China's "American card") to be played.

3.

The Japanese Relationship

As discussed in earlier chapters, the American relationship with Japan after World War I was at first uneasy and then antagonistic. After Japan was first opened to the outside world in the last third of the nineteenth century after centuries of isolation, it modernized rapidly. Going to war with China in 1894, Japan ended Chinese influence in Korea and gained Taiwan and the Pescadores. In 1904, in a new war with Russia, Japan ended Russian encroachment on Korea (annexing Korea in 1910) and forced Russia to return Manchuria to China. Fighting on the Allied side in World War I, Japan gained the German islands: the Marshalls, the Carolines, and the Marianas. Japan joined, too, in the Allied occupation of Siberia, though ultimately withdrawing its forces under American pressure. We saw already how Japan gradually encroached militarily on China in the 1930s, creating the puppet state of Manchukuo to which U.S. Secretary of State Stimson, uneasy about the gradual increase in Japanese power, addressed his "nonrecognition" doctrine.

Japan came to a strategic crossroads in 1941, when Germany attacked Russia. Counterbalancing interests led in two entirely different directions: either to attack Russia or attack the United States.

The latter offered Japan the most lucrative possibilities. If a Russo-German war exhausted Russia, which seemed likely, Russia could not thwart Japan's conquest of a huge mainland empire. And the chances for enormous gains in the Pacific for a resource-poor Japan were unlikely ever again to be so great. So Tokyo prepared for total war with the United States.

---

[2]China's detonation of its first nuclear device in October 1964 added another element to the equation. By 1966 four devices had been exploded and a limited-range missile capability was evidenced.

[3]By "revisionism" Mao meant an advocacy of capitalism.

Hostilities had to be initiated in a manner that would cripple American offensive power. If such a blow were to be successful, the Pacific would be in Japan's hands: major fleet units could not be replaced in less than three or four years. Surely, once the new empire was consolidated and it was evident that the continental United States was not threatened, the Japanese thought, Washington would make peace rather than undertake the enormous effort of conquering the Pacific islands one by one until finally the home islands could be subdued. This was the thought behind the Japanese attack on the U.S. fleet at Pearl Harbor on December 7, 1941. The Japanese underestimated American economic strength and badly misunderstood the American character.

As a result of the loss of World War II, Japan was stripped not only of the territorial conquests made after 1931 but also of the possessions it had gained in the late nineteenth century. Foreign occupation of Japan began. In form an Allied venture, in practice it was an almost purely American operation. All real power was in the hands of the Supreme Commander of the Allied Powers, General Douglas MacArthur, who, although ruling through the existing government, reintroduced liberal democracy and sought to reconstruct the country in the victor's image of the good society. A new constitution was promulgated, Japan renouncing armed forces and "war as a sovereign right of the nation."

With the development of the Cold War, Japan became essential to American security plans in Asia. In 1951 the Japanese Peace Treaty was signed, and with it a mutual security treaty between Japan and the United States. American troops were to be based in Japan until Japan could "assume responsibility for its own defense." The Japanese assumed no obligation *to defend American interests* outside of Japan's immediate area. During the Korean War, however, Japan became the main forward United States base, and the occupation of Japan came to an end.

From the time Japan regained sovereignty, Japanese foreign policy was set essentially within the framework of American tactics and objectives. Although Japan restored diplomatic relations with Russia in 1956, the relationship remained cool; and whereas some trade agreements were concluded with China, official Japanese relations were with Taiwan. There was some opposition to this policy. Socialists argued for freedom from U.S. policy and for diplomatic recognition of, and greater trade with, Beijing, but they could not overcome the more conservative Liberal-Democrats. Even in 1960, when in the aftermath of the U-2 incident rallies and riots protested a new Japanese-American security treaty and forced Premier Kishi to resign, the Socialists were unsuccessful. Though 50,000 demonstrators assembled outside the Diet, on June 19, 1960, the treaty was ratified.

Japan's economy expanded greatly in the 1960s, making it one of the most important industrialized nations in the world. In fiscal 1966 Japan's GNP was over $100 billion. But its growth depended heavily on continued world prosperity and an upward trend in world trade. And because Japan imported 99 per cent of its oil it was extraordinarily vulnerable to foreign politico-military pressures, particularly because its navy was totally inadequate to protect vital sea lines of communication (SLOCs). With "self-defense" forces of only about 250,000 Japan had to rely almost entirely on the United States for security against military attack.

4. _____

The Indian and Pakistani Relationship

The contact of the United States with India and Pakistan, unlike that with China and Japan, has essentially all taken place since World War II, since these nations achieved independence.

More than a thousand years earlier, prior to the eighth century, the Hindu civilization already dominated India, with primary "loyalties focused on kinship, caste, and village," and

MAP 6

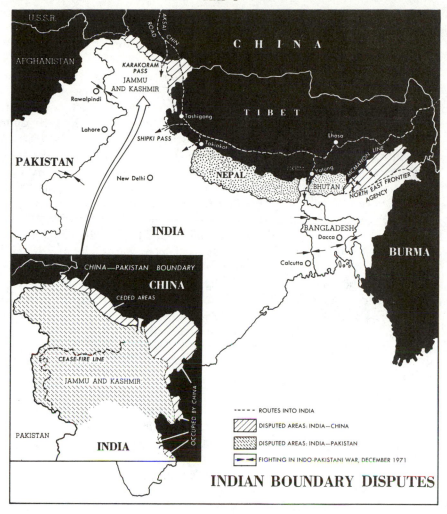

INDIAN BOUNDARY DISPUTES

ties usually being "based on blood relationships."[4] Into this atomized setting came the Muslims. Gradually increasing their influence, by the early 1500s the Muslims dominated almost the entire subcontinent. Against this backdrop of Hindu-Muslim hostility next came the Western powers intent on establishing trade and colonization, first Portugal and then Britain, Holland, and France. The Portuguese soon were driven out and the Dutch found the East Indies more lucrative. With the termination of the Seven Years War (1756–1763), France was eliminated, leaving Britain firmly in control. Although the Indians at times resisted strongly, London eventually conquered the entire subcontinent.

Although Hindu-Muslim enmity continued, from the late nineteenth century all Indian factions began strongly to demand national independence. With the end of World War II Britain, exhausted and nearly bankrupt, chose to leave. At first London had hoped to retain political unity in India, but Hindu-Muslim antagonism made that impossible. By early 1947 incredibly

[4]C. I. Eugene Kim and Lawrence Ziring, *An Introduction to Asian Politics* (Englewood Cliffs, N.J.: Prentice-Hall, 1977), p. 122.

brutal fighting between Hindus and Muslims was occurring, and over the next several months many hundreds of thousands were slain. On August 14, 1947, Pakistan became an independent state. Because the Muslims were concentrated at either end of the subcontinent, Pakistan was divided into two pieces separated by approximately one thousand miles of Indian territory. On August 15 India became independent.

Because the British had moved toward Indian independence in a relatively orderly way, relations with both new states were fairly good. Indian-Pakistani relations, in contrast, were acrimonious, and conflicts arose over the status of the princely states whose future Britain had left unsettled, especially Kashmir. Kashmir was a heavily Muslim state with a Hindu maharajah. After British rule ended, Hindu-Muslim clashes occurred in Kashmir and the maharajah requested Indian occupation and annexation. India agreed, but Pakistani irregular troops were present and fighting occurred. As hostilities continued a UN-sponsored cease-fire was agreed upon, but the armies remained and the situation was deadlocked. Neither India nor Pakistan would agree to a vote until all forces were first withdrawn, and there things remained. New fighting in 1965 solved nothing, ending in agreement to restore the previous dividing line.

Against this background of tension, Pakistan and India followed different paths in the first two decades after independence. Pakistan, smaller and more vulnerable, moved close to the United States, joining SEATO and the Baghdad Pact (CENTO) and receiving considerable economic and military aid. India, however, initially chose a nonalignment orientation, believing that true independence could be achieved only by avoiding identification with rival Cold War blocs. Indeed, India viewed American policy in Asia with a good deal of disquiet, fearing the conversion of Asia into a Cold War battlefield. On regional issues, though, India took a very active stance, especially relations with Pakistan and (after 1962) with China. In either case, Indian policy was heavily larded with moralistic pronouncements and in 1961 India forcibly took the Goa enclaves in India from Portugal. But on Cold War matters New Delhi studiously avoided making commitments.

Despite India's stance and America's containment strategy, for much of the period United States–Indian relations were quite good. Various American leaders, especially Eisenhower and Kennedy, saw India as the primary alternative to the Chinese model of development for the area, a "showcase" of democracy and capitalism in the struggle with communism for the allegiance of the Third World. From 1946 to 1968, India received approximately $7 billion in military and economic aid, more than any other state outside of Europe except South Korea.[5]

The 1965 Indian-Pakistani hostilities in some ways were a watershed. Existing preconceptions and mutual antagonisms were strengthened, but now accompanied by a substantial and decided shift in American and Soviet fortunes. Soviet influence in India already had been increasing steadily, helped by Moscow's support in the 1962 conflict with China. The United States with some difficulty had maintained good relations with both India and Pakistan to this point, supplying economic and military aid to both (much to Pakistan's irritation). But when the fighting broke out in the summer of 1965, Washington, because the weapons it supplied were supposed to be used only against Communist aggression, cut off aid to both parties. (Washington in the process violated the principle of conservation of enemies by creating antagonism all the way around.) Pakistani-United States relations cooled markedly, the Pakistanis sharply criticizing America's Vietnam policy and becoming more cooperative with Beijing. And New Delhi, seeing Moscow's growing influence and reliability as an arms supplier, began to cultivate more harmonious relations with the Soviets.

[5]Cecil V. Crabb, Jr., *American Foreign Policy in the Nuclear Age,* 3rd. ed. (New York: Harper & Row, 1972), p. 362.

5.

Nixon-Kissinger-Ford: Designing a New Approach

Richard Nixon and Henry Kissinger came to power at a time when these and other changes in the international system had brought about a radical transformation of the problems faced by the United States. Recognizing that the American political consensus on which post–World War II policy had been built lay in ruins, and confronted with a world in which effective power was ever more diffused and relationships were increasingly fluid, the new administration was determined to alter course.

Nixon and Kissinger believed that the changes currently underway in the international system could not be stopped. What was necessary in the design of a new approach was to make those changes work for the United States. As in the past, the Soviets had to be contained, but this had to occur within a stable multilateral equilibrium. To obtain such an equilibrium an interlinked web of bilateral and multilateral pressures would have to be fashioned, a web that took advantage of the natural "rules" and tendencies in the system and the propensities and interests of the major players. Diplomatic solutions would be emphasized as much as possible, but the Soviets would also have to know that Washington was willing to fight to protect its vital interests if necessary.

In immediate terms that meant that the United States must withdraw from Vietnam (in a manner that would satisfy public opinion but not harm United States credibility) while moving toward a normalization of relations with China (but do so in a way that would not unduly provoke the Soviets) and at the same time strengthen the defensive arrangements with Japan.

America's number one problem in Asia was to revamp relations with China. Nixon and Kissinger came to office convinced that rapprochement with Beijing was imperative (though they were not exactly sure how they would do it). Reciprocally, in a clear illustration of the impact of third-party influences, the Soviet invasion of Czechoslovakia in 1968 had convinced Mao Zedong that American-Chinese reconciliation was imperative; Beijing had to reduce its enemies so it could concentrate on the Moscow threat.

As might be expected given the historical legacies, early American efforts toward China were somewhat tentative and ambiguous. But after Sino-Soviet border clashes occurred in March 1969, Nixon and Kissinger acted boldly, issuing a series of unilateral signals and communications to third parties that made it apparent that the United States wanted better relations with China. Though not responding directly, Beijing subtlely signaled that it understood and agreed. To facilitate the dialogue Washington set up a secure communication channel to Beijing through Pakistan. When new Sino-Soviet fighting broke out in August, and the Russians inquired what the United States would do in the event of a Soviet military strike against Chinese nuclear facilities, the Nixon administration decided that in the event of a Sino-Soviet war the United States would have to support China.[6]

After more signals, direct contacts were established, and in early 1970 ambassadorial discussions were resumed at Warsaw.[7] Each side, without foreknowledge of the other's plans, had prepared a proposal for direct high-level talks. Though subsequently there were interruptions in the process because of the U.S. incursion into Cambodia and other current events, the stakes were too high for either side to be deflected by lesser matters. In January the possibility of a presidential visit to Beijing was broached. After further messages concerning the timing, venue,

---

[6]See Henry Kissinger, *White House Years* (Boston: Little, Brown, 1979), pp. 183ff.

[7]From 1955 to 1969 the United States and China had conducted ambassadorial level talks, first in Geneva, then in Warsaw. They had been in abeyance since February 1969.

agenda, and the like of a meeting or meetings, on April 27, 1971, Beijing extended an official invitation for either a special envoy or the President, or both, to come to Beijing, the modalities to be worked out through the Pakistanis.[8]

From July 9–11, 1971, Kissinger, provided with a "cover" by Pakistan President Yahya Khan, held secret talks with Zhou Enlai and Mao Zedong in Beijing. Recognizing that little concrete business could be accomplished, the parties concentrated on building confidence, clearing away the misperceptions and distrust that had been dominant in their mutual relations for so long, and examining the nature of fundamental interests and needs. It was evident that, specific differences aside, there was considerable similarity in terms of what the parties thought necessary to produce equilibrium, and in the strategic advantages to be obtained from reducing mutual enmity. Upon Kissinger's return and favorable report, Nixon issued his announcement of the trip and the plans for a Chinese-American summit.

6.

Nixon-Kissinger-Ford: Implementing a New Approach

To make sure the Soviets could not torpedo the new approach, Washington increased its contacts with China by a secret channel in Paris. The Nixon administration even went so far as to keep the Chinese informed of all its moves with Moscow, and its assessments of Soviet intentions. In October, Kissinger undertook a second preparatory trip, settling as many of the details of the summit as possible prior to the actual meeting itself, including the drafting of most of the communiqué that was to be issued at the summit's completion.

On February 21, 1972, Richard Nixon arrived in China, the first time an American President had visited the Chinese People's Republic. In conversation with Chinese leaders Nixon stressed that America's diplomacy was based on other state's *policies,* not their domestic structure or ideology. Neither China nor the United States was a threat to the other, he said, and their national interests generally were compatible. For their part, the Chinese made it clear that the Soviets had become their major security concern. There were, of course, many policy differences. As pointed out in Chapter 14, the Shanghai communiqué format of stating separate points of view allowed the parties to state their positions on subjects on which they disagreed. On Taiwan, for example, each side reaffirmed its existing position, in effect postponing the issue until later. But the differences were not allowed to obscure the strategically more important compatibilities. Significantly, the parties agreed that they were opposed to "hegemony," hegemony being a code word for Soviet domination.

The opening to China and the beginning of the process of normalization constituted a fundamental turning point in American foreign policy. But whether the promising beginning ultimately would prove as beneficial as it first appeared was not self-evident. And in the eyes of some, progress for the Nixon, Kissinger, and then Ford years was disappointing. Although in 1973 the two countries established liaison offices in each other's capitals, the improved communications did not immediately lead to further agreements; trade and personnel exchanges expanded, but not at the rate optimists had expected. China was concerned about and highly critical of détente, believing that it involved appeasement of the Soviets. There was also no movement toward a convergence of views on Taiwan.

It was not only the state of American-Chinese relations that was unclear as 1976 drew to a close. There also was enormous uncertainty over China's domestic situation in the wake of the deaths earlier in the year of Mao and Zhou. In the struggle for succession Hua Guofeng had

[8]For message text, see Kissinger, *White House Years,* p. 714.

been named Premier and Chairman of the Chinese Communist party and the "Gang of Four"—radicals led by Mao's widow—had been arrested. But it was not certain on the one hand that the "Gang" had been eliminated permanently. Neither was it clear on the other hand whether the pragmatic Deng Xiaoping, who had been dismissed in April and who many times previously had risen from seeming oblivion, would regain power. It would make a lot of difference.

Though the opening to China was the centerpiece of the Nixon-Kissinger new Asian policy, strengthening Japanese-American relations was almost as important. At issue in the late 1960s were the continued occupation of Okinawa and the scheduled renewal in 1970 of the mutual security treaty.

Okinawa had become one of the United States' most important military bases in Asia. But Japanese domestic pressures were such that to maintain the status quo would be more risky than negotiating Okinawa's reversion while arranging for use of the bases under Japanese sovereignty. And that is just what was done. In November 1969 Nixon and Japanese Prime Minister Sato agreed that Okinawa would be returned to Japan by 1972, while the United States would maintain military bases on the island with only minor restrictions on their use in conventional conflict. On the sensitive nuclear issue Washington yielded, and all such weapons were removed. Following this agreement, the mutual security treaty was renewed as scheduled.

To keep the separate pieces of the new U.S. policy in tandem was not easy—especially since Sino-Japanese relations still remained cool. In 1971, one of what became known as the "twin shocks" originated in this asymmetry, causing a decided cooling in United States–Japanese relations. Since regaining its sovereignty Japan had followed America's lead on the Taiwan issue, despite the obvious strategic and commercial advantages that closer relations with mainland China would have obtained for Japan. The Japanese were entirely unaware of the secret American negotiations with China from 1969 to 1971, and had been assured several times that there would be close prior consultation by the United States and Japan on major policy moves. Thus, when on July 15, 1971, Nixon revealed what had been happening, Tokyo was shocked and angered. There was a second shock in August, having nothing to do with China, when Nixon suddenly announced a 10 per cent import surcharge and restrictions on the dollar's convertibility into gold. Secretary of State Rogers gave Sato less than thirty minutes' prior notice of this announcement. For the next several months the United States took pains to assuage Japanese feelings and continually stressed the overarching importance of the alliance, but Japanese-American relations did not quite regain their previous warmth.

American actions did, however, produce an important and desired shift in Japanese policy—normalization of Japanese relations with the Chinese. By late 1971, the China problem for Japan had already become acute, Zhou saying that Japan had to choose between Taiwan and the PRC. Confronted with this dilemma and having long pursued a minimal nonalignment orientation in the Sino-Soviet dispute, the Japanese were hesitant, but Nixon's visit to China forced the issue. The choice was for normalization. After Tanaka Kakuei succeeded Sato as Prime Minister in July 1972, preliminary negotiations began. Soon diplomatic relations were agreed to, and Japan announced that it understood and respected the Chinese position that Taiwan was an "inalienable part" of China, describing the People's Republic as the "sole legal government in China." Diplomatic relations with Taiwan were suspended by Japan, although nondiplomatic ties were maintained. Sino-Japanese trade increased dramatically, and negotiations commenced for a treaty of peace and friendship. Concerned about the growing Soviet threat, China also strongly supported the U.S.–Japan mutual security treaty.

The Sino-Japanese normalization produced a distinct cooling in Japanese-Soviet relations. As Chinese-Japanese negotiations continued the Kremlin criticized Japan's willingness even to consider China's antihegemony demands. Meanwhile, Japanese-Soviet talks on a peace treaty remained deadlocked over the "northern territories" problem, four strategic ("Japanese") islands in the Kuriles held by the Russians since World War II.[9] Soviet Foreign Minister Gromyko was told bluntly in a January 1976 visit that the return of the islands was a prerequisite for a peace treaty. Given no encouragement, after Gromyko's departure Prime Minister Miki defiantly announced that Japan was prepared to sign a treaty with China that included an anti-hegemony clause.[10] Another irritant in Japanese-Russian relations was Tokyo's handling of a Soviet pilot's defection in a MIG-25. Making a series of lame administrative excuses, Japanese and American experts thoroughly examined the aircraft before returning it, dismantled and neatly packaged in crates.

Washington was pleased over both the growing closeness in Japanese-Chinese relations and Japan's willingness to adopt a somewhat stronger position vis-à-vis Moscow. There was less to cheer about in defense matters as the Nixon administration's efforts to persuade the Japanese to increase defense spending substantially, yielded little result. In 1976 Tokyo adopted a Defense Program Outline designed to produce improvements in both quality and functional capability, but because the plan foresaw neither quantitative increases nor major increases in defense spending, most Americans believed that its impact would be minimal. Although American-Japanese relations had rebounded substantially from the twin shocks, there still were quite different perceptions of the security threat and, consequently, asymmetrical views of defense requirements.

Turning to the third leg of the strategic triangle, the Indian subcontinent, the Nixon administration originally did not intend to become involved in disputes there. Avoidance or minimal nonalignment were the planned policy orientations. But events soon brought about a change in this plan. In the 1970 elections in Pakistan, the Awami League of Sheikh Mujibur Rahman, which advocated complete regional autonomy for East Pakistan, won an overwhelming victory. It was evident that once the National Assembly convened it would vote the League's program. To prevent this, Pakistan's President Yahya Khan postponed the Assembly session, arresting Mujibur. Widespread violence broke out in the east, followed by full-scale rebellion. The independent state of Bangladesh was proclaimed, and brutal violence followed as the Pakistani army sought to crush the rebellion.

The United States believed that an independent Bangladesh was inevitable, given the strong nationalism sweeping the area. No 40,000 troops could permanently subdue 75,000,000 people. Nixon and Kissinger's concern was the aid being given the rebels by India. In the Nixon administration's eyes, India was seeking not just an independent Bangladesh but the dismemberment of *West* Pakistan. When New Delhi in August signed a friendship treaty with the Soviets, American policymakers saw in it a calculated effort by Moscow designed to humiliate China (Pakistan's close friend) while simultaneously freeing India of worry about third-party influences on its security (i.e., a possible two-front threat). American attempts to mediate failed, Indian aid increased, and the conflict escalated.

In late November 1971 India launched an all-out offensive in the east. Washington, though believing India's wish to dominate the subcontinent to be the reason behind the war, was still more concerned about the Russians. The real issue was seen as how to respond to a Soviet effort to encourage "India to exploit Pakistan's travail in part to deliver a blow to our system of alliances, in even greater measure to demonstrate Chinese impotence."[11] The White House believed that the appropriate response was to *tilt* toward Pakistan to preserve West Pakistan as an independent state and to thwart Soviet intentions.[12] An American carrier task force was ordered into the Bay of Bengal and a hotline message was sent to Moscow calling for a cease-fire in both east and west and immediate negotiations. India, with its victory already complete in the east, on December 16 accepted the cease-fire.

[9]Russia had never signed a peace treaty with Japan after World War II.
[10]Miki had replaced Tanaka in December 1974.
[11]Kissinger, *White House Years,* p. 886.
[12]The State Department disagreed.

The United States believed it had achieved important objectives: India had stopped, West Pakistan was intact, Bangladesh was independent, and China had not lost faith in the United States' ability to react. But serious questions remain about the nature of the crisis itself. Although Washington identified the Soviets as a key actor, there is much to show that India was acting on its own. There is reason to think that India's immediate objective was only to detach East Pakistan, thereby weakening India's primary enemy in the process, rather than dismembering *West* Pakistan. Whether American policy was "successful" in this episode remains a matter of controversy. The U.S. actions certainly embittered relations with India.

Turning to U.S. policy toward Southeast Asia, it was soon evident that the Paris Peace Agreements had not really solved the problems of Indochina. Although the United States withdrew its forces on schedule, the Vietnamese combatants redeployed and reequipped. A number of small-scale skirmishes began, followed in December 1974 by a heavy North Vietnamese attack in the Mekong Delta area. In March 1975 came an all-out North Vietnamese offensive. Simultaneously, in Cambodia, the Communist Khmer Rouge increased pressures on Lon Nol's regime. Ford and Kissinger, seeking to prevent collapse in both Vietnam and Cambodia, asked Congress for emergency funds, but Congress disagreed. On April 30, 1975, with all remaining Americans evacuated (plus nearly 50,000 South Vietnamese), the Saigon government surrendered.

A few days earlier the Khmer Rouge had taken over in Cambodia, while in Laos the North Vietnamese were the power behind the Pathet Lao, which on December 3 abolished the monarchy and established a People's Democratic Republic. The "reunification" of the Socialist Republic of Vietnam was proclaimed on July 2, 1976. Despite a tremendous effort by the United States, all Indochina had now "fallen" to the Communists.

7.

Carter and the Shift Toward a Lesser Presence

When Jimmy Carter took office, the problem of maintaining an appropriate security balance in Asia appeared to require less immediate attention than it had in previous years. The Nixon and Ford administrations, confronted with the specific issue of how to manage the Chinese relationship, had opted to conserve enemies and had chosen to pursue the counterbalancing interest of limited cooperation with Beijing rather than continuing its alternative, with an orientation of confrontation.

Except for the Philippines, Jimmy Carter wanted to lessen the U.S. military presence in Asia.[13] To do that would entail (1) further normalization of relations with Beijing, (2) transferring greater responsibility for Korean defense to Korea, and (3) prodding Japan toward a larger defense effort.

Chinese relations were key and the increase in Chinese internal stability paved the way as the Central Committee restored Deng Xiaoping to all his previous posts in July 1977, and elected a relatively moderate Politburo. To exploit this, in August 1977 Secretary of State Vance was dispatched to Beijing to assure the Chinese leadership of Carter's wish to make progress. Washington specialists began drafting a briefing on legislation that would be needed to preserve nondiplomatic ties with Taiwan once diplomatic relations were shifted to Beijing.

By April 1978 Vance and National Security Adviser Brzezinski were able to specify January 1, 1979, as a target date.[14]

---

[13]The continued U.S. use of Subic Bay and Clark airfield were agreed in December 1978.
[14]Stanley Karnow, "East Asia in 1978: The Great Transformation," *Foreign Affairs: America and the World, 1978* (New York: Pergamon Press, 1979), p. 598.

Talks now proceeded at several levels and locations. Beijing's three conditions for normalization were difficult to satisfy: (1) the shift of diplomatic relations from Taipei to Beijing; (2) the withdrawal of all American forces from Taiwan; and (3) the abrogation of the U.S.–Taiwan mutual security treaty. For domestic political reasons and the impact the treaty abrogation might have on other allies, the United States hesitated. But the Carter officials were ultimately able to draft modifications that preserved the essential thrust of Beijing's conditions while altering their adverse impact, and Beijing's pragmatic leadership accepted the compromise.

By December 1978 all was in place. Formal diplomatic relations would be shifted as China demanded, but the United States would be allowed to maintain unofficial representation with Taiwan. Though both sides agreed that there was only one China and it included Taiwan, Beijing privately agreed not to contradict a public U.S. statement that Washington understood China had no intention of invading Taiwan. China also agreed that the United States did not have to abrogate the Taiwan treaty but could simply allow it to lapse in one year (as per Article 10). Finally, though Washington promised not to make new commitments to furnish military aid to Taiwan in 1979, deliveries in the pipeline could continue and fresh sales of defensive weapons could begin again in 1980. On this point of weapons sales the parties really "agreed to disagree," it being clear that the issue was not settled. On January 1, 1979, the United States and China resumed diplomatic relations.

Although the establishment of diplomatic relations between the United States and China was a seminal event, it was only one of the significant developments resulting from Chinese initiatives in the late 1970s. Beijing's new leadership was determined both to modernize dramatically China's economic system and to fashion a broad anti-Soviet coalition. In February 1978 Hua Guofeng outlined the "four modernizations," a program for major advances in agriculture, industry, science and technology, and defense that clearly would require help from the West. Diplomatically, China moved vigorously to consolidate ties with Japan. A February 1978 trade agreement worth over $20 billion was followed by an intensification of negotiations on the peace and friendship treaty. Tokyo, increasingly angered by Moscow's refusal to discuss the northern territories issue and its fortification of the islands, was receptive, and on August 12, 1978, the treaty was signed.

Increasingly isolated in the region, the Russians responded by strengthening ties with an equally receptive Vietnam, for Hanoi had been confronted by deteriorating strategic circumstances in the 1976–1978 period as relations had become increasingly strained with its fellow Communists in both Kampuchea and China. China made it clear that it considered Vietnam to be working hand-in-glove with Moscow in an effort to establish hegemony in Asia, and in August there was heavy fighting along the border. Thus Vietnam welcomed the Soviet initiative, and on November 3 a Soviet-Vietnamese Treaty of Peace and Friendship and Cooperation was signed.

Its flank presumably now protected by the Soviets, on December 17, 1978, Vietnam launched a major offensive against its erstwhile Communist allies in Kampuchea, easily expelling the brutal Pol Pot regime and occupying most of the country. A new Kampuchean government was installed under Heng Samrin and it appeared that the Vietnamese were settling in for a lengthy stay.

Meanwhile, Deng Xiaoping was in Washington to celebrate the normalization of American-Chinese relations. He indicated that the Vietnamese occupiers of Kampuchea (Russia's "Cubans" in Asia) needed to be taught a lesson and informed President Carter that China had tentative plans to attack. Concerned, Carter sought to persuade Deng not to go ahead, but his effort was unavailing. Choosing to risk the invocation of the Soviet-Vietnamese Friendship Treaty (which called for mutual assistance against aggression), in February 1979 China invaded Vietnam. The Chinese made it evident they did not intend either conquest or territorial acquisition. The goal was to "punish" Vietnam; once that had been accomplished the Chinese would withdraw (which they did). Whether Vietnam was sufficiently "punished" in the sequel is a matter for conjecture. Although China had made clear its willingness to fight to prevent Soviet-Vietnamese hegemony (and the Soviets had not intervened), Vietnam nonetheless remained the dominant military power in Southeast Asia, firmly in control of most of Kampuchea.

Events inside China prepared the way for continued "businesslike relations" with the West. China faced economic difficulties, and in 1979 Hua Guofeng announced, applying the "four modernizations," that the next three years would be a period of "readjustment" in the national economy. China's major problems, such as insufficient technology, skills, infrastructure, and capital could not be solved without Western help. The political situation reflected these economic realities and ideology took a back seat. By the end of 1980 the pragmatic Deng Xiaoping had reasserted substantially full control. All the remaining radicals were purged from the Politburo, and Hua was replaced (September) by Deng's choice, Zhao Ziyang, as Premier. Following their show trial, the Gang of Four were convicted (December). By the end of 1980, Deng's ascendancy seemed complete.

The second Carter hope, of withdrawing ground combat troops from Korea, was opposed both by the JCS and Japan. Only about 3,000 men were withdrawn before the growing fear that North Korean strength had been underestimated brought a halt to further withdrawal. Meanwhile, as we saw in Chapter 14, the violence in Asia, the continued Soviet military build-up, and events in Africa and the Persian Gulf persuaded the Carter administration by 1979 to reappraise entirely the directions and emphases of its defense policy. More and more, Washington perceived an overall, serious Soviet threat; U.S. policymakers felt it necessary to alter course accordingly. As a consequence, Washington began a cautious exploration of defense cooperation with China.

In 1979, although Washington did not sell China arms, it encouraged China to investigate possibilities in Western Europe. And in January 1980 U.S. Secretary of Defense Brown visited Beijing, stating that the United States and China shared similar strategic assessments and would strengthen contacts between their defense establishments. In the wake of Brown's visit, the United States announced it was prepared to sell China "nonlethal" military equipment—communications equipment, trucks, helicopters, and the like. The movement toward greater defense cooperation, the granting by Congress in January 1980 of most-favored-nation trading status (denied the Soviets), and a host of personnel exchanges and visits demonstrated a clear warming in Chinese-American relations.

The United States also sought to strengthen defense ties in South and Southeast Asia. In 1979, because of Thailand's anxiety over Vietnam's invasion of Kampuchea, Carter sold military equipment to Bangkok. A year later Vietnamese forces raided across the Thai border from Kampuchea to disrupt Thailand's repatriation of refugees and its toleration of sanctuaries for the Khmer Rouge. In the aftermath, more American aid was forthcoming.[15] The United States, seeking to beef up defenses on the subcontinent, also offered Pakistan a $400 million aid package over two years. Pakistani President Zia ul-Haq contemptuously dismissed the offer as "peanuts," both because of the size of the package and the fact that only "defensive" arms would be supplied. Carter was no more successful with India, Mrs. Gandhi rejecting an offer of military sales and saying that the measures the United States was taking in response to the Soviet invasion of Afghanistan were "disproportionate."

Carter's program made more (although limited) progress with Japan. Tokyo's gradually growing interest in defense problems, as reflected in the 1976 White Paper, implied an expanded effort. The new Prime Minister, Takeo Fukuda, lobbied vigorously against Carter's plan to withdraw troops from South Korea, that "dagger pointed at the heart of Japan," and the 1977 White Paper voiced growing concern about the Soviet naval build-up. By 1978–1980 Tokyo had become more and more defense conscious. Changing attitudes of Japan's neighbors, especially

---

[15]Pleasing to the United States, ASEAN termed the Vietnamese incursion an "act of aggression."

Beijing's advocacy of a defense build-up, offered promise that Japan, responding to the Soviets, would add a third-party influence alongside U.S. efforts.

But the most important factor was the startling growth in Soviet strength in Asia (itself a reaction to the "China card" and China's increased freedom). The introduction of Backfire bombers and SS-20 IRBMs into the Transbaikal and Siberian Military Districts significantly augmented the Soviet nuclear threat, since the Soviets could now target Japan as well as China and the Philippines. At sea, the Soviet Pacific fleet could deploy new surface combatants and submarines. It had augmented its power projection capabilities through the use of Vietnamese basing and port facilities. Most significantly from Tokyo's viewpoint, Soviet strength had been built up systematically in the northern territories, the most sensitive area of all for Japan.

In 1980, the Carter administration, reappraising its alternatives (maintaining or increasing pressure), stepped up its campaign for an increased Japanese defense effort. When Prime Minister Ohira visited Washington in May he pledged a serious effort to improve Japanese capabilities. But in Japanese politics major initiatives can be taken only *after* a supporting consensus is achieved. Although the Japanese agreed that the strategic circumstances were changing adversely, there was no consensus on the appropriate policy response. Following Ohira's untimely death, Zenko Suzuki, the new Japanese Prime Minister, suggested that defense spending would be increased significantly, but this turned out to mean a contemplated 9.7 per cent increase—which to Washington was not nearly enough. But even for a 9.7 increase, there was no real consensus and on December 19, 1980, the Suzuki cabinet adopted a FY 1981 budget with only a 7.6 per cent increase. Table 8 shows the 1972-1982 trend.

It was not only in defense matters that things did not go smoothly in U.S.–Japanese relations; there was also the matter of trade. From the ruins of World War II Japan had built the second largest market economy in the world. To a considerable extent this progress was dependent on foreign trade. For several years Japan had had a significant trade surplus with the United States, exceeding $5 billion in 1976. President Carter recognized that part of the problem arose from disparities in productivity, wage rates, and technology, and in some areas the Japanese had a competitive edge. These were not problems that could be solved by negotiation. But there also were issues of access to Japanese markets, the changing direction of Japanese trade (to China and "developing" Asia), and a lack of sufficient recognition in Japan that the trade problem might provoke an American protectionist reaction or even reconsideration of the security relationship. Eschewing a confrontation orientation, Carter chose to initiate low-key talks with Japan to address these issues, but despite some reduction in trade barriers by the end of the decade the U.S. trade deficit with Japan was $10 billion-plus and growing.

As the Carter years drew to a close there not only was unease in Washington about relations with Japan but there was also growing concern about China, especially the unresolved problem of Taiwan. After diplomatic recognition had been extended to China nondiplomatic relations had been instituted with Taiwan, and trade and cultural relations continued. Under the 1979 Taiwan Relations Act, Washington had undertaken security commitments nearly as strong as

TABLE 8 United States and Japanese Defense Expenditures, 1972–1982

	$ MILLION					$ PER CAPITA					% GNP				
	1972	1976	1978	1980	1982	1972	1976	1978	1980	1982	1972	1976	1978	1980	1982
United States	83.4	91.0	105	142.7	215.9	399	423	481	644	938	7.2	5.4	5.0	5.2	7.2
Japan	2.7	5.0	8.5	8.9	10.3	26	45	75	75	87	0.9	0.9	0.9	0.9	1.0

Source: International Institute for Strategic Studies, appropriate annual volumes of *The Military Balance*. All figures rounded.

those it had had under the old defense treaty. And in 1980 the United States had resumed sales of "defensive" military equipment. As we shall see, the Taiwan arms issue would bedevil U.S.–Chinese relations even more in the next administration.

8. The Reagan Administration and Beyond

Ronald Reagan took office with almost a reverse image of how to deal with the security balance in Asia. He was determined to halt what he saw as a serious decline both in the elements of American power and the willingness to use it. Because the Soviets were perceived as the major threat, Moscow would be the focal point of his efforts. In Asia, this "get tougher with the Russians" confrontation orientation could easily translate into closer relations with China. But Reagan, a longtime friend of Taiwan, had attacked the Carter agreement on normalization during the presidential campaign. When Reagan took office, many worried that his disposition would be toward a major shift back toward Taiwan. But, taking a middle course, the new Reagan administration quickly indicated that it recognized the tangible strategic benefits that could be derived from closer relations with China. Secretary of State Haig in June 1981 announced that the United States was now willing even to consider the sale of "lethal" weaponry to China.

Despite Reagan's assurances to Beijing, he sought simultaneously close relations with Taiwan. In the fall of 1981, when Taiwan asked for new aircraft, the United States was sympathetic and Beijing objected strongly. Perhaps to convince the United States that arms sales to Taiwan were unnecessary, in September Beijing published a nine-point program for peaceful reunification. Combining the stick with the carrot, the Chinese warned that, if the United States continued to follow a dual policy, China might introduce more warmth into Soviet relations. But despite Beijing's efforts, Reagan adhered to the middle course he had charted. Although he rejected Taiwan's requests for more sophisticated planes such as the F-16, Reagan also refused the demands of China to cut off new aid. In early 1982 Washington announced that more F-5Es would be sold to Taiwan.

At the same time though, Reagan recognized the adverse effects his policy was having on relations with China and sought to reduce the friction as much as possible. For nearly six months talks with China were conducted almost continuously, and in August 1982 the United States pledged eventually to terminate arms sales to Taiwan, although sales would be continued at a level not to exceed that of 1979 for a time.

It soon was evident that the two parties interpreted the American pledge very differently. The United States claimed it meant only that transfers would be ended once Beijing and Taiwan resolved their differences, i.e., once "the China problem" was settled. Beijing said that was not what had been agreed to; the United States, China said, had pledged to sell arms to Taiwan at the present level only for a short time and soon to phase out the program entirely. In March 1983 the disagreement took more concrete form when Washington announced that arms sales to Taiwan were expected to total $800 million and $780 million in 1983 and 1984, respectively. Furious, Beijing charged that sales of this magnitude patently violated the August understanding since sales in the base year of 1979 were $598 million and the projected sales to Taiwan in both 1983 and 1984 would be more.[16] The United States countered that the real value of the projected sales was less if inflation since 1979 were taken into account, and thus there was not any violation. Although Reagan was not trying to implement a "two Chinas" policy and was aware of

[16]China's reaction on July 23, 1983, was more specific still, and vehement, China claiming that the United States, by including three types of advanced antiaircraft missiles, was actually improving Taiwan's defenses *qualitatively. New York Times,* July 24, 1983.

the strategic advantages accruing from Sino-Soviet enmity, it was obvious that he nevertheless held Taiwan in much higher esteem than his recent predecessors had, and believed he could deal with Taiwan extensively without alienating Beijing. Although the record shows that in one sense Reagan was correct and Beijing was not *alienated,* it also reveals that American-Chinese relations were very difficult in this period. To China the status of Taiwan was a matter of vital interest, and as Foreign Minister Wu Xueqian put it, "As far as bilateral relations between China and the United States are concerned, the principal obstacle is the issue of Taiwan."[17]

In part in response to the cooling of relations with Washington but in part just because it was in its interest to do so, in 1982 and 1983 China was carefully reappraising its relations with the superpowers. The Soviets, only too aware of PRC–U.S. unease, for a long time had been seeking a new round of negotiations with the Chinese. In late 1982, Beijing responded favorably and talks began. When China then raised its long-standing demands for Soviet withdrawal from Afghanistan, a loosening of Moscow's relations with Vietnam, and the reduction of Soviet forces near their common border, the talks were stalemated, as was a new round in March 1983. That progress in these talks was difficult, given the fundamental features of the Sino-Soviet conflict, should surprise no one. The fact that little progress was made is less important than the fact that with changing strategic circumstances the parties continued to be willing to talk. Both parties remained aware that alternatives to the policy contents currently being implemented existed. Under certain circumstances, substitutions of "shelved" interests might become both feasible and advantageous. Though the Chinese remained convinced of the Soviet threat, they also believed that certain compatibilities might exist. And as Prime Minister Zhao Ziyang told Secretary of Defense Caspar Weinberger during the latter's visit to China in September 1983, China would not attach itself to any power or bloc. China would go its own way.

Reagan's relations with Japan differed little from Carter's: defense sharing and the trade deficit were major issues, and little headway was made on either. Consider that (when Reagan took office) Japan was spending less than 1 per cent of its GNP on defense while the United States was spending over 5 per cent of *its* GNP. In per capita terms the United States was spending ten times more than Japan on defense. These facts increasingly rankled Washington. When Suzuki met Reagan in May 1981, the President very strongly urged the Japanese to increase their defense efforts. Suzuki told Reagan that the Japanese would comply with his request, but the sensitivity of the defense issue in Japan was great. This sensitivity was illustrated by the uproar that was caused by the use of the term *alliance* in the communiqué after the Suzuki-Reagan meeting. (By the provisions of the mutual security treaty the United States was obligated to defend Japan, but Japan has no reciprocal obligations.) Foreign Minister Ito, who was responsible for the language in the communiqué, was forced to resign in the face of opposition claims that the term *alliance* implied a larger Japanese role and reciprocal obligations.

Several other incidents marred Japanese-American relations in 1981: an American submarine collided with and sank a Japanese merchant ship, and failed to rescue survivors; American naval vessels in a joint training exercise damaged the nets of Japanese fishermen; and former U.S. Ambassador to Japan Edwin Reischauer said that United States warships long had transited Japanese waters carrying nuclear weapons (with Japanese consent). In each case a great public furor resulted in Japan.

In December 1981 the Suzuki cabinet did increase defense spending somewhat, but government spokesmen emphasized the singular nature of the decision, saying any further increases would be "very small."

In November 1982 Yasuhiro Nakasone was elected Prime Minister. Much to Washington's

---

[17]*New York Times,* September 27, 1983, p. A3. In a visit to America in January 1984, Prime Minister Zhao Ziyang reaffirmed this theme, using the phrase "the main obstacle." *New York Times,* January 17, 1984, p. A12.

pleasure, Nakasone indicated clearly his determination to increase Japanese defense capability; expenditures on defense would increase more than 4 per cent in *real* terms, he said. Moreover, in January 1983 Tokyo reversed a long-standing policy and decided to make it possible to transfer military technology to the United States. Even more pointedly, during a visit to Washington, Nakasone deliberately used the word *alliance* to describe the American-Japanese relationship. Nakasone went on to stress the need for a strong defense posture to counter the Soviets. Not surprisingly, the Soviets reacted strongly. Already upset by American plans to base F-16s in northern Japan in the late 1980s, Moscow now deplored what it said was a return to Japanese "militarism," even suggesting that as a result Japan might someday be the target of a nuclear strike. But Nakasone seemed unimpressed.

Though the Soviet response did not persuade Nakasone to alter his course, whether in fact he actually would be able to implement significant changes in Japanese defense policy was an open question. Japanese public opinion might support a gradual enhancement of capability, but there was no consensus for a major step-up in spending, Japan showed no enthusiasm to accept a larger role in regional security affairs, and the competition for scarce funds from nondefense sectors of the government continued severe. Outside Japan—and a factor in Japanese thinking— there remained deep concern in Asia about the possibility of a revival of Japanese militarism. These internal and external restraints made more than gradual change unlikely, no matter what Nakasone's intentions were. And, indeed, the 1984 budget adopted by the cabinet contained only a 6.55 per cent increase for the military, far less than senior American officials had wanted. Whether Japan would ultimately implement U.S. Secretary of Defense Weinberger's suggestion that the Japanese should defend the air space and sea lanes up to a thousand miles from Japan's borders was not known.

Early in the Reagan years the other major issue in American-Japanese relations, the trade deficit, seemed on the verge of improvement. Washington chose a limited cooperation orientation and, after intensive negotiations, in May 1981 Tokyo agreed to a "voluntary" reduction in auto exports to the United States. Other negotiations brought a reduction in the prior restrictions on the import of American tobacco products to Japan. In response to requests from an American trade mission in November 1981, Japan agreed to an acceleration of the tariff reduction schedule earlier specified in the GATT Tokyo round. On January 30, 1982, Japan took other conciliatory measures. But the United States believed that the total Japanese moves were nowhere near sufficient; Japanese exports continued to flow, and though the restrictions on American imports had been reduced slightly in selected areas, a vast network of nontariff barriers in Japan still discriminated against U.S. (and other Western) products. Worse, sometimes the Japanese moves seemed downright misleading (in American eyes). In May 1982 Tokyo promised some sixty-five more liberalization measures, but many remained unimplemented.

The Japanese argued they were doing everything they could, given domestic economic and political pressures; anyway, why should they be punished for their technological superiority and America's inefficiency? As Hondas, Toyotas, and Subarus crowded American streets while American autoworkers saw their unemployment benefits run out, as Japanese steel invaded American markets, and as Japanese electronic and microprocessing capabilities expanded at an astounding rate, tension inevitably grew. Meanwhile, the underlying structural problems only got worse. The trade deficit, $18 billion in 1981, grew to more than $19 billion in 1982 and jumped to $21 billion in 1983. Few saw any reason why it would not continue to grow. American-Japanese relations were much less promising in trade matters than they were in defense.

Reagan's primary emphasis in Asia was on relations with China and Japan, as just discussed. Elsewhere, Reagan generally followed policies similar to those of the last years of the Carter administration. For example, on the Korean Peninsula, Reagan strongly affirmed America's commitment to the security of South Korea. Determined to maintain a strong forward deployment posture, Reagan emphasized the necessity of keeping American troops in Korea to counter the threat from the north.[18] Continuing Carter's low-key approach to the Kampuchean conflict, Reagan followed the UN majority in refusing to seat the Heng Samrin government and gave diplomatic support to ASEAN's attempt to find a political solution to the conflict.

In those areas in which Reagan's policies did differ from Carter's, he almost always adopted a position more reminiscent of the Cold War policies of the 1950s. Arms sales were stepped up, for example, and included the transfer of some of the most sophisticated weapons in America's inventory, such as the sale of F-16s to Pakistan. But these matters were distinctly secondary in significance to U.S. relations with China and Japan.

9.

Summing Up

Our discussion shows that as the United States confronts security problems in Asia in the next several years, it may have serious difficulties in continuing to balance and reconcile these divergent tendencies. Central as always to the Asian balance are the relations of Russia and Japan to China. China hold the major key to the security balance, with Japan playing an important though secondary role. Other actors have some importance, but their primary significance derives from their relationship to the major actors in the balance: China, Russia, and Japan. The United States must keep its priorities straight and not again design its policy toward Asian nations as if ideology and abstract moral principle were more critical than straightforward security issues.

The Sino-Soviet dispute will remain the core balance around which other relationships revolve. But this does not mean it will be static. Policymakers in both Moscow and Beijing will remain alert to the possibility of utilizing counterbalancing interests and redressing their differences if Washington is maladroit enough to encourage it. Although this is an unlikely development unless forced upon the Communist giants, it is not an impossible development. Washington must keep the principle of the conservation of enemies very much in mind and not yield any points in the game of keeping Chinese-American hostility limited. If this is done, it will continue to restrict the strategic freedom of the Soviets more than any single other policy action anywhere in the world possibly can. Secondary issues, such as arms sales to Taiwan, must not be permitted to interfere with the prime objective.

Although its role is secondary to China's, Japan is also a major player on the Asian scene. If Japanese-American relations are not to decline, the United States will have to make a greater effort not to be too blunt with Japan. Although the Japanese are prepared to accept that greater defense efforts are needed, they are not prepared to go so far as the United States wishes. The Japanese, too, see a growing Soviet threat, but not one so massive or imminent as the United States suggests. Therefore, they conclude that although Japanese military capability should be enhanced, given the nature of the threat and the capabilities of American air- and seapower, a major policy shift is unnecessary.

If Washington will have to modify its outlook to avoid a serious decline in Japanese-American relations, so too will Japan. Tokyo must recognize that Washington is deeply upset over the combination of Japan's limited defense efforts and the worsening trade balance, and this will not be tolerated indefinitely. Although not all aspects of the trade problem are susceptible to negotiation, some are. And Tokyo could, if it wanted, increase significantly its defense spending.

The United States should not be expected to bear the burden of defending Japanese inter-

---

[18]Although the content of Reagan's Korean policy was similar to Carter's of 1980, his style was very different. Human rights received little attention and Chun Doo Hwan was treated cordially.

ests to the extent it has in the past. If Japan cannot be persuaded by negotiation to play a larger role, the United States may have to choose the alternative of reducing its commitments and deployments unilaterally. This would probably compel Japan, just to protect its own interests, to increase its military strength substantially. There would be some danger in that case of a gulf being created, but in the most fundamental sense Japan will be the United States' "ally" for the foreseeable future no matter what the state of Japanese-American relations, because Tokyo is determined to resist Soviet efforts at domination. In the end, the Japanese also know that the vital sealines of communication on which Japan's trade-dependent economy so heavily relies cannot likely be defended anyhow unless the Japanese expand their air- and seapower substantially.

As Sino-Japanese relations warm further and Japanese-Soviet relations remain cool, and as Japanese military capability increases (whether "willingly" or not), the United States should find it possible to choose less involved, less risky orientations and still have a stable security balance. The Asian balance, after all, is essentially Asia's affair. The United States should transfer responsibility to Asian shoulders at every opportunity, encouraging settlements guaranteed by substantial Asian support. Any other course will not only be costly, ultimately it will be futile. Avoidance must be the orientation adopted toward military conflict on the continent, forward deployment to be replaced by offshore positioning that takes advantage of the flexibility guaranteed by the U.S. favorable location. The basic principles of international relations and the balance of power process, as well as the historical legacy of the long Asian struggle against foreign domination, guarantee that (ultimately at least) America's "natural allies" will band together to oppose any Soviet aggression. (In the same way, any major Chinese efforts at border revision will encounter strong opposition.) These facts permit the United States to make carefully considered, situation-specific choices about whether and how to become involved, and to adopt an essentially supportive stance that will add stability to the balance as and to the extent necessary. Conserving enemies via the appropriate mix of low involvement orientations, the United States thus will be able to achieve its fundamental objective in Asia—the prevention of domination by a single hostile power—at minimal cost and risk.

19

Area in Ferment:
The Middle East

There are moments in the lives of nations and peoples when it is incumbent upon those known for their wisdom and clarity of vision to survey the problem, with all its complexities and vain memories, in a bold drive toward new horizons.

Anwar Sadat
Speech to the Israeli Knesset,
November 20, 1977

An attempt by any outside force to gain control of the Persian Gulf region will be regarded as an assault on the vital interests of the United States of America, and such an assault will be repelled by any means necessary, including military force.

Jimmy Carter
State of the Union Address,
January 23, 1980

The Middle East is a critically important region, and one very much in ferment. It is the transportation and communication crossroads of Europe, Africa, and Asia, commanding the strategic approaches to all three continents. It was the cradle, and remains the center, of three great world religions: Judaism, Christianity, and Islam. And, it has the largest concentration of proven oil reserves in the world, and is the leading oil-producing region as well.

United States national interests in the Middle East have remained clear and consistent since World War II, despite differences in style or emphasis by successive administrations. Fundamental policy objectives include preventing the control of the area by any hostile power, not allowing regional disputes to lead to a nuclear confrontation, ensuring access to the area's oil for the United States and key friends at tolerable prices, and (because it affects so much of the foregoing) minimizing area instability and the negative consequences it produces. It is especially important to the United States not to allow Middle East developments unduly to degrade the United States–Soviet global security balance.

The *design* of U.S. policy is therefore clear—what is intended. *Implementing* the policy effectively, though, is by no means easy because the problems faced are quite intricate and hard to deal with in isolation. Identifying the actors involved (the first of the four operational steps) is particularly difficult in this area.

1.

Five Interlinked Problems

Five interlinked problems have confronted the United States in the Middle East for almost the entire post–World War II period: the Arab-Israeli conflict, difficulties caused by inter-Arab disputes, oil imports, Soviet efforts at penetration, and building Persian Gulf stability. Each of these problem areas by itself is complicated and difficult to deal with, but the complexities are compounded by the fact that each affects and is affected by the others. And each of these five problems raises one or more distinct issues. Since the Vietnam War, affairs in the region have been complicated even further by (1) a growth in prominence of the Palestinian issue, and (2) the greatly enhanced importance of the Persian Gulf and the Arabian Peninsula as a result of America's dependence on foreign oil.

The first and in some ways the core problem confronting the United States in the Middle East is the Arab-Israeli conflict. It is self-evident that although the resolution of this problem would not automatically produce regional stability, unless the Arab-Israeli conflict is settled stability is impossible. The Arab-Israeli problem is important also because of Washington's and Moscow's ties to local actors and the possibility that one of the area's frequent outbursts of violence might lead to U.S.–Soviet confrontation. Resolving the conflict would significantly reduce such dangers, and also might lessen Soviet influence in the region. After all, the Russians have made their most impressive inroads by adopting a very pro-Arab stance. Would the Arabs be so anxious for Russian help if there was peace with Israel? Settling the Arab-Israeli problem would be beneficial in another way: it would contribute to the achievement of stability in the Persian Gulf and the Arabian Peninsula. The Saudis' concern with establishing Arab sovereignty over East Jerusalem and developing an appropriate vehicle for Palestinian self-determination (as well as its broader concerns over Israel's role in the area as a whole) make it very interested in a satisfactory Arab-Israeli settlement. The degree to which the Saudis are willing to accommodate American oil and other interests is in part a function of their view of U.S. policy on the Arab-Israeli conflict. The issue of how to deal with that conflict remains a major one in the post-Vietnam era.

In the post-Vietnam era the Arab-Israeli problem has been complicated further by the rising salience of the Palestinian issue. From the "end" of the 1948–1949 Palestine War through the 1967 hostilities, the major parties in the Arab-Israeli dispute were Israel and the surrounding Arab states. The Palestine Liberation Organization (PLO) had been created in 1964, but until the June War it was essentially a creature of the Arab states. As a result of that war, however, many Palestinians concluded that the Arab states would never succeed in "liberating" Palestine. Accordingly, Palestinian guerrillas began to act independently, launching a variety of low-level military actions from bases in the states surrounding Israel. On the diplomatic front, the PLO rejected UN Security Council Resolution 242 because it did not deal with the issue of Palestinian self-determination. Over the next several years the Palestinian cause gained strength, and many policymakers came to believe that the Palestinian issue was the heart of the Arab-Israeli problem. In 1974 the Arab heads of state recognized the PLO as the "sole legitimate representative" of the Palestinian people. The Israelis, however, continued to believe that no accommodation was possible with the PLO.

How is the United States to handle this complicated Palestinian problem and the even more complicated "Arab"-Israeli dispute of which it is a part?

The second problem confronting American policy is inter-Arab relations. Although the Arabs (sometimes) act in concert toward Israel, they frequently disagree strongly on other matters. Fluid relationships, uncertainty and the switching of alliances, and the manipulation of counterbalancing interests are typical in inter-Arab affairs. It is risky for the United States to assume that any situation will last very long, or to put too much faith in any one Arab leader or state.

These inter-Arab conflicts enormously complicate the U.S. problem, not only because of their impact on the Arab-Israeli dispute but also because of the tactical opportunities they may provide for Soviet penetration. In 1967 Egypt's President Nasser felt he had no choice but to blockade the Gulf of Aqaba in large part because of inter-Arab concerns. This action not only created a situation in which Israel felt it had no choice but to attack; it also helped ensure Egyptian dependence on Soviet arms. In 1948, inter-Arab enmity precluded effective coordination of the Arabs' effort to prevent the creation of Israel. The 1970–1971 Jordanian civil war resulted in the resettling of many Palestinians in southern Lebanon, which soon became a base for attacks against Israel, using Soviet weapons. During the same conflict the United States and Soviets came near to confrontation in support of their client states. Inter-Arab conflicts are a permanent part of the Middle East scene; they overlap the other conflicts, and to many Arab leaders, *inter-Arab relations are equally or more important* than the Arab-Israeli conflict. (Israel almost never has been the *primary* focus of Saudi concern, for example.) Such inter-Arab relations therefore importantly affect both the Arab-Israeli conflict and U.S.–Soviet relations, raising the policy issue for the United States of how to establish priorities among these problems.

The third problem of the post-Vietnam era, unlike the first two that had long historical roots, is a relatively recent one: United States dependence on foreign oil. Prior to the 1970s the United States was not a net oil importer. By the time of the Arab embargo in the 1973 Arab-Israeli war, though, the United States was importing more than 25 per cent of the oil it consumed, and after that time the level was increased, at times ranging upwards of 40 per cent. Moreover, Japan and Western Europe import more than 90 and 60 per cent of their oil needs, respectively.

It is not only a question of supply; it is also a matter of money. After the shock of 1973–1974, oil prices stabilized for a while at about $11–12 per barrel, increasing very little through 1978. In 1979, however, oil prices rose to the $30–34 per barrel range, a level that many experts had thought would not come before the end of the century. Although oil prices declined slightly in the early 1980s, there was no guarantee they would not jump significantly again. Such price hikes contributed massively to economic dislocation, involved great transfers of wealth to the oil producers, created strong inflationary pressures in the consuming states, and added to balance of payments problems.

The United States and most of its major allies will continue to be vulnerable to oil shortages until at least the year 2000. The dependencies are great, and despite occasional fluctuations in demand the long-term prospects are not encouraging. Although U.S. imports of oil have shifted to greater reliance on African and Latin American sources, imports from the Persian Gulf in the early 1980s still exceeded what would be prudent, and Japanese and European dependence on Middle East oil remained high. These developments have greatly enhanced the significance of the Persian Gulf and Arabian Peninsula, and increased concern over the possibility of regional unrest and the potential for oil flow disruption, dispute escalation, and the outside intervention that may entail. The issue here is how either to ensure oil supplies or lower dependence.

This brings us to the fourth problem: United States–Soviet relations. Although the Arab-Israeli conflict, inter-Arab disputes, and Peninsula and Persian Gulf oil and location issues also have intrinsic importance, to the United States their greatest significance lies in their impact on United States–Soviet relations. Washington's fundamental objective, in the post-Vietnam era as earlier, had to be the prevention of control of the Middle East and its strategic positions and oil resources by a single hostile power. The only state with the potential now to achieve such control is the Soviet Union. The issue here is the straightforward but difficult one of how to keep Soviet influence in the region within tolerable bounds.

The fifth problem is how to create some stability in this volatile area. This concern lay behind much of U.S. policy toward Iran. The issue in Iran, as we shall see in Section 6, was primarily how to encourage development at a pace that did not lead to chaos. Decreased stability, in Iran or elsewhere in the area, would only enhance Soviet opportunities for penetration.

2.

Background: The Arab-Israeli Wars of 1956 and 1967

From the time of their "final" dispersion from Judea by the Romans in 135 A.D. until the twentieth century, the Jewish people had no independent state of their own. Scattered throughout the world, though there were many good experiences, at many times and in many locations the Jews were subject to intense persecution. The Jewish people never gave up their hope of returning to the Middle East and setting up their own state, and in the nineteenth century the Zionist movement developed with a determination to achieve that objective. During World War I Britain promised help in establishing a "national home" for the Jewish people in Palestine.

But there also was another claimant to the land, the Arabs of Palestine. Constituting more than 90 per cent of the area's inhabitants at the time, the Arabs, too, received wartime promises from the British: Arab national self-determination and independence in exchange for help in fighting the Turks (who had controlled the area for hundreds of years). Obviously, these promises were incompatible.

When World War I ended, instead of independence Palestine became a League of Nations Mandate under British control, and small-scale Jewish immigration to Palestine began. Arab-Zionist conflict was frequent and bitter. Once the "holocaust" commenced in Europe in the 1930s the immigration trickle of European Jews to Palestine turned into a torrent. Arab-Zionist enmity continued, and at the end of World War II it became even more bitter. Unable to solve the problem, in early 1947 Britain turned the whole mess over to the UN, and on November 29, 1947, the UN General Assembly, with strong United States support, resolved 33–13 to partition Palestine into independent Arab and Jewish states, with the city of Jerusalem internationalized (see Map 7).

The Zionists rejoiced, but the Arabs had all been opposed to partition and now pledged to prevent the resolution's implementation. Limited clashes and small battles occurred, and with the end of the British Mandate on May 14, 1948, war began in earnest. Though the Arabs were numerically superior their attention was divided, with the Arab governments (Arabs other than Palestinians) being more concerned about their domestic problems and in ridding their own states of foreign influence. Accordingly, the Israelis triumphed easily. Four armistice agreements were signed, the last on July 29, 1949.

As a result of the war, Israel acquired far more territory than it would have obtained under partition. But the Palestinian Arabs got nothing, the West Bank being annexed by Transjordan (now Jordan) and Egypt retaining the Gaza Strip as an administered territory. So much for Arab unity. Jerusalem was divided, with Jordan ruling the old city and Israel the new. And nearly three-fourths of a million Arabs who had left their homes during hostilities soon were crowded into UN refugee camps near Israel's borders, to become a malignant cancer. The Arabs said this was only the first round; a second round was coming, and they would win.

The most important Arab leader in the 1950s was Egypt's Gamal Nasser. Nasser was much less concerned with the Cold War than with eliminating foreign colonial influence from the region and countering the Israelis. Using the orientation of participatory nonalignment, Nasser

MAP 7

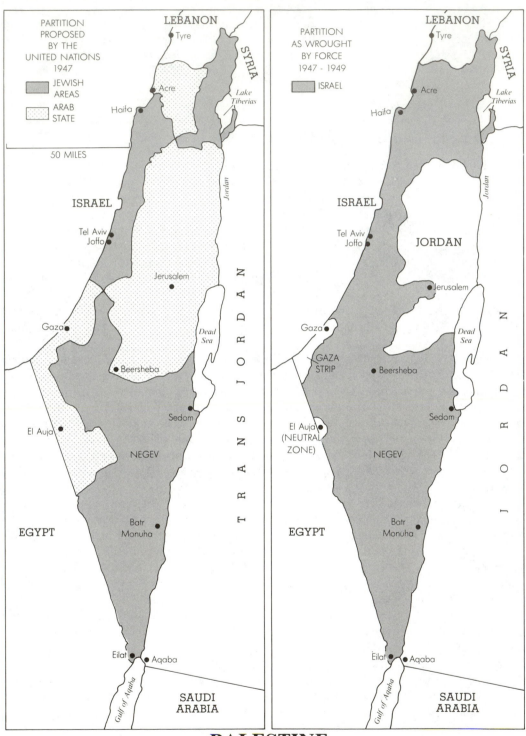

PALESTINE

frequently sought to play the United States and the Soviet Union against each other for Egypt's benefit. After bargaining with the West and not being able to obtain the terms he wanted, in September 1955 Nasser signed the now famous arms deal with Czechoslovakia (which was acting as a Soviet agent), enabling Moscow to leapfrog NATO's southern flank and establish a presence in the Arab heartland. The United States responded by agreeing in principle to help finance the construction of Egypt's High Aswan Dam. To Washington's chagrin though, Nasser continued to deal with the Soviets. When negotiations with the United States over the precise details on the Aswan loan dragged on and Nasser intimated that if the details of the Aswan loan were unsuitable he would get the money from Moscow, an infuriated U.S. Secretary of State John Foster Dulles withdrew the offer.[1] Nasser retaliated by nationalizing the Suez Canal Company, pledging to use operating proceeds to finance the dam's construction.

Britain, the largest stockholder in the Suez Canal Company, convinced that Nasser wanted to destroy its influence throughout the region, was determined not to allow him to succeed. Because of Nasser's assistance to the Algerian rebels, the French also were adversarial, as were the Israelis. On October 29, 1956, Israel attacked Egypt, followed two days later by Britain and France.

U.S. policy had been based on incompatible moral abstractions since the Suez crisis began. Because Britain was anti-Communist and democratic, there had been pressure on Washington to take its side, but Britain also had a second image as Egypt's former colonial master, now considering military actions that might or might not seem justified to third parties. Because there are no criteria for prioritizing such absolutes, Washington had shifted first this way, then that. But now a decision had to be made. Choosing to oppose "colonialism" and "aggression," the United States led the fight against its NATO allies and Israel and for a UN-sponsored cease-fire and withdrawal. Under intense pressure from Washington and amid threats of rocket warfare from Russia to "crush the aggressors," on November 6 Britain accepted a cease-fire, and the French and Israelis reluctantly followed suit. To the Arab masses Nasser again was a hero, this time having successfully defied *both* the colonialists and Israel.

The United States, evaluating the Suez affair essentially in Cold War terms, saw the drastic decline in Western strength that Suez had brought and perceived enhanced opportunities in the Middle East for the Soviets. Alarmed, in early 1957 Washington proclaimed the Eisenhower Doctrine, the President stating that the United States would aid any nation that sought assistance against "overt armed aggression from any nation controlled by international communism," that aid to include, if necessary, the use of military force. But Arab reaction to the Eisenhower Doctrine was almost entirely negative. It was the West and Israel that had just attacked, and Moscow had supported the Egyptians. Washington's failure to empathize was monumental.

Very slowly now the United States began to realize how counterproductive was its preconception that all problems in the Middle East resulted either from Nasser's tactics or from Communist machinations. Accordingly, when in early 1958 Egypt and Syria united to form the United Arab Republic, Washington reacted very cautiously. But when a crisis erupted in Lebanon in May the U.S. preconceptions emerged to inhibit careful analysis; Eisenhower and Dulles assumed that Nasser and the Communists were behind the unrest. After what Washington saw as a "Nasserist" coup in Iraq on July 14, the United States answered Lebanese President Chamoun's call for help by landing the marines in Lebanon. But once the marines arrived, it became clear that the dispute *had* been essentially internal in nature, and soon the American troops were pulled out.

After the Lebanon crisis ended, Middle East politics entered a new phase. Washington and

---

[1]Contingent offers by Britain and the World Bank were withdrawn also.

Moscow adopted less confrontational orientations, and instead of Cold War or Arab-Israeli issues being the focus, inter-Arab disputes now occupied center stage. Within the Arab world, between 1959 and 1966 inter-Arab alignments exhibited exceptional fluidity: Iraq and Egypt went from friends to bitter adversaries; Syria seceded from the United Arab Republic; Egyptian troops served alongside those from Saudi Arabia, Jordan, and the Sudan and thwarted Iraq's claim to Kuwait; and in the civil war in Yemen Egypt backed the republican government while the Saudis and Jordanians supported the deposed Imam. Many Arab states exhibited significant internal instability, also adding to the uncertainty.

In 1966 there was another major shift in focus when, following a coup in Syria, a chain of events began that eventually led to war. Determined to "liberate" Palestine, the new Syrian regime orchestrated an intensive guerrilla campaign against the Israelis by El-Fatah. Predictably the Israelis retaliated, and throughout the spring of 1967 tension escalated in a mounting cycle of attack and retaliation. Nasser, with more than forty thousand troops supporting the republican regime in the Yemen civil war, was accused by Jordan, Syria, and other Arabs of being willing to kill Arabs but afraid to fight the Israelis. After being informed by Syria and the Soviets in mid-May that Israel was preparing to attack the Syrians, Nasser ordered a partial mobilization and sent a small force into the Sinai.

When the Egyptians asked the UNEF contingent positioned at the Sinai border (since the Suez crisis) to redeploy, quite unexpectedly UN Secretary-General U Thant said that any repositioning would also have to include the units in the Gaza Strip and at Sharm el-Sheikh. Nasser had avoided mentioning Sharm el-Sheikh, because if UNEF forces were so withdrawn inter-Arab pressure to reoccupy it and subsequently close the Gulf of Aqaba would be enormous, and the Israelis repeatedly had said that closure of the straits would mean war. Nevertheless, when confronted with U Thant's all-or-nothing approach, largely for reasons of inter-Arab credibility, Nasser felt compelled to ask the UNEF to pull out, and on May 22 the straits were closed.

The issue for Washington was how to restrain diplomatically both Israel and Egypt. But Washington was acting from a position of limited leverage, and its efforts had little impact.

In late May, Nasser increased the tension by concluding an alliance with Jordan and saying that if war came the Egyptian objective would be to destroy Israel. On June 2, Moshe Dayan was appointed Israel's Defense Minister. Nobody had expected war, but events had snowballed to a point at which they had a momentum all their own, and, with choices increasingly limited, hostilities came. On June 5 Israeli aircraft launched a devastating attack that in three hours destroyed two thirds of Egypt's air force on the ground and rendered most of its airfields inoperative. Over the next five days the remaining Egyptian forces, plus those of Syria, Jordan, and Iraq, were decisively defeated. When the hostilities had ceased, Israeli forces were occupying the entire Sinai Peninsula (including Sharm el-Sheikh), the Gaza Strip, the West Bank (including the old city of Jerusalem), and the Golan Heights (see Map 8). Again Israel had won a crushing victory.

Many expected Nasser to have to sue for peace, but he was able to avoid it. Eager to recoup some of the prestige it had lost with the Arabs because of its lack of involvement during the war, Moscow quickly provided vast quantities of economic and military assistance to Egypt. And the Saudis, Libya, and Kuwait pledged $266,000,000 yearly for as long as the "consequences of aggression" remained. The Arabs further agreed that there would be no peace, no negotiations, and no recognition of Israel. So much for any hopes of compromise.

After lengthy negotiations, on November 22, 1967, the Security Council passed what was to become the famous Resolution 242. It recognized the "inadmissability of the acquisition of territory by war and the need to work for a just and lasting peace in which every state in the area can live in security," and called for "withdrawal of Israeli armed forces from territories occupied in the recent conflict" (it did not say "all" territories), termination of belligerency, and "respect for and acknowledgement of the sovereignty, territorial integrity and political indepen-

MAP 8

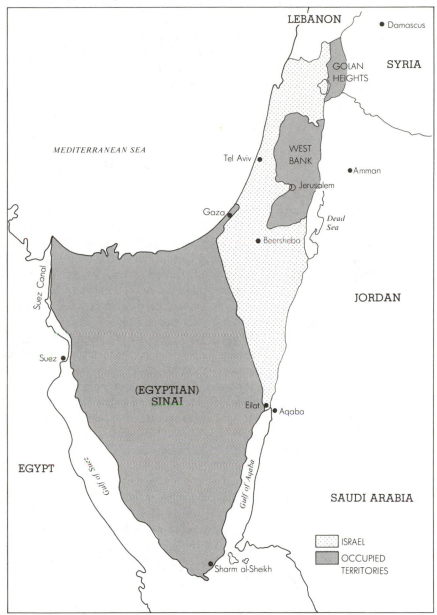

"ISRAEL" AFTER THE 1967 WAR

dence of every state in the area and their right to live in peace within secure and recognized boundaries. . . ."[2]

Because of the complex and interlinked nature of the various issues and the depth of the passions they aroused, the parties had recognized that a comprehensive agreement with precise provisions was not possible. Resolution 242 was sufficiently vague that each party could interpret

[2]For the complete text of this important document, see United Nations, Security Council, S/RES/242 (1967) (S/8247), November 22, 1967.

its provisions as it saw fit. And, indeed, there were different views. Egypt saw 242 as a definite plan for complete Israeli withdrawal from the lands it occupied in 1967. Whereas Israel saw it only as a set of principles providing a foundation for talks.

President Johnson, at this time, was preoccupied with Vietnam, and did not believe outsiders could do much to settle the Arab-Israeli dispute, anyway. Understandably, therefore, his primary orientation was avoidance. There was one important exception, though: Determined to maintain a "favorable balance of power," the United States replaced France as Israel's major arms supplier.

3.

The Nixon-Ford Policy and Shuttle Diplomacy

President Nixon took office determined to have the United States play a more active role in the Middle East. As he saw it, following an orientation of avoidance simply allowed the situation to deteriorate, and the lack of peace benefited only the Soviets. Confidential exchanges were initiated with Moscow and four-power talks were commenced at the UN, the objective in each case to develop parallel views that could provide the catalyst for constructive negotiations. But there was no progress. Nixon's activism yielded no more benefits than did Johnson's avoidance.

On the military front in 1969, Nasser sought to pressure the Israelis by launching a war of attrition against positions along the Suez Canal. Israel responded furiously. When air raids across the Suez Canal failed to halt the bombardment, late in the year American-supplied Phantom jets carried out bombing raids deep into Egypt's interior. In response, Nasser obtained advanced Soviet surface-to-air missiles manned by Russian crews, and new Soviet aircraft with Russian pilots. Concerned about the escalating conflict and the enhanced Soviet involvement, on June 19, 1970, Secretary of State Rogers proposed a standstill cease-fire and the initiation of indirect peace talks under the auspices of UN special representative Gunnar Jarring. Nasser accepted unconditionally. Although first rejecting the proposal, following assurances from Washington on arms deliveries and the acceptability of avoiding any withdrawal prior to a final settlement, the Israelis agreed and talks began. But almost immediately, Israel charged Egypt with massive cease-fire violations and walked out.

In September 1970 another crisis arose. Palestinian organizations using Jordan as a base of operations against Israel had become almost a "state within a state," presenting a severe challenge to Hussein's ability to rule. Following a series of incidents Hussein ordered his army to attack the guerillas. Just as it seemed Hussein would be victorious, tanks from the Syrian-trained Palestine Liberation Army intervened, but by September 22 they began to withdraw.

Most observers today believe that the Syrians withdrew from Jordan because of a militarily decisive Jordanian air strike against the tanks, coupled with a growing threat of Israeli intervention. But Washington was convinced that American military maneuvers and threats, and its support for possible Israeli intervention, had been crucial. In Kissinger's view, American policy had both deterred possible Soviet intervention and persuaded the Soviets to rein in their clients. The idea that in the face of an adverse military balance the Soviets could and would prevent their regional clients from acting thus took firm root in the thinking of American policymakers.

Early in 1971, new efforts were made to resuscitate the dormant Israeli-Egyptian talks. In an attempt to move things off dead center Ambassador Jarring suggested that Israel promise complete withdrawal from the occupied territories in the context of reciprocal security pledges. A few days later Egypt's new President, Anwar Sadat, declared his willingness to sign a *peace agreement* with Israel if Resolution 242 was implemented fully. On the diplomatic defensive, the Israelis fought back. Secure and recognized boundaries were items to be negotiated, they said, not unilaterally determined in advance. Israel claimed the Egyptian version of Resolution 242 "would have Israel restore its past territorial vulnerability," which Israel would never allow. American officials, worried about the lack of progress, subsequently tried to initiate negotiations on a step-by-step basis, but their efforts were fruitless.

Sadat became increasingly frustrated. The diplomatic front was stalemated. And although Moscow was making massive arms deliveries, because of its concern over confrontation with the United States, the Kremlin was refusing to supply weapons to Egypt that were capable of striking Israel. After the United States–Soviet summit brought no positive results and further negotiations with the Soviets proved unproductive, in July 1972 Sadat suddenly ordered the Soviets expelled from Egypt.

American officials believed that the expulsion of the Soviets, set in the context of Washington's massive aid to the Israelis, wholly foreclosed Egypt's military option. But it was in just this situation late in the year that Sadat began exploring with Syria the feasibility of a limited war against Israel. As their preparations continued throughout the summer and early fall of 1973, there was much available intelligence to indicate that hostilities were indeed possible, but Nixon and Kissinger, and most components of the intelligence community, continued to think Sadat was bluffing. After all, if the military balance precluded an Arab victory, surely the Arabs would not begin a war they knew they could not win. Past-future linkages contributed their part also: three wars seemed to have clearly established Israeli superiority. Even the Israelis, with the best intelligence in the area, were not worried. Moreover, the Soviets had agreed not to take unilateral advantage, and Nixon and Kissinger did not think Moscow would be willing to jeopardize détente by encouraging rash actions. Finally, the Jordan crisis had shown that the Soviets could and would rein in their clients when necessary. The case in logic was complete, but, defying this logic, on October 6, 1973, Egypt and Syria attacked.

The course of the conflict is discussed in Chapter 14 and need not be repeated here. The results are our concern.

The October war produced a psychological paradox. Although ultimately the Arabs began to lose the war, they acted as if they had won. Because their military proficiency had so far surpassed their previous efforts and vastly exceeded the Israeli (and American) expectations, the limited objective of enhancing their bargaining position had been achieved and the "myth of Israeli invincibility" destroyed. Conversely, the Israelis, who had begun to "win," acted as if they had lost. The "victory" had been so unexpectedly difficult and required such a dreadful expenditure of blood and treasure. Perhaps it was time to be more flexible.

When hostilities terminated, the Egyptian Third Army on the east bank was surrounded, and the Israelis had cut the Suez-Cairo road. Sadat and the Soviets could not tolerate this indefinitely. In Kissinger's view the tenuous military situation, the psychological paradox, and the fact that there was neither victor nor vanquished created a propitious context for negotiations.

The issue was how to get negotiations going. Mediation was the logical orientation, and after some preliminary meetings and a brief session of the Geneva Conference, Kissinger undertook what became known as "shuttle diplomacy," traveling back and forth between Egypt and Israel in an effort to get both parties to compromise.[3] As a result of Kissinger's skillful mediation (and the propitious circumstances) on January 18, 1974, Egypt and Israel signed a disengagement agreement providing for Israeli withdrawal ten to twenty kilometers into the Sinai, a UN buffer zone, and a series of restricted forces areas. Washington privately promised to be "fully responsive on a continuing and long-term basis" to Israel's military needs. Following this success Kissinger turned to the Syrian front, and on May 31 a disengagement agreement providing for partial withdrawal, limited forces zones, and a UN controlled area, was signed there, too.

---

[3]The Geneva Conference was held under UN auspices. The United States and the Soviet Union were co-chairmen, the other participants being Egypt, Jordan, and Israel. Syria refused to attend. There was only one brief session and then the conference recessed.

MAP 9

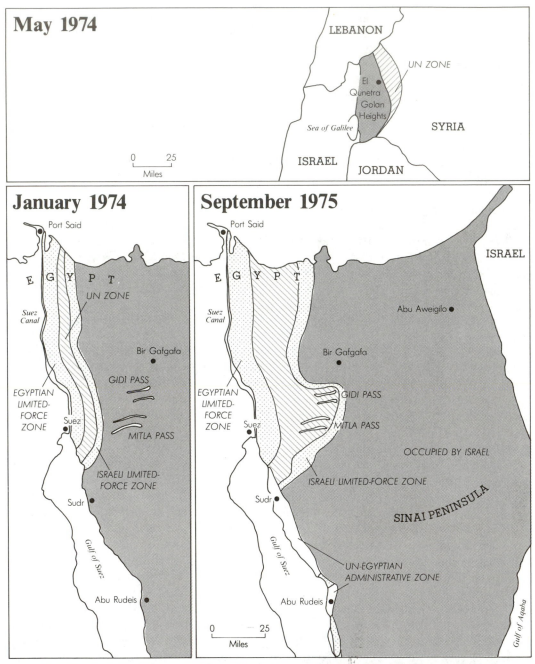

MIDDLE EAST DISENGAGEMENT ACCORDS

Although administration attempts to bring about further Egyptian-Israeli negotiations proved unavailing throughout the remainder of the year, aid programs to both parties continued at a substantial rate and for the time being at least there did not seem to be great urgency.[4]

4.

The Rise of the PLO and the Lebanon Connection

But another factor now was complicating American efforts to resolve the Arab-Israeli dispute: inter-Arab rivalry and the growing prominence of the Palestinian issue.

In the spring of 1975 President Ford and Secretary Kissinger were worried, convinced that the "negotiating dynamic" had to be restored if war was to be averted. But in October 1974 Arab leaders had declared that the PLO was the "sole legitimate representative" of the Palestinians, thereby foreclosing any Jordanian option, and both Egypt and Israel now seemed unwilling to make any important concessions. Believing that Israel was the primary obstacle to progress, Washington began to apply pressure, even saying that if the Geneva Conference were reconvened the United States would favor "substantial restitution of the 1967 frontiers." After receiving promises from Washington that Israel would not be short-changed, Tel Aviv relented and talks started anew. On September 4, 1975, the Sinai II Accords were signed. Israel pledged to withdraw from the Sinai's strategic mountain passes and to return the oil fields. Egypt would advance to the eastern edge of the old UN zone. A new buffer zone would be created, surveillance stations established, and limited force zones set up. Crucially, the *United States* would establish warning facilities between the parties, stationing two hundred civilian technicians on the ground. Privately, Washington also promised Israel more military aid, guaranteed it would receive enough oil to make up for the loss of the oil fields, and promised not to recognize the PLO or to negotiate with it until the PLO recognized Israel's right to exist and accepted Resolutions 242 and 338.[5]

Kissinger and Ford were pleased. The slide toward war had been halted. The United States had produced an agreement and the Soviets had been shut out. The Israelis, though unhappy at relinquishing the strategic passes and the oil fields, had received unprecedented promises of aid, guarantees of oil supplies, and a virtual veto over United States action *re* the PLO. Furthermore, Washington now was physically involved, making an Arab attack much less likely. Sadat, too, was well pleased, recovering land and oil and preparing the way for increased economic assistance.[6]

The Soviets opposed the agreement strongly, as did the PLO, and Syrian President Hafez Assad denounced Sadat for concluding partial agreements that would divide the Arabs and perpetuate "Zionist occupation." With Syria in opposition, Jordan out of the picture, Israel unwilling to talk to the PLO, and Sinai II just having been signed, the possibilities of further step-by-step progress were at least temporarily finished. For the remainder of the Ford-Kissinger term, Arab-Israeli concerns generally did not receive priority treatment.

But the PLO's transfer of the bulk of its fighting forces into Lebanon now began to destroy the uneasy equilibrium by which Muslims and Christians there had accommodated to each other. Lebanon's domestic situation long had been unstable. The central government was weak, unable to assert its will effectively unless its constituent elements would compromise. This lack

---

[4]The Egyptians also were soothed by Nixon's private revelation to Sadat that "the American objective in the Sinai was to restore the old Egyptian international border." See Edward R. F. Sheehan, "How Kissinger Did It: Step by Step in the Middle East," *Foreign Policy* (Spring, 1976), p 44.

[5]Resolution 338 was the cease-fire resolution the Security Council passed in the October War. It also called for negotiations and the implementation of Resolution 242.

[6]$700 million was promised.

of power at the center, combined with deep Christian-Muslim antagonisms and a variety of intersect rivalries, the existence of private militias that in total outnumbered the army, and the presence of 300,000 Palestinian refugees and 5,000–10,000 Palestinian guerrillas who raided Israel and brought forth Israeli retaliation, produced a highly inflammable context. Following a number of what at first seemed to be minor incidents in 1975, a full-scale conflagration developed.

Ford and Kissinger interpreted the Lebanon civil war primarily in terms of its impact on the Arab-Israeli conflict. They felt it was significant only to the extent it invited outside intervention or threatened to escalate. Since the conflict in Lebanon was not yet that dangerous, Washington urged restraint on Syria and Israel and offered its good offices and mediation, but it carefully avoided becoming heavily involved. In mid-summer 1976 Syrian forces invaded Lebanon in strength to compel some solution, and by late fall most of Lebanon except the area along Israel's northern border was under Syrian control. In late October the United States watched as Arab heads of state agreed on a (Syrian-dominated) Arab peacekeeping force. There the matter rested—temporarily.

5.

Carter and the Camp David Accords

When Jimmy Carter took office in 1977, the most urgent of the five problems the United States confronted in the Middle East seemed to be the Arab-Israeli confrontation itself. Less worried than his predecessors about communism, Carter did not see merit in operating apart from the Soviets, à la Kissinger. At first Carter did not have a coordinated Middle East policy in mind, but by midsummer a new implementing strategy had been developed. Carter was convinced that the step-by-step method was dead. He wanted to reconvene the Geneva Conference and negotiate a comprehensive settlement. If this objective were to be achieved the Russians would have to be involved and some formula discovered for Palestinian participation. Soon efforts were made in both directions. But the new Israeli government of Menachem Begin (elected in the spring) made it painfully clear it would never negotiate with the PLO, and Jerusalem charged that Washington was violating the Sinai Accords by hinting that if the PLO modified its views it might be invited to Geneva.

All efforts to devise an acceptable formula for Palestinian participation proved fruitless. But on October 1, 1977, the United States and the Soviets agreed to what they considered mutually acceptable principles for settlement. They included a reconvening of the Geneva Conference, negotiations involving all parties (including representatives of the Palestinians), ensuring the legitimate rights of the Palestinian people, withdrawal from occupied territories, and the establishment of normal peaceful relations. The United States believed the package was fair and balanced, and pointed out that the Soviets had made an important concession by dropping their previous insistence on Israeli withdrawal from *all* territories. But both Egypt and Israel were furious. The Israelis attacked the phrase "legitimate rights" as code words for a Palestinian state, and pointed to the failure to mention Resolution 242. Cairo, whose relations with Moscow had been frigid since Sadat had abrogated the Treaty of Friendship and Cooperation in 1976, was concerned about Washington's effort to upgrade the Soviet role. (It was certainly a legitimate question to raise.)

With no progress in sight and the possibility of greater Soviet influence in the area, on November 9, 1977, Anwar Sadat summed up what Egypt had lost and what it had gained by its impasse with Israel. Sadat then stunned observers by proclaiming his willingness to go "to the end of the world" to obtain peace, even "to the Israeli parliament itself." The cardinal principle of counterbalancing national interests had led Sadat to propose one of the boldest diplomatic moves in history. A surprised Begin immediately invited Sadat to Israel and on November 19 the Egyptian leader landed in Jerusalem. In a historic address before the Knesset the following day, Sadat told the Israelis "we accept living with you in permanent peace." For peace to be achieved though, Israel would have to withdraw from *all* territories occupied in 1967 and the Palestinians would have to have a right to create an independent state.

Reactions were mixed. Jordan and Saudi Arabia were noncommittal, wanting to see what would happen next. But Syria, the PLO, Iraq, Libya, Algeria, and South Yemen bitterly denounced the move at a "rejectionist" summit in Tripoli, and the Soviets, too, were highly critical. Sadat reacted by breaking diplomatic relations with the rejectionists and ordering the Soviets to withdraw a number of their cultural and consular officials.

Egyptian-Israeli negotiations began almost immediately, but progress was minimal and by August 1978 the negotiations were deadlocked. Believing it imperative that talks continue, President Carter offered to mediate, and Sadat and Begin agreed, both coming to the United States, to Camp David. After exhaustive bargaining facilitated by Carter's effective mediation, on September 17, 1978, the Camp David Accords were signed.

There were two agreements, each in part procedural: the "Framework for the Conclusion of a Peace Treaty between Egypt and Israel" and the "Framework for Peace in the Middle East." The former, which was relatively straightforward, was an agreement to conclude a final treaty providing for total Israeli withdrawal (in phases) from the Sinai, to establish various security and restricted zones, and to bring about full Egyptian-Israeli peace. The latter, which was more complicated, provided arrangements for negotiating the procedures for the election of a transitional self-governing authority on the West Bank and Gaza, for the termination of Israeli military administration there and a partial withdrawal and relocation of forces, and for negotiations on the "final status" of the West Bank and its relation to its neighbors. Jordan and representatives of the Palestinians were to be invited to participate in these negotiations.

The West Bank–Gaza agreement avoided the core issues of sovereignty, territorial boundaries, and the status of Jerusalem. It was designed as a stepping-stone toward more comprehensive negotiations. Whether success ultimately would be achieved would depend in part on whether Egypt and Israel could reach satisfactory compromises, in itself a very difficult task. But the problem was much more complicated than that, because none of the Arabs most concerned with the West Bank—the Palestinians and Jordanians—were parties to the Camp David agreements and they had not authorized Sadat to be their spokesman.

Most Arabs believed that if Sadat signed a peace treaty with Israel, the Arab coalition would be badly split and Arab capability would be reduced severely. This would allow Israel to strengthen its hold on non-Egyptian territory and make the possibility of a Palestinian-Arab state even more remote. Inside Egypt opposition to the Camp David agreements was widespread, ranging from former ministers in the regime to elements on both the left and right. In addition, nearly all the other Arab states were opposed, and major efforts were undertaken to isolate Sadat and compel a change in policy. Even the Saudis, who had supplied vast financial assistance to Egypt since the October War, and in 1977 had promised to bankroll all of Egypt's military development for the next five years, were upset. But Sadat had invested too much to turn back now. He hoped that once concrete results were achieved by Camp David, Saudi Arabia, Jordan, and perhaps even Syria ultimately would find it was in their interest to join the peace process.

The Israelis generally were pleased. For them, too, the principle of counterbalancing interests applied: if a peace treaty could be achieved and their most capable enemy, Egypt, be isolated, the Israelis would end their encirclement, thereby greatly enhancing their security. Though the Israelis would have to give up major territorial and petroleum assets, it would be worth the trade (assuming the United States once again would be supportive). How better could Israel implement the principle of conservation of enemies?

Intensive negotiations followed, and on March 26, 1979, the Egyptian-Israeli Peace Treaty was signed, terminating the state of war between them (with the exchange of instruments of ratification). Israel promised to withdraw completely from the Sinai in phases over a three-year period (which it did). Egypt would resume full sovereignty in the area, deploying limited forces separated by UN buffer zones. Because Israel had to turn over the remaining oil fields under its control, the United States made a new commitment to serve as a last-resort source of Israeli petroleum requirements for a 15-year period. In addition to maintaining its existing economic and military aid programs of $1.785 billion and $1 billion annually to Israel and Egypt, respectively, Washington also promised to make one-time grants to the two countries of $3 billion and $1.5 billion, respectively.

Throughout 1979 implementation of the treaty took place on schedule, and on February 25, 1980, Egypt and Israel exchanged ambassadors. Egypt was getting its land back, and Israel had virtually eliminated any near-term threat of a Arab attack. The risk of a United States–Soviet confrontation was reduced correspondingly, and Soviet influence in Arab-Israeli matters was at an all-time low.

But there still were serious problems. Though Egypt and Israel began negotiations on the Palestinian issue, the talks got nowhere. Meanwhile, the number of Israeli settlements on the West Bank continued to increase, making compromise even less likely. On the inter-Arab front, after the treaty was signed most of the Arab states broke diplomatic relations with Cairo, and most Arab aid commitments to Egypt (including the Saudis') were terminated. Egypt was expelled from the Arab League, and the league's headquarters was moved from Cairo to Tunis. Sadat was almost entirely isolated, under pressure at home and abroad. For the Carter administration, though, nothing could diminish the importance of peace in the Middle East having been achieved.

6.

The Oil Problem and the Stability Problem

As noted at the beginning of this chapter, the United States in the Middle East has been confronted by five interlinked problems. We traced the essential development of two of these five problems through the Carter administration, showing especially the connections between the Arab-Israeli problem and the Soviet influence problem, with some attention also being given the problem of inter-Arab differences.

In the early 1970s another problem began to develop: the United States was becoming a net importer of oil. At first, the gravity of the problem was not understood. But it became painfully clear in the October 1973 war. To apply pressure to those countries supporting Israel, on October 16, 1973, the Arab members of OPEC drastically increased their oil prices, and shortly thereafter they announced a total embargo on all oil exports to the United States. All of the OPEC states soon joined in the price rise, and by the end of the year oil prices were four times what they had been before the war.

By October 1973 the United States was importing more than 25 per cent of its oil needs (Western Europe 60+ per cent, Japan more than 90 per cent), and its vulnerability was apparent. The Saudis promised they would ease the embargo if progress were made on the disengagement talks, and would work to convince the others to go along. Sadat also indicated he would help. With the signature of the Egyptian-Israeli agreement in January 1974, and strong evidence that a Syrian-Israeli agreement would be forthcoming, the Saudis and Egyptians went to work, and on March 19, 1974, the embargo was suspended.

The OAPEC oil embargo stimulated Nixon and Kissinger to intensify their (existing) efforts to improve relations with the two nations (apart from Israel) who were most closely attuned to U.S. interests. These "twin pillars" of the Persian Gulf region were Iran and Saudi

Arabia. With Britain withdrawing all its forces "East of the Suez" from South Arabia and the Persian Gulf, and the United States involved in Vietnam and unwilling to take on new commitments, Iran and Saudi Arabia seemed the logical candidates to maintain stability in the Gulf region. It was not only oil that made these countries important but also geography. Situated at the head of the Gulf, Iran has an extended boundary with the Soviet Union, possesses nearly half the Gulf's shoreline, and borders the crucial Strait of Hormuz. Saudi Arabia is a large country about the size of the United States east of the Mississippi, overlooks most of the Red Sea connecting the Suez Canal and the Bab el-Mandeb Strait, and has common boundaries with Jordan, Iraq, Kuwait, Qatar, the United Arab Emirates, and both Yemens. Both countries were pro-Western and seemed to be politically stable.

Meanwhile, the Soviets, excluded from the Arab-Israeli peace process and witnessing Washington cementing relations with Egypt, Israel, Saudi Arabia, and Iran, prudently altered course to exploit the counterbalancing interests of Iraq, which feared the growth of Iranian power.

The Soviets had cultivated good relations with Iraq since the late 1960s, and had signed a fifteen-year treaty of friendship and cooperation in 1972. But now Soviet-Iraqi cooperation was increased. The Russian navy obtained regular access to the port of Umm Qasr in the Gulf, and major arms agreements were concluded. On the latter count, by 1976 Iraq was "first among current recipients of Soviet military hardware."[7]

Moscow complemented these moves with a determined program focused on the region's strategic rimlands and littorals. The Soviets had had good relations with South Yemen for several years, providing generous amounts of economic and military aid. But in the late 1970s Soviet ties here, too, were strengthened and the strategic port of Aden became a virtual Soviet base, providing a staging area and stop-off point for operations in the Arabian Peninsula and the Horn of Africa. Across the Red Sea, Moscow supported Marxist Ethiopia, being willing to accept a loss of influence in Somalia in return. At the same time that these political and aid initiatives were undertaken, the Soviets were vastly increasing their maritime and power projection capabilities. Many Americans believed there now was a major Soviet threat to the critical SLOCs of the Persian Gulf and Indian Ocean.

Early in 1978, as the Carter administration continued its "twin pillars" program, it acceded to Saudi wishes for more advanced weapons systems by promising to sell them F-15s (although with certain armament and basing restrictions), while Riyadh responded by continuing to use its influence in OPEC to maintain relative price stability and ensure adequate oil supplies. Even the signs from Iraq were encouraging, as Baghdad continued (a process begun in 1975) to diversify its arms sources and trade patterns, thereby decreasing its dependence on the Soviets.

But in Iran developments were beginning that eventually would undermine one of the "twin pillars." The fall of the Shah (already discussed in Chapter 10) had serious ramifications. Many U.S. allies were very disturbed, with anxiety especially severe in Saudi Arabia. Anxious to maintain regional stability, and having provided financial aid to regimes from Bahrein to North Yemen, Egypt, and even Somalia, Riyadh was dismayed by the unwillingness of the United States to support strongly a long-time friend. The fact that the Khomeini government was of the Shiite sect and might seek to undermine orthodox Sunni Muslim regimes in the area was an additional concern. And the conclusion of the American-mediated Egyptian-Israeli Peace Treaty in March produced even further disenchantment with Washington.

Illustrating the cardinal principle of third-party influences, these factors resulted in evident unease in United States-Saudi relations. Previously Saudi opposition to the Camp David frameworks had been quite limited, but after the peace treaty the Saudis became a leading force in

[7]United States Central Intelligence Agency, "Communist Aid to the Less Developed Countries of the Free World, 1976," p. 30.

isolating Sadat. In April, the Saudis broke diplomatic relations with Cairo, and in July they cancelled plans to finance Egypt's purchase of 50 F-5E fighters.

These events had an important effect on oil prices. From 1974 to 1978, with the Saudis playing a major role in ensuring relative price stability, the price of crude had risen only from $10–11 per barrel to $12–13 (a decrease in real terms when corrected for inflation). But in 1979 in the context of (1) increased demand by consuming countries, (2) decreased production in Iran as a result of the revolution, (3) a weakening of Saudi influence in OPEC because of its previous support of Egypt and close association with the United States, and (4) less inclination in Riyadh to be so accommodating, along with the conclusion in many countries that oil in the ground was more valuable than more capital for development, oil prices rose to the $30–35 per barrel range mentioned before.

Things soon went from bad to worse. In late October 1979, President Carter agreed to let the Shah come to New York for medical treatment. In response, on November 4 armed "students" seized the American Embassy in Teheran and took its incumbents hostage. Defying the "Great Satan" (i.e., the United States), the captors said the American hostages would not be released unless the Shah was returned to stand trial for his crimes and the United States apologized.

The President moved cautiously, first freezing Iranian assets held in American banks and seeking to mobilize support at the United Nations. Though avoiding precipitous military action, privately the President informed Khomeini that if the hostages were put on trial or harmed the United States would attack.

Hardly had Washington had time to catch its breath when on December 27, 1979, the Soviet Union invaded Afghanistan. Although the Soviet invasion can be understood best in terms of the deteriorating geostrategic circumstances around the Soviet periphery (discussed in Chapter 14), the timing and bald nature of the attack, plus the fact that it was the first use of regular Soviet forces outside the Soviet bloc since World War II, combined to shock American policymakers. Indeed, President Carter said the invasion of Afghanistan changed his view of Soviet behavior more than any other event during his tenure in office.

The invasion of Afghanistan and the hostage crisis led to changed priorities in Washington, provoking a truculence far beyond what the Soviets had anticipated. These events led to the "Carter Doctrine," quoted in the headnote to this chapter. Believing that Soviet control of Afghanistan could threaten both Iran and Pakistan and the Strait of Hormuz, Carter accelerated efforts to increase American power projection forces and established the Rapid Deployment Joint Task Force (RDJTF). A number of nonmilitary pressures soon were applied to the Soviets including a partial grain embargo, halting the sale of high-technology and other strategic items, and a boycott of the Olympic Games in Moscow. Over the next several months, however, there was no evidence to indicate that the Soviets would change course.

The President also sought to influence Iran by political and economic pressures. Oil imports were halted, diplomatic relations were severed, and military exports were impounded. Here, too, success appeared unlikely, so on April 24, 1980, the United States attempted a military rescue mission. But because of mechanical failures in three of the eight helicopters involved in the rescue attempt, the mission was aborted without ever reaching Teheran. To the frustration in Washington was added the spectacle of incompetence.

No progress was made in the hostage crisis for several months after the rescue debacle, but in September Khomeini signaled that he might be more flexible on the hostages when he omitted any mention of an American apology in stating the conditions for settlement. And by this time the Shah had died of cancer, removing another of the obstacles.

But the crucial factor was the operation of two of the cardinal principles. In late September, intermittent fighting, which had been occurring along the Iraq-Iran border since May 1979, burst into war with a major Iraqi assault. Confronted with a vastly changed power problem Iran chose to conserve its enemies, and because of the third-party influence of Iraq, Iran became much more cooperative with the United States. Strenuous negotiations still were required, but the gap was narrowed as Washington and Teheran sought a prestige-saving solution that still would achieve the substantive objectives. Eventually (with Algerian help) agreement was achieved, the United States pledging to free Iran's frozen assets, forego claims for damages, help identify the Shah's assets in the United States, and not interfere in Iran's internal affairs. But the Iranians had to agree to a procedure to settle financial counterclaims, the wealth of the Shah was not "returned" as Teheran long had demanded, and no "apology" was offered. On January 20, 1981, after 444 days of captivity, the 52 American hostages were released.

7.

The Reagan Administration and Beyond

Within hours of the release of the hostages, Ronald Reagan became President. Reagan was determined to "restore" American leadership, take a "tougher"stance toward Moscow, strongly support the friends of the United States, and resolutely oppose its enemies.

As applied to the Middle East, Reagan's ideas (in combination with Secretary Haig's) led to an effort to create a "strategic consensus"—meaning that the Reagan administration worked vigorously to persuade countries in the area to agree on the existence of a significant Soviet threat and cooperate in developing the capabilities essential either to deter Soviet action or counter it effectively. To implement this concept, access to onshore military facilities already obtained in the Carter administration (in Oman, Kenya, Somalia, and Egypt) was strengthened, and numerous joint exercises were conducted. Military aid to regional friends was increased, including the sale to Saudi Arabia of five AWACs aircraft as well as conformal fuel tanks for their F-15s (much to Israel's chagrin). Unilaterally, the United States greatly stepped up its efforts to enhance power projection capabilities by means of the RDJTF, and maintained the continuous deployment in the Indian Ocean of two carrier task forces.

American policymakers did not ignore problems other than the Soviet threat, but they received much lower priority. In early 1981 and 1982, efforts were made to enliven the Palestinian autonomy talks and to defuse the continuing crisis in south Lebanon, but there was little sense of urgency. When specific developments occurred that exacerbated Arab-Israeli tensions Washington usually sought to minimize the difficulties. Not that all was smooth sailing. Following the destruction of Iraq's nuclear reactor by Israeli aircraft in June 1981, Washington temporarily held up shipments of additional F-16s to Israel and supported the UN Security Council's condemnation of the raid. In the same way, when in December 1981 Israel unilaterally annexed the Golan Heights, an angry United States suspended a bilateral strategic cooperation agreement that had been signed only three weeks earlier; and after the Israeli strike against the PLO in south Lebanon in June 1982 President Reagan hesitated in submitting for congressional action a plan to sell seventy-five more F-16s to Israel. But in each case it was evident that no further sanctions against Israel would be forthcoming. Indeed, despite the administration's chagrin at some of the Israelis' methods, privately many Americans were pleased when Israeli Defense Forces attacked the PLO strongholds. Instead of applying meaningful sanctions, after the Israelis had driven the PLO from the south of Lebanon the United States mediated a "settlement" providing for the guerrillas' expulsion from West Beirut as well. In order to maintain the strategic assets necessary to counter the Soviets, Washington felt it was imperative that cooperative links be maintained with the Israelis. The concept determined the content. All that mattered was implementation. The danger was that Saudi Arabia and Egypt might believe that Israel could do whatever it wanted without incurring serious opposition from the United States.

The difficulty with the strategic consensus approach was that it did not square with the basic features of the Middle East political environment. As our analysis has shown, the major problems the United States confronts in the Middle East stem from the various interlinked regional conflicts and the impact they have on America's geostrategic, resource, and balance of power interests. The strategic consensus approach failed to execute step 1 correctly: determining who is seriously involved. The Soviets are not the primary cause of these problems, and seldom are they even a major actor. Although the United States must be concerned with the increased Soviet military capability, a Soviet military attack is not the *primary* threat in the Middle East. The primary threat is Soviet exploitation of regional conflicts and instability, and it is on these matters that Washington must focus.

The strategic consensus approach had several other drawbacks. First, it gave insufficient emphasis to the various regional power problems that regional actors faced and to the fact that to those actors these other problems were the most important. Second, it underestimated the still enormously important past-future linkage of antiforeign nationalism. Most regional actors still possess an almost obsessive sensitivity to actual or perceived foreign efforts at domination, and a too-apparent United States presence in the region often is just not welcome. Third, because the strategic consensus approach required the cooperation of specific regional actors for its implementation, Washington had an enormous stake in preserving the status quo. But the currents of change are strong and unpredictable all throughout the Middle East, as the assassination of Anwar Sadat in the fall of 1981 clearly highlighted, and a strategy requiring stability is very unsatisfying in such a volatile region. Fourth, it prevented maximum use of the cardinal principle of third-party influences. The lack of recognition of the significance and nature of the many linkages between problems led the United States in some cases to view those problems too bilaterally. It therefore had to forego opportunities for influence that altering policies toward third parties would have provided.

By early 1982 the United States began to realize that the highly visible strategic consensus approach was not yielding beneficial results. Therefore, although planning for use of the Rapid Deployment Force in the new Central Command continued apace, the Reagan administration generally adopted a lower profile in both rhetoric and action. Instead of loudly stressing the Soviet threat and engaging in highly visible efforts to obtain onshore facilities, informal cooperation and quiet assurances that the United States could be relied on for support became the order of the day. Indeed, Washington's fundamental concern in the early part of 1982 was not the Soviets but the completion of the Israeli withdrawal from Egypt under the terms of the 1979 Peace Treaty. Much to the administration's relief, although there were minor irritations the Israelis pulled out on schedule. To help meet Israeli security concerns, the President agreed to American participation in the multinational peacekeeping force organized to patrol the Sinai.

After the Sinai withdrawal was completed, the United States hoped to reinvigorate the Palestinian autonomy talks, but efforts soon were sidetracked by events in Lebanon. On June 6 in "Operation Peace for Galilee" Israeli forces moved northward across the border, determined to secure the twenty-five-mile zone in southern Lebanon from which Palestinian forces in the past had attacked Israeli settlements. But the Israelis did not stop once that objective had been achieved, instead fighting their way to the outskirts of Beirut. It was clear that the Israeli goal had changed. No longer was it just to secure southern Lebanon; now the objective was to eliminate the PLO. The United States dispatched Ambassador Philip Habib, who had mediated the cease-fire in southern Lebanon in 1981, and as a result of his painstaking efforts another agreement was reached. PLO leaders and combatants in Beirut, equipped only with side weapons, closed their offices and bases and departed for nine different Arab countries (although PLO units in northern and eastern Lebanon stayed in place). American, French, and Italian forces were dispatched to assure safe implementation of the withdrawal and to protect the Palestinians who had been left behind. While the pullout was in process, Bashir Gemayel was elected the new President of Lebanon.

After the PLO withdrawal was completed the multinational force also departed. Tragedy soon followed. On September 14 Bashir Gemayel was assassinated. Then Israel allowed Lebanese Christian forces to move into the Palestinian refugee camps at Sabra and Shatila, following which these forces massacred hundreds of Palestinian men, women, and children. Lebanon's new President, Amin Gemayel, requested outside assistance and the United States, France, and Italy again dispatched troops to Lebanon. In light of the evident turmoil and uncertainty, it was not at all clear how long the peacekeeping forces would have to stay. With the multinational force in place the United States, hoping to restore Lebanese government sovereignty while still ensuring Israeli security, undertook an intensive mediation effort to bring about the full withdrawal of all foreign forces from Lebanon.

As 1982 went on Washington more and more believed that progress on the stalled West Bank autonomy talks was of fundamental importance. With the strong advice and encouragement of Secretary of State George Shultz, on September 1, President Reagan launched a major new peace initiative. The President suggested that the most appropriate way to solve the Palestinian problem was eventually to have complete Israeli withdrawal from the West Bank and Gaza Strip, and the development of Palestinian self-government "in association" with Jordan. Reagan said there should not be an independent Palestinian state, however, and that Jerusalem should remain undivided. Israeli Prime Minister Begin summarily rejected the Reagan proposals, but at an Arab summit meeting in Fez, Morocco, Arab leaders, though reiterating their call for an independent Palestinian state, hinted at some flexibility on the issue of the recognition of Israel. And rather than rejecting the Reagan Plan, the Arabs meeting at Fez just avoided mentioning it. King Hussein, too, showed some flexibility, calling the Reagan proposals "constructive," though he made it clear he would not join the negotiating process unless the other Arabs, including the PLO, authorized him to do so. Even Yasir Arafat was not entirely negative (which caused him trouble *inside* the PLO and with the Syrians).

But it was evident that little progress could be made on the Arab-Israeli problem as long as the troubles in Lebanon consumed so much diplomatic energy, so it was Lebanon that held center stage for most of 1983. The American commitment gradually deepened, changing from enabling the Lebanese government to resume full control of Beirut to bringing about the total withdrawal of foreign forces, helping the government obtain sovereignty over the entire country, and achieving security for Israel's northern border. Throughout the first half of the year efforts were focused on the withdrawal issue, and through the extensive mediation of Ambassador Habib and Secretary of State Shultz a Lebanese-Israeli accord was reached in May. Pleased, the United States lifted its suspension of F-16 shipments to Israel.

But no further progress was made. Israel said that implementation of the accord was conditional on the withdrawal from Lebanon by Syria and the PLO and they both refused, demanding that the Israelis leave first. Meanwhile, the American commitment in Lebanon continued to deepen. As discussed in Chapter 6, Congress authorized deployment of American marines for an additional eighteen months. After the bombing of marine headquarters in October, Reagan said keeping American marines in Lebanon was "central to our credibility on a global scale." As the shelling of marine positions continued, terrorist incidents mounted, and American reconaissance planes were fired on from Syrian-controlled territory, the United States responded with naval bombardments and air strikes. Determined not to be "driven out," the President, in language reminiscent of the domino theory, stated:

> We cannot pick and choose where we will support freedom. We can only determine how. . . .
> If others feel they can intimidate us . . . in Lebanon they will become more bold elsewhere. If Lebanon ends up under . . . forces hostile to the West, not only will our strategic position in the eastern Mediterranean be threatened but also the stability of the entire Middle East including the vast resources of the Arabian Peninsula.[8]

[8] *New York Times*, October 24, 1983, p. A10.

As if things were not already sufficiently complex and volatile, in the fall of 1983 elements of the PLO, wounded and humiliated by the expulsion from Beirut and south Lebanon in 1982, rebelled against Yasir Arafat. Castigating Arafat for his unwillingness to reject completely the Reagan initiative and for what were alleged to be other signs of "moderation" toward Israel, Syrian-supported rebel units launched a full-fledged military onslaught, driving Arafat and his supporters from Tripoli and throwing the entire Palestinian movement into disarray.

Throughout the remainder of 1983 and into early 1984 the Lebanese situation continued to deteriorate in a seemingly unending cycle of violence. With his political base disintegrating and the territory under the control of the central government continuing to shrink, in March President Gemayel, following talks with Syrian President Hafez Assad, cancelled the May 1983 troop withdrawal agreement with Israel. Assad, who had opposed the agreement because of the new relationship it would have established between Israel and Lebanon and the diplomatic achievement it signified for the United States, had won a major victory. American marine members of the multinational peacekeeping force, meanwhile, were withdrawn to their ships in frustration, and the European members of the peacekeeping force soon departed also.

The United States' efforts to help the Lebanese government obtain sovereignty over the entire country and to bring about the removal of all foreign forces had failed, and American prestige declined accordingly. Syrian influence, on the other hand, had never been higher. What would happen next was not clear. What was clear, though, was that the United States again had not correctly determined who was involved or assessed operational power relationships accurately, and again had chosen a higher level of step 4 (involvement) than was wise.

8.

Summing Up

As the United States looks forward and confronts the interlinked problems of the Middle East in the 1980s and 1990s, if it is to design and implement a cost-effective policy it will need to operate from a considerably different concept. For the United States to protect its national interests in the Middle East in the optimal manner, the action-oriented "can do" determination to plunge in and solve the region's problems must be replaced by a prudent, discriminating policy designed to involve the United States in a much more selective and low-key fashion.

Certain guidelines seem clear. To begin with, it is important for the United States to decrease even further its foreign oil dependency. Some progress already has been made. In mid-1984 oil imports from OPEC were only 60 percent of what they had been in 1973, and only one-fourth as much as in 1977.[9] Indeed, by 1984 only about 10 percent of U.S. oil imports came from the Persian Gulf. Moreover, there were nearly 400 million barrels in the Strategic Petroleum Reserve. While these developments are laudable, there is still much to do. The United States needs to diversify further its sources of oil supply, with special emphasis on the Western Hemisphere. The Strategic Petroleum Reserve should be fully filled. With regard to protecting Gulf supplies and the vital sealines of communication, the United States, though it cannot withdraw entirely, should not play such a dominant role. Because *allied* dependence on Gulf oil is so very real, in the very nature of international relations Japan and Western Europe will *have* to play a larger role in ensuring access, just to protect *their* interests, if the United States does not do it for them.

In dealing with the Arab-Israeli, inter-Arab, and Persian Gulf stability problems it will be essential for the United States to take into account the cardinal principles and implementing

---

[9]The year 1977 was a watershed for oil imports. Net imports, net imports from OPEC sources, and net imports from Arab OPEC states were higher than in any year prior to 1984.

guidelines developed in Chapters 4 and 5. Because there are so many interlinked conflicts most regional actors' policy choices will be made by very narrow margins. If one recognizes the trade-offs that are available, frequently it will be possible to take advantage of counterbalancing interests and produce a favorable change in policy through the careful use of third-party influences. Past-future linkages will continue to be important, and a major effort must be made to empathize with regional actors to understand their interests and priorities. Soviet-American relations simply are not the most vital concern of the Middle Eastern states. Washington cannot base its policies toward key states such as Saudi Arabia or Egypt primarily on the Soviet threat if it hopes to maximize cooperation. Because of the fluidity and complexity of regional relationships, more than ever it will be imperative for Washington to investigate thoroughly to determine who is involved and who holds the key to the outcome of regional conflicts, and not assume it is the Russians. Rigid preconceptions must not blind policymakers to the fact that most of the region's problems are neither Soviet-produced nor essentially military.

Because the five problems the United States faces are interlinked, another prescription is in order: the United States must not deal with Middle Eastern issues separately, in isolation one from the other. Whereas the Arab-Israeli conflict is clearly central to regional stability (although its resolution would not eliminate all other problems), it cannot be addressed effectively without considering its multifaceted, multidirectional linkages with Persian Gulf, inter-Arab, oil, and United States-Soviet concerns, for example. The best *net* cost-benefit policy must be sought, recognizing that no policy will be perfect. And certainly Washington cannot productively view the region's problems only in terms of moral abstractions (although it would be foolish to assume that the emotional attachment to Israel will not continue to be important).

Having given these general prescriptions, we must at the same time inject a note of caution. There is a quite natural, very "American" tendency at this point to want to lay out specific policy proposals, proposals that, if implemented effectively, presumably would lead to a resolution of key regional problems. Such a tendency carries within it the assumptions that these regional problems can be solved satisfactorily, and that the United States can play a major role in their resolution. But as the analysis in this chapter has made clear, in our view such assumptions are at best questionable, and probably are just plain wrong. In many regional situations America's operational capability can be only minimal. The United States can*not* unilaterally solve the Arab-Israeli conflict, for example, nor can it decisively influence the course of many of the inter-Arab disputes. Similarly, whether the Persian Gulf will or will not be stable is largely beyond America's power to determine. Washington must accept these limitations and tailor its policies accordingly. Low-involvement orientations, such as avoidance or minimal nonalignment, often will be the most suitable, or efforts at mediation (that are not disguised attempts to impose American solutions). Moderate aid should be provided to key friendly states such as Israel and Egypt, but too much of an effort to shape events (especially if it is made without sufficient regard for regional quarrels and antiforeign nationalism) will be extremely counterproductive among the highly "sovereignty-conscious" actors of the area and will increase instead of lessen the enmity confronted. Given the depths of regional conflicts, the passions involved, and the irreconcilable nature of many of the parties' interests, the United States must accept the fact that many of the Middle East's problems will not be solved soon, and be prepared to live with uncertainty, volatility, and tension for the foreseeable future.

Though it may not be to America's *liking,* this lack of operational capability is not automatically inimical to America's *interests.* It is very important to remember that although the U.S. leverage is limited, *the Soviet Union's is too.* Since the problem of Soviet influence is the most important of all for American interests, and since the most fundamental American objective is to prevent Soviet control, and not to achieve American dominance, the general inability of outside powers to exercise controlling influence also can be seen as a plus. If Washington is in no position to dominate the Middle East, neither is Moscow.

The United States has valuable assets as it deals with the Middle East. It really *does* want the states of the region to remain independent. It really does not want any one state to become dominant or indigenous governments to become subservient to foreign masters. It desires economic progress and stability and has an unmatched capacity to provide technological assistance. It has strong regional friends who, although they do not always see eye to eye with Washington (or each other), generally act in ways beneficial to United States interests. Surely Moscow would trade its footholds in South Yemen and Syria, and its tenuous relationship with Iraq, for friendly relations with Israel, Egypt, Saudi Arabia, Jordan, and Oman. Although the list of friends and adversaries may change, there is no reason it should not remain of equivalent value. Given its strengths, and the region's characteristics, if the United States will reduce further its oil dependency and employ prudently a policy approach that utilizes the cardinal principles and takes appropriate operational steps within the context of the Middle East's basic features, it can achieve the objective of preventing control of the region by a single hostile power, and do so at reasonable cost and risk.

The Developing Nations:
Africa and Latin America

It is impossible to draw a line anywhere on the map of Africa which does not violate the history or future needs of the people.

President Julius Nyerere
Tanzania, 1963

If, after Nicaragua, El Salvador is captured . . . who in Central America would not live in fear? How long would it be before major strategic U.S. interests—the canal, sea lanes, oil supplies—were at risk?

Thomas O. Enders
Assistant Secretary of State for Inter-American Affairs
February 2, 1982

Relations with the developing nations of Africa and Latin America only rarely were crucial to the United States before the Vietnam War.[1] In the post-Vietnam era, though, the situation gradually changed, and the United States more and more found itself confronted with problems in these regions that seriously impacted important interests.

1.

Three Interlinked Problems

The problems confronting the United States in its relations with the developing nations span a range from geostrategic to economic. In theory, the distinction is clear. Geostrategic problems involve politico-military interests, and economic problems, obviously, involve economic interests. But, as we shall see, these problems ultimately tend here, as elsewhere, to blend together so that it is hard to treat them separately.

[1]We broaden our coverage to include Asia as appropriate when discussing economic issues. Politico-military matters related to Asia were discussed in Chapter 18.

Change and ferment are the common hallmarks of the developing world. In Africa, most of the states have only recently become independent and have little experience managing the complex affairs of modern government. Moreover, few African states have a stable sense of nationalism and societal cohesiveness is rare, most states containing a wide variety of tribal, ethnic, and religious groupings whose primary allegiance is either sub- or transnational. Added to this is the fact that many of the newly independent African states are socially, economically, and politically stratified, a situation highly conducive to disruption and violence. On top of everything else, most of these states lack economic viability.

Internal unrest has been rife in such conditions, as one would expect. In the five years preceding the advent of the Nixon administration, for example, military coups took place in fourteen different African countries. A bloody civil war broke out in the Congo (Zaire) in the early 1960s, and in 1968 brutal fighting was raging in Nigeria. Adding further to African instability was the fact that the boundaries of many African states have no intrinsic logic, having been established decades earlier by one colonial power or another primarily to suit imperial interests. Although frontier disputes before the 1960s were relatively infrequent, with the progress of decolonization they were increasing, with severe risks of escalation and external intervention.

In Latin America, most of the states (except for several in the Caribbean) have a longer period of national identity than the new states of Africa, which reduces one source of instability. And, because of their location, prior to the 1960s most Latin American states generally remained outside the main areas of global tension (although after Castro took power in Cuba the Caribbean sometimes has been a flash point). But, like Africa, many Latin American states also have had a history of regime change by military coup, and economic and social conditions often have bred turmoil.

The first problem the United States encountered in Africa and Latin America after the Vietnam War was the widespread *instability and ferment* in these areas. It provided numerous opportunities for foreign exploitation. The problem raised the issue of how, over time, the vital interest of preventing these regions from being controlled by a single hostile power could be implemented? Such instability and ferment also had a negative impact on *the second problem* Washington had to confront, the rapidly growing U.S. deficiency in *strategic resources* (see Diagram 15). Because many of the primary sources of these crucial materials are developing nations in Latin America and Africa, particular LDCs thus will increase greatly in geostrategic significance to the United States. South Africa with its diamonds, platinum-group metals, gold, manganese, fluorspar, and antimony; Nigeria and Venezuela with their oil; Zaire with vast quantities of cobalt, copper, and uranium; and Brazil with its manganese and tantalum, are but a few examples. The issues here are how best to see to it that control or significant influence over such major resource suppliers or producers does not pass into the hands of a power hostile to the United States and how to ensure free access on a normal commercial basis?

The likely trend in the development of the resources problem could find the United States confronted by a crucial *third problem*—ensuring the security of *supply routes*. The issue here is how to protect those raw material and resource imports to the United States which must be transported over vulnerable sealines of communication (SLOCs)? For the United States (and Western Europe), the primary SLOCs from Africa and Latin America involve the Indian Ocean and the South and Eastern Atlantic. Maritime and power projection capabilities, bases and overflight rights, the use of port facilities, and the like thus become matters of concern. South Africa is especially critical, for around the Cape of Good Hope passes most of the West's internationally exchanged oil, plus a vast quantity of strategic materials. Cuba, by virtue of its location and military strength, can threaten transit of the Windward and Yucatan Passages. It is thus potentially able to dry up ocean traffic from the Panama Canal, South America, and the Caribbean to the East Coast or the Gulf of Mexico. Most Americans tend to underestimate U.S. vulnera-

DIAGRAM 15 Net Import Reliance as a Per Cent of Apparent Consumption. Source: U.S., *Department of Defense, Annual Report Fiscal Year 1982*, p. 22.

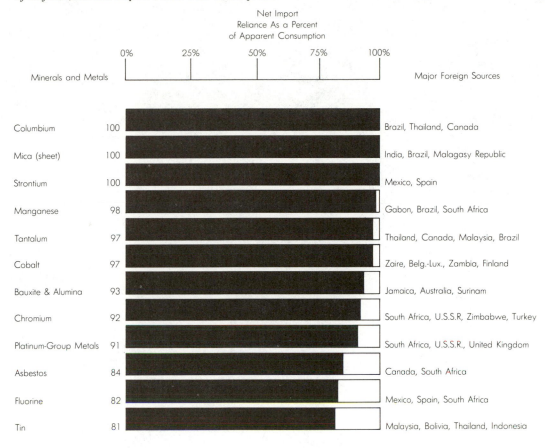

Net Import
Reliance As a Percent
of Apparent Consumption

Minerals and Metals		Major Foreign Sources
Columbium	100	Brazil, Thailand, Canada
Mica (sheet)	100	India, Brazil, Malagasy Republic
Strontium	100	Mexico, Spain
Manganese	98	Gabon, Brazil, South Africa
Tantalum	97	Thailand, Canada, Malaysia, Brazil
Cobalt	97	Zaire, Belg.-Lux., Zambia, Finland
Bauxite & Alumina	93	Jamaica, Australia, Surinam
Chromium	92	South Africa, U.S.S.R, Zimbabwe, Turkey
Platinum-Group Metals	91	South Africa, U.S.S.R., United Kingdom
Asbestos	84	Canada, South Africa
Fluorine	82	Mexico, Spain, South Africa
Tin	81	Malaysia, Bolivia, Thailand, Indonesia

bilities here, but a glance at a map showing German submarine sinkings in World War II would make them revise that view.

Of course, LDCs have geographical significance for more than just SLOC reasons. Brazil is the fifth largest country in the world and would be important for that reason if no other. Location makes states strategically signficant and proximity influences the degree of concern. Clearly this is one reason the United States is so interested in developments in the Caribbean and in Central America. And certain states automatically acquire importance because they share borders with a number of states. Mozambique, having common frontiers with Tanzania, Malawi, Swaziland, Zambia, Zimbabwe, and South Africa, is an example.

The United States must cope with these geostrategic problems and must do so within the special context of the ardent desire of the developing nations for rapid economic development.

Economic development is a major objective of all LDCs, often being the primary concern. By whatever indicator one employs—GNP, or GNP per capita, percentage of the labor force in agriculture, or the like—three fourths of the states in the world are very poor, as Table 9 shows. These countries are not identical, of course. The countries of Latin America generally have had a per capita product two to three times larger than that of the African states. And there have been variations in the rate of growth, technological sophistication, and so on. But there are broad similarities, and they are significant. The LDCs are extremely poor, and seek rapid growth; they

TABLE 9 Economic Status of Less Developed Countries

	GNP PER CAPITA		GDP*		% OF LABOR FORCE IN AGRICULTURE	
	1979 Dollars	Average Annual Growth (%) 1960–79	Millions of Dollars, 1979	Average Annual Growth (%) 1970–79	1960	1979
Venezuela	3,120	2.7	48,970	5.5	35	19
Argentina	2,230	2.4	95,120	2.5	20	13
Brazil	1,780	4.8	204,480	8.7	52	40
South Africa	1,720	2.3	52,920	3.6	32	30
Chile	1,690	1.2	20,920	1.9	30	20
Mexico	1,640	2.7	121,330	5.1	55	37
Cuba	1,410	4.4	—	6.0	39	24
Panama	1,400	3.1	2,770	3.4	51	34
Ivory Coast	1,040	2.4	9,130	6.7	89	79
Peru	730	1.7	14,770	3.1	53	38
Nigeria	670	3.7	75.170	7.5	71	55
Nicaragua	660	1.6	1,560	2.6	62	40
Honduras	530	1.1	1,900	3.5	70	63
Zimbabwe	470	0.8	3,640	1.6	69	60
Angola	440	−2.1	2,490	−9.2	69	60
Kenya	380	2.7	5,280	6.5	86	78
Indonesia	370	4.1	49,210	7.6	75	59
Niger	270	−1.3	1,710	3.7	95	91
Zaire	260	0.7	6,020	−0.7	83	75
China	260	—	252,230	5.8	—	71
Mozambique	250	0.1	2,360	−2.9	81	67
India	190	1.4	112,000	3.4	74	71
Somalia	—	−0.5	1,030	3.1	88	84
Ethiopia	130	1.3	3,530	1.9	88	80
Chad	110	−1.4	570	−0.2	95	85
Bangladesh	90	−0.1	7,670	3.3	87	74

Source: The World Bank, *World Development Report 1981* (New York: Oxford University Press for the World Bank, 1981), pp. 134–139, 170–171.
*GDP means Gross Domestic Product.

want the gross world product to grow, and they want their share to increase. They see the disparity of output and wealth between the LDCs and the developed nations, and they want these gaps significantly narrowed.

For most of the LDCs, though, the obstacles to sustained, vigorous growth are massive. Insufficient capital is available, domestic savings being too meager. External sources can and do provide a second source of capital, but when the sums are large enough to make a difference, debt service itself can become a problem—as Table 10 shows for Mexico, Brazil, and others in 1982. Economic infrastructures (marketing, distribution, transportation and communication systems and the like) usually are inadequate, modern work skills are minimal, the technological level is low, and the majority of the work force is employed in subsistence agriculture. Problems are compounded in many of these countries because of great population pressures. Indeed, in some areas population growth is almost like a tidal wave. The stark reality is that many poli-

TABLE 10 International Monetary Fund Loans to LDCs

COUNTRY	TOTAL LOAN* (in millions)	UNDRAWN BALANCE	DATE OF AGREEMENT	EXPIRATION DATE
India	$5,500.00	$3,520.00	Nov. 81	Nov. 84
Mexico	3,960.00	3,410.00	Dec. 82	Dec. 85
Yugoslavia	1,828.20	609.40	Jan. 81	Dec. 83
Turkey	1,375.00	319.00	June 80	June 83
Rumania	1,212.75	1,047.75	June 81	June 84
Pakistan	1,010.90	521.40	Dec. 81	Nov. 83
Peru	715.00	649.00	June 82	June 85
Ivory Coast	532.95	211.60	Feb. 81	Feb. 84
Jamaica	525.47	205.81	April 81	April 84
Hungary	522.50	390.50	Dec. 82	Jan. 84
South Africa	400.40	225.50	Nov. 82	Dec. 83
Morocco	309.38	92.81	April 82	April 83
Thailand	298.65	246.51	Nov. 82	Dec. 83
Sudan	217.80	140.80	Feb. 82	Feb. 83
Kenya	166.65	67.65	Jan. 82	Jan. 83
Uganda	123.75	82.50	Aug. 82	Aug. 83
Costa Rica	101.53	75.90	Dec. 82	Dec. 83
Honduras	84.15	67.32	Nov. 82	Dec. 83
Somalia	66.00	49.50	July 82	Jan. 84
Liberia	60.50	55.00	Sept. 82	Sept. 83
Madagascar	56.10	33.66	July 82	July 83
Togo	52.25	44.28	Feb. 81	Feb. 83
Senegal	51.98	51.98	Nov. 82	Nov. 83
El Salvador	47.30	26.26	July 82	July 83
Haiti	37.95	24.75	Aug. 82	Sept. 83
Gabon	37.40	37.40	June 80	Dec. 83
Barbados	35.07	24.55	Oct. 82	May 84
Mali	33.42	13.00	May 82	May 83
Mauritius	33.00	8.25	Dec. 81	Dec. 82
Panama	32.67	32.67	April 82	April 83
Malawi	24.20	13.20	Aug. 82	Aug. 83
Gambia	18.59	0.0	Feb. 82	Feb. 83
Dominica	9.40	3.14	Feb. 81	Feb. 84

*Interest charged on loans varies according to loan size, market conditions and source.
Source: International Monetary Fund

cymakers in these countries have to devote much of their time to simply keeping their people fed.[2]

What complicates the problem of the LDCs is the fact that their trade often is heavily dependent on the sale of one or two products. Fluctuations in the quantity and price of the sales of that product can have an enormous impact.[3] If the product is exported primarily to one or two countries, and if the economy is significantly dependent on exports for the capital necessary

[2]According to the UN Food and Agriculture Organization, in 1983 twenty-two countries faced *catastrophic* food shortages in Africa alone. *New York Times,* October 18, 1983, p. 1.

[3]Consider the price history of coffee, which has been controlled by international agreement between producers and consumers ever since the early 1960s and is thought to be the most successful such commodity agreement ever made. The world price of coffee per pound, under $.50 in the late 1960s, shot up after 1975 very steeply to about $2.30 and then began falling after 1977 to a June 1983 average of $1.26. See *New York Times,* July 18, 1983.

for development (or the foreign exchange with which to purchase imports), the LDC is in a highly vulnerable position.

2.

The Historical Legacy: Latin America

As always, it is necessary to see how things came to be what they are. In both Latin America and in Africa, historical development has left a strong legacy of antiforeign nationalism, a nationalism that conditions and strongly complicates United States-developing nation relations. We look at Latin America first.

Throughout much of the nineteenth and early twentieth centuries, as our discussions in Chapters 2 and 11 showed, the United States, basing its policies on the Monroe Doctrine, treated Latin America more or less as its private backyard, to do with as it wished. At times, substantial U.S. intervention took place in Latin America, sometimes to protect hemisphere security, and sometimes just to preserve U.S. hegemony. In the first thirty years of the twentieth century, U.S. forces intervened repeatedly in Nicaragua, Haiti, the Dominican Republic, Mexico, and Panama.

Three points stand out about United States-Latin American relations during this period. First, the United States' heaviest involvements were in Central America and the Caribbean, the regions closest to its frontiers. Geographical proximity and the Panama Canal combined to make this "northern zone" of Latin America the sector most crucial to U.S. vital interests. Second, because of Washington's intervention, many Latin Americans over time came to view the Monroe Doctrine as just a cover for Yankee imperialism, although it is fair to point out that the Monroe Doctrine also shielded Latin America from *European* ambitions. Third, although U.S. intervention and its dominating presence provoked much enmity, at the same time the United States *did* gain concrete strategic advantages from its control of the Caribbean and the Panama Canal and from its possession of the lands it had acquired by war from Mexico and Spain. Hemispheric hegemony *did* produce both U.S. national and hemispheric security.

But because U.S. policies were producing much enmity American policymakers in the 1920s and 1930s began a reappraisal. On March 4, 1933, President Roosevelt announced the "good neighbor" policy: the United States would be a good neighbor, "the neighbor who resolutely respects himself and, because he does so, respects the rights of others." Gradually relations between the United States and Latin America improved. Troops were withdrawn from Nicaragua and Haiti, the Platt Amendment was abrogated, nonintervention was pledged, trade barriers were reduced, and cooperation was increased in various functional areas. It became correct to speak of an evolving inter-American system.

Once World War II broke out it became clear that there was still a major weakness: there was no political-military framework for collective diplomacy and defense. To remedy this an overhaul and expansion of the inter-American system began, and in September 1947 the Rio Treaty of Reciprocal Assistance was signed by twenty American states. The following year the Charter of the Organization of American States (OAS) was approved.

In the early years of the Cold War the United States accorded Latin America very low priority. Washington was preoccupied with Europe, Asia, and the Middle East, regions where the threat of Communist bloc expansion was perceived to be greater. The only major exception occurred in Guatemala, where in 1954 the CIA (on instruction from the President) helped overthrow the government of Colonel Jacobo Arbenz, believing it to be controlled by, and be a base for, international communism. But such intervention was very much the exception to the rule, the United States generally paying little attention to Latin American developments. Avoidance was the most frequently chosen orientation.

In fact, it was the very lack of United States attention that most irritated some Latin leaders. Many Latin Americans believed that the United States was the primary *cause* of the area's problems and that it "owed" them assistance. Certainly the problems Latin governments faced were severe: a very high population growth; feudal political structures; one-product trade-dependent economies; and insufficient capital, skills, and technology for economic growth. And regardless of "whose fault" their problems were, there was no gainsaying the importance of the United States to Latin American economic development. At the end of the 1950s, for example, more than 40 per cent of Latin American exports went to the United States. Although Latin America was not of much interest to the United States, the United States was of great interest to Latin America. By 1960 social, economic, and political pressures were such as to create a region in ferment.

Another factor was added to the cauldron in 1959 when Fidel Castro overthrew Cuban dictator Fulgencio Batista. Castro's revolution raised the specter of a wave of rebellion throughout the region, and put the future of United States–Cuban relations at risk. But it was also a clear sign that unrest in the region was increasing, that unless programs were devised to deal with some of the underlying causes conditions there would become even more explosive and the appeal of violent revolution would increase.

President Kennedy took office concerned both about these deteriorating conditions and the increasingly close Cuban-Soviet relationship. As Soviet arms shipments poured into Cuba and Castro proclaimed his allegiance to the Communist cause, the President, after listening to key advisers from State, the CIA, and the JCS, chose confrontation and accepted a plan that had been developed under the Eisenhower administration for an invasion of Cuba by a small group of CIA-trained anti-Castro forces. On April 17, 1961, these rebels landed in the Bay of Pigs, but were quickly and decisively defeated. Because all parties knew of Washington's role despite the pretense of noninvolvement, the United States suffered a humiliating defeat. Additionally, the Bay of Pigs operation revived the specter of United States interventionism in Latin American affairs. Most Latin leaders, being strongly anti-Communist, abhorred Castro's growing ties with Russia, but they did not favor an interventionist policy by Washington.

The Bay of Pigs operation was one facet of the Kennedy administration's determination to pay more attention to Latin America, but the showpiece of the new policy was the Alliance for Progress. Washington believed that fundamental changes were irrevocably altering the status quo, that conditions demanded the United States take the lead in shaping the future. Stressing the need for self-help and social reform, President Kennedy called for all people in the hemisphere to join together in a vast cooperative effort, pledging $20 billion in U.S. economic assistance to help make the project a success. But progress was slow, and by 1968 the Alliance had come to a dead end, its dreams shattered against the hard rock of reality.

Despite Kennedy's early interest in Latin American affairs and the Alliance for Progress, for most of the 1960s the United States gave Latin America only intermittent attention. Using an indirect opposition orientation, inconspicuous efforts were made to influence domestic affairs in countries such as Honduras, Chile, and Brazil, and there was concern over the open support of insurrection by Castro in various countries (especially Bolivia), but generally Latin American developments received low priority. The major exception occurred during the revolt in the Dominican Republic in April 1965. Although intelligence and diplomatic reports were incomplete and contradictory, President Johnson believed he knew the answer to the question in step 1—who is involved. Johnson believed that the rebels were Communist controlled, and the crisis thus became part and parcel of the struggle against the Communist bloc. The crisis was seen as a test of American resolve, so some 30,000 American troops were dispatched, most of whom subsequently were put under the command of an Inter-American Peace Force formed by the OAS. The fact that the United States did not seek OAS action until *after* the marines had landed, and probably would have acted as it did with or without the OAS, did not escape attention. Although the OAS retroactively endorsed the action, the affair angered almost all Latin American leaders, raising suspicions about Washington's intentions and costing much of the goodwill that had been built up in prior years through the "good neighbor" policy.

Although U.S. policies did little to resolve basic Latin American problems in the 1960s, the Latin governments themselves made progress in some areas. There was general if varying economic growth throughout the region, GNP rising by more than 5 per cent a year, and GNP per capita rising more than 3 per cent annually. There were other encouraging economic developments, as industrial production increased and manufactures began to account for a significant percentage of regional exports. But the negatives outweighed the positives because very little had been done to remedy the most fundamental problems, and the causes of unrest continued to grow and fester. Continued turmoil seemed the most likely course.

3.

The Historical Legacy: Africa

When World War II ended Africa was almost entirely under foreign control, as it had been since before the turn of the century. The United States had paid little attention to "the dark continent" before, and had no inclination to do so now.

But strong winds of change were beginning to blow. African nationalism, though inchoate and variable, was growing rapidly, making it increasingly difficult for the colonial powers to maintain their positions. Where prior to 1957 only Ethiopia, Liberia, Sudan, and South Africa were independent, in that year the dam broke and a flood of new independent African states followed. By 1969 there were thirty-eight independent states in Africa, providing nearly one third of the entire membership of the UN. Led by individuals such as Kwame Nkrumah of Ghana, Sékou Touré of Guinea, and Kenya's Jomo Kenyatta, the new states generally adopted nonaligned policy orientations, demanded the elimination of what remained of foreign control on the continent, tackled the enormous problems of economic development, and worked to establish viable, stable entities.

But as the rapid decolonization occurred, trouble abounded. The new states had no stable sense of nationalism behind them and societal cohesiveness was rare. Hundreds of tribal units existed, frequently claiming a higher allegiance than the new government; the new states' boundaries usually were artificial; more than eight hundred languages and dialects were spoken on the continent; and there were nearly as many religious variations as there were languages and ethnic groups. To this enormous diversity and fragmentation and the lack of sovereign experience were added other difficulties. Many Africans had believed that once independence was achieved progress would be swift and sure, because their problems had been "caused" by the colonialists. But progress seldom was as rapid as expected, and great frustrations and tensions resulted. The lack of trained personnel, infrastructures, technology and capital, and the like prevented the rapid development many had foreseen (and promised). Since people had expected substantial progress with independence the lack of progress placed regimes under severe pressure, and often there were major struggles for power, rapid changes in government not being unusual.

The pervasive instability frequently manifested itself in secessionist efforts and civil war. Tribally or religiously based separatist efforts were evident in Ghana, Chad, Kenya, and Zambia, for example. Following Belgium's abrupt grant of independence to the Congo (Zaire) in 1960, a full-scale civil war developed. It was almost five years before order was restored there; the attempted secession by the mineral-rich Katanga province was prevented after a substantial UN intervention supported by U.S. money and material. Zaire's borders were unchanged. In 1962 Ethiopia formally absorbed Eritrea, but immediately an Eritrean secessionist movement began, a movement that continued year after year. In 1966 tribally based unrest began in Nigeria, and

MAP 10

AFRICA

in May 1967 the Ibo-dominated Eastern Region proclaimed itself the independent state of Biafra. Soon a bloody civil war was in progress there, ending finally in a central government victory. Nigeria's borders were unchanged.

Despite, in many cases, very arbitrary frontiers, the tendency to preserve the status quo in Africa was clear.

Exacerbating and overlapping all the foregoing difficulties in this period was a set of racial/colonial problems. To black Africa, the racial and colonial factors were inseparably linked. In cases such as Portuguese Africa, the reason is clear. Whereas in the 1950s and 1960s, Britain, France, and Belgium were relinquishing their possessions, white Portugal continued to hold black Angola, Mozambique, and Guinea tenaciously.

To outsiders the Southern Rhodesian situation seemed less clear. Southern Rhodesia had defied the British and broken away from the Commonwealth in 1965, after which the UN imposed economic sanctions. Thus in the late 1960s Britain no longer controlled Rhodesia. To black Africans though, the issue was still as much colonial as racial, because the white domination and racial discrimination in Rhodesia were the product of a system developed under Britain's tutelage. The same sort of reasoning applied to the dominant position of whites and to the segregation of apartheid in South Africa. And, as it had been since World War I, South-West Africa was controlled by South Africa.

Even as late as 1969 it was difficult to predict the near-term future of any of these cases. In Portuguese Africa stubborn insurgencies were continuing, but Lisbon seemed to be unyielding. The situation in Rhodesia was explosive, but the UN sanctions appeared to be having little impact and there was no reason to assume that major changes would occur soon. South Africa seemed too strong to be overcome militarily by those who most might wish it done and too solid economically to be affected seriously by economic sanctions. And although in 1966 the UN declared South Africa's mandate over South-West Africa terminated and renamed the territory "Namibia," the UN actions had little practical effect.

In this change and ferment economic development would have been difficult even if the economic base had been strong, but in most African states it was pathetically weak. African leaders were well aware of this weakness, so despite the historically developed anti-Western coloration of many of their nonalignment stances a number found it necessary to maintain strong trade and aid linkage to the industrialized West, and in many instances the interest was reciprocal. French and British links to their former colonies were especially strong.

But although a number of cooperative economic relationships were established with the industrialized states, most African LDCs believed that until they increased their bargaining power the amount of aid they received would be insufficient and their terms of trade would be unfavorable. Many LDC leaders in Latin America and Asia shared this view and the result was the formation at the 1964 United Nations Conference on Trade and Development (UNCTAD) of the Group of 77. The Group of 77 became a permanent organization and soon became a major player in the growing North-South dialogue.

The United States usually played only a minor role in Africa in the 1950s and 1960s (with the exception of the UN Congo operation, noted previously). Although generally supportive of African independence and the end of colonialism, Washington's primary concern was the Cold War and in that context events in Africa usually seemed unimportant. Because of this, in the Eisenhower years, with the United States trying to deter Soviet expansion while maintaining a balanced budget, an avoidance orientation most often was chosen.

President Kennedy was more interested in Africa than Eisenhower had been, and in the early 1960s it looked as if the United States would play a larger role in Africa. The Peace Corps, established in 1961, definitely was oriented toward Africa, foreign aid funding was increased, and the United States played a major part in supporting UN activity in the Congo. But the interest was short-lived. Aid programs did not produce the desired gratitude or leverage and economic development was minimal, so by the mid-1960s aid was decreased substantially. Even more important than the lack of progress was the fact that events in other areas were taking precedence, the Vietnam War overshadowing all else. By the late 1960s the United States again was adopting a very low profile in African affairs.[4]

4.

African Affairs Under Nixon, Ford, and Carter

U.S. policy toward Africa during most of the Nixon administration might be labeled "benign neglect." Although the President was sympathetic to African desires for self-determination and economic development, and he strongly denounced white racism in southern Africa, such matters were distinctly secondary in importance to maintaining stability. The administration believed

[4]The United States was much less reliant on the import of strategic resources in 1968 than it is today and the matter was not yet perceived to be a major problem.

that more often than not an active U.S. role would be destabilizing and the priority of maintaining stability was demonstrated many times. In March 1970 the United States vetoed a UN Security Council resolution that condemned Britain for not overthrowing the white-minority regime in Rhodesia; in 1972 Washington joined with the United Kingdom, South Africa, and Portugal in voting against a resolution that proclaimed support for the domestic opponents of the South African regime and the legitimacy of their struggle against apartheid "by all available means"; and there were many other examples.

Washington was not against change as such. It welcomed the independence of Guinea-Bissau in 1974, and despite the leftist leanings of President Machel it did not oppose the 1975 independence of Mozambique. What the United States was against was *violent* change, because it raised the issue mentioned in connection with the first of the three problems. Change should come in an orderly, peaceful manner *in order to maintain stability* and minimize the potential for Soviet intervention and a "Cold War" confrontation.

There could be no better illustration of this way of approaching the first problem than the fact that in 1971, in exchange for continued use of air bases in the Azores, the United States promised Portugal, the leading colonialist state in Africa, aid of almost half a billion dollars. This was nearly as much as all Africa combined would receive. Inevitably, black Africa interpreted such action as support for Portuguese colonialism. Aid to Portugal, the passage by Congress in 1971 of the Byrd Amendment (allowing the importation of chrome from Rhodesia despite UN sanctions), U.S. votes at the UN opposing radical change, and the general unwillingness to play a major role on self-determination and development matters, increased significantly African suspicion of U.S. policy.

The second problem (resources) by 1974 was forcing Washington to increase its attention to developing nations traditionally receiving a very low priority. Washington began to alter course. At the UN, though strongly opposing the Group of 77's demands for a (pro-LDC) New Economic Order and the General Assembly's Charter of the Economic Rights and Duties of States, American policymakers offered new proposals on economic and other North-South problems. But it was the Angolan crisis that was the real turning point for the United States, for the way in which that crisis developed made the first two of the three problems merge. Though the dispute had a long history, it burst forth in full-throated crisis only in 1975. In January, Portugal and the major nationalist organizations signed an agreement stipulating the procedures for Angolan independence. The agreement soon broke down, and fighting broke out among the guerrillas. Angola, with its major oil and mineral resources, and occupying a key geographical position on the border between white-ruled southern Africa and independent black states, could not be dismissed as being of no strategic significance.

The instability-Soviet foreign exploitation problem and the resource vulnerability problem overlapped as the Soviets increased their activity.

The Soviet Union had supported the Popular Movement for the Liberation of Angola (MPLA) since organized resistance to the Portuguese had started in 1961. As intra-Angolan hostilities escalated, Russian aid was now increased. The United States, which through the CIA had been providing quite limited support to the National Liberation Front of Angola (FNLA), responded by increasing economic and military assistance on a clandestine basis to the newly formed FNLA/UNITA (National Union for the Total Independence of Angola) coalition. But the increase only provoked a counterescalation by Moscow. Determined that their client should win, after South African forces intervened on behalf of the FNLA/UNITA in October, the Russians introduced more than 10,000 Cuban combatants into Angola. This counterescalation could not be countered by covert means and Ford and Kissinger went to Congress in a plea for funds to aid FNLA/UNITA. Congress refused to appropriate monies to match Soviet escalation, and by mid-1976 the MPLA had gained the upper hand.

The success of the MPLA stimulated Kissinger into a flurry of activity. A stable equilibrium, the Secretary believed, could be established only if the Soviets could be properly restrained and if Soviet-Cuban intervention were precluded elsewhere in the region, but that would not be possible if the United States had alienated most of an Africa increasingly polarized on racial matters. Therefore, during a visit to sub-Saharan Africa in early 1976 Kissinger set forth a ten-point program providing for majority rule in Rhodesia, and declared that until majority rule was obtained the Salisbury regime "will face our unrelenting opposition." Kissinger also urged that a timetable be set for independence for South-West Africa, condemned apartheid in South Africa, promised to work for repeal of the Byrd Amendment, and pledged "positive" new aid programs.

At first, there were some encouraging responses. Rhodesian Prime Minister Ian Smith indicated a willingness to negotiate, and in Namibia, at talks organized by South Africa, black and white delegates announced the territory would become independent on December 31, 1978. In September, after private talks with leaders of "front-line" black states, Kissinger's negotiations with Ian Smith produced a plan for majority rule within two years and the immediate convening of a conference to form an interim government. But while nationalist leaders applauded Smith's acceptance in principle of majority rule, they rejected several specific elements of the package. Smith, in response, said the terms were not negotiable, and soon there was deadlock again. By year's end a negotiated solution once more seemed far off.

Jimmy Carter took office believing that his predecessors' policies had been misguided and ineffective, and he promised major changes. Reassessing American counterbalancing interests, he concluded that Soviet-American relations would remain important, but would not dominate. The United States would be freed from an "inordinate fear of Communism" to work on building a new world order, encourage economic development, protect human rights, enhance North-South cooperation, and so on. In Secretary of State Vance's view, in "no other aspect of foreign policy did our administration differ so fundamentally from that of our predecessors."[5]

Although Carter attached a high priority to improving United States–African economic relationships, in general the results proved disappointing. By 1980 sub-Saharan Africa still was receiving less than 3 per cent of U.S. exports, and total American economic assistance was only about $2 billion annually, approximately 10 per cent of all donor assistance to the continent. Direct private investment, too, was small. There were a number of developments that partly qualify this assessment, though. First, although overall economic assistance was low, it was growing at rates averaging more than 20 per cent per year and it was becoming an increasing share of the total AID budget. Second, although the overall magnitude of trade was not large, trade relations with specific countries such as Nigeria and Zambia were expanding rapidly. Third, U.S. imports from black Africa came to exceed imports from South Africa. Crucial in this development was the Nigerian connection. Nigeria, influential with the other independent black states, possessing the largest black population on the continent, and having the second largest armed forces and a GNP equal to South Africa's, was a major oil producer. By the time Carter left office, Nigeria was the second-largest supplier of imported crude oil to the United States, and by far its largest trading partner in sub-Saharan Africa.

On racial-colonial questions the Carter administration took a hard line, believing that identification with the cause of majority rule was both the best way of preventing Soviet-Cuban exploitation of racial conflicts, and necessary as a matter of fairness and basic human rights. Determined to demonstrate unity with black aspirations, the President persuaded Congress to overturn the Byrd Amendment. On the Rhodesian issue the administration utilized an orientation of neutral problem solver. Coordinating frequently with the "front-line" states bordering on

[5]Cyrus Vance, *Hard Choices: Critical Years in America's Foreign Policy* (New York: Simon & Schuster, 1983), p. 256.

South Africa and Rhodesia, Washington advanced a joint plan with Britain to hand power back to London which, in turn, would supervise free elections while a UN force supervised a cease-fire. Smith rejected the proposal, instead negotiating a modified majority rule internal settlement with moderate black leaders. The President refused to accept Smith's "solution" though and fought vigorously against congressional pressures to lift economic sanctions against the new government.

But because it was unable to bring about progress, Washington eventually reduced its involvement. Others did not, however, and they had better luck. While the fighting continued in the fall of 1979, the British government convened another in the long series of conferences on the matter, and in early December an agreement was reached on free elections. A cease-fire followed, and in elections held in February, Robert Mugabe was elected Prime Minister. On April 17, 1980, the new state of Zimbabwe was born.

Although the United States had played no direct role in the Rhodesian settlement, the outcome was warmly welcomed by Washington. Results were less pleasing on the Namibian issue. Here, too, at first President Carter pushed hard. Fearing that the independence earlier agreed to by South Africa would result in a government strongly discriminating against blacks, in 1977 the five Western members of the UN Security Council formed a "contact" group to negotiate simultaneously but separately with South Africa and the guerrilla organization SWAPO (South West Africa People's Organization). By July 1978 both parties had accepted in principle a UN plan for a cease-fire, the election of a constituent assembly, and Namibian independence. But in September the South African government withdrew its support, and in December Pretoria, working in coordination with the Democratic Turnhalle Alliance (a coalition of Namibian groups opposed to SWAPO), held elections under its own auspices. With no settlement in sight, SWAPO, which had been as uncompromising as Pretoria, and which had received increasing aid from the Soviets and Cubans at bases in Angola, escalated the war. Though more talks were held and several times agreement seemed near, South Africa, concerned about a spillover effect, the loss of a buffer, and the ultimate objectives of an independent Namibia dominated by SWAPO, always found ways to avoid agreement.

The United States was no more successful in persuading South Africa to modify apartheid, all attempts to exert influence proving unproductive. Building on the 1963 ban on arms sales, an embargo was placed on all items used by the South African military and police, and limited economic pressures were applied. But because of South Africa's enormous geostrategic importance, even the Carter administration was unwilling to adopt a confrontation orientation. The second and third problems blended at this point (resources and supply routes). To move too strongly might destabilize South Africa, around whose southern periphery many large supertankers transited daily carrying oil to Western Europe. Moreover, with trade continuing at nearly $4 billion a year, South Africa continued to be the primary U.S. supplier of such strategic materials as chromite, diamonds, and antimony. By the end of 1980 Washington seemed at least as concerned with South Africa's potential cooperation on political-military issues as it was with apartheid.

Developments in the Horn of Africa raised the third problem (supply routes) in connection with the first (Soviets). In July 1977, Somalia invaded Ethiopia in support of guerrilla activity by ethnic Somalis of the Western Somali Liberation Front. From the early 1950s through 1976, Ethiopia had been the United States' most important ally in Africa, and strong links had been maintained even after the overthrow of Emperor Haile Selassie in 1974. But in early 1977 the United States had suspended aid on the ground that human rights were being violated by the new regime, and Colonel Mengistu, the new Marxist-leaning Ethiopian leader, subsequently had followed up on previous contacts for aid from Moscow. The Soviets, long the major supplier of Somalia, for a while uncomfortably straddled the fence, but eventually they opted for Ethiopia.

As in Angola, Cuban soldiers were employed, perhaps 20,000, along with 3,000 Soviet military technicians, perhaps $2 billion in aid, and several Soviet generals on the ground. By the spring of 1978 the Somalis were repelled.

Because of its anti-interventionist inclinations and the simple point that, after all, the Soviets *were* helping defend Ethiopia's territorial integrity, the United States could do little immediately except to urge restraint and decry Soviet adventurism. Nevertheless, the Soviet action generated a great deal of debate in Washington about the "real" nature of the Soviet threat and perhaps the occasional need for direct involvement. When Angolan-based Katangan insurgents invaded Zaire's Shaba (Katanga) province in May 1978, the United States, concerned that its inaction in the Ethiopian-Somalian conflict (following on the Soviet-Cuban "success" in Angola) was being interpreted as a lack of resolve, provided eighteen C-141 transports to ferry Belgian and French troops in their bailout of the Mobutu regime.[6] Whether the United States ultimately benefited from even this limited involvement is open to question though, since African reactions were mixed and some of Washington's friends, such as Nigeria, were sharply critical. Such developments, however, powerfully pushed forward American contingency plans to be able to deploy significant military forces quickly wherever a need appeared.

By 1979 the Carter administration was increasingly concerned with such geostrategic and military matters. Although the North-South, "African solutions for African problems," frameworks were important, they were losing ground to concerns over the tendency of all three problems to blend together. Soviet-Cuban interventionism made it increasingly difficult to separate the issues of the East-West conflict, resource dependencies, and protection of SLOCs. When the Iranian and Afghanistan crises occurred geostrategic factors all but took over, with the (typically American) concomitant assumption that a forward deployment stance would be necessary. As mentioned in Chapter 19, major programs were undertaken to enhance power projection capabilities, and the administration pursued efforts to acquire military access rights (in Africa) in Kenya and Somalia. Seeing the Soviet-Cuban footholds in Angola and Ethiopia, Moscow's treaties of friendship with Ethiopia, Libya, Congo, Angola, and Mozambique, and Russian advisers in fourteen African countries, by the end of its term the Carter administration viewed Africa from what was nearly a 1950s Cold War perspective.

5.

Latin American Affairs Under Nixon, Ford, and Carter

In the Nixon-Kissinger years relations with Latin America received little attention except as they affected the administration's efforts to fashion détente and create a new global equilibrium with the Soviets. The United States deliberately reduced its visibility on the hemispheric stage, hoping the Latin Americans themselves would play more active roles in solving regional problems. A clear indicator of Washington's lower profile was that whereas at one time the United States had been the principal source of military equipment for Latin America, from 1969–1972 it provided less than one sixth of the arms transfers.[7]

There were a few exceptions to Washington's lack of attention in this period. For example, occasional disputes occurred over the policies of Latin American maritime nations toward the issue of territorial waters (discussed in Chapter 21). There also was a minicrisis over Soviet

---

[6]When Shaba province had been similarly invaded in 1977, the United States had limited its involvement to the shipment of a few spare parts.

[7]Richard Nixon, *U.S. Foreign Policy for the 1970s: Shaping a Durable Peace,* A Report to the Congress by Richard Nixon, President of the United States, May 3, 1973 (Washington, D.C.: U.S. Government Printing Office, 1973), p. 119. Congressional determination to restrict arms transfers also was important in this regard.

efforts in 1970 to construct a submarine base in Cuba. Both DOD and the JCS believed that a submarine base in Cuba would significantly worsen the strategic threat. Kissinger shared this view, but he also "saw the Soviet move as going beyond its military implications; it was part of a process of testing under way in different parts of the world."[8] Adopting a confrontation orientation, Kissinger informed Soviet Ambassador Dobrynin that the United States simply would not tolerate a submarine base in Cuba. Within two weeks construction of the base slowed down, and soon thereafter it ceased entirely.

Concern about the Communist threat was also driving United States policy vis-à-vis Chile. Assuming that similar ideology produces similar interests and that all leftist-Marxist governments actually or potentially are Soviet proxies, since 1964 the United States intermittently had implemented an indirect opposition orientation to prevent Salvador Allende from being elected Chile's President. In the early stages of the 1970 campaign the policy was continued but at a very low level because Washington was convinced that Allende would lose. The Nixon administration's actions were essentially ineffective though and Allende received 36 per cent of the vote, more than any other candidate. Since a majority was required for election the scene then shifted to the Chilean Congress for a run-off. Exactly what the United States did next remains a matter of controversy, but it seems clear that Washington again was involved in a moderate covert effort to prevent Allende's election. Again its efforts were unsuccessful, and on October 24 Allende was voted President of Chile.

Following his victory the United States was determined to make Allende's life difficult. Export-Import Bank grants and credits were cut off, and Washington played a major role in shutting off financing from the World Bank, IMF, and Inter-American Development Bank. All nonmilitary foreign aid was withheld following Chile's expropriation of United States copper companies (although military aid continued).

Although the American opposition was not very effective, Allende nevertheless had severe problems. Inflation in Chile was rampant, increasing from "163 per cent in 1972 to 508 per cent in 1973."[9] The coalition of disparate elements supporting Allende soon fragmented badly, extreme factionalism developed, and the Chilean economy was in shambles. Not surprisingly, domestic discontent became widespread. In June 1973 an army coup was prevented, but in September the military seized power and Allende was killed. Although the CIA was not directly involved in the overthrow of Allende, because of Washington's outspoken opposition and the fact that the Agency to some extent had been supporting opposition to his regime, the United States drew considerable criticism for alleged participation in the coup, both at home and abroad. The direct involvement of the United States in Chilean affairs had been very counterproductive. Much unnecessary enmity was created, and the fact that Allende's difficulties were primarily of his own making was lost in the shuffle.

Except for the submarine base and Chile cases the Nixon-Ford-Kissinger years were largely free of Latin American crises, and the administrations, indeed, did reduce United States involvement in the region. This deliberate policy, combined with the growing diffusion of power in the international system, contributed to declining U.S. influence in the region and the increased independence of the Latin American states. Much to Washington's chagrin, both Brazil and Mexico voted for the 1975 UN resolution identifying Zionism as "racism"; Venezuela played a not always friendly role in OPEC; and Brazil signed an agreement with West Germany for nuclear reactors and enrichment, fabrication, and reprocessing facilities. In the economic sphere, too, relations were changing. Once dominated by the United States' share, by the mid-1970s Latin America sent only about one third of its exports to the United States, importing a similar percentage. A similar diversification could be found in foreign direct investment (and in arms

[8]Kissinger, *White House Years* (Boston: Little, Brown, 1979), p. 641.
[9]International Institute for Strategic Studies, *Strategic Survey 1973* (IISS: London, 1974), p. 81.

transfers). When Jimmy Carter took office in 1977, Latin America was no longer the United States' private backyard, to do with as it wished.

Carter, rearranging the priorities of the three problems confronting American policy, was determined to pursue a new approach to Latin America. Instead of the "special (i.e., security) relationship" that had existed for so long, Latin American policy would be incorporated into a global framework that emphasized equality and respect and dealt with fundamental problems of economic growth, the protection of human rights, and North-South relations. In 1977 the two key issues to be addressed by the new approach were the Panama Canal Treaties and improving relations with Cuba. In each case, limited cooperation was the orientation chosen.

Since 1903 the United States had controlled a ten-mile wide Panama Canal Zone and operated the Panama Canal as, in the language of the 1903 treaty, "if it were the sovereign of the territory." The treaty rights obtained by the United States had been granted "in perpetuity." Over the years anti-American feeling over this situation had grown in Panama, and in 1964 bloody riots had erupted in the Canal Zone. Negotiations had commenced shortly afterwards, and had continued intermittently for the remainder of the decade and into the 1970s. By the time Carter took office, it was clear that for much of Latin America this was not just an American-Panamanian issue. It was a symbol of United States-Latin American and North-South relations in general.

Economically, by the late 1970s, with changes in world trade patterns and shipping technology, the canal, although still important, no longer gave the United States the great benefits it had for so many years. Indeed, less than 10 per cent of United States waterborne traffic transited the canal. Strategically though, the Panama Canal retained considerable value in facilitating naval deployments between the Atlantic and Pacific oceans, especially for use in limited contingencies or prior to the outbreak of general war.

For Carter the military advantages of retaining control over the canal were more than counterbalanced by the political gains he believed would be obtained by achieving a settlement, and as soon as he took office negotiations were reinvigorated. As a result, as we saw in Chapter 6, on September 7, 1977, Panama and the United States signed two new treaties. One provided for continued United States operation and control of the canal until the year 2000, but with progressively greater Panamanian participation. The United States also would have primary responsibility for the canal's protection and defense during this period. On the effective date of the treaty *Panama* (not the Organization of American States, as would have seemed appropriate) would assume general jurisdiction over the Canal Zone, and at the end of 1999 Panama would assume control of canal operations. The second agreement provided for the permanent neutrality of the canal, gave both parties the right to act to defend that neutrality, and provided United States warships a right of "expeditious passage."[10] Obviously, these treaties were poorly drawn from a technical viewpoint, and they immediately produced divergent interpretations by Panama and the United States.

Carter viewed these Panama Canal Treaties as a great success (though many critics charged that their strategic costs outweighed the political gains). His efforts to improve relations with Cuba were more of a disappointment to him. Negotiations did result in the opening of Cuban and United States Interest Sections in Washington and Havana in September 1977. The United States halted reconnaissance overflights and Castro released a few political prisoners. But continued Cuban involvement in Angola and Havana's participation with the Soviets in the Ethiopia-Somalia war precluded further progress. When the Shaba invasion occurred in mid-May 1978 the United States, convinced that the Cubans were deeply involved, suspended efforts toward achieving better relations.

Perhaps the most characteristic feature of Carter's approach was its emphasis on human

[10]Meaning, to move as quickly as possible, to "go to the head of the line."

rights, a point of view not directly centered on any of the three major problems the United States confronted. The President, utilizing broad moral abstractions as the basis for policy in typical American fashion, set up an NSC Interagency Group on Human Rights and Foreign Assistance to review all proposed projects in the light of the recipient's human rights record. Soon foreign aid to Uruguay and Argentina was cut off because of human rights violations in those countries. El Salvador and Guatemala, aware that they were scheduled to be on the *verboten* list, beat Washington to the punch by rejecting aid. Brazil, the most powerful country in Latin America, knowing that cuts in U.S. aid were coming, did likewise. It was almost as if the United States had set out deliberately to violate the cardinal principle of conservation of enemies. Only in the Dominican Republic, where in 1978 the combined protests of the United States and several Latin American governments prevented the military from overturning the election process, did the human rights approach signally contribute to a useful result.

In the economic sphere in the Carter years, military assistance declined noticeably. As Latin American nations diversified their world markets, the impact of U.S. trade policies and practices lessened somewhat also. The United States still was the most powerful economic actor in the region though, and its trade still constituted nearly one third of both Latin America's imports and exports.

Though the overall economic role of the United States in terms of Latin America declined somewhat in the Carter years, trade with Mexico defied the trend. By 1980, Mexico was the third largest trading partner of the United States.[11] Two-way trading now exceeded $27 billion, up from $9 billion in 1977. Partly, this great growth stemmed from the administration's recognition that Mexico's abundance of oil and natural gas was available by wholly secure transit routes.[12] This fact helped resolve the second and third of the three problems in a very efficient way.

Carter's globalist human rights–North-South emphasis left him unprepared for the complications of the real world. Nowhere was this more evident than in the crisis in Nicaragua, where General Anastasio Somoza Garcia had been strongly entrenched since 1936. The United States had maintained strong ties with the Somoza regime over the years, grateful for the stability it brought, if also concerned over its heavy-handedness. But by the mid-1970s opposition to Somoza in Nicaragua was pronounced. Several small revolutionary groups combined into the Frente Sandinista de Liberación Nacional (FSLN); the Sandinistas.[13] As Carter cut aid to Nicaragua in 1977 because of human rights violations, the FSLN increased guerrilla operations. When the moderate editor of *La Prensa,* Pedro Chamorro, was assassinated on January 10, 1978, demands for Somoza's resignation were loud. Order disintegrated, and the FSLN took the lead in opposition.

The United States now had to weigh two counterbalancing interests: to support Somoza (prevent "another Cuba"—a victory by a Marxist-oriented, partly Cuban-supported FSLN), or to oppose Somoza (in the name of human rights). The United States could not effectively pursue any middle ground. When ferocious fighting in the fall convinced Washington that Somoza could not win, Carter nonetheless tried to settle by means of an internationally supervised plebiscite that no one was enthusiastic about, including Somoza. The United States also terminated military aid. When the United States called for an OAS peacekeeping force to police a cease-fire in Nicaragua, the OAS rejected the plan. On July 17, 1979, Somoza fled into exile. Carter at first tried to work with the Sandinistas, but by the end of his term he was convinced that Nicaragua was more and more fueling the revolution in El Salvador, and all remaining aid to Nicaragua was suspended.

[11]Behind only Canada and Japan.
[12]Mexico's proven oil reserves were said to be about 50 billion barrels, sixth largest in the world.
[13]Named after Augusto Cesar Sandino, a guerrilla leader assassinated by the government in 1934.

Many saw the fall of Somoza as a distinct defeat for the United States. In a broad context, when combined with events in Iran, Washington's refusal to act in Ethiopia and Angola, the growing Soviet military capability, and the like, the revolution in Nicaragua could be seen as part of a general American decline, an inability to solve the first of the three problems. Viewed more narrowly, the revolution symbolized a significantly lessened American position in Central America and the Caribbean, and because Cuba had trained some of the FSLN leaders and supplied matériel, a corresponding gain for Castro. There were other events in this perceptual chain. In March there had been a leftist coup in the Caribbean ministate of Grenada. Then in mid-July 1979, United States intelligence discovered in Cuba what appeared to be a Soviet combat brigade. Carter insisted that that status quo was "unacceptable." Moscow claimed there was no combat brigade, only a "training force." Eventually it appeared that the Carter administration had overreacted, that most of the Soviets had been in Cuba for years and were there primarily for training purposes. After increasing modestly military aid and intelligence activities in the Caribbean and receiving Soviet promises not to alter the status quo, Carter declared that the brigade had been effectively "neutralized"; the "unacceptable" was now acceptable. To much of the American public, this was yet another setback.

There also were problems in El Salvador. In October 1979 a junta of Salvadoran colonels and civilians overthrew General Carlos Humberto Romero. Because of Romero's record on human rights Washington was not displeased at this turn of events, but throughout 1980 a climate of almost pathological violence developed in El Salvador as government forces and guerrilla groups clashed with unbridled ferocity. The Carter administration worked vigorously to moderate the violence and to bring about social and economic reforms, and to move the government toward a more democratic political structure, but without much success.

6.
The Reagan Administration and Beyond

The Reagan administration saw Africa and Latin America primarily as theaters in a zero-sum global struggle against Soviet communism. Other matters could be important, but they could not be primary.

Let us look first at Latin America. Ronald Reagan was fully convinced conceptually of the primacy of problem number one, instability and the opportunities it provided for Communist exploitation. Embracing the concept that similar ideology inevitably breeds similar interests, friends, and enemies, and believing that "the Communists" were actively seeking to foment world revolution, Reagan perceived a Soviet-Cuban axis constituting a major threat to U.S. interests throughout the hemisphere. As part of their global strategy, as Secretary Haig put it, the Soviets had developed a "hit list" designed to lead to the "ultimate takeover" of Central America. In December 1981 Washington charged that Cuba was seeking to exploit and control the revolution in Nicaragua and trying to induce the overthrow of governments in El Salvador and Guatemala. Washington charged that elsewhere in the hemisphere Castro was working to destabilize regimes in Colombia, Chile, Argentina, and Uruguay.[14]

Because concept governs content and affects the means of implementation, and because Reagan subscribed to the domino theory, the President felt it was necessary to choose a confrontation orientation, to halt "the Communists" before the dominoes began to fall. The dispute in El Salvador was a test of the U.S. ability and determination to draw the line against Com-

[14]See U.S. Department of State, "Cuba's Renewed Support for Violence in Latin America," Special Report no. 90, December 14, 1981.

munist aggression. If El Salvador fell, who in Latin America would be safe? Convinced that the main source of guerrilla strength was the training and weapons supplied by the Communist bloc countries, almost immediately on taking office Reagan countered by stepping up American economic and military aid. At first there were hopes in Washington for a quick military victory, but these soon proved to be illusory. Hoping that a democratic system could take root the United States then pushed vigorously for elections, and in March 1982 a constituent assembly was elected (with presidential elections scheduled to occur within two years). To Washington's chagrin the relatively moderate Christian Democrats received only 40 per cent of the vote, however, as a host of more conservative elements allied against them. The risk of an extreme polarization of Left and Right remained high, and the outlook for democratic institutions was uncertain at best.

As the war in El Salvador showed no signs of ending, the Reagan administration again stepped up its military aid to the Salvadoran government, certifying to the Congress that El Salvador was advancing toward democracy and generally showing greater respect for its citizens' human rights. Seeking to interdict the arms flow to the guerrillas in El Salvador from Cuba-

MAP 11

THE CARIBBEAN

Nicaragua through Honduras, military aid to Honduras was increased severalfold, joint military exercises were conducted, a U.S.-controlled training facility was established, and the CIA provided covert support for Nicaraguan exiles operating from Honduran bases against the Sandinistas. Concerned about Soviet-Cuban-Nicaraguan exploitation of other revolutionary situations, in January 1983 Reagan lifted the five-year-old embargo on arms sales to Guatemala. In late October the United States, in conjunction with several tiny eastern Caribbean nations, even undertook military action, invading the island nation of Grenada. Reagan was convinced that Grenada was, or soon would become, a Soviet-Cuban "colony," which would be used as a base for exporting terrorism and revolution throughout the hemisphere. Though the major stated objective at first was to rescue American medical students endangered by developments in the aftermath of a recent coup on the island, most observers saw the Soviet-Cuban "threat" as the major source of the President's action. Third-party efforts to moderate American-Cuban-Nicaraguan hostility, meanwhile, such as the February 1982 offer of Mexico's Lopez Portillo to act as a "communicator," a September 1982 initiative by Mexico and Venezuela, and the 1983 efforts of the "Contadora Group"—Mexico, Venezuela, Colombia, and Panama—were encountering skepticism in official Washington. No significant progress was being made in any of the disputes, although the 1984 election of José Napoleon Duarté as El Salvador's President was a positive development.

Although Central American and Caribbean conflicts took top priority in the Reagan administration, they were not the only important issues with which the administration had to deal. Two other issues of significance were the Argentine-British war over the Falkland (Malvinas) Islands and the Latin Americans' massive foreign debts.

On April 2, 1982, Argentina invaded the British-controlled Falkland (Malvinas) Islands. Before the commencement of hostilities, the United States, confronted as it was by a dispute between two states with which it wished to maintain good relations, had adopted a nonaligned orientation. As hostilities appeared more and more probable, President Reagan even personally telephoned the Argentine leader, General Leopold Galtieri, imploring him not to use force. But it was all for nought.

Washington's first response was to call for a cease-fire and try to mediate the dispute, but it soon became clear that no peaceful resolution was possible. Faced with the dilemma of choosing between unpleasant alternatives (a dilemma that generated serious clashes between Secretary of State Haig and UN Ambassador Jeane Kirkpatrick) after considerable internal debate the administration chose to support the British. Limited economic sanctions were imposed on the Argentines while London was supplied with fuel, intelligence assistance, and matériel.

As hostilities developed the British quickly established their superiority, and on June 14 Argentine forces in the islands surrendered. Only too aware of the damage its position on the war had caused in its relations with Argentina, in July 1982 the United States authorized the export to Buenos Aires of a computerized control system for a sensitive facility that was crucial to Argentina's nuclear energy programs, even though the Argentines consistently had refused to sign the Nuclear Nonproliferation Treaty. Several additional moves followed, and with the lifting of the arms embargo after the election of President Raúl Alfonsín in December 1983, U.S.–Argentine relations were almost back to normal.

The Reagan administration also undertook some initiatives to help certain of the Latin American countries deal with the massive external debts they had accumulated. Because of their strategic importance and the size of their debts (in both cases more than $80 billion), Brazil and Mexico received particular attention. In 1982 the United States negotiated a $1 billion advance purchase of oil for its Strategic Petroleum Reserve from Mexico, approved $1 billion in Commodity Corporation Credits, and worked with the International Monetary Fund to put together a new loan package. Reagan also worked with the Brazilians. In November 1982 he announced a $1.2 billion emergency loan, with an additional $300 million in December, and in Brazil's case, too, the United States helped obtain new funding from the IMF. Although these moves, in and of themselves, could not solve the debt problems, they helped, and they were important in easing political relationships. (And in early 1984 Reagan agreed to provide Brazil with sophisticated technology for its rapidly-growing arms industry, reestablishing the military relationship suspended during the Carter years.)

In the Caribbean, Reagan's economic policy was centered around what he called the "Caribbean Basin Initiative." Launched in February 1982, the Caribbean Basin Initiative was designed to be an "integrated program" that would "help our neighbors help themselves." Hoping to create conditions under which free enterprise could flourish, Reagan called for special tax incentives for U.S. private investment in the region, no protective tariffs against Caribbean products for a period of twelve years (except textiles and apparel), a moderate amount of U.S. development assistance, and technical assistance and training programs for the private sectors of the Caribbean nations' economies. Because of the mixed socialist-capitalist nature of most of the region's economies, the magnitude of the problems they confronted, and the unrest that was so prevalent in the area, reaction to the President's proposal was, to say the least, rather restrained. Congress, too, was less than enthusiastic, and although it passed the Caribbean Basin Economic Recovery Act in July 1983, implementation of the proposal was both slow and sporadic.

More generally, as would be expected, the Reagan administration's economic policy toward Latin America as a whole emphasized free market principles and sought to stimulate private investment—American and indigenous—through agencies such as AID, the Overseas Private Investment Corporation, and various multilateral development banks.

But the administration's efforts in all these areas really were rather minimal. International economic policy clearly was subordinate to domestic interests, and all attempts of Latin American states (and the Third World as a whole) to negotiate new North-South economic structures and relationships were vigorously resisted. Although the President did attend the Cancun Summit in October 1981, he went only on condition that there would be no detailed negotiations, no concrete agreements would be achieved, and there would be no Cuban presence. In such a situation, little concrete progress could be made in solving LDC economic problems, and little was.

One fact was glaringly evident: Although matters of economic growth and foreign debt were serious and the Reagan administration was willing to take a few limited steps to help relieve some of the pressures, because of Reagan's conceptualization of the forces at work and the primacy of the Communist threat, economic concerns, though they would have to be dealt with, would continue to be of secondary priority (whether the Latin Americans agreed or not).

Africa, like Latin America, was assessed by Reagan primarily in terms of its impact on the struggle against the Communists. Geostrategic interests thus were primary. As pointed out previously, in the late 1970s the United States had begun a major effort to deal with problem number three, the security of the vital SLOCs circumscribing southern Africa, by increasing its maritime capability and developing the RDJTF. Reagan stepped up both programs substantially. Economic and military assistance were increased, with Somalia, the Sudan, and Kenya (nations providing facilities for the RDJTF and/or working with Washington in joint military exercises) topping the list. Washington made no bones about the rationale with which it dealt with the issues. The states along the Indian Ocean littoral needed aid to "defend our interests in the Indian Ocean/Persian Gulf area. . . . Most countries in this region face severe economic difficulties, and several face serious, Soviet-inspired threats from Ethiopia or South Yemen."[15]

The resource-dependency problem was also on Reagan's mind. Unilaterally, efforts were

[15]U.S. Department of State, "International Security and Economic Cooperation Program FY 1983," Special Report no. 99, March 1982, p. 4.

made to increase stockpiles, and in April 1982 the President transmitted to Congress a National Materials and Minerals Plan. Resource interests and concern for stability also drove Washington's southern Africa policy. Worried that turmoil in mineral-rich South Africa would provide enormous opportunities that the Soviets or their proxies or clients might exploit, the United States declared it would not be forced to choose between black or white in South Africa or undertake actions that might exacerbate Pretoria's problems. In a move to reduce bilateral tension, Reagan eased the curbs on exports of nonmilitary goods that Carter had imposed. At the same time, of course, the President could not support apartheid. For geostrategic reasons, therefore, minimal nonalignment was the orientation adopted toward South Africa's internal affairs.

Namibia was a thornier issue; for much of black Africa it was a litmus test of U.S. policy. The Reagan administration was wholly aware of this, of course. Being action-oriented, the President decided that the United States should play a leading role in seeking a settlement; the United States would become "constructively engaged" in the search for a negotiated solution. Because all three problems of United States policy in the area were interlinked by the nature of events in the region, Washington's concern for stability, and the Soviet-Cuban presence on the continent, the United States sought a plan that would not unduly offend South Africa, one that would link Namibian independence with a Cuban withdrawal from Angola. The administration worked hard to convince South Africa of its intention to cooperate in the future if a Namibian settlement could be achieved. In consequence, in September 1981 South Africa and the members of the Contact Group agreed to achieve consensus on constitutional principles and then move on to negotiate the modalities of a transition period and free elections. Several other procedural difficulties were resolved also, and in early 1982 there were hopes that a solution was in sight. But as had happened so many times before stumbling blocks developed, and by midyear the situation again looked bleak.

In an effort to restore some momentum the United States initiated discussions with Angola on the linkage between the removal of the Cubans from Angola and the departure of South Africans from Namibia, but the talks got nowhere; and though in September Reagan warned the front-line states (Angola, Mozambique, Botswana, Zimbabwe, Zambia, and Tanzania) that the United States might withdraw from the Contact Group unless the evacuation of the Cubans was accepted as a precondition for negotiations, this too had little effect. American operational power was, to say the least, minimal. Decreasing even more the chances for a negotiated settlement, South Africa with increasing frequency launched military raids against suspected SWAPO bases in Angola, Mozambique, and Lesotho, implementing what many black Africans saw as a policy designed to destabilize the whole southern region. And within Namibia, itself, the South Africa-supported provincial government resigned and Pretoria resumed direct control. There seemed little reason to think a solution would be found soon. In the meantime, in early 1984 South Africa signed a nonaggression pact with Mozambique and a cease-fire agreement with Angola, mutually to diffuse the military tension.

Elsewhere on the continent, problem number one, instability and the opportunities it provided for Soviet exploitation, and its relationship to problem number three, the security of the vital SLOCs, continued to be major concerns. Political and military conflicts abounded, and though the United States was not involved in all of them, in those it considered geostrategically significant it played an important role. In northwest Africa in the former Spanish Sahara, where hostilities had occurred off and on since Spain's withdrawal in 1975, Reagan tilted strongly toward Morocco against the Libyan-backed Polisario movement. Immediately after taking office the President released $230 million worth of arms transfers that had been delayed by Carter, and soon more sales were made as well as agreements reached for a joint military commission and U.S. access to Moroccan air bases in time of crisis. In the strategically significant Horn, fighting broke out again in 1982 between Ethiopia and Somalia and the United States airlifted more weapons to the Somalis. And in Chad, Washington helped finance the successful guerrilla war of Hissene Habre against the Libyan-backed leader, Goukouni Oueddei. Reagan was determined to preserve some degree of stability in key areas, and was willing to commit American strength to do the job.

Economic difficulties added to the instability. *No* African state really did well economically in the early 1980s, and many actually regressed. Worldwide recession, high interest rates, weakened demand and lower prices for primary products (and oil), a tightening of the supply of foreign capital, all combined with the already heavy burden of foreign debt which many African countries had to carry, added up to economic conditions that in many cases were little short of catastrophic. Even Nigeria, whose future seemed so promising, was in severe straits, and these conditions there triggered a military coup in early 1984.

The Reagan administration's economic policy toward Africa appeared to be guided by three basic considerations. First, the United States should be selective in choosing whom to help, focusing primarily on states that were both geostrategically significant and anti-Soviet. Second, as much as possible, projects should be both economically sound and emphasize the role of the private sector. And third, economic difficulties, though important, were less significant than politico-military matters, and economic problems and the possible responses thereto should be evaluated in a larger geostrategic context. Many African states disputed this last point. As a result of these considerations, as we noted earlier, United States aid grew only modestly, and development aid shrank proportionately while military assistance increased. The Reagan administration also encouraged private efforts and those activities of international financial institutions such as the International Development Agency that particularly emphasize private enterprise. Partly because of the relatively small amounts of aid provided, but more importantly because of the magnitude of the problems being confronted, Reagan's policies did little to relieve Africa's economic troubles.

In addition to the ongoing disputes in southern Africa, continuing conflicts elsewhere on the continent, and widespread economic travail, Washington perceived a fourth source of instability, the machinations of Libya. Colonel Qaddafi was financing, training, and possibly directing terrorist organizations on a broad scale; covertly financing some of the Arab states' transactions with the Soviets; "meddling" in some of his neighbors' affairs (especially Chad, Egypt, and the Sudan); and acting as a munitions depot and providing the use of certain facilities for the Russian military. Reagan was determined to curb Qaddafi's influence and early he chose a confrontation orientation, expelling the Libyan diplomatic mission from Washington and undertaking a major effort to isolate Libya diplomatically. When in August 1981 Libyan warplanes challenged the U.S. Navy's F-14s over the Gulf of Sidra, they were promptly shot down. Although many in and out of Washington thought that Reagan overestimated Qaddafi's significance, there was no gainsaying that the Libyan leader was a destabilizing factor, nor was there any doubt of Reagan's determination not to let his influence grow.

Although it was impossible to predict with confidence the outcome of the major disputes in Africa and Latin America, it was evident that the Reagan administration's focus on geostrategic concerns in both regions was an important corrective to Carter's overemphasis on North-South issues and moral abstractions. Unfortunately, Reagan, in the fashion of many previous American presidents, placed far too much emphasis on the importance and binding power of a similar ideology with the result that he viewed all leftist governments with suspicion, as if they constituted an actual or potential bloc controlled directly or indirectly by Moscow. In a like vein, the Soviet hand was seen almost everywhere as causing or exploiting conflict, with regional and global causative factors seriously underestimated and problems too often viewed in essentially military terms. As a corollary, the interests and capabilities of regional actors tended to be insufficiently understood or empathized with.

7.

Summing Up

Putting together a coherent foreign policy for dealing with the developing nations is a difficult task at best. It seems clear that the importance of the LDCs to the United States will increase in the next several years. But although the United States has many interests in the developing world, some are much more important than others. A few countries are vital for geostrategic and/or economic reasons, others may be moderately important depending on the contingency, but some are essentially irrelevant. Judgments must be made about relative importance, and priorities established. Overall, the fundamental objective must be to prevent the control of Latin America and Africa, and the specific geostrategically important countries therein, by a single major power hostile to the United States.

This framework for objectives and interests does not dictate any particular policy stance or orientation, though. Just because the United States has a major stake in relations with many developing nations, it does not follow automatically that an active involvement, forward-deployment strategy and its associated orientations are called for. In Section 1, when we discussed the three problems confronted, we said that each raised an issue: how to prevent foreign domination of these areas, how to have free access to important raw materials, and how to ensure the security of vital sea routes. The answers given to these issues by successive U.S. administrations clearly revealed that neither the problems faced nor the issues to be decided show clearly which alternatives would make the best policy choices. They do not point automatically or obviously to *when, where, how,* and *to what extent* the United States should become involved.

Several basic factors explain why there are no easy answers. *First,* the widespread instability and minimal economic development of the developing world will continue to exist for the foreseeable future, creating unforeseeable difficulties. This may be regrettable, but it *is* what the future holds. The United States needs to recognize and accept this, and be prepared to adjust its policies accordingly. *Second,* most regional actors do not attach the same significance to the first problem: they do not perceive a major Soviet threat, and even those who do usually judge it as a matter of lower priority than their other concerns. Washington has not always, as our account shows, known how to empathize with and understand the regional actors' perceptions and priorities. To many LDCs, for example, economic problems *are* the number-one priority, and if it is to exercise power effectively the United States will have to recognize and deal with this fact. Because of their own interests, many LDCs will utilize participatory nonalignment in an effort to play Washington against Moscow and extract maximum benefit from both. Given these tendencies and the widespread instability and conflict, the Soviets occasionally will be able to exploit situations, and in some cases even have their aid sought. Nevertheless, and this is the *third* point, nationalism in the LDCs, inchoate and fragmented though it sometimes may be, is an extremely powerful antiforeign force. Past-future linkages are very important in this regard. The LDCs of Africa did not throw off the yoke of European colonialism in order to be controlled by Moscow, and the Latin Americans have no desire to have the Russian Bear replace the Colossus of the North. To assume that the United States sees the threat to the independence of these states better and cares more about their independence than they do hardly makes sense.

The three factors just described will limit United States operational capability in many situations. U.S. power will not always be pertinent to specific situations, or it may be too costly or risky to use. Moreover, the developing nations may not be "responsive" to U.S. preferences. The LDCs have their own perceptions and priorities, they confront very intractable problems, and they vary enormously in their culture and history. All of this suggests that the United States must be extremely cautious about attempting to play a leading role in resolving LDC problems. Ultimately, whether it is in Namibia or Nicaragua, local or neighboring parties usually will hold the key, and frequently there will be more to lose than gain for the United States by becoming heavily involved.

At the same time, because of its strategic materials requirements, it is important for the United States to step up its unilateral efforts to reduce its resource vulnerability, thus reducing the need or temptation to jump in. The Reagan program is a good start, but only a start. Militarily, it is important that the effort to enhance maritime capability to protect vital SLOCs be continued. Here the United States must make it clear that it will not single-handedly protect the SLOCs used by Western Europe and Japan. Like it or not, to protect their own interests, friends of the United States must play a larger role, and this they are likely to do in a substantial way only if it is evident Washington will not do it all for them.

Power projection capability will have to be upgraded also, but much caution and judgment will be needed. Because of the danger of unwanted entanglements, onshore facilities should be sought sparingly. And politically, in many cases efforts to obtain onshore basing, rights of access, and the like can be counterproductive. Forces must be built and deployed accordingly, and the sensitive issue of onshore access must be approached with great care. Second, and even more crucially, the enhanced military strength, once achieved, must *not* become an *excuse* to become involved. A *very selective, supportive* stance is called for, with regional forces generally providing the first line of defense against external attack. The United States should not deploy in front of those it is only supporting or be too trigger-happy in its readiness to react.

In complicated situations like so many we have described, where the three problems so often are interlinked, avoidance and/or minimal nonalignment frequently are excellent orientations for the United States. The question always must be asked whether the direct power of the United States must be utilized, for in the largest sense what the United States wants to see prevail in these areas is fully consistent with their own most basic preferences: to be free politically and to prosper economically. Although the United States in a strategic sense may have to shield these areas, if necessary, from the potential hegemony of a hostile superpower, the real nature of the issues, most of the time, is much more likely to be of less dramatic stuff. Here patience and a more consistent attention to the interests of the LDCs, as *they* express them, may in the end pay large dividends.

21

Mushrooming Technology and the Changing Global Environment

Apart from oil spills and the continual dumping of rubbish, untreated sewage, chemical wastes and spent nuclear fuel, the seas are exposed to contaminated rain and rivers. . . . With an estimated total volume of 360 million cubic miles, for long the ocean seemed big enough to digest or dilute without trace any amount of pollution. But, contrary to popular assumptions, [the seas] do not comprise a single entity. They are formed by separate bodies of water kept apart . . . largely without mixing. Hence the local pollution disasters. . . .

Thomas Land[1]

In considering the problems faced by the United States, the issues to be decided, and the alternatives that represent the effective range of choice, we have thus far proceeded area by area, geographically. But there are four fundamental problems, functional in nature rather than specific to one geographical area, which need to be addressed before we, in Part Five, summarize and conclude. Just as the U.S. Department of State has to be organized to deal with both geographical and functional (i.e., cross-regional or worldwide) problems, so too must any study of foreign policy cover both types of problems.

The four problems we discuss are *overarching* in a dual sense. First, they are of fundamental importance, not only to the American people but to all the peoples on Planet Earth. Second, although these problems can be discussed separately, they have an impact in some degree also on each other, for these four overarching problems are concerned especially with the physical conditions under which we live and the changes taking place in our environment. This environment has been changing swiftly under the impact of an ongoing technological revolution, which, gaining new momentum after World War II, bids fair to transform our lives.

The first problem is how to cope with what might be called "quality of life" issues—such

---

[1]"Taking a Regional Approach for Caribbean Development," *International Perspectives,* July-August 1981 (Ottawa, Canada), p. 25.

as food supplies, pollution, and potential shortages of raw material resources, especially as the surge in world population continues and puts pressures on living standards. The second problem is how to deal with the growth of terrorism, as the essentially indiscriminate use of violence increases. The third problem is how to adjust to the revolution in the approach to the uses of the seas, as the "open" ocean rapidly shrinks around the world. The fourth problem is how to deal with the uses of outer space, especially as the utility of space for warfare increases. As this listing of problems implies, technological change has an impact on all the other problems.

Each of these four problems, although linked to the others, also has a distinctive and separate character. Therefore, as we address each problem, we consider the issues that each problem raises and (usually) the choices each makes necessary for the United States.

Because the technological revolution provides the background that all four problems to a degree share, we begin our considerations with it and then move on to a discussion of the four problems.

1.

The Technological Revolution

The technological revolution today continues its momentum and its consequences. What are the nature of these changes and how do they affect the issues in this chapter?

In the eighteenth century, it took almost as long to deliver a message across Europe as it did in Julius Caesar's time. Two thousand years after Rome the roads in Europe were often in no better condition, while the method of transportation (horses at "stageposts" along the way) was the same. Then came change—in abundance. James Watt was not the first to produce a steam engine but his inventions in the 1760s made steam really usable. By 1829, George Stephenson's "Rocket" had outdistanced other early locomotives, and before that in 1807, Robert Fulton fitted out a steamer and ran it successfully on the Hudson River. From then on, man could move faster about the earth regardless of the winds and tides.

Closely associated to these changes in transportation were the changes the steam engine brought to industry and to production. The power of steam could be harnessed to perform work. Machinery meant labor-saving devices, greatly multiplying the productive capability of all who came to possess them. In time, steam from coal was supplemented by power from oil and then from nuclear fission. Electricity made the utilization of machinery simpler, altering forever the need for man to do most of his work during the daytime.

Communication was also revolutionized. The Battle of New Orleans in the War of 1812 was fought in the Americas *after* the peace treaty between the United States and Great Britain had already been signed. In Europe by this time Napoleon had installed a system of land semaphore stations on hills, which could send messages from Milan to Paris or Toulon in hours instead of days. The telegraph, the telephone, and the cable, made enormous changes and the radio freed man from the confines of landlines and cables, so that messages went through the skies.

With these gains in control over the environment, mankind acquired the ability to influence that environment much more significantly than ever before. With scientific progress came discoveries as to how to increase food supplies, how to cure illnesses, and how to prolong life. The population of the world, once held within the iron bounds of limits on food and medical care, began to spurt upward. From a population of one billion in 1800, world population almost doubled by 1920 to 1,810,000,000, and more than doubled by 1940 to 2,245,000,000. These increases were almost insignificant as compared to the population growth that took place over the next decades: 3,632,000,000 in 1970; 3,889,000,000 by 1975; and forecasts of 6,000,000,000 by the year 2000. The population growth was coming faster and faster. Population kept pressing

DIAGRAM 16 Population Projections, 1970–2000, By Major Regions (Source: U.S., Department of State, *World Population: The Silent Explosion,* 1978, p. 5.)

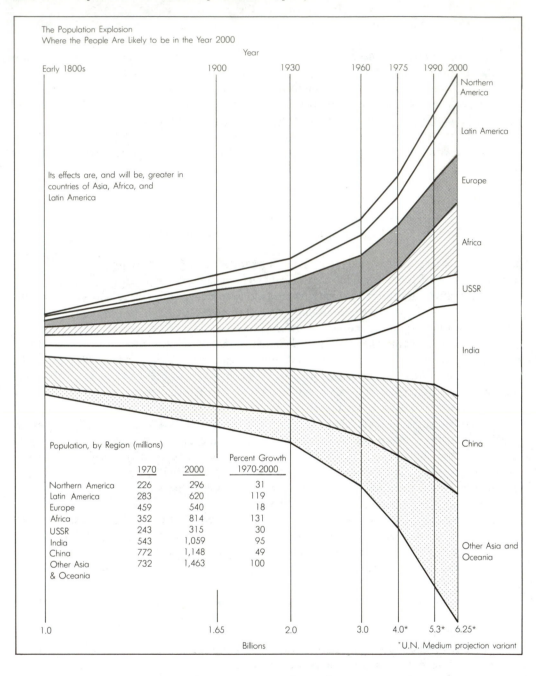

The Population Explosion
Where the People Are Likely to be in the Year 2000

Year

| Early 1800s | 1900 | 1930 | 1960 | 1975 | 1990 | 2000 |

Northern America

Latin America

Its effects are, and will be, greater in countries of Asia, Africa, and Latin America

Europe

Africa

USSR

India

China

Population, by Region (millions)

	1970	2000	Percent Growth 1970-2000
Northern America	226	296	31
Latin America	283	620	119
Europe	459	540	18
Africa	352	814	131
USSR	243	315	30
India	543	1,059	95
China	772	1,148	49
Other Asia & Oceania	732	1,463	100

Other Asia and Oceania

| 1.0 | 1.65 | 2.0 | 3.0 | 4.0* | 5.3* | 6.25* |

Billions   *U.N. Medium projection variant

Europe
Africa
China
Other Asia & Oceania

on food supplies but food supplies increased steadily and sufficiently on a worldwide basis so that famines were less frequent and the effects of famines were far less severe.

Catastrophe caused by food shortages, such as Victoria Brittain commented on in 1982, are much more avoidable today, provided the political will exists. She wrote: "Drought is an old and well-known enemy of people [in the Horn of Africa]. Emergency relief efforts . . . have been enough to save most people except when the droughts have been on an immense scale . . . or deliberately hidden by the responsible government, like the Welo famine that began the downfall of Emperor Haile Selassie of Ethiopia." That government having fallen, the new Marxist regime "has similarly destroyed the livelihood of thousands of peasant families . . . to stamp out resistance. . . . Resources of men and money no longer go into agriculture, but into war."[2]

Looking ahead, the enormous population increases anticipated by the first years of the next century constitute a problem which may have no desirable solution at all. The U.S. expertise in agricultural production is of great utility for furthering U.S. policy in this area in a humane sense.

In no area of technological change have developments exceeded those occurring in the development of new weapons. The remarkable "advances" of the second half of the nineteenth century brought mechanization to the armed forces—a trend that has since continued. At sea, the shape of things to come was foreshadowed by the battle between the Union ironship *Monitor* ("the cheesebox on a raft"—a reference to its flat deck profile with its revolving gun turret) and the Confederate ironclad *Virginia,* on March 9, 1862. Railroads were used for the first time during the American Civil War to transport troops and supplies in an organized way. Breech-loading rifles began to replace old-fashioned muskets. The first effective naval submarine was launched in 1888, and the machine gun, improved cannon, and better armor plate all also came along before the century ended. In World War I, when the old infantry tactics of the charge were still being followed, the British suffered 60,000 casualties in one day during the Battle of the Somme (1916) as flesh was pitted against machine guns. Then, in turn, came tanks to overcome the machine guns. Eventually, by World War II, airplanes came to overcome tanks. By the "fourth round" of the Arab-Israeli War, surface-to-air missiles (SAMs) came to overcome airplanes. Later came stand-off air-to-ground missiles and electronic countermeasures to counter the SAMs. And the process continues.

In the meantime, in 1945, nuclear weapons added an entirely new dimension of destruction. The first U.S. hydrogen bomb exploded in November 1952 over the Marshall Islands made a crater a mile in diameter with a maximum depth of 175 feet (equal to the height of a seventeen-story building). It became possible to fire ICBMs across oceans from one continent to another. Naturally, since these weapons could cause virtually an unlimited number of deaths, they remained the most feared development of all in the technological revolution. Although man had soared into space and visited the moon, it was space as a battleground that continued to arouse both the most intense hopes and extreme fears—as we see later in this chapter.

Thus, what Will Herberg once said about the upsurge of democracy and of nationalism might well be said of the *ultimate* consequences of this technological revolution: that it "is not a simple, unmitigated good, but rather an historical development of dubious character, presenting two faces, looking in very different directions."[3] Technology can have very positive or very negative results. But technology itself is neutral about the uses to which it is put by people.

The United States, as a leader in technology, has much that is positive and useful to offer a world with always more mouths to feed. We will be more specific after we have stated the first of the four problems.

[2] *Britannica Book of the Year, 1982,* p. 162.
[3] In a rebuttal to Arnold Toynbee, *The Intercollegian* (February 1955), p. 10.

2.

The Quality of Life on Planet Earth

The first overarching problem is the present and prospective quality of modern life on this globe, what one study called "Global 2000 issues."[4] The technological revolution just noted impacts directly on people everywhere, especially by raising issues in terms of food, pollution, and raw material resources.

Food as an issue provides one focus of the problem, intimately related to the numbers of mouths to feed. It was technology which permitted the very spurt forward in population. Longer life for all is now possible with modern medical techniques. But the big difference is infant survival. A hundred years ago in a family of ten children, only three might survive to full adulthood; now all ten may. In this same last hundred years the development of scientific agriculture has permitted the far more intensive planting of crops. Yields have grown to many times the amount per acre that was possible two hundred years ago. Fishing has become perhaps too efficient, endangering long-run supplies—which is one of the more positive reasons why nations have been establishing regulated fishery zones two hundred miles out to sea (as we see in Section 4). There is simply no way of foreseeing whether increases in food supplies will keep pace with the already projected increases in population, in general. For particular regions or nations, however, the outlook is probably more predictable.

With few exceptions the pressures of population will be greatest in the LDCs of Africa, Asia, and Latin America where economic development already is problematical for some, leading to increased disparities between rich and poor nations and growing domestic instability. In some of these areas agricultural capability is *declining* because of soil erosion, poor crop practices, deforestation, salination, and the like, and only a few areas have the capacity to produce foodstuffs at a rate commensurate to their needs. And maldistribution, poor administration, political problems, and the like complicate matters even more. Advances in transportation will allow the continued shipment of food, but if the world's supply and demand for food are in tighter balance the surpluses to deal with famines will be much harder to find. Birth control would appear to be the most effective alternative to starvation. One or the other is likely, and either is more likely than that technology will provide the answer.

There are, within this somewhat dismal picture, options that could change the course of events. The Soviet Union, for example, if it turned away long enough from its preoccupation with weapons, and turned to the solution of its problem in the agricultural area, especially if more free market operations were permitted, might make a significant difference in the overall picture. The variable here is the system of government and restrictions or lack of restrictions on free market forces. In the shorter run, it would be dangerous to neglect natural effects, such as drought and rainfall, which are unpredictable for any given year. If rainfall declined or rose even a small amount, or if the average temperature fell or rose even a little bit, it would have far-reaching effects on food supplies. (As it is, because of a warming trend, the oceans are rising at a quarter of an inch a year.) Technology can affect these variables only slightly.

A second quality of life issue is pollution. As more people fill the earth and technological change continues, it becomes more difficult to utilize policy to prevent a degradation of the environment. Industrialization, hailed as the panacea for providing improving standards of living, also brings with it pollution of the atmosphere, contamination of drinking water, even the threat of destruction of the ozone layer.

Pollution is an evil that costs money to correct. As with everything else, one deals here with trade-offs. To industrialize, in a fundamental sense, is to pollute. The newly developing countries

---

[4]The phrase is drawn from a United States government study titled *The Global 2000 Report to the President: Entering the Twenty-first Century* (Washington: U.S. Government Printing Office, 1980).

Problems and Issues Facing the United States

have, in general, not worried about the pollution as they industrialize, any more than the earlier industrializing nations did. Even to collect people in large cities is almost the same as saying, "to pollute." When one flies into Mexico City, the pollution often effectively obscures a view of the city from the air. A hundred miles from Los Angeles one encounters the first smog. In both cases, air currents increase the problem. The same is true of Ankara, where only houses up on the hillsides are above the yellow smog. These problems are not easy to cure. Putting controls on automobile emissions decreases the effect of the gasoline, and removing lead from gasoline does the same. Each effect is both a gain and a loss. As New England has begun to use more wood for fuel to conserve oil, smog has appeared in formerly clear skies. Nations worried about fundamentals such as the race between population growth and food supplies will probably put pollution control further down the list. Yet pollution can also spread across frontiers, as the Canadians complain is the case of "acid rain" coming from the United States. It seems probable that in this case, as in so many others, the richer nations will be able to afford more freedom from pollution than the poorer ones.

A third quality of life issue is raw material supplies. As many of the newer nations push forward in a headlong effort to industrialize they simultaneously fear that there will not be enough to go around, to meet the supply demands of all.

We have touched on raw material supplies earlier, but from a particular standpoint—whether monopolistic controls could be achieved by producing states. Here the issue is broader: *if* supplies will equal demand, what about the equity of some nations consuming far more than others?

This offhand approach to the supply-demand equation can be misleading. A fundamental law of economics quite rightly insists that supply and demand have an interlocked relationship and the glue that binds is price. If automobiles sold for $100, the demand would always far exceed the supply. If all automobiles were priced at $30,000 at today's prices, few could be sold and few would therefore be produced. Oil from shale can be produced in enormous quantities if the price were high enough and remained high enough.

This point is often forgotten as people speculate whether there will be "enough" for future generations. In one sense, the problem solves itself. If demand remains high or increases but the supply remains constant or decreases, the price will go up and a new balance will be struck. So in this sense there is always in general "enough." In another sense, as we said of food, there may not be enough in that, if prices rise, the poorer will suffer. And in a third sense, there is the possibility of the exhaustion of minerals or particular raw materials. Presumably, when all the copper is mined, there will be no new copper. (But the supplies of copper and manganese and cobalt in the seas are immense!)

Solutions to the problem of scarcity in the first sense turn around price. Solutions to scarcity in the third sense turn around technological ingenuity in finding substitutes. It is scarcity in the second sense that troubles the conscience. Or to put the point as it was expressed previously, what about the equity of some nations consuming far more than others? This issue is not primarily technological; it is philosophical or ethical or political.

Three general reactions to poverty can be observed, whether we speak of individual poverty or comparative national poverty. A first reaction is to ignore it. A second reaction is to take individual and personal action to deal with it—making a gift or contribution to alleviate the distress if Bangladesh is devastated by a tidal wave. The third reaction is to try to rearrange the division of resources; take from the rich and give to the poor, or shoot the rich and give to the poor. World history is full of the third reaction. In time, even in a short time, after a redistribution of wealth, the same old division recurs. (In the Soviet Union, for example, the rich today are the senior bureaucrats of the Communist party, who enjoy every kind of special privilege.) Whether this redistribution could be halted and real equity achieved and maintained—even *if* desirable—is very questionable. Some people are more intelligent, and some work harder or longer or more effectively than others. One might teach those who could do better how to do better, but there is no way to ensure some kind of high average general performance so that each person would "earn" an equal share of wealth.

This conclusion seems repugnant to the idealistic, but there is no evidence that the world would function better if wealth were evenly divided and there is certainly no evidence that that can be done or maintained.

The outlook is for continued disparities in wealth, with some nations consuming (and producing) more than others. There is no formula by which the poorer nations can achieve the standard of living of the richer nations, and certainly not by the transfer of wealth, whether outright or by "loans" which have no productive effect. What *can* be transferred, however, to some extent, is the technology for raising one's own standard of living. Even that is only itself a resource, to be used well or not.

One special reason for the creation of OPEC was the conviction of the oil-producing nations that only their former colonial or neocolonial subservience to "Wall Street" (or Exxon) had really been responsible for the lower standard of living they have known, and that they could bring about permanent change by amassing dollars now. (Their efforts increased pressures even more on the very poor nations.) Other raw material-producing countries have moved in the same way to try to create manipulated markets in tin or copper or coffee or sugar, though generally with limited success in affecting long-term prices.

Efforts to raise the standard of living are understandable and they confront the United States with a difficult set of choices on how to address these hopes. These efforts are probably doomed to disappointment in most cases, because the reasons for success or failure in terms of high standards of living in the United States, Sweden, and the like are not really appreciated. The combination of fertile land, a variety of raw materials, abundant water, a large and well-educated population, an appropriate role for government, and a beneficial climate is not one which is replicated very often outside the frontiers of the United States.[5]

There is some evidence that many of the newly developing countries realize that there are limits to what technological change is likely to do for them. They can see that the standard which Americans have enjoyed may not necessarily be replicable in their own nations where the sources of that standard mostly do not exist. But it is also in these poorer nations that population pressures are being felt most keenly, and it is also where the tendency is now unmistakable to devote resources disproportionately to armaments. (In 1979 all of the nations of the world spent a total of nearly $570 billion on their military forces—a vast sum and one contributed to disproportionately by the developing nations, especially given their other needs.) Disillusionment and bitterness in these nations are almost bound to increase in the future, and the accumulation of arms in their hands is almost as certainly going to result in more armed conflicts to settle disputed boundaries.

Quality of life problems, matters of technology and population pressures, pollution, resources, and so on have not been high on the list of American priorities except in a few isolated instances where they were perceived to affect seriously a specific relationship or crisis. Indeed, one really cannot say that in any broad sense there has been an American "policy" toward these problems; avoidance has been the most frequently utilized orientation. In part, this has been the result of the evident press and importance of other matters; in part, it is because it has only been recently that any number of policymakers (in *any* country) have recognized that a serious problem may exist and that unless policy changes occur in the next several decades the world as a whole, including the United States, may face a serious decline in the quality of life. Though it is not evident exactly what U.S. policy should be in these spheres, it is evident that a major

---

[5]Much of the discussion in Chapters 2 and 3 is relevant here.

complex of problems exists, a complex that is likely to constitute a significant part of the foreign policy agenda for years to come.

Given this situation, the most promising choice for the United States is to provide technical experts on a subsidized basis in such areas as agriculture (food), medicine (population control), and engineering (infrastructure for development). To the maximum extent possible, all aid should be offered in cooperation with existing multilateral organizations such as the United Nations and its specialized agencies. This approach avoids a direct giver-receiver relationship which can curry resentments. Technical development also has important financial implications, and financial relations between the United States and the developing countries represent a very delicate area, even via the multilateral route. Without the imposition of controls, money loaned to developing countries can easily be wasted in showy projects and also contribute to worldwide inflation. Aid should be provided only if it has real promise of producing economic gain. Again, interlinked to the financial question is that of arms supplies. The United States, under President Carter, tried to cut back the supply of arms to developing nations. It did not work very well as a policy. At the same time, it would be foolhardy to *encourage* heavily indebted nations associated with the "Free World" to spend disproportionately on arms. It is these nations that the United States can hope in practice to influence, even if only to a certain extent.

3.

Terrorism

The second overarching problem is increasing terrorism. One of the more negative aspects of change is the increasing resort to terrorism in the contemporary world. People have always felt fairly free to inflict bloodshed on other people in the name of politics, and the availability of television multiplies and extends the audience for such events. There is little doubt that terrorism is worse today than it was decades ago. One principal change is the less focused, more impersonal approach taken now by terrorists. Once it was an Austrian archduke and his wife who would be assassinated, as in 1914, or the King of Yugoslavia, as in the 1930s. Today it is more likely to be a school bus filled with children who were hit by a rocket, a plane load of tourists who were hijacked to Cuba or Entebbe, or Olympic athletes who happen to come from some hated country. Innocent bystanders are much more often involved in terrorist acts, there are more incidents, and the targets are less discriminated. In the U.S. State Department, the "roll of honor" of diplomats who have lost their lives in the course of their official duties has been lengthening rapidly in the last decades, only partly because the United States now sends more diplomats to more places.

The now frequent practice of kidnapping or assassinating members of diplomatic missions raises an issue that finds little precedent before World War II. The idea of taking a whole diplomatic mission as hostage as in Iran finds little parallel since the days of the Borgias, if we leave out the Boxer seige of the Western legations in Beijing. The deliberate shooting from the sanctuary of the Libyan London Embassy in April 1984 is practically unprecedented.

What are the sources of these very undesirable changes?

A first source of change is simply a built-in consequence of the proliferation of nation-states after World War II, as colonialism was dismantled. It is often overlooked today that one of the effects of colonialism was to fix responsibility for affairs in many fewer hands. In the days when the sun "never set on the British flag," and the French and others were not far behind in their territorial ubiquity, the number of sovereign units in the world was less than a third of what it is now. Responsibility and accountability was far more centralized, and the standards were nearer one another since all of the colonial powers were Europeans. This effect does not justify colonialism, but the effect existed.

But once colonialism was defunct and dismantled, many dozens of brand new nations came quickly into existence. These new nations very frequently were ruled by newly improvised governments without deep roots in the nations they governed. The lack of settled political customs encouraged resort to violence and the prizes of political power were as always tempting. Under these conditions the armed forces often prevailed, either in a sometimes naive attempt to provide reform or alternately to provide a platform for exploitation and personal aggrandizement for an ambitious colonel or sergeant. In any effort, responsibility and accountability was scattered widely. Merely as the probable offshoot of the effect of increased numbers of sovereign units, one could expect some maverick rulers in some of these new states—such as Idi Amin of Uganda, or the Emperor of Central Africa (who feasted on children), or a Colonel Muammar al-Qaddafi of Libya (who alone spent $2.1 billion on military goods and services in 1979 in a nation of 2,933,000 people, or $700 for each man, woman, and child!)

A second source of these changes was closely connected to the first, in that it was not likely that a host of newly independent states would spring into existence in a uniformly peaceful fashion, each with frontiers acceptable to themselves and to their neighbors. Although a widespread problem, the leading case was undoubtedly Israel. When the British mandate over Palestine was terminated after World War II, and an area contested over by Jew and Arab alike became a battlefield, the recurrent strife detailed in Chapter 19 began. That strife resembled very much the no-quarter conflict recorded in the Old Testament. A good deal of contemporary terrorism arises out of that one unresolved problem, as the PLO fights for its survival by every means at its disposal.

A third source of terrorism is the lack of unity in dealing with it. Because many of the newer members of the UN are disposed to condone some acts of violence and terrorism (if carried out under the right sponsorship and against the right targets), the practice itself has been hard to control. Even actions against commercial aircraft, involving hijacking, have not received the universal condemnation they deserve, as Cuba, Algeria, and Libya, to name a few, at different periods have been disposed to welcome such hijackers. The lag in achieving effective international common action and sanctions against transgressors provides an issue that may be beginning to be overcome as the new nations increasingly come to appreciate the shortcomings of international law applied only on a case-by-case basis. The universal condemnation by the United Nations of Iran's seizure of the U.S. Embassy in Teheran may be a turning point.

A fourth source of terrorism is the Soviet Union, which lends aid to what it terms "national liberation movements." Since the world is full of unrest and the rich in many countries do exploit the poor, there is a great market for subversion. In 1979 the Soviets exported $9.6 billion in acknowledged arms sales, compared to U.S. deliveries of $5.1 billion. Many of the Soviet weapons are cheap, crude, highly effective, and lethal. Along with arms in many instances come Soviet military advisers, instructors, and technical personnel, while guerrillas are sent to Moscow for training. In theory, the Soviet leaders must believe in this form of "doing good" but it may be that they are simply plodding forward along routine lines under the inspiration of outmoded slogans—meaning that it takes unbounded optimism to anticipate in the face of all the evidence already accumulated that the governments which come to power with these arms will bring great blessings to their peoples. (The alternative explanation for Soviet behavior is even less flattering; that they do not mind the slaughter, provided it worries the United States.)

Finally, there is the technological factor itself. With a host of governmental and nongovernmental arms suppliers available along with modern communications, electronics, and transportation systems, it is simply easier today to obtain the means of carrying out terrorist operations than it used to be. In a world in which states are highly permeable and interdependent, terrorism to implement orientations such as exacerbater or indirect opposition sometimes can be very effective.

The United States in facing this problem has sought to develop an effective counterterrorism policy and to devise effective mechanisms of implementation without a good deal of success. The Nixon administration employed an Inter-Agency Working Group, whereas Carter utilized the NSC working through the Special Coordination Committee and two subgroups. Dissatisfied with previous arrangements, President Reagan established an Interdepartmental Group on Terrorism in the State Department, which would work with the appropriate SIG in the NSC system. And within State, the Office for Combatting Terrorism played a more important role. Effective counterterrorist policy demands accurate timely intelligence, incisive evaluation, appropriate dissemination, precise action, and, in most cases, international cooperation. Such criteria are not easily met.

The orthodox interpretation of the terrorist problem today is that things will get worse before they get better as more actors use orientations of exacerbater or indirect opposition and take advantage of the capabilities of modern technology and the vulnerabilities of modern states. And this may be correct. But our examination of the sources of terrorism indicates the possibility at least that an alternative projection is equally plausible: the peak of this kind of violence may be near or even past. The newer nations are gaining in sophistication as they gain in experience, and many are beginning to understand the drawbacks of departing from principle to favor special parties. And the honeymoon with the Soviet Union may be about over, as the recipients of Soviet arms consider all the effects of that aid. In short, it also is possible that the ending of the postcolonial phase may bring with it the beginning of the end of the unbridled terrorism of the 1970s.

4.

The Seas

The third overarching problem has to do with the regime of the seas.

Nowhere has the difference of approach of the industrialized powers, especially the United States, and the developing nations been more pronounced than over the resources and uses of the seas.

As pressures toward reducing the "high seas" have increased, these two groups have often argued for very diverse positions. After eight years of intense negotiations, a convention on the law of the sea, sponsored by the United Nations, was accepted for signature in April 1982 by an affirmative vote of 130, with 4 against and 17 abstaining. On the face of things, those against were only the United States, Turkey, Israel, and Venezuela. But those *abstaining* included the Soviet bloc (except Rumania), Belgium, Britain, Italy, Luxembourg, the Netherlands, Spain, Thailand, and West Germany. Of the key industrial nations, only France, Canada, and Japan actually voted with the majority. When the treaty was opened for signature, 117 states (including the Soviet bloc) signed on the first day. Initially, however, there were few ratifications.

The nature of the arguments that took up eight long years is illuminating, especially the issue on which unanimity in the end could not be found. They reflect how technology had affected the global environment.

For centuries the general principles governing the law of the sea existed unchanged. Off one's shores there was the narrow territorial sea; beyond were the open oceans where no nation's rule extended. It would be easy to overstate the degree of unanimity that prevailed over the width of the territorial sea, some nations claiming a four-mile width or more. Even so, the three-mile sea was fairly standard (supposedly originally the range of a cannon ball—which considerably overstates the technology of the eighteenth century!). Indentations such as bays were governed

MAP 12

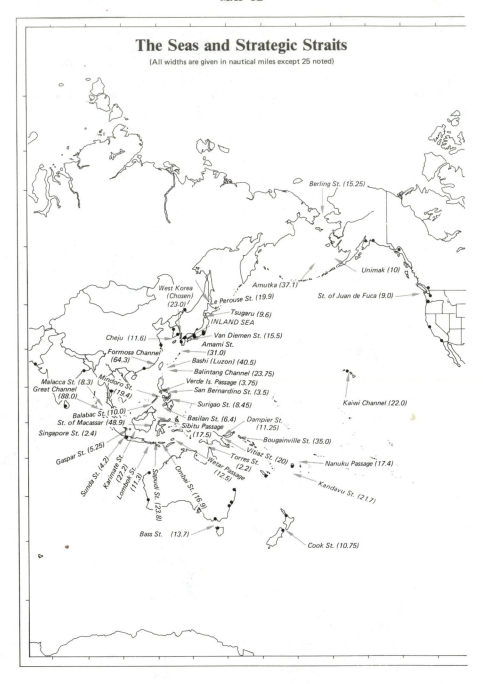

The Seas and Strategic Straits

(All widths are given in nautical miles except 25 noted)

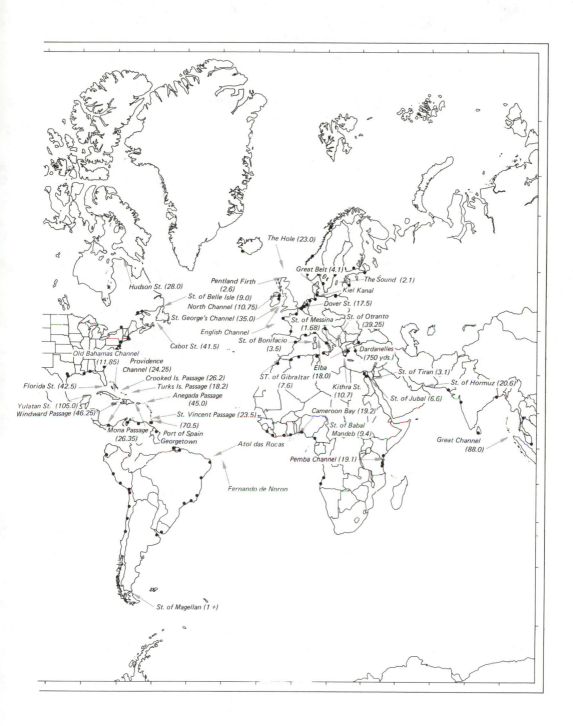

The Hole (23.0)

Great Belt (4.1)

The Sound (2.1)

Pentland Firth
(2.6)

Kiel Kanal

Hudson St. (28.0)

St. of Belle Isle (9.0)

Dover St. (17.5)

North Channel (10.75)

St. George's Channel (35.0)

St. of Messina
(1.68)

St. of Otranto
(39.25)

English Channel

Cabot St. (41.5)

St. of Bonifacio
(3.5)

Dardanelles
(750 yds.)

Old Bahamas Channel
(11.85)

Providence
Channel (24.25)

Elba

St. of Tiran (3.1)

Crooked Is. Passage (26.2)

ST. of Gibraltar
(7.6)

St. of Gibraltar
(18.0)

St. of Hormuz (20.6)

Florida St. (42.5)

Turks Is. Passage (18.2)

Kithra St.
(10.7)

St. of Jubal (6.6)

Anegada Passage
(45.0)

Yulatan St. (105.0)

St. Vincent Passage (23.5)

Cameroon Bay (19.2)

Windward Passage (46.25)

Great Channel
(88.0)

(70.5)

St. of Babal
Mandeb (9.4)

Mona Passage
(26.35)

Port of Spain

Georgetown

Atol das Rocas

Pemba Channel (19.1)

Fernando de Noron

St. of Magellan (1 +)

by special rules; and straits and other such passageways, even if less than six miles wide, if customarily used for passage, were open to the peaceful passage of all ships of all nations.

Very little thought was given to controls exercised out at sea. Ships were governed by the flags they flew, and international regulation was virtually nonexistent. The few rules that came into existence in the nineteenth century arose over slavery, seal hunting, and whaling. Denmark, on May 16, 1792, abolished slavery in its possessions as of the end of 1802. The United States in 1794 forebade any U.S. citizens from participating in the slave trade to foreign countries; on March 2, 1807 (taking force on January 1, 1808) importing slaves into the United States was prohibited. The British took similar action at about the same time. By the 1830s international cooperation at sea in restraint of the slave trade was common, and the U.S.–British Ashburton Treaty of 1842 provided for joint squadrons on the west coast of Africa. Seal hunting in the North Pacific was regulated by treaty in 1911. Whale hunting was controlled by voluntary whaling company agreement in the 1930s and by treaty in 1946. Piracy on the high seas was outlawed by traditional rules. It is astonishing but true that very few other regulations governed the open seas.

This condition changed rapidly after World War II. Inspired by the "sea safety zones" which a Pan-American Conference at Panama on October 2, 1939, proclaimed for an area three hundred miles from shore, and by the 1945 U.S. claim to the continental shelf resources beyond the territorial sea, the Latin American nations, particularly on the west coast, began to declare 200-mile fishing zones. Some even claimed 200-mile territorial seas, raising a serious issue from the viewpoint of the United States. Their argument was that the lack of any real continental shelf (in the Pacific, the sea is deep immediately offshore) restricted their control of adjacent resources such as nations with continental shelf areas were beginning to exploit. So they claimed exclusive jurisdiction or sovereign rights primarily for the purposes of fishing. (The United States, after arguing vainly against the rapid spread of this idea to nations with ample continental shelf, followed suit in 1976, proclaiming an exclusive *fishing zone* of 200 miles to sea.)

In 1958 the Geneva Convention produced an agreed legal definition for the continental shelf that was to be available for national exploitation (while preserving the navigational rights of other nations). This legal "continental shelf" extends from the outer edge of the territorial sea to the 200-meter isobath (depth line) or beyond, to the limits of exploitability. The physical continental shelf does not always match this definition. It starts at low tide and extends to where the ocean bottom slopes abruptly downward. The shelf varies from zero to 938 miles in width, for an average width of 48 miles. Depth at the outer edge varies from 65 to 1,800 feet, for an average depth of 436 feet. Drilling operations for oil and mining operations multiplied on the continental shelf while nation after nation proclaimed fishing areas off its coasts. There was an interplay here between advances in technology, the need for expanded food supplies, and a defense against the modern sea-going fishing factories of the Soviet Union and Japan that were overharvesting fish.

All of these developments naturally encouraged the landlocked states and those who could not themselves exploit an adjacent sea to defend joint international ownership and control of what was left, thus raising the issue of deep-seabed mining. Since the 1982 Law of the Sea Convention's provisions on standardization of the territorial sea at a twelve-mile width, and its provisions for transit passage rights through international straits, were acceptable to the United States and the other industrial states, it was on this point of the seabed and its control that the United States finally voted against the pact. The ultimate issue and real point of contention was the convention's proviso that later changes could be made in the regime of the sea which would be *binding* upon all signatories, *even without their consent*. Although the Soviet Union eventually abstained on adopting the final treaty to open it for signature, rather than voting against, their vote was on the same side with the United States on many of the key issues, such as the free passage of the straits. Once the treaty was actually opened for signature, however, in contrast to the United States, the Soviet bloc signed.

So, in a few short decades the open ocean has shrunk drastically and all sorts of special regimes for portions of adjacent coasts have now sprung up, developments clearly following in the train of their technological possibilities. The United States, reacting to this situation, has taken a conservative (and generally well-founded) stand toward the issues. Although the trend toward exclusive domains confers control over a large part of the adjacent ocean on the United States, it is noteworthy that the United States delayed the movement toward expropriation of the seas as long as it could. Some day the developing countries are very likely to realize that they have in general by these pressures forced the rich to get richer without much in return. It is fortunate that the U.S. record is so clear on these points.

5.

Space

The fourth overarching problem is space and the uses to which it should be put.

Just as with the regime of the seas, changing technology has also affected outer space. But to this point, because only the United States and the Soviet Union have successfully put spaceships into orbit and men in space, they have been able to set the stage on which the problem has been addressed. Other nations have no fulcrum as yet from which to influence how space would be used by mankind.

From the first ability of man to launch controlled satellites into space, the military potentialities of space technology have been recognized. If it had not been for "national means of verification," based largely on spy satellites, progress in the direction of SALT and agreements on arms control for nuclear weapons, as discussed in Chapter 16, would have reached a dead end long ago. For the Soviet Union has never been willing to agree to anything but a very modest on-the-ground site inspection, and the United States has never been willing to agree to controls whose observance could not be effectively monitored.

In 1966 both nations agreed in principle on a draft treaty to control the military uses of outer space. This treaty received UN endorsement, was ratified by the United States after a unanimous consent vote on April 25 in the U.S. Senate, and entered into force on October 10, 1967. Its main provisions are in Article IV, which restricts military activity in two ways. First, it prohibits placing in orbit or on the moon or other celestial body, or otherwise stationing in space, nuclear or other weapons of mass destruction. Second, it limits the use of the moon and other celestial bodies exclusively to peaceful purposes and expressly prohibits their use for military bases or installations, for testing weapons, or for conducting military maneuvers.[6]

Notice that spy satellites are not excluded by the terms of the treaty.

If one looked only this far into the situation, one might conclude that this is one area where mankind has been early in dealing effectively with a problem. But there are two other considerations. The first is the military conviction on both sides that the side which was the first to utilize outer space for weapons purposes would have an enormous, perhaps decisive advantage. This conviction creates a certain tension and the newspapers recurrently contain speculation about what would happen if the Soviet Union began a war by destroying the U.S. satellites whose information about Soviet activities and whose role in ensuring command communications

---

[6]For text of the treaty see the convenient collection published by the United States Arms Control and Disarmament Agency, *Arms Control and Disarmament Agreements: Texts and Histories of Negotiations,* 1980 Edition (Washington, D.C., 1980), pp. 51–55.

between U.S. activities widely scattered around the globe is so essential. (Although it is not clear that the Soviet Union would be serving its own interests to do this, it is a possibility.)

The second consideration is even more sobering and without question needs to be confronted. Somewhat perversely, the restrictions on the military use of outer space may not continue to be advantageous in terms of retarding a further acceleration in the arms race. Why that is so is somewhat complicated. To understand the connection we must begin from the fact that the emphasis in the arms race has been on *offensive* missile systems. SALT has tried to keep the number of launchers from rising but has *restricted* antimissile defense efforts. Specifically, the Anti-Ballistics Missile (ABM) agreement that entered into force on October 3, 1972, *limits* ABM systems to two sites (subsequently reduced to one site).

The thinking behind this approach to arms control is that the offense has such a great advantage over the defense that defense is not worth really attempting. Instead, an offensive ICBM should be offset by the existence of a similar ICBM on the other side. Then if these weapons are mutually considered to be fairly equivalent, the incentive to use them is removed since, although the initial *attack* cannot be effectively stopped, neither can the retaliatory strike. So each will suffer equally and no one has an advantage in starting a war unless they can somehow be assured that they will not suffer that retaliatory blow.

This thinking, which lay behind SALT I, was also fundamental to SALT II, which the United States did not ratify after the completion of negotiations in President Carter's administration. The number of allowable missiles allowed by SALT II exceeded the SALT I totals and hardly represented stopping a race, only slowing up its advances, as it were. One reason SALT II was not ratified, though, was the substantial American opinion that it gave the Soviet Union too many other offensive advantages, in regard to such systems as their long-range Backfire bombers and heavy ICBMs. When START was coined in the Reagan administration to give a name to the renewed arms talks (Strategic Arms Reductions Talks), it immediately became clear that there was still a very significant body of American opinion which wanted more intense arms developments (such as MX missiles, Pershing II deployments) to "catch up" with the "lead" of the Soviet Union as well as to close "the window of vulnerability." It is here that we get nearer the nub of the problem.

The "window of vulnerability" argument holds that the Soviet Union is approaching an ability to destroy the U.S. main-arsenal Minuteman IIIs in their silos as a result of a combination of great thrust (and large warheads) with improved accuracy. Given such large Soviet missiles, MIRVing (equipping a launcher with multiple warheads) has acted further to the Soviet advantage, since they can mount more warheads on each missile. One ten-headed Soviet missile, launched without warning, could (so the scare scenarios put it) take out five or ten U.S. launchers with fifteen to thirty or so U.S. warheads. So the United States, it is argued, must develop a whole series of responses to end this vulnerability. The MX missile, if it could be "hidden," or moved around, or clustered in packs, might be one solution; cruise missiles might be another.

Critics of such new and supposedly "invulnerable" U.S. missiles argue that their development would be "destabilizing." Since from the Soviet viewpoint such weapons would be "first-strike" weapons, the United States would possess exactly what the United States fears is already in Soviet hands. Proponents of such missiles point out that, if the Soviets launch first in a preemptive strike, the only conceivable way otherwise to go *unless a defense is possible* is to allow U.S. ICBM "launch on warning," *after* Soviet missiles are fired but *before* they land. The danger of firing on a false alarm is obvious. Following this path in almost any of its variations tends to put the premium on firing a preemptive strike. It will keep tensions higher and trigger fingers tighter. It represents what is correctly called a vicious cycle, with each retaliatory move met and raised by the opponent.

The argument can be given in much greater detail, but without changing any of the essentials. There are, however, defects in this argument. For example, it would be difficult to prove that nations resort to wars when they perceive advantages in weapons ratios. There is surely more to it than that.

The idea of a surprise attack is itself seldom rigorously examined, since its feasibility is usually thought to rest on the weapons ratio involved: given enough advantage in weapons, one can attack. This viewpoint is really the reverse mirror image of the idea of deterrence: that an equal number of weapons deters attack unless one side can gain an advantage by a preemptive attack. Both propositions avoid dealing with the complications of the real-world environment. Suppose the plan does not work? Suppose the war is not over quickly? Suppose third parties intervene? Examined in this light, one quickly sees that any weapon ratios that are at all likely will not alone be the decisive factor in unleashing war.

But it is best to go back to where the argument first begins: with the assumption that offense has inherent superiority in the missile age over defense.

Looking at the long history of warfare, what strikes one is the alternation between offensive advantage and defensive advantage. Many centuries ago, the offense held few cards against fortified cities with prudent supplies of food and water. Gunpower, applied eventually to the problem, blew great holes in stone walls, breaching them. In World War I, until an effective counter to the machine gun was invented, the defense was king. In World War II, Hitler's *blitzkrieg* signaled the resurgence of the offensive.

When the nuclear age began, what impressed analysts was the thought that unless a foolproof defense could be developed, money and effort devoted to that purpose was thrown away since one or a few missiles, if they got through, would create all the destruction needed. So the money and effort should be put into offensive programs to deter the enemy.

Now deterrence is either a psychological imponderable (before the act) or a success or failure (after the act). In plainer English, deterrence is a hope until one sees whether it in fact worked or not. By then, if it did not work, it is too late and one faces an accomplished fact. So one has to ask about deterrence, when looked at prospectively (before we know whether it worked) whether we are dealing in hard likelihoods or soft likelihoods. Are there weapons ratios, "hardware" arrangements, guaranteed to deter no matter what the nationality of the prospective enemy, its history and experience, degree of national frustration, impatience or tolerance, and the like? Would, for example, that set of weapons which would deter the United States also deter the Soviets? Does the same amount of weapons deter both nations? Do we assume, to complicate the problem a little further, that any given nation at least has some "deterrence" susceptibility or vulnerability, so that, facing such deterrence, it would always refrain from striking out, regardless of the importance of the issue? Calculations about matters such as these quickly lead to a feeling of uneasiness about assured conclusions.

Now suppose that a foolproof defense can be managed—but only from outer space. Would it then be more sensible to continue as is?

It is here that we reach the crux of an issue reflecting the evolving situation, for the new laser technology and particle beam technology offer a serious prospect of neutralizing offensive ICBMs by destroying them shortly after launch. If that can be done on an assured basis (i.e., enough to blunt an effective attack), it would remove any real incentive for any nation to attempt a preemptive strike for the radioactivity and the rest of it would occur in their own skies, over their own country. If the defense is really assured,[7] it even removes the incentive to maintain much of an offensive ICBM force. If it worked out, the incentive would shift in all cases to assured defense.

It is now clear why restrictions on the military use of outer space may not continue to have a retarding effect on the arms race. When it was evident that the offense had an unbeatable

---

[7]"Assured" here does not mean "perfect" but rather sufficient to blunt the attack on the defending forces who would retain the ability to attack in retaliation.

superiority over the defense and the defense, "useless" as it was, was restricted; when it was feasible to limit offensive weapons by just counting launchers; and when agreements could be monitored satisfactorily by national technical means, the restrictions did have a retarding effect. But as new systems threaten to destabilize the balance and more accurate and lethal weapons are accumulated, as doubts appear about the utility of agreements that control no more than a share of offensive systems, and as the technological obstacles to effective defensive systems become less forbidding, restrictions on the military use of outer space may actually increase pressures to obtain either offensive advantage or enhanced deterrence by the accumulation of more ICBMs, SLBMs, cruise missiles, and the like. The arms race may actually be speeded up, not retarded.

Two groups today, then, are especially interested in weapons in space. The first, stymied by the standoff in the competition for a meaningful edge in offensive weapons systems (or frustrated over how to control such weapons in some agreed ratio, reliably), want to move the competition to outer space. (Or fear the enemy will do that if the United States does not.) The second group, convinced that an arms race in offensive weapons leads to inherently unstable results, wants to shift to a defensive orientation. And that means using outer space for the lasers and other new weapons. It was this alternative for the issue that President Reagan chose in principle in 1983 when he directed accelerated research and development in this area.

The arguments are still taking shape because the technology is not yet sufficiently developed. Once technology goes where it very apparently is heading, the issue will have to be faced squarely. Yet there are no guarantees, if the arms race is thus extended to outer space, that the promises will prove reliable, that defensive systems only will be installed, and that such defensive systems will prove reliable. Here is an area where the possibility exists for Soviet-American cooperation, since the mutual advantage of taking the sting out of offensive weapons transiting space is easily apparent, and cooperation would not involve bringing the nationals of the other nation inside one's own frontiers.

6. Summing Up

In this chapter we have seen some of the drastic changes which technology has brought to mankind in recent decades, for better or for worse. These changes have given new dimensions to old problems, such as the race between food and population, and they have added new problems to old problems, such as the threat of nuclear annihilation. In neither case is it appropriate for us to assume that these technological changes, affecting the global environment, will in themselves trigger foreordained responses. Instead, such changes pose problems to be solved, some in novel guises, some novel per se, by man's ingenuity. Bismarck once said that man cannot control the currents; he can only steer. Thus as the problems become more complex and the dangers grow, the premium on steering well increases. In today's more crowded, less abundant, and far more dangerous world, intelligent policy decisions are what separate us from danger, bloodshed, and even destruction of the world and all that is in it. The paradox that confronts us here is the same we sketched out in the beginning in Part One: that issues of life and death for the people of the United States are settled by decisions made in Moscow and other national capitals as well as in Washington. Americans can *influence* decisions taken abroad by the quality of American decisions taken at home—and that says much—but Americans cannot *control* the rest of the world—and that says something significant, too.

In the next and final chapter we focus on what we consider those decisions should involve.

PART FIVE

Policy for the Time Ahead

22

Conclusions and Evaluation

Our talks that afternoon [in China] focused on the Soviet Union. The Soviets, Mao said, wanted world domination, and if their drive was ever to be stopped, the United States would have to stand up to them.

President Gerald Ford[1]

Throughout this book we have made specific and explicit judgments as to the policy needed to preserve the Republic. We have arrived at such judgments through the use of equally specific theoretical propositions, which we shall shortly sum up. Since the conditions abroad that the American people face constantly change, along with the American appraisal as a people of what needs to be done, the recommendations given in these chapters will need revision (and should need revision) as time goes on. After all, what is to be done in policy has to reflect two sides of a single coin: both the internal as well as the external, both aspirations and fears about problems developing abroad and willingness at home, amid distractions, to face these problems effectively. The exact fluctuations in these two variables are not very predictable.

What we hope will *not* change is the usefulness of the theoretical and analytical tools we have provided. Hopefully they will be as applicable to the future as it shapes itself as they are in the present analysis. Let us begin this final chapter, then, by reviewing the principal theoretical and analytical points made.

1.

The Theory Reviewed

We ended Chapter 1 by saying that one major theme was that policy has two faces: that the policymaker has to reconcile the "internal" and the "external." The policymaker has to reconcile what his people are willing to do, with what he thinks the problem faced abroad needs by way of response.

What a people are willing to do depends, in turn, very much on how they perceive the problem faced. In Chapter 12 we saw an anxious President Roosevelt trying to rally a reluctant American people to deal with a triumphant and arrogant Hitler instead of taking refuge behind

---

[1]Gerald Ford, *A Time to Heal* (New York: Harper & Row, 1979), p. 336.

the frail barrier of a series of neutrality acts. This was a time when the draft was extended by one vote—although that American mood was to change dramatically under the impact of Pearl Harbor.

Problems have an objective character; they exist in a real world. Adolf Hitler was a real person who brought down real death and destruction upon his own people and many others. He proved to be bent upon altering the world in his own image. But this description is ex post facto. We know this all now, beyond a reasonable doubt. Roosevelt was historically right that Nazi Germany was a real problem, that it would not go away, that it had to be faced.

But Roosevelt was talking to a people whose history showed a wonderful degree of immunity from foreign physical threat, at least after colonial times. He presided over a nation that was used to the security conferred by distance from danger, and one disillusioned by the idealistic hopes with which it embarked on its crusade in the latter years of World War I: "the war to save civilization," as the U.S. victory medals proudly proclaimed. Chapters 2 and 3 gave the background necessary to understand the special attitudes with which Americans tend to approach problems, and Part Three showed the main features of American policy into contemporary times. These chapters show graphically the vital role of *perception*. They show specifically how Americans in different periods of time looked out on problems—problems whose real nature was not altered by the American version of those problems but was affected, sometimes drastically, by what American administrations chose to do or not to do about those problems. Such policy choices reflected and reflect the momentary appraisal of what is faced, and like the attitude at first toward the threat of Hitler, it may or may not be adequate or sufficient. The choices are made always in terms of the problem as it is perceived at a time—which, by definition, is normally before all the evidence is in. In Chapters 16 and 21 we showed how the judgment must be made about the implications of the continuing Soviet arms build-up before the American people have the solid historical records and evidence as to what the Soviets are really up to at the present moment.

In Part Four, we showed problems that had to be faced, issues that had to be decided, and the alternatives which represented the choices available. But stating that these *are* the problems, that these *are* the issues, that these *are* the choices assumes a perspective and outlook by the American people which is consistent with our analysis. No matter how real these problems may be, how much the issues cry out for handling, no matter how imperative the choices, all of it has to be perceived as that—or nothing will happen.

In Chapter 1 we said that policy has three parts: concept, content, and implementation. We also said that policy has two phases: design (phase 1) and implementation (phase 2), with content the bridge between. We have just made the same point another way, for the design of policy leads to content from a concept, and concept *means* how a people visualize in advance the connections between problems existing in the state system toward which some stance needs taking, and what they are willing to do about it. Concept *means* what they think will happen as a result of their action or inaction. What will other nations be doing or not doing? What will be the presumed consequences?

We described all of this in Chapters 1 and 4 and in a series of diagrams. We elaborated our conceptional or design yardstick in Chapter 4 in describing four cardinal principles. These principles remind us that in forecasting policy effects, four aspects are critical: (1) to remember third-party influences on a bilateral relationship, (2) to bear in mind that past-future linkages as a principle translates into each party having nation-particular perceptions of a "common" problem, (3) to keep in mind that counterbalancing national interests means that whereas one alternative is chosen as the content for present policy, possible future policy content is best summed up by looking at the "shelved" interests in reserve (which collectively also describe what the total system may *become*), and (4) to remember that the amount of enmity encountered is not fixed but in important ways is the product of the policy followed and the approach made to the idea of the conservation of enemies.

In Chapter 5 we added the important considerations that affect policy implementation as we described the four operational steps of phase 2, implementation. Once a policy content is chosen, we still have to do four things in a concrete situation calling for implementation. We have to identify the actors in the particular instance. Who is really involved? We must in the specific case determine the objectives of each party involved. What do they want and what might the United States want? In step 3 we need to analyze the net capability. What is the operational power relationship? And in step 4, as a result, the policymakers have to choose an orientation. What involvement is really necessary?

The link between the cardinal principles and the operational steps is *content*. But what does that mean in the light of the preceding discussion? Content is the result on the one hand of a perception and on the other hand of the consequence of a debate. Choices of content will reflect a people's appraisal of a problem faced and will usually in the United States, on important issues, spark some kind of a debate leading to some kind of a decision. So the debate gives meaningful clues by its length and intensity to the degree of popular consensus. Policy content, reflecting a particular concept or problem appraisal, will be implemented without much further debate until the results encountered seriously depart from the results anticipated when the content was first chosen.

So, to say it very simply, policy design (phase 1) does not come in very often for review. Once formulated, it tends to be implemented more or less automatically along those lines until real difficulties appear. (That is why the thought process is frequently perfunctory at that stage and bureaucratic procedures govern.) But even when design expectations are essentially matched by actual results, the steps in phase 2 have to be taken quite deliberately and quite specifically since the content of a policy (or even the concept of a policy) does not automatically describe in a specific instance who is involved and how heavily and what net resources can be brought to bear. We may determine as concept to ensure the rule of law and as content to protect the oil routes to Japan from the Arabian Peninsula, but a specific threat by Iraq or Iran to close the Strait of Hormuz has to be evaluated in terms of what U.S. and other naval units can be deployed and what is happening elsewhere at the same time.

2.

The Substantive Analysis Reviewed

With these kinds of thoughts and theoretical propositions in mind, we examined in Part Two how Washington makes foreign policy. We began in Chapter 6 by observing the formal division of powers and the political interplay between President and Congress as they approach policy issues. We saw a more recent tendency by Congress to challenge the "imperial" presidency approach of Nixon, fixing limits to presidential initiatives in the fields of international agreements, the conduct of intelligence operations, the use of military force, and approaches to nuclear nonproliferation and foreign aid. These congressional initiatives are the political results of the failure of the post–World War II consensus. They are the normal trappings which accompany the redesign of foreign policy.

In Chapter 7 we explored the bureaucracy, showing how some of its characteristics (such as information processing) derive from the very nature of its tasking, with little effect from policy content. We showed how difficult it is to keep such an elaborate mechanism as the executive departments of the U.S. government moving in a coordinated fashion.

In Chapter 8 we looked at public opinion and interest groups from all the perspectives thus far covered in this chapter: as an influence on policy design and implementation in the broadest sense, as a specific influence creating or dissolving policy consensus, as a specific effect on specific governmental actors. We found that the most important effect of the media is to circulate and communicate reactions to policy events rather than specifically to cause changes in policy. We found that interest groups have rather limited influence on policy compared to what is generally assumed.

In Chapters 9 and 10 we turned to the Department of State and the national security system, since these are the organs of government that are most specifically concerned with policy design and implementation. We showed the coordination and communication problems inherent in a necessarily complicated apparatus and we noted the interplay between the mechanics of the national security system and presidential style. We closed Part Two with a case study of the Iranian fiasco.

We have already discussed the purpose of Part Three. In giving a succinct review in Chapters 11, 12, 13, and 14 of the evolution of American policy (emphasizing deliberately its security aspects as always a prime policy concern), we found the United States first struggling with the typical (and obvious) problems of a small, weak nation, surrounded by powerful neighbors and struggling to survive. We found a second period, of inaction and invulnerability, when the United States was essentially immune from foreign attack but indifferent to foreign involvements. That second period began about 1850 and lasted to 1898. Then began a third period, of involvements but on a sporadic basis, from 1898 to 1941 and Pearl Harbor. Typical of this period was the conviction that the United States had the power to achieve what was necessary and the lack of conviction that the American people knew what that was. The fourth period of U.S. policy began with U.S. involvement in World War II and continued until the evacuation from Vietnam. It was typified by a consensus that the United States must play a leading part in global affairs, particularly in frustrating Communist aggression wherever it occurred.

We are now in the fifth period—the one that Part Four specifically covers. Americans still believe they have the power (or can amass it) and they are agreed that the old isolationism is not a feasible option. But Americans are not fully agreed on just how and where and when to play a leading part and carry most of the burden. The old containment consensus has fragmented and dissension has reasserted itself over most of the problems and issues and alternatives which policy today involves.

In examining the sequential development of American approaches and the resulting policies, we illustrated how the observations of Chapters 2 and 3 applied. From colonial times on through the Vietnam War, we saw certain American tendencies in approaching policy issues that do not serve the United States well, such as the tendency to moralize or to utilize moral and abstract principles as guideposts to decision making. In Chapter 15 we pointed out particularly the U.S. tendency to avoid specifics and approach problems by categories ("We will not ship war materials to nations which bomb women and children from the air"). We pointed to the American preference for some more or less automatic basis for commitment (anytime, for instance, an "X" attacks a "Y").

In Part Four we examined a whole series of policy problems and issues as they are perceived, and the alternatives these issues frame today for our choice, beginning in Chapter 16 with that overriding problem, U.S.-Soviet relations. In Chapters 17, 18, 19 and 20 we looked at each major geographical area for which we must frame and choose between policy alternatives. We pointed out how often the problems (and therefore the issues) were interlinked. After looking at each main geographical area we then, in Chapter 21, examined the sweep of technological change as it has influenced the nature of four overarching problems—problems such as the global quality of life, terrorism, the uses of the seas, and the possible uses of space, problems which are not specific to any one geographical area and evade geographical confines.

There now remains to us one task: to emphasize not so much the *specific* policy recommendations that are clearly set forth in each chapter of Part Four but rather to highlight the most important concerns which the analysis in Part Four reveals. We sum these up in two sections, looking at so-called East-West (superpower-related) issues and then North-South (industrialized vs. LDC) issues in terms of recommended U.S. objectives.

3.

East-West and Security Concerns

In approaching East-West security concerns it is necessary to have a strategic-political grasp of the real nature of the problem the Soviets present and what might be done about it, as well as a sense of its military implications.

The relationship to the Soviets is the single most important security problem confronting the United States because the Soviets hold the keys to life or death for millions of Americans. The United States does not have the realistic option of making the Soviet Union a friend or an ally. For numerous reasons, including divergent historical experiences, contrasting social and economic systems, ideological disagreements, and balance of power relationships, there is no reasonable hope or expectation that the fundamentally antagonistic relationship can change.

That is not the same as to say (1) that the United States cannot defuse the resulting tension in some degree, or (2) that the United States cannot adopt policies inhibiting the most objectionable or dangerous or threatening Soviet behavior.

Worst of all as an attitude toward the problem would be a perception by the American people that the two superpowers have *no* common interests; they obviously do. Avoiding nuclear war heads the list, but there are many other issues, too. Both superpowers benefit by preventing the demise of the United Nations, feeble and partial as that forum sometimes is as an agent for peaceful settlement. Both superpowers can benefit through realistic and reliable arms control agreements. Both superpowers are badly served if their policymakers encourage their peoples to regard each other only and simply as threats.

President Carter was absolutely right when he argued that the overriding stress American policy had placed on *communism* as the main determinant of U.S.–Soviet relations was wrong, that there were many other problems and issues which needed addressing, and that the ideological emphasis was overdone. Unfortunately, as we have seen, Carter, in his concern over human rights, at first downgraded the implications of the continued, high-gear Soviet defense effort (whether it stemmed from communism, ambition, or just plain fear). In the next administration, President Reagan, redressing Carter's initial priorities, came near at first reviving the entire Cold War psychology of approach. This emphasis put the U.S.–Soviet relationship into deep freeze, to no great advantage to either side. (The sullen Soviet response did not help things, either.)

The middle ground here should be clear: even though the Soviet Union *does* represent a military threat to the United States, that threat (which is mutual) does not rule out collaboration and cooperation.

Ironically, cooperation is even made possible by elements in the arms race. It is sometimes overlooked that, in the nature of the problem, no nation can ever remain 100 per cent ready for war. Impressive as Soviet arms expenditures may be, they fall far short of that level. The same is even truer of the United States. To be fully mobilized and armed and ready for war is impossibly expensive in peacetime (unless war for certain is right around the corner). But that mutual lack of sufficient preparedness gives mutual enemies or antagonists a mutual interest in negotiating an agreed level of preparedness which stabilizes the risk from which each suffers. Provided the agreement is realistic and reliable, arms-control agreements are particularly desirable between enemies, providing the psychological and technological problems we saw in Chapters 16 and 21 can be overcome.

Conclusions and Evaluation   **405**

The United States can also adopt policies that inhibit Soviet adventurism and risk taking. What does accomplishing that entail? We are speaking here only in a minor key of military or deterrence measures. The major resources open to the United States are, as indicated previously, psychological, economic, and political.

The psychological and political dimensions of East-West tensions are often appraised rather superficially. The Soviet Union's expansion of power and influence in the 1950s, 1960s, and 1970s was partly the result of natural growth and the repairs of war losses. It was also partly the result of the lack of strong opponents at first in Europe and in Asia. It was strongly aided for many years by the U.S.–Chinese antagonism that safeguarded Russia's vulnerable rear. It was assisted by America's embroilment in the Vietnam War, which limited U.S. freedom to act elsewhere. It was given easy triumphs in the Third World by the initial and almost reflexive anticolonial stances of the newly emerging nations as they castigated the West for past sins and blamed their present problems on that historical past. We saw in Chapter 16 how many of these windfall assets have now been removed from the Soviet balance sheet. The United States has discontinued its most self-damaging options, restoring more natural relations with China and disengaging from Vietnam. Many Third World nations are less convinced that the Soviets hold the keys to the future.

Economic assets are also largely in the hands of the United States and its industrial allies. In the heart of Moscow, "hard-currency" shops still exist where the native Russian ruble has no purchasing value for the scarce commodities on sale there but American dollars do. The U.S. dollar, flanked by the Japanese yen and the German mark, are the key currencies for trade and finance around the world.

But it is only through a sense of overall strategic direction that the United States can capitalize on these abundant assets in the drive to limit Soviet ambitions or actions to safe levels. The American people need to think through how to play their cards to achieve a tolerable relationship with the Soviets at a decent price. The first clue is in the cardinal principle of the conservation of enemies. One primary reason why the containment consensus in the American public broke apart under the impact of Vietnam was that the United States, which had started out to contain the Soviets, had with that war embarked also not only on the containment of Level 2 Communist nations like China but of Level 3 Communist states such as North Vietnam (or even Level 4 Communist forces such as the Viet Cong in South Vietnam). These are—with a vengeance—indeed more enemies than the United States could usefully use. The flagrant disregard of the cardinal principle of the conservation of enemies eventually and inevitably brought its own punishment and a return to a search for prudence.

The United States, if it would limit Soviet adventurism (or temptations in that direction), must remove so far as possible any important third-party support for such Soviet purposes, especially third states who are immediate or near neighbors of the Soviet Union. And this for a plain reason: the more the "frontal" preoccupation of the superpowers with each other, the more attention they must pay to their vulnerable flanks and rear. If the historical record shows anything clearly about the state system, it is that the amount of hostility and degree of threat a nation encounters are in part variables. Choices can be made that modify both threat and hostility. So that, whereas the nature and intensity of the Soviet threat must be countered in part by military or defense preparations, that threat also can be shaped and altered by a well-designed and implemented policy that takes carefully into account the counterbalancing interests of third states.

China is a first vital key. It is unlikely that the United States and China will become allies and from the standpoint of U.S. interests it is even conjectural whether it would benefit the United States. But it is highly important that the Chinese continue to have more reasons why they cannot ally again with Russia than they have reasons to do so. The U.S. relationship with China has to focus on increasing an active Chinese sense that their best course is a positive relationship with the United States.

The same principle of counterbalancing national interests must govern U.S. relations with other countries whose friendship or alliance or even benevolent neutrality toward the Soviets assists the Soviets to believe that they can concentrate on a hostile relationship with the United States without great fear for their political-military flanks and rear. The primary countries here are those who have a frontier bordering on the Soviet Union. Poland is a leading example of a nation whose basic and innate orientation is hostile to the Soviets and where it is important for the United States to use its financial resources to increase and strengthen Polish-American ties. (From this point of view, economic sanctions, although designed to influence the regime, may have been counterproductive in weakening Poland.) Rumania and Czechoslovakia are other illustrations in the same area of nations open to influence from outside the Soviet orbit. Small countries in and of themselves, they retain prime psychological (and even strategic) significance in this connection.

Although it is ultimately necessary, if a natural order and peace and the relaxation of tension are ever to return to Europe, for the Soviets to withdraw altogether or at a minimum, permit its satellites a great degree of independence, it is not in America's interests to try to force this occurrence or to contrive it through direct pressures. The remarks made previously about depriving Russia of assurances of third-party support are not made in the interests of *pressuring* the Soviets so much as *dissuading* them from pressuring the West under the impression they could make gains. But neither can the Soviets nor the West in the long run have real peace if the Soviets attempt the permanent occupation of Eastern Europe and the permanent division of Germany.

We must recall that the most basic reason the tension level remains high in Europe is because Soviet forces are deployed beyond Soviet borders, deep into the heart of Europe, and NATO's counterdeployment makes the heart of Europe an armed camp. These deployments, in turn, exist only because of Europe's arbitrary and unnatural division. The first priority for the United States is to change its policy focus from the symptom to the cause, to address seriously the problems of divided Europe and divided Germany. Most of the current difficulties are symptoms of deeper problems, and those deeper problems just must receive greater attention. Europe will not stay divided forever. The United States must design a long range program that will help produce conditions that will shape inevitable change in a way that is beneficial to American interests.

At the same time that such a long range program is being designed and implemented, the United States still will have to deal with the more immediate problem of troop deployments, of course. As we saw in Chapter 17, the United States has two basic alternatives if the Soviets maintain their advanced position. One is to continue its own forward deployment. Although forward deployment has been basic policy for almost four decades and has certain advantages, in our view the other option, reducing deployment, deserves further study. The United States must remain committed in world affairs and continue to play a responsible role, but in many areas that can be done without sizable and permanent troop deployments abroad.

But there may be still another possibility: mutual withdrawal of U.S. and Soviet forces. This would be far preferable to a unilateral U.S. drawdown. How might mutual withdrawal be peacefully accomplished? Here, again, there are two alternatives. There could be a withdrawal of troops from both Germanies, leaving two German states. That would seem to be inviting all kinds of troubles. Or such a mutual withdrawal could be made in conjunction with German reunification. In that event the need would exist for the Soviets to be convinced that their withdrawal would not allow an aggressive anti-Soviet orientation to spring up in the evacuated areas.

To say that there are risks for the Soviets does not rule out the possibility that they would agree to it, particularly if Poland and the other nations in the Soviet bloc become more and more ungovernable short of continual armed coercion. The point here for American policy is to realize that the emphasis in Europe has to be placed on changing the present status quo *with Soviet consent.* So long as it is simply assumed that the Soviets have no possible interest in mutual withdrawal, it remains largely unexplored—as decades of negotiations over German reunification clearly show.

In the long run stationing American forces in Europe, keeping Germany forever divided and Poland subjugated to Soviet interests, represent attempts by outside influences to preserve unnatural arrangements at high costs in tension and associated enormous expenditures for armaments on both sides. If the United States cannot allow Europe to be controlled by the Soviets, it can work to produce conditions whereby the present unnatural and dangerous division can be changed peacefully, reducing costs and risks for Washington and Moscow alike.

Before turning to the other areas in which the interests of East and West impinge, we should reflect that, although changes in America's European policy are advisable, in light of the problems being faced and the interests involved it is unrealistic to expect change to occur very rapidly. This is not the case with respect to the other areas, however. The general circumstances in which the United States finds itself elsewhere permit much more discretion.

In general, because of its physical location, the United States enjoys a priceless strategic asset: *flexibility.* Although not immune from attack, it can only be invaded after an aggressor has first suppressed effective resistance in Europe and in Asia. Therefore, the United States to a considerable extent is free to choose where and when to draw the line, and particularly where to deploy its forces. It can answer the question of how to become involved by recognizing the desires of states to protect themselves and taking advantage of its enormous geographical good fortune. Instead of a forward deployment strategy, which often in Asia has found the United States deploying in front of those it was presumably only supporting, *the United States can readily afford to adopt an essentially supporting role* in most areas of the world. It can afford more than most nations to choose its involvements selectively, becoming deeply involved only infrequently. As a general proposition, therefore, the United States should make commitments and deploy its forces essentially on a back-up basis to maintain the overall stability of the balance of power in every major area of the world.

One cannot say that the United States never should deploy at the front, or that it never should intervene. In selected cases, when considering the proper operational orientation (phase 2, step 4), there may be critical situations that require a quick and perhaps massive involvement. It is essential to have the capability available (phase 2, step 3) to undertake such action. But this will be very much the exception to the rule. Given its geographical advantages, the United States can think about what it would like to see done, what will happen if it does not act, what others may do, and so on, *before* committing. This will prevent unnecessary, costly, often counterproductive actions. Most often, a supportive role will be the most cost-effective means of ensuring the preservation of the Republic.

To argue that the United States should take full advantage of its geographic assets is not to overlook how the world has grown smaller with technological changes which permit missiles to cover thousands of miles in minutes. We addressed this problem in Chapter 21. Nor is it to argue for a neoisolationism, an abandonment of commitments, and a return to unilateralism. We are not then referring to the severing of alliance links but to the optimum patterns of military deployment available to the United States. Many people tend to confuse these two quite different things.

Such thoughts are very pertinent in addressing the Middle East.

In the Middle East-Persian Gulf area, as the 1980s began, the United States was showing a distinct tendency to *increase* its military commitment. Part of the rationale for the Rapid Deployment Joint Task Force was the assumed need to confront any Soviet advance in this critical area. Proponents of the RDJTF pointed to the ease with which the Soviets might advance southward in Southwest Asia, as they had already done in Afghanistan. Proponents also pointed to the ease with which friendly governments with small defense forces in the area might be overthrown.

If the United States was being forced to maintain troops along the Iron Curtain as the result of NATO's unwillingness to take over the whole initial burden of the front line, the same United States with far less reason was strengthening its ability to deploy in the Middle East because the area was considered vital to Europe and Japan. If the area was so vital to Europe and Japan it seemed reasonable that they show far more interest in defending it. Much less of the American oil imports came from the area, in any case—assuming this was really relevant. After all, protecting the area from a Soviet armed attack assumes the Soviets have sufficient reason to mount one. Defending against a Soviet attack there by deploying American forces there assumes a very limited war confined to that local area. Neither assumption can be branded outright as impossible but both are clearly improbable. If the Soviets want to control Middle East oil, they will use surrogates and subversion, rather than direct military attack. But if the Soviets did mount a direct military attack, they would be beginning a war that would quickly assume worldwide dimensions. There would be no sense in the United States allowing significant forces to be lured into an area that militarily would be a sideshow and logistically would strain American reinforcement capability.

The Middle East is one area of considerable concern to the Soviets in which their presence is presently highly restricted. Given the crosscurrents of fears and hatreds in the area (Jordan vs. Syria, Iraq vs. Iran, and so on), it would be relatively easy for the Soviets to again increase their profile in the area if American forces become too prominent. Residual and standby base rights are one thing, semipermanent stationing of forces is another.

By 1982–1983 this problem was further complicated by the ultranationalistic tendencies of the Begin government toward Samaria and Judea (i.e., the Arab West Bank). Since it was open to the United States to attempt to encourage the maintenance of a minimal superpower military profile in the area, it appeared only sensible to restrain the impulse to move in the opposite direction. Since the Middle East was the Third World area most full of weapons and riddled with unsolved political problems, prudence was highly desirable.

Asia offered even greater flexibility from this point of view than did the Middle East, since there was no great need for American military forces to be maintained in any strength in the area. China and Japan were certainly capable of imposing restraint on Soviet behavior so that American intervention could take the form of a back-up force (or nuclear umbrella). Undoubtedly, comparing the 1980s with the 1960s or 1950s, this was the area in most marked contrast, for the United States in those earlier decades had fought two onshore wars in Asia, neither of which could have been long continued without arousing active Chinese opposition. But with Chinese strategic attention subsequently directed *westward* at the Soviet frontier, there was little reason to anticipate any resumption of the 1950s fighting and 1960s tension between the United States and China. Only one possibility could turn this desirable situation into something else, and that would be a continued U.S. insistence on arms aid to Taiwan. Fortunately, by mid-1982 the Reagan administration appeared to have recognized this fact and pledged eventually to end all such aid (although as we showed in Chapter 18, the issue was not entirely dead).

The U.S. role in Africa has been highly restricted from a military and even a political point of view. Here it would seem only politic to preserve some detachment. Many of the issues that are most volatile on the African continent are of no direct concern to the United States. It is only of peripheral interest to the United States whether Africa resolves the black-white issue or it is left unresolved; it is in no sense a problem the United States brought about. The U.S. interest is that Africa should arrive at some workable solution. In the same way the disputed African frontiers concern the United States only if they bring on war and even then, only if the war assumes broader connotations. These are issues in which sympathy and understanding as well as the offer of good offices can be brought to bear, but they are not issues in which American national interests are seriously involved. The most significant exceptions are oil from black Nigeria and the strategic metals and geographical position of white South Africa.

Latin America (and the Caribbean) are areas of significant importance to the United States, especially from a negative viewpoint—meaning the implications for the United States of these areas being subject to hostile control or even serious influence. This is not true of the whole area in the sense that those Latin nations furthest removed are less important in a strategic sense, but since the whole area is essentially a cultural unit, distinctions of this sort also rapidly prove unusable. This is one of the notable implications of the Falkland–Malvinas Islands crisis of 1982. That dispute, as in the Greek-Turkish tensions, showed clearly that issues may arise between nations which are both friendly to the United States and that, when they do, the United States may have to choose between counterbalancing interests.

In a larger and more permanent sense the developing nations of South America or Central America or elsewhere are likely to be plagued for years by incipient unrest or violent armed struggles, for one of the great "gifts" of modern culture is cheap weapons easily available for everyone. It would be naive for the United States to expect that it can promote and maintain good relations with all of these states by having one ear to the ground to detect approaching change as the status quo is overthrown by some armed group claiming to have the interests of the masses more at heart.

4.

North-South and Economic Development Concerns

The United States, as a very wealthy nation, has both an interest and obligation to promote economic growth and development worldwide. This interest and obligation can easily be sentimentalized or reduced to proposals for grants of aid ending up in the pockets of some oligarchy. There are no painless or easy ways to development, even where the intention is sincere and the abilities are present. Foreign capital can be a blessing or a curse. Money in and of itself, like national power, is neutral. It is a resource to be used but its simple availability cannot assure its wise application to a problem. Loans, pumped into an economy, may simply produce inflation rather than productive growth.

In the early 1980s many of the LDCs clamored for someone else to solve their problems by satisfying the demands of their citizens. Loans increased drastically as nation after nation sought to live above its means (to consume more than it produced). The very spread of this philosophy across the world was one significant reason for worldwide inflation. (The other significant reason was the sudden increase in the costs of energy, which caught the industrial world unprepared.) The world economy is much more fragile than most people assume. Because of the overextension of credit worldwide, the United States in the decade of the 1980s would fare quite well if it could avoid a repetition of the Great Depression of the 1930s.

In this situation the United States would be well advised to approach money solutions to foreign problems, especially in the LDCs, with very great caution, insisting on prospects for real gains in the GNP to accompany any infusion of funds. The United States would be equally wise to insist candidly that it did not introduce poverty into the world, that it would like to see poverty abolished everywhere, that it is ready to assist with aid, but that it can only provide (some of) the tools for those ready to do the work. If low tariffs can be maintained and credit be controlled, the significant threatening dangers may be averted and the world may prosper.

It would be wrong to ignore the great advances already made (much of it under U.S. sponsorship) in liberalizing world trade through the abolition of tariff barriers. Between 1948 and

1969, world trade expanded from $121.1 billion to $553.0 billion. Although this expansion did not benefit all equally, it undoubtedly benefited most a great deal.

The point to remember in considering these economic developments and frustrations, is that much has already been done to permit greater prosperity worldwide even though much remains undone, and further advances are difficult. Results are bound to run behind inflated expectations of what can be done since the most obvious changes that might be made in U.S. policy also create built-in additional difficulties. For example, if the U.S. government moves to relax pressures on foreign borrowers by expanding the money supply in the hope of lowering interest rates, it may bring on either a renewed inflation at home and abroad or a dumping of some of the hundreds of billions of dollars now floating around the world as an international currency. Either result on any large scale would be a disaster for the LDCs, let alone the United States. Caution is desirable, even at the price of frustration.

5.

Final Thoughts

Anyone who has lived behind the Iron Curtain or even visited there can hardly avoid noticing the stifling of initiative, the sense of restriction that prevails. Conversely, even the most casual visitor to the United States quickly takes in the freedom in the air—to make individual choices as one pleases, to move, to change jobs, even to leave the country. The United States, just by the nature of its society, has a priceless asset in dealing with the world: that it projects this air of freedom for all to arrange their own affairs. The United States has no "Brezhnev Doctrine" that asserts, in effect, that once in the socialist bloc you are never allowed out without bloodshed. Although the United States in its history has not been immune to the temptation to direct the affairs of its smaller neighbors, its own Monroe Doctrine took the opposite tack: declaring the whole of the Americas free from European recolonization.

Perhaps one day the Soviets will take a more generous view. In the meantime this one difference is a critical reason why the United States, if it does not make foolish policy choices, will survive and prosper in the competition. Sometimes people say that the United States "has an enormous reservoir of goodwill abroad," and that, to some extent, is true. (There is also a second reservoir of ill will out there, among those who envy the United States, and a third reservoir, of those who hate the United States.) To stress goodwill is really the wrong thing to stress as significant; that is simply the sentimental version of the more practical point that no nation likes being under the control of another, and foreigners quite correctly tend to assess that on this point the superpowers are not just Tweedledee and Tweedledum. In the film, *The Mouse That Roared,* the plot idea turns on having a war with the United States in order to get postwar aid. Whoever made a film about the Soviet Union with the same plot idea?

If we look closely at the American national character we realize a second important point— that Americans are "doers" and impatient doers at that. Americans are action-oriented more than speculative and are used to organizing themselves for activity. The combination of traits is formidable. It accounts for the elasticity and energy with which Americans can regroup and address themselves to new problems in new ways. As such, these traits are a great strength. Americans respond well to problems. But such traits are also a source of weakness, since they encourage Americans to work out solutions quickly and carry them out themselves if others are too slow in responding. Americans tend temperamentally to want to deploy on the front line because they see there is a need. So the American temperament encourages a too-forward, too-active role even while the American geopolitical position confers the option of *supplementing* rather than *preempting* the resources of others. Nothing was more striking about the U.S.

involvement in the Vietnam War than that Americans, seeing what they thought was a serious and pressing need (to frustrate a Communist aggression on a weak flank of the "Free World"), quickly sent a half-million troops halfway around the world. They spent billions of dollars to save nations from a "domino effect" those nations showed little concern about. In exchange for this U.S. export of troops, presumably to help save Japan, the Japanese exported automobiles and computers to the United States!

This book shows clearly how difficult it is for a nation able, by nature of its great wealth and power, to decide what *ought* to be attempted in its policy. The United States in its history has vacillated between two extreme roles: from a conviction that it ought to go strictly its own way, to the heady thought after World War II that the United States should play a global role. The sobering effect of having tried both extremes indicates that neither is an appropriate principle by which to decide American involvement in world affairs.

In these pages we have sought to provide the intellectual apparatus for deciding *where* to draw the line of the extent of U.S. involvement and *how* such decisions can be arrived at. The concepts in this book provide guidelines to a prudent and moderate policy for the United States as Americans face the new challenges and opportunities that lie ahead.

INDEX

413

European Economic Community
  budget disputes, 310
  and Falklands, 311
"Ex Comm," 124, 125, 176, 176*n*
Export-Import Bank, 143, 371
Exxon Oil Company, 19, 142

F

Falkland Islands crisis, 69, 86, 149, 261, 311, 376
Farewell Address of President Washington, 189, 267
Fashoda crisis, 74, 194
Federation of American Scientists, 141
First Opium War, 24
Fishing zones, 394
Force de frappe, 308
Ford, Gerald, 96, 106–107, 108, 178, 178*n,* 181, 285, 345, 367, 401
Foreign Service Act of *1980,* 156
Formosa, 226. *See also* Taiwan
Forrestal, James, 167
40 Committee, 174, 176, 178
Four-Power Treaty, 205
"Fourteen points" of Woodrow Wilson, 44, 201–202
France, 24, 26, 30, 66, 74, 108, 189, 190, 192, 196, 292, 298, 299–300
Frankel, Charles, 151*n*
French and Indian War, 190
French Revolution, 28, 191
Frente Sandinista de Liberación Nacional (FSLN), 373
"Friday Breakfasts," 120, 179
Fulbright, William J., 241, 242

G

Gadsden Purchase, 26
Galbraith, John Kenneth, 239
Gallup, George H., 129*n*
Galtieri, Leopold, 376
Galucci, Robert L., 243, 244
Gang of Four, 323, 327
Gandhi, Indira, 327
Gates, Thomas, 167
Gaza, 337, 347
Gelb, Leslie H., 84*n,* 112, 112*n,* 113*n,* 115*n,* 130*n,* 160*n*
Gemayel, Amin, 353, 354
Gemayel, Bashir, 352, 353
General Accounting Office, 101
Geneva Convention on continental shelf, 394

Geneva Peace Conference of *1973,* 256
Germany
  absorbs Czechoslovakia, 54
  Basic Treaty between West and East Germany, 297
  formal creation of two German states, 296
  geographical position of, 23
  implications of division of, 407, 408
  inroads in China, 31, 196
  and the Munich Conference of *1938,* 46, 53, 54
  nuclear cooperation with Brazil, 108, 371
  in World War I, 198–201
  zones of occupation, 218, 219
Geyelin, Philip, 240
Ghengis Khan, 17
Glenn Amendment, 108
Golan Heights, 351
Great Britain, 17, 24, 25, 26, 27, 30, 43, 66, 69, 73–74, 190, 191, 192, 194, 196, 198–201, 205, 206, 211, 212, 214, 215, 216, 218, 219, 227, 286, 292, 300, 304, 305, 308, 310, 319–320, 337, 339, 349, 365, 367, 369, 376
Great Depression, 208
Greeley, Horace, 35
Grenada, 19, 96, 131, 133, 289, 374, 376
Grew, Joseph, C., 208
Grey, Sir Edward (Viscount of Fallodon), 73
Gromyko, Andrei
  and Cuban missile crisis, 233
  Kissinger's opinion of, 256, 257
Ground Launched Cruise Missiles (GLCMs), 302
Group of *77,* 366, 367
Guatemala, 59, 173, 362, 373, 376
Gulf of Aqaba, 336
Gulf of Sidra, 379
Gulf of Tonkin incident, 109, 241
Gulf of Tonkin Resolution, 50, 109–110, 241–242
Guzman, Arbenz, 173

H

Habib, Philip, 352, 353
Habre, Hissene, 379
Haig, Alexander, 135, 148, 149, 168, 180, 182, 261, 285, 329, 374, 376
Haile Selassie, Emperor, 369, 385
Halberstam, David, 52*n,* 133, 242, 242*n*
"Hamlet" concept in Vietnam, 243
Harding, Warren G., 202, 203
Hay, John, 196
Hay-Bunau-Varilla Treaty, 197
Hay-Pauncefote Treaty, 31, 195

Hayakawa, S. I., 95
Hayter, Sir William, 275
Helms, Richard, 115
Helsinki Agreements, 297
Heng Samrin, 326, 332
Herberg, Will, 385
Hickenlooper Amendment, 143
Hilsman, Roger, 151*n*, 232, 232*n*, 233, 242, 242*n*, 243
Hitler, Adolf, 17, 23, 46, 50, 53, 54, 64, 66, 72, 202, 212
Holmes, Oliver Wendell, 38
Honduras, 59, 376
Hoopes, Townsend, 50, 50*n*, 51, 51*n*, 240, 240*n*, 242, 242*n*
Horn of Africa, 349, 369, 378
Hua Guofeng
    becomes Premier and Chairman, 322, 323
    and the "four modernizations," 326
Huerta, Victoriano, 198
Hughes, Charles Evans, 204, 205
Hughes-Ryan Amendment, 101, 104, 105, 174
Hull, Cordell, 149, 207, 208, 212, 215
Hume, David, 3
Hunter, Robert, 115, 115*n*, 120, 120*n*, 178, 179*n*
Hussein, King of Jordan, 78, 353
Huyser, Robert, 116, 184

I

Implementation (of policy), 5, 7, 12, 13, 21, 57, 58, 76–90, 186, 265, 266
India
    becomes independent, 320
    explodes nuclear device, 108
    post-independence policies of, 320
    war with Pakistan, 252, 253, 320, 324–325
"Inevitability of war," 281, 283, 284
Intelligence Authorization Act for Fiscal Year *1981*, 104–105
Intelligence Producers Council, 170
Interagency Groups (IGs), 181, 373
Interdepartmental Group on Terrorism, 391
Interdepartmental Groups, 176, 177
Interdepartmental Regional Groups (IRGs), 176
Interest groups, discussed, 138–143, 144
International Development Cooperation Agency, 154*n*
International Energy Review Group, 178
International Monetary Fund, 376
"Interventionists," pre-World War II, 64
Iran crisis, 10–11, 13, 96, 107, 116, 120, 131, 158, 173, 178–179, 180, 182–185, 350–351, 390

Iraq, 45*n*, 349, 350–351
Israel
    annexes Golan Heights, 351
    bombs Iraqi nuclear reactor, 351
    creation of, 337
    disengagement agreements with Egypt or Syria, 343, 345
    and Jordan, 78
    and June War of *1967*, 340
    and Lebanon, 149, 351, 352–354
    and Palestine Liberation Organization, 335, 345, 346, 351, 352–353
    Peace Treaty with Egypt, 347, 348
    and October War of *1973*, 255, 343
    and Security Council Resolution *242*, 342, 343, 346
    and Suez crisis of *1956*, 227, 339
    war of attrition with Egypt, 342

J

Jackson, Andrew, 24
Japan
    annexes Korea, 317
    and defense budget, 328
    establishes relations with China, 326
    and Manchurian affair, 45, 50
    "northern territories" problem with Soviets, 323–324, 326, 328
    oil dependence of, 318
    and Pearl Harbor attack, reasons for, 317, 318
    Perry's visit, 31
    renounces armed forces and war, 318
    security treaty with U.S., 45, 318, 323
    seizes German islands, 204, 317
    signs peace and friendship treaty with China, 326
    takes Taiwan and Pescadores, 317
    third-party influences on and Pearl Harbor, 67–68
    and trade restrictions, 331
    Twenty-one Demands of, 204
    and the U.S. "shocks," 323
    war with China, 207
    war with Russia, 29, 197
    and Washington Naval Disarmament Conference, 205–206
Jarring, Gunnar, 342
Jaruzelski, Wojciech, 305
Jefferson, Thomas, 25, 26, 96
Jewish lobby, 140–141, 142, 144
Johnson, Hiram, 206

Kissinger, Henry (cont.)
    dominance of National Security Council
        system, 115, 125, 177, 178
    and EC-121 incident, 124
    Nixon's confidence in, 148
    priority of security in foreign policy, 189
    and purpose of China move, 312
    replaced as National Security Adviser, 178
    secret trip to China, 322
    shuttle diplomacy of, 86, 343
    and Soviet submarine base in Cuba, 371
    and State Department, 160–161
    ten-point program for southern Africa, 368
    tilt toward Pakistan, 252, 253, 324, 325
    use of "back channels," 13n
    view of conflict in Jordan, 342
    and Vietnam peace, 245–248
Knapp, Harry S., 206
Kohl, Helmut, 301
Kommunist, on war theory revision, 284
Korea
    annexed by Japan, 317
    strategic location of, 54
Korean War, 13, 14, 18, 45, 46, 47–49, 50, 55,
    57, 61, 64, 78, 123–124, 140, 166, 172, 173,
    175, 224–226
Kossuth, Louis, 43
Kredit Anstalt collapses, 304
Kruger, President of South African Boer
    Republic, 194
Krulak, Victor, 116
Krulak-Mendenhall mission, 116

L

Laird, Melvin, 168
Land, Thomas, 382
Lansing, Robert, 199, 199n, 204
Lansing-Ishii Agreement, 204
Law of the Sea Convention, 8, 391
League of Women Voters, 139
Lebanon
    American marines in, *1958,* 96, 227, 339
    civil war, 345, 346, 354
    domestic situation of, 345–346
    Israeli invasion of, *1982,* 149, 351, 352–354
    multinational peacekeeping force in, 107,
        352–353
    1958 crisis, 96, 227, 339
    Palestinians in, 336, 345, 346
    PLO evacuation from Beirut, 352
"Lend-Lease" Act, 215

Lenin, V. I., 281, 281n, 283, 284
Leopold, Richard W., 192, 192n, 201n, 203n
Less Developed Countries (LDCs)
    arms spending, 388
Liberty Lobby, 139
Libya, 378, 390
Lincoln, Abraham, 26, 27, 121
Lindbergh, Charles A., 212, 215
Lippman, Walter, 203
Lodge, Henry Cabot, Sr., 193
Lodge reservations, 202
Louisiana Territory, 26
Loyalists, 24
Ludlow Amendment, 212
Luns, Joseph M. A. H., 291
Lusitania, 199

M

MacArthur, Douglas, 13, 49, 225, 318
McCarthy, Joseph, 37, 49
McElroy, Neil, 167
McFarlane, Robert, 180, 181
McKinley, William, 96, 195–196, 268
McNamara, Robert S., 117, 123, 124, 167–168,
    175, 176
Madero, Francisco, 198
Mahan, Alfred Thayer, 193, 193n
Maine, 193, 195
Malenkov, Georgi, 307
Malvinas Islands crisis. *See* Falkland Islands
    crisis
Manchukuo, 317
Mansfield Resolution, 308
Mao Zedong, 251, 281, 321, 322
Marco Polo bridge incident, 208
Maritime "choke points," 278
Marshall, George C., 49, 217
Marshall Plan, 47, 306
Marx, Karl, 35, 280
Mass media, discussed, 132–136
May, Ernest, 238
Maximilian, 26, 30, 192
Mayaguez incident, 96, 107, 124
Meese, Edwin, 180, 182
Melville, Herman, 40n
Mendenhall, John, 116
Mengistu, Haile, 369
Mexican cession, 26
Mexican War, 31, 32, 96
Mexico, 26, 30, 31, 32, 96, 192, 197, 198, 289,
    371, 373, 376

Truman, Harry S. (cont.)
    refuses to recognize China, 98
    on relations with Congress, 93
    relieves MacArthur, 13
Truman Doctrine, 46–47, 53, 109, 221, 306
"Tuesday lunch bunch," 123, 174, 176
Turkey, 108, 126, 140, 292, 300
Turner, Stansfield, 173, 183*n*
Twenty-fifth Congress of the Communist Party
    (Soviet Union), 257
"Twin pillars" concept, 349

U

U-2 incident, 113, 230
Uganda, 108
"unconditional surrender" formula, 216
Undersecretaries Committee, 176, 177
Unilateralism, 203–207, 209
United Arab Republic, 85, 339
UN Conference on Trade and Development
    (UNCTAD), 366
UNEF, 340
UN Security Council Resolution *242,* 340, 341,
    342, 345, 346
United Rubber, Cork, Linoleum and Plastic
    Workers of America, 139
United States. *See also* American
    "acquires" Panama Canal Zone, 197
    acquisition of Philippines, 193, 195–196
    allies with Taiwan, 226
    arms deliveries, figures, 390
    army strength, nineteenth century, 27
    bombing campaign in Vietnam, 84
    Caribbean vulnerabilities of, 358, 359
    "Central Command," 286, 352. *See also*
        Rapid Deployment Joint Task Force
    conceptual basis of Cold War policies, 45–
        46, 221
    continental expansion of, 26
    disregards Sino-Soviet friction, 55, 65–66,
        81, 240–241
    efforts to be neutral, World War I, 198–200
    establishes diplomatic relations with China,
        326
    Europe's importance to, 291, 292, 294
    expansion in Caribbean, 196
    first century developments, 189–192
    forces compared to Soviets, 300
    geographical isolation, effects of, 22–25, 67
    grants China most-favored-nation status, 327
    as guarantor of Latin American
        independence, 362
    has priceless strategic asset, 408
    historical experience, effects of, 25–28, 30–
        33, 42
    immigration's effects on, 33–35
    and "loss" of China, 49, 52
    modest dimensions of nineteenth century
        policy, 31–32
    national security organization, pre-World
        War II, 28, 163–164
    no comment on UAR break up, 85
    oil imports, by *1984,* 354
    Pacific expansion, 196
    and Persian Gulf oil dependency, 336
    plays great role in UN, 44–45
    policy formulas lead to Vietnam, 50–52
    population diversity, World War I, 198
    population growth, until Civil War, 191
    rejects Versailles settlement, 44, 97
    Rules of Land Warfare of *1914,* 219
    Security Treaty with Japan, 318, 323
    shift from isolationism to globalism, 44,
        227
    and Spanish-American War, 22, 27, 31,
        195–196, 268
    and Suez crisis, *1956,* 310, 339
    surrounded by great powers, early years, 43,
        190, 267, 404
    "tilts" toward Pakistan against India, 252,
        253, 324, 325
    and Undeclared War with France, 32, 190*n*
    unique experience of, 22–37
    unlike much of world, 40–41
    and War of *1812,* 24, 32, 191, 192
United States Information Agency (USIA), 154
United States Intelligence Board, 169
United States v. Curtiss-Wright, 99*n*

V

Vance, Cyrus, 119*n,* 120, 121, 146*n,* 179, 180,
    183, 185, 325, 368, 368*n*
VBBs (Vance-Brzezinski-Brown lunches), 120,
    179
Venezuela, 289
Venezuela boundary dispute, 31, 73, 194
Venezuela debt crisis, 197
Vergennes, Charles, 267, 268
Verification Panel, 176
Versailles Treaty, 44, 97, 202
Viet Cong, attack Pleiku, 242
Vietnam War
    CIA advice about, 113, 173
    FSO suggestions about, 160

Gulf of Tonkin Resolution, 50, 109–110,
241–242
hamlet concept in, 242
identification of enemy problem in, 59, 78,
238–239
mass media coverage of, 136, 136n
peace negotiations, 245–248
policy formulas leading to U.S. involvement
in, 50–52
road to U.S. commitment in, 235–240
standard operating procedures in, 112, 248
Tet offensive in, 7, 51, 136, 243, 244
U.S. confusion in, 243–245
Villa, Francisco "Pancho," 32, 198
Virginia, 385
Vulnerability of missiles argument, 288

W

Waldheim, Kurt, 256
Walesa, Lech, 306
Wallace, Henry, 279
War of *1812,* 24, 32, 191, 192, 383
"War Powers Resolution," 100, 106–107
Warnke, Paul, 84
Warsaw Pact
forces compared to NATO, 300
reliability of various forces in, 82
signed, 223, 224
Washington, George, 7, 25, 189, 191, 267
Washington, Treaty of, 31, 192
Washington, Treaty of, 31, 192
Washington Naval Disarmament Conference,
204–206
Washington Special Action Group (WSAG), 124,
134, 176
Watergate scandal, 7, 37, 101, 104, 131, 261
Weigley, Russell F., 193n, 206, 206n
Weinberger, Caspar, 149, 168, 330, 331
Wells, H. G., 203
West Bank, 347, 409
Western Somali Liberation Front, 369
Westmoreland, William, 243
Whaling, 394
Wheeler, Burton, 215

Wheeler, Earle, 52, 242, 244
Wilde, Oscar, 55
Wilhelm II, Kaiser, 30, 194
Wilson, Charles, 167
Wilson, Woodrow
arguments for League of Nations, 32–33, 44,
203
on balance of power, 33, 44, 201, 203, 263
on causes of World War I, 32–33
and entangling alliances, 32–33
Fourteen points of, 44, 201–202
mistake of linking League Covenant to
Versailles Treaty, 202
policy toward Mexico, 198
reelection campaign of, 200
requests declaration of war, 200–201
sends troops into Caribbean, 96
a study in contrasts, 197
uncompromising toward Senate, 202
use of diplomatic recognition, 98
and Versailles Conference, 97
and Versailles Treaty, 97, 202
World Trade expansion, 410, 411
World War II, begins, 212
Wu Xueqian, 330

Y

Yahya Khan, 322, 324
Yalta Conference of *1945,* 97, 137, 217
Young, Andrew, 183

Z

Zaire, 364
"Zero option," 309
Zhao Ziyang, 330
Zhou Enali, 322
Zia ul-Haq, 327
Zimbabwe, 369
Zimmermann note, 200, 201
Zionism, 371
Zorin, Valerian, 234
Zumwalt, Elmo, 253, 279

Duplicate.

In the Name of the most Holy and undivided Trinity:

It having pleased the Divine Providence to dispose the Hearts of the most Serene and most potent Prince George the Third, by the Grace of God, King of Great Britain, France and Ireland, Defender of the Faith, Duke of Brunswick and Luneburg, Arch Treasurer and Prince Elector of the Holy Roman Empire &c.ª And of the United States of America, to forget all past Misunderstandings and Differences that have unhappily interrupted the good Correspondence and Friendship which they mutually wish to restore, and to establish such a beneficial and satisfactory Intercourse, between the two Countries upon the Ground of reciprocal Advantages and mutual Convenience as may promote and secure to both perpetual Peace & Harmony, and having for this desirable End already laid the Foundation of Peace and Reconciliation, by the Provisional Articles signed at Paris on the 30.th of November 1782, by the Commissioners empowered on each Part, which Articles were agreed to be inserted in and to constitute the Treaty of Peace proposed to be concluded between the Crown of Great Britain &